Series Editors:
George H.S. Singer
Ann P. Turnbull
H. Rutherford Turnbull, III
Larry K. Irvin
Laurie E. Powers

Families and Positive Behavior Support

Other books in the
Family, Community, & Disability series:

Children with Acquired Brain Injury:
Educating and Supporting Families
edited by George H.S. Singer, Ph.D.,
Ann Glang, Ph.D., and Janet M. Williams, Ph.D.

Redefining Family Support:
Innovations in Public–Private Partnerships
edited by George H.S. Singer, Ph.D.,
Laurie E. Powers, Ph.D., and Ardis L. Olson, M.D.

Family,
Community,
&Disability

Families and Positive Behavior Support

Addressing Problem Behavior in Family Contexts

edited by

Joseph M. Lucyshyn, Ph.D.
University of British Columbia

Glen Dunlap, Ph.D.
University of South Florida

and

Richard W. Albin, Ph.D.
University of Oregon

·P·A·U·L·H·
BROOKES
PUBLISHING Co®

Baltimore • London • Toronto • Sydney

Paul H. Brookes Publishing Co.
Post Office Box 10624
Baltimore, Maryland 21285–0624

www.brookespublishing.com

Typeset by Integrated Publishing Solutions, Grand Rapids, Michigan.
Manufactured in the United States of America by
Hamilton Printing Company, Rensselaer, New York.

The stories in this book are based on the authors' experiences. In some cases, permission
has been granted to use actual names and details. In other cases, individuals' names and
other identifying information have been changed to protect their identities. Still other
vignettes are composite accounts that do not represent the lives or experiences of specific
individuals, and no implications should be inferred.

The photographs on this book's cover and throughout the text have been graciously
provided by many families that have found improved quality of life through positive
behavior support.

Library of Congress Cataloging-in-Publication Data

Families and positive behavior support : addressing problem behavior in family contexts /
edited by Joseph M. Lucyshyn, Glen Dunlap, and Richard W. Albin.
    p.   cm.—(Family, community & disability)
    Includes bibliographical references and index.
    ISBN 1-55766-574-5
    1. Developmentally disabled children—Services for.   2. Parents of children with
disabilities—Services for.   3. Behavior disorders in children.   4. Problem children—
Behavior modification.   5. Family social work.   I. Lucyshyn, Joseph M.   II. Dunlap, Glen.
III. Albin, Richard W.   IV. Series.

HV891 .F35 2002
362.7′086′9—dc21

                                          2002016406

British Library Cataloguing in Publication data are available from the British Library.

Contents

Series Preface

The purpose of the *Family, Community, & Disability* series is to provide a forum for contemporary work on the challenges and issues that families face, as well as effective ways of supporting families as they fulfill their roles in the lives of people with disabilities. The authors for each volume strive to create a vehicle for making state-of-the art theory, research, and practice readily accessible to a diverse audience.

In North America, the institution of the family underwent revolutionary changes during the last half of the 20th century. Fundamental changes took place in the rates of women's employment outside of the home, the prevalence of divorce and remarriage, and the numbers of single and never-married mothers, as well as in the traditional roles of men and women in homes and in geographic mobility. Demographic changes, including the rapid growth of non-European ethnic populations and the burgeoning numbers of older adults, also contributed to the transformation of North American families. At the same time as these trends were evident, the percentage of people with long-term disabilities grew dramatically—a trend that will continue as we move into the first quarter of the 21st century. Families are the primary source of day-to-day assistance for people with disabilities. They are crucial to the quality of life for people with developmental disabilities, chronic illnesses, mental illnesses, and disabilities associated with aging.

Much progress has been made in recognizing the key roles of families in early intervention, education, transitions to adulthood, and supported living for people with disabilities. However, the knowledge base about practical ways to strengthen and support families in their multiple roles is still in a nascent stage. Theories of family change, adaptation, and life-span development need to be tested against the phenomena of modern family life. Ethical and social policy issues need to be articulated and analyzed. And, perhaps most important, effective ways of supporting families need to be tested and disseminated. We endeavor to address these topics in this series.

No single discipline has a primary claim to the field of family and disability studies and much is to be gained by the cross-fertilization of ideas from many traditions, including psychology, history, anthropology, education, sociology, economics, medicine, law, and philosophy. It is also essential that the voices of family members and people with disabilities be heard in this forum.

Editorial Advisory Board

Foreword

Many times in my career people have asked me whether I find it difficult to work with individuals who have disabilities and their families. In fact, I find the work meaningful and rewarding, which is why I have been doing it for the past 30 years. The only times that have been difficult are those periods when I have had to face the gaping chasm that far too often exists between academic research and traditional services, on the one hand, and the practical needs of families who have a loved one with a disability, on the other hand. Reading *Families and Positive Behavior Support: Addressing Problem Behavior in Family Contexts* has been both therapeutic and inspirational. The authors have elaborated on an approach to research and service that is sensitive to the hopes, needs, and concerns of families. In my opinion, this book is the gold standard against which all future work in the field must be judged. It is a watershed document that articulates a vision that is sure to be influential for many years to come.

The first section of the book could have been titled "Everything you ever wanted to know about the fundamental nature of positive behavior support (PBS), including many things you never even thought of." The authors, however, chose the more succinct title of "Characteristics and Context of Positive Behavior Support with Families." Although the approach has many dimensions, all admirably detailed, the two that most stand out in this section, and indeed throughout the book, involve quality of life and systems change. The focus on quality of life represents a sea change for the field. For decades, there have been endless microanalyses of problem behavior as well as countless demonstrations of specific interventions and their effects. Yet, ultimately, none of this matters unless it leads to an outcome greater than the mere reduction of problem behavior. Let me illustrate. At the beginning of my career, I worked with a 9-year-old girl residing in an institution who had autism and engaged in a high rate of tantrum behavior. When Thanksgiving came, all of the other children went home to their families. She remained on the psychiatric ward, having tantrums. Later, we developed an intervention procedure for her and the tantrums stopped. The following Thanksgiving, all of the other children went home again. She remained on the psychiatric ward quietly, with no tantrums. Her problem behavior had stopped, but good quality of life had not even begun. Anecdotes like this one, no doubt, have led the authors of this book to argue repeatedly that the fundamental nature of PBS involves bringing about substantive changes that result in families being able to enjoy life together in the community. The reduction of problem behavior is an important side effect, but the enhancement of quality of life is the critical main effect.

The authors also eloquently argue for the centrality of systems change and its pivotal role in ensuring that the PBS enterprise is successful. Traditionally, the field has focused on identifying specific interventions and evaluating their effects. The central question has been "What intervention(s) can be useful?" The PBS approach has a very different focus, leading to the new question: "How must we change social, cultural, health, legal, financial, and policy contexts so that interventions that work in the circumscribed settings of clinic, laboratory, and institution will also work in the complex community environments in which families must function?" More exciting still, sometimes systems change itself may be the "intervention" of choice—such as when a family is able to make financial and legal arrangements for their child with disabilities to move from a restrictive group home setting that is conducive to problem behavior to a supported living situation that is conducive to friend-ships, preferred activities, and freedom of community participation. This molar approach to intervention is one of the most encouraging developments detailed in *Families and Positive Behavior Support.*

The second section, which deals with issues of assessment and intervention, is a tour de force concerning best practices in the field. One idea stands out above all: If you want to understand challenging behavior and improve peoples' lives, then focus on problem contexts, not on problem behavior and certainly not on problem people. In many ways, our society's devotion to a label-segregate-drug approach for people with disabilities is tantamount to blaming the victim. Rather than adopting this unfair philosophy, it is better to recognize that people typically show problem behavior because they are enmeshed in problem contexts. Improve the context and you are likely to improve the behavior. A person who is given few choices, who is involved in meaningless activities, who is surrounded by "professionals" who are often inadequately trained, and whose future is planned by functionaries of service agencies rather than loved ones is a victim and not a problem. The remedy, as author after author notes, involves ecologically valid intervention (contextual goodness of fit), person-centered planning, teaching the communication of needs, home–school collaboration, cultural sensitivity, and addressing issues that pertain to the whole family and not just the person with disabilities. Above all, professionals must acquire humility by understanding that families are partners, not helpers. Families and professionals educate one another to promote goals and interventions that are worthy of pursuit and that, in the end, produce a consensus that the outcomes achieved are meaningful in preserving and enhancing the quality of family life.

The third section consists of multiple case studies, many written by parents, that describe the implementation of PBS philosophy with respect to assessment, intervention, and outcomes. The information presented is such that the reader gains a detailed appreciation for how to implement a comprehensive PBS program in the home and community. Abstract principles and ideas come to life in a series of compelling descriptions and systematic but practical plans. The power and necessity for partnerships and collaborative teaming is made clear throughout. Particularly impressive are the accounts of failures and setbacks and how families and their supporters work to overcome these difficulties and get on with life. The hopeful message here is that families do not have to take it anymore. PBS is all about empowerment and self-determination. This insider's view of PBS in action is a uniquely informative and uplifting aspect of the book, and the poignant case studies written by parents attest to the courage, imagination, and humanity that ultimately shape the goals and tactics that constitute PBS.

The fourth section deals with collaborative research with families. The key word is *collaboration.* That is, families are not viewed as passive participants; rather, they are seen as active partners in the research process. It has been noted elsewhere (Carr et al., 2002) that family members can play at least four important roles in research. Specifically, they can 1) provide valuable qualitative perspectives that help shape the nature of assessment; 2) screen and alter proposed intervention strategies to increase their relevance to problematic situations; 3) evaluate whether the selected approach meshes well with family values, needs, and structures; and 4) define the nature of desired outcomes to ensure that they are congruent with personal perceptions of improved quality of life. The final chapters are outstanding in the way that they address each of these four roles. These chapters, as a group, provide a model for the next generation of researchers to follow, helping to propel the field toward greater relevance, practicality, and feasibility.

Whether you are a family member, a teacher, a service provider, a policy maker, a researcher, or a student, *Families and Positive Behavior Support* is a book that you will want to own and read again and again. It is a path to the future filled with hope and encouragement that proves it is possible to combine serious science with humanistic values in order to do some good for the world.

Edward G. Carr, Ph.D.
Leading Professor
Department of Psychology
State University of New York at Stony Brook

REFERENCE

Carr, E.G., Dunlap, G., Horner, R.H., Koegel, R.L., Turnbull, A.P., Sailor, W., Anderson, J.L., Albin, R.W., Koegel, L.K., & Fox, L. (2002). Positive behavior support: Evolution of an applied science. *Journal of Positive Behavior Interventions, 4,* 4–16, 20.

Foreword

Families who have children with developmental disabilities and problem behaviors learn quickly to trust the professionals who help plan for the realities of life: How can I manage the trip to the supermarket that has become impossible? How do we improve the family dinner that usually ends in tears? How do I cope with ongoing sleep deprivation and still be a good mom? Who can I talk to about a persistent sense of alienation in the most ordinary community circumstances? Professionals learn quickly that their relationship with a family is most productive when the family feels comfortable enough to answer difficult questions truthfully: What is day-to-day life like? How do you feel about it? What seems to make things work better?

Sometimes, we parents don't know the answers to those questions ourselves. Sometimes, we need to be helped to explore our feelings and responses. Sometimes, we parents need to be taught that, yes, we are still valued and valuable human beings; yes, we can be not only good parents but great parents; no, we are not supposed to be crying ourselves to sleep at night; yes, our knowledge of our own family rhythms and our love for our children means a lot—but we shouldn't expect it to be enough by itself; and, yes, we need partnerships and collaborations.

I have never met a parent who didn't want to be a better parent. Nothing makes one feel this impulse more deeply than having a child with "severe and profound" disabilities or behavior problems. The impulse to be a better parent quickly makes us say, "I will do anything. I will try anything." Today, parents looking for answers on problem behavior have many approaches available to them. On the Internet, parents can find references and arguments for almost any model that can be imagined. With so many models available to us to help with problem behaviors, how can we choose? "Well," a dear friend with disabilities says, "if you have to choose between severe and profound, choose profound."

It is fair to say that some approaches to problem behaviors are severe. These are based on deprivation or punishment, minute-by-minute programming, or other kinds of force. Sometimes, severe models seem okay because that is how we ourselves were raised. Yet, we can do better.

Positive behavior support is not a severe model—it is a profound model, based on respect and caring and the dignity of the family and of the person who has disabilities. It is profound because it helps families understand and cope with fundamental shifts that disability brings to the family ecology. Positive behavior support looks at the foundations of the whole family system and is based on clear-eyed assessment of what works for each family. It is profound because it is based on love and helps families deepen their understanding of what love is and how it works.

Learning to respond more fully to our children and ourselves—to focus on what is good in our relationships with each other—is good for each of us. Whether you are the parent of a child with disabilities or the professional who supports a family, it is possible you may one day realize that a child's disability has given you the most amazing access to the deepest treasures of life. No, disability is not magic. Our children are not little shamans. But we may learn, for example, that our own calm heartbeat somehow speaks directly to a child's frantic heart and calms him. Or we may learn that a child who "does not make eye contact" has a clear picture of her world, even if it is based only on a fleeting glance from the corner of her eye.

However we may learn it, the lesson is simple: We are connected to each other, deeply and organically, in mutual relationships of care, love, and respect that can transcend many challenges. From a child with disabilities and behavior problems, we may learn that in this life our own imperfections are irrelevant. The fact that we don't know everything, or cannot do everything, doesn't matter. What is wanted is not perfection of the self but the courage to connect and to care.

Families and Positive Behavior Support: Addressing Problem Behavior in Family Contexts is written by collaborative teams of professionals and parents who had the courage to connect with each other in new ways. The research collaboration is clear and is even more important because it is so unusual. Collaboration between parent researchers and professional researchers creates solutions that are practical—and collaboration is an inherent part of the positive behavior support model.

Collaboration is easily misunderstood. It is easy to say, "Yes, our team is collaborative," and difficult sometimes to demonstrate. Over and over again, *Families and Positive Behavior Support* demonstrates that true collaboration is the key to creative, innovative, reality-based, useful, practical research. This is not research designed to hold a shelf down or even to add weight to a résumé. It is research that is useful because it is informed by real collaboration between parents and professionals. In every chapter, the collaboration and the resulting innovation are clear.

Collaboration takes many forms in this book and in the world at large. The first way to collaborate is to communicate, to share words and ideas—to say the same thing. Communication is a key step, because it is important to have a sense of agreement. Yet, if that's all you do, then sooner or later someone on your team will remark that a partner says all of the right things but doesn't walk the talk.

The second kind of collaboration is coordination—to share expertise or, more literally, to share leadership. Each person manages his or her part of the work depending on his or her expertise. For example, the psychologist does the assessment, the therapist designs the plan, and the family implements the plan under the direction of the appropriate professional. Of course, it is great to have a team, but sooner or later certain people feel that their expertise is overburdened or undervalued. Or they will feel that their teammates' contributions are overvalued—or, worse, that their teammates' work is not properly connected to reality or a theoretical framework (depending on their perspective).

The third way to collaborate is to dig a little deeper, to truly cooperate—to share actions. You have to share a mission if you are going to "operate with" someone else. A cooperative team is one in which members understand the goal so well that a team member can act in another's place and that members can speak for each other in a pinch.

Full collaboration happens when members share real work—when the members come to the team ready and willing to change not just what they do but who they are. Think of working out with partners at a gym: Everybody's capabilities change as a result of the effort. When you work together collaboratively, the work changes you and what you are capable of—and it changes the other person, too.

Families and Positive Behavior Support shows what research can be when the research team is collaborative. Positive behavior support is a model based on collaboration and, most important, on the active engagement of the whole team—including the child with problem behaviors. That makes it real . . . and that is the best thing that can be said about any model or research.

Sue Swenson
Executive Director
The Joseph P. Kennedy, Jr. Foundation
Washington, D.C.

Contributors

Richard W. Albin, Ph.D.
Associate Professor
Educational and Community Supports
College of Education
University of Oregon
1761 Alder Street
Eugene, OR 97403

Anjali Barretto, Ph.D.
Assistant Professor
Department of Special Education
Gonzaga University
502 West Boone
Spokane, WA 99258

Leasha M. Barry, Ph.D.
Assistant Professor
College of Professional Studies
University of West Florida
Post Office Box 758
Gulf Breeze, FL 32562

Kathy R. Ben, B.A.
Family Support Specialist/Consultant/
   Advocate
TASH
The Arc
Family Support Council
Division of Developmental Disabilities,
   District III
1731 East Water Street
Tucson, AZ 85719

Nila F. Benito
Education and Training Director
Center for Autism and Related Disabilities
University of South Florida
13301 Bruce B. Downs Boulevard
Tampa, FL 33612

E. Richard Blumberg, Ph.D.
Instructor of Pediatrics
The Elizabeth M. Boggs Center on
   Developmental Disabilities
University of Medicine and Dentistry
   of New Jersey
335 George Street
New Brunswick, NJ 08903

Claire Chapman
Parent of a son with autism
Stafford, VA

Deborah Chen, Ph.D.
Professor
Department of Special Education
California State University, Northridge
18111 Nordhoff Street
Northridge, CA 91330

Lisa S. Cushing, Ph.D.
Research Associate
Peabody College
Vanderbilt University
Box 328
Nashville, TN 37203

K. Mark Derby, Ph.D.
Associate Professor
Department of Special Education
Gonzaga University
502 West Boone
Spokane, WA 99258

June E. Downing, Ph.D.
Professor
Department of Special Education
California State University, Northridge
18111 Nordhoff Street
Northridge, CA 91330

Glen Dunlap, Ph.D.
Professor
Department of Child and Family Studies
Louis de la Parte Florida Mental
   Health Institute
University of South Florida
13303 Bruce B. Downs Boulevard
Tampa, FL 33612

Susan Fake, M.A.
Positive Behavioral Support Consultant
P.A.C.T.
Post Office Box 78042
Seattle, WA 98178

Lise Fox, Ph.D.
Research Associate Professor
Department of Child and Family Studies
Louis de la Parte Florida Mental
    Health Institute
University of South Florida
13303 Bruce B. Downs Boulevard
Tampa, FL 33612

Connie Ginsberg, B.S.
Executive Director
Family Connection of South Carolina
2712 Middleburg Drive
Suite 103-B
Columbia, SC 29204

Sara E. Goldberg-Hamblin, Ph.D.
Assistant Professor
Department of Educational Psychology,
    Administration, and Counseling
College of Education
California State University, Long Beach
1250 Bellflower Boulevard
Long Beach, CA 90840

Jay W. Harding, Ed.S.
Program Associate
Center for Disabilities and Development
The University of Iowa
100 Hawkins Drive
Room 251
Iowa City, IA 52242

Joshua K. Harrower, Ph.D.
Assistant Professor
Department of Child and Family Studies
Louis de la Parte Florida Mental
    Health Institute
University of South Florida
13301 Bruce B. Downs Boulevard
Tampa, FL 33612

Meme Hieneman, Ph.D.
Assistant Professor
Department of Child and Family Studies
Louis de la Parte Florida Mental
    Health Institute
University of South Florida
13301 Bruce B. Downs Boulevard
MHC 2–113A
Tampa, FL 33612

Robert H. Horner, Ph.D.
Professor
Educational and Community Supports
College of Education
University of Oregon
1761 Alder Street
Eugene, OR 97403

Larry K. Irvin, Ph.D.
Professor
College of Education
University of Oregon
Eugene, OR 97403
Research Professor
Teaching Research (Eugene)
99 West 10th Avenue
Suite 337C
Eugene, OR 97401

Maya Kalyanpur, Ph.D.
Associate Professor
Department of Reading, Special Education,
    and Instructional Technology
Towson University
8000 York Road
Towson, MD 21252

Anne T. Kayser, B.A.
Math teacher
Parent of a child with autism
8095 Southwest Fairway Drive
Portland, OR 97225

Shannon Kelly-Keough
Designer
Made by Mom Creations
2250 Gale Avenue
Coquitlam, British Columbia V3K 2Y8
Canada

Don Kincaid, Ed.D.
Research Assistant Professor
Department of Child and Family Studies
Louis de la Parte Florida Mental
    Health Institute
University of South Florida
13301 Bruce B. Downs Boulevard
Tampa, FL 33612

Joseph M. Lucyshyn, Ph.D.
Assistant Professor
Department of Educational and Counselling
   Psychology, and Special Education
Faculty of Education
University of British Columbia
2125 Main Mall
Vancouver, British Columbia V6T 1Z4
Canada

Teresa MacGregor
Behavior Consultant
CBI Consultants
103 Cedarwood Drive
Port Moody, British Columbia V3H 4W2
Canada

Ursula Arceneaux Markey
Co-Director
Pyramid Parent Training Program
4120 Eve Street
New Orleans, LA 70125

Joyce Metzger
Early Intervention Section
1600 Kapiolani Boulevard
Suite 1401
Honolulu, HI 96822

Pat Mirenda, Ph.D.
Associate Professor
Department of Educational and Counselling
   Psychology, and Special Education
University of British Columbia
2125 Main Mall
Vancouver, British Columbia V6T 1Z4
Canada

Carol Niederhauser, B.A.
Training Coordinator
South Carolina Autism Society
652 Bush River Road
Suite 203
Columbia, SC 29210

Charles D. Nixon, Ph.D. (deceased)
Lane County Direction Service
Counseling Center
576 Olive Street
Suite 307
Eugene, OR 97401

Catherine C. O'Leary, Ph.D.
Psychology Fellow
Division of Child and Adolescent Psychiatry
Boston Medical Center
One Boston Medical Center Plaza
Boston, MA 02118

Stephanie M. Peck Peterson, Ph.D.
Assistant Professor
Special Education
School of PAES
The Ohio State University
1945 North High Street
375A Arps Hall
Columbus, OH 43210

Kathryn D. Peckham-Hardin, M.A.
Lecturer
Department of Special Education
California State University, Northridge
18111 Nordhoff Street
Northridge, CA 91330

Shridevi Rao, Ph.D.
Assistant Professor
Department of Special Education
The College of New Jersey
Post Office Box 7718
Ewing, NJ 08628

Susan Rocco
Coordinator
Special Parent Information Network
919 Ala Moana Boulevard
Room 101
Honolulu, HI 96814

Grace Ellen Santarelli, M.A.
School Psychologist
Doctoral Student
Gevirtz Graduate School of Education
University of California at Santa Barbara
Santa Barbara, CA 93106

Betsy Santelli, M.Ed.
Director of Outreach
Beach Center on Disability
2415 Brookridge Avenue
Golden Valley, MN 55422

Karen Scandariato, B.A.
923 Griffis Street
Cary, NC 27511

Carol Schall, M.A.
Virginia Autism Resource Center
549 Southlake Boulevard
Richmond, VA 23236

Patrick Shannon, Ph.D.
Assistant Professor
Department of Social Work
University of New Hampshire
50 College Road
PeHee Hall
Durham, NH 03824

George H.S. Singer, Ph.D.
Professor
Gervitz Graduate School of Education
University of California at Santa Barbara
2321 Phelps Hall
Santa Barbara, CA 93106

James R. Skouge, Ed.D.
Assistant Professor
Center on Disability Studies
University of Hawaii
1776 University Avenue UA 4–6
Honolulu, HI 96822

Steve Sullivan
1431 Assembly Street
Columbia, SC 29201

Sharleen Tifft
170 McIntosh Hill Road
Foley, MO 63347

Ann P. Turnbull, Ed.D.
Co-Director
Beach Center on Disability
The University of Kansas
1200 Sunnyside Avenue
3111 Haworth Hall
Lawrence, KS 66045

H. Rutherford Turnbull, III, LL.B., LL.M.
Co-Director
Beach Center on Disability
The University of Kansas
1200 Sunnyside Drive
3111 Haworth Hall
Lawrence, KS 66045

Bobbie J. Vaughn, Ph.D.
Assistant Professor
Department of Child and Family Studies
Louis de la Parte Florida Mental
    Health Institute
University of South Florida
13301 Bruce B. Downs Boulevard
Tampa, FL 33612

Tom Weddle, M.A.
Intervention Specialist
7018 North Belt
Spokane, WA 99208

Renee M. Whaley
Director
Parent Education Network
11260 Deed Street
Spring Hill, FL 34609

Brennan L. Wilcox, M.S.W., J.D.
Attorney at Law
210 Southwest Jewell Avenue
Topeka, KS 66606

Terry Williams, B.A.
Mental Health/Substance Abuse Counselor
2019 Bob White Court
Mary Ester, FL 32569

Angela Zangerle
Sea of Dreams Foundation
87–370 Kulahanai Street
Waianae, HI 96792

Volume Preface

The purpose of *Families and Positive Behavior Support: Addressing Problem Behavior in Family Contexts* is to present current theory, practice, and research on positive behavior support (PBS) with families of children and youth with developmental disabilities and problem behavior. PBS is a collaborative, assessment-based approach to addressing problem behavior that integrates behavioral science with person-centered values and a systems perspective. The goals of the approach are to improve the behavior and quality of life of people who engage in problem behavior and to do so in ways that are effective, acceptable, feasible, and durable when implemented by educators, families, and other support providers in typical home, school, and community settings. Within the approach, functional assessment results are used to develop PBS plans that emphasize lifestyle improvements, proactive and educative strategies, and reinforcement-based procedures. The aim is to build effective environments in which positive behavior is more functional than problem behavior. PBS initially began in the 1980s as an alternative to aversive interventions for people with severe disabilities. Since the 1990s and early 2000s, it has grown to address the behavioral support needs of a wide range of individuals across a diversity of home, school, and community contexts.

This book focuses on PBS with families of children and youth with disabilities who engage in problem behavior in natural family contexts. A central theme of the book is the way in which the philosophy and practices of PBS can guide assessment, behavior support plan design, and implementation in family settings. Additional themes are the importance of a practical empiricism that directly benefits families of children with disabilities and the need for professionals to listen and learn from families as well as to guide and support. The book also addresses how a process of PBS can be augmented and adapted to more fully meet the support needs of a greater diversity of families. A key assumption is that families and the natural contexts of family life are qualitatively different from professional contexts in which positive behavior support may be implemented, such as schools, workplaces, and group homes. Practitioners recognize that if the technology of PBS is to reach and help families in meaningful and substantial ways, then it needs to be enhanced and adapted to better accommodate the characteristics, ecology, and culture of family life in all its depth, richness, and diversity. For these reasons, a process of PBS with families takes into account the characteristics of family systems and the unique ecologies and cultures of families. With families, the goals of PBS are to empower parents and other family members to improve the behavior and lifestyle of the child or youth with a disability, to strengthen the family as a whole, and to do so in ways that are congruent with family ecology and culture.

Families and Positive Behavior Support has four specific goals. The first is to enhance understanding about the complexities and subtleties of family life and to incorporate this broadened view into a process of positive behavior support with families. The second goal is to influence professional practice in behavioral family intervention by presenting examples of successful PBS with families. The third goal is to promote the participation of families in leadership roles in the development and dissemination of knowledge about PBS with families. The fourth goal is to encourage partnerships between researchers and families by describing and illustrating different approaches to collaborative research.

A unique feature of *Families and Positive Behavior Support* is the way in which the perspectives and experiences of families are interwoven with the perspectives and experiences of professional practitioners and researchers. In addition to chapters by professionals, the book includes chapters and essays written by parents. Integration of the voice and knowledge of researchers, practitioners, and family members in one edited volume reflects three aspects of the development and dissemination of the science and technology of PBS. First, PBS has been developed in collaboration with key stakeholders who are responsible for implementing the technology in typical home, school, or community settings. Families have been important members of this ongoing collaboration. Such partnerships are essential to bridge the gap between research-based knowledge and its practical use in daily life. The inclusion of professional and parent authors reflects this partnership and research-to-practice linkage. Second, practitioners of PBS with families recognize that if families are to truly value and effectively use the technology to benefit their child and family, then it is not helpful to impose a hierarchical relationship in which parents and other family members are viewed as passive consumers of expert knowledge. It is much better to develop an egalitarian relationship in which families are viewed as colleagues and practitioners of the approach and to work from an empowerment framework to realize this relationship and level of expertise. Case study chapters and essays by parent authors reflect this aim and its realization. Third, chapters and essays written by parents reflect an important higher order outcome of an empowerment approach to behavioral support with families: the natural movement of some families into leadership roles in the practice and dissemination of PBS.

This book and its contents represent many years of research and practice by behavioral scientists and family support professionals working in concert with parents and other family members. This joint effort has led to the development of a practical technology of behavioral support that is proving to be acceptable, effective, and feasible within the daily lives of families. Much of the scientific advancement of PBS with families has taken place under the auspices of the Rehabilitation Research and Training Center on Positive Behavior Support (RRTC-PBS). The RRTC-PBS is funded by the National Institute on Disability and Rehabilitation Research of the U.S. Department of Education through the University of South Florida in partnership with five affiliate universities: University of Oregon, University of California at Santa Barbara, State University of New York at Stony Brook, The University of Kansas, and California State University at Hayward. Together, the RRTC-PBS represents a unified effort of six research and training sites that involves active collaboration with state training teams, national researchers, family organizations, schools, and service agencies. For more information on such resources, visit web sites connected to the University of South Florida (www.rrtcpbs.org), the University of Oregon (www.pbis.org/english), or the Beach Center on Disability at The University of Kansas (www.beachcenter.org).

Families and Positive Behavior Support is organized into four sections that reflect its purpose and goals. Section I includes three chapters that address the characteristics and context of positive behavior support with families. An introductory chapter presents the theoretical and values foundations of the approach, describes twelve key features of the approach with families, and summarizes research on the efficacy of functional assessment and PBS with families. In the next chapter, a parent offers a poignant account of 20 years of experience raising a son with a disability and challenging behavior and of the evolution of behavior management practices toward PBS during this span of time. A third chapter describes recent special education law on the provision of functional assessment and positive behavioral supports in schools and discusses opportunities for families to use the law to secure effective behavioral support services.

Section II presents six chapters and two essays that focus on assessment and intervention in family contexts. In the lead chapter, three parents present their perspectives and insights on professional assessments, interventions, and parent–professional interactions. Subsequent chapters discuss and illustrate ways that a process of PBS can be augmented and adapted to reach a wider diversity of families. Topics include 1) how to design effective and contextually appropriate behavior support plans, 2) ways to promote culturally responsive services, 3) strategies for teaching communication skills in family contexts, 4) additional supports for highly distressed families, and 5) ways to facilitate home–school collaboration. Essays linked to two chapters offer family experiences and perspectives on developing behavior support plans and on home–school collaboration.

Section III includes six chapters and three essays that present a broad range of case studies of family-centered behavioral support. Case study chapters and essays are organized to follow the life cycle of children from early childhood to adulthood. Through narrative accounts by parents and data-based summaries by behavioral researchers and interventionists, evidence and testimony is presented for the relevance, effectiveness, and generalizability of functional assessment and positive behavior support across a diversity of children and families. Represented across case study chapters are children with different disabilities, families with different compositions and ethnic backgrounds, and interventionists using different variations of a process of PBS.

Section IV is composed of four chapters that focus on collaborative approaches to research in PBS and family support. The section's opening chapter presents issues and considerations for collaborative research in PBS. Subsequent chapters illustrate different approaches to collaborative research with families. They include 1) a longitudinal, single case analysis of comprehensive behavioral support; 2) a multimethod case study that integrates single subject and qualitative research methods; and 3) a participatory action research study of Parent to Parent, a nationwide family support organization. Together, these chapters offer behavioral and family researchers examples of methodologies that can contribute to forming research partnerships with families, to conducting research in natural family settings, and to developing knowledge about behavioral support with families that is characterized by both scientific rigor and practical relevance.

Families and Positive Behavior Support is intended for professionals, families, researchers, students, and all individuals who are concerned with the delivery of positive behavior support services to families. We hope that all readers recognize the features of the approach that unite these chapters and essays, including the development of collaborative partnerships, the use of functional assessment to guide the design of positive behavioral supports, a focus on improving behavior and quality of life for the child and family, and the provision of implementation support that empowers family members to support the child with a disability in a manner that is effective, acceptable, and sustainable. It is our deepest wish that the book and its contents contribute to improvements in the quality of services to families raising children with disabilities and problem behavior, to an expansion of research on PBS with families, and to enhanced lives for children and families.

Acknowledgments

We thank the parents and professionals who contributed chapters and essays to the book. Their experiences, insights, and wisdom have helped to define current best practices in positive behavior support with families and to create an edited volume that comprehensively addresses the challenge of problem behavior in family contexts. We offer hearty thanks to all of the contributors for their patience during a long process of completing the book for publication.

We also thank several colleagues who offered advice and guidance during the original development of the structure and content of the book and who provided additional support during the process of its completion. These colleagues include George H.S. Singer at the University of California at Santa Barbara, Ann P. Turnbull at The University of Kansas, and Robert H. Horner at the University of Oregon. For assistance and advice related to editing specific chapters, we extend thanks to Bonnie Todis at Western Oregon University, Pat Mirenda at the University of British Columbia, Ursula Arceneaux Markey at Pyramid Parent Training Program in New Orleans, and Elizabeth Nakazawa at Nakazawa Communications in Portland, Oregon.

We thank Dr. Edward Carr and Sue Swenson for contributing forewords to the book. Dr. Carr, Leading Professor in the Department of Psychology at the State University of New York at Stony Brook, is a founding father of the applied science of positive behavior support. Over the past 30 years, he and his colleagues have published seminal research in the areas of applied behavior analysis and positive behavior support. Sue Swenson is the parent of a child with a physical disability. She also is Executive Director of the Joseph P. Kennedy, Jr. Foundation. Ms. Swenson has played an important role in bringing the voice and experience of families to policy makers and research scientists at the national level and has thus helped to influence the quality of services to people with disabilities and their families. We are honored to have their voices and perspectives grace the book.

We are grateful to the staff at Paul H. Brookes Publishing Co. for their patient and diligent assistance with the production of this book. We thank Jessica Allan, Jennifer Kinard, and Theresa Donnelly for their work as Acquisition Editors and also Nicole Schmidl and Lisa Rapisarda for their work, respectively, as Book Production Editor and Production Manager. We also thank Melissa Behm for her helpful assistance.

It also is important to acknowledge the numerous small but essential ways that our respective institutions of employment have helped to support the production of the book. Joseph M. Lucyshyn thanks the Department of Educational and Counselling Psychology, and Special Education of the Faculty of Education, University of British Columbia, and also his previous affiliation, the Teaching Research Division of Western Oregon University. Glen Dunlap thanks the Division of Applied Research and Educational Studies, Department of Child and Family Studies of the Louis de la Parte Florida Mental Health Institute, University of South Florida. Richard W. Albin thanks Educational and Community Supports at the College of Education, University of Oregon.

Joseph M. Lucyshyn also thanks his wife Yoko and his daughter Misa for their support and forbearance during the production of the book, as well as for the many lessons that they have taught about the gift of a child and family life.

To all families supporting children with disabilities and challenging behavior

*To all professionals who are committed to working with families as equal partners in the
implementation of positive behavior support in typical family contexts*

and

*To the late Charles D. Nixon, a gifted counseling psychologist, as well as a friend
and colleague, who dedicated his life to supporting families of children with disabilities
and problem behavior and who possessed in ample measure the self-discipline, wisdom,
and humility necessary to truly help families*

Section **I**

CHARACTERISTICS AND CONTEXT OF POSITIVE BEHAVIOR SUPPORT WITH FAMILIES

CHAPTER 1

Positive Behavior Support with Families

Joseph M. Lucyshyn, Robert H. Horner,
Glen Dunlap, Richard W. Albin, and Kathy R. Ben

This chapter describes a positive behavior support (PBS) approach to helping families of children and youth with developmental disabilities and problem behaviors. This population includes children and youth with the diagnosis of autism spectrum disorder, mental retardation, and other disabilities that are characterized by cognitive impairment (e.g., Down syndrome, Cornelia de Lange syndrome). Many features of the approach may also apply to families of children with other kinds of challenges, such as attention-deficit/hyperactivity disorder or acquired brain injury.

The chapter begins with a positive view of children and youth with disabilities and their families. Discussion follows about family diversity, the challenge of problem behaviors to family life, and parent perspectives on problem behavior and behavioral support. The chapter then defines the PBS approach; the goals of the approach with families; and its foundations in applied behavior analysis, values-based advocacy movements, and family ecology theory. In the heart of the chapter, 12 features that characterize the approach are described and illustrated. This is followed by a summary of family-based research in functional assessment and PBS that offers empirical evidence for the efficacy and acceptability of the approach.

A POSITIVE VIEW OF CHILDREN WITH DISABILITIES

PBS begins with a positive view of children and youth with disabilities living with their families. A traditional deficit model of family life emphasizes the caregiving burdens that children[1] with disabilities place on their families and the dysfunction that families experience as they strain to support the child within the family system (Gartner, Lipsky, & Turn-

---

[1]In this chapter, the terms *child* and *children* refer to both young children and older children (youth).

bull, 1991). However, a more positive view of children with disabilities and their families has emerged in the literature. Summers, Behr, and Turnbull (1989) described the positive contributions that children with disabilities make to their families. As reported by parents (Abbott & Meredith, 1986), these contributions may include increased happiness, strengthened family ties, expanded social networks, and expanded career development. Parents of children with disabilities who write about their experiences (Featherstone, 1980; Ferguson & Asch, 1989; Turnbull & Turnbull, 1985) consistently view their child with a disability first and foremost as a son or daughter. At the same time that they acknowledge caregiving challenges, these parents underscore the intrinsic worth of the child as a member of the family. As one mother wrote, "Jeff is neither my burden nor my chastisement, although his care requires more than I want to give at times. He is not an angel sent for my personal growth . . . He is a son" (Pieper, 1977, p. 88).

By holding a positive view of children with disabilities and problem behavior, practitioners of PBS also emphasize the intrinsic value and integrity of the child independent of problem behavior. This perspective has an important corollary: If families can solve problems of child behavior and learning in family contexts, then they can begin to overcome myriad caregiving challenges. In so doing, they can build a life with their child that is characterized by less stress and more happiness and success.

THE IMPORTANCE OF THE FAMILY

PBS also holds a positive view of the family. The family is profoundly important to the development, education, and behavioral support of a child with a disability (Erwin, 1996; Singer & Irvin, 1989). First, the family is a child's most valuable and durable resource and exerts the most powerful influence on the child's development (Dunlap & Fox, 1996). The culture and ecology of the family, including the child's neighborhood and school, provide the overall context for child development (Bronfenbrenner, 1986). Throughout early childhood intervention and public school education, the family is the primary source of continuity for the child or youth with a disability. This family involvement and influence may continue undiminished for older adolescents and young adults with more severe disabilities (Ferguson & Ferguson, 2000).

Second, parents are experts about their child with a disability and about their family's culture and ecology (Dunlap & Robbins, 1991; Turnbull & Turnbull, 2001). Parents possess in-depth knowledge about their son or daughter's strengths, needs, preferences, idiosyncrasies, and learning history. Through years of experience in raising the child, reading literature about children with disabilities, and interacting with professionals, parents typically acquire much information about supporting and accommodating the child in the context of family life (Dunlap, Robbins, & Darrow, 1994; Gallimore, Coots, Weisner, Garnier, & Guthrie, 1996). Parents also have unique knowledge about their family's culture and ecology, such as family goals and values, daily and weekly family routines, resources, social supports, and stressors (Lucyshyn & Albin, 1993).

Third, federal disability laws in the United States recognize parents as key decision makers in their child's development and education (Turnbull, Turnbull, Stowe, & Wilcox, 2000). For young children, the Individuals with Disabilities Education Act (IDEA) Amendments of 1991 (PL 102-119) mandated the provision of early intervention services in natural environments, including family homes. When developing individualized family service plans, the law requires professionals to address family concerns, priorities, and resources that are related to enhancing child development (Bailey & McWilliam, 1993;

Gallagher, 2000). For school-age children, the 1997 amendments to IDEA (PL 105-17) expanded and strengthened the role of parents as members of their child's education team. As a result, parents are included as members of evaluation teams that make decisions about their child's educational placement and the general provision of special education and related services. The law empowers parents and other team members to request a functional assessment and to design positive behavioral interventions for children and youth whose challenging behavior impedes their participation in a school's general curriculum (Turnbull, Wilcox, Stowe, & Turnbull, 2001). When professionals who offer behavioral support recognize, accept, and value the importance of the family, they are more likely to work with families as partners and colleagues. In addition, professionals and family members are more likely to participate in a reciprocal process of listening and learning about ways to best educate and support children or youth with disabilities and problem behaviors.

THE CHALLENGES THAT PROBLEM BEHAVIORS POSE IN FAMILY CONTEXTS

Problem behaviors are not unique to children with developmental disabilities. Before their language, cognitive, and social skills have developed fully, typically developing children engage in a variety of problem behaviors, including whining, crying, noncompliance, aggression, and tantrums (Dishion & Patterson, 1996). These behaviors, however, typically diminish to low, normative levels as the child develops communication skills, conceptual knowledge about the world, and greater self-sufficiency in the daily tasks and activities of family life (Carr et al., 1994).

In contrast, for many children with developmental disabilities, problem behaviors that begin in early childhood do not diminish naturally with age. An array of developmental and learning deficits—language, cognition, sensory, social, emotional, and/or motor—set the stage for the continuation and further development of problem behaviors into middle childhood and adolescence (Hunt, Johnson, Owen, Ormerod, & Babbitt, 1990; Walker, Colvin, & Ramsey, 1995).

Children with developmental disabilities exhibit a wide range of problem behaviors. Those that commonly concern parents are noncompliance; verbal and physical aggression; self-injury; and a variety of destructive (e.g., breaking, tearing), dangerous (e.g., running away, pica), and disruptive (e.g., screaming, hand flapping) behaviors (Hunt et al., 1990). In addition, a wide range of irritating, worrisome, or embarrassing behaviors (e.g., moaning, incessant demands, inappropriate comments) is a source of stress for families (Turnbull & Ruef, 1996). Basic developmental problems that are of concern include toileting, eating, and sleeping problems (Durand, 1998; Kedesdy & Budd, 1998; Wheeler, 1998). This array of problems has an enormous impact on the life of the child and the family as a whole. Thus, an inherently positive view of the child with a disability is necessarily tempered by an understanding of the challenges that families face when their child engages in problem behaviors (Koegel et al., 1992; Pahl & Quine, 1987).

Problem behaviors diminish a child's quality of life. He or she may be exposed to fewer natural learning opportunities, become isolated from family members and peers, or experience little involvement in community life. For example, a 5-year-old with autism who screams every time his parents prompt him in simple tasks experiences fewer and fewer parental teaching attempts. A teenager with multiple disabilities who engages in embarrassing, disruptive behavior whenever her parents take her into the community may no longer go with her family to a favorite store or restaurant.

Problem behaviors equally affect the family's quality of life. Family members' well-being may suffer, daily routines and activities may be disrupted, and community life may become almost nonexistent (Fox, Vaughn, Dunlap, & Bucy, 1997; Turnbull & Ruef, 1996). For instance, the mother of a boy with Cornelia de Lange syndrome may be consumed with worry, anticipating her son's next episode of aggression. The parents of a girl with autism may be exhausted because of their daughter's late night self-injurious episodes. When behavior problems pervade family life, the consequences to the family system can be negative and far reaching. Parents may experience stress-induced health or psychological problems, marriages may be strained, and/or the child may be placed out of the home (Anastopoulos, Guevremont, Shelton, & DuPaul, 1992; Blacher, 1994). Professionals who provide behavioral support to families need to understand how problem behaviors affect the child and family's life. By doing so, interventionists are more likely to reduce problem behavior *and* improve the quality of life of the child and family.

FAMILY DIVERSITY

Families of children with disabilities and problem behaviors vary in ethnic and cultural background, family composition, socioeconomic status, age, and parenting experience and knowledge (Kalyanpur & Harry, 1999; Lynch & Hanson, 1998). Their communities also vary widely in the quality of educational services, family support resources, neighborhood safety, and economic opportunity. In addition, demographic changes—including an increase in dual-income families, an increase in single-parent families, and a decrease in social support from extended family members—have made parenting, particularly parenting children with disabilities, more difficult (Singer, 1996).

These differences may affect a family's ability to adapt successfully to a child with a disability who engages in problem behavior. A two-parent family that lives in a middle-class neighborhood with excellent school services and family support resources may find it easier to raise a child with a disability than a single mother who has a low income and lives in an underserved community (Markey, 2000). Professionals who provide behavioral support to families need to understand the implications of this diversity. Doing so increases the likelihood that assessment and intervention activities will be culturally sensitive and feasible within the family's ecology (Harry, Kalyanpur, & Day, 1999).

FAMILY PERSPECTIVES ON PROBLEM BEHAVIOR AND BEHAVIORAL SUPPORT

In qualitative studies with 17 families of children with disabilities and problem behavior, Turnbull and Ruef (1996, 1997) illuminated family experiences and perspectives related to problem behaviors and behavioral support. This research provided invaluable insights into the difficulties that families experience in addressing problem behavior, supporting an inclusive lifestyle, and receiving effective behavioral support services. It also clarified the qualities of behavioral support and parent–professional interaction that parents find most helpful or desire to receive.

In their synthesis of qualitative themes, Turnbull and Ruef (1996) indicated that families want 1) assessments that help them better understand the reasons for their child's problem behavior, 2) assistance in structuring family routines, 3) strategies to enhance parent–child communication, and 4) strategies to reduce stress. In a companion analysis with the same families, Turnbull and Ruef (1997) offered additional insights into lifestyle issues and concerns. Significant themes included the following:

1. Parents having to exclusively take the roles of initiator, catalyst, and choreographer of lifestyle changes and supports for their child with a disability

2. Families wanting to work in collaboration with professionals and community members to address the challenges of creating an inclusive lifestyle for their children

3. Families experiencing the task of building friendships across the life span as challenging but important

Based on these findings, Turnbull and Ruef reflected that families want and need "a custom-designed, multi-component, comprehensive system of supports and services" that addresses, in a collaborative and practical fashion, the full range of problem behaviors and lifestyle needs of their child with problem behavior (1996, p. 290). In terms of professional assistance, they concluded that "families need a reliable alliance with dependable, trusted, and nonjudgmental helpers who provide assistance in the home and community" and are available to offer support across the entire day, week, and life cycle of the family (p. 291).

As noted by Turnbull and Ruef (1996), these family perspectives and needs are compatible with a PBS approach. Consequently, they have served to both validate and inform the development and refinement of the approach with families. Thus, embedded within PBS are values, guidelines, procedures, and activities that are informed by science in concert with the voice and experience of families raising a child with a disability and problem behavior.

POSITIVE BEHAVIOR SUPPORT DEFINED

Positive behavior support is a collaborative, assessment-based approach to developing effective, individualized interventions for people with problem behavior. Behavior support plans emphasize the use of proactive, educative, and reinforcement-based strategies to achieve meaningful and durable behavior and lifestyle outcomes (Horner, Albin, Sprague, & Todd, 2000; Koegel, Koegel, & Dunlap, 1996). The approach eschews the use of aversive consequences that deliver physical pain or compromise an individual's dignity (Carr, Robinson, & Palumbo, 1990; Luiselli & Cameron, 1998; Scotti & Meyer, 1999). At its core, PBS integrates valued outcomes, behavioral science, empirically validated practices, and systems change (Sugai et al., 2000). A brief summary of these core features is provided in Table 1.1.

With families, PBS takes into consideration family perspectives and family systems when defining meaningful and durable outcomes, and when deigning behavior support plans (Dunlap, Newton, Fox, Benito, & Vaughn, in press; Lucyshyn, Albin, & Nixon, 1997; Vaughn, Clarke, & Dunlap, 1997). Thus, the approach is both child and family centered. Practitioners of PBS work in partnership with families to develop a vision of the child's inclusion in family and community life and to develop PBS plans that are a good fit with the cultural and ecological features of the child's family and community (Albin, Lucyshyn, Horner, & Flannery, 1996; Moes & Frea, 2000; Vaughn, Dunlap, Fox, Clarke, & Bucy, 1997). The approach also assumes the need for parent education and support so that families are empowered to implement behavior support strategies with fidelity, to promote durable improvements in behavior and in child and family lifestyle, and to solve new or recurring behavior problems with little to no professional assistance (Dunlap et al., 2000).

PBS with families has been shaped by behavioral and family researchers, education and family support professionals, and family members who have informed and evaluated the ap-

Table 1.1.   Core features of positive behavior support (PBS)

Valued outcomes	PBS is concerned about both reductions in problem behavior and lifestyle change. Change in problem behavior without change in learning, living, working, and leisure outcomes is insufficient. A focus on behavioral outcomes emphasizes that PBS is more concerned with the effects of intervention than with reliance on a particular technique or method. A focus on valued outcomes emphasizes that the goals of PBS are driven by people in the support context (e.g., family, child, support staff) rather than by the expert or by an external system.
Science of human behavior	In PBS, behavioral interventions are based on a functional assessment of problem behavior (O'Neill et al., 1997). Within this process, the fundamental principles of behavior are the cornerstone that guides intervention (Bijou & Baer, 1978; Wolery, Bailey, & Sugai, 1988). The big message here is that PBS technology is not medically driven (i.e., diagnosis driven) but function driven.
Empirically validated practices	PBS emphasizes the use of empirically validated intervention procedures (Repp & Horner, 1999). Positive behavior support plans are comprehensive, integrating multiple strategies. Key among these are ecological design, antecedent modification, instruction, consequences that eliminate rewards for problem behavior, and consequences that enhance rewards for appropriate behavior.
Systems change	PBS recognizes that effective practices do not endure if they are implemented outside the context of supportive and nurturing systems. This is true whether interventions are being used in the school, in the community, or in a family's home. It is as important to make sure that there is sufficient time, resources, and expertise as it is to make sure that effective practices are selected.

proach since the early 1990s. PBS also is a dynamic approach that can be expected to evolve, expand, and improve as new research-based knowledge is gained, as new and more efficient service delivery methods are developed, and as a wider range of children and families are introduced to the approach (Hieneman & Dunlap, 2001; Koegel, Koegel, & McNerney, 2001; Ruef, Turnbull, Turnbull, & Poston, 1999; Sailor et al., 1999; Vaughn, Fox, & Dunlap, 2000).

GOALS OF THE APPROACH

The broad goals of PBS are to help parents and other family members achieve meaningful and durable improvements in the child's behavior and lifestyle and in the quality of family life as a whole (Fox, Dunlap, & Philbrick, 1997; Lucyshyn & Albin, 1993). Specific goals are defined in partnership with families and reflect their preferences and vision. Goals range from modest to ambitious, depending on the extent of the child's problem behaviors, the time and resources that are available to the family and the interventionist, the level of interest and energy of family members, and the extent to which additional family-centered supports may be needed.

Child-centered goals include durable reductions in problem behavior across the contexts of family life, promotion of the child's health and safety, and improvements in functional skills such as communication and daily living skills. Lifestyle goals for the child or youth include successful participation in valued daily and weekly routines and activities in the home and community (e.g., getting ready for school in the morning, eating dinner together as a family, joining a parent on a shopping trip), the development of friendships with typical peers, and successful inclusion in the child's neighborhood school. Core family-centered goals are empowering parents and other family members to effectively implement behavioral supports, to build valued family routines and activities in the home and community, and to use PBS to solve new or recurring problems.

For many families, additional family-centered goals may be needed (Lutzker & Campbell, 1994; Singer & Powers, 1993). Family members who are exhausted from caregiving may need respite care services. A mother who is experiencing debilitating worry or stress-induced migraine headaches may benefit from learning stress-reduction techniques. Parents in underserved communities may be taught advocacy skills that can help them improve their child's education or gain access to family support services. Parents whose marriages are strained may benefit from marital counseling. In each of these examples, family-centered goals and interventions focus on teaching individual family members new skills, extending resources and social supports, and strengthening the family system. The aim is to help parents and other family members become more capable of supporting the child and contributing to a balanced, meaningful, and fulfilling life at home and in the community.

FOUNDATIONS OF THE APPROACH

PBS with families has developed from four broad foundations: 1) applied behavior analysis (Baer, Wolf, & Risley, 1987; Horner, 1999), 2) behavioral family intervention (Lutzker & Campbell, 1994; Sanders, 1996; Webster-Stratton, 1994), 3) community living and family support advocacy movements (Turnbull & Turnbull, 2001; Singer, Powers, & Olson, 1996), and 4) ecological/family systems theories about child development and family life (Gallimore, Weisner, Kaufman, & Bernheimer, 1989; Minuchin, 1974). These foundations are discussed next.

Applied Behavior Analysis

The technology of PBS is firmly grounded in and inextricably linked to applied behavior analysis, the science of behavior change (Baer et al., 1987). PBS is a natural development in the evolution of applied behavior analysis toward a science that 1) helps consumers (e.g., families, educators, psychologists) understand the full range of variables that influence problem behavior and adaptive behavior; 2) provides consumers with a technology that is effective and acceptable in natural contexts; and 3) promotes meaningful and durable changes in the behavior and lives of individuals with disabilities and in the lives of parents, educators, and others who support them (Carr, 1997; Koegel et al., 1996; Scotti & Meyer, 1999).

Three developments in applied behavior analysis have informed the approach. First, since the 1980s, functional assessment has reemerged as an essential tool for understanding problem behavior and for designing effective interventions (Horner & Carr, 1997; Iwata, Dorsey, Slifer, & Bauman, 1982/1994; O'Neill et al., 1997). Second, the field of applied behavior analysis has expanded its empirical examination of the variables that influence behavior. In addition to the influence of consequences on human behavior, behavior analysts have begun to more fully examine the influences of ecological variables (i.e., setting events) and immediate antecedent events on behavior (Horner, Vaughn, Day & Ard,

1996; Luiselli & Cameron, 1998; Smith & Iwata, 1997). This has led to the empirical development of a wide range of antecedent-based interventions such as enhancing activity patterns, offering choices, and using visual schedules to enhance predictability (Repp & Horner, 1999; Scotti & Meyer, 1999). Third, behavior analysts have grown concerned about the gap between the technology of applied behavior analysis and its actual use by consumers in typical home, school, and community settings (Dunlap & Kern, 1997; Johnston, 1991). To bridge this gap between research and practice, there has been an increasing emphasis on 1) implementing research in natural settings with typical consumers, 2) developing effective and socially valid interventions, 3) identifying contextual variables and outcomes that affect the "survivability" of the technology in natural settings, and 4) forming collaborative research partnerships with families and other consumers of behavioral technology (Baer et al., 1987; Fawcett, 1991; Lucyshyn et al., 1997; Markey, 2000; Schwartz & Baer, 1991; Turnbull, Friesen, & Ramirez, 1998; Vaughn, Dunlap, et al., 1997).

Behavioral Family Intervention

The behavioral family intervention literature makes four contributions to the practice of PBS with families. First, behavioral family interventionists are encouraged to develop a "non-blaming, supportive, reciprocal relationship" with parents and other family members (Webster-Stratton & Herbert, 1993, p. 410). Such a collaborative relationship is viewed as essential for building trust and commitment, for teaching parents more effective parenting practices, and for promoting the generalized use of behavioral interventions (Sanders & Dadds, 1993; Webster-Stratton, 1998). Second, interventionists recognize the need for family-focused supports when contextual factors such as social isolation, marital discord, or daily stressors impede the ability of parents to effectively support their child (Patterson, Reid, & Dishion, 1992; Singer, Irvine, & Irvin, 1989). Potential family-focused supports include advocacy, respite care, stress-reduction training, and marital counseling (Lutzker & Campbell, 1994; Singer & Irvin, 1991). Third, behavioral parent training research offers empirically validated strategies for teaching family members to implement interventions, such as written instruction, behavioral rehearsal, manual- or video-based curricula, self-evaluation checklists, and modeling or coaching in natural family settings (Koegel, Glahn, & Nieminen, 1978; O'Dell, 1985; Sanders & Dadds, 1993; Webster-Stratton, 1994). Fourth, behavioral parent training research indicates that parents of children with developmental disabilities are more likely to promote positive outcomes when training and support activities are individualized, practical, and action oriented (Graziano & Diament, 1992).

Community Living and Family Support Movements

The child- and family-centered values that are embedded in PBS are based in the community living movement of the 1960s, 1970s, and 1980s (Taylor, Biklen, & Knoll, 1987; Wolfensberger, 1972) and the family support movement of the 1980s and 1990s (Moroney, 1986; Singer et al., 1996) The community living movement, through changes in federal law and public policy, strengthened the rights of people with developmental disabilities to be raised at home with their families, to be educated in their neighborhood schools, and to experience the full range of benefits of citizenship and community life. The family support movement has helped to strengthen and empower families in their traditional caregiving roles (Singer & Powers, 1993). The movement has moved social policy away from a traditional model of family services that emphasized professional dominance and family pathology toward a model of family support that is family driven and strengths based (Allen & Petr, 1996; Dunst, Trivette, & Deal, 1994). In this model, families define their aspirations and needs, professionals work in partnership with families, and principles of empowerment guide help-giving behavior (Rappaport, 1987; Salisbury & Dunst, 1997).

Ecological/Family Theories

For many families, applied behavioral science and family-centered values may not be sufficient conditions for promoting meaningful and durable behavior and lifestyle changes for a child with a disability. Knowledge about the family system or ecology may be necessary as well (Egel & Powers, 1989). For this reason, PBS with families incorporates practical, action-oriented knowledge from three influential ecological theories of the family: 1) family systems theory, 2) family stress and adaptation theory, and 3) ecocultural theory.

Family Systems Theory   Family systems theory (Minuchin, 1974; Turnbull & Turnbull, 2000b) recognizes that a child with a disability exists within a larger family system with the following elements: family structure, family interaction patterns, family functions, and family life cycle. Efforts to change problem behavior and parenting practices without considering the family system can lead to negative side effects for other family members and to unacceptable or unsustainable interventions (Harris, 1982). In contrast, knowledge about the family system can aid in the selection of child- and family-focused interventions that improve family structure and functioning, strengthen relationships within the family (e.g., relationships between spouses, siblings, and other relatives), and address changing needs at different points in the life cycle (Lutzker & Campbell, 1994; Turnbull, Summers, & Brotherson, 1986).

Family Stress and Adaptation Theory   Family stress and adaptation theory (McCubbin & Patterson, 1983; Singer & Irvin, 1991) provides a useful framework for understanding how families of children with disabilities adapt to caregiving stress. The theory offers a positive view of the ability of families to adapt to stressors such as a child's behavior problems, chronic caregiving demands, and social isolation. Positive coping strategies that are used by families include focusing on child strengths, working together more closely as a family, and remaining thankful for the many gifts of life (Bristol, 1984; Singer & Powers, 1993). Understanding the stressors that a family is experiencing, validating positive adaptations, and helping families identify additional coping strategies can enhance a family's ability to adapt successfully to the challenges of raising a child or youth with a disability and problem behaviors.

Ecocultural Theory   Ecocultural theory (Gallimore, Coots, Weisner, Garnier, & Guthrie, 1996; Gallimore et al., 1989) is derived from cross-cultural ethnographic studies of family life (Whiting & Edwards, 1988). It provides a useful framework for understanding ecological influences on child development within the family. The theory supposes that families socially construct child activity settings to accommodate the needs of children within the constraints and opportunities of the family's environment. Parents proactively strive to construct activity settings that are meaningful to the family, congruent with child characteristics, and sustainable over time. The activity setting is viewed as a primary unit of analysis and intervention. When interventions are carefully embedded within activity settings, they are more likely to be family centered, culturally sensitive, and sustainable (Bernheimer & Keough, 1995).

Marrying Science and Values

PBS with families builds on a long history of behavioral and family research, but it is guided by human values and the real-life problems that confront families raising children and youth with disabilities and problem behaviors. In essence, the approach marries science and values. The aim of this union is to make the technology of PBS highly accessible and useful to families. A second aim is to ensure that PBS does not perpetuate a history of professional dominance over families (Darling, 1988); instead, it is to serve parent goals and aspirations for the child and family and to empower family members with the confidence and skills that are necessary to achieve these goals (Rappaport, 1987; Turnbull & Turnbull, 2001; Webster-Stratton, 1998).

TWELVE KEY FEATURES OF POSITIVE BEHAVIOR SUPPORT WITH FAMILIES

PBS with families is characterized by 12 key features that compose the values, assumptions, and activities of the approach. These are summarized in Table 1.2 and described in the following subsections.

1. Collaborative Partnerships

Practitioners of PBS are committed to developing collaborative partnerships with family members and other key stakeholders in the support process (e.g., educators, psychologists, related services providers, family advocates) (Dunlap & Fox, 1999; Horner et al., 2000; Lucyshyn & Albin, 1993; Vaughn, Dunlap, et al., 1997). Within this book, *collaborative partnership with families* is defined as the establishment of a truly respectful, trusting, caring, and reciprocal relationship in which interventionists and family members believe in each other's ability to make important contributions to the support process; share their knowledge and expertise; and mutually influence the selection of goals, the design of behavior support plans, and the quality of family–practitioner interactions. In the finest unfolding of this relationship, the traditional expert–client dichotomy is transformed into an equal partnership in which family members and practitioners offer complementary expertise, solve problems together, and acknowledge each other's contributions to meaningful behavioral and lifestyle outcomes (Singh, 1995; Turnbull & Turnbull, 2001).

Necessity of Partnership with Families   The development of collaborative partnerships with families reflects egalitarian values but also practical necessity (Hieneman & Dunlap, 1999; Webster-Stratton, 1998). The superordinate goal of promoting meaningful and durable behavior and lifestyle changes for the child or youth with a disability, and for the family as a whole, is more likely to be achieved within the context of a truly collaborative partnership. During assessment, in-depth knowledge about the child and family, which is necessary to develop an effective and contextually appropriate support plan, is more likely to be acquired if the interventionist listens to family members. During the de-

Table 1.2. Twelve key features of positive behavior support with families

1. Build collaborative partnerships with families and other professionals who serve the child or youth with a disability.

2. Adhere to family-centered principles and practices throughout assessment, support plan development, and implementation support activities.

3. Help families identify and achieve meaningful lifestyle outcomes for their child with a disability and the family as a whole.

4. Recognize that problem behaviors are primarily problems of learning.

5. Understand that communication is the foundation of positive behavior.

6. Conduct functional assessments to understand the functions of problem behavior and the variables that influence behavior and to improve the effectiveness and efficiency of behavior support plans.

7. Develop individualized, multicomponent support plans that help families create effective family contexts in which problem behaviors are irrelevant, ineffective, and inefficient at achieving their purpose.

8. Ensure that positive behavior support plans are a good contextual fit with family life.

9. Utilize the family activity setting as a unit of analysis and intervention that can help families embed interventions into family life.

10. Provide implementation support that is tailored to family needs and preferences.

11. Engage in a process of continuous evaluation of child and family outcomes.

12. Offer support to families, professionals, and other members of a support team in a spirit of sincerity and humility.

sign of a behavior support plan, the reciprocity that is inherent in an equal partnership greatly facilitates the mutual exchange of ideas, suggestions, and concerns. During implementation support, the partnership makes it easier for parents to adopt new parenting practices and for interventionists to modify support strategies that prove to be unacceptable or ineffective.

The development of a collaborative partnership with families begins with assessment activities and continues throughout the design of a support plan and the provision of implementation support. During assessment interviews, practitioners balance the formal aspects of the information-gathering process (e.g., asking about behaviors of concern, identifying events that are associated with problem behavior) with a conversational style that reflects nonhierarchical patterns of discourse (e.g., asking open-ended questions, listening to stories about child strengths or problem behavior, validating the expression of emotions) (Bernheimer & Keough, 1995; Singer & Powers, 1993; Turnbull & Turnbull, 1991). Practitioners also moderate the use of professional jargon by substituting scientific language with more common usage and by defining key terms (e.g., *antecedent stimuli* = *triggers*). Interviews usually take place in the family's home unless an alternative place is more convenient for the family.

During plan development, behavior support strategies are designed to fit well with family routines and activities in the home and community. To do so, families help determine the routines or problematic contexts that they wish to improve and define the features of successful contexts (Clarke, Dunlap, & Vaughn, 1999; Lucyshyn et al., 1997; Vaughn, Clarke, & Dunlap, 1997). The interventionist also cautions parents to only choose behavior support strategies that from their point of view will be acceptable, feasible, and effective in family contexts. This dialogue helps family members see the interventionist as a reliable ally who is committed to improving the child's behavior and the family's life in ways that are meaningful to the family (Singer & Powers, 1993; Turnbull & Ruef, 1996). During implementation support, the partnership is maintained and further strengthened by shared control over the choice of implementation support activities (e.g., modeling, role-playing, engaging in telephone consultation), by the interventionist's support of parent efforts to modify strategies to better fit family contexts, and by the interventionist's effort to empower parents to solve problems without professional assistance. This may involve, for example, teaching parents to conduct functional assessments and to develop or adapt behavioral supports for family contexts that continue to be problematic (Lucyshyn & Kayser, 1998; Mullen & Frea, 1995; Vaughn, Fox, & Dunlap, 2000).

Importance of Partnership with Professionals   Practitioners of PBS also develop collaborative partnerships with educators and other professionals who are members of the child or youth's education team. Because PBS emphasizes comprehensive lifestyle improvement, practitioners of PBS are committed to including children and youth with disabilities in their neighborhood schools (Sailor, Gee, & Karasoff, 2000; Weigle, 1997). The neighborhood school is viewed as the best possible educational setting because of the rich opportunities that it offers for meaningful learning activities, language and social development, friendships, and lifelong community membership (Goetz, Anderson, & Laten, 1989; Harrower, 1999).

As with families, the formation of partnerships with members of the child or youth's educational support team at school is a necessity if the broad lifestyle outcomes of PBS are to be achieved. Students with developmental disabilities and problem behaviors often have learning or developmental problems that cut across different disciplines and areas of expertise. In addition to a cognitive disability, a student may have a visual or hearing impairment, may have a need for augmentative and alternative communication (AAC), or may have physical disabilities that require the services of a physical therapist or an occupational therapist. Typically, a behavioral consultant does not possess the interdisciplinary knowledge necessary to design a behavior support plan that addresses all of the challenges that a student may face. The expertise of related services professionals may also be needed. In addition, educators who work directly with the child or youth in the school, such as the child's teacher or a teaching assistant, commonly possess insights about positive strategies that help the child or youth succeed in the classroom. Incorporating these ideas into a behavior support plan can increase the likelihood that the plan will be acceptable and feasible to school personnel as well as to family members. Honoring the expertise and insights of school-based team members may also contribute to a sense of shared ownership and commitment as the support plan is implemented across home and school settings.

Supporting Home–School Collaboration   Practitioners of PBS also are committed to supporting and facilitating home–school collaboration. These efforts are approached with respectful attention to the structural impediments in schools that may hinder truly collaborative partnerships. These impediments may include a traditional expert–client view and hierarchical organizational processes that do not lend themselves to collaborative decision making. Although IDEA has strengthened the role of parents in their child's education and has created a presumption in favor of functional assessment and PBS in schools (Turnbull et al., 2001), these impediments may interfere with the full implementation of new roles and activities.

Within this context, practitioners of PBS do several things to support and facilitate home–school collaboration. First, practitioners communicate respect to both parents and educators, recognizing the best intentions of each stakeholder to meet the educational needs of children in the midst of the constraints and opportunities present in a school or community. Second, practitioners work within the natural decision-making structures that are already in place in schools. For example, decisions about functional assessment activities and the design of behavioral supports may be made during individualized education program (IEP) meetings with members of the child or youth's interdisciplinary team. Practitioners also 1) work closely with school principals to coordinate meetings, 2) serve as facilitators of behavior support plan development meetings, and 3) represent the interests and preferences of educators as well as those of families. Throughout the process, practitioners are mindful to nurture positive and constructive views of parents and educators toward each other. For example, the interventionist may inform the teacher of a father's strengths or inform a mother of the creative ways in which the teacher supports her child. These efforts are aimed at increasing mutual understanding and amity, which are at the heart of all successful home–school collaborations.

If a school resists including parents as decision-makers in a process of PBS, then the interventionist may play a stronger advocacy role on behalf of the family (Morin, 2001; Turnbull, 1999). Depending on the level of resistance, this may involve encouraging parents to advocate for their rights under the law, discussing with administrators and educators the new roles of parents as defined by law, providing information to schools about functional assessment and PBS, or serving as a parent advocate during a mediation process.

2. Family-Centered Principles and Practices

Practitioners of PBS adhere to family-centered principles and practices in the delivery of support services to families. As defined by Allen and Petr, "Family-centered service delivery, across disciplines and settings, views the family as the unit of attention. This model organizes assistance in a collaborative fashion and in accordance with each individual family's wishes, strengths, and needs" (1996, p. 64). Two family-centered practices have been described previously: 1) building family–professional partnerships that are characterized by respect and equality and 2) including families as key decision makers about child and family goals for behavioral support and intervention. Four additional family-centered practices are described next.

Build on Family Strengths and Capabilities   During initial assessment activities, interventionists encourage family members to identify family strengths and positive adaptations to their child's disability. These insights may then be incorporated into the development and implementation of a behavior support plan. For example, a parent with excellent advocacy skills may be encouraged to take a lead role in building a collaborative partnership with the teacher and principal at her son's school. During a functional assessment interview, family members share their knowledge and insights about problem behavior and strategies or adaptations that appear to help (e.g., offering choices, using visual systems, positively redirecting problem behavior). When these insights are consistent with functional assessment information and a positive approach, they are incorporated into a child's behavior support plan and the family's contribution is acknowledged.

Employ Competency-Enhancing and Empowering Practices   Practitioners of PBS employ several practices that enhance a family's self-confidence in supporting a child with a disability and empower parents to understand and solve problems. First, as parents and other family members begin to use behavioral supports effectively, the interventionist encourages them to attribute improvements in behavior to their own efforts (Dunst et al., 1994). The interventionist does so because this recognition is essential if parents are to understand and solve problems in the future. Second, the interventionist also works to "give away" the knowledge of PBS (Riley, 1997) by teaching parents how to assess problem behaviors and develop effective behavioral supports. This may involve showing a family how to adapt a successful support plan for use in a new family context or coaching parents in how to conduct a functional assessment and build a behavior support plan for an unsolved, problematic family context. Rather than "train and hope" that parents generalize the use of interventions to new family settings (Stokes & Baer, 1977), the interventionist directly coaches family members in how to understand and solve new or recurring problems on their own (Carr, Levin, et al., 1999; Lucyshyn et al., 1997; Vaughn et al., 2000). Third, practitioners also support parents in becoming effective advocates for their child with a disability. This may include informing parents about their rights under the law, coaching parents in how to prepare for meetings with professionals, and offering tips on how to contribute to a mutually beneficial partnership with their child's teacher.

Mobilize Informal and Formal Supports and Resources   Family-centered interventionists seek to incorporate into behavioral support informal and formal supports and resources that can help sustain a family's implementation of PBS. Through a person-centered planning process or a family ecology assessment, social supports and resources are identified and incorporated into a support plan (Albin et al., 1996; Kincaid, 1996). Informal supports and resources may include assistance from siblings and grandparents in the implementation of behavioral supports or mentoring from a parent who has experience using PBS (Lucyshyn & Kayser, 1998). Formal supports and resources may include AAC strategies from a speech-language pathologist or respite care services from a local nonprofit organization.

Provide Behavioral Support in a Flexible and Responsive Manner   Family-centered interventionists organize behavioral support activities flexibly and responsively, based on family preferences and changes in family circumstances (Salisbury & Dunst, 1997). During a process of PBS, interventionists typically visit a family's home when it is convenient for the family. If a parent expresses discomfort with an otherwise effective behavioral support strategy (e.g., the use of positive contingencies), then the interventionist engages in a dialogue that results in one of three outcomes: 1) regaining parental informed consent for the use of the intervention, 2) adjusting the strategy in a way that is more acceptable or feasible for the family, or 3) replacing the intervention with one that is both effective and acceptable to the family. Overall, when interventionists adhere to family-centered principles and practices, families are more likely to trust them, commit to a process of PBS, and sustain the use of behavioral supports over a long period of time.

3. Meaningful Lifestyle Outcomes

Lifestyle of the Child or Youth   For many children and youth with developmental disabilities, problem behaviors develop in the context of a lifestyle that lacks the qualities of life typically developing children and youth take for granted. These qualities include valued friendships with peers at school and in the community, active participation in a variety of enjoyable family and community activities, and a developmentally appropriate level of choice and control in one's life. When these qualities of life are absent in a child or youth's experience, problem behaviors tend to flourish (Risley, 1996). For this reason, a central aim of PBS with families is to help parents create a richer and more meaningful lifestyle for their child with a disability (Koegel et al., 1996; Turnbull & Turnbull, 2000a). The term *meaningful lifestyle outcomes* is defined as improvements in family and peer relationships, home and community activity patterns, and/or choice and self-determination that are consistent with the preferences and resources of family members and other key stakeholders in the child's support system. Within this definition, meaningful lifestyle changes may range from modest to extensive, depending on the child, family, and community.

Family Quality of Life   A focus on meaningful outcomes also takes into consideration the quality of the family's life. Problem behaviors constrain not only the lives of children but also the lives of their families (Fox, Vaughn, et al., 1997; Koegel et al., 1992). For example, a mother of a boy with multiple disabilities may be homebound, a father may be estranged from his teenage daughter with a mild cognitive disability, or a younger brother may feel afraid to come home after school because of aggression toward him by an older brother with autism. Improvements in the child or youth's lifestyle should include reciprocal improvements in the lives of other family members. As a result of PBS, a family should be able to enjoy a weekend trip together to a favorite park. A father and his teenage daughter should be able to engage in activities that are mutually enjoyable and that strengthen their relationship. A younger brother should be able to feel safe in his own home in the presence of his older brother with a disability.

Person-Centered Planning   The importance of promoting meaningful lifestyle outcomes for the child and family has led to incorporating person-centered planning methods in PBS (Fox, Philbrick, & Dunlap, 1997; Harrower, Fox, Dunlap, & Kincaid, 1999). *Person-centered planning* is a collaborative approach to developing a vision of an inclusive lifestyle for a person with a disability and to developing an action plan to achieve the vision. Person-centered planning processes (e.g., Vandercook, York, & Forrest, 1989; Pearpoint, O'Brien, & Forrest, 1992) offer several benefits to a process of PBS. Assessment activities that are embedded in person-centered planning are strengths based and child centered, so participants are more likely to identify child strengths and abilities as well as lifestyle goals that are meaningful to the child and family. The informal and egalitarian nature of the process helps to establish collaborative partnerships between family members and professionals. Follow-up meetings facilitate the development of a support network for the child and family. Operating in concert with a PBS plan, the person-centered plan offers a vision of an inclusive lifestyle and an action plan for pursuing it. The behavior support plan provides the strategies and tools necessary to help the family and team achieve the vision.

4. Functional Assessment

Functional assessment is the process of identifying the events that reliably predict and maintain problem behaviors (O'Neill et al., 1997). Functional assessment places problem behavior in environmental contexts and facilitates identification of the changes in these contexts that may relate to behavioral improvement. The overriding purpose of functional assessment is to improve the effectiveness and efficiency of behavior support plans (Carr et al., 1994; Repp & Horner, 1999). A large body of empirical literature has clearly established that problem behaviors serve a purpose for people with disabilities (Carr & Durand, 1985; Derby et al., 1994; Iwata et al., 1982/1994). These functions fall into four broad categories: 1) avoid or escape nonpreferred or aversive demands, tasks, or people; 2) obtain social attention; 3) gain access to a preferred item, activity, or situation; and 4) obtain self-stimulation or automatic reinforcement (O'Neill, et al., 1997; Repp & Horner, 1999). In addition, a growing body of intervention research offers substantial evidence that functional assessment is invaluable for developing effective behavior support plans for children and youth with disabilities across a wide range of home, school, and community contexts (Carr, Levin, et al., 1999; Dunlap, Kern-Dunlap, Clarke, & Robbins, 1991; Vaughn, Clarke, & Dunlap, 1997; Wacker, Cooper, Peck, Derby, & Berg, 1999).

During a functional assessment, interventionists and family members learn the meaning of problem behavior from the child's point of view. For example, when it is time to wake up and get ready for school, a 7-year-old with autism may scream and kick his father to escape the aversive task of getting out of a bed. While her mother is preparing lunch, a 16-year-old girl with multiple disabilities may knock over potted plants in the living room to get her mother's attention. At the grocery store, a 12-year-old boy with a mild cognitive disability may engage in verbal threats to get his grandmother to buy him a preferred item.

In addition to revealing the purpose of problem behavior, a good functional assessment offers insights into the lifestyle or ecological issues that may contribute to problem behavior, identifies child strengths and preferences, and brings to light family knowledge about effective interventions. Furthermore, if during the assessment a parent expresses shame or guilt about the occurrence of problem behavior, the interventionist responds in a manner that helps to normalize the experience for the family (Hawkins, Singer, & Nixon, 1993). When a functional assessment is conducted in such a collaborative and respectful manner, family members typically find it to be helpful. Functional assessment typically involves five steps:

1. Conducting a functional assessment interview with family members at home, school, or another location that is convenient for the family

2. Identifying home and community contexts, routines, or activities in which problem behavior occurs

3. Developing summary hypothesis statements (also referred to as *summary statements*) about the functions of problem behavior and the variables that influence problem behavior

4. Completing functional assessment observations in at least one or two problematic family contexts (e.g., morning routine, grocery shopping) to confirm hypotheses

5. Developing a competing behavior pathways diagram for each function of problem behavior that identifies a) desired behavior and b) alternative replacement behavior (Marshall & Mirenda, in press; O'Neill et al., 1997)

A good functional assessment leads to a consensus about the functions of problem behavior that is essential to the design of a technically sound behavior support plan. Products include: 1) operational definitions of the behaviors of concern, 2) a description of ecological or lifestyle factors (i.e., setting events) that set the stage for problem behavior or that promote desirable behavior, 3) a description of antecedent stimuli that predict or trigger problem behavior or that promote desirable behavior, 4) a description of the consequences that maintain problem behavior, 5) direct observation data that support the link between behavior problems and their controlling antecedents and consequences, and 6) summary hypothesis statement(s) and competing behavior pathway diagram(s) that guide the design of interventions (Horner et al., 2000).

Consider the previous example of the 7-year-old boy with autism who disliked having to get out of bed in the morning. The functional assessment interview and observations would show that 1) the behaviors of concern are screaming and aggression, 2) the child's continued sleepiness 5–10 minutes after being awakened is a setting event that decreases the value of getting up and ready for school, 3) parental demands and physical prompts are triggers for problem behavior, and 4) the function of the problem behavior is to escape getting out of bed and completing the morning routine (e.g., using the bathroom, getting dressed). The desired behavior for the routine is for the child to cooperate in getting up and completing the morning routine. An alternative replacement behavior that is acceptable to the family is for the child to request a 5–10 minute delay in getting out of bed and starting the routine. The summary statement/competing behavior pathways diagram for this problematic family context is presented in Figure 1.1.

These functional assessment results provide the foundation for the development of a behavior support plan. Through a collaborative dialogue between family members and the interventionist, behavioral supports are generated that are 1) logically linked to each feature of the problem, as identified in the functional assessment; 2) technically sound (i.e., consistent with established principles of behavior change); 3) likely to render problem behaviors "irrelevant, ineffective, and inefficient at acheiving their purpose"; and 4) acceptable and feasible to the family (Horner et al., 2000; O'Neill et al., 1997, p. 66).

5. Problem Behaviors as Problems of Learning

Practitioners of PBS view problem behaviors as problems of learning. Although it is recognized that developmental disabilities have a biological basis and that pharmacological or nutritional interventions can help moderate problem behavior for some individuals

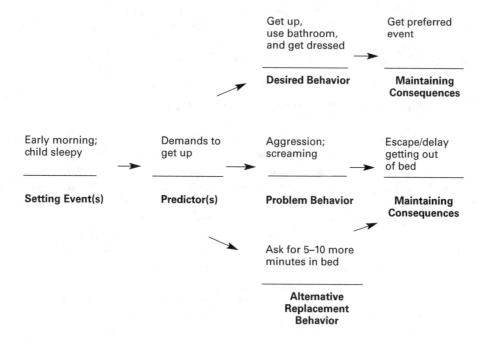

Figure 1.1.   Summary statement and competing behavior pathways diagram for problem behaviors during morning routine. (From *Functional Assessment and Program Development for Problem Behavior: A Practical Handbook, 1st edition,* by R.E. O'Neill, R.H. Horner, R.W. Albin, J.R. Sprague, K. Storey, J. Newton © 1997. Reprinted with permission of Wadsworth, an imprint of the Wadsworth Group, a division of Thomson Learning. Fax 800-730-2215.)

(Kennedy & Meyer, 1998; Pace & Toyer, 2000), it also is widely understood that the etiology of problem behavior lies primarily in processes of social interaction and learning (Patterson et al., 1992; Taylor & Carr, 1994).

Children or youth develop problem behaviors in family contexts because their disability has interfered with the development of communication and social skills; limited their conceptual and practical knowledge about the world; or distorted their ability to interpret everyday visual, auditory, or tactile stimuli (Greenspan & Wieder, 2000; Wetherby, Prizant, & Schuler, 2000). Given these encumbrances, children often learn that problem behaviors are an effective means for getting specific wants and needs met and for controlling positive or aversive interactions and events. For example, a 5-year-old with autism screams whenever she wants a new videotape placed in the VCR. She screams for a change in activity because she does not have the language skills to ask for help or the performance skills needed to change the videotape herself. A 10-year-old with Down syndrome engages in destructive behavior while his mother is preparing supper because he does not have the communication skills to request parental attention or the independent play skills to organize and manage his free time.

Certain responses to problem behavior may teach children and youth that problem behaviors "work." For example, the father of the child with autism may respond to his daughter's screams by changing the videotape. The mother of the boy with Down syndrome may respond to her son's destructive behavior by leaving the kitchen, scolding her son, and then helping him find a new activity in which to engage. Although these parenting practices are quite common and may reduce problem behaviors in the short term, they also are likely to maintain problem behaviors in the long run. The central message here is that such patterns of parent–child interaction can be transformed and problem behaviors can be reduced by teaching new behaviors and skills that make problem behaviors irrelevant. For example, the child with autism could be taught to ask a parent for help in changing videotapes or even to do so herself. The child with Down syndrome could be taught to ask for parental attention and to play with a variety of toys for extended periods of time.

6. Communication as the Foundation of Positive Behavior

Practitioners of PBS with families recognize that the foundation of positive behavior is an effective communication partnership between the child with a disability and his or her parents as well as with other important people in the child's life (e.g., siblings, grandparents, friends, teachers, respite care providers) (Beukelman & Mirenda, 1998; Butterfield, Arthur, & Sigafoos, 1995). Family members work closely with the interventionist and other key stakeholders (e.g., a speech-language pathologist, an AAC specialist) to identify the communicative functions of problem behavior, to select functionally equivalent responses to replace problem behaviors, and to teach the child to use language or AAC instead of problem behaviors to communicate wants or needs (Carr et al., 1994; Fox, Dunlap, & Buschbacher, 2000; Reichle & Wacker, 1993).

Consider a young child with pervasive developmental disorder (PDD) who bangs his head on the floor and other surfaces at home. A functional assessment indicates that the child engages in self-injurious behavior to get his mother's attention. The mother, the interventionist, and the speech-language pathologist agree to teach the child two ways to get parental attention that are functionally equivalent to self-injurious behavior. He is taught to communicate his desire for attention by saying "Mom" or "Help" or by handing his mother a card with one of these symbols on it. He is also taught to use these language skills in each family context in which his mother is unable to give him her undivided attention.

Because parents cannot always be at the beck and call of their children, the team agrees that after the child consistently uses language instead of problem behavior to get his mother's attention, he will be taught to endure increasingly longer periods of time (e.g., 1 minute, 3 minutes) before his mother responds (e.g., "Yes, sweetie, I hear you—I will be there in a minute"). In addition, the child's older sister, grandparents, and respite care provider are informed of these communication goals and encouraged to use the strategies to support and maintain the child's use of language instead of problem behavior to get attention.

As illustrated, understanding the purpose of problem behavior is essential for identifying the language skills and tools that a child may need to communicate (e.g., speech, sign language, picture symbols, a voice output communication aid). Identifying effective ways to communicate and teaching language skills is at the heart of an effective PBS plan. In the example of the child with PDD, this involved selecting language skills that 1) are easy for the child to use (e.g., one-word phrases, picture symbols within easy reach), 2) are effective at gaining attention or assistance, and 3) require less effort than self-injurious behaviors. The central message here is that a well-designed behavior support plan ensures that a child's use of language achieves wants and needs more effectively and efficiently than problem behavior.

7. Multicomponent Support Plans

PBS with families involves designing comprehensive, multicomponent behavior support plans. These plans integrate ecological, preventive, teaching, and consequence strategies into a well-balanced whole that addresses each function of problem behavior and the setting events and triggers for problem behavior. The goal is to design effective family environments or contexts in which problem behaviors are no longer relevant, effective, or efficient at achieving their purpose (Horner et al., 2000; O'Neill et al., 1997). A good behavior support plan defines changes in family environments and in parent and other family member behavior, and it is these changes that result in change in the behavior of the child.

Because a functional assessment typically reveals several features of the problem in family contexts (e.g., one or more setting events, triggers, or functions), behavior support plans in family contexts necessarily include multiple components (Lucyshyn et al., 1997). These components may include up to five intervention categories: 1) setting event (i.e., lifestyle or ecological) strategies, 2) preventive strategies, 3) teaching strategies, 4) effective consequences, and 5) emergency procedures. Each component of the plan is logically linked to a feature of the problem as identified in the functional assessment. Figure 1.2 presents a multicomponent behavior support plan that is based on the functional assessment results described previously for the 7-year-old with autism during his morning routine.

An effective support plan emphasizes lifestyle enhancements, ecological adjustments, and proactive strategies that create a rich pattern of activities and relationships but avoids the features of situations that set the stage for or trigger problem behavior. Here, the aim is to design environments or contexts in which problem behaviors are no longer relevant. Consider an 8-year-old with autism and a hearing impairment who is enrolled, after school, in a child care center near his home. His stepfather arrives in the late afternoon to take the boy home, usually at the final snack time or while his stepson is playing with toys. His stepfather uses sign language to say that it is time to leave. To avoid the transition, the boy has a tantrum and runs away. From his point of view, leaving the child care center at that time is aversive because it interrupts preferred activities. Also, he cannot predict what will happen after leaving the center. That is, he cannot easily imagine future events that are equal to or better than those that he is currently experiencing. Having a tantrum and running away serve to delay his departure.

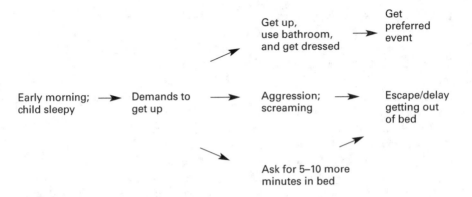

Strategies that will Make Problem Behavior Irrelevant, Ineffective, and Inefficient

Ecological/Lifestyle Strategies	Preventive Strategies	Teaching Strategies	Consequence Strategies
Place alarm clock with snooze button next to child's bed Arrange schedule so child has choice of 5–10 extra minutes in bed Before introducing prompts to get up, spend 5 minutes engaged in preferred interactions with child (i.e., gentle interactions that help child wake up)	Use a visual schedule that helps child predict both steps in routine and preferred events (e.g., Peanut Butter Panda Puffs cereal for breakfast, *Magic School Bus* on TV) Use natural positive contingencies instead of demands to motivate getting up and doing steps in routine	Teach child to press snooze button and/or ask for 5 more minutes, let child do this twice	Let child stay in bed contingent on pressing snooze button and/or asking for 5 more minutes Give child favorite cereal or let child watch favorite TV program contingent on getting up, using bathroom, and getting dressed If child aggresses, prompt language 3 times; give time but do not give reinforcing event

Figure 1.2.   Summary statement/competing behavior pathways diagram and positive behavior support plan logically linked to features of problem in morning routine. (From *Functional Assessment and Program Development for Problem Behavior: A Practical Handbook, 1st edition,* by R.E. O'Neill, R.H. Horner, R.W. Albin, J.R. Sprague, K. Storey, J. Newton © 1997. Reprinted with permission of Wadsworth, an imprint of the Wadsworth Group, a division of Thomson Learning. Fax 800-730-2215.)

For each feature of the problem, a behavioral support is developed. To avoid the aversive interruption, the stepfather prompts his stepson to leave after snack time is over or after spending a few minutes playing with him. To increase predictability and motivation for leaving, a picture schedule is developed that depicts the steps in the routine as well as a positive event that is contingent on leaving cooperatively (e.g., receiving a healthy snack in the car, visiting a duck pond on the way home). Before prompting the boy to go to the car, the stepfather reviews the picture schedule and offers a choice of one positive event that will occur after leaving the center. If the boy leaves cooperatively, then his stepfather praises him and keeps his promise. Following implementation of this plan, the boy eagerly gets his backpack, puts on his jacket, and runs *to* the car.

A good plan also includes effective consequences that make problem behaviors ineffective or inefficient at achieving their purposes. Consider, for example, a 4-year-old with a moderate cognitive disability who spits at her mother when her mother is busy with household chores. The girl does so to regain her mother's attention. From the child's point of view, parental reprimands and physical restraint that follow spitting are just as interesting as maternal praise and hugs. Based on this assessment, the mother and interventionist develop a consequence that is logically linked to the function of the child's behavior. When the daughter spits, her mother refrains from any emotional display or physical contact. Instead, she immediately turns away from her daughter, briefly but firmly says, "No, that's not okay," and walks away for at least 10 seconds. After this brief time-out from parental attention, the mother, without any comment about the spitting, redirects her daughter in a neutral tone of voice back to a preferred activity (e.g., a puzzle, a drawing board). Once the girl is reengaged, her mother returns to the use of proactive and positive strategies (e.g., reminders to request attention, parental attention contingent on independent play). After several days of implementing this procedure in conjunction with other supports, the mother reports that her daughter no longer spits at her. Effective consequences in family contexts may involve mild forms of punishment, such as brief reprimands or a temporary loss of privileges, but never procedures that cause physical pain, loss of dignity, or humiliation (Horner et al., 1990).

Before finalizing a multicomponent support plan with families, practitioners of PBS strive to ensure that interventions are both *necessary* and *sufficient* for rendering problem behaviors irrelevant, ineffective, and inefficient. A plan that does not address the major features of a problematic context may fail because it is insufficient. One that includes strategies beyond what is necessary may fail because it overwhelms the family. Finding the golden mean between these two errors in plan design is significantly easier when parents are included as equal partners in plan development. Doing so can help in the design of multicomponent plans that are simple and elegant in terms of their ease of use and precision of fit with the problem (see, for example, Derby et al., 1997; Moes & Frea, 2000; Vaughn, Clarke, & Dunlap, 1997).

8. Contextual Fit with Family Life

In addition to developing behavior support plans that are technically sound, family practitioners are equally concerned with designing plans that are a good fit with family life. The terms *contextual fit* or *contextually appropriate* refer to behavior support plans that are congruent with child, implementor, and setting variables and, thus, are likely to be acceptable, feasible, and sustainable (Albin et al., 1996; Harrower et al., 1999). The concept of contextual fit acknowledges the difficulty that families may have in implementing and maintaining multicomponent plans. The concept also speaks to the cultural and ethnic diversity of families and the need for interventions that are culturally sensitive and appropriate (Harry, Kalyanpur, & Day, 1999; Lynch & Hanson, 1998). When behavior support plans possess a good contextual fit with family life, parents are more likely to view the plan as acceptable and important, to implement the plan with fidelity, and to use the plan over a long period of time.

Until recently, the primary method for gaining implementation fidelity and maintenance was to provide more and better parent training (O'Dell, 1985). Although parent training and support remain vital aspects of PBS with families, the concept of contextual fit suggests that fidelity and maintenance also may be enhanced by proactively designing better support plans. Such improved support plans are designed to better fit the goals, values, resources, and skills of families, as well as the structure and cultural patterns of family life.

For many practitioners, the collaborative process of conducting a functional assessment and designing a behavior support plan is often sufficient for developing contextually appropriate support plans. The reciprocal process of listening and learning together about the child's problem behaviors, discussing family goals in problematic family contexts, and generating solutions based on functional assessment information can lead to a plan that is contextually appropriate as well as technically sound (Clarke, Dunlap, & Vaughn, 1999; Moes & Frea, 2000).

For other families, a more in-depth understanding of family ecology may be necessary to ensure the contextual fit of a behavior support plan. This may be the case particularly for families experiencing multiple stressors or for families of culturally diverse backgrounds (Lucyshyn, Nixon, Glang, & Cooley, 1996; see also Chapter 6). Family ecology information that may enhance the contextual fit of behavior support plans includes knowledge of parent goals for the child and family, family strengths, available resources and social supports, sources of stress, and daily routines in the home and community (Lucyshyn & Albin, 1993).

Consider a 6-year-old with autism who engages in attention-seeking, aggressive behavior. Supplemental to a functional assessment, a family ecology assessment indicates that his mother is exhausted from caregiving responsibilities and is experiencing a stress-induced illness. On the positive side, the mother is deeply committed to caring for her son and has two older daughters who are willing to help with caregiving responsibilities. This family ecology information determines three additional supports that are aimed at alleviating parental stress and fortifying caregiving resources. First, the interventionist assists the family in connecting with a local nonprofit agency that offers respite care services to families of children with disabilities. After-school and weekend respite care services are arranged. Second, the boy's older sisters agree to provide child care for 1 hour per day on a predictable weekly schedule. They also agree to participate in training and support activities during plan implementation. Finally, because of the serious nature of the mother's stress-induced illness, the interventionist contacts the family's service coordinator to acquire funds for long-term, in-home support services. All of these measures relate to contextual fit because for this family, the effectiveness, acceptability, and long-term sustainability of positive behavioral interventions in the home require that the mother is rested and healthy, that the child's siblings are informed and helpful, and that the family's long-term needs for assistance are addressed.

Evidence of contextual fit only is manifest after implementation support has been provided and families have begun using the plan on a regular basis. If the plan possesses a good contextual fit, then family members are likely to 1) implement behavioral support strategies accurately and effectively, 2) successfully use the strategies in new family contexts, 3) continue to use plan procedures for an extended period of time, and 4) view the plan as being acceptable and helpful.

9. Activity Setting as a Unit of Analysis and Intervention

In PBS with families, the family activity setting is viewed as an important unit of analysis and intervention (Gallimore, Goldenberg, & Weisner, 1993; Lucyshyn & Albin, 1993; Vaughn, Clarke, & Dunlap, 1997). *Family activity settings* are home and community routines and activities that include the child with a disability and one or more family members; occur on a regular basis, whether daily, weekly, or yearly; and are important to the child and/or family. Examples of valued activity settings include mealtimes at home, shopping with parents, visiting grandparents, taking day trips, going on vacations, or participating in seasonal celebrations. For families raising children with disabilities, many of these activity settings are unsuccessful due to child problem behavior.

The importance of the activity setting as a unit of analysis and intervention is based on its empirical grounding in ethnographic studies of child development in the context of family life (Gallimore et al., 1993), its compatibility with best practices in teaching functional skills in natural learning environments (Dunst, Hamby, Trivette, Raab, & Bruder, 2000; Snell & Brown, 2000), and its congruence with ecological systems theory (Bronfenbrenner, 1986). Activity settings represent a microcosm of family ecology. They are composed of several elements: 1) time and place, 2) people, 3) tasks and their organization, 4) resources, 5) goals and values, and 6) child–parent interaction patterns. By addressing problem behavior in the context of valued family activity settings, interventionists support the natural efforts of families to construct routines that are consistent with child characteristics, meaningful to the family, and sustainable within the context of the family's culture and ecology (Bernheimer & Keough, 1995).

Working in the context of valued but problematic routines can have several benefits. First, when functional assessment–based interventions are embedded in valued routines, interventionists simultaneously address child problem behavior and family goals and visions for the future. Second, because routines include both objective and subjective elements of family ecology (e.g., people, tasks, goals and values) they provide an ideal context for developing contextually appropriate and culturally sensitive interventions. For example, in a dinner routine, other people (e.g., siblings) who are part of the routine are included in the design and/or implementation of behavioral supports. For a shopping routine, the tasks in which the parent and child will engage are identified and behavioral supports are designed to facilitate completion of these tasks. A visit to the home of relatives may include cultural goals and values about ways to show respect to elders.

Third, family members lead busy, complex lives. In addition to caregiving responsibilities, parents devote time to other tasks, such as purchasing food and preparing meals, transporting family members, participating in recreational activities, and engaging in social activities with friends and relatives (Turnbull & Turnbull, 2000a). Intervening in the context of problematic routines and activities can help parents better support their child with a disability in the midst of these other functions of family life. Beginning intervention in only one or two valued routines at a time can make the process of PBS more feasible and less overwhelming for families.

Finally, as families succeed in transforming problematic routines into successful ones, they experience behavioral technology not as a burdensome intrusion but as a practical tool for achieving the simple but sacred necessities of family life: sending a son off to school well rested and nourished, going on a worry-free shopping trip with a teenage daughter, visiting a beloved grandparent in a nearby town. When interventionists help families achieve such outcomes, parents are more likely to continue using behavioral supports because the supports have been woven into the fabric of everyday family life (Bernheimer & Keough, 1995).

10. Implementation Support

Practitioners of PBS are committed to helping families successfully implement behavior support plans in family contexts. To do so, they work closely with parents and other family members to develop an implementation plan. This plan defines training and support activities that the interventionist and family agree are necessary to support the implementation of behavioral interventions in family contexts (Horner et al., 2000; Lucyshyn & Albin, 1993). In our experience, although some families can implement a behavior support plan with little additional assistance, most families require some form of implementation support to do so successfully.

An implementation plan typically includes a description of training and support activities, a summary of roles and responsibilities, and a time line for completing the process of training and support. Training and support activities that are commonly used with families include a written plan that provides clear guidance for using plan components, a one- or two-page implementation checklist for parents to self-manage the use of interventions, and regularly scheduled home visits. During home visits, activities that families find particularly helpful include developing intervention materials (e.g., making a picture schedule, setting up a play room to encourage language use), modeling of and coaching on plan strategies, and engaging in problem-solving discussions.

Implementation support has three distinct phases: 1) an initial "intense" period of training and support; 2) a transition phase that leads to self-direction and self-sufficiency; and 3) a sustaining phase, in which key interventions and problem-solving strategies are integrated into the family's cultural practices. These phases are discussed in detail next.

Initial "Intense" Phase   During the initial phase of implementation, the key consideration is providing families with the breadth and depth of training and support necessary to ensure the successful implementation of the support plan and the resolution of problem behaviors (Carr, Levin, et al., 1999; Lucyshyn et al., 1997; Vaughn, Dunlap, et al., 1997). This can be a very intense experience for families (Fox, Vaughn, et al., 1997). To be sure, some families may need no more initial support than a written plan and telephone consultation to succeed in improving child behavior. For other families to succeed, however, the interventionist may need to visit the home several times, coach the family in the use of interventions, and engage in several problem-solving discussions with family members.

Along with this intense level of initial activity, families also experience a myriad of emotions that need to be acknowledged and respected. Some may hold doubts and fears about whether the plan will work or whether they will have the ability to succeed. Initial efforts by parents to change discipline practices can generate dissonance and discomfort. Validating and working through such emotions can build trust, generate hope, and overcome obstacles toward the attainment of child and family goals (Walker & Singer, 1993). As parents experience their first successes in improving child behavior and in creating effective family contexts, their confidence begins to grow. During this phase, the family and the interventionist also discover which interventions work or do not work, are unnecessary, and/or go against family cultural values and practices. Through problem-solving discussions, these issues are raised and efforts are made to improve the plan's effectiveness and contextual fit.

Transition Phase   As parents and other family members become proficient at implementing behavioral supports and improving their child's behavior, the interventionist turns her or his attention to a longer-term goal: empowering family members to become self-sufficient at building effective family contexts in which child problem behaviors are irrelevant, ineffective, and inefficient. The overall process of collaboratively conducting brief functional assessments, generating summary hypothesis statements, and building behavioral supports that are tailored to individual routines plays an important role in helping families develop this capacity (Albin, Dunlap, Horner, & Sailor, 2000; Vaughn, Fox, & Dunlap, 2000). Every problematic context that is solved helps families understand and practice the art and science of building a good behavior support plan. After several reiterations of this process, families may be encouraged to take the lead in diagramming a summary hypothesis statement and generating behavioral supports that are linked to the features of the problem. The interventionist provides assistance as needed but emphasizes the family's ability to understand and solve behavior problems.

Sustaining Phase   When family members succeed in improving problem behavior and family life and can solve new or recurring problems, they enter a sustaining phase that is measured in years (Carr, Levin, et al., 1999). At this time, the interventionist who initially helped the family may be less involved or no longer available to provide support. This support role may be assumed by other members of the family's support network, such as the child's teacher or a local service provider. Several experiences characterize this phase. Parents embed into the daily practices of family life a minimal set of core interventions that are necessary to maintain desirable behavior. For example, parents may use picture schedules, language prompts, and positive contingencies as daily means to support a child with autism (Fox, Dunlap, & Philbrick, 1997). Parents also may work with other members of their support network to adapt and improve behavioral supports for new problematic contexts. Finally, when a family experiences major changes (e.g., parent illness, a move to a new town, divorce) or a child experiences a life cycle transition (e.g., childhood to adolescence) (Ferguson & Ferguson, 2000), parents may seek additional professional assistance to weather or recover from these disruptions to the continuity of child progress and family life. In these circumstances, adjustments or changes to the child's behavior support plan are often necessary.

Because families face many potential obstacles to the long-term maintenance of behavioral interventions (Griest & Forehand, 1982; Hieneman & Dunlap, 2001), we encourage practitioners and service agencies to establish a "dental model" of longitudinal support. In this model, families and service providers arrange periodic "checkups" to monitor progress, and practitioners offer additional training and support as needed. If a checkup shows that all is going well, then the interventionist offers encouragement and collegial regard. If old problems have returned or new problems have arisen, then the interventionist provides reminders about effective intervention, arranges brief "booster sessions" to support families in their use interventions, or conducts a problem-focused functional assessment that helps to update the behavior support plan. If major behavior problems flare up and threaten child and family gains, then a more comprehensive functional assessment may be reinitiated and revised child-centered and/or family-centered supports may be introduced. Such a longitudinal model of support may extend the generalization and maintenance of behavioral supports from years to decades, a time frame that is more compatible with the life cycle of families (Carr, Levin, et al., 1999).

11. Continuous Evaluation

Practitioners are committed to evaluating the short- and long-term outcomes of a process of PBS with families. Emphasis is on the use of meaningful and multiple measures of child and family outcomes (Meyer & Evans, 1993). Care also is taken to select or design measures that parents and other caregivers (e.g., grandparents) find to be "family friendly"— that is, easy to use and helpful.

Key measures of interest include 1) problem behavior, 2) adaptive behavior, 3) family implementation of behavioral supports, 4) child and family lifestyle changes, 5) social validity (i.e., the acceptability of goals, procedures, and outcomes), and 6) contextual fit. The singular purpose of any outcome measure is to provide the family and the interventionist with relevant information for evaluating progress and improving the effectiveness, acceptability, and contextual fit of behavioral supports and implementation support activities.

Measures of problem behavior may include the daily or weekly frequency of individual behaviors of concern or major incidents of problem behavior. Measures of adaptive behavior may include the frequency and/or type of language used by the child or the number of times that the child successfully participates in targeted family routines. Families also may self-monitor and self-evaluate their level of plan implementation with a one- or two-page implementation checklist (Lucyshyn &, Albin, 1993; Sanders & Dadds, 1993).

Measures of lifestyle outcomes for a child may include the number of community activities in which he or she participated or the number of same-age friends with whom he or she spent time during the previous month (Malette et al., 1992). Quality of life measures for the family may involve a formal stress index or parent verbal report of changes in quality of life. Measurement of social validity or contextual fit typically involves a brief questionnaire on which family members rate the acceptability and importance of the support process or the goodness of fit of the behavior support plan (Clarke et al., 1999; Lucyshyn et al., 1997).

Evaluation of child and family outcomes is made family friendly by including parents in the selection of evaluation procedures, by choosing or designing measures that are relatively easy to use, and by ensuring that instruments not only measure problems but also child progress and family success. For example, to evaluate improvements in child behavior, families may complete a simple "indicator behavior" form one to three times per week to describe the frequency of major behavior incidents (Albin et al., 2000). Alternatively, parents may keep track of behavior incidents by filling out small index cards that measure frequency and provide continuous insight into environmental triggers and the functions of behavior (Carr, Levin, et al., 1999; Vaughn, Fox, & Dunlap, 2000). To evaluate a young child's adaptive behavior, interventionists may administer on a yearly basis formal instruments that measure child development, such as the Battelle Developmental Inventory (BDI; Newborg, Stock, & Wnek, 1984; see also Dunlap & Fox, 1999). To assess lifestyle outcomes, interventionists may employ instruments such as the Resident Lifestyle Inventory (RLI; Kennedy, Horner, Newton, & Kanda, 1990).

Continuous evaluation of child and family outcomes is essential for the long-term sustainability of a support plan. Plan design is viewed as being inseparable from plan evaluation. The reiterative process of plan development, evaluation, and improvement helps the family and the interventionist recognize and overcome problems with interventions, obstacles to implementation, and changes in life circumstances that disrupt progress. Initial evaluation activities provide information necessary for plan adjustments and revisions. Further evaluation shows the interventionist and family whether these changes have had the desired effect. Long-term follow-up can identify changes in the child or in family life that require reassessment and redesign of supports. Throughout the evaluation process, evidence of child progress, parent efficacy, and lifestyle improvement gives occasion for the acknowledgment and celebration of the child and family.

12. Support with Sincerity and Humility

In our work with families and other members of a child's behavior support team, we have found that the goals of PBS are much more likely to be achieved if interventionists relate to families and to other team members in a spirit of sincerity and humility. Several qualities characterize this spirit: 1) truly listening; 2) validating emotions and experience; 3) being responsive to parent and professional knowledge and suggestions; 4) admitting what we do not know and valuing assistance from those who do; 5) correcting errors in the design or implementation of support plans; and 6) encouraging parents and other members of the child's team to make decisions, solve problems, and eventually take the lead.

Like collaboration, the practice of humility is more of a necessity than a choice. The thoughtful interventionist recognizes that a child's family and educators who work with the child possess valuable knowledge for designing an effective behavior support plan. This knowledge can only be utilized if the interventionist takes the time to listen and learn. Errors in plan design or implementation are not uncommon. When interventionists and other team members readily acknowledge these errors, shortcomings in plan design are resolved, team members master behavioral support strategies more quickly, and parents feel more at ease because they know that they are not alone in experiencing their child's behavior as challenging.

A spirit of humility also encourages interventionists to be mindful of the many threats to the long-term maintenance of interventions in family settings. These include, for example, relatives disagreeing with a parent's use of positive discipline strategies, a child's extended illness, or parental fatigue during a long school holiday. When interventionists are mindful of these threats, they are more likely to take proactive steps to fortify the family against potential setbacks to child progress and parent effective use of interventions.

EMPIRICAL SUPPORT FOR
THE EFFICACY AND ACCEPTABILITY OF
POSITIVE BEHAVIOR SUPPORT WITH FAMILIES

PBS represents an evolution of applied behavior analysis toward a new applied science that 1) views consumers of research as collaborative partners, 2) values ecological and social validity as well as internal validity, 3) seeks to promote lifestyle changes, and 4) views social systems as units of analysis and intervention (Carr, 1997; Carr et al., 2002; Turnbull et al., 1998). The purpose of this science is to develop a technology of behavioral support that is effective, acceptable, and feasible when used in typical home, school, and community environments by families, professionals, and other care or service providers (Carr, Horner, et al., 1999).

Carr, Horner, and colleagues (1999) completed a comprehensive meta-analysis of the efficacy of positive behavioral interventions for people with developmental disabilities who engage in serious problem behavior (e.g., self-injury, aggression, property destruction, tantrums). The authors examined single subject intervention studies (Barlow & Hersen, 1984) that were published between 1985 and 1996 and used stimulus- and/or reinforcement-based interventions. The analysis indicated that PBS was effective for all examined problem behaviors and across a wide variety of participants, settings, interventionists, and intervention strategies. Effect sizes (i.e., magnitude of changes) were large and associated with reductions in problem behavior that usually exceeded 80%. The analysis also indicated that PBS was more effective when a functional assessment was completed and used to design interventions.

Although these results are encouraging, few of the 109 studies included in the meta-analysis were conducted in typical family settings with parents as interventionists. In addition, only a few of the studies extended beyond a year, so there is little evidence of the long-term durability of PBS. Because PBS is a relatively new enterprise, there is only a modest body of behavioral research that assesses the efficacy of PBS with families. These studies are briefly reviewed next, with attention to the contributions that they have made to a new applied science of PBS.

Arndorfer, Miltenberger, Woster, Rortvedt, and Gaffaney (1994) conducted one of the first descriptive and experimental functional analyses in which families were actively involved in assessing the problem behavior of their children with developmental disabilities. Functional assessment interviews and observations in home settings generated hypotheses about the functions of problem behavior. These hypotheses were then confirmed under experimental conditions, which the parents conducted at home under researcher direction. This study demonstrated that functional analysis procedures can be practical and helpful in home contexts and that parents can actively participate in their use within natural, routine activities with their children.

In a longitudinal study with young children exhibiting problem behavior in the home, Derby and colleagues (1997) extended the usefulness of functional analysis. The authors also documented the effectiveness and durability of functional communication training (FCT) for children and parents in family contexts. Four young children with multiple disabilities participated in a long-term, in-home intervention project that focused on building positive reciprocal interactions between parents and their children (Wacker, Peck, Derby, Berg, & Harding, 1996). Descriptive and experimental analyses conducted in the home identified the environmental antecedents and consequences that controlled problem behavior. This information guided the development of an individualized, multicomponent intervention plan that included FCT, reinforcement strategies, and extinction procedures. Results for each child evidenced long-term reductions of problem behavior and functional use of requests. In addition, nontargeted social and toy play behaviors by the children increased during treatment and were maintained at 9, 12, and 17 months follow-up.

Fox and colleagues (Dunlap & Fox, 1999; Fox, Dunlap, & Philbrick, 1997) documented the effectiveness of a comprehensive early intervention approach for families of young children with autism that combined functional assessment and positive behavioral supports with lifestyle and family systems considerations. The Individualized Support Project (ISP) integrated functional assessment and behavior support plan design with person-centered planning activities. The goal was to develop individualized behavioral and family supports that help parents achieve their vision of an inclusive lifestyle for the child. Parents were regarded as essential partners in the development of goals and interventions. Results from single subject analyses of the ISP project with six young children with autism offered preliminary evidence of the approach's efficacy. Multiple-baseline probe observations in the home across time periods ranging from 3 to 6 months indicated reductions in problem behavior to minimal or zero levels. In additions, these changes were associated with clear gains in overall child development as measured by the BDI (Newborg et al., 1984).

Lucyshyn and colleagues (1997) conducted a longitudinal, descriptive, and experimental analysis of comprehensive PBS with the family of a teenager with multiple disabilities and severe problem behavior (see Chapter 17). The study introduced two innovations into a process of PBS with families: 1) the activity setting as a unit of analysis and intervention and 2) contextual fit as a guide to the design of contextually appropriate behavior support plans. Innovations in research methods included the integration of participatory action research (PAR) procedures with single subject research methods (Barlow & Hersen, 1984; Whyte, 1991) and the measurement of lifestyle changes. Following a functional analysis and the collaborative design of a comprehensive multicomponent PBS plan, the teenager's parents were taught to implement the plan in four valued routines in the home and community. A multiple-baseline probe design across settings (Horner & Baer, 1978) documented a functional relationship between the introduction of the support plan and improvements in behavior and routine participation across a 26-month period of base-line, intervention, and follow-up. Repeated measures of social validity and goodness of fit indicated the acceptability of behavioral and lifestyle outcomes and the contextual fit of the behavior support plan. These results were replicated and extended by Lucyshyn and colleagues (2000) in a 46-month longitudinal study of comprehensive PBS with the family of a young child with autism.

In a series of investigations, Vaughn and colleagues (Clarke et al., 1999; Fox, Vaughn, et al., 1997; Vaughn, Clarke, & Dunlap, 1997; Vaughn, Dunlap, et al., 1997) further extended the efficacy of a collaborative process of functional assessment and PBS with families in the context of activity settings. They also contributed to the definition of a new applied science by employing multiple research methodologies to study community-based, family-centered PBS.

Vaughn, Dunlap, and colleagues (1997) developed a research partnership with the parent of a 9-year-old with Cornelia de Lange syndrome who engaged in intense problem behaviors in three community contexts: 1) a drive-through bank, 2) a grocery store, and 3) a fast-food restaurant (see Chapter 18). They collaborated with the family to complete a functional assessment, to experimentally verify hypotheses about the functions of the problem behavior, and to develop positive behavioral supports for each routine. A quasi-experimental, single subject design was employed to evaluate outcomes. Results suggested that implementing behavioral supports in each setting reduced problem behaviors to min-imal or zero levels and increased the child's cooperative responses. A social validity meas-ure indicated that the interventions were acceptable and easy to use. In a companion qual-itative study, Fox, Vaughn, and colleagues (1997) illuminated the family's subjective experience of the process of PBS. The mother kept an audiotaped journal from which the authors analyzed transcripts. Themes that emerged from the analysis included the negative impact of problem behaviors on the family, the positive impact of the support plan on the family's quality of life, and the importance of the trusting relationship that developed be-tween the interventionist and the family.

Subsequent single subject experimental analyses by Vaughn and colleagues strength-ened the efficacy and acceptability of their approach to PBS. Vaughn, Clarke, and Dunlap (1997) collaborated with a parent to develop a PBS plan for an 8-year-old with a severe in-tellectual disability. The boy engaged in problem behaviors in a bathroom routine at home and during outings to restaurants with his family. A multiple-baseline design across set-tings clearly documented the intervention's effectiveness in rapidly and durably reducing problem behaviors and in improving the child's positive engagement. The results of this study are presented in Figure 1.3. In a study with the family of a 10-year-old with Asperger syndrome who engaged in problem behavior during an early morning routine, Clarke and colleagues (1999) used a single subject withdrawal design to document the effectiveness of PBS in reducing problem behavior and increasing on-task engagement during the routine. Each of these studies also evidenced high indices of social validity.

Koegel, Steibel, and Koegel (1998) demonstrated that PBS effectively helps families ameliorate aggression by children with autism toward their younger siblings. Koegel and colleagues collaborated with three families in which a 4- or 5-year-old child with autism displayed serious aggression with an infant or toddler sibling. Following a functional as-sessment with each family, the authors designed an individualized, multicomponent sup-port plan that addressed the multiple functions of each child's aggressive behavior. The parents were taught to implement the plan in home routines in which aggression fre-quently occurred. A multiple-baseline design across the families documented a functional relationship between parent implementation of the intervention and meaningful and dur-

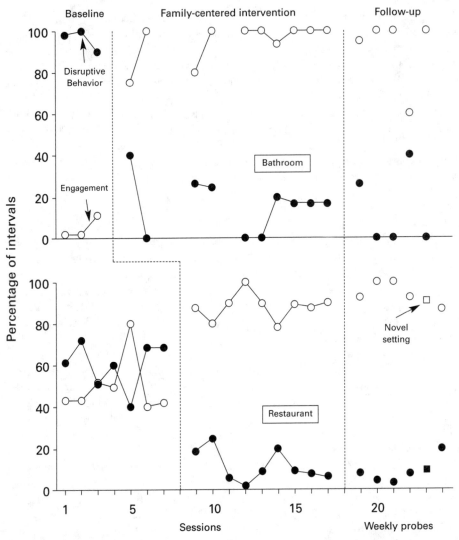

Figure 1.3. Percentage of intervals with disruptive behavior and engagement across the bathroom and restaurant routines. Connected data points represent sessions that occurred approximately two times per week. Disconnected points span a period of 1 week. The square data points during follow-up in the restaurant routine depicts a probe session that was conducted in a different restaurant environment. (From Vaughn, B.J., Clarke, S., & Dunlap, G. [1997]. Assessment-based intervention for severe behavior problems in a natural family context. *Journal of Applied Behavior Analysis, 30,* 715; reprinted with permission).

able decreases in problem behavior. In addition, the children with autism showed increases in their spontaneous use of appropriate behavior. Naïve observer ratings of parent and child levels of happiness during videotaped observation sessions indicated that the parents and children were happier during the intervention phases of the study. Multiple-baseline results are presented in Figure 1.4.

Barry and Singer (2001) conducted a longitudinal case study of PBS with a family of a 10-year-old with autism who engaged in life-threatening aggressive behavior toward a younger sibling. The study demonstrated that repeated functional assessments and plan revisions are important for addressing problem behaviors across the life cycle of childhood. It also illustrated a family-centered approach to plan development that was acceptable and feasible

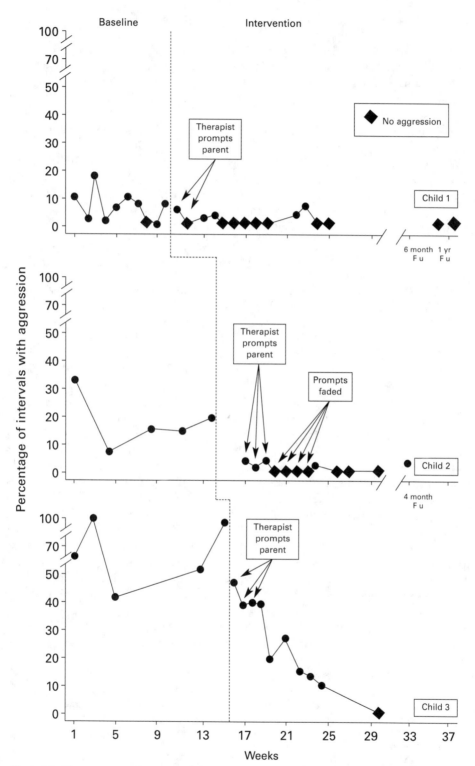

Figure 1.4. The percentage of intervals during which the children exhibited aggression (circles) toward their infant or toddler sibling during baseline, intervention, and follow-up (F u). *Arrows* indicate sessions when the parents were prompted to provide the intervention. *Diamonds* indicate sessions with zero aggression. (From Koegel, L.K., Steibel, D., & Koegel, R.L. [1998]. Reducing aggression in children with autism toward infant or toddler siblings. *The Journal of The Association for Persons with Severe Handicaps, 23,* 116. Copyright © *The Journal of The Association for Persons with Severe Handicaps*; reprinted by permission.)

to a family that was under extreme duress. An initial functional assessment indicated that the child engaged in aggression (e.g., choking) toward his infant sibling to obtain attention. The authors devised a multicomponent support plan that included teaching the child to gain attention in more appropriate ways. To conform with family preferences, the interventionists first implemented the intervention at home with the child. They taught his parents to implement the plan only after improvements in behavior were established. As the infant sibling grew into a toddler (between the ages of 3 and 20 months), the older brother's aggression returned in new forms (e.g., prompting the toddler to climb to the top of a staircase), necessitating reassessment and plan revisions. A 26-month-long, nonconcurrent multiple baseline across types of aggression indicated that the plan and its revisions were associated with decreases in problem behavior to zero levels and increases in appropriate attention-seeking behavior. These improvements were maintained at 1 and 4 months follow-up.

In the most extensive demonstration of comprehensive PBS to date, Carr and colleagues (Carr, Levin, et al., 1999) collaborated with a wide range of stakeholders to develop and implement a multicomponent support plan for three people. The individuals—who were 14, 17, and 38 years old—had severe cognitive disabilities and engaged in severe problem behaviors. The two youth lived at home with their families, and the adult lived in a group home. Intervention partners included parents, siblings, teachers, therapists, group-home staff, and job coaches. Settings consisted of home, school, community, and work. Problematic contexts in which interventions were implemented included self-care or chore routines at home, academic tasks at school, and a variety of community activities.

Following a comprehensive functional assessment, a multicomponent approach was implemented with each individual. Plan components included building rapport, providing FCT, building tolerance for reinforcement delay, providing choices, and embedding easy tasks within difficult tasks (Carr et al., 1994). In addition, strategies to promote generalization and maintenance were implemented. A longitudinal, multiple-baseline probe design across participants demonstrated the efficacy of the comprehensive approach for reducing problem behaviors, improving spontaneous communication, and promoting task engagement. Long-term maintenance of intervention effects was observed for up to 2 ½ years. This study made two additional contributions to the empirical literature on PBS with families. First, it illustrated developing, monitoring, and coordinating multicomponent behavior support plans with many stakeholders across the multiple settings of a person's life. This level of comprehensiveness may be necessary to truly assist families in improving the behavior and lifestyle of their child with a disability. Second, it reiterated the need for a life-span perspective to promote the long-term maintenance of PBS. Similar to the study by Barry and Singer (2001), changes that occurred in each participant's life situation required additional assessments and revisions in intervention strategies. As stated by Carr and colleagues,

> Ultimately, maintenance does not refer even to the time period of our study but, rather, to periods measured in decades as the individual progresses from childhood through adolescence to adulthood. This life-span perspective has become the new measure of maintenance and will require research into methods for identifying and achieving meaningful change over protracted periods of time. (1999, p. 23)

A final study reviewed in this chapter presents the first empirical evidence of contextual fit's relative contribution to the design of behavior support plans for family contexts. In a descriptive case study, Moes and Frea (2000) compared child and family outcomes of a prescriptive intervention approach with outcomes of a contextualized intervention approach. The study was conducted with the family of a 3-year-old with autism and a mood disorder. A functional assessment indicated that the child engaged in escape-motivated disruptive behavior in two home routines that involved parental demands. During the prescriptive approach, the researchers selected an intervention package from the research literature, and they systematically taught the child's parents to implement it in one routine. Results indicated that this approach was associated with initial improvements in problem behavior and functional communication (e.g., asking for a break), but no improvement in on-task behavior. These improvements also deteriorated during the course of intervention and did not generalize to the second routine. The researchers then introduced the contextualized approach. This involved assessing family routines and parent–consultant collaboration in designing a support plan. The contextualized plan included strategies that reflected parent preferences and adaptations that better fit parent goals, values, and resources. Implementation in the first routine was associated with immediate and stable reductions in problem behavior, a substantial increase in on-task behavior, and little to no use of functional communication to escape the task. These outcomes generalized to the nontrained routine, and all outcomes were maintained at 3 months follow-up. A measure of contextual fit indicated that the contexualized plan was sustainable and highly compatible with the family's goals, values, resources, and abilities.

Taken as a whole, these studies offer preliminary empirical evidence of the acceptability, effectiveness, and durability of PBS with families of children and youth with developmental disabilities. They also offer initial evidence for the external validity of the approach—that is, its applicability across diverse problem behaviors, children with disabilities, families, and home and community settings. In addition, the studies contribute to an emerging science of PBS that is characterized, with respect to families, by the following qualities: 1) assessment and intervention in typical home and community settings with family members as interventionists, 2) the establishment of research partnerships with families, 3) the measurement of multiple child and family outcomes, 4) respect for and use of multiple research methodologies, and 5) attention to both scientific rigor and practical relevance.

Many more replications and extensions of this preliminary research are necessary before a PBS approach with families can be widely regarded as having a solid empirical foundation. Additional research with families is also needed to broaden and deepen knowledge about PBS in family contexts and to improve its effectiveness, efficiency, durability, and generality. As reflected in the previously reviewed studies, the scientific advancement of PBS with families should prove to be an exciting and fruitful endeavor.

CONCLUSION

This chapter has described the foundations, characteristics, and empirical basis of a positive behavior support approach to helping families of children and youth with developmental disabilities and problem behavior. The approach is grounded in a positive view of the child and the family. While acknowledging the challenges that families face in raising a child with a disability and problem behaviors, the approach also recognizes the strengths that families bring to bear on these problems. The goals of the approach are to improve the child's behavior, enhance the child's participation in family life, and enhance the quality of life of the family as a whole. Central to this mission is the empowerment of family members to build effective home and community contexts in which 1) problem behaviors are irrelevant and ineffective, 2) parent–child interactions are positive and constructive, and 3) new or recurring problems are resolved with minimal professional assistance. The foundations of the approach include applied behavior analysis, behavioral family intervention, the family support movement, and ecological theories of family life. Core features of the approach include 1) the development of collaborative partnerships with families, 2) the application of family-centered principles and practices, 3) the functional assessment of problem behavior, 4) the design of multicomponent behavior support plans that emphasize functional communication training and antecedent-based interventions, 5) the design of plans that possess a good contextual fit with family culture and ecology, 6) the provision of implementation support that is tailored to family preferences and needs, and 7) the practice of professional humility. A growing body of empirical research has begun to establish the effectiveness, acceptability, and generality of the approach across a diversity of children and families.

For families, the central message of this chapter is that a new approach to behavioral support has emerged that has been shaped by families as well as by scientists and practitioners. The approach recognizes family expertise, focuses on understanding why children engage in problem behavior, and emphasizes the design of behavioral supports that are both effective and a good fit with family life. The approach encourages parents to work with professionals as equal partners, to develop a vision of a more successful life for their child with a disability, and to become experts in their own right in using behavioral supports to improve child behavior and the quality of family life.

For professionals who support children and families, the central message is that positive behavior support offers a comprehensive set of values and practices that helps achieve professional goals for children and families in a more collegial, effective, culturally sensitive, and lasting manner. The marriage of science and values that characterizes positive behavior support encourages professionals to work with families as collaborative partners during a process of behavioral assessment, intervention design, and implementation support. By conducting family-friendly assessments, developing effective and contextually appropriate interventions, and working in an empowerment framework, professionals are more likely to succeed in helping families overcome problem behaviors and in strengthening the family.

As the following chapters and essays in this book attest, when families and professionals take these messages to heart and put them into practice, families experience considerably more of the comfort, happiness, and depth of meaning that characterize a successful family life. It is these human outcomes that validate the collaborative, family-centered approach of positive behavior support to which this volume is devoted.

REFERENCES

Abbott, D.A., & Meredith, W.H. (1986). Strengths of parents with retarded children. *Family Relations, 35*, 371–375.

Albin, R., Dunlap, G., Horner, R., & Sailor, W. (2000). *Longitudinal research in the community: Case study demonstrations of the effects of implementation of positive behavior support.* Paper presented at the 25th annual meeting of The Association for Persons with Severe Handicaps, Miami Beach, FL.

Albin, R.W., Lucyshyn, J.M., Horner, R.H., & Flannery, K.B. (1996). Contextual fit for behavioral support plans: A model for "goodness of fit." In L.K. Koegel, R.L. Koegel, & G. Dunlap (Eds.), *Positive behavioral support: Including people with difficult behavior in the community* (pp. 81–98). Baltimore: Paul H. Brookes Publishing Co.

Allen, R.I., & Petr, C.G. (1996). Toward developing standards and measurements for family-centered practice is family support programs. In G.H.S. Singer, L.E. Powers, & A.L. Olson (Vol. Eds.), *Redefining family support: Innovations in public–private partnerships* (pp. 57–86). Baltimore: Paul H. Brookes Publishing Co.

Anastopoulos, A.D., Guevremont, D.C., Shelton, T.L., & DuPaul, G.J. (1992). Parenting stress among families of children with attention-deficit hyperactivity disorder. *Journal of Abnormal Child Psychology, 20*, 503–520.

Arndorfer, R.A., Miltenberger, R.G., Woster, S.H., Rortvedt, A.K., & Gaffaney, T. (1994). Home-based descriptive and experimental analysis of problem behaviors in children. *Topics in Early Childhood Special Education, 14,* 64–87.

Baer, D.M., Wolf, M.M., & Risley, T.R. (1987). Some still-current dimensions of applied behavior analysis. *Journal of Applied Behavior Analysis, 20,* 313–327.

Bailey, D.B., & McWilliam, P.J. (1993). The search for quality indicators. In P.J. McWilliam & D.B. Bailey (Eds.), *Working together with children and families: Case studies in early intervention* (pp. 3–20). Baltimore: Paul H. Brookes Publishing Co.

Barlow, D.H., & Hersen, M. (1984). *Single case experimental design: Strategies for studying behavior change* (2nd ed.). Elmsford, NY: Pergamon.

Barry, L.M., & Singer, G.H.S. (2001). A family in crisis: Replacing the aggressive behavior of a child with autism toward an infant sibling. *Journal of Positive Behavior Interventions, 3,* 28–38.

Bernheimer, L.P., & Keough, B.K. (1995). Weaving interventions into the fabric of everyday life: An approach to family assessment. *Topics in Early Childhood Special Education, 15,* 415–433.

Beukelman, D.R., & Mirenda, P. (1998). *Augmentative and alternative communication: Management of severe communication disorders in children and adults* (2nd ed.). Baltimore: Paul H. Brookes Publishing Co.

Bijou, S.W., & Baer, D.M. (1978). *Behavior analysis of child development.* Upper Saddle River, NJ: Prentice Hall.

Blacher, J. (Ed.). (1994). *When there's no place like home: Options for children living apart from their natural families.* Baltimore: Paul H. Brookes Publishing Co.

Bristol, M.M. (1984). Family resources and successful adaptation to autistic children. In E. Schopler & G.B. Mesibov (Eds.), *The effects of autism on the family* (pp. 289–310). New York: Kluwer Academic/Plenum Publishers.

Bronfenbrenner, U. (1986). Ecology of the family as a context for human development: Research perspectives. *Developmental Psychology, 22,* 723–742.

Butterfield, N., Arthur, M., & Sigafoos, J. (1995). *Partners in everyday communicative exchanges: A guide to promoting interaction involving people with severe intellectual disability.* Baltimore: Paul H. Brookes Publishing Co.

Carr, E.G. (1997). The evolution of applied behavior analysis into positive behavior support. *Journal of The Association for Persons with Severe Handicaps, 22,* 208–209.

Carr, E.G., Dunlap, G., Horner, R.H., Koegel, R.L., Turnbull, A.P., Sailor, W., Anderson, J.L., Albin, R.W., Koegel, L.K., & Fox, L. (2002). Positive behavior support: Evolution of an applied science. *Journal of Positive Behavior Interventions, 4,* 4–16, 20.

Carr, E.G., & Durand, V.M. (1985). Reducing behavior problems through functional communication training. *Journal of Applied Behavior Analysis, 18,* 111–126.

Carr, E.G., Horner, R.H., Turnbull, A. Marquis, J., Magito-McLaughlin, D., McAtee, M., Smith, C.E., Anderson-Ryan, K.A., Ruef, M.B., & Doolabh, A. (1999). *Positive behavior support for people with developmental disabilities: A research synthesis.* Washington, DC: American Association on Mental Retardation.

Carr, E.G., Levin, L., McConnachie, G., Carlson, J.I., Kemp, D.C., & Smith, C.E. (1994). *Communication-based intervention for problem behavior: A user's guide for producing positive change.* Baltimore: Paul H. Brookes Publishing Co.

Carr, E.G., Levin, L., McConnachie, G., Carlson, J.I., Kemp, D.C., Smith, C.E., & McLaughlin, D.M. (1999). Comprehensive multisituational intervention for problem behavior in the community: Long-term maintenance and social validation. *Journal of Positive Behavior Interventions, 1,* 5–25.

Carr, E.G., Robinson, S., & Palumbo, L.W. (1990). The wrong issue: Aversive vs. nonaversive treatment. The right issue: Functional vs. nonfunctional treatment. In A.C. Repp & N.N. Singh (Eds.), *Perspectives on the use of nonaversive and aversive interventions for persons with developmental disabilities* (pp. 361–380). Sycamore, IL: Sycamore.

Clarke, S., Dunlap, G., & Vaughn, B. (1999). Family-centered, assessment-based intervention to improve behavior during an early morning routine. *Journal of Positive Behavior Interventions, 1,* 235–241.

Darling, R.B. (1988). Parental entrepreneurship: A consumerist response to professional dominance. *Journal of Social Issues, 44,* 141–158.

Derby, K.M., Wacker, D.P., Berg, W., DeRaad, A., Ulrich, S., Asmus, J., Harding, J., Prouty, A., Laffey, P., & Stoner, A. (1997). The long-term effects of functional communication training in home settings. *Journal of Applied Behavior Analysis, 30,* 507–531.

Derby, K.M., Wacker, D.P., Peck, S., Sasso, G., DeRaad, A., Berg, W., Asmus, J., & Ulrich, S. (1994). Functional analysis of separate topographies of aberrant behavior. *Journal of Applied Behavior Analysis, 27,* 267–278.

Dishion, T.J., & Patterson, S.G. (1996). *Preventive parenting with love, encouragement, and limits: The preschool years.* Eugene, OR: Castalia.

Dunlap, G., & Fox, L. (1996). Early intervention and serious problem behaviors: A comprehensive approach. In L.K. Koegel, R.L. Koegel, & G. Dunlap (Eds.), *Positive behavioral support: Including people with difficult behavior in the community* (pp. 31–50). Baltimore: Paul H. Brookes Publishing Co.

Dunlap, G., & Fox, L. (1999). A demonstration of behavioral support for young children with autism. *Journal of Positive Behavior Interventions, 1,* 77–88.

Dunlap, G., Hieneman, M., Knostser, T., Fox, L., Anderson, J., & Albin, R.W. (2000). Essential elements of inservice training in positive behavior support. *Journal of Positive Behavior Interventions, 2,* 22–32.

Dunlap, G., & Kern, L. (1997). Behavior analysis and its relevance to special education. In J.L. Paul, M. Churton, H. Roselli-Kostoryz, W. Morse, K. Marfo, C. Lavely, & D. Thomas (Eds.), *Foundations of special education: Basic knowledge informing research and practice in special education.* Pacific Grove, CA: Brooks/Cole Thomson Learning.

Dunlap, G., Kern-Dunlap, L., Clarke, S., & Robbins, F.R. (1991). Functional assessment, curricular revisions, and severe behavior problems. *Journal of Applied Behavior Analysis, 24,* 387–397.

Dunlap, G., Newton, S., Fox, L., Benito, N., & Vaughn, B. (in press). Family involvement in functional assessment and positive behavior support. *Focus on Autism and Other Developmental Disabilities.*

Dunlap, G., & Robbins, F.R. (1991). Current perspectives in service delivery for young children with autism. *Comprehensive Mental Health Care, 1,* 177–194.

Dunlap, G., Robbins, F.R., & Darrow, M.A. (1994). Parents' report of their children's challenging behaviors: Results of a statewide survey. *Mental Retardation, 32,* 206–212.

Dunst, C.J., Hamby, D., Trivette, C.M., Raab, M., & Bruder, M.B. (2000). Everyday family and community life and children's naturally occurring learning opportunities. *Journal of Early Intervention, 23,* 151–164.

Dunst, C.J., Trivette, C.M., & Deal, A.G. (Eds.). (1994). *Supporting and strengthening families: Methods, strategies, and practices.* Cambridge, MA: Brookline Books.

Durand, V.M. (1998). *Sleep better! A guide to improving sleep for children with special needs.* Baltimore: Paul H. Brookes Publishing Co.

Egel, A.L., & Powers, M.D. (1989). Behavioral parent training: A view of the past and suggestions for the future. In E. Cipani (Ed.), *The treatment of severe behavior disorders: Behavior analysis approaches* (pp. 153–173). Washington, DC: American Association on Mental Retardation.

Erwin, E.J. (Ed.). (1996). *Putting children first: Visions for a brighter future for young children and their families.* Baltimore: Paul H. Brookes Publishing Co.

Fawcett, S.B. (1991). Some values guiding community research and action. *Journal of Applied Behavior Analysis, 24,*621–626.

Featherstone, H. (1980). *A difference in the family.* New York: Basic Books.

Ferguson, P.M., & Asch, A. (1989). What we want for our children: Perspectives of parents and adults with disabilities. In D. Biklen, D. Ferguson, & A. Ford (Eds.), *Schooling and disability* (pp. 108–140). Chicago: University of Chicago Press.

Ferguson, P.M., & Ferguson, D.L. (2000). The promise of adulthood. In M.E. Snell & F. Brown (Eds.), *Instruction of students with severe disabilities* (5th ed., pp. 629–656). Upper Saddle River, NJ: Prentice Hall.

Fox, L., Dunlap, G., & Buschbacher, P. (2000). Understanding and intervening with children's challenging behavior: A comprehensive approach. In S.F. Warren & J. Reichle (Series Eds.) & A.M. Wetherby & B.M. Prizant (Vol. Eds.), *Communication and language intervention series: Vol. 9: Autism spectrum disorders: A transactional developmental perspective* (pp. 307–331). Baltimore: Paul H. Brookes Publishing Co.

Fox, L., Dunlap, G., & Philbrick, L.A. (1997). Providing individual supports to young children with autism and their families. *Journal of Early Intervention, 21,* 1–14.

Fox, L., Vaughn, B.J., Dunlap, G., & Bucy, M. (1997). Parent–professional partnership in behavioral support: A qualitative analysis of one family's experience. *Journal of The Association for Persons with Severe Handicaps, 22,* 198–207.

Gallagher, J.J. (2000). The beginnings of federal help for young children with disabilities. *Topics in Early Childhood Special Education, 20,* 3–6.

Gallimore, R., Coots, J., Weisner, T., Garnier, H., & Guthrie, D. (1996). Family responses to children with early developmental delays II: Accommodation intensity and activity in early and middle childhood. *American Journal of Mental Retardation, 101,* 215–232.

Gallimore, R., Goldenberg, C.N., & Weisner, T.S. (1993). The social construction and subjective reality of activity settings: Implications for community psychology. *American Journal of Community Psychology, 21,* 537–559.

Gallimore, R., Weisner, T.S., Kaufman, S.Z., & Bernheimer, L.P. (1989). The social construction of ecocultural niches: Family accommodation of developmentally delayed children. *American Journal of Mental Retardation, 94,* 216–230.

Gartner, A., Lipsky, D.K., & Turnbull, A.P. (1991). *Supporting families with a child with a disability: An international outlook.* Baltimore: Paul H. Brookes Publishing Co.

Goetz, L., Anderson, J., & Laten, S. (1989). Facilitation of family support through public school programs. In G.H.S. Singer & L.K. Irvin (Eds.). *Support for caregiving families: Enabling positive adaptation to disability* (pp. 239–251). Baltimore: Paul H. Brookes Publishing Co.

Graziano, A.M., & Diament, D.M. (1992). Parent behavioral training: An examination of the paradigm. *Behavior Modification, 16,* 3–38.

Greenspan, S.I., & Wieder, S. (2000). A developmental approach to difficulties in relating and communicating in autism spectrum disorders and related syndromes. In S.F. Warren & J. Reichle (Series Eds.) & A.M. Wetherby & B.M. Prizant (Vol. Eds.), *Communication and language intervention series: Vol. 9: Autism spectrum disorders: A transactional developmental perspective* (pp. 279–303). Baltimore: Paul H. Brookes Publishing Co.

Griest, D.L., & Forehand, K.C. (1982). How can I get any parent training done with all these other problems going on? The role of family variables in child behavior therapy. *Child & Family Behavior Therapy, 4,* 73–80.

Harris, S.L. (1982). A family systems approach to behavioral training with parents of autistic children. *Child & Family Behavior Therapy, 4,* 21–35.

Harrower, J.K. (1999). Educational inclusion of children with severe disabilities. *Journal of Positive Behavior Interventions, 1,* 215–230.

Harrower, J.K., Fox, L., Dunlap, G., & Kincaid, D. (1999). Functional assessment and comprehensive early intervention. *Exceptionality, 8,* 189–204.

Harry, B., Kalyanpur, M., & Day, M. (1999). *Building cultural reciprocity with families: Case studies in special education.* Baltimore: Paul H. Brookes Publishing Co.

Hawkins, N.E., Singer, G.H.S., & Nixon, C.D. (1993). Short-term behavioral counseling for families of persons with disabilities. In G.H.S. Singer & L.E. Powers (Eds.), *Families, disability, and empowerment: Active coping skills and strategies for family interventions* (pp. 317–341). Baltimore: Paul H. Brookes Publishing Co.

Hieneman, M., & Dunlap, G. (1999). Issues and challenges in implementing community-based behavioral support for two boys with severe behavioral difficulties. In J.R. Scotti & L.H. Meyer (Eds.). *Behavioral intervention: Principles, models, and practices* (pp. 363–384). Baltimore: Paul H. Brookes Publishing Co.

Hieneman, M., & Dunlap, G. (2001). Factors affecting the outcomes of community-based behavioral supports: II. Factor category influence. *Journal of Positive Behavior Interventions, 2,* 67–74.

Horner, R.D., & Baer, D.M. (1978). Multiple-probe technique: A variation of the multiple baseline. *Journal of Applied Behavior Analysis, 11,* 189–196.

Horner, R.H. (1999). Positive behavior supports. In M. Wehmeyer & J. Patton, (Eds.), *Mental retardation in the 21st century* (pp. 181–196). Austin, TX: PRO-ED.

Horner, R.H., Albin, R.W., Sprague, J.R., & Todd, A.W. (2000). Positive behavior support for students with severe disabilities. In M.E. Snell & F. Brown (Eds.), *Instruction of students with severe disabilities* (5th ed., pp. 207–243). Columbus, OH: Charles E. Merrill.

Horner, R.H., & Carr, E. (1997). Behavioral support for students with severe disabilities: Functional assessment and comprehensive intervention. *The Journal of Special Education, 31,* 84–104.

Horner, R.H., Dunlap, G., Koegel, R.L., Carr, E.G., Sailor, W., Anderson, J., Albin, R.W., & O'Neill, R.E. (1990). Toward a technology of "non-aversive" behavioral support. *Journal of The Association for Persons with Severe Handicaps, 15,* 125–132.

Horner, R.H., Vaughn, B.J., Day, H.M., & Ard, W.R. (1996). The relationship between setting events and problem behavior: Expanding our understanding of behavioral support. In L.K. Koegel, R.L. Koegel, & G. Dunlap (Eds.), *Positive behavior support: Including people with difficult behavior in the community* (pp. 381–402). Baltimore: Paul H. Brookes Publishing Co.

Hunt, F.M., Johnson, C.R., Owen, G., Ormerod, A.J., & Babbitt, R.L. (1990). Early intervention for severe behavior problems: The use of judgment-based assessment procedures. *Topics in Early Childhood Special Education, 10,* 111–121.

Individuals with Disabilities Education Act Amendments of 1991, PL 102–119, 20 U.S.C. §§ 1400 *et seq.*

Individuals with Disabilities Education Act Amendments of 1997, PL 105–17, 20 U.S.C. §§ 1400 *et seq.*

Iwata, B.A., Dorsey, M.F., Slifer, K.J., Bauman, K.E., & Richman, G.S. (1994). Toward a functional analysis of self-injury. *Journal of Applied Behavior Analysis, 27,* 197–209. (Reprinted from *Analysis and Intervention in Developmental Disabilities, 2,* 3–20, 1982).

Johnston, J.M. (1991). We need a new model of technology. *Journal of Applied Behavior Analysis, 24,* 425–429.

Kalyanpur, M., & Harry, B. (1999). *Culture in special education: Building reciprocal family–professional relationships.* Baltimore: Paul H. Brookes Publishing Co.

Kedesdy, J.H., & Budd, K.S. (1998). *Childhood feeding disorders: Biobehavioral assessment and intervention.* Baltimore: Paul H. Brookes Publishing Co.

Kennedy, C.H., Horner, R.H., Newton, J.S., & Kanda, E. (1990). Measuring the activity patterns of adults with severe disabilities using the Resident Lifestyle Inventory. *Journal of The Association for Persons with Severe Handicaps, 15,* 79–85.

Kennedy, C.H., & Meyer, K.A. (1998). The use of psychotropic medication for people with severe disabilities and challenging behavior: Current status and future directions. *Journal of The Association for Persons with Severe Handicaps, 23,* 83–97.

Kincaid, D. (1996). Person-centered planning. In L.K. Koegel, R.L. Koegel, & G. Dunlap (Eds.), *Positive behavior support: Including people with difficult behavior in the community* (pp. 439–465). Baltimore: Paul H. Brookes Publishing Co.

Koegel, L.K., Koegel, R.L., & Dunlap, G. (Eds.). (1996). *Positive behavioral support: Including people with difficult behavior in the community.* Baltimore: Paul H. Brookes Publishing Co.

Koegel, L.K., Steibel, D., & Koegel, R.L. (1998). Reducing aggression in children with autism toward infant or toddler siblings. *Journal of The Association for Persons with Severe Handicaps, 23,* 111–118.

Koegel, R.L., Glahn, T.J., & Nieminen, G.S. (1978). Generalization of parent-training results. *Journal of Applied Behavior Analysis, 11,* 95–109.

Koegel, R.L., Koegel, L.K., & McNerney, E.K. (2001). Pivotal areas in intervention for autism. *Journal of Clinical Child Psychology, 30,* 19–32.

Koegel, R.L., Schreibman, L., Loos, L.M., Dirlich-Wilhelm, H., Dunlap, G., Robbins, F.R., & Plienis, A.J. (1992). Consistent stress profiles in mothers of children with autism. *Journal of Autism and Developmental Disabilities, 22,* 205–216.

Lucyshyn, J.M., & Albin, R.W. (1993). Comprehensive support to families of children with disabilities and problem behaviors: Keeping it "friendly." In G.H.S. Singer & L.E. Powers (Eds.), *Families, disability, and empowerment: Active coping skills and strategies for family interventions* (pp. 365–407). Baltimore: Paul H. Brookes Publishing Co.

Lucyshyn, J.M., Albin, R.W., Horner, R.H., Mann, J.C., Mann, J.A., & Wadsworth, G. (2000, February). *Positive behavior support with a family of a child with autism: A longitudinal, experimental, single-case replication.* Colloquium presented to the Faculty of Education at the University of British Columbia, Vancouver, Canada.

Lucyshyn, J.M., Albin, R.W., & Nixon, C.D. (1997). Embedding comprehensive behavioral support in family ecology: An experimental, single-case analysis. *Journal of Consulting and Clinical Psychology, 65,* 241–251.

Lucyshyn, J.M., & Kayser, A.T. (1998, February). *Helping families build successful routines: A group process in positive behavioral support.* Paper presented at the 7th annual Best in the Northwest Conference of the Autism Society of Washington, Bellevue.

Lucyshyn, J.M., Nixon, C., Glang, A., & Cooley, E. (1996). Comprehensive family support for behavior change in children with ABI. In G.H.S. Singer, A. Glang, & J. Williams (Vol. Eds.), *Children with acquired brain injury: Educating and supporting families* (pp. 99–136). Baltimore: Paul H. Brookes Publishing Co.

Luiselli, J.K. & Cameron, M.J. (Eds.). (1998). *Antecedent control: Innovative approaches to behavioral support.* Baltimore: Paul H. Brookes Publishing Co.

Lutzker, J.R., & Campbell, R. (1994). *Ecobehavioral family interventions in developmental disabilities.* Pacific Grove, CA: Brooks/Cole Thomson Learning.

Lynch, E.W., & Hanson, M.J. (Eds.). (1998). *Developing cross-cultural competence: A guide for working with children and their families* (2nd ed.). Baltimore: Paul H. Brookes Publishing Co.

Malette, P., Mirenda, P., Kandborg, T., Jones, P., Bunz, T., & Rogow, S. (1992). Application of a lifestyle development process for persons with severe intellectual disabilities: A case study report. *Journal of The Association for Persons with Severe Handicaps, 17,* 179–191.

Markey, U.A. (2000). PARtnerships. *Journal of Positive Behavior Interventions, 2,* 188–190.

Marshall, J., & Mirenda, P. (in press). Parent–professional collaboration for positive behavior support in the home. *Focus on Autism and Other Developmental Disabilities.*

McCubbin, H.I., & Patterson, J. (1983). The family stress process: The double ABCX model of adjustment and adaptation. In H. McCubbin, M. Sussman, & J. Patterson (Eds.), *Advances and developments in family stress theory and research* (pp. 7–37). Binghamton, NY: The Haworth Press.

Meyer, L.H., & Evans, I.M. (1993). Meaningful outcomes in behavioral intervention: Evaluating positive approaches to the remediation of challenging behavior. In S.F. Warren & J. Reichle (Series Eds.) & J. Reichle

& D. Wacker (Vol. Eds.), *Communicative approaches to the management of challenging behavior* (pp. 407–428). Baltimore: Paul H. Brookes Publishing Co.

Minuchin, S. (1974). *Families and family therapy.* Cambridge, MA: Harvard University Press.

Moes, D.R., & Frea, W.D. (2000). Using family context to inform intervention planning for the treatment of a child with autism. *Journal of Positive Behavior Interventions, 2,* 40–46.

Morin, J.E. (2001). Winning over the resistant teacher. *Journal of Positive Behavior Interventions, 3,* 62–64.

Moroney, R. (1986). *Shared responsibility: Families and social policy.* Chicago: Aldine.

Mullen, K.B., & Frea, W.D. (1995). A parent–professional consultation model for functional analysis. In R.L. Koegel & L.K. Koegel (Eds.), *Teaching children with autism: Strategies for initiating positive interactions and improving learning opportunities* (pp. 175–188). Baltimore: Paul H. Brookes Publishing Co.

Newborg, J., Stock, J.R., & Wnek, L. (1984). *Battelle Developmental Inventory (BDI).* Allen, TX: DLM Teaching Resources.

O'Dell, S. (1985). Progress in parent training. In M. Hersen, R.M. Eisler, & P.M. Miller (Eds.), *Progress in behavior modification* (9th ed., pp. 57–108). San Diego: Academic Press.

O'Neill, R.E., Horner, R.H., Albin, R.W., Sprague, J.R., Storey, K., & Newton, J.S. (1997). *Functional assessment and program development for problem behavior: a practical handbook.* Pacific Grove, CA: Brooks/Cole Thomson Learning.

Pace, G.M., & Toyer, E.A. (2000). The effects of vitamin supplement on the pica of a child with severe mental retardation. *Journal of Applied Behavior Analysis, 33,* 619–622.

Pahl, J., & Quine, L. (1987). Families with mentally handicapped children. In J. Orford (Ed.), *Treating the disorder, treating the family* (pp. 39–61). Baltimore: The John Hopkins University Press.

Patterson, G.R., Reid, J.B., & Dishion, T.J. (1992). *Antisocial boys.* Eugene, OR: Castalia.

Pearpoint, J., O'Brien, J., & Forrest, M. (1992). *PATH (Planning Alternative Tomorrows with Hope): A workbook for planning positive futures.* Toronto: Inclusion Press.

Pieper, E. (1977). *Sticks and stones: The story of loving a child.* Syracuse, NY: Human Policy Press.

Rappaport, J. (1987). Terms of empowerment/ exemplars of prevention: Toward a theory for community psychology. *American Journal of Community Psychology, 15,* 121–128.

Reichle, J., & Wacker, D.P. (Vol. Eds.). (1993). *Communicative alternatives to challenging behavior: Integrating functional assessment and intervention strategies.* Baltimore: Paul H. Brookes Publishing Co.

Repp, A., & Horner, R.H. (Eds.). (1999). *Functional analysis of problem behavior: From effective assessment to effective support.* Belmont, CA: Wadsworth.

Riley, D.A. (1997). Using local research to change 100 communities for children and families. *American Psychologist, 52,* 424–433.

Risley, T. (1996). Get a life! Positive behavioral intervention for challenging behavior through life arrangement and life coaching. In L.K. Koegel, R.L. Koegel, & G. Dunlap (Eds.), *Positive behavioral support: Including people with difficult behavior in the community* (pp. 425–437). Baltimore: Paul H. Brookes Publishing Co.

Ruef, M.B., Turnbull, A.P., Turnbull, H.R., & Poston, D. (1999). Perspectives of five stakeholder groups: Challenging behavior of individuals with mental retardation and autism. *Journal of Positive Behavior Interventions, 1,* 43–58.

Sailor, W., Freeman, R., Britten, J., McCart, A., Smith, C., Scott, T., & Nelson, M. (1999). Using information technology to prepare personnel to implement functional behavioral assessment and positive behavioral support. *Exceptionality, 8,* 217–230.

Sailor, W., Gee, K., & Karasoff, P. (2000). Inclusion and school restructuring. In M.E. Snell & F. Brown (Eds.), *Instruction of students with severe disabilities* (5th ed., pp. 1–30). Upper Saddle River, NJ: Prentice Hall.

Salisbury, C.L., & Dunst, C.J. (1997). Home, school, and community partnerships: Building inclusive teams. In B. Rainforth & J. York-Barr, *Collaborative teams for students with severe disabilities: Integrating therapy and educational services* (2nd ed., pp. 57–87). Baltimore: Paul H. Brookes Publishing Co.

Sanders, M.R. (1996). New directions in behavioral family intervention with children. In T.H. Ollendick & R.J. Prinz (Eds.), *Advances in Clinical Child Psychology* (Vol. 18). New York: Kluwer Academic/Plenum Press.

Sanders, M.R., & Dadds, M.R. (1993). *Behavioral family intervention.* Upper Saddle River, NJ: Prentice Hall.

Schwartz, I.S., & Baer, D.M. (1991). Social validity assessments: Is current practice state of the art? *Journal of Applied Behavior Analysis, 24,* 189–204.

Scotti, J.R., & Meyer, L.H. (Eds.). (1999). *Behavioral intervention: Principles, models, and practices.* Baltimore: Paul H. Brookes Publishing Co.

Singer, G.H.S. (1996). Introduction: Trends affecting home and community care for people with chronic conditions in the United States. In G.H.S. Singer, L.E. Powers, & A.L. Olson (Vol. Eds.), *Redefining family support: Innovations in public–private partnerships* (pp. 3–38). Baltimore: Paul H. Brookes Publishing Co.

Singer, G.H.S., & Irvin, L.K. (Eds.). (1989). *Support for caregiving families: Enabling positive adaptation to disability.* Baltimore: Paul H. Brookes Publishing Co.

Singer, G.H.S., & Irvin, L.K. (1991). Supporting families of persons with severe disabilities: Emerging findings, practices, and questions. In L.H. Meyer, C.A. Peck, & L. Brown (Eds.), *Critical issues in the lives of people with severe disabilities* (pp. 271–312). Baltimore: Paul H. Brookes Publishing Co.

Singer, G.H.S., Irvine, A.B., & Irvin, L.K. (1989). Expanding the focus of behavioral parent training: A contextual approach. In G.H.S. Singer & L.K. Irvin (Eds.), *Support to caregiving families: Enabling positive adaptation to disability* (pp. 85–102). Baltimore: Paul H. Brookes Publishing Co.

Singer, G.H.S., & Powers, L.E. (1993). Contributing to resilience in families: An overview. In G.H.S. Singer & L.E. Powers (Eds.), *Families, disability, and empowerment: Active coping skills and strategies for family interventions* (pp. 1–25). Baltimore: Paul H. Brookes Publishing Co.

Singer, G.H.S., Powers, L.E., & Olson, A.L. (Vol. Eds.). (1996). *Redefining family support: Innovations in public–private partnerships.* Baltimore: Paul H. Brookes Publishing Co.

Singh, N.N. (1995). In search of unity: Some thoughts on family–professional partnerships in service delivery systems. *Journal of Child and Family Studies, 4,* 3–18.

Smith, R.G., & Iwata, B.A. (1997). Antecedent influences on behavior disorders. *Journal of Applied Behavior Analysis, 30,* 343–375.

Snell, M.E., & Brown, F. (Eds.). (2000). *Instruction of students with severe disabilities* (5th ed.). Upper Saddle River, NJ: Prentice Hall.

Stokes, T.F., & Baer, D.M. (1977). An implicit technology of generalization. *Journal of Applied Behavior Analysis, 10,* 349–367.

Summers, J.A., Behr, S.K., & Turnbull, A.P. (1989). Positive adaptations and coping strengths of families who have children with disabilities. In G.H.S. Singer & L.K. Irvin (Eds.). *Support for caregiving families: Enabling positive adaptation to disability* (pp. 27–40). Baltimore: Paul H. Brookes Publishing Co.

Taylor, J.C., & Carr, E.G. (1994). Severe problem behaviors of children with developmental disabilities: Reciprocal social influences. In T. Thompson & D.B. Gray (Eds.), *Destructive behavior in developmental disabilities* (pp. 274–289). Thousand Oaks, CA: Sage Publications.

Taylor, S.J., Biklen, D., & Knoll, J. (Eds.). (1987). *Community integration for people with severe disabilities.* New York: Teachers College Press.

Turnbull, A.P., Friesen, B.J., & Ramirez, C. (1998). Participatory action research as a model for conducting family research. *Journal of The Association for Persons with Severe Handicaps, 23,* 178–188.

Turnbull, A.P., & Ruef, M.B. (1996). Family perspectives on problem behavior. *Mental Retardation, 34,* 280–293.

Turnbull, A.P., & Ruef, M.B. (1997). Family perspectives on inclusive lifestyle issues for people with problem behavior. *Exceptional Children, 63,* 211–227.

Turnbull, A.P., Summers, J.A., & Brotherson, M.J. (1986). Family life cycle: Theoretical and empirical implications and future directions for families with mentally retarded members. In J.J. Gallagher & P.M. Vietze (Eds.), *Families of handicapped persons: Research, programs, and policy issues* (pp. 45–65). Baltimore: Paul H. Brookes Publishing Co.

Turnbull, A.P., & Turnbull, H.R. (1985). *Parents speaking out: Then and now.* Columbus, OH: Charles E. Merrill.

Turnbull, A.P., & Turnbull, H.R. (1991). Family assessment and family empowerment: An ethical analysis. In L.H. Meyer, C.A. Peck, & L. Brown (Eds.), *Critical issues in the lives of people with severe disabilities* (pp. 485–488). Baltimore: Paul H. Brookes Publishing Co.

Turnbull, A.P., & Turnbull, H.R. (2000a). Achieving "rich" lifestyles. *Journal of Positive Behavior Interventions, 2,* 190–192.

Turnbull, A.P, & Turnbull, H.R. (2000b). Family–professional partnerships. In M.E. Snell & F. Brown (Eds.), *Instruction of students with severe disabilities* (5th ed., pp. 31–66). Upper Saddle River, NJ: Prentice Hall.

Turnbull, A.P., & Turnbull, H.R. (2001). *Families, professionals and exceptionality: Collaborating for empowerment.* Upper Saddle River, NJ: Prentice Hall.

Turnbull, H.R. (1999). Two case studies of functional assessment and functional support: IDEA compliance and capacity-building issues. In A.C. Repp & R.H. Horner (Eds.), *Functional analysis of problem behavior: From effective assessment to effective support* (pp. 321–337). Belmont, CA: Wadsworth.

Turnbull, H.R., & Turnbull, A.P., Stowe, M., & Wilcox, B.L. (2000). *Free appropriate public education: The law and children with disabilities* (6th ed.). Denver, CO: Love Publishing Co.

Turnbull, H.R., Wilcox, B.L., Stowe, M., & Turnbull, A.P. (2001). IDEA requirements for use of PBS: Guidelines for responsible agencies. *Journal of Positive Behavior Interventions, 3,* 11–18.

Vandercook, T., York, J., & Forrest, M. (1989). The McGill Action Planning System (MAPS): A strategy for building the vision. *Journal of The Association for Persons with Severe Handicaps, 14,* 205–215.

Vaughn, B.J., Clarke, S., & Dunlap, G. (1997). Assessment-based intervention for severe behavior problems in a natural family context. *Journal of Applied Behavior Analysis, 30,* 713–716.

Vaughn, B.J., Dunlap, G., Fox, L., Clarke, S., & Bucy, M. (1997). Parent–professional partnership in behavioral support: A case study of community based intervention. *Journal of The Association for Persons with Severe Handicaps, 22,* 186–197.

Vaughn, B.J., Fox, L., & Dunlap, G. (2000, December). *The family network project: Providing positive behavior support to families from underserved communities.* Paper presented at the 25th annual meeting of The Association for Persons with Severe Handicaps, Miami Beach, FL.

Wacker, D.P., Cooper, L.J., Peck, S.M., Derby, K.M., & Berg, W.K. (1999). Community-based functional assessment. In A.C. Repp & R.H. Horner (Eds.), *Functional analysis of problem behavior: From effective assessment to effective support* (pp. 32–56). Belmont, CA: Wadsworth.

Wacker, D.P., Peck, S., Derby, K.M., Berg, W., & Harding, J. (1996). Developing long-term reciprocal interactions between parents and their young children with problematic behavior. In L.K. Koegel, R.L. Koegel, & G. Dunlap (Eds.), *Positive behavioral support: Including people with difficult behavior in the community* (pp. 51–80). Baltimore: Paul H. Brookes Publishing Co.

Walker, B., & Singer, G.H.S. (1993). Improving collaborative communication between professionals and parents. In G.H.S. Singer & L.E. Powers (Eds.), *Families, disability, and empowerment: Active coping skills and strategies for family intervention* (pp. 285–315). Baltimore: Paul H. Brookes Publishing Co.

Walker, H.M., Colvin, G., & Ramsey, E. (1995). *Antisocial behavior in schools: Strategies and best practices.* Pacific Grove, CA: Brooks/Cole Thomson Learning.

Webster-Stratton, C. (1994). Advancing videotape parent training: A comparison study. *Journal of Consulting and Clinical Psychology, 62,* 583–593.

Webster-Stratton, C. (1998). Preventing conduct problems in Head Start children: Strengthening parenting competencies. *Journal of Consulting and Clinical Psychology, 66,* 715–730.

Webster-Stratton, C., & Herbert, M. (1993). "What really happens in parent training?" *Behavior Modification, 17,* 407–456.

Weigle, K.L. (1997). Positive behavior support as a model for promoting educational inclusion. *Journal of The Association for Persons with Severe Handicaps, 22,* 36–48.

Wetherby, A.M., Prizant, B.M., & Schuler, A.L. (2000). Understanding the nature of communication and language impairments. In S.F. Warren & J. Reichle (Series Eds.) & A.M. Wetherby & B.M. Prizant (Vol. Eds.), *Communication and language intervention series: Vol. 9: Autism spectrum disorders: A transactional developmental perspective* (pp. 109–141). Baltimore: Paul H. Brookes Publishing Co.

Wheeler, M. (1998). *Toilet training for individuals with autism and related disorders: A comprehensive guide for parents and teachers.* Arlington, TX: Future Horizons.

Whiting, B., & Edwards, C. (1988). *Children of different worlds: The formation of social behavior.* Cambridge, MA: Harvard University Press.

Whyte, W.F. (1991). *Participatory action research.* Thousand Oaks, CA: Sage Publications.

Wolery, M.R., Bailey, D.B., Sugai, G.M. (1988). *Effective teaching: Principles and procedures of applied behavior analysis with exceptional students.* Needham Heights, MA: Allyn & Bacon.

Wolfensberger, W. (1972). *The principle of normalization in human services.* Toronto: National Institute on Mental Retardation.

CHAPTER 2

Finding Positive Behavior Support One Piece at a Time

Living and Growing with David

Renee M. Whaley

Editors' Note

The following chapter is an account of the author's inductive discovery of the basic premises of positive behavior support. The author, Renee M. Whaley, acquired her knowledge through the life experiences of her son, David, and through her constant efforts to give him understanding and support. In the 20 years of David's life, a series of developmental events revealed important realities about the nature of David's behavior (and all of our behavior) and the implications that these truths have for person-centered, respectful, and effective interventions. The author's discovery of positive behavior support predated the field's formal declaration and description of the approach.

Renee M. Whaley has used the insights gained through her son's life to assist many families and professionals through her work with the Family Network on Disabilities, her involvement with many family and advocacy organizations, and her membership on Florida's State Training Team on Positive Behavior Support. We are grateful to Ms. Whaley for sharing the fruits of her experience.

Behavior was an issue with my son, David, from the hour of his birth. David was my only child. I cannot compare his birth to any other. I can say, however, that it was not the birth for which I prepared. He was delivered as an emergency C-section on a day in which the hospital delivered at least 30 infants. It was a very stressful environment.

I awoke before midnight on March 9, 1976, with contractions that did not seem as painful as I had expected. The contractions were increasing in frequency. Instinctively, I knew that my body was ready to deliver. Although I knew the contractions were far too painless, I also knew through some primal instinct that it was time for this baby to be born.

It was decided at the hospital that David was too large for me to deliver vaginally. I remember lying on the assembly-line tarmac, waiting to have the C-section and having assorted staff come by to discuss how big my baby would be. The guesses ranged from 11 pounds to 14 pounds. I remember thinking, "Oh, dear God, don't let this be a girl; I cannot put on the birth announcement that the Whaleys are the proud parents of a 14-pound girl." An intern said, "Well, Mrs. Whaley, I think you are delivering a Green Bay Packer." I remember saying, "We aren't talking athlete here; I want 5 pounds of pure intelligence!" That phrase echoed in my head for years. In the illogical way that we try to make sense of the unthinkable, I wondered if I had challenged the fates.

When David was delivered, he was just under 10 pounds and full of kicking, screaming fury. I asked immediately about his Apgar scores. The answer was a clear 10–10. He had passed his first test. He would be bright, and all things were possible. He was a strawberry blond with fair skin and looked 3 months old. I had no idea that I could feel the intensity of emotion I felt for this newborn child.

David and I spent the next 3 hours in recovery. Within minutes of our arrival in the recovery room, I felt that something was not right. David seemed highly agitated. He was thrashing about in the isolet. He screamed, squirmed, flailed, and had to be repositioned in the isolet frequently. If it is possible for an hour-old infant to experience rage, David was furious. I felt the first pangs of fear for my son.

After 3 hours, I was admitted to a room and David went to the nursery. Within the next 5 hours, David experienced an oxygen assault from ingesting formula into his lungs. His pediatrician was called. When the pediatrician came to my room after examining David, it was his opinion that David had sustained no permanent ill effect. His color was good and he was active. It was explained that any time foreign material is in the lungs, it must be treated as pneumonia. David would have to undergo an 8-day regimen of antibiotics. That did not concern me. What the doctor was not saying did concern me.

The pediatrician was reluctant to answer my questions. I was not comforted by his vague responses. At some point, he stated that he had no concrete evidence to indicate David was not fine. He said, "David may just be one of these FLK types." He told me an FLK was a "funny looking kid." He was referring to how David behaved and responded.

David was in the intermediate care nursery for the next 7 days. They were uneventful from a medical view, yet David was unlike any baby I had known. He was stiff to hold. He did not conform to your body when held. He seemed agitated and behaved how I imagined that a baby addicted to crack might respond. He did not nurse easily. He slept far less than other newborns. When he did sleep, his eyes were partly open and his head was thrown back at a 90-degree angle to his body. Every time the pediatrician saw David during the hospital stay, he made some comment about David's behavior. Although the doctor would reassure me David was doing fine, the word *behavior* was always there like a small, foreboding cloud. From the day of David's birth, I began to watch other infants and children and compare his behavior with theirs.

Like all new moms, I was going to provide every enriching experience for my son. I had placed him on a quilt in the middle of my living room so he could see the world around him. I left the room to get a bottle. When I returned, David was gone. David and I were the only people in the house. I was struck with terror. Someone had stolen David! Then, I heard muffled sounds in the hall. My 12-day-old son had rolled over and over and into the hall. I sat and cried. I understood enough to know it was not a good neurological sign. We saw David's pediatrician when David was 14 days old. I discussed my fears. The doctor produced a small drawstring bag with several items and tried to engage David's attention. I didn't know at the time, but he was administering a Bayley test. I asked him what he was testing to determine. His answer was vague and noncommittal. I had already been inventorying what I knew about my child's odd, distant behavior. I had experience with a child with autism in a previous job. Then, I said the words that had been forming in my mind for the first 2 weeks of my beloved son's life: "Are you looking for autism?" His answer was, "Mrs. Whaley, you read too much!" On some level, I knew that David had a high probability for a diagnosis of autism. I just knew.

The first year of David's life was a challenge. He grew at a phenomenal rate and physically looked 2 years old at 1 year of age. His teeth began to come in at 3 months. His development was all over the board. He did not sit up until 8 months but was pulling to a standing position and doing stepping motions. David was the most unhappy baby I had ever seen. I was heartbroken that I could not seem to meet the needs of my child. I was no comfort to him. He did not even want to look at me. Life simply seemed to anger him. He did no cooing, nor did he make baby sounds. He screamed with what looked like rage. At 6 months of age, I insisted that his pediatrician do a workup. Something was not right. The doctor sent us to Easter Seals. The staff's evaluation was as unsettling as David's development. His upper body control was at a 4-month level; his lower body was at an 8-month level. His receptive language appeared to be good, but his expressive language was nonexistent. The staff had no answers but wanted to do a follow-along.

When David was 3 months old, we moved to Ohio. Shortly after this move, David began turning pages in a book if it was held for him. He turned pages with a pincer grip, not the palm grip that children usually develop first. He remained fascinated by any printed material. He focused his attention on the TV screen anytime words scrolled. He watched large logos on billboards as we drove by them. It was clear that some billboards held greater interest than others. At 8 months, he sat alone and began to crawl on the same day. The only time David smiled was when a flash bulb went off. All his baby pictures have this brilliant smile because the flash had been activated. The smile ended the minute the flash was over.

Just prior to 18 months of age, David still was not walking. I insisted that he be evaluated again. This time, I was referred to a diagnostic and treatment center for crippled children. We did the intake in a huge therapy room with no furniture. As I gave information to the therapist, David stood holding my leg. As I was telling the therapist that David did not walk, she got an odd look on her face. I looked around and saw that David had walked approximately 15 feet away from me. I still think of our visit to that center as my miracle cure. Nevertheless, although the staff were pleasant, David was not the kind of child they were primarily equipped to serve.

It was that week that I discovered that David was reading. During this time, tantrums were ongoing and full blown. At times, he would scream for hours on end. David slept less than 8 hours a day. He was inconsolable when his distress was expressed. Nothing comforted him. His pediatricians were either condescending with the "now, now, mother" attitude or unresponsive when I told them of the nightmare childhood my son was experiencing. One particular morning, David had eaten breakfast and was settled in the living room with a number of his favorite toys. All of a sudden, he let out a piercing scream. I rushed into the living room and could not find any reason for him to be upset. I went through an entire list of every possible need he might have. Nothing quieted him. In frustration, I left the room. In a few moments, he became quiet and I came back to see him sitting with a magazine. He opened the magazine and took my finger and pointed to the word *Avon* in an advertisement. David loved commercials. Other mothers sang lullabies; I sang the Oscar Mayer jingle. When I saw the word *Avon,* I realized that the Avon jingle had been playing on TV when David screamed. I sang the jingle and he gave me a huge smile. I went through the magazine and found advertisements with jingles he knew. When I sang the wrong jingle, he would become agitated and verbalize "nananan." When I sang the correct jingle for the advertisement, he would smile. David was reading the logo names.

It occurred to me that David might just recognize logos because of their unique design and color. I tried writing products he liked on paper, and again he knew the product the names represented. David had loved books from 3 months of age. He particularly loved maps and atlases. I next tested writing the name of a prominent place and giving him the wrong name. The same response occurred: When I spoke the correct name, I got a big smile; when I gave a wrong name, I got the "nananan" response. I stopped testing David at 200 words. I was sure that he was reading single words.

Because David was reading, I knew that he must be diagnosed. His development was not normal. I surveyed the local area and found the most prominent pediatrician. His practice was closed. After I threatened to picket the office in true sixties fashion with my best Saul Alinsky tactics, the doctor agreed to see me for an hour-long consultation. David was placed in a Cleveland clinic for a full workup that included an EEG, an occupational therapy assessment, a physical therapy assessment, a speech-language evaluation, a full auditory assessment, and complete psychological assessment. It was 3 days of intense testing. The result was a diagnosis of moderate mental retardation. When I asked what I could do to help him, the neurologist simply said, "Take him home and practice benign neglect." I will never forget the sounds of those words nor fail to respond to the dangerous implications they might have had for David and our family. The neurologist did, however, refer us to a low-incidence clinic for additional assessment.

The staff at the clinic did testing across three environments: their facility, my home, and David's preschool. By this time, I had located a preschool program for David in Bay Village, Ohio. He had washed out of a county program and a Montessori program because of his behavior. At the time, David was the youngest and newest child in the class. The teacher was reluctant to take him at younger than 2 years old; most of the children began the program at 3 years old. I explained the level of his behavior and told her that if we did not get a handle on his behavior, we would be looking at such intensive intervention in the future that it frightened me. The teacher made the exception. I would take David to school and watch from behind a one-way mirror as David struggled to escape every human contact and activity presented. He raged and threw tantrums almost nonstop. He finished the day early and was wringing wet with sweat from fighting every attempt to engage him in an activity.

The clinic staff were as divided on their opinion of what David's true abilities were as I was. He presented high in some areas and very low in others. The assessment produced more questions than answers, but they were good questions—questions that I know today were the basis for a good hypothesis. I had told no one that I believed David was reading. He did not speak, and I suppose I wasn't sure that anyone would believe me. When the team members concluded the report, I asked if they had a yellow pages and a morning newspaper. I explained that I wanted to show them something about David, which they agreed to let me do. I asked them to show David any advertisement of their choice and ask David what it was. They chose a temporary secretarial service with a photograph of a rose in the advertisement. David took one look and pantomimed typing. He did this kind of pantomime for several advertisements. He clearly demonstrated he had some knowledge of each advertisement.

Next, I asked that they choose any city named in the newspaper that was not totally obscure and show it to David. After he was shown the name, I asked that they verbally give David the name of three cities—one being the correct name—and watch his response. He correctly identified all of the cities. It was confirmed that at 22 months of age, he was reading. They speculated that he might be hyperlexic, but a person with hyperlexic reading would not demonstrate understanding of the words read. David clearly understood. The group members were interested in David and decided to follow his progress. They wrote conflicting reports but agreed that his understanding was far greater than his ability to communicate. They expressed discomfort with this less-than-clear picture of David's disability and the level of his intellectual abilities. This was my first lesson in the value of a good baseline.

The preschool was beginning to have an impact on David. He required more speech-language intervention. By pure serendipity and utilization of the yellow pages, I began David in private speech-language therapy at a local hospital. The therapist was probably the person who taught me the most about understanding and shaping behavior.

At 2 ½ years of age, David still did not speak. No one could tell me if speech would ever develop, and for as much as I struggled with David's difficult behavior, I was equally concerned that he had no way to express himself. Instinctively, I knew that a lack of language contributed to David's anger and temper tantrums.

David was big enough and bright enough to get into things that were dangerous. He also was becoming an escape artist. If your attention was engaged anywhere else, he took the opportunity to escape the house or school or to conduct an experiment in flooding the bathroom. His curiosity led him to do things that I could not anticipate. He did not sleep more than a few hours a night, so keeping up with him became a major and tiring problem. Breaking, dumping, shredding, spilling, and destroying were favorite activities. He was noncompliant to most basic requests. He had a very restrictive diet and only ate mashed potatoes, applesauce, and rice cereal. He ate nothing that was not in a purée or baby-food consistency. He could not entertain himself and fought any attempt to engage him purposefully. He was now routinely biting himself on the wrist and chewing the sleeves off all of his shirts. If provoked sufficiently, he would bite the person who was the object of his tantrum. When being physically assisted through an activity, he would go limp and fall on the floor. I had no idea how to change his behavior. His behavior was escalating at a rapid rate. I was afraid for him.

His preschool teacher gave me my first lesson in ignoring unwanted behavior. It was circle time and David had no intention of joining the children for the lesson. The teacher decided it was time for David to join the group. She physically picked him up and sat him on her lap as she began to read *The Very Hungry Caterpillar*. David was not interested in the story and squirmed and yelled. The teacher was tall and leggy, so she simply crossed her leg over his kicking ones, enveloped him in her arms, and went on reading. He thrashed, arched, kicked, and screamed to no avail. She continued to read. Her voice did not show any awareness that he was raging. In what appeared to be absolute fury, he began to bite her. He bit her arm, her shoulder, and her breast repeatedly. She made no sign that he was affecting her. *The Very Hungry Caterpillar* continued. I watched my son wage this violent attack through a one-way glass and cried because I knew it would be his last day in school.

When the story was over, David was exhausted and soaking wet from perspiration. The teacher calmly sat him down on the floor and told him it was time to go home. She walked him out to me. I was shaking, sure she would tell me that he was impossible and his education at this school was over. Instead, she very calmly said she believed that he would do much better at the next storytime. I cried. He came back the next day and, for the first time, sat in his chair for storytime. It was my first lesson in ignoring "bad" behavior. To this day, I have no idea how the teacher endured David's onslaught without flinching. I can only say that I am grateful she did.

I really did not begin to understand how to help David shape better behavior until the speech-language therapist began working with David. She was young, full of life and energy, and had an absolute natural talent for working with challenging kids. She was a trained and practicing speech-language therapist, but I know today that she was a natural positive behavior analyst. She was the first one to tell me that David did things for a reason and that it was our job to understand why. That is pretty close to saying, "All behavior has a function." She taught me never to assume that I knew why David was doing something. She taught me to really look at all that was happening when I was trying to understand some behavior. She could see life from David's perspective. In fact, she would crawl under the table if that was where David could be reached. Without judgment, she worked with him whatever his emotional, physical, and intellectual state. I swear that she had great fun with this raging, unhappy child. She got him to do things no one else would even suggest for him. She always took the time to observe. She knew how to wait and how to motivate. Everything she did with David was based on the assumption that he was bright and would do what was in his best interest in the easiest way possible. She worked at giving David control over his life; so many others had worked to control him. She figured out what he wanted and taught him ways to attain those things. The speech-language therapist took her cues from David. She built on his skills and took him where he wanted to go. With that approach, David had less need to rage. Given what we know today, David's success with the speech-language therapist is hardly surprising. She never made him risk more than he could tolerate, and the final control was always with him and within safe limits.

The speech-language therapist first saw David at the hospital with two other little boys. Both boys were a little older and more advanced than David. One had emerging language and grew up to have a significant speech problem and some minor learning disabilities. The second boy was a beautiful, angelic-looking child who was later diagnosed as having autism. He was as passive and angelic as David was raging and aggressive. One day, I watched the three boys during therapy through the one-way mirror. David was clearly the most difficult. He threw the puzzle on the floor, crawled under the table, and yelled every time the therapist insisted that he do a task.

I was sharing the observation room with others who were watching speech-language therapy for a stroke patient. They began watching David, and I could tell by their expressions that they believed David was a "demon child." Finally, they left the room, and once again I cried. Their judgment clearly was that David needed discipline and I had failed in that duty. The speech-language therapist laughed at this idea. She said that she was more encouraged when a child was noncompliant; it means that he or she cares. She told me that if David cared, he would learn. She was right. Years later, it was clear that my son had accomplished more simply because he cared enough to get angry. We used that anger to shape his learning. His anger taught us what was important to him. When we knew this, we taught him alternative ways to express himself that were more acceptable and effective.

The speech-language therapist taught me the strong link between David's behavior and his lack of language. When I resisted learning sign language, she helped me understand the far greater importance of David's developing language. She taught me that language was more than speech and that my son needed to expand his language regardless of whether he ever spoke.

Because David had demonstrated both interest and capability in reading, the speech-language therapist and I began to increase his language potential by labeling everything in David's environment with cards that had a picture of the object and the name printed beneath it. These 4" x 4" cards were taped all over our house, identifying things as common as a sofa and as unique as Sophia, David's finch. The refrigerator was covered with food option cards, and the front door had a ring over the doorknob with cards of all the potential places we might visit, ranging from the grocery store to his grandmother's house. When we spoke to David, we used these cards wherever possible to illustrate what we were saying and signing. As we introduced more signs and cards, we began increasing our demand that his wants and needs be communicated in some formal manner (e.g., card, sign, point and gesture).

Both the speech-language therapist and the preschool teacher were sure that David was more cooperative when he knew what to expect. We began making a linear picture schedule for David's day. We allowed him to choose activities as rewards for completing tasks during the day. He was quick to grasp this concept and became tyrannical if anyone endeavored to change the order once it was determined for the day.

When it was clear to us as a family that predictability was important to David's ability to enjoy life, I began to illustrate all new events for him. I purchased a large newsprint pad. Because I have some art skills, I started drawing pictures of what I told him verbally. If we were going to a movie, I would draw the marquee, ticket booth, refreshment stand, popcorn, and the movie screen. I might add absurdities to illustrate the points. David came to love this activity. Often, I would illustrate our conversations.

David had an incredible sense of humor that emerged as his language increased. I often tell parents that David made puns before he could speak. The first two signs David was taught were SHOES and SAUSAGE. I cannot say that SHOES and SAUSAGE were the best and most functional signs to choose. Today, I would make different choices, but that was 20 years ago. David watched us explain and demonstrate the two signs, which are somewhat similar—which, again, was probably another mistake in choice of signs. SHOES is signed by tapping closed fists together at the thumbs. SAUSAGE is signed by holding fists in the same position but by opening and closing the fists as hands move from the center position. I had no idea if David understood what we were showing him. The next morning, David responded to the question, "What do you want for breakfast?" by pointing to the eggs card and signing SHOES. He laughed as though it was a great joke. For as long as he lived, a couple times a year he would tell me that he would have eggs and shoes for breakfast.

The fact that David was able to make a joke with a two-word sign vocabulary was important to my understanding of the importance of communication to his well-being and behavior. I remember thinking that my child is wonderfully aware of absurd humor but has had no way to share that humor. I began to understand the depth of his frustration and anger. It served to strengthen my resolve that David would have every access to language and that his dignity and choices would be respected to the extent I was able to affect his world. As David's language skills increased, his behavior improved in almost direct proportions.

It is my nature to stand back and look for the reason in a person's behavior. It was therefore an easy concept for me to begin to look at what was affecting David's behavior and to take notes. The notes were in the form of nonemotional journal entries that recorded exactly what was happening in David's life. The detail of life has always interested me, so my notes reflected all of the details. Sound, light, temperature, individuals present, and state of health were all things that found their way into my journals. As I read the journals over time, patterns would emerge. I began seeing similar responses in similar circumstances. Simple things became clear. Low light calmed David. Surprise was stressful for him. Certain textures were uncomfortable for him. Words like *soon, near,* and *in a while* only served to increase David's anxiety. By keeping good notes and recognizing similarities, I began slowly to understand what might trigger both good and bad behavior. I would test a supposition and then adjust his experience to reflect the good outcomes.

Even with all of the adaptations that we made for David's lack of speech, we were unable to provide him with all of the communication supports that he needed to reflect the full depth of his understanding. We could communicate concrete things, but we had little ability to communicate the more complicated concepts that are common to any conversation or humor that David appeared to have the intellectual ability to comprehend. Some things were simply impossible for David's family, teachers, and therapists to understand. We were unsure whether the problem was poor communication or failure to understand the concept. This "chicken or the egg" thinking was maddening. Did David not talk because he did not understand, or did he not talk because he was unable to process the mechanics of speech? Looking back, I am sure that both deficits were present.

David spent 2 years at another preschool that was operated by his speech-language therapist, who was also his primary teacher. Preschool was not guaranteed in the 1970s, so there were no legal guidelines and no individualized education programs (IEPs). Nonetheless, David spent time with typical children in both of his preschool experiences.

When David was 5 years old, we moved to Arizona. The foundation for our approach to learning had been formed by David's early experience with his first preschool teacher and his speech-language therapist in Ohio. In Arizona, after several abortive attempts to find the correct educational programs for David, we found a school for him. His primary teacher, a former ballerina, was also a speech-language pathologist. She was one of those people who naturally worked well with students who had autism. She understood how to teach in single concepts with a strong language base and to include enough drama to engage the students. She was ahead of her time in understanding the need for students with autism to move in space and to coordinate their movement with rhythm and music.

This teacher also reinforced the mind-set that David could do anything until he demonstrated that he could not. She was quick to recognize that even though David needed a lot of repetition, he had no tolerance for rote sameness. She was expert at adding novel elements to repetitive activities. She was expert at embedding language goals in instructional material that utilized all of his senses and increased his language development. She asked nothing of him that did not give him a way to be interactive in the area of language.

This teacher and the students would mount two drama performances each year. They were abbreviated forms of classical musicals. They produced *The Other Nutcracker, The Other Mikado,* and many more. There were no children enrolled in the school who did not have strong language and behavior issues, and many of the children had a diagnosis of autism or related disabilities, yet all of them participated in the productions. The productions included costuming, scenery, lighting, and music. The staff even wore tuxedos. Children with no speech and limited social awareness were, for two nights per year, stars in front-and-center productions attended by their families and friends.

At first, I was skeptical that David could tolerate performing. The reality was that not only could he perform, but he also enjoyed the applause as much as anyone. He basked in the attention that it brought him. One of my proudest moments was watching him be Mr. Banks in *The Other Mary Poppins.* I also will always remember him as a chimney sweeper in the same musical, pushing a broom across a dark stage full of chimney tops with a single spotlight on him. He stopped center stage, tipped his hat to the audience, and pushed his broom off the stage in that single spot of light. It was as charming as Chaplin's "Little Tramp." There was not a dry eye in that house. David was a star, and he knew it.

I learned that night that David needed the opportunity to be successful and that he could be with the right preparation. We took pictures of all of David's productions. All his life, he would look through the album of his plays and announce to us that he was going to visit his memories. The more opportunities David had to participate in the typical activities that other kids took for granted, the more acceptable his behavior became.

David found his voice at the school in Arizona. At 5½ years old, David finally began to use speech. By age 6, he was using full sentences. His language was first heard at this school, but it was born of the work begun by his previous preschool teacher and speech-language therapist. His new teacher in Arizona taught David the things that interested him in a way that he could internalize. She gave him the desire to know more and the willingness to share that knowledge in a way that demonstrated how much he truly knew. This teacher taught me to view David as a child first and to look at the autism second. She taught me to give him skills that met his needs, not mine. She taught me that I should not allow anyone to teach him dumb stuff. He didn't have the time or the need to learn things that did not improve his life. His teacher understood that David needed to control himself and taught him ways to do that. She always treated him as capable and as valuable. He understood that in her, and thus loved her as much as he loved his previous teacher and speech-language therapist.

David's development was consistently demonstrating that his academic strengths were his strongest assets. In the fifth grade, he began to attend public school. We moved to Maryland, where he was included in general education classes with strong support to assist in developing better speech and better social skills. We were transferred to Florida, where he entered public middle school in general education classes. His high school experience was in general education with community-based instruction.

I remember the first day David became his own advocate. We had moved to Florida, where the heat can be brutal and school buses are not air-conditioned. He came home on such a day. The bus driver stomped off the bus to greet me before David exited. She was visibly upset and stated that she was writing David up. I asked why. It seemed that the window by his assigned seat was broken and would not open. He elected to sit in another seat. I asked if he was sitting in someone else's seat. She said no; it was a vacant seat but not his assigned seat. She said she told David three times to move and take his assigned seat. Apparently, David ignored her. As we stood in the 100-degree summer heat I asked, "So, what happened?" She said she ordered him to move to the seat with no ventilation and he refused—this time by saying clearly, "Lady, you are full of s____!" I looked her in the eye and, as evenly as I knew how, said "What did he do wrong?" I am sure that according to bus regulations his behavior was inappropriate. Yet, frankly, it was one of the most appropriate demonstrations of David's understanding his right to be comfortable and his right to seek reasonable accommodation.

As the incident on the school bus shows, David apparently had done some incidental learning as the result of his inclusive education. His last teachers were other kids. He reached the point at which he was able to model some of the behavior of his typical peers in many important ways. I came to understand that only other teenagers could teach David what behavior was appropriate for that age. He had developed all the "teenitus" of any young, emerging adult. He liked to stay up late and had difficulty getting up early. He was messy and mouthy. He was lazy at times. Like all teenagers, he was angling as well as learning to take control of his life.

The final lesson for me was that David, because he had autism, was held to a different standard. Other people without a disability could be lazy, rude, or unmotivated. For David, it was "behavioral" and something someone wanted to include in an IEP. The truth

is that a disability is not a right to change a person's characteristics for model citizenship or the convenience of others. It was unfair to expect David to always do his "best." Who in the world always does his or her best?

David developed skills that allowed us to plan for his move to an apartment with a support team that would assist his transition from school to postschool life. Even though David was successful in so many ways, the medical profession used a different standard of care. Because of that difference, David died on December 3, 1996, at age 20, of a misdiagnosed ruptured appendix. Behavior that was not abhorrent but the result of abject pain was discounted.

As we try to change the behavior of people with disabilities, it is important that we also change our behavior. Behavior always has a function. If we do not understand that function, then we place people at risk. Maybe that is the ultimate lesson I have learned. Understand that lesson, and know that I will never love anyone more or miss anyone more profoundly than I do David, and you will have the legacy of my one and only beloved son.

Postscript

The philosophical tenets that drive the delivery of good and respectful behavioral support are the result of work by caring professionals who understand the need to respect the individual and to provide interventions that do not violate the right to have needs met. I did not know at the time that I was learning the underpinnings of what is now known as positive behavior support. When I was keeping notes and distancing myself from the actions of my child to better view what in the environment was triggering behavior, I did not know that I was doing what is now part of a functional assessment. The single validity for me of practicing positive behavior support is that it always respects the person. This respect on my part was driven by my absolute love of my son. It is not surprising to me that David was successful. He was respected in a way that required all who worked with him to never violate him by forcing a behavior change by external control. The control was always given to David. To be sure, it was not always easy to discern what David's behavior meant in terms of his interests or needs. When I think about his entire short life, however, it is clear that he was most forgiving when we attempted to understand him. When we finally understood what his behavior meant and could offer him a better alternative, I was amazed at his willingness to accommodate our desire to have him do things differently.

If I have one regret, it is the time I wasted teaching "dumb stuff"—stuff that accommodated society's preferences, not his. I must have spent, at the very least, 3 months of a 20-year life trying to stop David from rocking his head from side to side. It made him appear different in public. Today, the head-rocking goal would NEVER appear on his IEP. That goal served everyone else's goals but had nothing to do with his needs. It was clear that we did not have an alternative that helped David release stress more effectively. Yet, we demanded that he change a behavior simply to accommodate our desire to have him look "normal." Today, I would not spend the time on such trivial goals. I would spend time on things that improved the quality of David's life in a far more concrete manner.

For me, positive behavior support is a tool that enabled me to build a strong bridge to my son. I remain incredibly grateful to those who helped me understand how to support the most important person in my life. I know his quality of life was better for that help. I remain so proud and so grateful for having been David's mother. He remains in my heart.

CHAPTER *3*

Family Interests and Positive Behavior Support

Opportunities Under the Individuals with Disabilities Education Act

H. Rutherford Turnbull, III, Ann P. Turnbull, and Brennan L. Wilcox

This chapter describes how families of children with disabilities and accompanying challenging behavior are suitable beneficiaries of positive behavior support (PBS) under provisions of the Individuals with Disabilities Education Act (IDEA). Thus, the chapter's focus is three-fold. First, what are IDEA's basic provisions that authorize families to be involved in their children's education? Second, what are IDEA's basic provisions that affect children who are suitable beneficiaries of PBS? Third, what is the relationship of the family-participation provisions of IDEA to the PBS provisions of IDEA, and what are the consequences of that relationship for families, service providers, and researchers? This chapter does not review the research on family–provider relationships, especially as they revolve around PBS. We have done that elsewhere and have concluded that, as a general rule, the IDEA legal authority for a partnership between families and professionals is less than optimally realized (Turnbull & Turnbull, 2001). Despite these findings, the fact remains that parents are more fully involved with schools and the education of their children than ever before, and the IDEA structure that made that result possible was strengthened by the Individuals with Disabilities Education Act Amendments of 1997 (PL 105-17).

Those two statements are cause for celebration. Yet, the new IDEA provisions for PBS put an extraordinary burden on parents. Parents need to understand IDEA, PBS, and the relationship between them as well as be prepared to act on that knowledge base. Parents also must invest extraordinary amounts of time, incur emotional stress when advocating for a new technology, and, perhaps, shoulder the legal expenses to secure PBS.

Is the price too high for parents to pay? We think not. Even so, we continue to bemoan the fact that, as in the past, the burden of ensuring a free appropriate public education (FAPE) and using the newest technologies ultimately falls on parents (Turnbull & Turnbull, 2001). Nonetheless, as researchers into and users of positive behavioral interventions and supports, it is clear to us that PBS is worthy of hot pursuit by parents (Turnbull, Turnbull, Stowe, & Wilcox, 2000).

THE INDIVIDUALS WITH
DISABILITIES EDUCATION ACT'S SIX PRINCIPLES

Ever since IDEA was first enacted as the Education for All Handicapped Children Act of 1975 (PL 94-142), its six basic principles have governed the rights of students and the duties of schools (see Turnbull et al., 2000). The significance of these principles is that they have also authorized families and schools to enter into a special partnership (see Turnbull & Turnbull, 2001). This fact is particularly salient with respect to PBS.

The first of the six principles is zero reject. This is a rule against excluding any child with a disability from a FAPE. Among other things, it states that the student may be disciplined but may not be subjected to any cessation of educational services (IDEA, §§ 1412 [a][1], 1415 [k]). It also provides the student with a public education at no cost to his or her parents (IDEA, §§ 1412 [a][1], 1401 [8]).

The second principle is nondiscriminatory evaluation. This principle requires fair assessment of the student to determine whether he or she has a disability and, if so, what special education and related services are required (IDEA, § 1414 [a]–[c]). To carry out a fair evaluation, the school must conduct an interdisciplinary assessment of the student across a variety of domains (cognitive, behavioral, developmental, and physical) and in the specific areas in which the student is known or suspected to have a disability (IDEA, § 1414 [b]). Among other things, this principle also includes the student's parents as members of the team that evaluates the student. It also gives them the right to secure (sometimes at the cost of the school) and have considered evaluations conducted by qualified individuals who are not employees or contractors of the school (IDEA, § 1414 [b], [c]).

The third principle is a FAPE. This is a rule requiring the individualization of special education and related services (IDEA § 1414 [d]). Just as the student's parents are members of the nondiscriminatory evaluation team, so too are they members of the student's individualized education program (IEP) team. This team must base the student's IEP and related services on the student's evaluation. The purpose of a FAPE is to ensure specified outcomes for the student, including a productive, independent adult life to the maximum extent possible (IDEA, § 1400 [c][5][E][ii]). The linchpin of a FAPE is the student's IEP; the standards for determining whether a student has a FAPE are that the school follows proper IDEA procedure and that the IEP allows the student to benefit from special education and any other services provided (IDEA, § 1414 [d]; *Board v. Rowley*, 458 U.S. 176 [1982]). A FAPE includes, among other things, provisions regarding PBS, as explained more fully later in this chapter.

The fourth principle is the least restrictive environment (LRE). LRE is a rule of access to and progress through the general curriculum, which is comprised of the academic, extracurricular, and other school activities for students without disabilities (see 34 C.F.R. §§ 300.347, 300.553). To have that access and the opportunity to benefit, the student is entitled to receive supplementary aids and services as specified by his or her IEP team (IDEA, §§ 1401 [29], 1412 [a][5]).

Significantly, Congress regards special education as a service, not as a place to which students are sent (IDEA, § 1400 [c][5][C]). Accordingly, the legal presumption is that the student will be educated, to the maximum extent appropriate for the student, with students who do not have disabilities (IDEA, § 1412 [a][5]). This presumption may be set aside only if the "nature or severity of the disability is such that education in regular classes with the use of supplementary aids and services cannot be achieved satisfactorily" (34 C.F.R. § 300.550). Even in such cases, however, the local education agency (LEA) must provide a proper continuum of available services to ensure that the student is taught in the most inclusive environment possible (34 C.F.R. § 300.551). The student's IEP team, supplemented by general educators and school administrators, determines the student's placement and, if applicable, must justify why access with supports to the general curriculum should not be afforded (34 C.F.R. 300.347).

The fifth and sixth principles are, respectively, procedural due process (sometimes called *procedural safeguards*) and parent–student participation. These rules create checks and balances. They are ways to ensure that the student benefits from being in school and that the school provides the required services and placements (see Board v. Rowley; 34 C.F.R. §§ 300.500–300.589). They also ensure shared decision making concerning the student's education (IDEA, § 1414 [d][1][B][i]; 34 C.F.R. §§ 300.344 [a][1], 300.345).

POSITIVE BEHAVIOR SUPPORT: DEFINITION AND PURPOSE

PBS is a technology of intervention that is applied to and on behalf of students whose behavior is or is regarded as challenging or problematic (see Sugai et al., 1999). Its purpose is to produce "socially important behavior change" (IDEA, § 1414 [b]). Its focus extends beyond the student and includes systems change activities, environmental alterations, skill instruction activities, and behavioral consequence activities (IDEA, § 1414[b]). These four components combine to form what Sugai and colleagues described as

[A] behaviorally based systems approach [which is applied] to enhance the capacity of schools, families, and communities to design effective environments that improve the fit or link between research-validated practices and the environments in which teaching and learning occurs. Attention is focused on creating and sustaining school environments that improve lifestyle results (personal, health, social, family, work, recreation, etc.) for all children and youth by making problem behavior less effective, efficient, and relevant, and desired behavior more functional. In addition, the use of culturally appropriate interventions is emphasized. At the core, [PBS] is the integration of behavioral science, practical interventions, social values, and a systems perspective. (1999, pp. 6–7)

RELATIONSHIP OF IDEA'S SIX PRINCIPLES TO ITS PROVISIONS FOR POSITIVE BEHAVIOR SUPPORT AND RELATED INTERVENTIONS

Having briefly described IDEA's six principles and the characteristics and purposes of PBS, it is now appropriate to examine the relationship between the two. To do that, one must remember that IDEA's six principles create a seamless procedure: Enroll the student and keep him or her in school no matter what (zero reject), evaluate him or her fairly (nondiscriminatory evaluation), and provide a benefit from education (a FAPE).

It is also important to remember that PBS itself is a seamless process: Determine whether the student's behaviors warrant the technology and, if so, conduct a functional behavioral assessment (FBA)[1] (nondiscriminatory evaluation) as the basis for the intervention; develop a behavioral intervention plan (BIP) (an appropriate education) that details the intervention; and deliver services in the LRE and through the least drastic means (i.e., presumptively, through positive means). It is futile to separate these two seamless processes from each other; it is, however, fruitful to show their connections. The connections arise from two separate sets of IDEA's provisions. The first set deals with the IEP process, and the second deals with discipline.

---

[1]IDEA uses *functional behavioral assessment* and some professionals use *functional assessment*. These terms are synonymous. The former appears in this chapter because this is the IDEA term and IDEA is the topic of this chapter.

Provisions for the Individualized Education
Program Process and Positive Behavior Support

IDEA Section 1414(d)(3)(B)—which relates to the IEP—requires each IEP team to consider "special factors" when it develops a student's IEP. Section 1414(d)(3)(B)(i) provides that "in the case of a child whose behavior impedes his or her learning or that of others," the IEP team shall "consider, when appropriate, strategies, including positive behavioral interventions, strategies, and supports to address that behavior." This provision has several implications for families.

Definitions   It is significant that IDEA does not define what behavior impedes the student's or other students' learning. A consortium of university PBS research and technical assistance centers offered the following definition of *impeding behaviors* (Turnbull, Wilcox Turnbull, Sailor, & Wickham, 2001, p. 467):

1. impede the learning of the student or of others and include those behaviors that are externalizing (such as verbal abuse, aggression, self-injury, or property destruction), are internalizing (such as physical or social withdrawal, depression, passivity, resistance, social or physical isolation, or noncompliance), are manifestations of biological or neurological conditions (such as obsessions, compulsions, stereotypies, or irresistible impulses), are manifestations of abuse, neglect, exploitation or maltreatment, or are disruptive (such as annoying, confrontational, defiant, or taunting), and
2. could cause the student to be disciplined pursuant to any state or federal law or regulations, or could cause any consideration of a change of the student's educational placement, and
3. are consistently recurring and therefore require functional behavioral assessment and the systematic and frequent application of positive behavioral interventions and supports

Several comments about this definition are in order. First, the identified behaviors are associated with various types of disabilities. A parent should not be thwarted from seeking PBS for a child simply because the child's disability has not been subjected to PBS research (Sugai et al., 1999). A child who has a developmental disability, emotional disorder, physical disability, learning disability, or attention deficit/hyperactivity disorder can benefit from this definition, as its approach is pragmatic and not theoretical.

Second, we create a causal connection between the behavior and the consequences. If, as a result of the behavior, the student could be disciplined or if a change of placement might be considered, then PBS is appropriate. That is so because, as parents know, prevention is the best approach. Waiting until discipline or a change of placement is required may be waiting too long.

Third, we say that the behaviors must be "consistently recurring." This is a serious limitation, for it prevents consideration of PBS if there is only a single behavioral event. Some parents may want even the single event to trigger PBS. Yet, schools may argue that a single event may not be the reason for discipline (unless it is a weapons or drugs violation) or a change of placement debate. Parents, then, should respond that if the behavior is punishable under a school code of conduct, it is impeding. Or, they may agree that one occurrence may trigger requirements, but that the key is likelihood of recurrence.

Turning now from this proposed definition, let us consider what IDEA and the U.S. Department of Education (ED), which is responsible for implementing IDEA, say about PBS. Here, parents encounter some serious problems of interpretation. Two problems arise initially with respect to the term *impeding behavior.* First, *impeding behavior* has not been defined by IDEA, its regulations, or the ED. Second, IDEA itself and its regulations use only the term *impede* whereas the ED uses the terms *interfere* and *significantly impair* in phrases and manners that indicate that *impede, impair,* and *interfere* may have similar meanings (64 Fed. Reg. 12,479, 12,480, & 12,588, March 12, 1999). This is more than a matter of semantics. Whatever the ED says *impede* means is how most courts will interpret the word, for courts defer to agency interpretations unless these interpretations are clearly indefensible (see *Sutton v. United Air Lines, Inc.,* 527 U.S. 471 [1999]). Thus, for a parent who wants PBS for his or her child, the term *significantly impair* limits the opportunity for PBS to be provided. That is so because *significantly* qualifies *impair.*

Moreover, the ED seems to further limit the opportunity for PBS to be provided. This is so because of the following clarification regarding PBS: "School officials have powerful incentives to implement positive behavioral interventions, strategies and supports whenever behavior interferes with the important teaching and learning activities of school" (65 Fed. Reg. 12,588). In our judgment, the ED's clarification here is significant because it instructs courts, hearing officers, state and local school administrators and other professionals, parents, and advocates for students with disabilities concerning the interpretation and application of IDEA and its regulations.

Let us be precise. The term *incentive* is different from the term *requirement.* In our view, an incentive is a positive reason for acting; a requirement is a legal duty to act. Thus, despite the requirement to consider PBS, the ED clarifies that there is no requirement to implement PBS. However, it indicates that the PBS provisions do presume in favor of PBS. Therefore, a parent may at least argue that PBS should be used; it is presumptively the correct intervention for "impeding" behavior. Professional judgment will still prevail in determining whether PBS is the correct technology to use for any particular student.

The term *interferes* seems to us to be a synonym for *impede.* Yet, note what follows the term *interferes*—namely, the phrase "the important teaching and learning activities of the school." We believe that this phrase asks a decision maker (e.g., the student's IEP team, a hearing officer, a court) to determine what is an "important" activity and to distinguish it from an "unimportant" or "less important" activity. This seems to be a limiting or qualifying phrase: Unless the behavior interferes with something "important," it does not "impede" and, therefore, does not trigger the IEP team to consider the use of PBS. On the one hand, if the courts defer to the ED, the definition of *important* is all-important: On its meaning hang the opportunities for PBS. On the other hand, courts may disregard the ED's interpretation as being in conflict with the statute.

Moreover, the phrase also adds the phrase "teaching and," suggesting to us that not just the learning of the student and others is affected by impeding behavior. The teaching—the activities of the school staff—must also be impeded for educators or others to determine that behavior does indeed impede. Assuming, again, that the courts defer to this interpretation, the ED puts the burden on the parents to show that their child's behavior not only impairs his or her own learning and/or the learning of other students but that it also impairs the ability of the school faculty to teach. Thus, the parents face a two-pronged test.

In our judgement, this is a defensible interpretation because, if an educator cannot teach on account of a student's behavior, then that student's behavior impedes or interferes with the learning by other students. Yet, it also limits the ability of a student to receive PBS, and that is something that parents may well find objectionable. It gives the parents the unenviable task of asserting that the particular teacher(s) lacked competency to teach their child or to teach other children while their child was in the classroom. This makes the parents take the offensive against a teacher, requires the parent to document poor teaching and perhaps to even suggest how the teacher should have responded (i.e., to define good teaching), and subjects the child to possible teacher or administrator retaliation.

Moreover, it seems to us that the ED considers violation of a school code of conduct to be "impeding behavior." This reflects the language of Congress (IDEA, § 1414 [d][3][B] [i]). In its questions and answers on IEPs, the ED states that

> In most cases in which a child's behavior that impedes his or her learning or that of others is . . . repetitive, proper development of the child's IEP will include the development of strategies, including positive behavioral interventions, strategies and supports to address that behavior. . . . This includes behavior that could violate a school code of conduct. (64 Fed. Reg. 12,479)

Here, the limiting term—consistent with the consortium's definition—is *repetitive*. Again, the single behavior that impedes learning will not benefit the child or the parents who are seeking PBS. That is the thrust of the first sentence. Under the ED's interpretation, the impeding behavior must be repetitive, or there must be a significant chance that it will recur.

Yet, note that there may be an inconsistency within the interpretation. That is so because any violation—even the single violation of a school code of conduct—may trigger PBS. That is the thrust of the second sentence. The distinction between the first and the second sentences is significant, for it is not just the "high visibility/high risk" violations (e.g., assaults, verbal harassment, sexual harassment, property destruction) that trigger PBS's consideration; it is also for matters such as running in the hallways and talking during school assemblies—whether repetitive or not.

Thus, the severity of the impeding behavior is not the key element; the frequency or future likelihood are. Accordingly, parents seeking PBS will want to document how often their child has been written up for impeding behavior. In impeding cases, the count controls, and that may well be so with code violations as well.

Team Membership   Under IDEA, the IEP team must take the required action for PBS and impeding behavior. This fact necessitates discussion of two significant aspects. The first is that the IEP team members are fundamentally the same people who complete the student's nondiscriminatory evaluation (IDEA, § 1414 [d][1][B]). The second is that the IEP and evaluation teams include the student's parents.

The consequences of the evaluation and IEP teams having overlapping members are that the evaluation data are known to the IEP team (and to the parents as team members) and that the data must be taken into account when the teams decide whether to consider PBS. By being members of the evaluation and IEP teams, the parents are in a position to provide information that may be useful to the team, such as how the child behaves at home and in the community. The school personnel team members probably would not have this information. Yet, the "whole child" is the team's concern, and behaviors at home and in the community may well be relevant to behaviors at school (and vice versa). As members of the team, parents are in a position to describe the home and community behaviors and, thereby, to provide a more complete description of the child—the whole child perspective that is necessary for a full understanding of why behaviors occur and what can be done to ameliorate them.

Basing an Individualized Education Program and a Behavior Support Plan on the Nondiscriminatory Evaluation and Functional Behavioral Assessment   Any plan for PBS must be based on some form of evaluation: no evaluation means no defensible plan. This is the rule of the statute and the holding of the cases (see Turnbull et al., 2000). It is also a common-sense rule: The principle of nondiscriminatory evaluation precedes the principle of a FAPE because the purpose of the evaluation is to determine whether the child has a disability and, if so, the educational consequences of that finding

(IDEA, § 1414 [a][1][B]). The educational consequences can include a plan to address impeding behavior. Yet, that plan will be only as good as the evaluation on which it rests. Data must drive the development of any particular plan.

Therefore, a brief discussion about the evaluation and plan development is in order. No PBS plan should be developed, incorporated into an IEP, and implemented unless the LEA has first conducted an FBA (Sugai et al., 1999). The assessment should be conducted across all home and community environments. A written report should be prepared that documents the actions taken to conduct the assessment and the results of the assessment (34 C.F.R. §§ 300.530–300.543; see also Sugai et al., 1999).

Some might argue that a PBS plan is too complex and unwieldy to be included in the IEP because various minor changes may be required at different times and holding an IEP meeting regarding every change would be nearly impossible. Minor changes that do not affect the core components of the PBS plan, however, can be made without an IEP meeting if the IEP has a provision allowing such changes. For example, the IEP could include schedules for altering specified interventions or supports, or their frequency or duration, without requiring the IEP team to reconvene.

Incorporating Positive Behavior Support into the Individualized Education Program
As noted previously, PBS is among the special factors that IEP teams must consider in IEP development, review, and revision. If the IEP team determines during this development, review, or revision that the child is in need of "a particular device or service (including an intervention, accommodation, or other program modification) in order for the child to receive a FAPE, the IEP team must include a statement to that effect in the child's IEP" (34 C.F.R. § 300.346 [c]). Thus, if the IEP team determines that a student requires any positive behavioral intervention or support, then the student's IEP must include a statement to that effect. Indeed, if a student has a PBS plan, then the IEP team should incorporate that plan into the student's IEP. IDEA itself, the regulations promulgated under it, and the Office of Special Education Programs (OSEP) commentary imply that this should be the case (34 C.F.R. § 300.346 [c]; see also 64 Fed. Reg. 12,620). For this reason alone, parents should insist that the PBS plan and the IEP be merged or incorporated.

There is yet another reason why this is a sound recommendation: If the student exhibits behaviors that subject him or her to school discipline, then the parents will want to argue that the student's behaviors are manifestations of his or her disability. That argument may safeguard the student against various kinds of sanctions. If the IEP team itself has determined that certain behaviors are challenging or problematic—and if they have made this determination after conducting an FBA, developing a PBS plan, and incorporating the plan into the student's IEP—then it will be very difficult for the school to argue successfully that the student's behavior is not a manifestation of the disability. In effect, the FBA and IEP/PBS procedures may stop a school from applying certain types of discipline.

Considering and Documenting
Yet another implication of the parents' participation in the evaluation and IEP teams relates to the IEP team's duty to consider the use of PBS. The word *consider* is important. The word *consider* requires the IEP team to

- Understand what PBS is and how it works

- Have the ability to implement PBS

- Engage in a discussion about whether to employ PBS

- Detail the reasoning behind its decision on whether to employ PBS

These elements of the word *consider* are common-sensically defensible. The IEP team members cannot consider what they do not understand, and it is meaningless for them to consider a futile option—one they cannot implement, even rudimentarily. Furthermore, for them to consider anything, they must engage in a discussion, weighing the pros and cons of using PBS, and they must decide on one or more rationale for a decision. A result without a reason is indefensible and subject to attack as whimsical and not professionally sound. If any of these elements are absent, then it is questionable whether the IEP team has met its statutory duty to consider PBS.

Accordingly, parents should themselves be well versed in the meaning of PBS. They should also ask the other team members about the following:

- What training they have had in PBS

- How they define PBS

- What they believe are the purpose and methods of PBS

- How PBS may apply to the child

- How PBS is being used with respect to other children

- The capacity (training and experience) of school faculty and administrators to deliver PBS to the child and other children

- How the delivery of PBS will be evaluated for the child

In short, the parents should not only know their child and PBS but should also ensure that the school faculty and administrators know the child and PBS. In the absence of that kind of knowledge—both theoretical (about PBS) and applied (about the child)—it is not likely that PBS can be considered or effectively delivered.

Considering When Appropriate   The IEP team must consider positive behavioral interventions and supports "when appropriate," namely, when the student's behavior impedes learning (IDEA, § 1414 [d][3][B][i]; 34 C.F.R. § 300.346 [a][2][i]). Two questions that parents should always ask, and that the IEP team may be asked in a challenge to its decision-making process and the results of that process, are

- When is PBS not appropriate to be considered?

- What factors rule out PBS in the team's consideration?

These are entirely proper questions for parents and the entire team to ask. After all, IDEA identifies PBS as an intervention that must be considered. Therefore, the duty seems to be not only to consider PBS but also to decide whether it should not be used and, if not, why. It is advisable for the team to document its decision-making process, the result (i.e., not to use PBS), and the reasons for that result. If the parents so choose, they may make their own notes of the team's processes, results, and reasons, paying particular attention to why the team decided against using PBS. Was it because the child's behavior did not impede learning or teaching? Was it because the behavior was not likely to recur? Or was it for other reasons?

Considering Alternative Interventions   The team members are not required to use PBS. They are required only to think about (to consider) whether to use them or other interventions or no interventions at all. IDEA's language allows the IEP team to "consider" the use of PBS, other interventions, both, or none at all. Accordingly, we believe that a team may consider interventions such as a therapeutic drug regimen (relying on medical advice); the use of nonpositive interventions (which are hard to justify under the rebuttable presumption given to PBS; Turnbull et al., 2000; Turnbull et al., 2001); or the continuation, modification, or discontinuation of present (positive or other) interventions, if any. Note, however, that in every such case the IEP team is required to consider PBS, even if they are also considering other strategies.

Again, the parents, as members of the IEP team, are in an excellent position to request team members to justify any decision they make about PBS or other interventions. For one thing, the parent may have information about the child's medical history and medication. Unless the parent has authorized the child's physician to release medical records to the school and the doctor has complied, the IEP team would not have this useful information. Inasmuch as some behaviors may be caused by neurobiological conditions that only a physician can diagnose and treat, and inasmuch as the definition of *impede* includes behaviors that are traceable to underlying neurobiological conditions, it is helpful for the team to know what only the parents or the physician know. If a behavior does have a neurobiological basis, then PBS, coupled with medication, may be entirely warranted (although this is not to say it may not be warranted in other cases).

Addressing the Behavior   The IEP team must consider "strategies" to "address" the student's behavior (IDEA, § 1414 [d][3][B][i]; 34 C.F.R. § 300.346 [a][2][i]). This language comes within the "appropriate education" (FAPE) principle and means that the strategies must target preventing, reducing, replacing, or otherwise appropriately addressing the behavior or behaviors. The basis for this judgment is the Supreme Court's *Board v. Rowley* decision (458 U.S. 176). In that case, the Supreme Court interpreted IDEA's requirement of a FAPE to mean that the student must be given services that will enable the student to "benefit" from special education. This standard suggests that any strategy to address a student's behavior must be one that will benefit the student in the sense that it is efficacious for the purpose for which it is used—that is, the interventions change the student's behavior and, thus, enhance the student's ability to benefit from special education and related services.

Hence, the parents are in the position, as team members, to ask other team members to justify any intervention in terms of its outcomes. Will it effectively produce change in behavior (address the behavior)? If not, what is its justification? These are good questions for parents to ask. Moreover, in asking these questions, the parents must make it clear that their inquiry rests on the student's right to a FAPE. That is the principle that guides the address requirement.

In defining an "appropriate education" in *Board v. Rowley,* the Supreme Court created two key tests for determining whether a student has received a FAPE: the process test and the benefit test. *Board v. Rowley's* process test essentially requires LEAs to follow IDEA's procedural requirements to provide a FAPE. Thus, if proper IDEA procedures are not followed, then, in most cases, a court will hold that the student has not received a FAPE (Turnbull et al., 2000).

Board v. Rowley's benefit test requires that the student benefit from the services provided. Thus, even if the proper procedures are followed, a student is not receiving a FAPE if he or she is not receiving a benefit from the services. This need not be the maximum benefit, but the services provided must result in some substantive level of benefit, and the student's capacities must not regress (Turnbull et al., 2000).

Note that this benefit is only required when IDEA necessitates PBS consideration and behavioral intervention planning. In the absence of a situation in which behavioral intervention planning is required by IDEA, the student is not required to benefit from such planning for a FAPE to be established. For example, a student who requires other special education or related services but not individualized PBS may still receive PBS as part of a schoolwide program. The student will not have been denied a FAPE if the schoolwide PBS services fail to provide a benefit. For the student who requires individualized behavioral planning under IDEA, however, PBS and behavioral planning must provide a benefit.

Regardless of requirement by law, using PBS with any and all students, and attempting to provide a benefit therefrom, is best practice. Similarly, providing a higher level of benefit than that required by law is best practice. These best practices provide benefit not only for individual students but also provide schoolwide benefits, including environments that are more conducive to learning because of fewer class disruptions (Sugai et al., 1999; Turnbull et al., 2001).

In the team's consideration of PBS and of other interventions, parents can be very useful, providing information about the following:

- Their child's medical history, present diagnosis, and treatment (especially with respect to medication)

- What other forms of behavioral or educational interventions the parents have used in the past

- Whether the parents or other professionals have resorted to nonpositive measures (e.g., extensive time-out)

- What interventions have seemed to be effective and the conditions under which they were effective

Again, gathering such information is a matter of the team having a complete picture of the whole child.

Documentation and the Individualized Education Program Team Decision-Making Process   We also believe that it is advisable for the team to document their decision-making process by minutes (e.g., notes, audiotape recordings) that at least reflect the following matters: which interventions were considered, how much time did the team spend in consideration, who was on the team, how often did it meet, why it was not regarded as appropriate to consider PBS, which other strategies were considered, and which factors ruled out PBS in the team's consideration. The reasons for documentation are straightforward.

First, fair process tends to produce fair results. This legal maxim, incorporated into Section 1414 of IDEA, assures that, at the very least, there is documentation of the team's consideration (see Turnbull et al., 2000). Documentation tends to be a technique for accountability: If the team knows that the parents are documenting the team's actions, then the team itself may well engage in much more careful consideration of the interventions offered to the child.

Second, in a lawsuit or due process hearing, the team's decision-making process may be attacked on the grounds that a flawed process cannot lead to an acceptable result. In such a case, documentation of the process can be evidence of a defensible process. Under *Board v. Rowley*, a fair decision-making process is one defense to a claim that a school has not provided a student with a FAPE. By extension of the "process definition" of a FAPE, it seems to us that a similar standard probably will apply to the "consider" requirements related to PBS.

Provisions for Discipline

As noted previously, IDEA requires educators and parents to address PBS under two circumstances. The first relates to the IEP process. The second relates to the discipline of the student. Here, several of IDEA's six principles come into play. First, the principle of zero reject applies because IDEA prohibits "cessation" of services to any child with a disability; alternatively stated, the zero-reject rule and the IDEA no-cessation rule prevent the school from excluding the student on account of discipline. The principle of nondiscriminatory evaluation is also important because, as noted previously, any program for the child must be based on a nondiscriminatory evaluation, including one that consists of an FBA. The principle of a FAPE applies because there must be an opportunity for the child to benefit from whatever environment or program the child is offered. Furthermore, the school must follow proper procedure in providing or denying PBS. The principle of LRE comes into play because, even if the child is subject to discipline, the child must still have the opportunity to participate in the general curriculum and to progress through it. The student must also be able to progress in his or her IEP goals, regardless of disciplinary placement (34 C.F.R. § 300.121 [d]).

Removing the Child from the Current Placement   IDEA Section 1415(k)
(1)(A) gives LEAs the authority to remove a child from the current placement "to an appropriate interim alternative educational setting, another setting, or suspension, for not more than 10 school days to the extent such alternatives would be applied to children without disabilities" or

> To an appropriate interim alternative educational setting for the same amount of time that a child without a disability would be subject to discipline, but for not more than 45 days if:
> - the child carries or possesses a weapon to or at school, on school premises, or to or at a school function, under the jurisdiction of a state or a local educational agency; or
> - the child knowingly possesses or uses illegal drugs or sells or solicits the sale of a controlled substance while at school or a school function under the jurisdiction of a State or local educational agency.

Under IDEA Section 1415(k)(2), a hearing officer is given authority to

> Order a change in the placement of a child with a disability to an appropriate interim alternative educational setting for not more than 45 days if the hearing officer:
> - determines that the public agency has demonstrated by substantial evidence that maintaining the current placement of such child is substantially likely to result in injury to the child or to others;
> - considers the appropriateness of the child's current placement;
> - considers whether the public agency has made reasonable efforts to minimize the risk of harm in the child's current placement, including the use of supplementary aids and services; and
> - determines that the interim alternative educational setting meets [specified requirements].

Individuals with Disabilities Education Act Provisions   IDEA Section 1415
(k)(1)(B) imposes on LEAs a requirement concerning PBS when disciplinary actions for weapons or drugs are taken against a child with a disability. It states,

> If the [LEA] did not conduct a functional behavioral assessment and implement a behavioral intervention plan for such child before the behavior that resulted [in the discipline], the agency shall convene an IEP meeting to develop an assessment plan to address that behavior.

This meeting must take place "either before or not later than 10 [business] days after taking [the disciplinary action]." Furthermore, "if the child already has a behavioral intervention plan, the IEP team shall review the plan and modify it, as necessary, to address the behavior."

Department of Education Regulations   The statute describes FBA/BIP requirements in terms of the disciplinary actions described in Sec. 1415(k)(1)(A) (weapon and drug removals). The regulations in 34 C.F.R. § 300.520(b)(1) clarify that the FBA and BIP are required when "either first removing the child for more than 10 school days in a school year or commencing a removal that constitutes a change of placement under § 300.519, including [changes of placement for weapon or drug violations under § 300.520(a)(2)]." This would also trigger the FBA/BIP requirements in the case of removal by a hearing officer based on a substantial likelihood of injury to self or others in the current placement.

Defining "Change of Placement"   *Change of placement* is a technical term that refers to removals of two kinds. The first is for "more than 10 consecutive school days." The second is for a

Series of removals that constitute a pattern because they cumulate to more than 10 school days in a school year, and because of factors such as the length of each removal, the total amount of time the child is removed, and the proximity of the removals to one another. (34 C.F.R. § 300.519)

Interpreting the Statute and Regulations with Respect to Positive Behavior Support   Note that the FBA and BIP requirements make no mention of PBS in the event of disciplinary action. When the need for discipline arises, however, the IEP team is required to create, review, or revise any BIP for the sole purpose of addressing the student's sanctionable behavior (34 C.F.R. § 300.520 [b][c]). If it has to develop the plan in the first place, then it must do so by conducting an FBA before implementing a plan based on the assessment (34 C.F.R. § 300.520 [b][1][i]).

In our view, *FBA* and *PBS* are inseparable in the research and practice literature (Sugai et al., 1999; Turnbull et al., 2001). Furthermore, the impede provision requires the team to consider PBS to address learning-impeding behavior (IDEA, § 1414 [d][3][B][i]; 34 C.F.R. § 300.346 [a][2][i]). Thus, a fair reading of the statute and regulations is that the team must at least consider PBS as interventions to address the behavior for which the student is disciplined.

Discipline triggers FBA, BIP, and PBS. Parents whose children are being disciplined may assert this interpretation and its very practical implications—namely, that any discipline that triggers more discipline should be modified and that PBS is an effective intervention to change behavior. Indeed, although it is too late to use PBS as a prevention strategy because the student's behavior has already resulted in discipline, it is not too late to use PBS as a strategy to prevent further occurrences of behavior that are subject to discipline. The argument is that, although one incident triggering discipline has occurred, others can be prevented by PBS.

Positive Behavior Support as Part of a Behavioral Intervention Plan   The argument in favor of linking PBS to discipline is fortified by an explanation by OSEP in its commentary on 34 C.F.R. § 300.520 (a discipline regulation). In its commentary, OSEP states that a PBS plan may itself comprise the BIP:

If, under § 300.346 (a) and (c), IEP teams are proactively addressing a child's behavior that impedes the child's learning or that of others in the development of IEPs, those strategies, including positive behavioral interventions, strategies and supports in the child's IEP will constitute the behavioral intervention plan that the IEP team reviews under paragraph (b)(2) of [§ 300.520]. (64 Fed. Reg. 12,620)

Therefore, it seems that whenever the IEP team is required to examine an existing BIP (pursuant to 34 C.F.R. § 300.520), the team will necessarily reexamine the extent to which an FBA and possibly a BIP should be undertaken and developed.

The Manifestation Rule   The authority of LEAs to remove students with disabilities from the classroom is tempered by "the manifestation rule." In all but three circumstances (the student possesses weapons or illegal drugs or poses a substantial threat of injury to himself or others; see IDEA, § 1415 [k]; 34 C.F.R. §§ 300.520 [a], 300.521), a LEA may not change the placement of a student with a disability as a form of discipline if the student's behavior is a manifestation of his or her disability (*Honig v. Doe,* 484 U.S. 305 [1988]). As noted previously, *change of placement* is a term defined by the IDEA regulations.

Say that a school does propose discipline that the parents believe is a change of placement. In this circumstance, the school must conduct a "manifestation determination" to decide whether the behavior is a manifestation of the child's disability (34 C.F.R. § 300.523). The review must be carried out no later than 10 school days after the decision has been made to remove the child from his or her present placement. If this review determines that the behavior is not a manifestation of disability, then the child may be disciplined in the same manner as a child without a disability except that the no cessation protection will apply (34 C.F.R. §§ 300.524, 300.121 [d]). If the review determines that the behavior is a manifestation of disability, then the change of placement may not be used to discipline the child except in cases of weapons, drugs, injury to self or others, or parental consent (see *Honig v. Doe*).

If a parent challenges the school's decision to discipline the student and invokes the right to a due process hearing, and if the school proposes to change the student's placement as a form of discipline, then the parent may assert that the behavior was a manifestation of the disability and that the school's right to change placement is contingent on the school complying with the change of placement provisions. In particular, the school must repeat in whole or in part and, as appropriate for the student, the processes applicable to evaluation, the IEP, and placement decisions (see IDEA, § 1415 [k]; 34 C.F.R. §§ 300.519, 300.520). These rules apply to all discipline, including discipline imposed when the student possesses weapons or illegal drugs at school or when the current placement would result in a substantial likelihood of injury to the student or others. In these latter cases, however, the student is not eligible for "stay-put" rules and, therefore, may be removed from the current placement immediately (34 C.F.R. § 300.514). If the school does repeat the process, then it must perform the nondiscriminatory evaluation and FBA and use them to develop an IEP, a BIP, and, possibly, a positive behavior support plan.

Positive Behavior Support as Presumptively Correct Intervention (Intervention of Choice)   Just as the LRE principle creates a rebuttable presumption in favor of access to and progress through the general curriculum, so it seems that IDEA has created a rebuttable presumption in favor of the use of PBS. That is, PBS is presumed to be the intervention strategy of choice for the IEP team in the case of impeding behavior. This is so because PBS is the only intervention specifically required for consideration by IDEA and, although other interventions may be considered, only PBS must be considered. This provision inherently requires that if the IEP team considers other interventions, then it may do so only in comparison to PBS and must have adequate cause for adopting another intervention over PBS when both are appropriate. The significance of this interpretation for parents is simple and direct: Parents should assert that their children are entitled to PBS over any other intervention and that their child's IEP team has the burden of proving that PBS is not warranted.

Presumption Against Aversive or Nonpositive Interventions   A presumption in favor of PBS is also a presumption against the use of aversive interventions. PBS rewards desirable behavior, making it functional, and removes rewards from undesirable behavior to decrease its functionality. Aversive interventions do not reward desirable behavior; instead, they attempt to punish undesirable behavior until it is eliminated (Sugai et al., 1999; Turnbull et al., 2001). These two approaches are antithetical; thus, preference for one is preference against the other.

IDEA does not explicitly prohibit aversive interventions, but commentary by the ED supports the conclusion that there is a rebuttable presumption in favor of PBS and against aversive interventions. In this commentary, the ED explained,

> Regarding what behavioral interventions and strategies can be used, and whether the use of aversive behavioral management strategies is prohibited under these regulations, the needs of the individual child are of paramount importance in determining the behavioral management strategies that are appropriate for inclusion in the child's IEP. In making these determinations, the primary focus must be on ensuring that the behavioral management strategies in the child's IEP reflect *the Act's requirement for the use of positive behavioral interventions and strategies.* (65 Fed. Reg. 12,589; emphasis added)

Here, the significance of this interpretation is the same as with respect to the presumption in favor of PBS. Parents should assert that their child should be protected against nonpositive interventions, and the burden of proof is on the IEP team to justify nonpositive or aversive interventions.

FAMILIES, CHILDREN, AND THEIR CONTEXTS

Up to this point, this chapter has concentrated on IDEA's provisions, their interpretations by the ED, and interpretations of the statute and the ED's comments. Necessarily, the focus has been on the school as the context for PBS and on the parent–professional relationships within which PBS may be operationalized. A larger context is addressed next: the family and the community.

One of the premises of PBS is that it is useful in all environments that an individual with challenging behavior occupies (Sugai et al., 1999; Turnbull et al., 2001). This premise is consistent with the traditional precepts that education, particularly that which takes the form of behavioral interventions, should generalize across environments and individuals within various environments and that education and behavioral interventions should be durable across time.

Indeed, a consensus definition of PBS holds that one of the components of PBS is environmental alterations—changing the environments in which the student receives special or general education. Those educational environments can well include the student's home, especially given the emphasis on home–school collaborations and the generalization of interventions from school to home (Turnbull, Turnbull, Shank, Smith & Leal, 2002). Moreover, there is consensus that the FBA, which underpins the PBS plan, should include an ecological analysis of the environments and interactions in which targeted behavioral events occur, including the home and family interactions (Turnbull et al., 2001).

These precepts, consensus statements, and facts about the sites of research and application of PBS have implications for families. There can be no doubt but that families are significant "environments" in which PBS can be applied; indeed, the precepts of generalization and durability command that whenever a family is willing to use PBS, the family should be competent to deliver it. The implication of "willing and able" is, quite simply, that the family is entitled to receive training in PBS: what it is, what its purposes and outcomes are and should be, and how it may be delivered. Indeed, under IDEA, families or other third-party surrogates for the child or other person with challenging behavior have the right to be trained in PBS matters.

Parent and family education in PBS is available under two different sets of provisions within IDEA. The first set is the related services provisions. A related service is any developmental, corrective, or other supportive service necessary for the student to benefit from special education (IDEA, § 1401 [22] [1999]; 34 C.F.R. § 300.24 [b]). Among the related services that benefit not just children but also families and can be associated with PBS, are

- Counseling, especially by social workers and psychologists, whom the ED identifies as being qualified to provide PBS

- Medical services

- Parent counseling and education

- Psychological services, which include assistance "in developing positive behavioral intervention strategies"

- School health services

- School social work services, which include assistance "in developing positive behavioral intervention strategies"

The second set of provisions covers Parent Training and Information Centers (PTIs) (IDEA, 42 U.S.C. § 1482) . PTIs exist in each state; some states have more than one. Their purpose is to provide information and education to parents concerning IDEA. To carry out this duty, PTIs should provide information about PBS. To fail to do so is to fail to capitalize on this new technology. Moreover, the ED recognizes that it is desirable to "export" technologies such as PBS from the school environment to family and community environments to better aid the student in IEP or individualized family service plan (IFSP) goal attainment (see 64 Fed. Reg. 12,549 & 12,588).

Finally, some children are served by schools and other agencies (e.g., mental health, developmental disabilities, juvenile justice, or child protective services agencies). Thus, the precepts of generalization suggest that PBS should be delivered in each of those agencies if it is also being delivered in school and that it should be delivered in the same way. Accordingly, parents should advocate for PBS generalization across these agencies and for representatives of these agencies to attend and contribute to the FBA and the IEP team meetings at which a BIP or PBS plan is being considered, developed, reviewed, or revised.

CONCLUSION

A new technology is only as effective as those who know about it, know how to deliver it, and are committed to delivering it. It is only as effective as it spreads—whether in schools as they consider positive behavior support as part of their required attention to impeding behavior or as part of their discipline-imposing procedures or whether in the individual's home or community environments. Given their membership on the school evaluation and IEP teams, their legal rights under IDEA to collaborate with schools in other aspects of their child's education, their legal rights to consent on behalf of their children, and their interests in securing generalized and durable interventions—and, in turn, universal changes of behavior in their children—it seems to us as if parents are in an excellent position to advocate for positive behavior support in service-delivery environments and, thus, to benefit from it. Of course, the hitch is that, as with most innovations in education or other service delivery, the burden of persuasion—the job of making sure that agencies do their job—too often falls, and falls too hard, on the parents.

REFERENCES

Board v. Rowley, 458 U.S. 176 (1982).

Education for All Handicapped Children Act of 1975, PL 94-142, 20 U.S.C. §§ 1400 *et seq.*

Honig v. Doe, 484 U.S. 305 (1988).

Individuals with Disabilities Education Act (IDEA) Amendments of 1997, PL 105-17, 20 U.S.C. §§ 1400 *et seq.*

Individuals with Disabilities Education Act (IDEA) of 1990, PL 101-476, 20 U.S.C. §§ 1400 *et seq.*

Sugai, G., Horner, R., Dunlap, G., Lewis, T., Nelson, M., Scott, T., Liakupsin, C., Ruef, M., Sailor, W., Turnbull, A.P., Turnbull, H.R., Wickham, D., & Wilcox, B.L. (1999). *Applying positive behavioral support and functional behavioral assessment in schools.* Lawrence, KS: Office of Special Education Programs (OSEP) Technical Assistance Center.

Sutton v. United Air Lines, Inc., 527 U.S. 471 (1999).

Turnbull, A.P., & Turnbull, H.R. (2001). *Families, professionals, and exceptionality: Collaborating for empowerment* (4th ed.). Upper Saddle River, NJ: Prentice Hall.

Turnbull, A.P., Turnbull, H.R., Shank, M., Smith, S., & Leal, D. (2002). *Exceptional lives: Special education in today's schools* (3rd ed.). Upper Saddle River, NJ: Prentice Hall.

Turnbull, H.R., Turnbull, A.P., Stowe, M., & Wilcox, B.L. (2000). *Free appropriate public education: The law and children with disabilities* (6th ed.). Denver, CO: Love Publishing Co.

Turnbull, H.R., Wilcox, B.L., Turnbull, A.P., Sailor, W., & Wickham, D. (2001). IDEA, positive behavioral supports, and school safety. *Journal of Law and Education, 30*(3), 445–504.

Section II

ASSESSMENT AND INTERVENTION

Three Families' Perspectives on Assessment, Intervention, and Parent–Professional Partnerships

Susan Rocco, Joyce Metzger,
and Angela Zangerle with James R. Skouge

When we were approached to write a chapter for a book on positive behavior support (PBS), we were flattered and more than a little intimidated. After all, what special knowledge could we have that would help other families and professionals? True, we had survived, and occasionally triumphed over, the behavioral challenges that our children with disabilities brought to our families. Our children are now young adults; they face a new set of challenges. Each of our experiences has involved a series of struggles, some of which have been long and difficult. Along the way, we have also experienced moments of grace and insight. Yet, none of us have felt uniquely enlightened. It was not until we sat down over sodas and snacks and started telling each other our own stories that a number of shared insights emerged.

First, we wish to introduce ourselves. Susan Rocco is the mother of Jason, a charmingly eccentric 20-year-old who recently graduated from high school and is starting his own business. Joyce Metzger is the mother of Glen, a computer-savvy 28-year-old who lives at home with Joyce and his pet parakeets. Angela Zangerle is the parent of Odee, a vivacious 19-year-old college freshman and accomplished hula dancer. Although we have difficulty viewing our children through the filter of disability, it will be useful to the reader to know that Jason is diagnosed as having autism, Glen has a mild to moderate cognitive disability, and Odee has experienced a traumatic brain injury (TBI). James R. Skouge, the fourth author, is a professor of special education at the University of Hawaii and a colleague and friend to each of us. In this chapter, he has served in the role of editor, pulling together our different experiences and weaving them into one cloth.

Each of us writes differently. Our experiences differ. Yet, the insights we identified, the truths we uncovered, we hold in common. Our purpose in writing this chapter is to provide family perspectives on assessment and intervention related to behavioral and educational supports for our children. We also wish to share our perspectives on parent–professional relationships, particularly our experience of partnerships that have been empowering and synergistic.

Like so many families, we experienced years of "professional" assessments and interventions. These included diagnostic assessments for identifying disability and making placement decisions, educational assessments of our children's learning problems, and behavioral assessments and interventions. The quality of these experiences has ranged from devastating to sublime. Through it all, we have learned many lessons. In this chapter, we distill our experiences and insights into eight themes about assessment, intervention, and parent–professional partnerships, which are presented in Table 4.1. After introducing a theme and its key points, the theme is illustrated by one or two vignettes from our experiences as parents.

Before beginning, a brief point for clarity is in order regarding the use of authors' names and pronouns. When we introduce and discuss a theme, the pronouns *we* and *us* are often used. During these discussions, the pronouns refer to the three parent authors, Susan, Joyce, and Angela. They also reflect the views of James, the professional member of the writing team. The author of each vignette that illustrates a theme is noted. Within a vignette, the pronouns *we* and *us* are also used, as well as the pronouns *myself* and *I*. In these instances, the pronouns refer to the author of the vignette and her family.

We hope that these themes contain lessons and points for improved practice so that the next generation of children and their families have it a little easier than ours. If they validate your own experience, spare you a step or two, or help you sidestep an obstacle, then we will have achieved our purpose. Our experiences include both pain and joy, tears and laughter. Through our journeys in the world of disability, our family bonds have grown stronger and stronger. We have become empowered. If a child in your family has a disability, then we expect that you can become empowered, too. If you are a professional serving children and families, then we hope that your relationships with families and your assessment and intervention practices are empowering for families. To the extent that they are, we applaud you. To the extent that they are not, we ask that you take to heart the insights and lessons herein. Doing so may give families more joy and less pain, more laughter and fewer tears.

Table 4.1. Lessons learned about assessment, intervention, and parent–professional partnerships

Families are greatly affected by the tone and emphasis of assessment information about their children's functioning, as well as by the means of sharing this information.

Futures planning is essential; families need to build new and meaningful dreams for their children.

When conducting a behavioral assessment, professionals should listen to and value parental knowledge and expertise about the purpose of the child's behavior and about the child's preferences and reinforcers.

Interventions should not focus on "fixing" children; rather, interventions should help family members and educators change what they do and improve the quality of children's lives.

Interventions should be developed collaboratively, taking into account family knowledge, culture, and lifestyle.

Good behavior support plans include communication strategies and tools that improve children's abilities to express their feelings, wants, needs, and interests.

Behavior support plans used by families should be based on assessments conducted with families in their homes and communities. Such plans are more likely to be proactive and practical.

Positive outcomes for children and families are more likely when professionals work with families as equal partners and aim to empower family members.

THEME 1

Families are greatly affected by the tone and emphasis of assessment information about their children's functioning, as well as by the means of sharing this information. Although we would prefer to begin the chapter on a more positive note, the truth is that we have not had very many positive experiences with the assessment of our children. For too long, we have been frustrated by assessments that focus on our children's problems and that artificially separate assessment from intervention. Some experts, such as school psychologists or social workers, have exclusively played roles in the initial assessment of our children, never to be seen again. Acting from a medical, pathological model, these experts intermittently "measured" our children, wrote detailed reports, delivered the invariably bad news, and prescribed various pull-out programs and therapies. These experiences left us—and, as often as not, our children's teachers—isolated and unsupported.

From these experiences, we have come to value assessments that offer a more positive view of our children and that offer helpful insights about their learning and behavior challenges. The lack of such strengths-based assessments is something that many families we encounter in our current advocacy work continue to experience and lament. Many parents know that their children, regardless of their cognitive or physical disabilities, possess many strengths and bring intangible gifts to the family. Yet, we continue to see an emphasis on deficits. For this reason, we strongly encourage the next generation of professionals and parents to build a new paradigm—one in which professionals conduct assessments that build trust with families, uplift the spirits of parents, and help families understand and support their children. In the first two vignettes, Susan and Joyce, respectively, describe their negative experiences with deficit-based assessments for their sons, Jason and Glen. In the third vignette, Joyce describes a brief but positive experience with an assessment that highlighted Glen's strengths.

Jason's First Diagnostic Assessment: Doomed From the Start

When I enrolled Jason in preschool, he was clearly in need of special education services. A postoperative lack of oxygen when he was 4 months old had resulted in gross and fine motor delays, as well as significant learning delays. At age 3 ½ Jason still did not have a functional communication system, and his frustration over not being able to express his needs resulted in head banging and occasional aggressive behaviors, such as pinching and hair pulling.

Because of his behaviors and communication delays, we were sent by the district to a private psychiatrist for an assessment. We spent about 30 minutes in his office, with me answering questions and Jason acting out, and we left without a diagnosis. I thought that meant that Jason did not have a behavioral or emotional disorder. It was quite a shock to get a copy of the letter the psychiatrist sent to the school 2 months later, which gave a diagnosis of atypical pervasive developmental disorder. I asked the teacher what that meant, and she could not tell me. Ultimately, I had to go to the medical library and look it up in the *Diagnostic and Statistical Manual of Mental Disorders, Third Edition, Revised* (American Psychiatric Association, 1987).

I was furious! The psychiatrist had not had the courtesy to tell me of his diagnosis. Nor had he supplied Jason's teachers and therapists with any recommendations on how to meet his needs. I was also devastated. I believed that his diagnosis meant that Jason's behavior was due to an organic imbalance, that there was nothing I could do to influence his behavior, that we were doomed to a life of head banging.

Glen's Educational Assessments: Enduring the "Can't Do Reports"

Professional teams met every 3 years to assess Glen's functioning and to determine his school placement. These reports, although useful to the professionals, were meaningless to me. I called them Glen's "can't do reports." When Glen was 12 years old, the clinical reports sent me into a rage. They were no more than snapshots of a few moments in Glen's life, bits and pieces of his knowledge, distorted pictures of my son, who was so much more. Family input was not sought.

After looking up the word *clinical* in the dictionary, I realized why I disliked reading these sterile writings. One of its definitions—"scientifically detached and dispassionate"—left no room for humanization. I resented the professionals' degrading descriptions of Glen: "lanky physique" (meaning that he was ungracefully tall and thin), "awkward gait," "drooling," "lethargy," and "drooping eyelids." No report mentioned Glen's medical history of daily seizures and medication side effects (fatigue, slurred speech, confusion, mental slowness, poor concentration).

At the meetings, the assessment team members read aloud their reports and recommendations. Since the last assessment, Glen's performance (at age 9) regressed from 36 to 27 months—thus labeling him severely mentally retarded. The occupational therapist stated that Glen had made no progress. She recommended a change from direct services to consultation with the teacher. Glen's "no progress" and "poor cooperation" led the physical therapist to discharge him from services.

For my family, assessments planted fear, discouragement, and lower expectations in our minds. Professionals' comments, such as "children bring their lifestyle to school" and "much of Glen's energy is spent in avoidance behaviors," triggered feelings of guilt and incompetence. As a result, we intensified our efforts to make Glen "normal." Family members individually spent 15 minutes daily alone with Glen to expand his attention and to improve his response to instructions. Glen's spontaneous and playful experiences with us were replaced by serious, structured activities. We were determined to change Glen! Instead, burnout struck.

Planting Seeds of Hope: A More Positive Assessment of Glen

Throughout Glen's school years, no individualized education program (IEP) ever addressed behavioral supports. As Glen grew older, problem behaviors emerged, from hugging too much to lying down on the ground and screaming. Because the role of the school psychologist was strictly to conduct assessments, the teachers had no one to turn to for advice. Despite our sharing of ideas and methods of what occasionally worked, we could not change Glen.

Dr. Daniel Overbeck, a behavioral psychologist from Arizona, entered our lives about this time. He was in our state as the guest speaker at an Easter Seals' parent meeting. His genuine understanding of the impact of disabilities on family life was presented so gently that we all felt comfortable sharing our feelings and experiences.

During his visit to Hawaii, Dr. Overbeck offered to do a behavioral assessment of a child attending the Easter Seals after-school program. Glen was chosen. From this assessment, Glen was found to be a very social, altruistic young man who engaged in meaningful activities and displayed much awareness of his environment and friends. This suggested mild to moderate delays. I was not ready for that "good" news and, oddly enough, took it with a grain of salt. I had just started giving in to the school's "severely retarded" label—and now this! After much discussion within our family, our spirits and energies slowly began to rise.

THEME 2

Futures planning is essential; families need to build new and meaningful dreams for their children. No one feels the pain of loss and broken dreams like a parent who has just learned that his or her child has a serious disability. Likewise, no one is more passionate about creating new dreams and holding high expectations for a child with a disability than a mother or father. Once these new dreams and expectations are formed, no one will pursue them with as much commitment and energy as the child's immediate family. For these reasons, we believe that personal futures planning is very important for families of children with disabilities.

Personal futures planning is a process of supporting families and professionals to nurture and define new hopes and dreams for children with disability. At the center of futures planning is an ongoing commitment by a team of individuals to envision and plan supports for the growth and inclusion of children in the home, school, community, and workplace. We think of this as team building, dream building, and community building. In the following vignette, Susan describes her introduction to personal futures planning for her son, Jason.

The Joy of "Mapping" Jason's Future

In the sixth grade, Jason and I were exposed to the wonderful experience of the McGill Action Planning System (MAPS; Vandercook, York, & Forrest, 1989). We used the MAPS process to plan Jason's transition to intermediate school. A facilitator guided Jason's educational team through a series of questions. The team included Jason's general education peers who had been supporting him in a pilot inclusion program. Seven questions were addressed:

1. What is Jason's history?

2. What is your dream for Jason?

3. What is your nightmare?

4. Who is Jason?

5. What are Jason's strengths, gifts, and abilities?

6. What are Jason's needs?

7. What would Jason's ideal day at school look like and what must be done to make it happen?

When it came time to list gifts, I had a whole list of them to contribute, but I waited to hear what others were going to say. My heart sang! They said the following things:

- He is a good friend to everyone.

- He makes us feel better when we are sad.

- He has a great sense of humor.

- He does not tattletale.

- He can sing.

- He is able to get even bullies to be nice.

Here was Jason's generation—his future—celebrating his strengths! When we got to the section on dreams, I was amazed at how normal everyone's expectations were for Jason. His peers envisioned Jason with his own family, a job, a "low-rider" to drive, and lots of friends. It made me realize how low my expectations had sunk given all the negative input up to that time.

THEME 3

When conducting a behavioral assessment, professionals should listen to and value parental knowledge and expertise about the purpose of the child's behavior and about the child's preferences and reinforcers. Because problem behavior is communication, we believe it is misguided to suppress problem behaviors without understanding the child's communicative intent or identifying positive communication alternatives. Given the intimacy of our knowledge about our children, we believe that professionals should listen to us and be responsive to our insights about the meaning or purpose of our children's problem behavior. As parents, we also know the importance of positive reinforcement. We know what motivates our kids and what we value as a family. In terms of reinforcers or motivators, we know what will be acceptable and feasible for us. For these reasons, we believe that it is very important that parents be included in the identification and selection of preferences and reinforcers. Because all families may not feel comfortable or confident about sharing their knowledge and insights, we encourage professionals to seek out and validate parental expertise during assessments. In the first vignette, Joyce describes how a service provider's deference to Joyce's knowledge about Glen's behavior may have saved Glen's life. In the second vignette, Angie shows how a hospital staff's willingness to work with her to determine Odee's preferences contributed to a pivotal step in Odee's progress after having sustained a TBI.

Glen's Aggressive Behavior and the Health Problem Beneath the Surface

Sick people are not happy people. They want to lie down and do nothing. Like anyone else, Glen's health dictates his state of mind and cooperation. Glen is a gentle person. Aggressive behavior immediately tells us that he is feeling rotten. One day, his program supervisor at his work site reported that Glen was screaming, kicking, and refusing to leave with the yard crew. I picked him up and took him directly to his medical doctor. He found no apparent physical ailment. That evening, Glen went into stasis. I asked the emergency doctor for a chest X-ray. The results showed that Glen was seriously ill with a collapsed lung. He was immediately hospitalized. He had been in great pain and could tell us only through aggressive actions. How sad. Again, Glen is so much like us. I am so very glad that the program supervisor realized that and called me. I would rather not think about what might have happened if he had treated my son's aggressive behavior as something that needed to be managed or controlled.

Collaborating to Nourish Odee: Finding "Da Bomb"

On April 1, 1992, Odee, who had sustained a TBI, was flown by air medevac to Kaiser Hospital in Vallejo, California. Kaiser in Vallejo has an excellent brain injury unit; however, it is for adults only. Therefore, Odee stayed in the pediatric ward and was wheeled to the TBI unit for daily treatment.

During Odee's stay at Kaiser, her left vocal cord was completely paralyzed. She was being tube fed. The speech therapist was trying daily to introduce Odee to soft solids, but Odee refused. Nothing would entice Odee to start eating. They tried Jell-O and pudding, hoping that she would give in and start eating. It was not until I remembered Odee's love of poi (a Hawaiian food that is made from taro root) that she began to eat again. "It's da bomb," Odee had always said. Because we were far from Hawaii, we had our family back home mail us poi in plastic bags. To the credit of the hospital staff, they allowed us to try this Hawaiian staple with Odee. Once she saw the poi, it was downhill from there. She would eat anything as long as we mixed it with poi. Soon, we were able to wean her off the tube feedings as she increased her tolerance for solids with poi. To this day, Odee waters the taro plants that grow next to the plumeria in the backyard. "It's da bomb," she says.

THEME 4

Interventions should not focus on "fixing" children; rather, interventions should help family members and educators change what they do and help improve the quality of children's lives. When we think about intervention, we no longer think in terms of "fixing children." Rather, we view intervention as the things that parents and professionals alike do to rebuild the contexts that surround children's lives: our homes, classrooms, schools, communities, and workplaces. Rebuilding these contexts requires creative and effective strategies and supports for living and learning. Successful intervention also requires parents and teachers to reflect on what does not work and to begin practicing more effective ways of supporting their children or students. Self-reflection, humility, and hard work are always part of the package. From our perspective, intervention should lead to a child's successful participation and inclusion in the activities and responsibilities of home, school, and community life. We do not, in fact, see intervention as separate from participation and inclusion. We believe that they go hand in hand. In the first vignette that follows, Joyce talks about the importance of personal change as a prelude to improvements in Glen's behavior. In the second vignette, Susan describes how she improved Jason's behavior and life by rebuilding some of the contexts around him.

Improving Glen's Behavior: Learning to Manage and Control Myself

At the age of 13, Glen's behavior (e.g., refusals to cooperate, lying on the ground, having tantrums) not only affected the family and the school but also his after-school program at Easter Seals. I forever will be grateful to the staff of Easter Seals for inviting me to attend a 2-day in-service workshop on addressing problem behaviors—a training that, at the time, was only offered to professionals. I was eager to learn what I thought would be physical ways to manage Glen, such as restraining holds and physical assistance. I learned these techniques, but it was the philosophy that changed our life with Glen—a philosophy that there was nothing wrong with Glen. We were challenged, instead, to design supports for Glen that would allow him to communicate and to participate in the everyday life of our family.

Over the years, my husband and I have learned that Glen is more like us than different from us. His response to his environment often mirrors our own responses. We pout, we give silent treatments, and we get mad. With Glen's limited communication skills, he has more difficulty expressing intentions and feelings such as, "I need help," "Leave me alone," "I don't understand," or "I'm scared." At times, we all have difficulty communicating some of these things in positive ways. Appreciating that Glen is more like us than different from us has helped us foster positive changes in his behavior and in our lives together.

One of the outcomes of this viewpoint is that I have realized that I cannot change my situation with Glen without first changing myself. When I learn to control and manage myself, I can better manage Glen. Now, I first see Glen as a "regular" person; before I viewed him as a person with disabilities. It makes me sad to reflect on the many years that we, his family, believed that Glen was different and that, as a result of this difference, we had to change him and control him.

I enthusiastically shared these insights with my family. I also undertook my own personal transformation with the hope that my success would demonstrate to my family the reality of this viewpoint. Needless to say, change is difficult. With great effort and many failures, I learned consciously to become aware of my own facial expressions, voice tone, and body language when faced with one of Glen's sudden and dramatic behavioral episodes. I learned that I can create an atmosphere for better communication with Glen by maintaining a relaxed body position, making eye contact, and speaking in soft tones. Whenever I failed to do so, I saw a sharp contrast in outcomes. Loud, angry responses escalated Glen's emotional state and provoked problem behaviors. As my new way of responding became more natural to me, the intensity, duration, and number of Glen's behavioral incidents declined.

Discovering the Joys of Natural Supports for Jason: Pizza, Tennis, and *Baywatch*

When Jason was 4 years old, I went back to work and began the frustrating search for after-school care. I tried several "generic" sitters, primarily because they said they really wanted to work with a child with disabilities. That zeal didn't last long. As soon as Jason began misbehaving (e.g., pulling the baby's hair for attention), I'd have to start looking for a new caregiver. Somehow both the sitters and I had a lack of confidence in our ability to problem-solve. We saw Jason's disability first. It didn't take too many failed sitters to decide that Jason needed "specialized" care.

So I started to take him to an after-school program for children with disabilities. They were providing care for about 40 other kids with disabilities, ranging in age from 4 to 20, and they had that confidence for which I was looking. Jason would spend 1½ hours on the bus in the afternoons getting from school to the program. Once there, Jason would be placed in a group of kids near his own age and given a choice of activities. Unfortunately, many of the choices were not things that Jason enjoyed. I'd often get reports that Jason was stubborn or that he did not want to participate. I guess that is why a look of pure salvation appeared on his face when I turned up at 5:29 P.M. to collect him.

After 11 years of this routine, I finally developed the courage to have a peer pick Jason up after school and bring him to our home, then take him to a pizza parlor or bowling alley to hang out together. The young people I recruited were not knowledgeable about PBS. Basically, they just paid close attention to Jason's preferences and signals. They went with the flow. In the process, they have introduced Jason to some age-appropriate fun and friendship that he had been missing out on. Each young caregiver is different. Jan is an athlete and likes to take Jason bowling or out on the field to kick a soccer ball around. Gina is a natural nurturer. She reads Jason his favorite books and fixes his favorite foods. Rodney is intent on teaching Jason to appreciate *Baywatch,* a popular TV show about scantily clad lifeguards in California. Eric takes Jason out to his tennis practices and introduces him to his team members. Each young person has contributed immensely to Jason's social life; he, in turn, has contributed to theirs.

I am struck by the contrasting reports of Jason's behavior at the center-based program and at home and in the community with his buddies. At the after-school program, Jason was described as being stubborn, inappropriate, uncooperative, and self-abusive. At home or in the community, he is cheerful, friendly, cooperative, and gentle. In retrospect, what appears obvious is that a lack of choice and control contributes to Jason's becoming a difficult person. It is not in his genes. It is in his surroundings. When Jason is with young people who give him some control over the things he does, who offer him choices, and who introduce him to new and interesting activities, he begins to relax and enjoy himself. When he senses that he is valued, his positive qualities come out and shine.

THEME 5

Interventions should be developed collaboratively, taking into account family culture and lifestyle. Living and working in Hawaii, we are intimately aware of the need to understand and accommodate differences in culture and lifestyle. Because classrooms and communities in Hawaii include so much ethnic diversity, we have grown in our sensitivity to differing ways of living and valuing. Some diversity issues are more obvious than others. How we dress and celebrate are often recognized as overt markers of culture. How we raise our children may be less visible, but it is just as cultural. In the following vignette, Angie describes how knowledge of her family's culture played a key role in developing effective strategies and supports for Odee.

Hula: The Healing Dance

Physical therapy, for Odee, was unpleasant. She loved her therapist, Herb Yee, and his staff. They became our extended family. However, therapy was not what Odee wanted to do. Now, I need to shift focus a little. Disability does not only happen to an individual. It happens to the entire family. At the time of the accident Odee's older sister, Kanani, was at her side. Kanani lives with the guilt of being responsible for Odee's accident. In addition, as much as we love Kanani, our focus as parents is on Odee because of her special needs.

For Kanani, who was 11 years old at the time of the accident, this was hard to understand and comprehend. Kanani became withdrawn and depressed, so we had to make a conscious effort to focus on Kanani's needs. The approach we took was to enroll Kanani in a hula class. On Thursday nights, Kanani and I went to hula lessons. This was our time together. Kanani developed into a beautiful dancer and this improved her self-esteem. After about 1½ years, Odee started accompanying us to practice. Watching Kanani dance inspired Odee to want to dance, too. This was an absolute blessing. Hula is an excellent means of getting exercise and strengthening muscles.

Herb encouraged us to enroll Odee in hula. The 2 years of hula became Odee's therapy. We took her to Herb for official examinations and to chart her progress. The hula was a

wonderful, fun way for Odee to work with her peers. She became part of the hula family. She was a hula sister. This type of therapy was much more powerful and effective than clinical therapy in accomplishing our goals for Odee.

THEME 6

Good behavior support plans include communication strategies and tools that improve children's abilities to express their feelings, wants, needs, and interests. Because we understand the importance of language for our children's development and success in life, we have asked professionals many questions: "How can I teach my son or daughter to ask for help instead of hit herself?" "Would sign language help?" "Can picture-board strategies be devised?" "What about electronic talkers or computer software?"

When we find professionals trained in language promotion or in the use of augmentative and alternative communication (AAC) strategies, we are very appreciative of their expertise and their assistance. We know that answering these questions and building effective communication strategies and tools takes much skill, time, and effort. Yet, too often we have encountered special education professionals who are unknowledgeable about AAC. When such expertise is available, we have sometimes found that the effort necessary to meet our children's unique language challenges is not expended. Accordingly, we challenge university-based teacher-training programs and speech-language therapist programs to do a better job of preparing professionals so that they meet the communication needs of children with disabilities. Two vignettes illustrate these points. First, Susan describes her personal effort to overcome Jason's self-injurious behavior by devising a uniquely effective communication intervention. Next, Joyce describes how a daily video chronicle of Glen's experiences has given him a means to share his experiences with others, develop a sense of self-identity, and decrease his overall level of anxiety.

Using Language to Replace Jason's Self-Injurious Behavior: Finding Our Own Way

Up until about kindergarten or first grade, Jason had a distressing habit of hitting or slapping himself immediately after he skinned a knee or bumped his head. His reaction was lightning fast, and neither his teachers nor I had a strategy to prevent him from inflicting pain on top of pain. Then one day a light bulb clicked on. I was listening to David Viscott, a popular media psychiatrist who liked to boil down complex situations to reveal simple (and predictable) motivations. He talked about the importance of expressing your hurt as soon as you experienced it. He said if you didn't express your hurt, it would turn into anger, which, if not expressed outwardly, would be turned inward. That was it! Jason was experiencing hurt, did not have a way to express it, and was turning his anger on himself.

My strategy was to teach him the sign for *hurt*. Each time he experienced a bump or scrape, I would catch his attention, acknowledge his hurt (i.e., say "Oh, you hurt yourself" while signing HURT), and then express my condolences (i.e., signing and saying *sorry*). I found through trial and error that the condolence part was as important as acknowledging his accidental injury. Once he was able to express his hurt and receive sympathy, he no longer lashed out at himself.

This is an example of a strategy or piece of wisdom that came outside of the special-education circle. I was not often given the "whys" of Jason's behavior by his teachers or even by the two psychiatrists with whom we visited along the way. Yet, I was always looking for clues so that I could be a better parent and intermediary. Finding an answer from the larger community was comforting because it gave me hope that I could figure things out on my own.

Glen and His Video Camera: Pictures Tell a Thousand Words

After Glen graduated from high school in 1992, he had a loving caregiver/attendant named Clyde. Both Clyde and Glen were in their twenties. They spent their days at home or out in the community. They enjoyed public transportation, the beach and parks, zoos and animals, lunch at the mall, bowling, movies, television and computers, and errands to the store or post office. In short, they spent quality time together.

Glen and Clyde had a video camera. As their day unfolded, they filmed brief video vignettes to capture the highlights of their day. The video came home in the evenings for Glen to share with the family. Just as we talk about our day, Glen did so through his videos and Clyde's narration. We saw the little things (e.g., Glen licking a stamp, sticking it in the top right corner of the envelope, and posting it in the box), the exciting things (e.g., horseback riding, bowling), and even the humorous and unexpected. In one such vignette, Clyde stood in the lobby of our high-rise condominium with the camera aimed at a closing elevator door—wondering aloud when, if ever, he would see Glen again. Glen had just disappeared on the elevator without him. They did reconnect and, as the video showed, Glen was delighted by the trick that he had played on Clyde.

Glen always has wanted to communicate his experiences with his family and with others. During his high school years, Glen demanded that we read out loud to him what we wrote to the teacher and what the teacher wrote to us. It was really important to him

that we knew what was happening with him away from home. Now photographs and videotapes helped Glen tell us and others about his life experiences. Every week, he eagerly shared videotapes with us of his and his caregiver's daily adventures. In fact, without a visual means of reflecting on and sharing his experiences, Glen grew anxious. After returning from a weekend on a Neighbor Island with his father, Glen appeared restless and agitated. His father, discerning why Glen was becoming anxious, quickly drove over to the 1-hour photo developing center and returned with pictures of their time together. As he shared the pictures with the rest of the family, he glowed. For Glen and for us, what it has all come down to is our family's efforts to help Glen with his communication needs.

THEME 7

Behavior support plans used by families should be based on assessments conducted with families in their homes and communities. Such plans are more likely to be proactive and practical. We lead busy lives, just as do other families raising children. In addition to raising a child with disability, some of us have other children, a spouse or a partner, an apartment or a house to maintain, and a full- or part-time job. This is the context in which we provide behavioral support to our children with disability. Given this context, it really helps us if behavior support strategies and plans are as proactive and practical as possible. We want and need strategies that prevent problem behaviors rather than require us constantly to react to problem behaviors. We need strategies that are doable in our daily lives.

To this end, we believe that it is helpful during behavioral assessment and planning activities for professionals to spend time with families in their homes and communities where problem behaviors occur—to see firsthand the challenges and successes that families experience, to ensure that recommended support strategies are feasible in a child's home and community. Doing so might ensure that behavior support plans work for families. In the following vignette, Joyce describes such a productive home visit by a professional.

Teaching Glen to Keep His Clothes On, Among Other Things: The Home Visit that Worked

In our experience, social workers and psychologists working for the Hawaii Department of Education are responsible for conducting assessments of our children rather than providing ongoing behavioral consultation. So, with no guidance, the teachers and I struggled daily with Glen's array of challenging behaviors. With nothing left to lose and remembering how 8 years previously Dr. Overbeck (more than any other person) had seen Glen's positive attributes, I telephoned him in Tucson. Fortunately, Dr. Overbeck told me that he was soon returning to Hawaii to provide additional behavioral consultations for the Hawaii Department of Health. I explained to him that having visitors in our home had become a source of anxiety for us, as we worried about Glen's unpredictable outbursts. Removing him to time-out only worsened the situation. At our family's expense, Dr. Overbeck agreed to make a home visit.

The family, Glen's teacher, and Glen were present for the consultation. This was the first time that Glen's teacher had visited our home. Just as it had been years before, Dr. Overbeck's soothing personality established a friendly, calm atmosphere for all of us, especially for Glen. One of the behavior problems we first addressed, as a matter of necessity, was Glen's habit of walking naked into a room full of guests in our home.

Shortly after discussions began, Glen disappeared and a short time later quietly re-entered the room completely naked. In embarrassed silence, all eyes turned to Dr. Overbeck. His response was, "Glen, I'm glad you're here, but you seem to have forgotten your robe." Glen then cooperatively followed me to his room, got dressed, and returned fully clothed. The incident faded as calmly as it had appeared. We followed Dr. Overbeck's lead in not discussing it in Glen's presence. His written report elaborated on how we could respond the next time: Redirect him with positive phrases, avoid scolding him, and refrain from showing any shock or surprise when he engages in such attention-seeking behavior.

The effectiveness and simplicity of Dr. Overbeck's plan impressed us. What proved to be the most helpful intervention, however, began with a departing question: "Does Glen have a belt?" We realized at that moment that Glen did not own a belt; as a result, it was very easy for Glen to slip out of his pants. Once his pants were off, the rest of his clothes followed. We immediately bought Glen a belt! Ever since Glen started wearing his belt, he stopped taking off his clothes in the house. The behavior simply disappeared! This was, by far, the easiest lesson learned about changing Glen's environment, not Glen.

The strategies that Dr. Overbeck taught us also proved helpful for another chronic problem that we had at home with Glen. For the longest time, whenever friends visited our home, Glen would determine their time of departure. In our house, guests take off their shoes upon entering the house, leaving them in the entryway. Usually after about 20 min-utes, Glen would quietly take our guests shoes, put them in front of each guest, and then point to the door. He would not budge until they left, and so visits with friends were al-ways short. Using the lessons we learned from Dr. Overbeck, we devised our own plan. First, everyone was asked to leave their shoes outside the apartment rather than visibly in the doorway. For Glen, once the shoes were out of sight, they were out of mind. He stopped prompting guests to leave. We also recognized that Glen wanted guests to leave because they dominated our attention. We were less available to Glen when our friends visited. For this reason, we also began to make extra effort to include Glen when friends called. We now make a point of including him in conversations by directing comments his way and by ask-ing him questions. We also give him opportunities to show visitors his birds, to serve guests coffee, or to demonstrate his computer skills. After a while, Glen usually shows less interest in our guests or in us and returns to his own interests.

Dr. Overbeck also helped us with Glen's chronically difficult bedtime routine. He taught us to use nonverbal cues instead of commands to increase Glen's cooperation and guide him through the routine. For example, when I carry Glen's parakeets into the bath-room, that is his cue to take a shower. When I brush my teeth, it is Glen's cue to brush his. When I move the birds into Glen's bedroom, that is the signal for puzzles and other quiet activities before turning in. Our evenings are now void of bedtime refusals. Dr. Overbeck also addressed my need to take respite, to do something for myself. It took a professional to convince me that I needed a life, too. I decided to make a commitment outside of the home. I signed up for an art class at the university twice per week. It was wonderful! The respite from caregiving uplifted both Glen and me. I will be forever grateful for Dr. Over-beck's wisdom and guidance.

THEME 8

Positive outcomes for children and families are more likely when professionals work with families as equal partners and aim to empower family members. We hope that by this point in the chapter, the reader understands that we want to work in partnership with professionals—partnerships that are equal but also empowering. By *empowerment,* we mean working with us to identify goals that are important to us and our children and providing information, skills, and resources that help us achieve these goals. Where professionals have joined with us in equal partnership and have worked to empower us, our children have experienced tremendous growth. When professionals have not worked as equal partners with us, our children have developed less and we as parents have experienced frustration, anger, and sadness.

We have also observed the following phenomenon: When families and professionals enter into balanced partnerships, communities strengthen and grow. When families are empowered with knowledge, skills, and resources, they often give back to their communities. They become strong and respected allies to professionals. They become effective advocates for other families. When there is an opportunity to do so, they may act as responsible community leaders, sharing information, knowledge, skills, and resources with other families and professionals. We see this phenomenon as one of the creative and synergistic outcomes of parent–professional partnership and empowerment. In the final two vignettes, Angie describes how, in partnership with professionals, she was able to help Odee relearn how to walk and was able to transform private pain and tragedy into healing and public education.

How Pogs Helped Odee Relearn to Walk

Within 8 months of Odee's accident, our insurance coverage was already running out. Odee was in a wheelchair, unable to care for herself—stubborn and uncooperative. Therapists would ask her to do her exercises and she would refuse. One by one, the "experts" gave up on the likelihood that Odee would walk again. "Accept the facts, Angie. Odee is about as good as she's going to get," the professionals began saying with increasing volume. I would not hear of it. I had been told that the first year after a TBI would define the likelihood of recovery. A year had not yet passed. In my view, these experts were jumping ship long before Odee's fate was sealed.

In this discouraging context, I found a physical therapist (Herb Yee) within our home community of Waianae who was willing to listen to me and share his expertise in partnership with Odee and me. In fact, Herb is the one who discovered the "magic" reinforcer that reawakened Odee's desire to overcome her disabilities.

Herb began seeing Odee three times per week. After our third visit, Odee was still stubborn. She did not cooperate with anything Herb had to offer. We were stuck. Suddenly, Herb said, "Odee, I will give you this Pog if you stand up from this chair." Odee stood up. Pogs were the craze in Hawaii at that time—cardboard disks with pictures and sayings. Kids were collecting them like baseball cards. They were expensive; you could pay as much as $5–$10 for collector's Pogs. All of them were highly motivating to Odee. She began to comply with physical therapy: For Pogs, she would stand, walk, climb stairs, do sit-ups, and use a stationary bicycle.

Once we found a reinforcer that worked, the next question was, "How were we going to afford all these Pogs?" Our medical bills were bankrupting us. The extra expenses we had incurred were outrageous. Fortunately, a local newspaper ran Odee's story. Pogs began pouring in by the hundreds from as far away as Illinois and Japan. Odee had Pogs to work for. Within 2 months, Odee was out of her wheelchair. At first, she sort of flopped around, dragging her left leg. She was so sincere in her efforts. She wanted every Pog Herb had to offer. Many an hour at Herb's clinic flew by. Herb stayed on, letting Odee earn her Pogs.

At some point, Odee began opening up to Herb. She told him, "I want to participate in the 'Jump for Your Life' contest" (a fundraising campaign for a local health organization;

students get pledges for the amount of jumps that they will complete). So Herb and I worked with the school. Odee couldn't do her jumps at school, so we did them at Herb's clinic. Odee was able to submit her card with the number of jumps accomplished. Odee was stoked. She was participating again in a school activity.

Then, she asked to learn to ride a bike again. "You have to gain your balance with me first," cautioned Herb. Everyone at the clinic was now interested. Herb got together with some of the maintenance personnel to build a balance beam from scrap lumber. After months of practice and hundreds of Pogs, Odee mastered the beam! At Herb's encouragement and with great fear, we presented Odee with a bike. What a scary first step! While practicing, she fell twice. Then it was freedom. She mastered bike riding!

I have often wondered what it was about Herb that set him apart from all the previous therapists. It wasn't that he "knew" kids. In fact, he doubted that he knew enough. Nor was it that he had any radically different approach. The other therapists had asked the same things of Odee. It must be that he listened to us, believed us, and worked with us.

Watch It! Don't Dodge It!: Angie, Odee, and Kanani Make a Video About Traffic Safety

Four years after Odee's accident, we were approached by Mary Kelly, a University of Hawaii graduate student in public health, who wanted us to help in the production of a traffic safety videotape. The Injury Prevention Unit of the Hawaii State Department of Health had allocated money to get children involved in making our highways safer. They wanted to use Odee's story, as it was tragic but not fatal (25% of Oahu's fatalities happen on the same road where Odee was hit). Our family was eager to help. Mary's team and I invited local kids to participate in scripting, acting, and making the videotape. Our goal was to capture the children's voices. The videotape was one of the most powerful activities that we have done for our community. For the first time, Kanani was willing to speak about her sister's accident. *Watch It! Don't Dodge It!* is now shown in every elementary school in Hawaii. It has received recognition from both Honolulu's mayor, Jeremy Harris, and Hawaii's governor, Benjamin Cayetano. In addition, during the year of our campaign, more than 600 students and parents were trained on traffic safety, and our community installed 10 new traffic lights, reducing the number of fatalities by 10%.

This experience of giving youth a voice was so powerful that Mary and I teamed up with James Skouge at the Hawaii University Center on Disability Studies. The three of us now sponsor a youth television program that is regularly broadcast on Hawaii Public Television. The program integrates children with and without disabilities, including children with attention-deficit/hyperactivity disorder, TBI, visual impairments, hearing impairments, and their typically developing peers. The kids are the producers, directors, writers, editors, and hosts of the show called *Through the Viewfinder.* The program content includes a mix of "disability awareness" storytelling, cultural celebration, and science. The kids are learning technical skills as well as social skills. Our intent is that they discover career choices for their futures. Odee is also a participant in this project.

Odee's social behavior needs improvement. It is difficult for her to maintain friendships. As parents, it is hard to be the bad guy, always correcting our children. This project has made a big difference in our lives because it has assisted in building Odee's self-esteem. The other children are helping her sort out appropriate behavior from inappropriate behavior. We are having fun and helping our daughter become a productive part of her community.

This project represents what community partnerships can do. No one person could have done it alone. Working together as a team, however, we have been able to coach our kids into leadership roles. Our once-shy kids are now grabbing the microphone to do the interviews because they know their product will be aired and perhaps the local paper will carry yet another story about their work.

CONCLUSION

We hope that the perspectives and insights that we have shared in this chapter offer a path that families and professionals can take together to improve the quality of assessment and intervention in the lives of children with disabilities and their families. In some communities, this path may be easier to find and walk along than in other communities. We think it is important to anticipate that in your own community, you may have to work very hard to create the path while you also begin to walk along it.

For us, the process of assessment and intervention did not come in a tidy package. More often than not, we have stood outside of professional circles. Throughout our efforts, we have found that any progress in improving assessment and intervention services to our children occurred in the context of a relationship with professionals that included mutual regard and shared commitment toward improving services.

At this stage in our families' development, we are looking for partners: people who appreciate our children; who can truly imagine opportunities that are not here until we make them; and who understand that families are for a lifetime and that "goals and objectives" must be referenced to hopes, dreams, and positive futures for children. We are looking for partners who use their knowledge and expertise to help build communities that include children with disabilities—respecting their individuality, recognizing their strengths, and honoring their cultural diversity.

Now that our kids have entered adulthood, we face a new set of challenges with a mix of anxiety and enthusiasm. We are cautiously optimistic about their futures. Both Jason and Glen have had their share of health problems. They get sick. They have seizures. They spend time in hospitals. They do not communicate in typical ways. They live their lives one day at a time. Jason returned from the hospital after Thanksgiving 1998 with a pacemaker. Glen spends most of his time at home because of health problems. Odee wants to be just like everybody else; she loves swimming, biking, studying science, and interviewing rock stars.

We appreciate the opportunity to contribute to this book. The collaborative writing has prompted much dialogue and reflection among us. Our stories have differed; yet, the lessons we have learned have been the same. We hope that they may be of some use to you in your role as family member or professional. We wish you well. Aloha.

REFERENCES

American Psychiatric Association. (1987). *Diagnostic and statistical manual of mental disorders* (3rd ed. rev.). Washington, DC: Author.

Vandercook, T., York, J., & Forrest, M. (1989). The McGill Action Planning System (MAPS): A strategy for building the vision. *Journal of The Association for Persons with Severe Handicaps, 14*(3), 205–215.

A Mother's Perspective on Developing and Implementing Behavior Support Plans

Anne T. Kayser

My son Tom was diagnosed with autism shortly before his third birthday. At the time of his diagnosis, Tom understood and used very little language. He rarely made eye contact with people outside his immediate family and usually ran away from people who tried to talk or play with him. His play was perseverative rather than imaginative: He lined up toy cars or figures instead of pretending with them; he spilled and threw blocks instead of building with them. He seemed to have a high tolerance for pain, as he almost never cried when he scraped his knee or bumped his head. In fact, he often hit himself on the place where he was scraped or bumped immediately after the injury. His father and I could not understand why Tom did this. The only thing we found that soothed him and stopped him from making a sore spot more sore was to embrace him, holding back his fists and pressing firmly on the place that hurt. Holding Tom firmly also became our standard method of dealing with his frequent tantrums.

As Tom grew, he hit his head more often, especially when someone tried to command his attention and teach him something. He also hit me, his teachers, and his therapists sometimes, but this behavior was easier to ignore and redirect. Seeing my child strike himself on the head and even occasionally on the face was terribly upsetting to me. I would plead with Tom to stop hitting himself. When my words failed to change his behavior, I would catch and hold his fists tightly or wrap my arms around his so that he could not hit himself for a while. Often, I would weep and kiss the place on his handsome head that he had just pounded. Sometimes I would sing one of Tom's favorite songs as I held him, hoping that the music would calm him. These responses to Tom's self-injurious behavior usually did calm him down, but only for a short time. With increasing frequency, as soon as I (or another adult) insisted that he sit and attend to instruction, Tom started hitting himself again.

It was during this time of escalating self-injurious behavior, when Tom was about 4½ years old, that I first contacted a specialist in positive behavior support (PBS). I had heard that this consultant was experienced in helping parents overcome problem behaviors in children with severe developmental disabilities. I called him and explained the problems that we were having. I expected that he, like so many of the other specialists we had taken Tom to see, would have a particular therapy or treatment to sell us, but I found his approach to be much more individualized than others that I had seen or read about. He listened carefully and asked many specific questions about the setting in which Tom was most likely to hit himself, as well as the things that usually preceded and followed his self-injury. After gathering this information, the consultant hypothesized that Tom was hitting himself to escape demands to sit and look at nonpreferred materials (e.g., flashcards, books, craft projects). He also surmised that Tom might find my strong emotional reaction to his head hitting rather entertaining, and I realized that Tom probably enjoyed the deep pressure he was getting when I held his fists or his whole body immediately after he hit himself. Although Tom had my mental attention throughout a teaching session, after he hit his head he enjoyed my physical and emotional attention as well. Thus, it became clear to me that in my effort to prevent my son's self-injury, I had inadvertently reinforced it.

What to do? The PBS consultant taught me that there were several proactive ways to prevent the negative behavior and to teach Tom a better behavior in its place. First, I would make the environment more predictable for Tom so that he would know how much work he had to do, when it would be over, and what he would get to do when the work was finished. These strategies were familiar to me because of my experience with structured teaching (through Project TEACCH, University of North Carolina at Chapel Hill), and they were fairly easy to implement. I made a simple visual system with multiple cards denoting "Tom's Choice" and "Mommy's Choice," and I put them in a row on the wall of the bedroom that was designated as our teaching room. When it was my choice, I either selected an activity with a clear ending (e.g., a small deck of flashcards to identify, a puzzle to assemble, a finite set of cups to name by color and stack) or I set a timer to show when a less-structured activity would be over.

The second strategy that the consultant recommended I liked less: reducing demands and the duration of instructional activities temporarily while Tom learned what the visual system and timer meant and if he used words instead of fists to communicate his desire for a break. I did not like this strategy because I felt that it would be a step backward in our instruction time. We had built up to naming 25 flashcards at a time, and the consultant wanted me to drop back to 8 or 10—even fewer if Tom said, "I want a break." In time, however, I began to see the wisdom of this strategy. Even though it would allow less time to teach Tom nouns, verbs, and adjectives for a while, it would give more opportunities to demonstrate how the new visual turn-taking system worked and how the timer worked. Tom would be reinforced more quickly and frequently for completing what I asked him to do. Gradually, as Tom became more cooperative, I would be able to add cards to the flashcard deck, pieces to the puzzle, or minutes to the timer. Indeed, this is what happened over the course of about a month after we introduced the new system.

The third strategy that the consultant proposed was the hardest but perhaps the most important for me to implement. I had to learn to reinforce desired behaviors and not to reinforce problem behaviors. Specifically, this meant giving Tom lots of hugs, kisses, favorite music, deep pressure play, and emotionally charged attention when he did the right things (which was relatively easy for me) and never when he hit himself (which was difficult for me). A math teacher by training, I found it natural to show excitement whenever a child edged toward a new skill; what felt unnatural, to say the least, was to ignore his violent outbursts. Before recommending this strategy, the consultant carefully probed as to whether my son's head hitting actually resulted in an injury to the head. After I reassured the consultant that it had not, he indicated that this opened up the possibility of using the technique of extinction. This procedure required me *not* to react in any noticeable way to Tom's head hitting. The consultant also cautioned that this technique would only work if it was used in tandem with the proactive, positive strategies in the plan.

Putting my son's head hitting on extinction (i.e., actively ignoring head hitting) took concentrated self-discipline on my part and on the part of everyone else working with him, but the payoff was well worth it. When we did not react to Tom's self-injurious behavior in any physically or emotionally detectable way but just blandly redirected him to complete the task at hand, we stopped playing his game. At first, as the consultant predicted, Tom was confused by our lack of response to head hitting; for 2 days this behavior increased as he tried to get our attention and get us to do what we used to do. I would sit silently, knowing that I must not react to the violent behavior but wishing I could grab those little fists before they struck my beautiful boy, willing my face not to betray my heart, praying that "this too shall pass." Then, on the third day of our new program, Tom stopped hitting himself during teaching sessions.

I wish that I could report that my son stopped hitting himself forever and in all situations, but this is not the case. He still has autism. He still has a high threshold for pain. He still has difficulty negotiating verbally. Thus, he still has an occasional outburst of head hitting when he is faced with too many changes, too many demands, not enough predictability, or a combination of these factors. I wish I could report that I always handle it well, that I remain emotionally neutral, calm, and rational. This is not the case either. Times that are stressful for my son are usually stressful for me, too, and in these times, I often let my guard down. I go back to catching his fists, to pleading for gentleness, to tears. The difference now is that I can recognize what I am doing and how it is affecting Tom's behavior, and this makes it possible for me to stop, rethink my response, and prevent myself from getting trapped in an unhelpful interaction pattern with Tom. Now, I have a tool for understanding and solving problem behaviors.

This tool, PBS, has been incredibly useful. With it, we successfully toilet trained Tom, helped him get over his fear of our VCR, got him to sleep through the night consistently in his own bed, taught him to cooperate with medical and dental professionals at checkups, helped him discover the fun of Halloween, and included him in his neighborhood school. The consultant guided my husband and me through several of these solutions, but as he did this he also taught us the process so that we could use it on our own. Now, for most of the challenges that we face with Tom at home and at school, I feel confident in my ability to perform a functional assessment and develop a workable support plan. Some problems are very complex, but the structure of the Functional Assessment Summary Statement that the consultant has taught us to use makes it possible for us to thoroughly comprehend and address all of the features of subtle or convoluted issues. Then, we are able to develop a combination of support strategies that set the stage for success, prevent problems, teach needed skills, and reinforce these skills powerfully. This approach has helped us create complete and lasting solutions to problems that used to drive us crazy!

Because there is so much suffering among families whose children have autism spectrum disorder and because positive behavior support has so much practical help to offer such families, the consultant wanted to start a support group to teach parents and professionals how to use this tool. My husband and I agreed to host monthly meetings in our home, at which the consultant or I led a discussion focused on one family's most pressing problem. Everyone who attended the meetings participated in analyzing and solving the

problem; in the meantime, all of us were learning a powerful process for solving problems with our own children. It was gratifying for me to watch other families experience successes similar to those that we experienced. Some of the problems that we solved together were life-threatening: A teenage girl with autism repeatedly opened the door of the family van as it sped down the freeway. Some problems were exhausting: A 12-year-old boy with autism continually did destructive things at home, like submersing telephones and computer keyboards in water when his mother tried to work in another room. Some problems were annoying or embarrassing: A 5-year-old boy with pervasive developmental disorder wet his pants on the school bus every morning. Regardless of the severity or complexity of the problems that families had to face, positive behavior support proved to be a really effective process for building practical plans that quickly brought desired results. For us and for many families in our support group, it brought about welcome changes in our children and in the quality of life that we enjoy with them.

> *Anne T. Kayser lives with her husband, Jeff, and their two children, Julia and Tom, in Portland, Oregon. Jeff and Anne hosted the Positive Behavior Support Group at their home from August 1996 to June 1999. Anne has presented information about positive behavior support at the Autism Society of Oregon's and the Autism Society of Washington's annual conferences, as well as at several workshops for parents and service providers. Since 1998, Anne has been consulting with other parents and teachers to address children's challenging behaviors. She has also helped an autism specialist in a small Oregon town start a Positive Behavior Support Group for families in that community.*

CHAPTER 5

Functional Assessment and Positive Behavior Support at Home with Families

Designing Effective and Contextually Appropriate Behavior Support Plans

Joseph M. Lucyshyn, Anne T. Kayser,
Larry K. Irvin, and E. Richard Blumberg

> *I have spread my dreams under your feet;*
> *Tread softly because you tread on my dreams.*
> —*W.B. Yeats*

The purpose of this chapter is to describe a family-centered approach to the development of positive behavior support (PBS) plans with families of children and youth with disabilities and problem behaviors. In this approach, practitioners work with families as collaborative partners during a process of assessment and plan design aimed at improving child or youth behavior and skills in the context of valued but problematic family activity settings. Functional assessment information is used to develop a plan that is technically sound, and family ecology information is used to ensure that the plan possesses a good contextual fit with the family's culture and ecology. The overall goal of the process is to empower families with the knowledge and skills necessary to more meaningfully and successfully include their son or daughter with a disability into the rich and myriad patterns of family and community life.

First, the chapter discusses the behavioral support needs of families, defines the goals and features of the family-centered approach, discusses the activity setting as unit of analysis and intervention, and summarizes preliminary empirical evidence for the efficacy and acceptability of the approach. Next, the chapter discusses four considerations for designing behavior support plans with families. Then the chapter presents a flexible, five-step process for designing effective and contextually appropriate positive behavior support plans for valued family routines and activities that are unsuccessful due to child problem behavior. The process is illustrated with two case study examples from our work with families as practitioners or researchers.

BEHAVIORAL SUPPORT NEEDS OF FAMILIES

Children and youth with developmental disabilities are increasingly being raised by their families at home and are attending local neighborhood schools (Singer, 1996; Sailor, Gee, & Karasoff, 2000). These advances in social policy have greatly improved the lives of children[1] with disabilities but have also placed significant caregiving challenges on many families (Singer & Irvin, 1989). Foremost among these challenges is the presence of problem behaviors such as aggression, self-injury, and property destruction. Problem behaviors are a major source of stress for families of children and youth with disabilities. They are associated with significant social costs, including physical exhaustion, social isolation and marital distress for parents, and out-of-home placement for the child with a disability (Blacher, 1994; Koegel et al., 1992; Singer & Irvin, 1991). Consequently, many families of children and youth with developmental disabilities have a tremendous need for behavior support services (Lutzker & Steed, 1998).

Despite this need, families continue to have difficulty obtaining effective behavior support services for problem behaviors in the home (Turnbull & Ruef, 1996). Families report the need for 1) services that promote meaningful behavioral and lifestyle change across all of the natural contexts of family life; 2) parent–professional relationships that are more collegial and less hierarchical; 3) assessments that help parents understand problem behaviors without assigning blame to the family; 4) interventions that are positive, practical, and culturally sensitive; and 5) outcomes that endure for many years (Ruef, Turnbull, Turnbull, & Poston, 1999).

FAMILY-CENTERED POSITIVE BEHAVIOR SUPPORT

Since the early 1990s, family-centered PBS has been developed in collaboration with families and family support professionals to address family interests and needs for behavior support services that are 1) collaborative and respectful, 2) effective and acceptable, 3) positive and practical, and 4) meaningful and durable (Dunlap & Fox, 1999; Hawkins, Singer, & Nixon, 1993; Koegel, Koegel, & Dunlap, 1996; Lucyshyn & Albin, 1993; Vaughn, Clarke, & Dunlap, 1997). The central goal of family-centered PBS is to empower families with the knowledge and skills necessary to

- Understand the causes of problem behavior

- Effectively implement positive behavioral supports in natural family contexts

- Ameliorate problem behavior and teach developmentally appropriate behaviors and skills

- Improve the quality of life of the child and the family as a whole

- Solve new or recurring problems in child behavior with little to no professional assistance.

Key features of the approach are summarized in Table 5.1.

---

[1]In this chapter, the terms *child* and *children* refer to both young children and older children (youth).

Table 5.1.   Features of family-centered positive behavior support

Collaborative partnerships
Family-centered principles and practices
Meaningful lifestyle outcomes
Functional assessment
Multicomponent positive behavior support plans
Contextual fit with family
Activity settings as a unit of analysis and intervention
Implementation support
Continuous evaluation
Support with humility

To achieve this goal, we have developed a collaborative process of functional assessment and positive behavior support plan development that utilizes the activity setting as a unit of analysis and intervention. In our experience as practitioners and researchers, activity settings, which are composed of the routines and activities of family life, provide an ideal context for the design of behavioral interventions that are technically sound and contextually appropriate. Preliminary research suggests that when positive behavior support plans are designed in collaboration with families to overcome behavior problems in problematic activity settings, interventions are likely to be experienced by families as effective, acceptable, feasible, and sustainable over time (Lucyshyn, Albin, & Nixon, 1997; Moes & Frea, 2000; Vaughn, Clarke, & Dunlap, 1997).

ACTIVITY SETTING AS A UNIT OF ANALYSIS

The activity setting as a unit of analysis was originally developed during early studies of child development in the family (Vygotsky, 1978; Whiting, 1980). The concept of the activity setting has since become a cornerstone of ecocultural theory, which is a cross-cultural, ecological theory of child development in family life (Gallimore, Weisner, Kaufman, & Bernheimer, 1989). *Activity settings* are the daily, weekly, and seasonal routines and activities of family life that provide essential contexts for child development and learning (Dunst, Hamby, Trivette, Raab, & Bruder, 2000). Examples of common activity settings in which child development takes place include morning routines, mealtime routines, shopping activities, gatherings that include extended family, and religious holidays and events. Cross-cultural ethnographic studies of family life indicate that parents proactively strive to construct activity settings that are congruent with their children's characteristics, consistent with their family's goals and values, and sustainable within the opportunities and constraints of their culture and ecology (Whiting & Edwards, 1988). Activity settings are composed of several common elements: 1) time and place, 2) people present, 3) resources, 4) tasks and their organization, 5) goals and values, and 6) common scripts or patterns of interaction. In the field of early childhood special education, the activity setting is viewed as an ideal context for the development of family-centered interventions and supports for families of young children with disabilities (Bernheimer & Keough, 1995; Dunst et al., 2000).

Lucyshyn, Irvin, and colleagues (2001) conducted an observational research study in typical but problematic activity settings with ten families of children with developmental disabilities and challenging behavior. The aim of the study was to validate the construct of coercive parent–child interaction patterns in valued but unsuccessful routines in the home. Preliminary sequential analysis results indicated that the children engaged in problem behaviors for a specific purpose (i.e., function), and this purpose was directly related to the goals and structure of family routines. During routines in which parental requests or demands were common (e.g., dinnertime, structured play, homework completion), children consistently engaged in problem behavior to escape the request or demand. During routines in which parents were busy with other tasks or chores (e.g., preparing supper, washing dishes, talking to another child), the children consistently engaged in problem behavior to regain parental attention. These results also indicated that the children only reduced or terminated problem behavior when parents reduced or terminated demands, delivered positive or negative attention, or terminated the routine all together. These preliminary results lend empirical support to the validity of the activity setting as an ecological unit of analysis that simultaneously addresses child behavior, parent–child interaction, and family ecology. The results also offer direction for the design of family-centered positive behavior support plans that are ecological in scope.

PRELIMINARY RESEARCH ON EFFICACY OF THE APPROACH

Intervention research on family-centered PBS has provided preliminary evidence for the effectiveness, acceptability, and durability of the approach. Lucyshyn and colleagues (1997; see also Chapter 17) collaborated with the family of a 14-year-old with multiple disabilities and severe problem behaviors in a 26-month, longitudinal study of comprehensive PBS. Functional assessment–based interventions were collaboratively developed with the youth's parents for four valued but problematic activity settings in the home and community: dinner at home, free time at home, grocery shopping at a neighborhood supermarket, and dinner at a favorite restaurant. A single subject, experimental design documented the effectiveness of a multicomponent behavior support plan for reducing problem behavior to near-zero levels and for promoting the youth's successful participation in targeted routines. Follow-up data at 3 months and 9 months indicated the durability of these outcomes. These results were replicated and extended in a 46-month, longitudinal study that was conducted in partnership with the family of a young child with autism (Lucyshyn et al., 2000).

Through a series of intervention studies, Vaughn and colleagues further extended empirical support for a family-centered approach that addresses problem behavior in the context of valued family routines. Vaughn, Dunlap, Fox, Clarke, and Bucy (1997; see also Chapter 18) collaborated with the family of a 9-year-old with Cornelia de Lange syndrome who engaged in problem behaviors in three community routines: grocery shopping, eating at a fast-food restaurant, and banking at a drive-through window. A single subject case study design combined with a qualitative study of family perspectives on the support process offered compelling evidence for the effectiveness and acceptability of the approach. These results were replicated and strengthened in two subsequent experimental studies with the family of an 8-year-old with a severe intellectual disability (Vaughn, Clarke, & Dunlap, 1997) and with the family of a 10-year-old with Asperger syndrome (Clarke, Dunlap, & Vaughn, 1999). Single subject research designs documented the effectiveness of functional assessment–based positive behavioral supports for improving one boy's participation in a bathroom routine at home and a restaurant routine in the community and for the other boy's participation in an early morning routine at home. Koegel, Steibel, and

Koegel (1998) offered additional evidence in a single subject experimental study with three families of children with autism who engaged in severe aggression toward younger siblings during play or meal routines in the home. A multiple-baseline design across families showed that individualized positive behavioral supports that matched the functions of problem behavior in each routine effectively reduced problem behavior to zero or near-zero levels. Across these studies, measures of social validity consistently indicated that the goals, procedures, and outcomes of the support process were viewed as acceptable and important to family members and to others who viewed randomly selected videotapes of parent–child interaction in the routines.

In a study with a family of a young child with autism, Moes and Frea (2000) offered preliminary evidence of the value of contextual fit for the design of effective and contextually appropriate behavior support plans in family routines. Using a case study design, the researchers compared the outcomes of a contextualized treatment approach versus a prescriptive treatment approach to ameliorate child problem behavior in one family routine. In the contextualized approach, the interventionists collaborated with the child's parents to select interventions that were consistent with the family's goals and values, the family's skills and resources, and the routine's tasks. Results indicated that the contextualized approach was associated with higher levels of implementation fidelity, maintenance of behavioral improvement, generalization to a nontrained routine, and high parental ratings of goodness of fit.

FOUR CONSIDERATIONS FOR DESIGNING POSITIVE BEHAVIOR SUPPORT PLANS IN FAMILY CONTEXTS

In their handbook on functional assessment and behavior support plan development, O'Neill and colleagues (1997) described four considerations for designing positive behavior support plans:

1. Behavior support plans define changes in our behavior (i.e., the people who support the child in the home, school, and/or community, including parents, teachers, behavioral consultants, and family interventionists)

2. Behavior support plans are built from functional assessment results

3. Behavior support plans should be technically sound

4. Behavior support plans should be contextually appropriate

In our work with families, we have applied and adapted these considerations to problem behaviors in family contexts. The next subsections discuss these considerations as they relate to families.

Behavior Support Plans Define Changes in Our Behavior

Positive behavior support plans that are used by families define changes in the behavior of family members who support the child or youth with a disability and in the behavior of others who support the family (e.g., a family interventionist). Behavior support plans also define changes or adjustments to family environments in the home and community. It is these changes in *our* behavior and in family environments that lead to improvements in child or youth behavior. For example, during dinnertime at home, a mother may offer her son with fragile X syndrome more choices of preferred foods to increase his motivation to eat and his cooperation at the dinner table. To make it easier for a girl with autism to go to bed in the evening, a family may put a night light in her room, turn off the TV in the adjacent living room, and send her brother and sister to bed at the same time. While shopping at the grocery store, a grandparent may offer a young boy with a mild disability the privilege of buying one item, with the offer being contingent on the child's cooperative and respectful behavior in the store. Across these examples, parents and other family members made changes in their behavior and changes or adjustments in family contexts. It is such changes that lead to improvements in the behavior of the child with a disability.

Behavior Support Plans Are Built on Functional Assessment Results

Functional assessment is a process of interviews and observations that leads to an understanding of the functions or purpose of problem behaviors, the variables that influence problem behavior and adaptive behavior, and the strengths and preferences of the focus person. The primary goal of functional assessment is to gather accurate information that leads to the design of an effective and efficient behavior support plan (Horner, Albin, Sprague, & Todd, 2000; O'Neill et al., 1997). During a functional assessment interview with families, parents and other family members describe the behaviors of concern and gain insights about the setting events that exaggerate the likelihood of problem behavior, the antecedent events that trigger problem behavior, and the consequences that maintain problem behavior (Mullen & Frea, 1995). During subsequent direct observations in the home or community, an interventionist or a parent gathers functional assessment data for the purpose of confirming the hypotheses generated during the interview. Consideration also is given to the desired behavior and the alternative replacement behavior that will successfully compete with or replace problem behavior. These results are then organized into a summary statement/competing behavior pathways diagram that is subsequently used to design a positive behavior support plan (Harrower, Fox, Dunlap, & Kincaid, 1999–2000; Horner et al., 2000). The format of a summary statement/competing behaviors pathways diagram and the way that it is linked to a behavior support plan is presented in Figure 5.1.

For each feature of the problem listed in a summary statement (also referred to as a *summary hypothesis statement*), a logically linked solution (i.e., intervention) is generated. Families are active partners in this problem-solving process. A good summary statement lays out the features of a problematic family context so clearly that the process of generating solutions can be quite democratic, with logical reasoning and common sense playing as much a role as technical knowledge. For example, a summary statement for a child with a moderate cognitive disability may indicate that a setting event during problematic transitions is a lack of predictability about what will happen next (e.g., returning home after an enjoyable car ride). A logical solution is to increase predictability about positive events that happen right after transitions (e.g., a snack in the kitchen). A summary statement for a boy with Asperger syndrome may indicate that parental demands to put away toys are triggers for problem behavior. A logical solution is to replace demands with strategies that promote cooperation, such as humor (e.g., "Let's try not to wake up the toys as we put them away") and choice (e.g., "You can put your cars away or your blocks away; take your pick"). As suggested by these examples, the collaborative problem-solving process, guided by an accurate summary statement, can lead to the selection of solutions to problem behavior in family contexts that are quite simple and relatively easy to use.

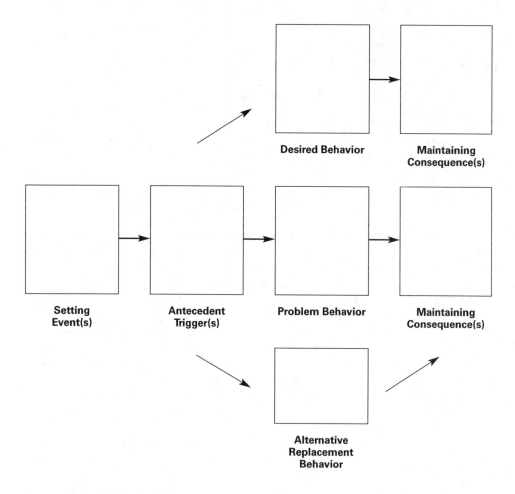

Desired Behavior

Maintaining
Consequence(s)

Setting
Event(s)

Antecedent
Trigger(s)

Problem Behavior

Maintaining
Consequence(s)

Alternative
Replacement
Behavior

Strategies that Make Problem Behaviors Irrelevant, Ineffective, and Inefficient

Setting Event Strategies	Preventive Strategies	Teaching Strategies	Consequence Strategies

Figure 5.1. Summary statement/competing behavior pathways diagram and its link to a multicomponent behavior support plan. (From *Functional Assessment and Program Development for Problem Behavior: A Practical Handbook, 1st edition,* by R.E. O'Neill, R.H. Horner, R.W. Albin, J.R. Sprague, K. Storey, J. Newton © 1997. Reprinted with permission of Wadsworth, an imprint of the Wadsworth Group, a division of Thomson Learning. Fax 800-730-2215.)

Behavior Support Plans Should Be Technically Sound

Positive behavior support plans that are designed for use in family contexts should be technically sound (Horner et al., 2000; O'Neill et al., 1997). This means that the procedures in the support plan are logically linked to features of the problem as identified by the functional assessment and are grounded in the basic principles of behavioral science (Bijou & Baer, 1978). A technically sound plan is one that, if implemented with fidelity, is likely to effectively and efficiently decrease problem behavior and improve adaptive behavior. In family contexts, such plans make problem behaviors "irrelevant, ineffective, and inefficient" at achieving their functions or purpose (O'Neill et al., 1997, p. 66).

Making Problem Behavior Irrelevant, Ineffective, and Inefficient   In this context, *irrelevant* means that the child or youth no longer needs to use problem behaviors to achieve his or her wants and needs. Consider a boy with Down syndrome who engages in attention-seeking problem behavior whenever his mother prepares supper. When he is allowed to help his mother with dinner preparation tasks (e.g., setting the table, making a salad), he does not engage in problem behavior. Because the boy receives parental attention for helping his mother, problem behaviors are no longer relevant to achieving this function.

Ineffective means that problem behaviors no longer enable the child or youth to achieve the function of his or her behavior. For example, a boy with attention-deficit/hyperactivity disorder (ADHD) engages in tantrums at home to get snacks before dinner is served. The family establishes a rule that if tantrums occur, then all snack privileges are removed for the rest of the day and are reinstated the next day. Thus, the tantrums are no longer effective at obtaining a snack.

Inefficient means that problem behaviors require much more effort and time to achieve their purpose compared with acceptable behavior. For example, if a girl with autism engages in problem behavior at home to escape using a fork or spoon during mealtimes, her parents may put her through the task two or three times before prompting her to ask for a break from using her utensils. If, however, she uses language to request a break from this task, her request is immediately honored.

Multicomponent Plans   Technically sound plans in family contexts typically include multiple components. This is because a functional assessment usually indicates several features to problem behavior in family contexts (e.g., more than one setting event, trigger, or function of problem behavior). For example, a functional assessment of problem behavior in a family dinner routine may indicate that a child engages in problem behavior to escape eating nonpreferred foods and to receive parental attention. Setting events that exaggerate the occurrence of these behaviors may include the child's limited food preferences and the absence of food choices during dinner. Triggers may include parental demands to eat nonpreferred foods and parental conversations with siblings. To improve child behavior in this routine, solutions need to address each feature of the problem.

Multicomponent behavior support plans in family contexts include up to five categories of intervention: 1) setting event strategies (i.e., lifestyle or ecological strategies); 2) preventive strategies; 3) teaching strategies; 4) consequence strategies; and 5) emergency procedures, if necessary. These are described and illustrated next.

Setting Event Strategies   Setting event strategies address child characteristics, physiological conditions, ecological events, or lifestyle issues that set the stage for problem behavior or exaggerate the occurrence of problem behavior in family contexts (Horner,

Vaughn, Day, & Ard, 1996). For example, a characteristic of children with autism that sets the stage for problem behavior is their inherent difficulty with verbal memory skills. An ecological strategy that typically ameliorates this problem is the use of visual systems that increase the predictability of tasks, activities, and schedule changes (Flannery & Horner, 1994). A physiological condition that exaggerates the occurrence of problem behavior for many nonverbal children or youth with disabilities is physical pain or discomfort due to illness (e.g., an ear infection, a cold, stomach pain). Ecological strategies that may neutralize this setting event and, thus, moderate the occurrence of problem behavior include appropriate and timely medical attention, pain-reducing medication, and the suspension of demands and tasks until the child or youth has recovered (Carr, Reeve, & Magito-McLaughlin, 1996). A lifestyle issue that people with severe cognitive disabilities commonly face is the absence of choice and self-determination in their lives. Having others direct and control one's everyday life can act as a pervasive aversive experience that exaggerates the occurrence of problem behavior in every aspect of the person's life. A lifestyle change that may greatly improve behavior in this situation is to increase the number of times each day that the person experiences choice and preference in daily tasks and activities, types of interaction, beverages and foods, and personal possessions (Malette et al., 1992).

Preventive Strategies   Preventive strategies address immediate antecedent events in the child or youth's environment at home or in the community that predict or trigger problem behavior. In family contexts, common triggers for problem behavior include parental demands, sudden interruptions, the absence of parental attention, difficult self-care tasks, parental attention directed toward another family member, transitions, and desired objects that are not immediately available to the child (e.g., a toy that a sibling is using). Common preventive strategies that are linked to these triggers for problem behavior include the following:

1. Strategies that motivate compliance and cooperation (e.g., choice giving, natural positive contingencies, high-probability requests)

2. Precorrections to prompt desired or alternative replacement behaviors (e.g., reminding a child to ask for attention, practicing with a teenager beforehand about how to ask a sibling to share time on the computer)

3. Safety signals that inform the child that he or she will reach a desired goal in a short time (e.g., "Eat three more bites and then you are finished," "Play with this toy for a few more minutes and then you can trade with your sister")

Teaching Strategies   Teaching strategies directly address the pivotal communication, social, and adaptive living skill deficits and needs of children with disabilities in family contexts (Fox, Dunlap, & Buschbacher, 2000; Koegel, Koegel, & McNeary 2001). These include 1) functionally equivalent language skills that replace problem behaviors as means to obtain wants and needs; 2) self-management skills to self-direct and self-control the completion of tasks and activities; and 3) social and daily living skills, such as negotiating compromises and playing independently or cooperatively. As with the other categories of intervention, teaching strategies for any given child are selected based on their direct link to relevant features of the problem as identified in a summary hypothesis statement. In this case, strategies are linked to the skill deficits that are associated with the occurrence of problem behavior. For instance, functional communication training (FCT) is an essential strategy for children who engage in problem behavior that is associated with language skill deficits. Cooperative play skill instruction may be an important strategy for children who engage in problem behavior during play time at home with siblings.

Consequence Strategies   Consequence strategies are aimed at strengthening desired behavior in family contexts, promoting the use of functionally equivalent language skills to replace problem behavior, and decreasing the occurrence of problem behavior (Horner et al., 2000). Positive reinforcement is the primary strategy used to strengthen desired behavior in family contexts. Families play a central role in the identification and selection of reinforcers for the child or youth. A strong emphasis is placed on using reinforcers that are naturally available in home and community settings and are acceptable and feasible to the family. For example, the parents of a young girl with autism may reinforce her for getting out of bed and getting dressed in the morning by contingently allowing her to watch a favorite children's program on public television. A boy with a moderate cognitive disability may be reinforced for staying with his mother during a trip to the mall by receiving the privilege of eating at a favorite restaurant in the food court.

Both positive and negative reinforcement strategies are commonly used to strengthen functionally equivalent language skills in family contexts (Derby et al., 1997). For instance, a mother who wishes to strengthen her child's ability to use language to request attention or help provides attention and assistance contingent on the child's use of language to communicate this want or need. A father who wishes to reinforce his child's use of language to escape difficult tasks at home (e.g., getting dressed, putting away toys) provides brief breaks or more assistance contingent on the child's use of language to request a break or help.

Consequence strategies to decrease problem behavior are designed in close consultation with families. The aim is to communicate one central message to the child or youth: Problem behaviors are no longer effective and/or efficient at achieving their function or purpose. How one effectively communicates this message can vary depending on the function of the child's behavior, the values and skills of the parents, and the specific contexts in which problem behavior occurs. One central strategy is extinction—that is, withholding or minimizing, to the greatest extent possible, the delivery of the consequence that maintains problem behavior. For example, if a boy engages in problem behavior to regain parental attention at home, then his parent actively ignores and redirects the behavior in a way that provides little attention (e.g., no eye contact, neutral affect). If a girl engages in problem behavior to escape a task, then her parent requires her to do the task three more times before letting her take a break. If a teenager engages in problem behavior to get a preferred activity, then his parent may withhold access to this activity for a period of time (e.g., 1 hour, 1 day). Effective consequence strategies may include the delivery of mild punishers such as verbal reprimands and the loss of privileges, but they never involve procedures that inflict pain, cause humiliation, or compromise the dignity of the child or youth (Horner et al., 1990).

Emergency Procedures   Emergency procedures are included in behavior support plans when severe problem behaviors, such as aggression or self-injury, cause property destruction or pose the risk of physical harm to the individual or others. The primary purpose of these procedures is to prevent or minimize injury or damage. Emergency procedures include strategies that 1) physically manage the environment to prevent or stop harm or damage and 2) physically block or restrain the individual from continuing to engage in harmful or destructive behavior. These procedures are never administered in a punitive or aggressive manner. In many areas, the use of such procedures requires formal training and approval by a special committee that monitors the use of behavioral supports with people who engage in severe problem behavior in home, school, and/or community environments (Sprague & Horner, 1991). Examples of emergency procedures used by parents in family contexts include briskly removing a youth to a "safe room" in the home, immediately removing the child from a community facility, physically blocking self-injury, or applying nonaggressive physical restraint until the child or youth is calm.

Behavior Support Plans Should Be Contextually Appropriate

Positive behavior support plans also should have a good contextual fit with family members and with family environments in which plan procedures will be implemented (Albin, Lucyshyn, Horner, & Flannery, 1996). Plans that are technically sound but do not possess a good contextual fit may be rejected by families, implemented inaccurately, or unsustainable over time. For these reasons, the behavior support plan's contextual appropriateness is as important as its technical soundness (Horner et al., 2000).

Variables that Are Relevant to Contextual Fit   Albin and colleagues (1996) suggested three variables that influence the contextual fit of behavior support plans: 1) target person variables, 2) implementor variables, and 3) setting or systems variables. Variables that are relevant to the child or youth with a disability are typically identified during a functional assessment and addressed during the design of a technically sound behavior support plan. These variables include the strengths and skills of the child or youth, the tasks and interactions he or she finds aversive, the items or activities that he or she finds reinforcing, and the purpose of problem behaviors. Variables that are relevant to the family members who are responsible for implementing positive behavioral supports include the goals and values of the family, the strengths and skills of family members, the resources and social supports that are available to the family, and the sources of family stress that may impede the implementation and long-term sustainability of plan procedures (Lucyshyn & Albin, 1993). Variables that are relevant to family settings and systems include 1) the daily, weekly, and seasonal activity settings of the child and family's life; 2) the accommodations families have made for the child with a disability; 3) the adaptability and cohesion of the family system and subsystems (e.g., spouse, sibling, extend family); and 4) the stage of the family life cycle (e.g., early childhood, adolescence, early adulthood) (Bernheimer & Keough, 1995; Turnbull & Turnbull, 2000).

Positive behavior support plans possess a good contextual fit when they reflect family goals and values, build on family skills and strengths, utilize family resources and social supports, and are embedded into the daily routines and activities of family life in ways that are acceptable and feasible to the family. These qualities of family-centered behavior support plans are associated with parental commitment to a process of change, high levels of implementation fidelity, sustained use of plans over a long period of time, and the generalization of support strategies to other nontrained family settings in the home and community (Barry & Singer, 2001; Clarke et al., 1999; Lucyshyn et al., 1997; Moes & Frea, 2000).

Ways to Establish Contextual Fit   Contextual fit with families may be accomplished in three ways. First, the collaborative partnership that is established between the interventionist and the family can go a long way toward enhancing the likelihood that a positive behavior support plan is both effective and contextually appropriate. The collaborative process of building an accurate summary hypothesis statement for a problematic family context and then generating logical, acceptable, and feasible solutions can often lead to the design of a plan that is a good contextual fit with family members and settings (Fox, Vaughn, Dunlap, & Bucy, 1997; Vaughn et al., 1997).

Second, the activity settings of daily, weekly, or seasonal routines in the home or community offer excellent contexts for developing effective and contextually appropriate behavior support plans. Activity settings include daily routines such as getting up in the morning and getting ready for school, free time while a parent is preparing supper, dinnertime, self-care routines, and going to bed at night. Activity settings also include weekly activities such as accompanying a parent on a shopping trip to a grocery store or mall, eating at sit-down or fast-food restaurants, participating in recreation activities at a community center, and visiting relatives and family friends. Less frequent activity settings that are also important to parents and children include birthdays and religious or secular holidays (Dunst et al., 2000). The activity setting represents a microcosm of family culture and ecology and, thus, contains many of the relevant person, implementor, and setting/systems variables that may need to be addressed. Activity settings are composed of ecological and cultural features such as time and place of occurrence, people involved, goals and values, resources used or available, tasks and their organization, and patterns of parent–child interaction. In addition, activity settings reflect the larger ecology of the family, including the family system, the family life cycle, and the constraints and opportunities of the family's neighborhood and community. Building behavior supports with families in the context of valued but problematic activity settings can greatly increase the likelihood that families will find the plan to be acceptable, feasible, and a good fit with their life.

For some families, a collaborative process of functional assessment and behavior support plan development that is focused on valued but problematic activity settings may still be insufficient for building a plan that is easily implemented and sustainable over time. Some families with whom we have worked experience stressors such as physical exhaustion, stress-induced illness, social isolation, marital distress, or poverty. In these circumstances, even the most sensitively designed behavior support plan may fail because the overarching problems overwhelm any attempt by the family to improve child behavior. For these families to succeed, additional family-centered supports may be needed.

For this reason, we have found it helpful at the start of a process of PBS to listen to families and learn about their lives in a way that extends beyond the specifics of child problem behavior and family activity settings. This involves a simple interview process in which we ask parents or other family members (e.g., grandparents) open-ended questions about their strengths as a family, the resources and social supports that are available to them in their community, the stressors that they are experiencing, and the overall goals that they have for the child and family. When the interview is carried out in an informal, conversational style, it is typically experienced by families as a helpful dialogue in which insights about strengths and resources are gained, hopes and concerns are voiced, and stressors that weigh heavily on the family are taken into consideration (Albin et al., 1996). The interview protocol is presented in Table 5.2.

If the interview indicates that the family is experiencing one or more major stressors, then the interventionist may, with the consent of the family, seek to directly address these issues as part of the process of PBS. For example, if a mother reports that she is exhausted from the chronic caregiving needs of her child with a disability, the interventionist may help the family secure respite care services from a local nonprofit agency. If stressors are reduced and family circumstances can be improved, then parents and other family members may be more capable of implementing positive behavioral supports in the home and community and, thus, more likely to improve the behavior and lifestyle of the child with a disability.

Table 5.2. Family ecology assessment

1. What would you characterize as your child's positive contributions to the family?

2. What would you characterize as your family's strengths?

3. What formal and informal resources have you used (or are available) to help improve your child's development and the quality of family life (e.g., help with child care from a family member, respite care from a local agency)?

4. What are your sources of social support (e.g., someone with whom you discuss and solve problems, someone with whom you participate in leisure activities)?

5. What are sources of stress?
    - What are the effects of your child's problem behaviors on you as a parent?
    - What are the effects of your child's problem behavior on your family as a whole?
    - Are there other sources of stress in the family that might affect your ability to implement a support plan or that affect your family's quality of life?

6. What are your goals for your child and for your family?

From Albin, R.W., Lucyshyn, J.M., Horner, R.H., & Flannery, K.B. (1996). Contextual fit for behavioral support plans: A model for "goodness of fit." In L.K. Koegel, R.L. Koegel, & G. Dunlap (Eds.), *Positive behavioral support: Including people with difficult behavior in the community* (p. 92). Baltimore: Paul H. Brookes Publishing Co.; adapted with permission.

STEPS IN BUILDING EFFECTIVE AND CONTEXTUALLY APPROPRIATE POSITIVE BEHAVIOR SUPPORT PLANS WITH FAMILIES

Based on the four considerations discussed previously, we have developed a flexible, five-step process for collaborating with families to develop technically sound and contextually appropriate positive behavior support plans. The process is flexible in that the number of steps that are implemented and the order of implementation can vary depending on the family's preference, the need to establish trust with the family, and the extent to which the child's problem behaviors are of crisis proportion or the family is experiencing other major life stressors. In addition, when families have successfully improved one or more problematic family contexts by using these methods, fewer steps in the process are necessary. Finally, the process becomes most streamlined and efficient when families have mastered it and can design their own behavior support plans without the assistance of a professional interventionist. The five steps are described in detail next (see Table 5.3 for a summary).

Step 1: Conduct a Functional Assessment

We typically begin the process of family-centered PBS with a functional assessment of child or youth problem behavior. This includes a comprehensive functional assessment interview with family members and functional assessment observations in one or more home or community settings in which problem behavior occurs. We use the functional assessment interview (FAI) form and the functional assessment observation (FAO) form developed by O'Neill and colleagues (1997). The interviews are typically conducted at the family's home. If a family prefers to participate in the interview at a place that is more convenient or acceptable to them, however, we defer to these preferences. After a functional assessment interview is completed, we develop hypotheses about problem behavior, review these hypotheses with the family, and later test the hypotheses during functional assessment observations in problematic family contexts in the home and/or community. These

Table 5.3. Steps for collaborating with families to build effective and contextually appropriate behavior support plans for problematic family activity settings

1. Conduct a functional assessment:
   a. Conduct functional assessment interview.
   b. Conduct functional assessment observations.

2. Conduct an assessment of family routines and ecology:
   a. Conduct an interview about family activity settings (routines/activities) in the home and community.
   b. Select and prioritize valued but problematic activity setting(s) for intervention and define vision of realistic and successful activity setting(s).
   c. Conduct a supplemental interview to ascertain child positive contributions, family strengths, resources and social supports, stressors, and goals.

3. Develop a summary hypothesis statement and a competing behavior pathways diagram for problem behavior in the targeted activity setting.

4. Design a technically sound and contextually appropriate behavior support plan:
   a. Identify strategies that are logically linked to features of the problem in the activity setting and that are likely to make problem behaviors irrelevant, ineffective, and inefficient at achieving their purposes. Brainstorm about:
      - Setting event strategies
      - Preventive strategies
      - Teaching strategies
      - Consequence strategies
   b. Finalize strategies that are likely to be effective and contextually appropriate:
      - Select necessary and sufficient strategies.
      - Select strategies that are acceptable, feasible, and a good fit with elements of the targeted activity setting.

5. As needed, select family-centered supports that may enhance implementation fidelity and long-term sustainability of the plan, as well as the overall quality of family life.

---

direct observations may be completed by the interventionist or by a family member. If a parent conducts the observation, then the interventionist sets up the FAO form for the parent and shows the parent how to use the form. Alternatively, if the family finds other observation formats to be easier to use, then the interventionist provides functional assessment forms that are in a checklist or note card format (Carr et al., 1994; Vaughn, Amado, et al., 1997). Throughout this process, the family and the interventionist engage in a collegial dialogue that is aimed at reaching a consensus of understanding about the functions of problem behavior, the events that set the stage for or trigger problem behavior, and the interactions and events that promote positive behavior. During this dialogue, every effort is made to acknowledge family insights, highlight parent strategies that promote desired behavior, and ensure that the experience is positive and supportive for the family.

If the functional assessment interview indicates that the family is in crisis due to child problem behavior, then immediate steps may be taken to institute emergency procedures in the home to reduce the level of crisis before other steps in the process are continued. For example, during one functional assessment, the parents of a boy with autism indicated that their son was engaging in aggressive behavior toward his newborn sister. A discussion of these behaviors indicated that some were life threatening (e.g., striking the infant on the head, putting a pillow over the infant's face). This information prompted the interventionist to request parental consent for immediately developing a behavior support plan that included emergency procedures to eliminate risk to the infant. The interventionist and parents then built a summary statement around this problem and generated procedures that were aimed at eliminating opportunities for the boy to be alone with his infant sister and solutions that were aimed at making aggression irrelevant and ineffective at achieving its functions (e.g., parental attention, escape from the infant's crying). Parent implementation of the plan across the next several days was associated with significant decreases in the boy's aggression against his sister. With this life-threatening situation abated, the wider process of behavior support to the family was rejoined.

Step 2: Conduct an Assessment of Family Routines and Ecology

Following the functional assessment interview, we take an in-depth look at the daily routines and weekly activities of the child in the home and community with family members (Lucyshyn & Albin, 1993). Because practitioners of PBS are committed to promoting both behavioral and lifestyle change, this assessment of broad patterns of problem behavior across daily and weekly routines and activities helps to define the challenge that families face and to organize a process of behavioral support in a manner that is congruent with family goals, needs, time, and energy levels (Horner et al., 2000). We use a family routine assessment form that provides information about daily routines and weekly activities in the home and community (Horner et al., 2000; Lucyshyn, Blumberg, & Irvin, 2001). For each routine, we ask about the 1) time of day and day of week, 2) type of routine, 3) behaviors of concern, 4) antecedent triggers, 5) maintaining consequences, and 6) extent to which the routine is typical and valued by the family. We also ask families to identify valued routines or activities that they once did with their son or daughter but can do no longer because of problem behavior. This information is used to prioritize and select valued but problematic routines and activities for intervention. Parents and other family members are encouraged to prioritize and select routines or activities for intervention that are most problematic to them, that may greatly improve the quality of the child and family's life together, or that can be resolved with a minimum of effort and commitment of time. By suggesting these criteria, parents are more likely to select initial settings for intervention that match their concerns and goals, daily or weekly schedule, level of energy, and degree of comfort with a process of change. If functional assessment observations have not been conducted in these problematic activity settings and doing so would strengthen hypotheses about problem behavior in the settings, then such observations are scheduled and completed by the interventionist or by a family member.

After family members have selected and prioritized problematic family contexts that they would like to improve, the interventionist asks the family what the first priority routine or activity would look like if it were successful. The structure of this vision is guided by the elements of activity settings as defined by Gallimore, Goldenberg, and Weisner (1993): 1) the time and place of the routine or activity, 2) the people who will be involved, 3) the material and social resources that will be used, 4) the tasks that will occur during the routine and how they will be sequenced and organized, and 5) the goals and values of the family that will be reflected in the routine. The interview guide that we use to generate a vision of a successful activity setting is presented in Table 5.4. This family-generated vision becomes the aim of the next step in the process: designing a technically sound and contextually appropriate behavior support plan for the envisioned routine or activity.

Depending on family circumstances or our initial relationship with the family, we also may introduce the supplemental family ecology assessment (see Table 5.2), which involves a semistructured interview about family strengths, resources/social supports, stres-

Table 5.4. Family vision of a successful activity setting

For the home routine, community activity, or monthly/seasonal/yearly event that you would like to improve,

- What would a realistic and successful routine, activity, or event look like?
- Where would it take place and when would it occur?
- Who would be there?
- What material and social resources would be available to support the routine, activity, or event?
- What would participants be doing? How would tasks be organized to support the routine, activity, or event's success?
- What family goals and values would be reflected by child and family participation in the successful routine, activity, or event?

From Albin, R.W., Lucyshyn, J.M., Horner, R.H., & Flannery, K.B. (1996). Contextual fit for behavioral support plans: A model for "goodness of fit." In L.K. Koegel, R.L. Koegel, & G. Dunlap (Eds.), *Positive behavioral support: Including people with difficult behavior in the community* (p. 92). Baltimore: Paul H. Brookes Publishing Co.; adapted with permission.

sors, and goals. This interview may occur at the start of the assessment process or soon after functional assessment information has been gathered. The interview serves two purposes. First, it can provide information that is helpful in selecting family-centered supports that improve quality of life and enhance family efforts to implement and sustain behavioral supports. Second, the interview can help to build rapport and trust with the family and to rekindle hope in parents whose spirits may have been worn down by challenging behavior. A discussion of family strengths, for example, may reveal to a mother sources of resilience in her family of which she was not aware. A discussion of resources may bring to light community resources that are yet untapped but of potentially great value to the family.

During a discussion of stressors, we ask parents to describe how the child or youth's problem behaviors affect each parent and how these behaviors affect the family as a whole. This information helps the family and the interventionist jointly decide whether other family-centered supports may be necessary to ensure the plan's success and to improve the family's quality of life. For instance, a mother may report that she is exhausted from the chronic caregiving that the child requires. A single parent who has a seizure disorder may indicate that she is having difficulty getting her seizure medication refilled every month. Information about family stressors prompts a discussion of additional supports and services that the family may need beyond PBS. From this discussion, decisions may be made, for example, to help secure respite care services for the family or to provide advocacy services.

Step 3: Develop a Summary Statement/Competing Behavior Pathways Diagram for the Targeted Activity Setting

After identifying and prioritizing valued but problematic family activity settings for intervention, a summary statement and competing behavior pathways diagram is developed for the first envisioned setting selected by the family. This diagram is then used to develop a multicomponent positive behavior support plan that makes problem behaviors irrelevant, ineffective, and inefficient within the activity setting of concern (Harrower et al., 1999–2000; Horner et al., 2000; Marshall & Mirenda, in press).

Build a Summary Statement of the Problem   The first step is to build a summary statement of the problem's relevant features in the targeted routine or activity.

The relevant features of the problem are 1) the setting events that set the stage for or exaggerate the occurrence of problem behavior; 2) the immediate antecedent events that trigger problem behavior; 3) the problem behaviors, listed by category of behavior (e.g., aggression, self-injury, destructive behaviors); and 4) the maintaining consequences for problem behavior. The summary statement is developed based on functional assessment interview information and direct observation results.

Build a Competing Behavior Pathways Diagram   Practitioners of PBS emphasize teaching adaptive behaviors that successfully compete with and, thus, replace problem behavior. A competing behavior pathways analysis highlights this emphasis. A competing behaviors analysis defines 1) the *desired behavior* in which a family would like the child to engage during a routine or activity that advances child participation and family success; 2) the *alternative replacement behavior* (i.e., functionally equivalent responses) that the child can use in the activity setting to achieve the same function(s) as the problem behavior; and 3) the *maintaining consequences* for desired behavior and alternative replacement behavior. After building a summary statement for the targeted routine or activity, the family and the interventionist identify desired behavior and alternative replacement behavior that are relevant to the routine or activity. Reinforcing consequences that will maintain desired behavior also are considered. These are combined with the summary statement of the problem to generate a summary statement/competing behavior pathways diagram (see Figure 5.1).

Step 4: Design a Technically Sound and Contextually Appropriate Positive Behavior Support Plan

The summary statement/competing behavior pathways diagram serves as the foundation for the design of a technically sound positive behavior support plan. The goal of the support plan is to empower parents and other families to ameliorate problem behavior and to successfully include the child or youth with a disability in the targeted family routine or activity. This process involves identifying behavioral supports that are logically linked to each feature of the problem, which is diagrammed in the summary hypothesis statement, that will make problem behaviors irrelevant, ineffective, and inefficient. The process also involves finalizing behavior support strategies in collaboration with the family to ensure that the plan is 1) technically sound, 2) as simple as possible given the features of the problem, and 3) a good contextual fit with the family routine or activity.

Identify Strategies that Make Problem Behaviors Irrelevant, Ineffective, and Inefficient   Once an accurate summary statement/competing behavior pathways diagram is built, the next step is to identify strategies that make problem behaviors irrelevant, ineffective and inefficient at achieving their purpose. To begin this process, the interventionist may first generate interventions that are logically linked to the summary hypothesis statement, then review these proposed interventions with the family for their consideration and input. Alternatively, the interventionist may develop the plan directly with the family during a "brainstorming" dialogue in which the interventionist and family jointly consider the features of the problem as diagrammed in the summary statement and generate interventions that they believe will make problem behaviors irrelevant, ineffective, and inefficient within the envisioned routine or activity. When the interventionist and the family repeat this collaborative problem-solving process for other problematic family contexts, parents often become quite familiar and comfortable with the process. When the interventionist takes time to teach parents how to implement the steps in the process, they also can become adept at using it on their own to solve new or recurring behavior problems (Lucyshyn & Kayser, 1999).

For each feature of the problem (e.g., setting events, antecedent triggers, problem behavior, maintaining consequences), one or more behavioral support strategies can be generated. Setting events direct the selection of logically linked ecological or lifestyle strategies that eliminate or neutralize aversive setting events and, thus, render problem behavior irrelevant. Immediate antecedent events direct the selection of preventive strategies that remove the aversive events that trigger problem behavior and introduce positive strategies that occasion desired behavior. The maintaining consequences for problem behavior direct the selection of consequence strategies that weaken or eliminate problem behaviors by rendering them ineffective or inefficient at achieving their functions. In addition, the desired and alternative replacement behaviors identified in the summary statement/competing behavior pathways diagram offer direction for teaching strategies and the specific content of instruction. Finally, the maintaining consequences for desired and alternative replacement behaviors direct the selection of strategies to strengthen and maintain these adaptive behaviors.

Finalize Strategies that Are Likely to Be Effective and Contextually Appropriate
Whether interventions are initially generated by the interventionist or by the interventionist with the family, the final step requires collaboration to distill the emerging plan into one that is likely to be both effective and contextually appropriate. During this dialogue, we encourage parents and other family members to agree only to a set of interventions that they believe will be effective, acceptable, feasible, and a good fit with the targeted routine or activity. As behavior analysts, we typically take the lead in guiding final decisions about interventions that are technically sound and, thus, likely to be effective. We defer to the knowledge of parents and other family members for the final selection and adjustment of strategies so that they are acceptable, feasible, and a good fit with the routine or activity. This egalitarian decision-making process is not simply informed by the value of collaboration. Experience has taught us that when key family members voice hesitation or concern about a particular support strategy (e.g., point systems, time-out), the intervention is less likely to be implemented with fidelity or to endure over time.

When making decisions about the contextual appropriateness of an emerging behavior support plan, the natural structure of family activity settings offers direction. Answers to questions about the contextual fit of the behavior support plan in relation to key elements of the routine or activity (e.g., time and place, people, resources, tasks, goals and values) can help to ensure the plan's contextual appropriateness. There are at least six questions of interest:

1. Do key family members believe that the support plan strategies can be implemented at the time(s) and in the place(s) that the problematic routine or activity occurs?

2. Does the plan take into consideration all of the individuals who may be involved or present during the routine or activity (e.g., siblings, extended family members, friends)?

3. Will the support plan strategies help the family achieve their goals for the child and the family as a whole during the routine or activity?

4. Are the support plan strategies congruent with the family values and beliefs that are part of the routine?

5. Does the proposed plan utilize the natural material and person resources that are available to the family during the routine or activity?

6. Does the plan adequately support child and family engagement in the tasks of the routine or activity, and are these tasks organized in a manner that supports the success of the routine?

Consideration of these questions by the family and the interventionist can lead to adjustments or additions to a behavior support plan that can increase the likelihood of family members successfully embedding interventions into problematic routines. A consideration of time and place may identify natural variations in the timing or location of a routine that can be addressed during a schedule of training and support to the family. For example, a home leisure routine for a youth with multiple disabilities may need to start 30 minutes later during weeks when her father works overtime and arrives home tired and in need of a break. Considerations about people present can ensure that interventions are feasible in the midst of social responsibilities during a routine. For instance, a grocery shopping support plan for a single mother of two young children may need to include plan adjustments for times when she has to take both children with her on a trip to the store. A review of goals and values may spark a discussion of the difference between incentives and bribes. Such a discussion may help all family members better understand and, thus, support the use of reinforcement procedures in the plan. Consideration of tasks and their organization in a routine may lead to adjustments that make the routine more efficient or conducive to success. During a morning routine, for example, parents may decide to leave the TV off until their daughter with a mild disability has completed self-care tasks and is dressed for school. As illustrated by these examples, the activity setting as a unit of analysis helps the interventionist and the family weave functional assessment–based behavior supports into the diverse fabric of family life. Doing so may contribute to the ease with which families can implement and sustain interventions (Bernheimer & Keough, 1995).

Step 5: Select Family-Centered Supports as Needed

For many families with whom we have worked, the previous four steps are sufficient for designing behavior support plans that are both effective and contextually appropriate when implemented in targeted family activity settings in the home or community. Nonetheless, some families face larger contextual challenges, including parental illness, major life transitions, employment problems, and marital distress. Such challenges can easily overwhelm any effort to improve child behavior in specific family contexts. For these families, additional family-centered supports may be needed to strengthen the family system; enhance informal and formal support networks; and allow parents to implement behavioral supports with greater ease, accuracy, and long-term success. In these cases, family ecology information about resources and social supports as well as sources of stress becomes relevant to the selection of family-centered supports. For example, the parents of a young boy with ADHD informs the interventionist that the father's swing-shift job precludes his involvement in child care and support of his wife during the week. This has created an untenable situation for the mother, who is suffering from chronic fatigue syndrome but has to care for their son by herself every weekday afternoon and evening. In this instance, a family-centered support may involve the interventionist's or a service coordinator's playing an advocacy role on behalf of the father. The aim would be to help the father acquire a day shift so that he could better support his wife and son. By ensuring that family-centered supports are in place for distressed families, the interventionist aims to enhance the quality of the family's life and to ensure that the family experiences the cohesion and stability that are necessary to implement and sustain a positive behavior support plan.

CASE STUDIES OF FUNCTIONAL ASSESMENT AND POSITIVE BEHAVIOR SUPPORT PLAN DESIGN WITH FAMILIES

This section presents two case studies of family-centered functional assessment and positive behavior support plan design. In these examples, variations of the five-step process were used to develop support plans for valued but problematic family routines or activities. In the first example, an interventionist collaborated with a single parent of a young girl with autism to build a positive behavior support plan for a problematic home routine in which the parent is busy with household tasks. In the second example, the interventionist collaborated with the parents of a boy with Cornelia de Lange syndrome to build a positive behavior support for a problematic grocery shopping activity. In each example, the interventionist and the family worked as collaborative partners to build an accurate summary statement/competing behavior pathways diagram for the activity setting and to design an effective and contextually appropriate positive behavior support plan for the targeted routine or activity.

For each family, information that is relevant to the design of a technically sound and contextually appropriate behavior support plan is presented. This information includes 1) a brief description of the child and the family; 2) an overview of family ecology; 3) a summary of functional assessment information about problem behavior in the activity setting; 4) the results of a functional assessment observation (O'Neill et al., 1997); and 5) a brief summary of each family's vision of a successful activity setting. Based on this information, the interventionist and the family collaboratively developed a summary statement/competing behavior pathways diagram for the problematic routine and then generated an effective and contextually appropriate positive behavior support plan. Contextual fit considerations guided enhancements or adjustments to the plan and/or the addition of family-centered supports. In each case, the family was able to implement the plan with fidelity, improve child behavior and participation in the routine or activity, and sustain these improvements for a long period of time.

Free-Time/Dinner Cleanup Routine

Child and Family   Emily was a bright and vivacious 6-year-old with the diagnosis of autism. She had well-developed language skills and could express herself in complete and grammatical sentences. Emily's family consisted of her mother, Susan, and her 17-year-old sister, Melissa. Emily's mother worked as a dispatcher at a city police department. The family lived in a two-bedroom, cottage-style home in a small, rural town in the Pacific Northwest. Susan sought behavior support services due to Emily's intense problem behaviors in the home, including yelling and screaming and disruptive, destructive, and dangerous behaviors.

Family Ecology   The interventionist's conversation with Susan about family ecology revealed many strengths, new opportunities to expand the family's support network, stressors associated with being a single mother, and well-defined child and family goals. In terms of strengths, Susan was resilient. She adeptly managed work life, child care, and household responsibilities from week to week with a tenacious sense of cheerfulness and a large reservoir of energy. Emily's older sister, Melissa, was mature and helpful. She regularly cared for Emily while their mother was at work. In terms of resources and social supports, Emily had recently made the transition from a preschool program in a nearby city to a kindergarten classroom in her neighborhood school. At the time that PBS services were initiated in the home, Emily had begun to receive special education support services at school within a wraparound service model (Eber, Osuch, & Redditt, 1996). A school psychologist had begun to coordinate the development of special education and family support services for Emily and her family. Until these services were in place, however, Susan continued to rely on her own personal and family resources (i.e., Melissa) to support Emily at home. Stressors for the family included Emily's constant demands for Susan's undivided attention; Susan's day in, day out experience of juggling work, child care, and household tasks and chores; and Melissa's lack of a typical teenager's life due to the need to care for her sister while their mother worked. Child and family goals included Emily's becoming less dependent on her mother and more independent at managing her free time, Melissa's establishing a more typical and satisfying personal life as a teenager, and Susan's finding a more family-friendly nine-to-five day job.

Functional Assessment and Family Routines Assessment   A functional assessment interview was completed at a location that was convenient for Susan—a restaurant near her daughter's former preschool. In a subsequent meeting, an assessment of daily and weekly routines and activities was completed to better understand the scope of the problem and to identify family priorities for intervention. Susan indicated that the most difficult contexts with Emily were home routines in the late afternoon and early evening, when Susan was busy with household and family responsibilities and could not give Emily her undivided attention. These included dinner preparation, after-dinner cleanup, and other household chores or parental tasks (e.g., laundry, conversation with Melissa). Functional assessment observations in these routines confirmed initial hypotheses about the functions of problem behavior and the antecedent triggers that were associated with problem behavior. Susan decided to begin intervention during the dinner cleanup routine. She envisioned a routine in which Emily would manage her free time with greater independence while Susan cleared the table and washed dishes after supper. It was also decided that after progress was made in this routine, Susan would expand her use of effective interventions to other problematic routines in the home (e.g., preparing supper, talking with Melissa). A summary of Susan's vision for the free-time/dinner cleanup routine is presented in Table 5.5.

Summary Statement/Competing Behavior Pathways Diagram   Functional assessment information and the family's vision of a successful free-time/dinner cleanup routine informed the development of a summary statement and competing behavior pathways diagram for the problematic home routine. The next subsection provides a narrative summary of functional assessment information for the routine, as well as the functional assessment observation results. The interventionist and the family used this information to build a summary statement diagram of the problem. Then, they identified desired behavior and alternative replacement behavior for the routine, and they added this information to complete the summary statement/competing behavior pathways diagram.

Table 5.5.   Family vision of a successful free-time/dinner cleanup routine

The free-time/dinner cleanup routine will take place in the early evening right after supper. Mom and Emily will be present. While Mom is clearing the dining room table and washing dishes in the kitchen, Emily will play independently and appropriately with favorite toys and activities in the living room. During the routine, Emily will learn to play independently and to tolerate an absence of mother's undivided attention, and Mom will keep up with household chores.

Building a Summary Statement of the Problem   Emily's mother cleared the table and cleaned up after supper 4–6 days a week. While Susan was busy cleaning-up, she expected Emily to play with her toys, look at her books, or listen to music in the living room or in her bedroom. When Susan began the routine, however, Emily initiated a wide range of problem behaviors. These included running out of her assigned area, yelling and screaming at her mother, and engaging in tantrums. Emily also engaged in destructive and dangerous behaviors, such as throwing toys and climbing on counters. Immediate antecedent events that triggered problem behavior included times when 1) Emily was alone and unoccupied, 2) Susan was busy with another task, and 3) Susan and Melissa talked with each other. When Emily engaged in problem behavior, Susan stopped what she was doing and attended to Emily. Her attention took the form of holding Emily, offering words of reassurance and affection, or helping her play with a toy. The primary function of Emily's behavior was to regain her mother's undivided attention. Two lifestyle/contextual factors appeared to set the stage for intense attention-motivated problem behavior. First, as a single parent, Susan was Emily's sole source of parental support. Consequently, Susan had to fulfill most of Emily's needs for affection and reassurance. Second, Susan's full-time job and variable work hours greatly reduced her availability to Emily and the predictability of her presence at home. The results from 2 days of functional assessment observation are presented in Figure 5.2. Based on interview and observation results, a summary statement diagram was built for the free-time/dinner cleanup routine (see Figure 5.3).

Identifying Desired Behavior and Alternative Replacement Behavior
After building a summary statement of problem behavior in the routine, Emily's mother and the interventionist identified desired behavior during the routine, as well as alternative replacement behavior in which Emily could engage to get parental attention. For desired behavior, Emily would engage in high-interest leisure activities that might compete effectively with her desire for Susan's attention. For alternative replacement behaviors, Emily would politely ask her mother for attention or help. The maintaining consequences for desired behavior would include the intrinsic reinforcement of high-interest leisure activities and quality time with Susan after the chores were completed. The maintaining consequence for alternative replacement behavior would be the delivery of brief parental attention or assistance that would be contingent on politely asking for attention or help. Based on this additional information, the summary statement/competing behavior pathways diagram for the free-time/dinner cleanup routine was completed. This completed diagram is presented in Figure 5.4.

Multicomponent Positive Behavior Support Plan Design   Using the summary statement/competing behavior pathways diagram as a guide, Susan and the interventionist generated a multicomponent positive behavior support plan that was aimed at making attention-seeking problem behaviors irrelevant, ineffective, and inefficient at achieving their function during the free-time/dinner cleanup routine. Beginning with setting events, Susan and the interventionist considered ecological and lifestyle strategies that might diminish Emily's intense anxiety, which was related to the availability and predictability of her mother's presence and attention. First, Susan decided to create a monthly calendar that would show Emily exactly when Susan would be home and when she would be at work. Second, Susan and the interventionist agreed to build a home picture schedule that would help Emily predict when she would receive Susan's undivided attention and when she would be expected to play independently. This schedule would include the free-time/dinner cleanup routine. Before initiating the dinner cleanup routine, Susan would review the schedule with

Functional Assessment Observation Form

Name: Emily

Starting Date: 11/20   Ending date: 11/22

Time	Behaviors			Predictors						Perceived Functions									Actual conseq.		Comments: (if nothing happened in period, write initials)
	Yelling/ screaming	Tantrums	Disrupt/destruct/ dangerous behavior	Demand/ Request	Difficult Task	Transitions	Interruption	Alone (no attention)	Talk with older daughter	Mom busy	Attention	Desired item/Activity	Self-stimulation	Demand/ Request	Activity ( )	Person	Escape/Avoid Other/ Don't know		Physical help	Verbal/ redirect	
Early evening routines at home											Get/Obtain					Escape/Avoid					
5:30 P.M.	1 12 2 13 13 3 14		1 12 2 3					1 12 2 3		1 12 2 13 3 14	1 12 2 13 3 14								1 12 2 13 3 14	1 12 2 13 3 14	Mom preparing supper
	4 5 15	5	4 15					4	5	4 15	4 5 15								4 5 15	4 5 15	
6:00 P.M.	16 17		16 17						16 6 17		16 6 17								16 6 17 17	16 6	Dinnertime
	18		18 19						18 19	18 19	18 19								18 19	18 19	
6:30 P.M.	8 20 9 21 10		8					8 20 9 21		8 20 9 21 10	8 20 9 21 10								8 20 8 20 9 21 9 21 10 10		Mom cleaning up after supper
	22 23		11 22 23							11 22 23	11 22 23								11 22 23	11 22 23	
Totals																					
Events:	1 2 3 4 5 6 7 8 9 10 11 12 13 14 15 16 17 18 19 20 21 22 23 24 25																				
Date:	11/20/99											11/22/99									

Figure 5.2. Functional assessment observation results for the free-time/dinner cleanup routine. (From *Functional Assessment and Program Development for Problem Behavior: A Practical Handbook, 1st edition,* by R.E. O'Neill, R.H. Horner, R.W. Albin, J.R. Sprague, K. Storey, J. Newton © 1997. Reprinted with permission of Wadsworth, an imprint of the Wadsworth Group, a division of Thomson Learning. Fax 800-730-2215.)

119

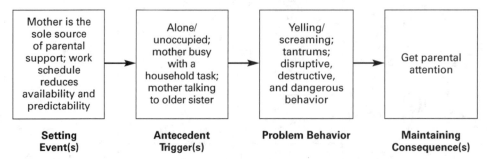

Setting Event(s) — **Antecedent Trigger(s)** — **Problem Behavior** — **Maintaining Consequence(s)**

Figure 5.3. Summary statement diagram for the free-time/dinner cleanup routine. (From *Functional Assessment and Program Development for Problem Behavior: A Practical Handbook, 1st edition,* by R.E. O'Neill, R.H. Horner, R.W. Albin, J.R. Sprague, K. Storey, J. Newton © 1997. Reprinted with permission of Wadsworth, an imprint of the Wadsworth Group, a division of Thomson Learning. Fax 800-730-2215.)

Emily, telling her what was expected, when she would regain Mom's attention, and what they would do together. To reduce the aversiveness of being alone while mother was busy, Susan would provide Emily with highly preferred toys and activities (e.g., a talking doll, computer-based educational activities and games, an audiotape of Susan reading a favorite children's book). Next, Susan and the interventionist generated preventive strategies to re-place triggers for problem behavior with proactive strategies that might occasion desired or alternative replacement behavior. These strategies included the proactive use of positive contingencies to motivate Emily to play independently (e.g., "Listen to your audiotape and let Mommy do her work, then I will come over and read you a story") and the use of verbal "safety signals" when Emily expressed anxiety about being alone or when she requested at-tention (e.g., "After I put these dishes in the sink, I will come over and help you").

To teach Emily desired and alternative replacement behavior, Susan agreed that be-fore beginning chores, she would use precorrections to teach Emily how to play with toys or politely ask for attention. Finally, Susan and the interventionist considered consequences to strengthen desired and alternative replacement behaviors and to weaken or eliminate problem behavior. They agreed that Susan's praise and other forms of brief attention would be contingent on Emily's playing independently, calmly waiting for attention, and politely asking for attention. When minor problem behaviors occurred, Susan would calmly redi-rect Emily while actively ignoring the behavior (i.e., not labeling or acknowledging the be-havior). If problem behavior escalated in intensity, then Susan would reduce her attention for several seconds before calmly but firmly redirecting Emily. If Emily initiated danger-ous behavior, then Susan would immediately redirect her while withholding the qualities of attention Emily sought (e.g., hugs, reassurance). As these decisions were made, the in-terventionist wrote each intervention under the appropriate column of the intervention section of the summary statement/competing behavior pathways diagram model (e.g., setting event strategies, preventive strategies, teaching strategies, consequence strategies). The multicomponent positive behavior support plan for the free-time/dinner cleanup rou-tine is presented in Figure 5.5.

Contextual Fit Considerations   In developing the behavior support plan for the free-time/dinner cleanup routine and in planning interventions for other home routines, several contextual fit considerations were taken into account regarding the routines' ele-ments (e.g., goals and values, resources, tasks and their organization). First, a priority goal for Susan was to teach Emily to play independently and not demand her mother's undi-vided attention. For this reason, it was decided to delay work on a second desired behavior

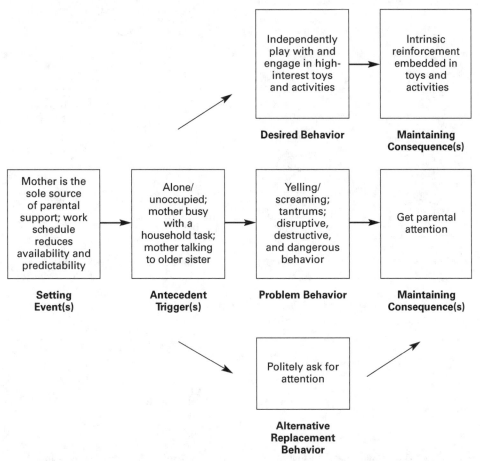

Figure 5.4. Summary statement/competing behavior pathways diagram for the free-time/dinner cleanup routine. (From *Functional Assessment and Program Development for Problem Behavior: A Practical Handbook, 1st edition,* by R.E. O'Neill, R.H. Horner, R.W. Albin, J.R. Sprague, K. Storey, J. Newton © 1997. Reprinted with permission of Wadsworth, an imprint of the Wadsworth Group, a division of Thomson Learning. Fax 800-730-2215.)

for Emily—helping her mother with chores. It was agreed that this goal would be worked on after Emily developed the ability to play independently while mother was busy. A second priority goal was for Melissa to establish a more typical teenage lifestyle (e.g., seeing friends after school, participating in extracurricular activities). Thus, Susan decided not to use Melissa as a source of informal support during the routine.

Considerations of the larger ecology of the family's life played a significant role in enhancing the feasibility and long-term sustainability of the positive behavior support plan. Although Susan had formidable personal resources at her disposal to implement the plan (e.g., a "can-do" spirit, organizational skills, self-initiative), attention to the quality of Susan's life suggested that it would be helpful to diminish her stressors and to make full use of formal resources that were newly available through the wraparound service team. The team was composed of Susan, Emily's kindergarten teacher, a school psychologist, a county service coordinator, a state family support specialist, a nonprofit agency respite care coordinator, and home and school-based behavior consultants. During a series of wraparound meetings that were coordinated by the school psychologist, the team generated additional services that were aimed at diminishing stressors, expanding the family's support network, and increasing the family's financial resources. The services and resources that the

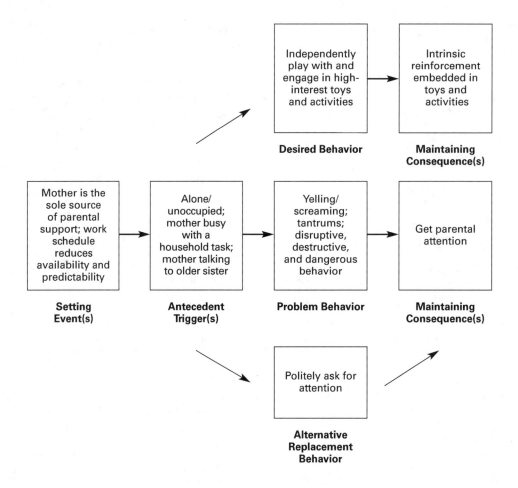

Independently play with and engage in high-interest toys and activities	→	Intrinsic reinforcement embedded in toys and activities
Desired Behavior		**Maintaining Consequence(s)**

Mother is the sole source of parental support; work schedule reduces availability and predictability	→	Alone/ unoccupied; mother busy with a household task; mother talking to older sister	→	Yelling/ screaming; tantrums; disruptive, destructive, and dangerous behavior	→	Get parental attention
Setting Event(s)		**Antecedent Trigger(s)**		**Problem Behavior**		**Maintaining Consequence(s)**

Politely ask for attention
Alternative Replacement Behavior

Strategies that Make Problem Behaviors Irrelevant, Ineffective, and Inefficient

Setting Event Strategies	Preventive Strategies	Teaching Strategies	Consequence Strategies
• Use visual systems to enhance predictability and expectations (e.g., monthly calendar, home routine schedule). • Set up Emily with high-preference toys and activities before starting chores. • Spend one-to-one quality time with Emily before initiating chores.	• Use positive contingencies to motivate independent play. • Use safety signals to motivate endurance (i.e., waiting for attention). • Offer choices to enhance motivation.	•Teach Emily to politely ask for attention or assistance. • Use safety signals to gradually teach Emily to tolerate an absence of attention.	• Give attention contingent on desired behavior. • Give attention and help contingent on politely asking. •Actively ignore and redirect minor problem behavior. • If problem behavior escalates, reduce attention and then redirect Emily.

Figure 5.5. Summary statement/competing behavior pathways diagram and positive behavior support plan for the free-time/dinner cleanup routine. (From *Functional Assessment and Program Development for Problem Behavior: A Practical Handbook, 1st edition,* by R.E. O'Neill, R.H. Horner, R.W. Albin, J.R. Sprague, K. Storey, J. Newton © 1997. Reprinted with permission of Wadsworth, an imprint of the Wadsworth Group, a division of Thomson Learning. Fax 800-730-2215.)

wraparound team generated included 1) school-based behavior support services in coordination with home-based services, 2) home- and center-based respite care services, and 3) money for respite care services and equipment and materials to support Emily at home (e.g., a computer, educational software, software for creating picture schedules).

Grocery Shopping Routine

Child and Family   Kyle was a charming and affectionate 11-year-old with the diagnosis of Cornelia de Lange syndrome. His language skills were limited to a modest repertoire of one- and two-word phrases to communicate simple greetings (e.g., "hello"), likes and dislikes (e.g., "toy," "loud"), and wants and needs (e.g., "Mom," "food"). Kyle's family included his mother, Brenda, his father, James, and his 13-year-old sister, Jessica. Both of Kyle's parents were business professionals: Brenda was an administrator at a publishing company, and James was a sales representative for a major credit card company. The family lived in a large, ranch-style home in a middle-class neighborhood of a mid-size city in the Pacific Northwest. The family sought behavior support services due to Kyle's infrequent but intense episodes of aggression, self-injury, and property destruction at home and in the community.

Family Ecology   The interventionist's conversation with Kyle's parents about family ecology revealed several strengths, a strong social support network, a good use of community resources, few but significant stressors, and clear goals for Kyle and his mother. In terms of strengths, Brenda and James had a strong marriage and equally shared child care tasks and responsibilities. As business professionals, they had excellent analytic skills and were good problem solvers. Jessica was mature for her age, had an affectionate relationship with her brother, and enjoyed helping her parents with child care and household tasks. In terms of social supports and resources, the family had a close relationship with extended family members, including grandparents, uncles, aunts, and cousins. Also, Brenda and James made full use of weekday and weekend respite care services, which were provided by a local nonprofit agency, and made a point of getting away together every few months to relax and recharge. A chronic stressor for Brenda was anxiety about Kyle engaging in the next incident of self-injury, aggression, or property destruction. Although these episodes were infrequent, they also were difficult to predict and psychologically devastating. As a result, Brenda and James severely limited Kyle's involvement in community activities and in family gatherings and events. A discussion of family goals indicated that the family wanted to eliminate problem behaviors and safely include Kyle in community and family activities. Brenda expressed a personal interest in reducing her level of anxiety so that she could better support Kyle, particularly in the community.

Functional Assessment and Family Routines Assessment   A functional assessment interview was completed in the home with Brenda and James, and functional assessment observations were completed in the home and community to confirm hypotheses about problem behavior (O'Neill et al., 1997). Following the functional assessment interview, an assessment of daily and weekly family routines and activities was completed. During this assessment the family indicated that their priority routines for intervention with Kyle were dinner at home and shopping in the community. The family then described what a realistic and successful dinner routine and grocery shopping routine would look like with Kyle. Before working on the grocery shopping routine, the interventionist and the family

Table 5.6.   Family vision of a successful grocery shopping routine

Kyle will accompany his mother or father to the neighborhood supermarket one or two times per week. During a trip to the store, up to 10 items will be purchased. While shopping, Kyle will help push the shopping cart, put items in the cart, and make at least one purchase for himself. He also will stay with his parent, wait in the checkout line patiently, and leave the store with his parent. A trip to the store with Kyle will be a safe and relatively stress-free experience.

first developed and implemented a positive behavior support plan for the dinner routine. The family successfully implemented this home-based plan, and, in doing so, gained confidence for addressing the far more challenging grocery shopping routine. The family's envisioned routine is presented in Table 5.6.

Summary Statement/Competing Behavior Pathways Diagram
Functional assessment information and the family's envisioned grocery shopping routine served as the basis for building a summary statement and competing behavior pathways diagram. As with the first case study, the next subsection provides a summary of functional assessment information for the problematic routine. Kyle's parents and the interventionist used this information first to build a summary statement diagram. Then, they identified desired behavior and alternative replacement behavior for the routine. This additional information completed the summary statement/competing behavior pathways diagram. Because Kyle's parents were familiar with the functional assessment and plan design process and had successfully improved one routine at home, they played a more active role in diagramming the summary statement and competing behavior pathways diagram for the routine and in generating behavioral supports. With support from the interventionist, Brenda completed the diagram for the grocery shopping routine, and both Brenda and James generated interventions that they believed would be effective and contextually appropriate. Brenda also agreed to be the primary implementor of the plan.

Building a Summary Statement of the Problem
Kyle accompanied Brenda to the grocery store one or two times per week. During these trips, Kyle bolted away from his mother, grabbed the arm of a stranger, or bit himself on the arm. On one harrowing occasion, he bit a shopper at the store. A setting event that appeared to exaggerate the occurrence of problem behavior was times when the store was crowded and noisy. Immediate antecedent events that appeared to trigger problem behavior included passing through a crowd of people, standing too close to strangers, sudden loud noises, and waiting in the checkout line. The maintaining consequences for problem behavior appeared to be Brenda's immediately moving Kyle away from crowded places, moving away from someone standing near Kyle, moving to a shorter line, or abruptly leaving the store. The primary function of Kyle's behavior appeared to be escape from aversive events in the store. A functional assessment observation completed in the store confirmed the functional assessment information that was acquired by interview. Based on these results, Brenda and James, with support from the interventionist, built the summary statement diagram for the grocery shopping routine (see Figure 5.6).

Identifying Desired and Alternative Replacement Behaviors
After building a summary statement of problem behavior in the routine, Brenda, James, and the interventionist identified desired behavior and alternative replacement behavior for Kyle in the store. For desired behavior, Kyle would actively participate in the steps of the shopping routine, helping his mother put items in the cart and selecting at least one item for him-

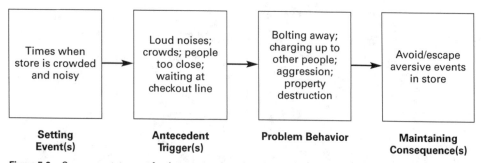

| Times when store is crowded and noisy | → | Loud noises; crowds; people too close; waiting at checkout line | → | Bolting away; charging up to other people; aggression; property destruction | → | Avoid/escape aversive events in store |

Setting Event(s)   **Antecedent Trigger(s)**   **Problem Behavior**   **Maintaining Consequence(s)**

Figure 5.6. Summary statement for the grocery shopping routine. (From *Functional Assessment and Program Development for Problem Behavior: A Practical Handbook, 1st edition,* by R.E. O'Neill, R.H. Horner, R.W. Albin, J.R. Sprague, K. Storey, J. Newton © 1997. Reprinted with permission of Wadsworth, an imprint of the Wadsworth Group, a division of Thomson Learning. Fax 800-730-2215.)

self. For alternative replacement behavior for escape-motivated problem behavior, Kyle would say, "too many," "too loud," or "all done." Respectively, these were requests to go around crowds, to move away from loud noises, or to leave the store. The maintaining consequences for desired behavior would be parental praise and the purchase of a favorite item (e.g., a banana) contingent on desired behavior. The maintaining consequence for the use of language to escape aversive events in the store would include walking away from these events or leaving the store, contingent on asking to do so. The completed summary statement/competing behavior pathways diagram for the grocery shopping routine is presented in Figure 5.7.

Multicomponent Positive Behavior Support Plan Design   Using the diagram as a guide, Brenda, James, and the interventionist generated a multicomponent positive behavior support plan that was aimed at rendering problem behavior irrelevant, inefficient, and inefficient in the grocery store. Beginning with setting events, Kyle's parents and the interventionist considered ecological and lifestyle strategies that would reduce the aversive features of being in the store. For the issues of too many people and too much noise, Brenda decided to go to the store on days and at times when it was less crowded and less noisy. To increase predictability, Brenda and James agreed to develop a picture story that informed Kyle of the steps in the routine, including positive events (e.g., buying a favorite item, returning to the car). Next, the family and the interventionist considered ways to replace triggers for problem behavior with strategies that promoted patience and cooperation. For example, instead of walking through a crowd, Brenda would walk around groups of people. If an unexpected loud noise occurred, then Brenda would immediately tell Kyle what the sound was and reassure him that they would move away from it. For teaching strategies, Brenda would also use the picture schedule to remind Kyle of each step in the routine and prompt him to "use his words" if he appeared anxious.

Final discussion focused on consequence strategies that would enhance rewards for desired behavior and alternative replacement behavior and diminish or eliminate rewards for problem behavior. The competing behavior pathways diagram largely determined the selection of specific strategies. To strengthen desired behavior, Brenda would praise Kyle when he participated in the steps of the shopping routine and when he remained calm in the presence of crowds and noise. Also, if Kyle completed the steps in the routine and did not engage in major problem behavior, he would be allowed to purchase the preferred food item that he had selected. To strengthen alternative replacement behavior, she would offer reassurance and/or move away from crowds or noise when Kyle used language to express his want or need. To weaken problem behavior, the family agreed that if minor problem

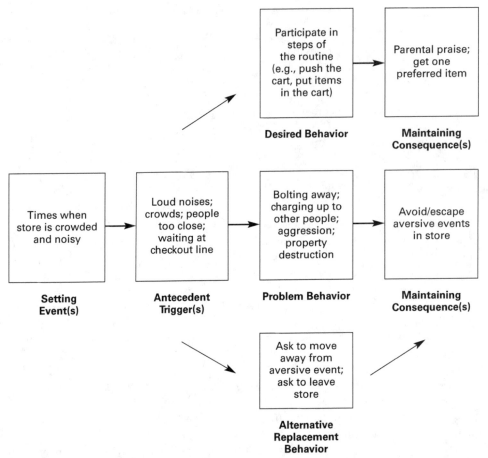

Figure 5.7. Summary statement/competing behavior pathways diagram for the grocery shopping routine. (From *Functional Assessment and Program Development for Problem Behavior: A Practical Handbook, 1st edition,* by R.E. O'Neill, R.H. Horner, R.W. Albin, J.R. Sprague, K. Storey, J. Newton © 1997. Reprinted with permission of Wadsworth, an imprint of the Wadsworth Group, a division of Thomson Learning. Fax 800-730-2215.)

behavior occurred (e.g., bolting away from the shopping cart), then Kyle would be calmly redirected back to the task. For major problem behavior, Brenda would deliver a brief reprimand, hurry Kyle out of the store, and not purchase the food item he had chosen. The multicomponent positive behavior support plan generated by the family, with the help of the interventionist, is presented in Figure 5.8.

Contextual Fit Considerations   The family and the interventionist discussed the plan's contextual fit with the ecocultural elements of the family's envisioned routine (e.g., time and place, goals and values, resources, tasks). This discussion suggested that the plan would be both effective and contextually appropriate. However, one aspect of the larger ecology of the family gave Brenda pause: She indicated that her anxiety when she was alone with Kyle in the community might interfere with her ability to implement the plan. Through this discussion, Brenda decided to explore techniques to control her anxiety and to remain calm in the midst of stressful situations. Shortly after implementing the plan in the grocery shopping routine with Kyle, Brenda began taking a yoga class for the purpose of reducing her stress level.

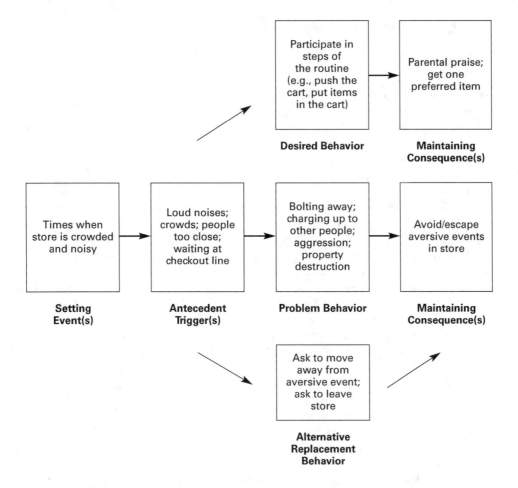

Strategies that Make Problem Behaviors Irrelevant, Ineffective, and Inefficient

Setting Event Strategies	Preventive Strategies	Teaching Strategies	Consequence Strategies
• Bring Kyle to store during less noisy/crowded times. • While in the store, minimize aversive events (e.g., go around crowds, walk away from crying infants).	• Review a picture schedule of shopping steps, emphasizing positive events. • Use positive contingencies natural to shopping to motivate cooperation in store. • Remind Kyle to use his words if he is feeling anxious in the store.	• Teach Kyle to help with steps in routine (e.g., push the cart, put items in the cart). • Teach Kyle to ask to avoid aversive events or leave the store. • Use safety signals to build tolerance.	• Offer praise and reassurance/give item contingent on desired behavior. • Avoid aversive events or leave store contingent on asking. • If minor behavior occurs, redirect Kyle and/or prompt language. • If major behavior occurs, leave store.

Figure 5.8. Summary statement/competing behavior pathways diagram and positive behavior support plan for the grocery shopping routine. (From *Functional Assessment and Program Development for Problem Behavior: A Practical Handbook, 1st edition*, by R.E. O'Neill, R.H. Horner, R.W. Albin, J.R. Sprague, K. Storey, J. Newton © 1997. Reprinted with permission of Wadsworth, an imprint of the Wadsworth Group, a division of Thomson Learning. Fax 800-730-2215.)

CONCLUSION

This chapter has described a collaborative, family-centered approach to designing technically sound and contextually appropriate positive behavior support plans in the context of valued but problematic family routines and activities in the home and community. In this approach, the interventionist works with the family as an equal partner in the completion of a functional assessment, in the development of a summary statement, and in the design of interventions and supports that are linked to relevant features of the problem in the routine or activity. The activity setting as a unit of analysis and intervention aids this problem-solving process because it helps the family and interventionist to understand the structural elements of valued routines and activities and to embed behavioral supports into the ecology of routines in ways that are acceptable and feasible to the family. The aim of this process is an effective and contextually appropriate positive behavior support plan that empowers families to improve child behavior and participation in valued activity settings in the home and community. This process has been illustrated in two routines (one in the home and one in the community) that are commonly problematic for parents of children with disabilities and challenging behavior.

Knowledge about the family system is important for the design of a contextually appropriate behavior support plan, as shown by Susan's support to Emily. With this information, a family and an interventionist can consider family-centered supports that may help parents implement and sustain a positive behavior support plan, as well as improve the quality of life for all family members. Kyle's parents played an active role in building a summary statement/competing behavior pathways diagram and in generating positive behavior supports for the grocery shopping routine; this illustrates the empowerment framework in which family-centered positive behavior support can operate (Turnbull & Turnbull, 2001). The interventionist strives to generate an *efficiency of outcomes* that reduces the family's need for his or her services in the future. He or she does so by including families from the start as partners in functional assessment and plan development and by directly teaching parents how to build summary statements and select interventions that are linked to the features of the problem.

We alert the reader to two limitations in this chapter. First, we have not described how to design a comprehensive positive behavior support plan that families can apply across all problematic contexts in the home and community. Rather, we have described a modest reiterative process for developing routine-specific positive behavior support plans. Readers who are interested in the design of comprehensive positive behavior support plans that address problem behaviors across home, school, and community contexts are referred to Carr and colleagues (1999), Horner and colleagues (2000), and Lucyshyn and Albin (1993). Second, the chapter has not described a process of implementation support, which may be necessary to support a family's implementation of a behavior support plan in family activity settings. Although the routine as a unit of analysis and intervention simplifies the implementation process for families, it does not preclude the need for an implementation plan. We refer the reader to Horner and colleagues (2000), Lucyshyn and Albin (1993), Sanders and Dadds (1993), and Webster-Stratton and Hancock (1998) for detailed information about implementation support.

This chapter offers three central messages to families and practitioners. First, family-centered positive behavior support recognizes families of children with disabilities and problem behaviors as equal partners in a process of functional assessment and positive behavior support plan design. Family participation is essential for the design of effective and contextually appropriate behavior support plans. Second, the activity setting of daily and weekly routines is a unit of analysis that lends itself to the design of behavioral supports that can be effectively embedded into the fabric of family life. Selecting valued but problematic routines and organizing behavioral support around solving them one or two at a time can empower families to take measured steps toward achieving their vision of family life with their child with a disability. Third, families are capable of becoming experts in their own right in the use of functional assessment and positive behavior support for their child with a disability. When the knowledge of positive behavior support has been firmly placed into the loving hands of family members, they are able to substantially improve the behavior and life of their child with a disability and the quality of family life as a whole.

Given the growing empirical evidence of the acceptability and effectiveness of family-centered positive behavior support, we conclude with recommendations to parents, professionals, researchers, and policy makers. We encourage parents of children with disabilities and problem behavior to seek and advocate for family-centered functional assessment and positive behavior support services such as those described in this chapter as well as in other chapters in this book. We encourage professionals who lead behavior support teams to include parents as valued members of the team and to incorporate family-centered positive behavior support practices into behavior support services. We encourage behavioral researchers to augment empirical knowledge about family-centered positive behavior support by conducting intervention research studies with families in natural family contexts and by using the activity setting of daily routines as a unit of analysis. We also encourage university-based educators to teach a new generation of professionals the interdisciplinary knowledge and skills of family-centered positive behavior support. Finally, we encourage administrators and policy makers to enhance or change organizational systems that involve assistance to families so that these systems support and nurture family-centered functional assessment and positive behavior support practices.

REFERENCES

Albin, R.W., Lucyshyn, J.M., Horner, R.H., & Flannery, K.B. (1996). Contextual fit for behavioral support plans: A model for "goodness of fit." In L.K. Koegel, R.L. Koegel, & G. Dunlap (Eds.), *Positive behavioral support: Including people with difficult behavior in the community* (pp. 81–98). Baltimore: Paul H. Brookes Publishing Co.

Barry, L.M., & Singer, G.H.S. (2001). A family in crisis: Replacing the aggressive behavior of a child with autism toward an infant sibling. *Journal of Positive Behavior Interventions, 3,* 28–38.

Bernheimer, L.P., & Keough, B.K. (1995). Weaving interventions into the fabric of everyday life: An approach to family assessment. *Topics in Early Childhood Special Education, 15,* 415–433.

Bijou, S.W., & Baer, D.M. (1978). *Behavior analysis of child development.* Upper Saddle River, NJ: Prentice Hall.

Blacher, J. (Ed.). (1994). *When there's no place like home: Options for children living apart from their natural families.* Baltimore: Paul H. Brookes Publishing Co.

Carr, E.G., Levin, L., McConnachie, G., Carlson, J.I., Kemp, D.C., & Smith, C.E. (1994). *Communication-based intervention for problem behavior: A user's guide for producing positive change.* Baltimore: Paul H. Brookes Publishing Co.

Carr, E.G., Levin, L., McConnachie, G., Carlson, J.I., Kemp, D.C., Smith, C.E., & McLaughlin, D.M. (1999). Comprehensive multisituational intervention for problem behavior in the community: Long-term maintenance and social validation. *Journal of Positive Behavior Interventions, 1,* 5–25.

Carr, E.G., Reeve, C.E., & Magito-McLaughlin, D. (1996). Contextual influences on problem behavior in people with developmental disabilities. In L.K. Kern, R.L. Koegel, & G. Dunlap (Eds.), *Positive behavioral support: Including people with difficult behavior in the community* (pp. 403–423). Baltimore: Paul H. Brookes Publishing Co.

Clarke, S., Dunlap, G., & Vaughn, B. (1999). Family-centered, assessment-based intervention to improve behavior during an early morning routine. *Journal of Positive Behavior Interventions, 1,* 235–241.

Derby, K.M., Wacker, D.P., Berg, W., DeRaad, A., Ulrich, S., Asmus, J., Harding, J., Prouty, A., Laffey, P., & Stoner, A. (1997). The long-term effects of functional communication training in home settings. *Journal of Applied Behavior Analysis, 30,* 507–531.

Dunlap, G., & Fox, L. (1999). A demonstration of behavioral support for young children with autism. *Journal of Positive Behavioral Interventions, 1,* 77–88.

Dunst, C.J., Hamby, D., Trivette, C.M., Raab, M., & Bruder, M.B. (2000). Everyday family and community life and children's naturally occurring learning opportunities. *Journal of Early Intervention, 23,* 151–164.

Eber, L., Osuch, R., & Redditt, C. (1996). School-based applications of the wraparound process: Early results of service provision and student outcomes. *Journal of Child and Family Studies, 5,* 83–99.

Flannery, K.B., & Horner, R.H. (1994). The relationship between predictability and problem behavior for students with severe disabilities. *Journal of Behavioral Education, 4,* 157–176.

Fox, L., Dunlap, G., & Buschbacher, P. (2000). Understanding and intervening with children's challenging behavior: A comprehensive approach. In A.M. Wetherby & B.M. Prizant (Eds.), *Communication and language intervention series: Vol. 9. Autism spectrum disorders: A transactional developmental perspective* (pp. 307–331). Baltimore: Paul H. Brookes Publishing Co.

Fox, L., Vaughn, B.J., Dunlap, G., & Bucy, M. (1997). Parent–professional partnership in behavioral support: A qualitative analysis of one family's experience. *Journal of The Association for Persons with Severe Handicaps, 22,* 198–207.

Gallimore, R., Goldenberg, C.N., & Weisner, T.S. (1993). The social construction and subjective reality of activity settings: Implications for community psychology. *American Journal of Community Psychology, 21,* 537–559.

Gallimore, R., Weisner, T.S., Kaufman, S.Z. & Bernheimer, L.P. (1989). The social construction of ecocultural niches: Family accommodation of developmentally delayed children. *American Journal of Mental Retardation, 94,* 216–230.

Harrower, J.K., Fox, L., Dunlap, G., & Kincaid, D. (1999–2000). Functional assessment and comprehensive early intervention. *Exceptionality, 8,* 189–204.

Hawkins, N.E., Singer, G.H.S., & Nixon, C.D. (1993). Short-term behavioral counseling for families of persons with disabilities. In G.H.S. Singer & L.E. Powers (Eds.), *Families, disability, and empowerment: Active coping skills and strategies for family interventions* (pp. 317–341). Baltimore: Paul H. Brookes Publishing Co.

Horner, R.H., Albin, R.W., Sprague, J.R., & Todd, A.W. (2000). Positive behavior support for students with severe disabilities. In M.E. Snell & F. Brown (Eds.), *Instruction of students with severe disabilities* (5th ed., pp. 207–243). Upper Saddle River, NJ: Prentice Hall.

Horner, R.H., Dunlap, G., Koegel, R.L., Carr, E.G., Sailor, W., Anderson, J., Albin, R. W., & O'Neill, R.E. (1990). Toward a technology of "non-aversive" behavioral support. *Journal of The Association for Persons With Severe Handicaps, 15,* 125–132.

Horner, R.H., Vaughn, B.J., Day, H.M., & Ard, W.R. (1996). The relationship between setting events and problem behavior: Expanding our understanding of behavioral support. In L.K. Koegel, R.L. Koegel, & G. Dunlap (Eds.), *Positive behavior support: Including people with difficult behavior in the community* (pp. 381–402). Baltimore: Paul H. Brookes Publishing Co.

Koegel, L.K., Koegel, R.L., & Dunlap, G. (Eds.). (1996). *Positive behavioral support: Including people with difficult behavior in the community.* Baltimore: Paul H. Brookes Publishing Co.

Koegel, L.K., Steibel, D., & Koegel, R.L. (1998). Reducing aggression in children with autism toward infant or toddler siblings. *Journal of the Association for Persons with Severe Handicaps, 23,* 111–118.

Koegel, R.L., Koegel, L.K., & McNeary, E.K. (2001). Pivotal areas in intervention for autism. *Journal of Clinical Child Psychology, 30,* 19–32.

Koegel, R.L., Schreibman, L., Loos, L. M., Dirlich-Wilhelm, H., Dunlap, G., Robbins, F.R., & Plienis, A.J. (1992). Consistent stress profiles in mothers of children with autism. *Journal of Autism and Developmental Disabilities, 22,* 205–216.

Lucyshyn, J.M., & Albin, R.W. (1993). Comprehensive support to families of children with disabilities and problem behaviors: Keeping it "friendly." In G.H.S. Singer & L.E. Powers (Eds.), *Families, disability, and empowerment: Active coping skills and strategies for family interventions* (pp. 365–407). Baltimore: Paul H. Brookes Publishing Co.

Lucyshyn, J.M., Albin, R.W., Horner, R.H., Mann, J.C., Mann, J.A., & Wadsworth, G. (2000, February). *Positive behavior support with a family of a child with autism: A longitudinal, experimental, single-case replica-*

tion. Colloquium presented to the Faculty of Education at the University of British Columbia, Vancouver, Canada.

Lucyshyn, J.M., Albin, R.W., & Nixon, C.D. (1997). Embedding comprehensive behavioral support in family ecology: An experimental, single-case analysis. *Journal of Consulting and Clinical Psychology, 65,* 241–251.

Lucyshyn, J.M., Blumberg, E.R., & Irvin, L.K. (2001). *Transforming coercive relationships in family routines.* Public Health Service Grant Proposal. National Institute of Child Health and Human Development, National Institutes of Health, Washington, DC.

Lucyshyn, J.M., Irvin, L.K., Blumberg, E.R., Laverty, R., Sprague, J.S., & Horner, R.H. (2001, May). Expanding the unit of analysis and intervention: Validating the construct of coercion in family routines. In B. Smith (Chair), *Applying sequential analysis to understand behavior in context.* Symposium conducted at the 27th annual meeting of the Association for Behavior Analysis, New Orleans, LA.

Lucyshyn, J.M., & Kayser, A.T. (1999, May).*Functional assessment and positive behavior support plan design at home with families.* Invited presentation/workshop at the Behavioral Consultant Forum, Mentorship Training Project, Specialized Training Program, University of Oregon, Lincoln City.

Lutzker, J.R., & Steed, S. (1998). Parent training for families of children with developmental disabilities. In J.M. Briesmeister & C.E. Schaefer (Eds.), *Handbook of parent training: Parents as co-therapists for children's problem behavior* (pp. 281–307). New York: John Wiley & Sons.

Malette, P., Mirenda, P., Kandborg, T., Jones, P., Bunz, T., & Rogow, S. (1992). Application of a lifestyle development process for persons with severe intellectual disabilities: A case study report. *Journal of The Association for Persons with Severe Handicaps, 17,* 179–191.

Marshall, J., & Mirenda, P. (in press). Parent–professional collaboration for positive behavior support in the home. *Focus on Autism and Other Developmental Disabilities.*

Moes, D.R., & Frea, W.D. (2000). Using family context to inform intervention planning for the treatment of a child with autism. *Journal of Positive Behavior Interventions, 2,* 40–46.

Mullen, K.B., & Frea, W.D. (1995). A parent–professional consultation model for functional analysis. In R.L. Koegel & L.K. Koegel (Eds.), *Teaching children with autism: Strategies for initiating positive interactions and improving learning opportunities* (pp. 175–188). Baltimore: Paul H. Brookes Publishing Co.

O'Neill, R.E., Horner, R.H., Albin, R.W., Sprague, J.R., Storey, K., & Newton, J.S. (1997). *Functional assessment and program development for problem behavior: A practical handbook.* Pacific Grove, CA: Brooks/Cole Thomson Learning.

Ruef, M.B., Turnbull, A.P., Turnbull, H.R., & Poston, D. (1999). Perspectives of five stakeholder groups: Challenging behavior of individuals with mental retardation and autism. *Journal of Positive Behavior Interventions, 1,* 43–58.

Sailor, W., Gee, K., & Karasoff, P. (2000). Inclusion and school restructuring. In M.E. Snell & F. Brown (Eds.), *Instruction of students with severe disabilities* (5th ed., pp. 1–30). Upper Saddle River, NJ: Prentice Hall.

Sanders, M.R., & Dadds, M.R. (1993). *Behavioral family intervention.* Upper Saddle River: Prentice Hall.

Singer, G.H.S. (1996). Introduction: Trends affecting home and community care for people with chronic conditions in the United States. In G.H.S. Singer, L.E. Powers, & A.L. Olson (Eds.), *Redefining family support: Innovations in public–private partnerships* (pp. 3–38). Baltimore: Paul H. Brookes Publishing Co.

Singer, G.H.S., & Irvin, L.K. (Eds.). (1989). *Support for caregiving families: Enabling positive adaptation to disability.* Baltimore: Paul H. Brookes Publishing Co.

Singer, G.H.S., & Irvin, L.K. (1991). Supporting families of persons with severe disabilities: Emerging findings, practices, and questions. In L.H. Meyer, C.A. Peck, & L. Brown (Eds.), *Critical issues in the lives of people with severe disabilities* (pp. 271–312). Baltimore: Paul H. Brookes Publishing Co.

Sprague, J.R., & Horner, R.H. (1991). Determining the acceptability of behavior support plans. In M. Wang, H. Walberger, & M. Reynolds (Eds.), *Handbook of special education* (Vol. 4). Elmsford, NY: Pergamon Press.

Turnbull, A.P., & Ruef, M.B. (1996). Family perspectives on problem behavior. *Mental Retardation, 34,* 280–293.

Turnbull, A.P., & Turnbull, H.R. (2000). Family–professional partnerships. In M.E. Snell & F. Brown (Eds.), *Instruction of students with severe disabilities* (5th, pp. 31–66). Upper Saddle River, NJ: Prentice Hall.

Turnbull, A.P., & Turnbull, H.R. (2001). *Families, professionals and exceptionality: Collaborating for empowerment.* Upper Saddle River, NJ: Prentice Hall.

Vaughn, B.J., Amado, R., Corker, M., Dunlap, G., Fake, S., & Lucyshyn, J. (1997, December). *The process of positive behavioral support with families in natural contexts.* Pre-conference workshop at the 22nd annual meeting of The Association for Persons with Severe Handicaps, Miami, FL.

Vaughn, B.J., Clarke, S., & Dunlap, G. (1997). Assessment-based intervention for severe behavior problems in a natural family context. *Journal of Applied Behavior Analysis, 30,* 713–716.

Vaughn, B.J., Dunlap, G., Fox, L., Clarke, S., & Bucy, M. (1997). Parent–professional partnership in behavioral support: A case study of community based intervention. *Journal of The Association for Persons with Severe Handicaps, 22,* 186–197.

Vygotsky, L. (1978). *Mind in society: The development of higher psychological processes* (M. Cole, V. John-Steiner, S. Scribner, & E. Souberman, Eds.). Cambridge, MA: Harvard University Press.

Webster-Stratton, C., & Hancock, L. (1998). Training for parents of young children with conduct problems: Content, methods, and therapeutic processes. In J.M. Briesmeister & C.E. Schaefer (Eds.), *Handbook of parent training: Parents as co-therapists for children's problem behavior* (pp. 281–307). New York: John Wiley & Sons.

Whiting, B. (1980). Culture and social behavior: A model for the development of social behavior. *Ethos, 8,* 95–116.

Whiting, B., & Edwards, C. (1988). *Children of different worlds: The formation of social behavior.* Cambridge, MA: Harvard University Press.

CHAPTER *6*

Working with Families of Diverse Cultural and Linguistic Backgrounds

Considerations for Culturally Responsive Positive Behavior Support

Deborah Chen, June E. Downing, and Kathryn D. Peckham-Hardin

The United States of America is one of the most culturally and linguistically diverse countries in the world. As of 2000, about one third of the population had Native American, African American, Hispanic, Asian, and other non-European backgrounds (Chan, 1990; Hodgkinson, 1992; United States Bureau of the Census, 2001). Furthermore, it is a country of immigrants, as 1 of every 10 people living in the United States was born elsewhere. In the 1950s, most immigrants came from Europe or Canada; however, by the end of the 20th century, most newcomers were from Central America, South America, and Asia (Knight, 1997). There are about 330 different languages being used in homes across the country (Census: Languages not foreign at home, 1993), and 1 in 7 people use a language other than English (Haedden, 1995). These statistics underscore the need for providers of behavior support services to develop skills in working with families whose culture and language are different from their own.

Upbringing, communities, and culture mold one's values, desires, and interactions. All behavior is influenced by culture and context. Certain situations and different expectations determine whether a particular behavior is considered appropriate. For example, in some families, children are expected to join in when adults are having a conversation and even argue their own point of view. In other families, these behaviors would be considered disrespectful. Because most service providers in special education belong to the mainstream culture, behavior that they consider unconventional or challenging is often behavior that deviates from mainstream culture and contexts. Depending on the child's family, socioeconomic status, and other cultural characteristics, however, these same behaviors may not seem unusual or particularly bothersome at home. When providing behavior support services to families from various cultural and linguistic backgrounds, service providers should recognize that families have diverse values, child-rearing practices, and behavioral expectations. These services will involve the complex interaction of at least two cultures, that of the family and that of the service provider or service organization.

Understanding differences in perspectives will influence the way in which a process of positive behavior support (PBS) is conducted, including 1) the development of a trust-

133

ing partnership with families, 2) the identification of behaviors of concern and problematic family contexts, 3) the completion of assessment activities, 4) the selection of behavioral support strategies, and 5) the provision of implementation support to families. The purpose of this chapter is to address this complex interaction of cultural perspectives through a discussion of the following:

1. The influences of family culture and values on child-rearing practices, discipline, and expectations of appropriate behavior

2. Cultural influences on a family's view of PBS

3. Considerations for enhancing family–professional relationships regarding PBS

4. Suggestions to assist service providers in more effective collaboration on positive behavior support plans with families from diverse cultural and linguistic backgrounds

This chapter does not describe specific cultural groups or provide information on how particular cultural groups view challenging behaviors. Although general information is available about traditional values of various cultures (e.g., Lynch & Hanson, 1998), each family's values and practices are colored by a complex interaction of many variables, including ethnicity, language, nationality, socioeconomic status, religion, educational level, and geographic location. Given this complexity, the intent of the chapter is to provide general considerations so that service providers working with families on behavioral issues can provide more culturally responsive services.

DIMENSIONS OF CULTURE

An individual's cultural identity comprises several dimensions, including ethnicity, race, gender, social class, religion, age, primary language, geographic location, and other factors such as profession and marital status (Gollnick & Chinn, 1994). Some of these characteristics are primary—that is, individuals are born with them or cannot change them easily (e.g., age, race, gender, ethnicity, disability, sexual orientation). Others are secondary—that is, individuals acquire them as they live (e.g., primary language, geographic location, religion, family status, education, work experience, profession, income) (Loden & Rosener, 1991). Differences in these cultural dimensions result in differing and even conflicting views between families and service providers toward child-rearing practices, children with disabilities, special education services, and related issues (Harry, 1992a, 1992b; Sileo, Sileo, & Prater, 1996; Turnbull & Turnbull, 1997). Therefore, when collaborating with families, it is essential for service providers to gather information about the individual family system, the family's view of the child's disability, and their culture's typical child-rearing practices.

Family Systems

The concept of *family* is defined by culture, economics, politics, and religion (Turnbull & Turnbull, 1997). Small nuclear families are typical of contemporary Anglo-European Americans; in contrast, traditional Hispanic, Asian, Indochinese, Middle Eastern, African American, and Native American families tend to be multigenerational and extended (Groce & Zola, 1993; Hanson, Lynch, & Wayman, 1990; Joe & Malach, 1998; Kallam, Hoernicke, & Coser, 1994; Kulwicki, 1996; Orlansky & Trap, 1987; Robbins, 1996; Sharifzadeh, 1998; Willis, 1998). To develop and implement effective behavior support programs, service providers should learn about the characteristics (e.g., composition, socioeconomic status, resources, special challenges) and the organization (e.g., roles and responsibilities of family members, how decisions are made) of the families they serve. Some families have very clear roles and responsibilities. For example, traditional Chinese families generally follow a patriarchal, vertical structure with well-defined interdependent roles. In this structure, fathers are responsible for supporting the family financially and representing the family in public, while mothers are responsible for the home and other domestic functions of the family (Chan, 1998; Chung, 1996). Children are taught to respect the line of authority pertaining to specific relationships, such as wife to husband or children to parents. In traditional Chinese families, filial obligation or duty to one's parents often results in having a large extended family living in one household. Moreover, the extended family is the primary support system because of the need to preserve the honor of the family name or to "save face." In contrast, in contemporary Anglo-European families, traditional male and female family roles are less obvious, and adults are likely to share child care, decision making, and household tasks (Hanson, 1998). In many Native American families, children are reared by grandparents or extended family members while their parents work (Joe & Malach, 1998). Thus, the characteristics and structure of each family system will influence how members of a particular family participate in their child's educational program and their relationship with service providers.

Perspectives on Disability

The Individuals with Disabilities Education Act (IDEA) Amendments of 1997 (PL 105-17) not only mandate services but also guide current approaches to the etiology and treatment of disabilities. These views typically reflect mainstream values. However, families from diverse cultural backgrounds may have very different perspectives, and these views influence their involvement in special education services. For example, some families may view the child's disability as a natural part of life and reject medical or educational intervention. Other families may believe that the child's disability is punishment from God, so they view the seeking of services as pointless. Yet other families from different cultures may believe that a disability is the result of a misdeed committed by the pregnant woman or by the child in a former life or is due to very bad luck (Chan, 1998; Groce & Zola, 1993; Willis, 1998). These beliefs often contribute to feelings of guilt and fatalism, so these families also may not seek services for their child (Chan, 1998).

   In contrast, other families may believe that the child is their God-given responsibility and that their duty is to do everything possible to care for the child (Alvarez, 1998; Sileo et al., 1996). Still other cultural groups may not acknowledge a disability in the child. Members of Deaf culture, for example, see a child's hearing loss as a linguistic difference rather than as a disability (Padden & Humphries, 1988). Consequently, their focus is on immersion of the child in Deaf culture and on access to American Sign Language. The family members' beliefs about the cause of the child's disability influence their expectations about how the child will behave, their goals for their child, and their participation in special education services, including the provision of PBS.

Child-Rearing Practices

Educational programs for students with disabilities, including PBS, are guided by theories and research derived from special education and psychology and tend to reflect mainstream values. Families from diverse backgrounds, however, may rely on tradition and culture to guide their child-rearing practices, including methods of discipline. Educational programs for children with severe disabilities tend to emphasize the development of independence and autonomy and focus on adaptive living skills and community-based instruction. In contrast, some families may place more value on interdependence and caring for each other (Groce & Zola, 1993). For example, traditional Asian families tend to be strict and protective of their children, and adult children live away from their families at a much later age than their Anglo-European American peers (Chan, 1998). In traditional Latino families, there is less emphasis on early attainment of self-help skills; a preschooler may still drink from a bottle and an older child may be accustomed to having someone tie his or her shoes (Zuniga, 1998). Furthermore, schools usually view schedules and routines as beneficial to promoting appropriate behavior. Families, on the other hand, may focus on natural biological rhythms where children are fed by family members when they are hungry and are put to bed when they are sleepy. Such differences between family and program practices can create obstacles to family–professional collaboration on positive behavior support programs for children with disabilities.

Expectations of Appropriate Behavior   Children learn manners and ways of interacting socially primarily from experiences in their families and communities. In some communities, children address adults more formally and use titles of respect; in others, interactions are very casual. For example, in traditional Iranian families, children are expected to be quiet when a guest is present, not to interrupt while adults are talking, and not to touch food without permission (Sharifzadeh, 1998). Some families engage in physical interactions (e.g., roughhousing, bear-hugging, wrestling) with other family members and with friends. Other families would find these interactions aggressive, threatening, or disrespectful. Some families typically yell at each other in everyday conversation. Others would interpret yelling as an expression of anger and a rude way to communicate. In some families, adults and children use swear words and seemingly vulgar language in their daily interactions. In contrast, these verbal interactions would be discouraged and even punished in other families. Children can be encouraged to be assertive to the point of aggressiveness in some families, which would be completely unacceptable in others. The value that different families place on certain behaviors depends on the need for the behavior to promote or maintain the family unit within the culture and geographic area. Therefore, behaviors that might be punished in one family and culture could easily be reinforced and supported in another. Similarly, children who have commonly engaged in a particular behavior at home may suddenly find that this same behavior is not tolerated by some teachers at school. For instance, African American children may appear to act more aggressively because such behavior is encouraged by their families as important for obtaining their civil rights (Grossman, 1995). Although differences in accepted behavior between home and school are probably experienced by all children, it may be easier for children without disabilities to learn when, where, and with whom they can engage in certain behaviors without getting into trouble.

Discipline   Families not only select different behaviors to encourage or discourage in children but also vary how children are disciplined. Families may reward desired behavior in extravagant and highly visible ways or resort to very subtle means of teaching the behavior. How families discipline children for exhibiting certain behaviors also varies by family. Some families may prefer to use guilt or loss of privileges as a consequence for misbehavior. Some African American, Asian, and Hispanic families may discipline their children in traditional ways that contradict the mainstream practices of the school program. In these families, punishment in the form of spankings, yelling, shaming, and isolation may be used to control behavior (Harry, 1992a). What might be considered abusive by members of mainstream American culture may be viewed as an expression of love or duty by parents in other cultures. For example, when a child misbehaves, families from Southeast Asia may pierce his ear to tether him to a doorknob, while others may lock their children outside for neglecting their responsibilities to the family (McIntyre & Silva, 1992, cited in Sileo & Prater, 1998). The manner in which children are taught to behave within their families will play a major role in their expectations of and responses to guidance at school. For example, if children expect adults to yell at or punish them when they engage in inappropriate behavior, then they may perceive anything they do as being acceptable if it does not elicit a loud reprimand or physical punishment. Similarly, the methods that families use to discipline their children will influence their participation in the development and implementation of behavior support plans. Service providers will need to identify ways to discuss proposed alternatives to physical discipline with families and to enlist their agreement to try alternative approaches (Forehand & Kotchick, 1996).

IMPLICATIONS FOR SERVICE PROVIDERS

For PBS to be both effective and efficient, service providers must acquire some understanding of the culture of the families with whom they work. A lack of cultural awareness and understanding can lead to difficulties in identifying behaviors of concern and the contexts in which they occur, in developing the necessary trust and rapport between family and service provider, and, ultimately, in providing timely and effective intervention. The following example involving a family from the Middle East highlights these difficulties:

> Ahmed's parents expressed a concern to a special educator regarding the 8-year-old's bedwetting. Accustomed to hearing about such problems for children with developmental disabilities, the special educator immediately suggested the use of special bed sheets to protect the bed and a systematic intervention plan to teach Ahmed to use the bathroom. The service provider later discovered that the parents and two children slept together in one bed and that it was considered inappropriate for children to sleep by themselves. The special educator had assumed that Ahmed slept in his own bed and in his own bedroom, and, therefore, did not recognize the full extent of the problem for the family. Ahmed's bedwetting was a more serious problem for all family members and was interfering with everyone's sleep. An immediate plan of action was needed.

In this example, the service provider had assumed that the family operated in a manner similar to her own culture and, thus, could not fully understand the depth of the problem for the family. Also, little understanding or rapport was present between the service provider and family. This may have accounted for the family's reticence to disclose their sleeping arrangement, and for the service provider's recommendation of a somewhat superficial intervention strategy (i.e., getting special sheets). Furthermore, this "strategy" simply delayed the discovery of a more effective intervention strategy for the family. This example illustrates how lack of knowledge about a family's cultural practices can interfere with effective intervention for problem behaviors in family contexts. To avoid this difficulty, service providers should invest time in getting to know and understand the families they serve, especially when the family represents a culture that is different from their own.

Overcoming Stereotypes

Although certain characteristics may be influenced by a family's particular cultural background, each family must be regarded as an individual and unique system. Making assumptions about a family's values and practices based merely on their cultural background can seriously interfere with effective collaboration. For example, not all Chinese families follow the traditional roles and responsibilities previously described. There is as much variation within any cultural group as there is between different groups. Thus, service providers should avoid stereotypes and get to know each member as an individual and each family as a unique system (Chen, Brekken, & Chan, 1997). Being aware of one's own biases and of the potential to stereotype family behavior is an important safeguard against treating families as cultural stereotypes. Gathering information about a family's roles and responsibilities, perspectives on disability, and child-rearing practices can contribute to an individualized and culturally responsive behavior support process.

Understanding Differences in Communication Styles

Typically, conducting a functional assessment and developing a behavior support plan involves probing questions and frank discussion about the family members' concerns, their child's behaviors, and contextual influences on behavior. Some families from Hispanic, Native American, and Asian backgrounds, however, may be offended by this approach to gathering information (Chan, 1998; Correa, 1987; Harry, 1992a; Orlansky & Trap, 1987). Families who were oppressed by authorities in their former countries may be reluctant to share information about their family with school or agency personnel (Ishii-Jordan & Peterson, 1994; Lowenthal, 1996). Some parents need to consult with extended family members before making decisions about a behavior support plan or other interventions. These examples suggest that service providers should first learn about the family's preferences related to sharing information and making decisions, then tailor their communication style to accommodate these cultural differences. Service providers can gain information on a family's preferred ways of communicating by 1) reflecting carefully on previous interactions (e.g., "How has the family participated in previous interactions?"); 2) asking other service providers about their experiences in serving the family (e.g., "Is there anything that you found to be helpful in working with this family?"); 3) asking the family directly, if appropriate (e.g. "Where would you like to meet?" "Who would you like at the meeting?" "What would be the best way for me to contact you?"); or 4) consulting with a cultural mediator, when available (e.g., "What would be the best way for me to learn about the child's learning needs and the family's concerns?").

Research also indicates that families from diverse cultures prefer individual and informal contacts with service providers rather than formal meetings (Harry, 1992a; Harry, Allen, & McLaughlin, 1995; Sileo et al., 1996). Moreover, families tend to trust service providers who are viewed as help providers rather than as agency representatives (Chan, 1990; Harry, 1992a, 1994). These findings suggest the need for service providers to develop relationships with families by identifying ways to interact individually with families. For example, the annual review of a child's individualized education program is a very formal meeting that usually involves a number of service providers and the signing of documents. In contrast, contacting families by telephone, making home visits, and working together on a shared activity are informal contacts that provide ongoing opportunities for a service provider to develop a trusting relationship with families. Through these interactions, families can recognize a service provider as an individual help provider rather than as an agency representative.

Cultural differences in the meanings of nonverbal communication can also lead to misunderstandings between families and service providers. For example, a service provider may be bothered by a parent's lack of eye contact during an interaction and attribute this behavior to a lack of involvement or respect, without understanding that eye contact is offensive in some cultures (Axtell, 1991; Chan, 1998; Dresser, 1996; Sileo & Prater,1998). Thus, service providers may misinterpret a parent's respectful behavior (i.e., averting eye contact) as disinterest or disrespect. Similarly, a service provider may interpret head nodding as an indication that parents agree to suggested goals and interventions. However, individuals from traditional Asian, Native American, and Middle Eastern cultures may be merely indicating that they are listening to rather than agreeing with the speaker. Consequently, service providers may become frustrated by a family's seeming lack of concern and commitment to their child's education when there is no follow-through at home on suggested interventions. Such misunderstandings may be avoided by learning about the family's communication style, clarifying the roles and expectations of service providers, and discussing what interventions the family is willing to implement at home.

Working with Interpreters

If the service provider does not speak the same language as the family, then a qualified interpreter is essential in the development and implementation of a behavior support plan. Unfortunately, in educational agencies, the majority of individuals in the role of interpreting between English and another language, with the exception of American Sign Language interpreters, have not received formal training.

Although it requires more effort and resources on the part of service organizations to train or locate qualified interpreters, family members (particularly children) should not be placed in the role of interpreting for their families (Arroyo, 1998). Furthermore, in special education services, interpreters not only translate from one language to another but also serve as liaisons or cultural mediators between two cultures (Chen, Chan, & Brekken, 2000; Dennis & Giangreco, 1996). However, service providers should not assume that an interpreter understands the family's culture just because he or she is fluent in the family's language (Arroyo, 1998). Thus, interpreters need specific training to be knowledgeable about the practices and values of both the family and the service system.

It is essential that service providers and interpreters plan together before meeting with the family and then again after the meeting to evaluate the interaction process (Chen et al., 2000; Langdon, 1994). First, service providers should be aware that educational acronyms and jargon are difficult to translate and that terms and procedures related to special education services are unfamiliar concepts to most families and in many cultures. For example, "positive behavior support" might be translated into "strategies for learning positive behavior" for a Spanish-speaking family. Furthermore, the concepts of PBS, functional assessment, antecedent-behavior-consequence (A-B-C) analysis (Bijou, Peterson, & Ault, 1968), and self-injurious behaviors require extensive explanation. Word-for-word translation between English and other languages may be difficult because of vocabulary differences (Chen et al., 2000). For example, in the Hmong language, there is not a word for *plan* so "positive behavior support plan" requires elaborate discussion. Second, service providers should discuss the use of terms related to the student's disability with the interpreter. On the one hand, words related to disability in many languages may seem derogatory by contemporary person-first language standards. On the other hand, some cultures do not even have a word for *disability* (Fowler, 1998). Third, service providers should emphasize professional ethics with the interpreter, including confidentiality. Interpreters may not have received formal training and may not be aware of their ethical responsibilities. They should understand that the interpreter does not participate in the conversation other than to provide accurate interpretation. Fourth, service providers should inform the interpreter when emotional issues, such as the diagnosis of a child's disability, will be discussed with the family. For example, the service provider and interpreter should discuss what might happen if the parent becomes extremely emotional, angry, or aggressive. In this way, both the service provider and the interpreter will be more prepared for the meeting. For their part, interpreters can assist service providers in knowing how to address family members, how to ask questions, and how to promote family participation in problem solving. Furthermore, by learning key phrases in the family's language, such as greetings, service providers can demonstrate respect for the families they serve (Correa, 1987; Hyun & Fowler, 1995).

Recruiting Bilingual/Bicultural Staff

Programs need not only qualified interpreters but also bilingual/bicultural staff to serve as cultural mediators as well as to serve families directly (Chan, 1990; Cleveland & Meyers, 1994; Harry, 1992a; Vincent, 1992; Yonemitsu & Cleveland, 1992). Agencies and service providers should consider how they can recruit and train qualified bilingual/bicultural staff to collaborate with families in the development and implementation of quality educational programs, including behavior support plans. A number of programs in other aspects of special education services have reported success in recruiting, training, and supporting bilingual/bicultural staff to work effectively with Puerto Rican families (Harry, 1992a); Spanish-speaking families (Vincent, 1992); Chinese, Korean, and Vietnamese families (Chan, 1990); and Cambodian, Hmong, Laotian, and Vietnamese families (Cleveland & Meyers, 1994; Yonemitsu & Cleveland, 1992).

STRATEGIES FOR DEVELOPING COLLABORATIVE RELATIONSHIPS WITH FAMILIES

Designing behavior support plans begins with getting to know the child, the immediate family, and, if relevant, extended family and friends. This process may take up to several weeks to complete but serves as the foundation to all subsequent interactions and activities. The importance of this step cannot be overstated and should be discussed carefully with families. During this phase, information is obtained about the structure of the family and its concerns and priorities, child-rearing practices, communication style, and expectations of service providers. The appendix at the end of this chapter outlines questions to assist service providers in gathering this type of information.

Some families, however, may find this process difficult to understand. For example, some families may be concerned that the service provider is not providing an immediate solution to the behavior problem. Others may even view the service provider's questions and hesitation to tell them what to do as a sign of incompetence. Some families also may be disturbed by the questions that are asked. To address these concerns, the purpose of the assessment process must clearly be explained. Emphasis should be placed on explaining that the process is a collective effort in which the family and the service provider work together to design an effective support plan. The service provider should also stress the critical role of the family members for developing a plan that makes sense to them and their child. Once the assessment process is explained, service providers can involve families by working with them to design an assessment plan. One strategy is to first obtain information about when problem behaviors are most problematic. This can help determine when, where, and how assessment information will be obtained. For example, a family may explain that problem behaviors are most troubling during trips to the grocery store. Given this, functional assessment observations may be limited to observing the child and family in this community environment. Yet, a family may report that problem behaviors occur across many different environments but express discomfort in having outsiders observe during certain family routines. In this case, observations may be arranged during carefully selected family contexts, and alternative data collection techniques (e.g., family videotapes, journals/daily logs, frequency count data sheets) may be used at other times. By collaboratively developing an assessment plan, both the family's concern for immediate action and the service provider's need to gather relevant information are addressed.

Everyone concerned with supporting the student at school, at home, or in the community should be considered a member of the support team. Nevertheless, family members typically will be more knowledgeable about what behaviors to expect and under what conditions. Collaboration between families and service providers is strongly supported in the literature (Dunlap & Fox, 1996; Lucyshyn & Albin, 1993; Turnbull & Turnbull, 1997; Vaughn, Dunlap, Fox, Clarke, & Bucy, 1997). Developing collaborative relationships takes time, communication, and effort. Collaborative relationships are achieved when all members of the team are perceived and treated as active and equal partners (Turnbull & Turnbull, 1997). However, establishing collaborative partnerships can be complicated and difficult to achieve. Differences in cultural backgrounds may further challenge this process (Harry, 1992a; Sileo et al., 1996; Turnbull & Turnbull, 1997; Walker & Singer, 1993). Some families may view the development and implementation of a behavior support plan with their child at home as the service provider's role and do not understand why they should be involved. For example, families from traditional Asian and Pacific Islander backgrounds typically rely on service providers and on their opinions to develop and implement programs that address their children's behavioral needs (Sileo & Prater, 1988).

Similarly, other researchers have noted that some families from Hispanic backgrounds view professionals as the experts and, therefore, assume passive roles in their interactions with them (Harry, 1992a; Harry & Kalyanpur, 1994). For instance, Harry (1992a) reported that Puerto Rican mothers often did not speak up during discussions concerning school placement and curricular issues, even though they held strong opinions regarding these matters. Similar patterns were found among Mexican American parents, who viewed educational decision making as the school's responsibility (Lynch & Stein, 1987). Furthermore, Ryan and Smith (1989) reported that Chinese American families in their study did not actively seek information related to their child's disability. The authors explained that many Chinese American families possess a strong deference to authority and expect others (e.g., health care professionals) to provide direction.

The service provider needs to enlist the family's involvement by explaining the family's essential role in the support process. For collaborative relationships to develop, service providers must first be aware of their own values and beliefs; acknowledge those of families, even if they are different or in conflict with their own; and find ways to resolve any differences in perspectives.

Providing Help That Is Helpful

To provide help that is actually helpful to families of diverse cultures, the service provider must be sensitive to cultural issues; work closely with families to address the concerns that they consider important; and design behavior support plans that will fit the family's values, beliefs, and practices. It is the family who ultimately decides what is helpful, so service providers must listen to what families want and work with them to find strategies that they will use. In this way, service providers will provide more culturally responsive and useful support. Albin, Lucyshyn, Horner, and Flannery (1996) emphasized the need to design support plans that fit within the contexts in which they will be implemented. As these authors noted, it is not helpful to design a support plan, no matter how technically correct, if the plan is not implemented. Support plans that are in conflict with the values of the people responsible for implementing the plan are not likely to be implemented. This concept of contextual fit is especially important when working with families from diverse cultures and backgrounds. Differences in how families view disabilities, child-rearing practices, and communication styles can serve as potential challenges to providing effective support.

One of the first steps to providing behavioral support for children and their families is, on the basis of the family's needs and wishes, deciding who should provide the support and how it should be provided. Service providers from Anglo-European backgrounds should understand that families from other cultures may need more time to become comfortable with them (Allen & Majidi-Ahi, 1989; Correa, 1987; Lowenthal, 1996). Furthermore, although service providers may assume the primary support role initially, research with families suggests that adequate and satisfactory social support networks play an important role in a family's adaptability to a child's disability (Albanese, San Miguel, & Koegel, 1995; Singer & Irvin, 1991). In addition, some families may rely primarily on natural support networks, such as family members, friends, and community. Traditional Hispanic families, for example, may enlist outside professional help only as a last resort (Harry, 1992b; Sileo et al., 1996; Zuniga, 1998).

Developing social support may be especially helpful for families with a child who exhibits significant behavioral challenges. These families may feel isolated from their friends, extended family, and/or communities. This may be especially true if the child's problem behaviors are so disruptive that family members stop involving the child in typical family and community activities (Fox, Vaughn, Dunlap, & Bucy, 1997). Some families may have recently immigrated and be without extended family or friends. Developing social supports may include helping the family reconnect with the natural supports of friends and family, when available, and/or helping the family connect with community resources, such as the child's school, religious affiliations, parent support programs, advocacy groups, or other community organizations. An assessment that identifies current and past support systems will help in the selection of appropriate resources and supports for families from diverse cultural backgrounds.

The second and perhaps more significant challenge that service providers face is providing support that is meaningful; productive; and respectful of a family's wishes, cultural and religious values, and lifestyle. Albin and colleagues (1996) identified three important considerations for designing behavior support plans that fit the context in which they will be implemented: 1) environment(s) in which the support plan will be used, 2) the characteristics of the individual for whom the plan is designed, and 3) the variables associated with the people who are responsible for implementation. The need to address cultural fit is shown in the following example:

Tien was a 16-year-old Vietnamese student who attended his local high school. He lived with his parents, grandparents, and five brothers and sisters. Tien was shy, had a great smile, followed some simple two-step directions, could count to 5, and said approximately six words in English. He had been given a special education label of "severely disabled." When he was upset or frustrated, Tien could become extremely aggressive and out of control.

A home–school conflict arose over Tien's behavior at mealtimes. The teacher at school informed the family that Tien refused to eat his lunch and would throw it at the teacher, an aide, or other students. When asked to pick it up, Tien hit, kicked, and screamed at others. School staff wanted to implement a behavioral intervention plan, and they wanted the parents to continue it at home. The parents and grandparents, however, could not understand the staff's difficulty with Tien at lunchtime. They had not experienced this at home and saw no real reason for a behavioral intervention plan. Frustration and misunderstandings were developing between the family and the school staff.

Tien's teacher and an interpreter asked to visit the family during dinner. After observing Tien at home, a possible explanation for his behavior at school became clear. At home, sticky rice was a staple food eaten at all meals—with the fingers, not with utensils. At school, although Tien had rice to eat, he had been made to eat it with a spoon or fork. Thus, Tien was allowed to eat his food like he did at home—with his fingers. The behavior problems immediately ceased. Given Tien's limited ability to explain what he found to be so frustrating (i.e., being required to eat with utensils), he resorted to a clearer way of communicating his preferences. Understanding cultural differences surrounding meal etiquette clarified the situation for everyone and resulted in a simple modification that made Tien's aggressive behavior unnecessary.

In summary, to provide help that is truly helpful to a family, service providers should consider the following:

1. Take the time to be aware of one's own values and beliefs and be open to other views as well. Be aware of differences in cultural perspectives and identify potential sources of conflict.

2. Respect the family's need to take more time to become comfortable with service providers from different cultures and backgrounds. Pace interactions accordingly.

3. Listen carefully to families about what is helpful and what is not. Follow their lead.

4. Respond to what the family defines as the problem.

5. Design support plans that fit within the family's values, beliefs and lifestyle. Involve family members in all aspects of designing the support plan (assessment through plan development and implementation support) to ensure that their goals and priorities are addressed.

6. During assessment, identify existing or potentially new natural supports and resources and assist families, as needed, to establish new support networks.

7. Develop supports for the whole family, not just for the child with a disability.

Culturally Responsive Practices During Functional Assessment and Positive Behavior Support Plan Development

To ensure that the support plan fits with the family's culture and lifestyle, culturally responsive practices should be incorporated into all phases of PBS. Specific considerations and practices are discussed next for completing a functional assessment and for developing a behavior support plan. Two vignettes, representing families from diverse cultural and linguistic backgrounds, illustrate how to include culturally responsive practices in PBS.

Functional Assessment   Designing a behavior support plan begins with gathering relevant information about the child and the people in his or her life. For families from culturally diverse backgrounds, information concerning the family's ecology (e.g., customs, child-rearing practices, communication style) should be gathered prior to or concurrent with the completion of a functional assessment (see the appendix at the end of this chapter). The previous example of the Middle Eastern parents who struggled with their son's bedwetting problem highlights the importance of gathering information that is related to family practices. In that example, information about the family's sleeping arrangements was essential for designing a support plan that fit the family's beliefs and lifestyle.

Although the basic steps involved in a functional assessment are the same for all families (e.g., complete a functional assessment interview, conduct observations to confirm hypotheses, determine the functions of problem behavior), certain cultural and linguistic differences among families may alter how information is collected and analyzed. Because language is culture bound, some words and phrases may connote very different meanings in different cultures. Misunderstanding the intent of a question or the meaning of a word can lead to misconceptions, which can in turn affect the gathering of accurate information. For example, in an effort to gather information about a child's skills during an interview with her parents, a service provider asked, "What gifts does your daughter have?" These parents responded, "She has no gifts." It is clear from this example that the parents misunderstood the intent of the question (i.e., to identify the child's strengths). Failure to recognize this miscommunication can lead service providers to draw incorrect conclusions about the child and family (e.g., the child has no skills, the parents cannot see their child's strengths).

To avoid cultural misunderstandings, service providers should take the time required to engage in a mutually informative conversation with the family about the child's problem behaviors and the family's ecology. During assessment activities, service providers should use easily understood words, define terms, clarify what is meant by questions asked, and verify the true intent of family responses. To this end, service providers should design interview and follow-up questions to ensure more accurate and culturally sensitive communication with families. As discussed previously, understanding the family's communication style and planning with an interpreter can greatly enhance the quality of interactions between service providers and families from diverse cultural and linguistic backgrounds.

Behavior Support Plan Development   Information obtained from the functional assessment is used to design the behavior support plan, which includes strategies to build and strengthen adaptive behaviors as well as to reduce problem behaviors. This requires intervention strategies that focus on what the child is and is not supposed to do as well as specify how the family and other team members will support the child (O'Neill et al., 1997). During this stage, family input is imperative. Information from family members regarding their goals for the child (e.g., follow simple directions, remain cooperative in the grocery store) and their family life (e.g., sleep through the night undisturbed, attend an entire church service together as a family) should guide the plan development process. O'Neill and colleagues discussed using strategies that result in making problem behaviors "irrelevant, inefficient, and ineffective" (p. 66). One or all of these intervention strategies may be used, depending on the child's needs and the family's willingness to implement different strategies.

Again, it is important to remember that when developing behavior support plans with families, special attention must be paid to designing interventions that are consistent with cultural patterns and lifestyles. Proponents of ecocultural theory suggest using the activity settings of daily routines as the unit of analysis in understanding family ecology (Gallimore, Weisner, Bernheimer, Guthrie, & Nihira, 1993; Gallimore, Weisner, Kaufman, & Bernheimer, 1989). Thus, during assessment activities, the service provider asks the family about typical activities in which the child participates at home (e.g. mealtimes, sleeping routines) and in the community (e.g., shopping, leisure routines). The purpose of identifying daily routines is to gain information about which activities are part of the child's family life, how the child currently participates in a given routine, what the family would like to change (if anything), and what resources are currently available to help make that change happen (Albin et al., 1996; Gallimore, Goldenberg, & Weisner, 1993; Lucyshyn & Albin, 1993). This information then can be used to design interventions that match the environmental and cultural features of each routine. Furthermore, support strategies that can be incorporated into established family routines are more likely to be implemented consistently over time, thus increasing the likelihood that meaningful change will occur.

Information about daily routines was imperative in designing culturally responsive interventions for Tien at school and for Ahmed and his family at home. For Tien, the assessment revealed that the family's mealtime routine included eating rice with one's fingers instead of utensils. Furthermore, the assessment revealed that all members of Tien's immediate and extended family ate this way, signifying a practice that was both important as well as culturally appropriate for this family. By respecting this cultural practice, Tien was allowed to eat with his fingers at school and the problem behavior was eliminated. Similarly, an assessment of Ahmed's daily routines disclosed that in this family, children and parents slept together in one bed. This family's bedtime routine involved all members of the family and represented a strong cultural belief that it is inappropriate for children to sleep by themselves. Given this information, traditional program strategies such as protective sheets and moisture detector alarms proved to be inappropriate.

IN-DEPTH VIGNETTES

The points discussed in the previous section are further illustrated by the following in-depth vignettes.

Emilio

Emilio was a 5-year-old Hispanic American boy who lived with his mother, father, 6-year-old sister, and 8-year-old brother. Emilio also had a large extended family, including a grandmother, aunts, uncles, and cousins. He was diagnosed with autism and was nonverbal. Emilio responded to some verbal directions (when motivated) and expressed himself through facial expressions, vocalizations and screams, gestures, objects, and pointing to pictures. He was very active, moving quickly from one activity to another. Emilio used pictures to communicate his interests and preferences. He attended a kindergarten class in his neighborhood school.

Situation   Emilio had difficulty following directions at home, at school, and in the community. He was also very impulsive and had a hard time handling materials in an appropriate manner. The primary problem, however, was that Emilio screamed loudly for several minutes when he did not want to do something and refused to do as he was told, especially during community outings. Emilio's father did not believe that his wife was strict enough with Emilio. He wanted her to clearly establish limits for Emilio. Emilio's teacher had similar problems with Emilio's behavior.

Hypothesis   The information collected at home and at school led to a plausible hypothesis. It was proposed that Emilio engaged in screaming behavior to escape an undesired activity. He also refused to follow directions for this same purpose, especially when he was asked to make a transition from a preferred activity.

Cultural Considerations   Emilio's father was clearly the head of the family. Although loving and concerned, he was strict with all the children and assumed the role of disciplinarian in the family. Emilio's father maintained that all his son needed for following directions was a stern, loud voice and physical guidance. Emilio's mother was soft spoken and deferred to her husband on all issues, but she did not feel comfortable with his approach to Emilio's challenging behavior. Furthermore, as Emilio's father worked at two jobs, it was Emilio's mother who spent the majority of time with the children. Although she had her extended family for support, Emilio's behavior made it difficult for these family members to offer much help. In addition, Emilio's screaming intensified when they were running errands in the community, and his mother found this very embarrassing. Given the family's values and practices, the service provider did not suggest that the father's approach was ineffective in helping Emilio learn appropriate behavior. Such a discussion would have destroyed any chance of building a partnership with Emilio's parents by 1) alienating the father from the service provider and any proposal for a behavior support plan and 2) placing the mother in the uncomfortable position of being disloyal to her husband if she tried the service provider's alternative suggestions. Consequently, the service provider needed to design strategies that would be helpful for Emilio and respectful of his father.

Behavioral Support Strategies   A simple picture schedule was devised for Emilio to use at home, at school, and in the community. The schedule was shown to him a few minutes before he had to make a transition (e.g., leaving home to go to the store). This procedure was implemented so that Emilio would have some idea of what was expected and could prepare himself for the change. Activities that Emilio disliked (e.g., helping to pick up his clothes) were interspersed with those he preferred (e.g., playing with toy cars) to improve his cooperation throughout the day. Whenever possible, Emilio was given a choice in daily living tasks (e.g., "Do you want to pick up your clothes or put your toys away?") and recreational activities (e.g., "Do you want to play with trucks, puzzles, or a Frisbee outside?") so that he had greater control over his activities.

Outcomes   After the behavioral support strategies had been consistently implemented for a month, Emilio learned to look at his schedule to see what activity was next.

Although he still screamed occasionally, his family reported that the frequency, duration, and intensity of this behavior had definitely decreased. Using pictures to help him make choices also appeared to be effective in reducing problem behavior. Emilio still displayed a very limited attention span and a strong need to move around, but offering him choices and giving him some control in situations appeared to have a calming effect. His siblings and cousins also had success in supporting Emilio when they used his picture schedule and pictorial/object choices. Emilio still screamed during community outings, but his family reported a decrease in the frequency, duration, and intensity of this behavior as well. During community outings, Emilio's mother brought highly desired toys to help keep him occupied, used his schedule, and kept outings as focused and short as possible. The program's success was related to both parents' agreement to use the picture schedule with Emilio and to provide choices. Furthermore, they believed this strategy fit fairly well into their family's daily life. In this way, the service provider was able to provide PBS that was culturally responsive to Emilio's family.

Tara

Tara, a 10-year-old with severe disabilities, was the only child of an Iranian couple. Tara attended public school and was fully included in her fourth-grade class. She had very limited speech, and she spoke mostly in Farsi. She liked exploring, being active, and being with other children.

Situation   Tara's parents reported that she often yelled to go to the bathroom throughout the night. They placed a great deal of emphasis on Tara's speech development, which was severely delayed. Therefore, her parents always responded to her requests by taking her to the bathroom, regardless of whether she had to use the toilet. They said that sometimes she simply played with the water at the sink. Her assistant at school also reported that Tara often stood up in class and yelled "bathroom" in Farsi. When the assistant took Tara to the bathroom, Tara frequently did not need to use it but instead tried to play with water in the sink. The assistant believed that the yelling behavior was a result of Tara's desire to escape classwork. Unfortunately, Tara's parents' prompt response to her loud demands to go to the bathroom at night not only interrupted their sleep but also may have contributed to yelling in the classroom. School personnel had no problem refusing Tara's repeated shouts to go to the bathroom when they were confident that she did not really need to go, but her parents felt differently. They wanted the teaching assistant to respond to Tara's demands to use the bathroom by taking her there despite the amount of time it would take away from her classwork.

Hypothesis   Given Tara's behavior in the bathroom (i.e., playing with the water), the team hypothesized that her request to go to the bathroom was a way to escape what she was doing (i.e., lying in bed) and to engage in a preferred activity (i.e., water play). The assistant who worked with Tara at school confirmed that yelling "bathroom" occurred when Tara was engaged in something that she did not like doing.

Cultural Considerations   Tara was the only child of two highly educated, professional parents who were devoted to their child. They were very concerned about her developmental delays, especially her lack of formal language. Although they did not like getting up frequently at night to respond to Tara's demands to use the bathroom, they believed that they were supporting her speech development by honoring all of her communicative efforts. They thought it was wrong to ignore these requests. Although both parents spoke English, it was their second language and they spoke Farsi at home. Tara's receptive and expressive communication skills appeared to be better in Farsi than in English. Therefore, they were uncomfortable ignoring any of her requests in Farsi.

Behavioral Support Strategies   As part of the assessment and plan design process, it was imperative to listen to what the family identified as important and to what they would and would not do as part of a behavior support plan. Tara's parents perceived her lack of speech as being a far more serious problem than her yelling during the night. A way to teach Tara to obtain what she wanted in a more accurate and conventional manner was needed. To help Tara be more specific in her communicative attempts, her parents agreed that they would respond to her calls to go to the bathroom, but once there, they only would allow Tara to use the toilet. She was no longer allowed to play in the water at the sink. Washing her hands was carefully controlled so that it did not involve any play time. In this manner, her parents believed that they still were supporting her communicative efforts. At various times during the day, her parents asked Tara if she wanted to play in some water. To avoid confusion, they allowed her to play outside in a wading pool or inside at the kitchen sink, not in the bathroom. School personnel also made the same distinction. When Tara asked for the bathroom, she was taken there but was not allowed to play in the water. There was a sink in the classroom, so the teaching staff gave Tara the break option of playing in the sink for a few minutes. Her parents and teachers used a picture card that said PLAY WATER to help Tara request this if she could not recall the actual spoken words. Tara was reminded of the card and shown how to use it during the day (e.g., touch it or give it to someone). If she asked to go to the bathroom, she was shown both a picture card for the bathroom and one for playing in water, and she was asked to make a choice between the two cards. When possible, she was allowed to play in the water if she chose the PLAY WATER card. When this was not possible, Tara was told that she could not play in water and was offered choices of other desired activities instead.

Outcomes   Within 2 weeks, Tara's yelling to go to the bathroom decreased considerably. In addition, she increased her use of the pictorial cards to indicate what she wanted. After 2 months, her parents and school staff reported further decreases in the frequency of yelling. During plan implementation, Tara's parents noticed that this behavior occurred most frequently right after she was put to bed, then again at around 2:00 A.M. Given this pattern, they sought medication to help regulate and increase Tara's sleep behavior. They also made adjustments in the amount and type of food she ate prior to bedtime. These additional interventions may have contributed to the overall success of the plan. Tara's behavior support plan demonstrates the importance of listening carefully to the family's priorities and developing interventions that address these concerns.

CONCLUSION

Cultural influences can have a profound influence on the interactions between families and service providers and in developing educational programs for children with disabilities. This chapter has sought to highlight this impact in an attempt to facilitate family–professional collaboration, especially with regard to behavior support plans. The chapter has discussed the incredible cultural and linguistic diversity of the United States and the influence of cultural perspectives on child-rearing practices, perspectives on disability, and family systems. This rich diversity requires that service providers recognize and overcome culturally based stereotypes, develop effective ways of communicating with families, and work with interpreters and cultural mediators to serve families more effectively and respectfully. There is no one correct way to interact with all families of a given culture, as each family has its own unique qualities and goals. Service providers can provide more effective services to families from diverse linguistic and cultural backgrounds by listening carefully to each family's needs and concerns; demonstrating the respect entitled to any family; and recognizing one's own cultural beliefs, biases, and values. Providing effective services to families involves a delicate balance between professional judgment and the family's values, beliefs, and practices. In this way, service providers can promote true partnerships with families in developing culturally responsive behavior support plans that are truly helpful to families and their children.

REFERENCES

Albanese, A.L., San Miguel, S.K., & Koegel, R.L. (1995). Social support for families. In R.L. Koegel & L.K. Koegel (Eds.), *Teaching children with autism: Strategies for initiating positive interactions and improving learning opportunities* (pp. 95–104). Baltimore: Paul H. Brookes Publishing Co.

Albin, R.W., Lucyshyn, J.M., Horner, R.H., & Flannery, K.B. (1996). Contextual fit for behavioral support plans: A model for "goodness of fit." In L.K. Koegel, R.L. Koegel, & G. Dunlap (Eds.), *Positive behavioral support: Including people with difficult behavior in the community* (pp. 81–98). Baltimore: Paul H. Brookes Publishing Co.

Allen, L., & Majidi-Ahi, S. (1989). Black American children. In J. Taylor & L. Huang-Nahame (Eds.), *Children of color: Psychological interventions with minority youth* (pp. 148–178). San Francisco: Jossey-Bass.

Alvarez, L.I.G. (1998). A short course in sensitivity training: Working with Hispanic families of children with disabilities. *Teaching Exceptional Children, 31,* 73–77.

Arroyo, W. (1998). Immigrant children and families. In M. Hernandez & M.R. Isaacs (Eds.), *Promoting cultural competence in children's mental health services* (pp. 251–268). Baltimore: Paul H. Brookes Publishing Co.

Axtell, R.E. (1991). *The do's and taboos of body language around the world.* New York: John Wiley & Sons.

Bijou, S.W., Peterson, R.F., & Ault, M.H. (1968). A method to integrate descriptive and experimental field studies at the level of data and empirical concepts. *Journal of Applied Behavior Analysis, 1,* 175–191.

Census: Languages not foreign at home. (1993, April 28). *USA Today,* p. 1A.

Chan, S. (1990). Early intervention with culturally diverse families of infants and toddlers with disabilities. *Infants and Young Children, 3,* 78–87.

Chan, S. (1998). Families with Asian roots. In E.W. Lynch & M.J. Hanson (Eds.), *Developing cross-cultural competence: A guide for working with children and their families* (2nd. ed., pp. 251–354). Baltimore: Paul H. Brookes Publishing Co.

Chen, D., Brekken, L., & Chan, S. (1997). *Project CRAFT: Culturally responsive and family-focused training* [video and booklet]. Baltimore: Paul H. Brookes Publishing Co.

Chen, D., Chan, S., & Brekken, L. (2000). *Conversations for three: Communicating through interpreters* [video and booklet]. Baltimore: Paul H. Brookes Publishing Co.

Chung, E.L. (1996). Asian Americans. In M.C. Julia (Ed), *Multicultural awareness in the health care professions* (pp. 77–110). Needham Heights, MA: Allyn & Bacon.

Cleveland, J.O., & Meyers, D.N. (1994). *Cultural aspects of southeast Asian refugee families. Guidelines for effective health intervention.* San Diego: San Diego Imperial Counties Developmental Services, Southeast Asian Developmental Disabilities Project (SEADD).

Correa, V.I. (1987). Working with Hispanic parents of visually impaired children: Cultural implications. *Journal of Visual Impairment and Blindness, 81,* 260–264.

Dennis, R.E., & Giangreco, M.F. (1996). Creating conversation: Reflections on cultural sensitivity in family interviewing. *Exceptional Children, 63,* 103–116.

Dresser, N. (1996). *Multicultural manners. New rules of etiquette for a changing society.* New York: John Wiley & Sons.

Dunlap, G., & Fox, L. (1996). Early intervention and serious problem behaviors: A comprehensive approach. In L.K. Koegel, R.L. Koegel, & G. Dunlap (Eds.), *Positive behavioral support: Including people with difficult behavior in the community* (pp. 31–50). Baltimore: Paul H. Brookes Publishing Co.

Forehand, R., & Kotchick, B.A. (1996). Cultural diversity: A wake-up call for parent training. *Behavior Therapy, 27,* 187–206.

Fowler, L. (1998). Native American communities. A more inclusive society? *TASH Newsletter, 24,* 21–22.

Fox, L., Vaughn, B.J., Dunlap, G., & Bucy, M. (1997). Parent–professional partnership in behavioral support: A qualitative analysis of one family's experience. *Journal of The Association for Persons with Severe Disabilities, 22,* 198–207.

Gallimore, R., Goldenberg, C.N., & Weisner, T. S. (1993). The social construction and subjective reality of activity settings: Implications for community psychology. *American Journal of Community Psychology, 21,* 537–559.

Gallimore, R., Weisner, T.S., Bernheimer, L.P., Guthrie, D., & Nihira, K. (1993). Family responses to young children with developmental delays: Accommodation activity in ecological and cultural context. *American Journal on Mental Retardation, 98,* 185–206.

Gallimore, R., Weisner, T.S., Kaufman, S.Z., & Bernheimer, L.P. (1989). The social construction of ecocultural niches: Family accommodation of developmentally delayed children. *American Journal on Mental Retardation, 94,* 216–230.

Gollnick, D.M., & Chinn, P.C. (1994). *Multicultural education in a pluralistic society* (4th ed.). New York: Macmillan.

Groce, N.E., & Zola, I.K. (1993). Multiculturalism, chronic illness, and disability. *Pediatrics, 91,* 1048–1055.

Grossman, H. (1995). *Classroom behavior management in a diverse society* (2nd. ed.). Mountain View, CA: Mayfield Publishing.

Haedden, S. (1995, September 25). One nation, one language? *U.S. News & World Report, 119*(12), 38–42.

Hanson, M.J. (1998). Families with Anglo-European roots. In E.W. Lynch & M.J. Hanson (Eds.), *Developing cross-cultural competence: A guide for working with children and their families* (2nd. ed., pp. 93–126). Baltimore: Paul H. Brookes Publishing Co.

Hanson, M.J., Lynch, E.W., & Wayman, K.L. (1990). Honoring the cultural diversity of families when gathering data. *Topics in Early Childhood Education, 10,* 112–131.

Harry, B. (1992a). *Cultural diversity, families, and the special education system: Communication and empowerment.* New York: Teachers College Press.

Harry, B. (1992b). Making sense of disability: Low income, Puerto Rican parents theories of the problem. *Exceptional Children, 59,* 27–40.

Harry, B. (1994). Behavioral disorders in the context of families. *Multicultural issues in the education of students with behavioral disorders* (pp. 149–161). Cambridge, MA: Brookline Books.

Harry, B., Allen, N., & McLaughlin, M. (1995). Communication versus compliance: African-American parents' involvement in special education. *Exceptional Children, 61,* 364–377.

Harry, B., & Kalyanpur, M. (1994). Cultural underpinnings of special education: Implications for professional interactions with culturally diverse families. *Disability & Society, 9,* 145–165.

Hodgkinson, H.L. (1992). *A demographic look tomorrow.* Washington, DC: Institute for Educational Leadership, Center for Demographic Policy.

Hyun, J.K., & Fowler, S.A. (1995). Respect, cultural sensitivity, and communication. *Teaching Exceptional Children, 28,* 24–28.

Individuals with Disabilities Education Act Amendments of 1997, PL 105-17, 20 U.S.C. §§ 1400 *et seq.*

Ishii-Jordan, S. & Peterson, R.L. (1994). Behavioral disorders in the context of Asian cultures. In R.L. Peterson & S. Ishii-Jordan (Eds.), *Multicultural issues in the education of students with behavioral disorders* (pp. 105–114). Cambridge, MA: Brookline Books.

Joe, J.R., & Malach, R.S. (1998). Families with Native American roots. In E.W. Lynch & M.J. Hanson (Eds.), *Developing cross-cultural competence: A guide for working with children and their families* (2nd. ed., pp.127–164). Baltimore: Paul H. Brookes Publishing Co.

Kallam, M., Hoernicke, P.A., & Coser, P.G. (1994). Native Americans and behavioral disorders. *Multicultural issues in the education of students with behavioral disorders* (pp. 126–137). Cambridge, MA: Brookline Books.

Knight, H. (1997). U.S. immigration at highest point since '30s. *Los Angeles Times,* pp. A1, A14.

Kulwicki, A.D. (1996). Arab Americans. In M.C. Julia (Ed.), *Multicultural awareness in the health care professions* (pp. 60–76). Needham Heights, MA: Allyn & Bacon.

Langdon, H.W. (1994). *The interpreter/translator process in the educational setting: A resource manual.* Sacramento, CA: Resources in Special Education.

Loden, M., & Rosener, J.B. (1991). *Workforce America! Managing Employee Diversity as a Vital Resource.* Burr Ridge, IL: McGraw-Hill/Irwin.

Lowenthal, B. (1996). Training early interventionists to work with culturally diverse families. *Infant-Toddler Intervention: The Transdisciplinary Journal, 6,* 145–152.

Lucyshyn, J.M., & Albin, R.W. (1993). Comprehensive support to families of children with disabilities and problem behaviors: Keeping it "friendly." In G.H.S. Singer & L.E. Powers (Eds.), *Families, disability, and empowerment: Active coping skills and strategies for family intervention* (pp. 365–407). Baltimore: Paul H. Brookes Publishing Co.

Lynch, E.W., & Hanson, M.J. (Eds.). (1998). *Developing cross-cultural competence: A guide for working with children and their families* (2nd ed.). Baltimore: Paul H. Brookes Publishing Co.

Lynch, E.W., & Stein, R.C. (1987). Parent participation by ethnicity: A comparison of Hispanic, Black, and Anglo Families. *Exceptional Children, 54,* 105–111.

McIntyre, T., & Silva, P. (1992). Culturally diverse childrearing practices: Abusive or just different? *Beyond Behavior, 4,* 1–11.

O'Neill, R.E., Horner, R.H., Albin, R.W., Sprague, J.R., Storey, K., & Newton, J.S. (1997). *Functional assessment and program development for problem behavior. A practical handbook* (2nd ed.). Pacific Grove, CA: Brooks/Cole Thomson Learning.

Orlansky, M.D., & Trap, J.J. (1987). Working with Native American persons: Issues in facilitating communication and providing culturally relevant services. *Journal of Visual Impairment and Blindness, 81,* 151–155.

Padden, C., & Humpries, T. (1988). *Deaf in America: Voices from a culture.* Cambridge, MA: Harvard University Press.

Robbins, M.J. (1996). Health care provision and the Native American. In M.C. Julia (Ed.). *Multicultural awareness in the health care professions* (pp. 146–165). Needham Heights, MA: Allyn & Bacon.

Ryan, A.S., & Smith, M.J. (1989). Parental reactions to developmental disabilities in Chinese American families. *Child and Adolescent Social Work, 6,* 283–299.

Sharifzadeh, V.S. (1998). Families with Middle Eastern roots. In E.W. Lynch & M.J. Hanson (Eds.), *Developing cross-cultural competence: A guide for working with children and their families* (2nd ed., pp. 441–482). Baltimore: Paul H. Brookes Publishing Co.

Sileo, T.W., & Prater, M.A. (1998). Creating classroom environments that address the linguistic and cultural backgrounds of students with disabilities: An Asian Pacific American perspective. *Remedial and Special Education, 19,* 323–337.

Sileo, T.W., Sileo, A.P., & Prater, M.A. (1996). Parents and professional partnerships in special education: Multicultural considerations. *Intervention in School and Clinic, 3,* 145–153.

Singer, G.H.S., & Irvin, L.K. (1991). Supporting families of persons with severe disabilities: Emerging findings, practices, and questions. In L.H. Meyer, C.A. Peck, & L. Brown (Eds.), *Critical issues in the lives of people with severe disabilities* (pp. 271–312). Baltimore: Paul H. Brookes Publishing Co.

Turnbull, A.P., & Turnbull, H.R. (1997). *Families, professionals and exceptionality: A special partnership* (3rd ed.). Upper Saddle River, NJ: Prentice Hall.

United States Bureau of the Census. (August 27, 2001). U.S. Census Bureau official statistics [On line]. Available: http://www.census.gov/population/estimates/nation/intfile3–1.txt.

Vaughn, B.J., Dunlap, G., Fox, L., Clarke, S., & Bucy, M. (1997). Parent–professional partnership in behavioral support: A case study of community-based intervention. *The Journal of The Association for Persons with Severe Handicaps, 22,* 186–197.

Vincent, L. (1992). Families and early intervention: Diversity and competence. *Journal of Early Intervention, 16,* 166–172.

Walker, B., & Singer, G.H.S. (1993). Improving collaborative communication between professionals and parents. In G.H.S. Singer & L.E. Powers (Eds.), *Families, disability, and empowerment: Active coping skills and strategies for family intervention*s (pp. 285–315). Baltimore: Paul H. Brookes Publishing Co.

Willis, W. (1998). Families with African American roots. In E.W. Lynch & M.J. Hanson (Eds.), *Developing cross-cultural competence: A guide for working with children and their families* (2nd ed., pp. 165–207). Baltimore: Paul H. Brookes Publishing Co.

Yonemitsu, D.M., & Cleveland, J.O. (1992). *Culturally competent service delivery: A training manual for bilingual/bicultural case managers.* San Diego: San Diego Imperial Counties Developmental Services, SEADD.

Zuniga, M.A. (1998). Families with Latino roots. In E.W. Lynch & M.J. Hanson, (Eds.), *Developing cross-cultural competence: A guide for working with children and their families* (2nd ed., pp. 209–250). Baltimore: Paul H. Brookes Publishing Co.

Questions to Guide
Culturally Responsive Practices

To develop effective behavior support plans in partnership with families, service providers need to gather information about the concerns, characteristics, attributes, preferences, and practices of families, as well as to communicate in ways that are clear and respectful. The questions contained in this appendix are intended to guide service providers in their interactions with families from diverse cultural and linguistic backgrounds. Some questions are intended for self-reflection or for discussion with a cultural mediator or interpreter; others are addressed directly to the family, as appropriate.

PLANNING

The first set of questions is designed to help plan for interactions with families. In planning, service providers should identify other service providers who have supported the family or cultural mediators who can provide helpful information; plan with an interpreter, as needed, before meetings and other contacts with the family; and consider how to acknowledge the family's point of view while offering information about the behavior support process. Service providers should ask themselves the following questions regarding planning:

1. How do I learn about the family's interactions and communication styles?

2. How do I ensure that the meaning of words I use are translated accurately from English into the family's language?

3. How will I discuss differences with families when their practices conflict with the program or mainstream values?

FAMILY ASSESSMENT

The second set of questions is designed to help service providers gain culturally relevant information. This information may be gathered indirectly through observations of family interactions and practices or through discussion with cultural mediators. For example, a service provider may see that a family does not wear shoes inside the house and, accordingly, take off his or her shoes before entering that home. In some situations, it may be appropriate to ask the family direct questions regarding how they would like to be addressed, what expectations they have of their children, who makes decisions in the family, and whether there are any cultural practices that they would like service providers to recognize. For example, some families may prefer to be addressed more formally (e.g., Mr., Mrs.), to use titles in addressing the service provider (e.g., Dr.), or to refer to a female service provider as "Auntie," particularly when speaking to the child. Service providers should ask themselves the following questions regarding family assessment:

1. Who are members of the family, including the extended family?

2. What is considered respectful and disrespectful in the family?

3. Who makes decisions in the family?

4. To whom does the family turn for support, assistance, and information?

5. What are the family's values and customs?

6. What are the family's child-rearing practices, forms of discipline, and expectations of children?

7. What are the family's concerns and priorities related to their child with a disability?

8. What community resources can I use to better serve this family?

9. What is the most efficient way for the family to collect data (e.g. writing, videotaping, audiotaping)?

SELF-EVALUATION

The final set of questions is intended to help service providers reflect on their interactions with families and guide the development of a true partnership with families during a process of positive behavior support (PBS). Families and service providers need to be clear about what they expect of each other, and they need information that will enhance their collaboration on the child's support plan. Service providers should ask themselves the following questions regarding self-evaluation:

1. What information do I need to help this family?

2. Have I clarified what the family expects of me and other service providers?

3. Have I discussed the roles and responsibilities of family members and service providers in a process of PBS?

4. Have I provided information on the family's legal rights regarding their child's educational program?

5. Are there any concerns about my interaction with the family that need to be discussed or clarified?

CHAPTER 7

Toward a Synthesis of Family Support Practices and Positive Behavior Support

George H.S. Singer, Sara E. Goldberg-Hamblin,
Kathryn D. Peckham-Hardin, Leasha Barry, and Grace Ellen Santarelli

This chapter provides a rationale for augmenting positive behavior support (PBS) with other interventions designed to assist families. PBS is a young movement, and family support services based on its principles and methods only have recently moved from research into practice. It is important not to repeat service design deficiencies in previous behavioral intervention programs with families. This chapter reviews some lessons learned from more than 30 years of research on behavioral approaches to helping families of children with challenging behavior. The chapter then examines how new ideas and practices can help create programs that avoid previous pitfalls. The review includes studies from the behavioral parent training (BPT) literature because PBS grows out of this research tradition. A body of evidence is presented that shows the limitations of traditional BPT and the benefits of combining it with family-focused supports, which are referred to as *supportive contextual interventions*.

Following this review is a discussion of contemporary, systemic approaches to supporting families that offer ideas and practices that may best fulfill the dual promise of PBS: ameliorating challenging behavior and improving quality of life for people with disabilities and their families. Supportive contextual interventions derive from ecobehavioral intervention programs, the family support movement, wraparound service methods, and other systemic approaches to child and family support. Each of these approaches is discussed. Suggestions follow for combining the elements of these practices to create a multimodal, multisystemic intervention model to help ensure that families receive maximum benefit from home-based positive behavior support services. The chapter also offers examples of how PBS plus supportive contextual interventions can help families implement behavior supports and improve the quality of child and family life. Throughout the chapter, we challenge practitioners of PBS with families to extend their analysis beyond the distal and proximal events that influence problem behavior in the home (i.e., the setting events, antecedents, and consequences that occasion or maintain problem behavior). Although this traditional analysis is necessary for the development of an effective behavior support plan, it may not be sufficient to help families that face contextual barriers to the successful implementation of behavior supports. We argue that the larger context that affects the family needs to be considered and that supportive contextual interventions, grounded in theory and research, need to be included in the array of supports for families.

THE NEED FOR SUPPORTIVE CONTEXTUAL INTERVENTIONS

Supportive contextual interventions are planned, ecological, family-focused methods that help families successfully implement behavior supports with their child and that contribute to an improved quality of life for the child and family. In the BPT literature, these additive methods are typically referred to as *adjunctive treatments.* Examples include problem-solving training, marital counseling, and stress management training (Kazdin, 2001; Sanders, 1996). This phrase from the literature, however, carries certain connotation. The word *adjunctive* implies that the BPT intervention is of foremost importance and additional kinds of assistance are meant primarily to improve training outcomes. Given the lifestyle focus of PBS, this emphasis requires adjustment. Also, we believe that many interventions do not need to be conceptualized as clinical treatments or therapies. They often have more to do with creating supportive social communities, helping families increase enjoyment in their lives, and assisting parents in defining and attaining their families' goals. Consequently, we have changed the term *adjunctive treatments* to *supportive contextual interventions.* We believe that such interventions should equally emphasize overcoming barriers to effective family implementation of behavior support and improving the quality of family life.

Approximately 30% of parents who seek help with their children's challenging behavior do not benefit from traditional BPT unless it is strengthened with supportive interventions that help family members deal with other problems in their lives (Lutzker & Campbell, 1994; Sanders, 1996; Singer & Powers, 1993; Webster-Stratton, 1997). In this chapter, we focus on this group of parents and argue that newer PBS methods are likely to be most successful when augmented by additional, integrally related interventions. Before making the case for expanding PBS, however, three background assumptions must be discussed.

First, PBS and its progenitor, BPT, have been extremely successful with many families. Parent education, formerly called *behavioral training,* is a preferred mode of treatment for behavior problems and skills deficits of children with developmental disabilities in the home and community. BPT has effectively allowed parents to address many forms of challenging behavior that are common to children with developmental disabilities (Koegel, Koegel, & Dunlap, 1996; Marquis et al, 2000). Furthermore, it has helped parents to teach children with mental retardation a wide array of home and community living skills and, in some cases, to maintain these skills for more than a year (Baker, 1996). Because of its extensive success, BPT has become a standard part of the service system for families in many parts of the United States.

There is a neighboring body of research on educating parents to address the behavior of typically developing children who act particularly oppositional and aggressive (Sanders, 1996; Webster-Stratton, 1998). This research has exceeded research on children with developmental disabilities in showing the benefits of supportive ecological interventions. Thus, this chapter draws on studies of BPT with parents of both typically developing children who are oppositional and children with disabilities. We assume that PBS and BPT are robust and effective treatments for many parents. We also assume that PBS may well be more effective than traditional BPT. For example, a meta-analysis of studies on PBS indicated that when positive treatments were enhanced with functional analysis, which is a core component of PBS, there was a 50% increase in effectiveness (Marquis et al., 2000). It is possible that some of the previous limitations of BPT will be less problematic in light of more robust PBS interventions. Nonetheless, we review and extrapolate from several BPT studies to conclude that PBS likely needs to include other interventions to be successful with 25%–30% of families (Webster-Stratton, 1998).

Third, it is important not to make overgeneralizations about families of children with disabilities. The roughly 30% of parents who do not respond successfully to BPT are likely to experience social and psychological stress that interferes with either learning or implementing positive parenting skills. There is simply no way to design methods to support these families without acknowledging and addressing such problems. Nonetheless, it is important to remember that this group is a minority among parents of children with disabilities. Raising a child with a disability can ultimately be a strengthening and enriching experience for family members, and it is a mistake to characterize the families as troubled and struggling (Turnbull & Turnbull, 2001). We do not wish to contribute in any way to the outmoded view that families of children with disabilities are pathological, inevitably troubled, or subjects of tragedy.

LIMITATIONS IN BEHAVIORAL PARENT TRAINING

Most of the problems that have traditionally interfered with successful BPT are associated with conditions that are not good for any family. Interfering variables include high levels of family stress, low socioeconomic status (SES), social isolation, negative social networks, marital discord, and parental depression. A body of research indicates that these problems hinder BPT; because of interference from internal or external factors in the family ecology, a sizable percentage of families do not respond to traditional BPT (Baker, 1996; Lutzker & Campbell, 1994; Singer & Irvin, 1989; Webster-Stratton, 1997). The following subsections review research on BPT that demonstrates the limitations in the approach. Because most of these studies examined group approaches to parent training and support, extrapolation to individual approaches to behavior support with families needs to be considered with caution.

Recruitment and Attrition Problems

Baker (1996) reviewed studies that reported on recruitment rates of parents of children with mental retardation who were invited to participate in BPT programs. These rates ranged from a low of 11% to a high of 54%. In studies that tried to determine why parents do and do not join BPT programs, those who do not join often have a lower SES, have received less education, perceive their children as being less troublesome than those who join, and have less confidence that they can learn new parenting skills (Baker, 1996). Researchers have made encouraging progress in this area, however, by using a combination of several different methods for improving the marketing, design, and implementation of BPT (Baker, 1996; Webster-Stratton, 1998).

Many parents who enroll in a program eventually drop out. Forehand, Middlebrook, Rogers, and Steffe (1983) reviewed 22 studies of interventions for parents of children with conduct problems and found that the average attrition rate was 28%. A later study reported that following baseline assessments, 22% of parents did not meet the attendance criteria necessary to adequately learn parenting skills (Webster-Stratton, 1998).

Acquisition Failure

Of those parents who join and remain in BPT programs, a sizable percentage fail to acquire new skills at adequate levels to change child behavior and maintain these changes. On a test of behavioral knowledge in three studies, Baker (1996) reported that approximately 45% of families of children with mental retardation failed to gain knowledge at a sufficient level to meet study criterion for understanding of behavioral concepts. O'Dell, Flynn, and Benlolo (1977) found that 32% of parents of children with oppositional behavior were not able to implement positive parenting methods successfully. Another study with parents of young children at risk for problem behavior reported an acquisition failure rate of 30% or more among parents who completed training (Webster-Stratton, 1997).

Lack of Maintenance

In regard to parents' continued use of positive parenting skills over time, Baker, Heifetz, and Murphy (1980) found that 14 months after attending BPT classes, 24% of parents failed to teach at least one new skill during the previous month. This finding was observed in two other studies of training for parents of young children with mental retardation. Extrapolating from the most optimistic data of the previously described studies, if a parent training program tries to recruit 100 parents, then it is likely to enroll 54. During the program, 5 parents are likely to drop out. Of the 49 remaining parents who complete the program, 37 are likely to continue effectively using parenting skills 14 months later.

In one study of mothers who were single and socially isolated and had a low SES, the researchers reported that none of the women who completed the clinic-based BPT were able to successfully implement BPT with their children with conduct disorders (Wahler, Cartor, Fleischman, & Lambert, 1993). Only those parents who received BPT *and* synthesis training, a form of counseling, were able to change their children's oppositional behavior and maintain these improvements 6 months postintervention. Maintenance was achieved only with the addition of a supportive contextual intervention. Webster-Stratton and Hammond (1997) reported that most of the children whose parents participated in a parent training program to address their children's conduct disorders maintained intervention effects 1 year postintervention. Nevertheless, 25% of the children in the most effective intervention conditions continued to exhibit clinically significant levels of problem behavior. In a study of predictors of treatment outcome, Webster-Stratton and Hammond (1990) indicated that these children's families were characterized by single-parent status, lower SES, and elevated levels of parental depression. Serketich and Dumas (1996) later conducted a meta-analysis of 26 studies of parent training with families of children who had conduct disorders. They concluded that interventions were effective in the short term but that there was not enough evidence to make the case for the durability of these effects over time.

Problems in How Behavioral Parent Training Is Presented

How parent training programs are organized and presented can negatively affect their acceptability and feasibility to parents (Webster-Stratton, 1998). If parents have to travel long distances or miss work to attend parenting classes, they may perceive the classes as being too inconvenient. Some parents, particularly those of low SES, may not be attracted to training opportunities that require transportation and child care. In addition, the hierarchical relationships that are often established between parents and professionals during traditional BPT is an important problem that has not yet been thoroughly researched (Lundquist & Hansen, 1998; Turnbull & Turnbull, 2001). Addressing this problem in her own work with families, Webster-Stratton described the difference between the traditional, professionally driven model and a more collaborative one:

> *Webster's New Collegiate Dictionary* defines collaboration as simply "to labor together"; the collaborative therapist labors with parents by actively soliciting their ideas and feelings, understands their cultural context, and involving the therapeutic process by inviting them to share their experiences, discuss their ideas, and engage in problem solving. The collaborative therapist works with parents to adapt concepts and skills to the circumstances of those parents and the temperament of their child. A noncollaborative approach is hierarchical, didactic, and nonparticipative—the therapist lectures, the parents listen. The noncollaborative therapist analyzes, interprets, and makes decisions for parents without incorporating their input. Principles and skills are presented to parents in terms of prescriptions for successful ways to deal with their children. Homework assignments are rigid and given without regard for the family's circumstances. (1997, p. 164)

These ideas are in keeping with current values in many disciplines that serve families and are often described as part of family-centered intervention (Allen & Petr, 1996). Additional research is needed to determine whether emerging democratic values about parent–professional relationships are empirically supported by evidence for improved efficacy. Webster-Stratton's intervention research on families of young children with conduct disorders suggests that this democratic setup is an important ingredient in preventing dropout and attrition, but this concept needs to be empirically tested (Webster-Stratton, 1998; Webster-Stratton & Hancock, 1998).

CONTEXTUAL THREATS TO EFFECTIVE PARENT TRAINING

Research on parents of children with and without disabilities repeatedly shows that parents who benefit the least from parent training must struggle with one or more of the following issues: poverty, low SES, social isolation, single parenthood, marital discord, and depression or other mental illness (Baker, 1996; Lutzker & Campbell, 1994; Sanders, 1996; Singer & Powers, 1993; Webster-Stratton, 1998). The variables that interfere with successful parent training are usually in the context of parent–child interactions, and they overshadow interventionist's efforts. Overshadowing factors all have the same functional effect: They impede the ability of parents to learn and/or carry out new parenting skills. Table 7.1 presents a list of some important overshadowing factors that threaten effective PBS with families.

For some families, several of these variables have been identified as factors that place children at risk for poor school achievement, problems with peers, and emotional and behavioral problems. These risk factors are multiplicative in their effects. That is, as families experience a larger number of factors, their risk increases in an exponential rather than in an additive fashion (Sameroff & Fiese, 2000). Moreover, risk factors often co-occur. For example, marital discord and maternal depression are highly correlated. Poverty and single parenthood are often linked through mother's loss of income after divorce (Singer, Irvine, & Irvin, 1989). Risk factors should be a major concern for PBS practitioners who work with children who have developmental disabilities and their families. The following sections review seven major risk factors that threaten effective parent support and training.

Table 7.1. Overshadowing factors that may interfere with effective PBS with families

Internal factors	External factors
Competing demands on parents' time and energy	Low socioeconomic status
Fluctuating stress levels	Social isolation
High levels of chronic stress	Major life changes (e.g., a move, divorce)
Parental depression	Changes in family activity settings due to changes in the surrounding ecology (e.g., the child care center closes, a respite care provider has an extended illness)
Marital discord	
Developmental changes in the child or the family	Cultural/linguistic differences among family members and service providers
	Inconsistent implementation at school or the workplace

Poverty

In 1999, 11.8% of adults and 16.9% of children 18 years and younger in the United States lived below the poverty level. This constituted approximately 32 million people (U.S. Census Bureau, 2000). There is a very strong association between poverty and children's risk of low birth weight, developmental disabilities, special education placement, chronic illnesses, learning disabilities, abuse and neglect, and severe behavior problems (Sherman, 1994). The link between poverty and childhood disability grew stronger during the 1990s, with children of single parents who had a low SES being at the highest risk (Fujiara & Yamaki, 2000). It is important to note that ethnicity is not a significant predictor of childhood disability when poverty is factored out. Families living in poverty are less likely to seek parent training, and when they do, they are less likely to complete it (Webster-Stratton, 1997). Upon completion of training, single mothers with low incomes have much more difficulty implementing PBS than middle-class parents (Wahler, 1980). Consequently, poverty both increases the risk of disability and decreases the effectiveness of treatment—a vicious cycle that needs to be broken. To effectively help parents who have a low SES and children with disabilities and challenging behavior, supportive contextual interventions have proven necessary (Lutzker, 1984; Lutzker & Campbell, 1994).

Social Isolation and Negative Social Networks

Mothers who have limited social support either make limited intervention gains or fail to maintain these gains at follow-up (Dumas, 1984; Dumas & Wahler, 1983; Webster-Stratton & Hammond, 1990). Social isolation interferes with the acquisition and maintenance of positive parenting skills (Wahler, 1988; Webster-Stratton, 1997). Studies on the link between social support and parenting suggest that parents who believe that they have social support benefit in a variety of ways (Cochran & Niego, 1995). Social networks provide instrumental support such as babysitting, advice on child rearing, and financial assistance. Without this kind of help, daily burdens may accumulate to the point that parents are overwhelmed and less able to carry out normal daily activities (Cochran & Niego, 1995). Singer (1993) studied the role of adult friends, extended family members, and supportive professionals in the lives of eight parents of children with serious challenging behavior. A mother in Singer's study reported how a neighbor regularly helped with her child's aggressive behavior. Whenever the mother was not at home at bedtime, her neighbor assisted in putting the child to bed because the child's father was unable to handle the boy's challenging behavior alone. A father in another family discussed how a friend covered for him when he had to leave work to take care of his daughter's behavior or medical problems. Bristol, Gallagher, and Schopler (1988) found that mothers who received the desired amount of household help from their husbands were happier in their marriages, less likely to be depressed, and more competent in parenting. Social support also can serve as a buffer from stressful events. For example, a mother who loses her job may be cushioned from this life stressor through help from friends in finding other employment or by financial assistance from her family.

Wahler and colleagues (Wahler, 1980, 1988; Wahler et al., 1993) focused their BPT research on mothers who have a low SES and are isolated. These women experience the stresses of poverty and have small social networks, which primarily consist of extended family members and social agency representatives. In the earlier research, Wahler (1980) found an association between days when mothers implemented BPT and the receipt of positive social support (Wahler et al., 1993). Wahler and colleagues argued that BPT is contraindicated for these parents unless additional counseling is provided.

A consortium of university researchers and parent leaders of Parent to Parent mutual aid programs conducted a randomized two-group comparison of parents who received help from experienced parents through structured parent-run programs compared with others on a waiting list (Ainbinder et al.,1998; Singer et al., 1999; see also Chapter 19). Support from experienced parents promoted perceived parental self-efficacy, helped parents gather believable and helpful information, helped parents solve the problem that initially led them to the Parent to Parent program, and promoted a sense of hope and acceptance about their children and families. Researchers who have reported success in serving isolated parents have made social support a major addition to BPT for children with disabilities (Lutzker & Steed, 1998; Singer, Irvine, & Irvin., 1989), for children with conduct problems (Sanders, 1996; Webster-Stratton, 1997), and for the prevention of child abuse and neglect (Lutzker, 1984).

Fluctuating Stress Levels

One way that contextual variables disrupt BPT is through inconsistency in family implementation of strategies (Harris, Peterson, Filliben, Glassberg, & Falvell, 1998; Kazdin, 2001). Elevated and fluctuating levels of stress in the home can aversively affect a parent's ability to implement parenting strategies. On a daily and weekly basis, family members experience changes in mood, energy levels, alertness, concentration, memory, and emotional availability. In studies by Singer and colleagues (Singer, Irvin, & Hawkins, 1988; Singer, Irvine, & Irvin, 1989; Singer & Powers, 1993), parents of children with severe disabilities kept daily journals in which they recorded stress levels during morning, daytime, and evening routines. Parents had consistent patterns of elevated stress levels according to the time of day, daily routine, and specific problems that occurred. Home life is not a steady state.

As part of a multicomponent service model for parents of children with severe disabilities, parents were taught both BPT and stress management skills (Singer, Irvine, & Irvin, 1989; Singer & Powers, 1993). As a weekly homework assignment, parents kept journals of the most stressful times of day and the times when children exhibited problem behavior. Mothers reported that their most stressful daily events required split attention and the completion of more than one task at once. Getting the family ready for school and work, preparing dinner while watching the children, and tending to children while talking on the telephone were common diary entries. For children whose challenging behavior is motivated by parental attention, times when parents are distracted can set the stage for behavior problems. One major task for parents is making arrangements to deal with the unexpected perturbations of daily and weekly routines. They must decide what to do when the babysitter does not arrive, the school bus is late, or the electricity goes out. While the parent is making and changing arrangements, a child with challenging behavior may continue to need consistent positive parenting.

Marital Discord

Some parents who experience marital discord are poor candidates for parent training in isolation of other forms of intervention (Sanders & Dadds, 1993; Webster-Stratton & Hammond, 1990). Certain kinds of conflict between spouses have a detrimental effect on typically developing children. Fighting that goes unresolved in ways that are acceptable to both parties and spousal physical violence are linked to increased emotional and behavioral problems in children (Cummings, 1994). This link has not been examined in regard to children with disabilities, which is an important missing piece in the literature because it is reasonable to assume that the same dynamic applies. Marital discord is also highly correlated with maternal depression (Christian-Herman, O'Leary, & Avery-Leaf, 2001). It, in turn, disrupts parent–child interactions with typically developing children, as discussed later in this chapter (Downey & Coyne, 1990).

A common source of disagreement between couples is child discipline. Mothers are the primary participants in parent training for children with metal retardation, and little is known about fathers' views on their wives' use of behavioral parenting skills (Baker, 1996). Clinical accounts suggest that if spouses do not agree on how to manage or prevent children's challenging behavior, then they may criticize each other and argue (Hawkins, Singer, & Nixon, 1993). Children with mental retardation may strain normal family problem-solving processes. Costigan, Floyd, Harter, and McClintock (1997) found that problem-solving sessions in these families were more negative compared with those of families with typically developing children. They also pointed out that single parents of children with mental retardation had the most difficulty in family problem-solving sessions.

Nevertheless, it is important to note that most families showed evidence of resiliency regardless of these problems. Adubato, Adams, and Budd (1981) demonstrated that under a therapist's supervision, the mother of a child with a developmental disability could teach her husband to carry out a behavior change program. Their skills maintained at a 2-year follow-up. Dadds, Sanders, Behrens, and James (1987), in a fine-grained analysis of the relationship between marital discord and child problem behavior, taught positive parenting skills to parents who were experiencing marital discord and had children with conduct disorders. Three of the four couples were able to administer child management methods with resultant decreases in challenging behavior, although there was little change in fighting between the parents. The authors then introduced partner support training, in which parents were taught to be less reactive and more positive with each other. After this supportive contextual intervention was added, child problem behavior and marital conflict were reduced. One finding in this study is of special importance: One of the four couples was not able to implement BPT until the partners learned to reduce their level of conflict. This is an example of families that are likely to require more than PBS alone.

The complexity of forming new combined families is another marital variable that can threaten effective parent education. In some cases, it can overshadow the implementation of positive parenting practices and the acquisition of new parenting skills.

Single Parenthood

Single parents constitute 25% of families with school-age children. They also are more likely to drop out of treatment prematurely and/or fail to benefit from it (Dadds & McHugh, 1992; Strain, Young, & Horowitz, 1981; Webster-Stratton & Hammond, 1990). Single parents are generally less responsive to parent training. This topic is complex, so generalizations must be made with caution. Single parents vary greatly, including whether they are single by divorce, death of a spouse, or never marrying. Perceived social support, SES, and emotional well-being also vary. Single parenthood is often linked to poverty and all of its stresses. A larger percentage of single mothers come from lower SES groups and begin parenthood without many of the resources that are available to parents who are in higher-income brackets and have more education. Recent divorce is associated for some women with loss of income, change of residence, and reorganization of everyday routines. Depression is a common reaction to the loss inherent in some divorces. The child care and workload demands of a single parent may be exceptional, requiring many tasks that compete with behavioral intervention skills.

Recent divorce can disrupt positive parenting in some mother–child relationships (Simons, Lin, Gordon, Conger, & Lorenz, 1999). Parents react to divorce in many different ways; the more negative reactions (e.g., severe depression) are often cause for concern. It should not be assumed, however, that these findings apply generally. Divorce can be a relief for some parents and children and may lead to reductions in parental distress. Also, many divorced parents eventually remarry.

Depression

Parents who are without supports and experience depression are also poor candidates for BPT by itself (Griest, Forehand, & Wells, 1981). A review of the literature on the prevalence of mild depression in mothers of children with disabilities suggested that approximately 25%–30% of these women experience elevated depressive symptoms compared with roughly 20% of mothers of typically developing children (Singer & Yovanoff, 1993). Compared with parents who are not depressed, parents with depression interact less with their children, have a more negative outlook, are less responsive to their children, are less contingent in their responses, and are prone to using harsh and inconsistent discipline (Downey & Coyne, 1990). When a positive mother–infant relationship is disrupted by depression, mothers tend to elicit more resistance and aggression in their children. In turn, problems with the children become another source of stress and a further cause for depression (Griest et al., 1982). When parents with depression seek help for their children's behavior problems, they are less responsive to parent education programs than parents who are not depressed.

Nevertheless, caution should be taken to avoid the assumption that depression in parents of young children with disabilities necessarily troubles the waters. Although these findings are well established for parents of typically developing children, there is some evidence to the contrary regarding the ways that depressed mothers of children with disabilities interact with their infants and young children (Smith, Innocenti, Boyce, & Smith, 1993).

Cultural and Social Class Differences

An area of difficulty that has yet to see much empirical progress is the barrier of cultural and social class differences between trainers and parents. These differences can reduce recruitment and successful outcomes for BPT (Forehand & Kotchick, 1996; Webster-Stratton, 1998). Cultural assumptions held by interventionists can clash with other underlying cultural assumptions. Differences between parents and interventionists regarding behavioral standards related to culture and/or social class can get in the way (Forehand & Kotchick, 1996). For example, a cultural belief that children should do what is expected without praise or recognition can be a barrier to BPT, with its emphasis on positive consequences. Families with standards for appropriate behavior that differ from those of the majority culture may have trouble understanding recommendations for changing behavior. For example, instructions to talk more frequently to infants and toddlers may make little sense to individuals from a culture that values silence over speech. Families in which older siblings, uncles, grandparents, or a nanny provide children's daily care probably do not benefit from BPT if it is taught only to mothers, as is the common practice.

IMPROVEMENTS IN THE CONTENT
AND DELIVERY OF BEHAVIORAL PARENT TRAINING

To overcome contextual barriers to effective parenting education, researchers have developed and tested several strategies that can be organized into two major categories. First, they have developed strategies to improve the content and delivery of BPT. Second, they have enhanced BPT with supportive contextual interventions that are aimed at assisting parents in overcoming obstacles to effective parent training. The important thread that runs through these strategies is a move into the context that surrounds parents and children to address these contextual barriers. The following sections review ways that family interventionists have improved the content and delivery of BPT.

Reducing Inconsistency in Family–Child Interactions

Inconsistency has been a common contextual problem in implementing behavioral parenting methods (Adubato et al., 1981; Harris et al., 1998). The focus of most behavioral intervention studies with parents has been interactions between mothers and their children with challenging behavior. Solely focusing on mothers may be problematic in some families. It can cause disagreements about how to parent a child, which subsequently raise marital tension and impede maternal use of new parenting methods. Consistency is a basic characteristic of behavioral intervention plans and is assumed to be essential. Untrained family members may employ new strategies inconsistently and, thus, jeopardize the effectiveness of BPT. Adubato and colleagues handled this problem by showing a mother how to teach her husband BPT techniques that she learned from the interventionists. The researchers first provided this mother of a child with a disability with written and verbal instructions, modeling, and immediate feedback. They instructed her to provide the same instruction and feedback to her husband at home. These strategies were successful in increasing effective parenting behaviors of both the mother and father from baseline probes. In this case, the contextual barrier derived from only one parent learning the new methods. Overcoming this barrier involved moving into the spousal context. In addressing the same problem of within-family inconsistency, Harris and colleagues (1998) taught spouses to provide feedback to each other when one of them implemented BPT techniques. The researchers used a modified multiple-baseline design to first train three couples in BPT techniques. The couples all participated in the BPT sessions together, but clinicians also came to the parents' homes to observe the parents and provide feedback. Then, the researchers showed the parents how to give their spouses specific, positive, immediate feedback. Results indicated that all of the parents showed improvement in BPT techniques after the BPT training. In addition, after the spousal feedback condition, five of the six participants showed an increase in average BPT performance from the previous condition. In this case, parent training expanded to include some family systems variables.

Addressing Fluctuating Stress Levels

Stress levels in the home fluctuate for parents and children. Sanders and Dadds (1982) identified stressful times of day for parents of children who had conduct disorder. They found that when parents learned to use behavioral techniques in a relatively low-key home environment (e.g., the kitchen at a low-stress time of day), they did not transfer the techniques to more stressful times in the home. When the interventionists provided parents with specific training on how to cope with their child during more demanding time periods, generalization improved.

One way that researchers have tried to improve parent training to deal with fluctuating stress levels is by teaching methods that are easy to adapt to changing conditions and settings. An example of one such technique is Planned Activities Training (PAT; Sanders & Glynn, 1981). Powers, Singer, Stevens, and Sowers (1992) taught parents of children with severe disabilities to plan ahead for times when children were likely to exhibit problem behavior. PAT was provided, during which parents learned to identify stressful times and places, to provide toys to the children during these times, to prompt them to play with the toys, and to periodically check on and reward the children. The researchers taught these skills in a comfortable home setting and then helped the parents problem-solve ways to use PAT at stressful times at home and in community settings such as shopping malls, grocery stores, parks, and churches. Two of three mothers were able to effectively generalize the use of PAT skills to more difficult settings; the third parent required coaching in the other settings before improvements in parenting practices and child behavior were observed. Huynen, Lutzker, Bigelow, Touchette, and Campbell (1996) obtained similar results in working with four mothers of children with severe disabilities. The multiple settings in their study contributed more evidence for setting generalization with PAT.

Planning for Generalization and Maintenance

Generalization has long been recognized as a major area of concern in applied behavior analysis (Stokes & Baer, 1977; Stokes & Osnes, 1989). Since the late 1970s, considerable progress has been made in improving generalization in behavioral interventions for people with disabilities (Horner, Dunlap, & Koegel, 1988). BPT researchers have identified several strategies that improve the generalization of parent training across settings. Koegel, Glahn, and Nieminen (1978) worked with parents of children with autism and found that general skills instruction was more effective than task-specific training for promoting the generalized use of new parenting strategies. Sanders and Glynn (1981) demonstrated that teaching self-management strategies (e.g., self-monitoring by using a checklist) to parents of children with conduct disorders helped promote the generalization and maintenance of new parenting skills to a wide range of social activities and settings. Other family interventionists developed easy-to-use methods, such as PAT, that parents can readily transfer from trained to nontrained settings in the home or community (Lutzker & Steed, 1998; Sanders & Plant, 1989). Other methods that have been used to help parents generalize and maintain the use of effective parenting strategies to new settings include the following:

- Diverse training by using sufficient stimulus-and-response exemplars of parenting strategies (Powers et al., 1992)

- Incorporation of common, salient stimuli during parent training by involving the entire family in assessment and intervention activities and by conducting training activities in natural family contexts (Webster-Stratton, 1994)

- Professional contact with the family through regularly scheduled telephone contacts or follow-up sessions, which can serve as reminders to continue using previously trained skills (Cordisco, Strain, & Depew, 1988)

- Periodic booster sessions when follow-up assessment indicates a regression in the child's behavior (Kazdin, 2001)

General case programming is one new method for promoting generalized positive parenting skills that holds promise but has not yet been applied to the design of parent training programs (Engelman, 1980; Horner & Albin, 1988). The aim of applying this approach would be to design a parent training curriculum that directly and efficiently teaches parents generalized skills for using positive parenting strategies. Advances also are likely to grow out of a better understanding of the way in which other stimuli overshadow positive parenting skills and the way in which previously learned parent behavior successfully competes with parental use of effective parenting strategies (Dunlap, 1993). Finally, for many families, improving generalized outcomes requires an expansion of the focus of BPT and PBS to include contextual supportive interventions. As noted by Dunlap, "In some instances, the generalized performance of skills learned in parent training curricula may be a function of lifestyle events that are not typically regarded as integral to generalized outcomes" (1993, p. 283).

ADDING SUPPORTIVE CONTEXTUAL INTERVENTIONS

Another important way that family interventionists have addressed barriers to effective parent training is to directly intervene in the contextual problems that interfere with parents' abilities to implement positive parenting strategies. In this approach, the interventionist expands his or her attention to the setting events and antecedent conditions that affect parent behavior and selects supportive contextual interventions that make it easier for families to implement and sustain positive parenting strategies. The next subsections review supportive contextual interventions that have been empirically validated as helpful to families.

Supportive Interventions for Single Mothers with Low Incomes

Single mothers who have low incomes and are in unhappy social relationships generally have been unresponsive to BPT by itself. Wahler and colleagues (1993) argued that BPT alone is contraindicated for this group of parents. They demonstrated the additive effect of a supportive contextual intervention for mothers who are isolated and have children with conduct disorders. They developed a supportive intervention, called *synthesis training*, in which they taught mothers to examine their conflicted relationships with adults and understand how these experiences relate to conflict with their children. They worked with single mothers, teaching them to distinguish stress caused by coercive adults from stress caused by their children. They also worked with the mothers to solve interpersonal problems. When these interventions were combined with BPT, parents were much more able to address their children's challenging behavior. Mothers who received the additional support were able to implement BPT at home and to reduce child problem behavior at follow-up, compared with a BPT-only group that did not transfer behavioral parenting skills from clinic to home and did not reduce child problem behaviors.

Supportive Counseling

An early example of a supportive contextual intervention to improve parent training is the work of Griest and colleagues (1981), who examined the additive effects of supportive counseling on parents of children with conduct disorders. Parents were assigned to either a BPT-only group or to a group that received BPT plus supportive counseling for personal and family problems. The supportive counseling addressed the parents' perceptions of their children's problem behavior, personal adjustment, marital adjustment, and extrafamilial relationships. The mothers in the group who received the additional counseling were more successful in implementing BPT methods, and their children showed significantly decreased problem behavior and increased compliance to requests.

Behavioral Marital Therapy

In another example of expanded services to improve parent training, Dadds, Sanders, Behrens, and James (1987) demonstrated the additive effects of supportive behavioral counseling for marital discord in mothers and fathers of young children with conduct disorders. They analyzed the functional effect of using BPT followed by a brief behavioral marital therapy session with four couples. In three of four families, the BPT reduced child problem behavior in home observations; however, for only two of the four couples did the reduction in child problem behavior also lead to reduced marital conflict. For the other two couples, marital conflict diminished only after the parents received instruction on how to prevent coercive exchanges and provide supportive comments to each other. For one of the four families, the child's problem behavior did not respond to BPT until the marital counseling was implemented. The study showed that to improve child outcomes in some families, a supportive contextual intervention for marital discord was necessary. The study also showed that parent training by itself can reduce marital conflict in some families, whereas others need specific help with marriage problems to improve both spousal interactions and children's challenging behavior.

Parents as Educators of Other Parents

One supportive contextual intervention attempts to link parents of children with disabilities to other parents of children with disabilities by training parents to become teachers of BPT. Neef (1995) assigned parents to either a peer–parent training condition or a standard parent training condition. In the peer–parent training condition, a professional provided standard parent training to the first tier of parents. Once these parents had achieved a criterion level of BPT techniques, they began to teach BPT techniques to another group of parents. Results from the study indicated that both the standard BPT group and the peer–parent BPT group improved parental use of BPT strategies and decreased child problem behavior. The peer–parent BPT group, however, had the highest gains in generalized outcomes.

Combining Behavioral Parent Training with Other Behavioral Interventions

Research suggests that using additive interventions for some parents works better than BPT alone for improving children's problem behaviors. Kazdin, Siegel, and Bass (1992) conducted a study that makes this point clear. Working with parents of children with aggressive and antisocial behaviors, they compared three conditions. Parents were randomly assigned to one of three groups. One group received skills training in problem solving using cognitive-behavioral methods. A second group received BPT alone. The third group received both interventions. Children from all three groups changed their behavior in positive ways. The group that received the combined interventions, however, outperformed the other two.

Behavioral family intervention (BFI) is one of the best-researched approaches to parent training that integrates additional interventions for targeted contextual problems (Sanders, 1996). BFI uses BPT methods plus family-focused treatments that are also based on the principles of applied behavior analysis (Baer, Wolf, & Risley, 1968). That is, additive interventions such as parent self-management training, anger management, and problem solving are taught as skills that can be learned and implemented through operant and social learning principles. In research, BFI has been effective for families of children with developmental disabilities, conduct disorders, anxiety disorders, chronic abdominal pain, sleep problems, and feeding problems (Sanders, 1996).

BFI also recognizes that different families need varying levels of assistance to enact positive parenting skills. Sanders (1996) presented five levels of complexity in BFI interventions, ranging from mass distribution of videotapes to videotapes plus therapist-led group discussions to problem-specific behavior therapy for family members plus home-based parent training. PBS practitioners should find BFI promising because the additive interventions are taught in ways that are consistent with the skills and concepts that are needed to learn positive parenting. BFI represents a bridge between parent training as a sole intervention and more complex ecobehavioral approaches to supporting families of children with challenging behavior.

INTEGRATING MULTIPLE METHODS IN A SOCIAL SERVICE CONTEXT

Up to this point, we have reviewed several studies that employed BPT interventions alone or combined with single supportive contextual intervention, such as counseling. Families under severe stress, however, sometimes need a larger set of supports, including (to name but a few) respite care, financial aid, transportation, Parent to Parent programs, support groups, and medical care. These families may require a broader range of interventions aimed at improving family functioning, such as marital therapy, problem-solving training, anger management instruction, and joint action planning. The research literature is primarily based on studies conducted by university professors and their doctoral students. In contrast, most services for families are provided by practicing clinicians who often work for social service agencies. When a family needs a combination of services, several agencies may be involved. In the following discussion, the authors provide evidence for the effectiveness of multiple component interventions and then discuss their place in community systems of care for people with developmental disabilities.

Ecobehavioral Approaches

In the research literature, multicomponent interventions are labeled *ecobehavioral*. *Eco-* comes from the word *ecology* and implies a focus on the family as a system that is embedded within a larger social and environmental context. *Behavioral* indicates that the approach derives from applied behavior analysis and emphasizes the importance of learning new skills and changing the environment as the basis for improving child behavior and parenting practices. A small group of researchers has shown that packages of several interventions can help solve complex family problems (Kazdin et al., 1992; Lutzker & Campbell, 1994; Singer, Irvin, Irvine, Hawkins, & Cooley, 1989; Singer & Powers, 1993; Webster-Stratton, 1997, 1998). Examples of such packages are discussed next.

Project 12-Ways   Lutzker and colleagues have worked consistently within the ecobehavioral framework since the 1970s (Lutzker & Campbell, 1994). They developed a multi-element, ecobehavioral approach while working with parents who were sentenced for abusing and neglecting their children. Parents who abuse and neglect their children often have multiple problems that are linked to social disruptions of family life. Trained in the practical, empirical tradition of applied behavior analysis, Lutzker and colleagues realized that to help parents change their parenting practices, it was necessary to assist them in overcoming the disruptive aspects of their daily lives, including many of the contextual problems previously described. The research group developed a set of intervention packages that were aimed at assisting parents in dealing with several problems that can overshadow parent training. They chose interventions that were created using applied behavior analysis. Initially, they used 12 such treatment packages—thus, the intervention program name of Project 12-Ways. These packages included training for relaxation, home safety and cleanliness, budgeting skills, problem solving, marital communication, and child care skills. Lutzker and colleagues (1994) also adapted their system to serve families of children with autism and other disabilities. Through a series of case studies and multiple-baseline investigations and a large program evaluation, they built a solid case for the efficacy of their approach (Lutzker, 1998). It is difficult to effect changes in parenting with parents who are under court-ordered surveillance for child abuse or neglect; therefore, the results of the Project 12-Ways approach are impressive.

Project SAEF   A second ecobehavioral program, the Support and Education for Families Project (Project SAEF) was developed by Singer and colleagues at the Oregon Research Institute (Singer, Irvin, Irvine, et al. 1989; Singer & Powers, 1993). They developed a family support program for parents of children with severe and multiple disabilities. This program also used an ecobehavioral approach in which the researchers targeted overshadowing variables in addition to teaching parents positive parenting skills. The program was designed to provide two levels of support according to the intensity of family needs. Differing from Project 12-Ways, the Project SAEF approach emphasized working with parents in groups to build social support and solidarity. In Level I, parents participated in group-based positive parenting classes (i.e., BPT) followed by group stress-management classes (Singer & Powers, 1993). Using support groups was central to the Project SAEF design. A study of Parent to Parent programs indicated that this kind of mutual aide can significantly and positively affect parents' perceptions of coping and self-efficacy, as well as aid in developing more hopeful and accepting attitudes and in obtaining practical assistance for particular problems (Singer et al., 1999). A second study indicated that parents provide a unique form of self-help that professionals cannot provide (Ainbinder et al., 1998). Shared life experience—that is, the 24-hour per day reality of having a child with severe disabilities— allowed parents to believe statements made by other parents.

Respite care is one of the most frequently requested forms of service. It was the first family support service offered by regional developmental disabilities programs in the United States and continues to be an important function of these centers (Bradley, Knoll, & Agosta, 1992). It is often difficult for parents to find trustworthy respite care for children with complex needs; thus, at Level I of Project SAEF, college student volunteers also provided weekly respite by accompanying the children with disabilities to community activities. The volunteers were given training. They were taught to interview parents to learn how to be good companions for their children. An evaluation of the Project SAEF model revealed that this component of the program was highly valued by participating families (Singer & Powers, 1993).

At Level I, all families also received service coordination from an independent agency. The agency was not a gatekeeper for funds but provided aggressive links to other needed services and advocacy. At the parents' request, agency staff helped parents apply for government subsidies, obtain medical care, and connect with a variety of community agencies to meet needs for home care, employment, substance abuse treatment, and economic assistance. The agency staff were an integral part of the interdisciplinary group that implemented the Project SAEF model.

Level II programs were for parents who needed more individualized or more intensive assistance. At this level, different forms of counseling and in-home services for challenging behavior were added. Four forms of short-term counseling also were provided: 1) treatment for depression, 2) communication skills–based marital counseling, 3) problem-solving training, and 4) intervention for excessive self-blame and guilt. The project focused on these areas because the research literature and clinical experience indicated that they were at least as common as in the general population and possibly somewhat more prevalent among families of children with challenging behaviors (Singer & Yovanoff, 1993). The program also provided in-home behavior management education when parents' class participation did not lead to a child's behavior change. (See Singer & Powers, 1993, for a detailed discussion of these interventions.) The individual behavioral counseling assisted parents in setting goals and solving problems that impeded goal attainment (Hawkins et al., 1993). Many of the goals that parents developed concerned wider contexts such as employment, loneliness and social isolation, substance abuse, conflict with extended family members, and major negative life events. This approach allowed for flexible individualized assistance. The researchers relied on behavioral and cognitive-behavioral methods and tailored the treatment to individuals and specific families. They emphasized skills training, problem solving, and group support.

The philosophy of Project SAEF was important to its design and implementation. Project staff made considerable efforts to develop partnerships with families, honor the families' goals, and work within the families' value systems. When the project staff provided individual or couples counseling, their express purpose was to assist parents in setting their own goals and choosing the means to reach them (Hawkins et al., 1993).

Project SAEF was evaluated through replicated, randomized experimental studies that compared groups of parents who received the traditional services available in the community and groups who received the full range of supports (Singer, Irvin, Irvine, et al. 1989; Singer & Powers, 1993). In both the original target community and in a replication site, the SAEF model led to significant improvements in parents' and children's well-being.

PARTNERS Parent Training Program   A third ecobehavioral intervention was developed and evaluated for its effectiveness in serving parents who were part of a Head Start program in the Seattle area (Webster-Stratton, 1997, 1998). The participating parents were socially isolated, had low SES, and came from a minority culture. Webster-Stratton (1998) described a comprehensive program that used several supportive contextual interventions to affect the context of family life. After she discovered that some families were not responding to her previously validated BPT programs, BASIC and ADVANCED, Webster-Stratton broadened her parent education program to include social support and community-building for isolated parents (Webster-Stratton, 1994, 1997). Webster-Stratton (1998) first addressed the problem of low recruitment rates and poor retention. She believed that the problem lay not with the parents but with the fact that services were not accessible to these families. To determine what to name the program, how to advertise it, how to deliver it, and what content to include, she conducted focus groups that were made up of parents and professionals who worked in these families' neighborhoods. Based on this input, the program was advertised as a means to help parents prepare their children for school success. Services were offered in evenings by people who had the same ethnic and linguistic background as the families, videotape examples included children of the same ethnic background as those who lived in the neighborhood, incentives were offered for participation, and services such as child care and transportation were provided. To meet the multiple needs of families, the new parent education program included problem-solving training, coping skills, interpersonal-communication skills, self-control skills, and instruction on support-building. The staff strongly emphasized establishing equal partnerships with parents and working to bring families into active, friendly relationships with Head Start personnel. Webster-Stratton concluded that her comprehensive program is best understood as community building.

The results of the program were impressive. In a randomized trial with 500 families who participated in Head Start, the mothers who attended the parenting program used more positive and fewer negative parenting strategies with their children when compared with mothers in the control group. Of the 296 mothers who participated in the intervention group, 232 (88%) completed 50% or more of the parenting sessions. Children who received the intervention engaged in significantly fewer problem behaviors and had more positive affect than children in the control group. At 1-year follow-up, most of these improvements were maintained.

IMPLICATIONS FOR POSITIVE
BEHAVIOR SUPPORT SERVICES TO FAMILIES

The empirical improvements to BPT and the ecobehavioral intervention approaches summarized previously offer practitioners of PBS an opportunity to design a service model that incorporates the lessons learned from 30 years of behavioral intervention with families. One initial design decision is whether the people who offer PBS services should provide supportive contextual interventions—such as stress management training, skills training in budgeting, depression treatment, economic supports, job search skills, and marital counseling—or whether these additional services should be delivered by closely linked agencies. An advantage to an in-house design is that PBS providers can offer additional services that are compatible with the values and methods of PBS. A disadvantage of this "one-agency-does-all" approach is that the scope that one organization can provide is necessarily limited. A comprehensive family support program may need to have access to many forms of formal and informal support that can be flexibly combined to meet individualized family needs. Alternatively, multiagency approaches that offer more practical models of service delivery and design have emerged from two areas: 1) the family support movement in the developmental disabilities service system and 2) wraparound services in the children's mental health service system (Bradley et al., 1992; Singer, Powers, & Olsen, 1996; VanDenBerg & Grealish, 1996).

Family Support Movement

Policy makers have recognized the necessity of comprehensive family support services for families of children with developmental disabilities and have established at least some services in every state (Bradley et al., 1992; Dunst, Trivette, & Deal, 1988; Singer & Irvin, 1989). Led by parent advocates and their professional allies, the family support movement has influenced policy in the developmental disabilities field. Although the movement is still very small, representing about 3% of the budget for services for people with developmental disabilities, it has forced reexamination of the service systems in some states and offers new, less bureaucratic methods of providing family support (Bradley et al., 1992).

Several states (e.g., Michigan, Illinois, Pennsylvania) have funded stipends for parents to reduce the fiscal costs of caring for children with severe cognitive disabilities at home. Programs have tried to build up the range of services available to families to include several different forms of support. These programs, however, may be available only in urban areas or a few regions within a state. Other states, such as California, are only beginning to experiment with formal family support programs through the developmental disabilities service system.

We believe that the PBS movement should ally itself with the family support movement to find sufficient resources for overcoming the many contextual problems that can overshadow effective parental implementation of PBS. The values of the two movements overlap to a large extent. PBS values effective intervention methods that are nonaversive and based on a careful functional analysis. A PBS intervention increases a person's choices, involves a complete package of interventions when needed, increases functional skills (with a particular emphasis on communication skills), and leads to improved quality of life for the person with challenging behavior and his or her family. PBS also stresses partnerships between professionals and parents as well as interventions that are designed to fit with the family's values and lifestyle (Lucyshyn, Albin, & Nixon, 1997). Several authors have emphasized that partnership is critical to successful professional involvement with families (Dunst, Trivette, & Deal, 1994; Singer & Irvin, 1989; Turnbull & Turnbull, 2001; Webster-Stratton, 1998.)

The values behind the family support movement are not only compatible with PBS beliefs but also go well beyond them. We believe that an understanding of these values is helpful to PBS practitioners when they set out to create PBS service delivery programs, a necessary step if PBS is going to become widely available. At the broadest level, family support values are based on communitarian beliefs: 1) those closest to a person who needs assistance are primarily responsible for that individual's support, 2) the community is responsible for supporting these caregivers, and 3) the federal and state governments are responsible for providing the necessary resources to local communities so that they can support those who provide day-to-day assistance (Singer, 1996). A system that is based on these ideas acknowledges the need for community-based supports to assist families (in this case, PBS services) and for fiscal support from the state and national levels.

Dunst, Trivette, Gordon, and Starnes (1993) summarized six important values for family support. First, family support services enhance a sense of community. Second, they mobilize resources and supports. Third, they are consumer driven, so responsibility is shared by the family and the family support program. Fourth, family support services protect family integrity. Fifth, they strengthen family functioning. Sixth, family support services are proactive and preventive These six values converge with the values of PBS.

Family support programs in some states rely on a family support worker to link families to other kinds of formal and informal supports. In New Hampshire, the family support system in each region of the state hires family workers who often are parents of children with disabilities and who live in the area that they serve. These family support workers have access to a pool of funds that can be used flexibly and quickly to meet needs that improve family well-being as it pertains to a family member with a disability. For example, the funds were once used to pay for a car repair so that a rural family could take its child to a clinic. The money has also been used to pay a handyman to repair leaks in a roof and to assist a family in building a wheelchair ramp and widening doors in their house. In some states (e.g., Michigan), the funds go directly to families; in others, the funds are managed by regional committees that are composed of family members. The family support workers mobilize resources for families while giving their service-linking skills to parents, which makes the receiving parents better equipped to deal with complex and confusing service systems. The workers also activate informal supports, such as talking to a church group about ways to support the family, recruiting volunteers to help make a house wheelchair accessible, and assisting the family governing boards in holding town meetings at which other families in the region can share their knowledge.

We suggest that PBS programs work closely with family support programs in the developmental disabilities community agencies. Because the PBS workers spend several hours in homes and build positive relationships with parents, they are likely to spot overshadowing factors that impede positive parenting and parent education. Family support workers can find resources to alleviate these problems and keep PBS program staff from needing to act as service coordinators for obtaining other kinds of support. For example, it became clear to a PBS interventionist working in one home that tensions related to parental unemployment overshadowed effective parent education. Rather than having the PBS worker serve as a link to employers and job readiness programs, a service coordinator who worked closely with the PBS program made these connections. When one or more services work together to serve a family, it becomes all the more important to keep the family in a equal role. As with the other aspects of family support, parents should participate in meetings with the PBS and family support workers, and parents should define their needs, function as the ultimate decision makers, work as equal partners, and serve as active problem solvers.

Wraparound Services

This chapter's description of ecobehavioral, multisystemic interventions and flexible family support systems naturally leads to a different level of analysis: service design. Contemporary work in the fields of children's mental health and early childhood intervention has created a new vision of service coordination. The following discussion presents newer thinking about how to design and coordinate service systems to meet the complicated needs of children and their families. A key dimension of concern in this discussion is the level of service coordination in a community. This can be conceptualized as a continuum, ranging from single agencies that have no contact with other programs to a comprehensive unified system that consists of several programs serving all children and families in a specific area.

The term *wraparound* refers to a set of organizational structures and practices that aim to overcome the many barriers to interagency communication, collaboration, and resource sharing (Clark & Clarke, 1996; Eber & Nelson, 1997). Anyone who has attempted to obtain services or funds from two or three agencies for the same family or child understands the difficulties of a service world that is characterized by compartmentalization, bureaucratic methods, and nonconversant agencies—each with different rules for eligibility, different internal cultures, and different limitations on resources. Wraparound programs are designed to overcome these problems. They create collaborative teams of field workers from each agency commonly involved in supporting children with emotional and behavioral problems and their families. Mapping backward from face-to-face interactions with families, wraparound designers move up the different levels of organization, regulation, funding, and agency design that influence successful multisystemic assistance. Teams can include both public and private agencies and can include as members informal support providers. One representative of the team is responsible for acting as the service coordinator and liaison to the family so that the family never has to deal with more than one support person. The parents and the service coordinator develop an action plan, which includes input from the individual with behavior problems, and they present this plan to the team to create a broader implementation plan.

In the best-developed systems, policy makers have created a way to pool a designated percentage of funds from each agency. This serves as a flexible source of money for creating supports that are tailored to the family and child's needs. At the administrative level, the agency directors work together to alter practices and regulations that pose unnecessary obstacles to collaboration. In some areas, such as Santa Barbara, California, the children's service agencies, including nonprofit organizations, are located in one building with shared space for conferences and informal discussions. Wraparound service models are becoming standard practice in some states, such as Alaska, Illinois, North Carolina, Pennsylvania, and Vermont.

Wraparound services do pose many problems that must be solved with a steady commitment over time. The people who staff these services come from varied professions and types of training. They need to learn to communicate and cooperate with team members who have different perspectives on the causes of problems and their solutions. The various agencies involved in wraparound programs have distinct regulations, funding streams, and organizational cultures. These differences must also be transcended to coordinate planning and intervention.

Nevertheless, experience with wraparound services since the 1990s is beginning to produce a growing body of evidence supporting their efficacy (Bruns, Burchard, & Yoe, 1995; Eber, Osuch, & Redditt, 1996). Several state and local agencies have accumulated substantial experience in creating systems of care for children and youth with mental health challenges. As awareness of the value and necessity of home-based PBS services grows, it will be important for these new programs to formulate close working relationships with other components of the service system for children with developmental disabilities. Wraparound offers a model for overcoming organizational and professional barriers to comprehensive family support.

ENSURING THAT PBS SERVICES
ARE PRACTICAL AND FAMILY CENTERED

So far, this chapter has referred to PBS as if it were a matter of applying certain methods and values to promote improvements in child behavior and lifestyle and to strengthen family efficacy, autonomy, and cohesion. It has been suggested in the chapter that supportive contextual interventions, including other community resources, are likely needed for 30% or more of families that receive services. Systems analysis has been discussed, as well as the importance of embedding PBS into a practical service delivery system. Yet, there are two other ideas that we believe can ensure that PBS services to families are effective, practical, and family centered. One comes from ecocultural theory (Gallimore, Weisner, Bernheimer, & Guthrie, 1993). The second is the concept and measurement of family quality of life.

Ecocultural Theory

Ecocultural theory provides a template for understanding families in their cultural contexts. Because the demographic makeup of both the United States and Canada is changing rapidly, it is essential that PBS programs work with a variety of cultural and subcultural groups. Although ecocultural theory has many facets, this section focuses on two elements: 1) the meanings that family members give to daily activities and 2) the way that families accommodate a child's disability within the cultural context of daily activity settings. These two lines of thinking suggest some nonbehavioral ways in which PBS workers can intervene to support a family while providing PBS through parent education. Some of these interventions focus on rearranging the environment and negotiating new roles for family members.

PBS and ecocultural theory interact most clearly in analyses of daily routines or activity settings. *Activity settings* are contexts that one or more family members construct and carry out to maintain the family's day-to-day functions. These include basic routines such as cooking meals, dressing, bathing, grooming, communicating, sleeping, and so forth. Routines also include the various ways in which families respond to external demands, such as establishing practices around school homework, paying bills, going to work or school, and participating in activities with neighbors and extended family members. Other regular but less frequent activity settings might include going to the park, eating at restaurants, and attending church. Activity settings also include symbolic activities that are repeated over longer periods of time, such as birthday celebrations, holiday practices, and seasonal practices (e.g., an annual family trip to pick blackberries).

Activity settings define the structure of daily life for most families. They vary considerably from one household to the next based on cultural practices, SES, family constellation, work, and other contextual factors. A key concept in the theory is *accommodation,* which refers to the ways in which families construct and modify routines to meet the needs of family members, including the child with a disability. According to ecocultural theory, families strive to live by a set of cultural ideas about the way that daily routines should be conducted. For example, many families in North America aim to make dinner a special family time, when family members meet and talk about their day. Sometimes, however, family members with disabilities cannot fit into these routines without special accommodations. The family that values shared conversation at dinnertime may need to modify its dinner scenario to accommodate the needs of a child who communicates with a voice output communication aid (VOCA). Family members may need to learn to talk more slowly; allow more time for the child to respond with the VOCA; and use other ways to communicate, such as touches and gestures. In this example, the family achieves its ideal family dinner by modifying the routine to meet the needs of the person who uses an augmentative and alternative communication device. The accommodations are relatively small and, consequently, are likely to be sustained over time.

Other accommodations may involve larger changes from the family's ideal, may tax limited resources, or may modify a routine to such an extent that it is no longer sustainable. For example, in studies of Korean American immigrants whose children had autism and other developmental disabilities, Cho, Singer, and Brenner (2001) found that parents made various accommodations in response to the uncomfortable experience of having strangers stare at their child in public. Some parents' accommodations were to remain at home and spend as little time as possible in the community. The costs of this modification to daily routines were a sense of isolation and a reduction in pleasurable events. Other families found places in the community to take their children, such as fast-food restaurants and uncrowded public parks. They also purchased cars to avoid public transportation. These accommodations appeared to be less taxing and were most likely to be sustainable.

Ecocultural theory and its concepts offer a practical, family-centered way to think about PBS plus supportive contextual interventions. If behavior support strategies move families further from their desired daily activity settings, then families are likely to drop the strategies over time. On the other hand, if the strategies help families restore desired activity settings and reduce day-to-day efforts to respond to challenging behavior, then they are more likely to be sustained over time. For example, most families have a morning routine of roles, tasks, and social interactions that are each aimed at completing the routine. Ecocultural theory points to the ways that a family structures the morning routine, the meanings that the family attaches to the routine, the ways that the child's disability affects the routine, and the communication patterns among family members during the routine. This nuanced attention to the ecology and culture of routines can help PBS workers select behavior support strategies that are practical, culturally meaningful, and sustainable.

Family Quality of Life

The real-life examples reported in this book suggest that PBS has a radiating effect, improving not only the behavior of the child with a disability but also the quality of life of the family. When a family's fundamental difficulty is a child's challenging behavior, an effective, child-focused intervention can have positive repercussions for the family system and result in major family benefits. These benefits may include stress relief, enhanced social networks, and an increased sense of parent self-efficacy. For example, in their intensive work with families of children with severe disabilities, Koegel, Bimbela, and Schriebman (1996) and Lucyshyn and colleagues (1997) found that effective, child-focused PBS can lead to meaningful improvements in the quality of family life. If a child's challenging behavior causes parental depression, family social isolation, marital discord, sibling conflict, and/or employment restrictions, then effective intervention for the behavior may very well resolve these other problems. For example, a parent whose stress-induced intense anxiety is associated with episodes of child aggression may begin to feel more at ease when the challenging behavior is greatly reduced. In turn, the parent may have more time and energy to recognize and meet the social needs of other family members, feel more confident taking the child into the community, or have time to pursue family goals that extend beyond care for the child with a disability (Lucyshyn et al., 1997).

We have argued from the evidence, however, that in many families problems can prevent parents from learning, implementing, and sustaining behavioral interventions. In such cases, it is necessary to help families with their ecological, social, and/or personal problems. In these instances, supportive contextual interventions are likely needed to improve the quality of family life.

PBS aims to achieve two major goals. The first is to prevent, reduce, and eliminate challenging behavior and to replace it with socially acceptable behavior that is generalizable and durable. The second goal centers on improving the quality of life of people with disabilities and their families. Family quality of life is a relatively new concept to define and analyze, and it is emerging as an important part of disability policy analysis (Turnbull, Summers, & Poston, 2000). One well-reasoned, large-scale initiative to define and measure quality of life comes from researchers at the Beach Center on Disability (Turnbull et al., 2000). Since 2000, they have been developing a family quality of life taxonomy and measure that is based on extensive interviews with parents and other family members. They have identified nine domains that, when combined, are meant to define family quality of life. Table 7.2 presents each of these domains.

We believe that this taxonomy of family quality of life can help move home-based PBS services toward the multimodal, multisystemic approach for which this chapter advocates. Again, we believe such an approach is essential if the myriad contextual obstacles to effective service delivery are to be overcome and if the quality of life for many families is to be improved. Consider a family that is raising a 10-year-old boy with a developmental disability and severe problem behaviors. After completing a functional assessment of problem behavior with the child's parents, a PBS worker conducts a semistructured interview with the family, which focuses on the nine quality of life domains. The interview indicates that the family is experiencing difficulties across several domains that require additional family-focused supports and wraparound service coordination. In the daily family life domain, the parents report that several family activities are disrupted by problem behavior, including

Table 7.2.   Quality of life domains and definitions

Domain	Definition
Daily family life	The daily, recurring activities that help meet the individual and collective needs of family members
Family interaction	The relationship among family members and the relational environment in which the family operates
Financial well-being	The financial means to at least pay for what the family needs and, in some cases, to pay for what the family wants
Parenting	The activities of adult family members that help children grow and develop in multiple areas of life, including the emotional, social, intellectual, productivity, physical, and spiritual realms
Advocacy	The advocacy activities required by family members to benefit the family member with disability
Emotional well-being	The individual emotional and internal aspects of life, or the "becoming" of life
Health	The physical and mental health aspects of life
Physical environment	The physical environmental aspects of life, including dimensions of space, access to needed services, safety, and comfort
Productivity	The skills and opportunities to participate and succeed in various activities of life, or the "doing" of life

Source: Turnbull, Summers, & Poston, 2000.

mealtimes, the morning routine, and grocery shopping. In the family interaction domain, the parents report that they argue over how to address their son's challenging behavior. In the domain of financial well-being, it is noted that the mother had to give up her job because, due to her son's problem behavior, the school often called her at work to take him home. In the domain of parenting, the parents are frustrated by their son's continual problem behaviors at home, and their other two children without disabilities have begun exhibiting challenging behavior. In the domain of physical environment, the family's lease for their rented house expires soon and will not be renewed. Within the next 2 months, they need to find new, low-income housing that is suitable for a family with three children.

Consider now that the PBS worker is a member of a wraparound service team through which multimodal, multisystemic supports are coordinated. The many problems facing the family are linked to an intervention that is associated with a different mode of service. For example, challenging behaviors identified in the daily family life and parenting domains are addressed by PBS and activity setting analysis. A behavior support plan targets problem behavior during mealtimes, the morning routine, and community outings with the children (e.g., grocery shopping). Parental conflict identified through the family interaction domain is ameliorated by the parents' agreeing to attend short-term family counseling that focuses on problem-solving skills. The provision of this supportive contextual intervention is coordinated with home-based behavior support services through the wraparound service team. In the domain of financial well-being, school demands for the mother to pick up her son are resolved through coordination across PBS, family support, and wraparound services. For example, the school district and family support services agree to share the cost of education about PBS and to include the child's parents, teacher, speech-language pathologist, and paraprofessional aide. Based on functional assessment information, which indicates that sending the boy home is a reinforcing consequence, the school also agrees to stop calling the mother to take her son home. Given this agreement, the mother decides to seek new part-time employment. Finally, in the realm of physical environment, the family support specialist on the wraparound services team agrees to connect the family with a low-income housing specialist who will assist the family in securing a new rental home in the vicinity of their children's schools.

The taxonomy of family quality of life can help PBS workers and other members of a wraparound service team identify, select, and coordinate the provision of PBS, family support, and wraparound services. Such a team identifies and coordinates behavioral supports and supportive contextual interventions around the full range of issues facing a family. In turn, this helps create substantial improvements in the family's quality of life.

CONCLUSION

Based on a review of the behavioral parent training literature, this chapter has made the case that supportive contextual interventions are needed for many families. The review has shown that a variety of social and ecological factors, ranging from depression and illness to social isolation and cultural differences, impede success for some families. It has also illustrated the way that researchers have expanded the focus of parent training interventions to address these obstacles. Examples have included the addition of marital counseling, stress management training, social support, self-management skills, treatment for depression, and behavioral family therapy. The chapter also has discussed ways in which researchers have improved recruitment and dropout rates, and it has demonstrated that many forms of supportive contextual interventions go beyond the normal purview of positive behavior support and psychological treatment. We have argued that comprehensive service models require attention to a larger unit of analysis—that is, systems design. We argued for some of the advantages of organizing services that are based on strongly linked service system models, such as the family support movement and wraparound services.

In addition, this chapter has stated that tools beyond those derived from behavior analysis and positive behavior support are needed. A primary example is activity setting analysis, which examines daily routines to understand the meanings of home life and examines the structure and content of routines to make accommodations more sustainable for families. We believe that a multisystemic, multimodal service system will help PBS to achieve its dual goals of replacing challenging behavior with durable, socially acceptable behavior and improving child and family quality of life. Based on these ideas, the authors make the following recommendations.

First, positive behavior support providers should design their services to include interventions and supports that deal with contextual overshadowing. This change will make positive behavior support interventions more successful and will improve the quality of life of families. Ecobehavioral and family support models are two possibilities. Whichever model is chosen, the positive behavior support team members should plan from the program's inception to deal with problems that have been empirically identified as overshadowing variables.

When families have complex needs, positive behavior support practitioners and researchers need to ally themselves with other efforts to improve family quality of life. The family support movement in the developmental disabilities field is a natural ally. In addition, when positive behavior support workers align themselves with family support programs, they should use a wraparound model for the coordination of interagency services.

In their first contact with parents, interventionists should make clear the program's mission. In this way, parents will understand from the beginning that, in addition to positive behavior support, the interventionists may suggest and provide supportive contextual treatments and/or support services. These interventions may involve work with the whole family. In addition, positive behavior support interventions ought to be designed, implemented, and evaluated with parents and/or other family decision makers serving as full partners. Allied family support programs should be consumer governed.

The interventionists should plan for long-term follow-up to promote maintenance. Follow-up methods might include periodic booster sessions, newsletters, telephone calls, and information about advice hotlines or web sites. Contracts with those supplying funds should include funds for follow-up contacts and services. Members of the positive behavior support team should anticipate that a family may require renewed brief assistance when developmental changes in the child, fluctuations in family stress, and major life events occur.

The positive behavior support program should account for ways to build supportive networks of parents who face similar challenges. Alternatives include Parent to Parent telephone-based networks, parenting classes, Internet chat rooms, and community-building activities. Alternatively, the program can ally itself closely with other organizations that provide these links among families facing similar challenges.

Activity settings provide a framework for conducting focused functional analyses. Interventions based on activity settings may involve changes in place of or in addition to positive behavior support. All interventions should take into account individual family goals and values.

Intervention evaluations should include quality of life indicators for the family as a whole. It is particularly important to ask about and deal with possible unwanted intervention side effects. Such side effects may include family arguments about how to deal with problem behavior or stress due to the extra work needed to implement an intervention.

Positive behavior support providers who take the ecobehavioral and ecocultural models to heart will likely discover that some key services or funds are not available to meet the needs of certain families. In these cases, positive behavior support providers should consider educating parents about advocacy. They also should consider working actively in the community to promote new supports and to organize new resources.

Researchers and program designers must pay more attention to the issue of long-term maintenance of positive behavior support for families. The quality of research evidence in this area needs to be improved. Service systems should devote resources to developing ways to promote maintenance over the long term. Finally, an expanded model for positive behavior support requires attention to systems analysis and service design. The units of analysis and the instruments for helping families must be enlarged.

REFERENCES

Adubato, S.A., Adams, M.K., & Budd, K.S. (1981). Teaching a parent to train a spouse in child management techniques. *Journal of Applied Behavior Analysis, 14*(2), 193–205.

Ainbinder, J.G., Blanchard, L.W., Singer, G.H.S., Sullivan, M.E., Powers, L.K., Marquis, J.G., & Santelli, B. (1998). Consortium to Evaluate Parent to Parent, USA: A qualitative study of parent to parent support for parents of children with special needs. *Journal of Pediatric Psychology, 23*(2), 99–109.

Allen, R.I., & Petr, C.G. (1996). Toward developing standards and measurements for family-centered practice in family support programs. In G.H.S. Singer, L.E. Powers, & A.L. Olsen (Vol. Eds.), *Redefining family support: Innovations in public–private partnerships* (pp. 57–85). Baltimore: Paul H. Brookes Publishing Co.

Baer, D.M., Wolf, M.M., & Risley, T.R. (1968). Some current dimensions of applied behavior analysis. *Journal of Applied Behavior Analysis, 1,* 91–97.

Baker, B.L. (1996). Parent training. In J.W. Jacobson & J.A. Mulick (Eds.), *Manual of diagnosis and professional practice in mental retardation* (pp. 289–299). Washington, DC: American Psychological Association.

Baker, K.L., Heifetz, L.J., & Murphy, D.M. (1980). Behavioral training for parents of mentally retarded children: One-year follow-up. *American Journal of Mental Deficiency, 85*(1), 31–38.

Bradley, J., Knoll, J., & Agosta, J. (Eds.). (1992). *Emerging issues in family support.* Washington, DC: American Association on Mental Retardation.

Bristol, M.M., Gallagher, J.J., & Schopler, E. (1988). Mothers and fathers of young developmentally disabled and nondisabled boys: Adaptation and spousal support. *Developmental Psychology, 24*(3), 441–451.

Bruns, E.J., Burchard, J.D., & Yoe, J.T. (1995). Evaluating the Vermont system of care: Outcomes associated with community-based wraparound services. *Journal of Child and Family Studies, 4*(3), 321–339.

Cho, S., Singer, G.H., & Brenner, M. (2001). Adaptation and accommodation to young children with disabilities: A comparison of Korean and Korean American families. *Topics in Early Childhood Special Education, 20*(4), 236–249.

Christian-Herman, J.L., O'Leary, K.D., & Avery-Leaf, S. (2001). The impact of severe negative events in marriage on depression. *Journal of Social and Clinical Psychology, 20*(1), 24–40.

Clark, H.B., & Clarke, R.T. (1996). Research on the wraparound process and individualized services for children with multisystem needs. *Journal of Child and Family Studies, 5,* 1–5.

Cochran, M., & Niego, S. (1995). Parenting and social networks. In M.H. Bornstien (Ed.), *Handbook of parenting, Vol. 3. Status and social conditions of parenting* (pp. 393–417). Mahwah, NJ: Lawrence Erlbaum Associates.

Cordisco, L.K., Strain, P.S., & Depew, N. (1988). Assessment for generalization of parenting skills in home settings. *Journal of The Association for Persons with Severe Handicaps, 13*(3), 202–210.

Costigan, C.L., Floyd, F.J., Harter, K.S.M., & McClintock, J.C. (1997). Family process and adaptation to children with mental retardation: Disruption and resilience in family problem-solving interactions. *Journal of Family Psychology, 11*(4), 515–529.

Cummings, E.M. (1994). Marital conflict and children's functioning. *Social Development, 3*(1), 16–36.

Dadds, M.R., & McHugh, T.A. (1992). Social support and treatment outcome in behavioral family therapy for child conduct problems. *Journal of Consulting and Clinical Psychology, 60*(2), 252–259.

Dadds, M.R., Sanders, M.R., Behrens, B.C., & James, J.E. (1987). Marital discord and child behavior problems: A description of family interactions during treatment. *Journal of Clinical Child Psychology,* *16*(3), 192–203.

Downey, G., & Coyne, J.C. (1990). Children of depressed parents: An integrative review. *Psychological Bulletin, 108* (1), 50–76.

Dumas, J.E. (1984). Indiscriminate mothering: Empirical findings and theoretical speculations. *Advances in Behaviour Research and Therapy,* *6*(1), 13–27.

Dumas, J.E., & Wahler, R.G. (1983). Predictors of treatment outcome in parent training: Mother insularity and socioeconomic disadvantage. *Behavioral Assessment, 5*(4), 301–313.

Dunlap, G. (1993). Promoting generalization: Current status and functional considerations. In R.V. Houten & S. Axelrod (Eds), *Behavior analysis and treatment* (pp. 269–296). New York: Kluwer Academic/Plenum Publishers.

Dunst, C.J., Trivette, C.M., & Deal, A.G. (1988). *Enabling and empowering families: Principles and guidelines for practice.* Cambridge, MA: Brookline Books.

Dunst, C.J., Trivette, C.M., & Deal, A.G. (Series & Vol. Eds.). (1994). *Supporting and strengthening families: Vol. 1. Methods, strategies, and practices.* Cambridge, MA: Brookline Books.

Dunst, C.J., Trivette, C.M., Gordon, N.J., & Starnes, A.L. (1993). Family-centered case management practices: Characteristics and consequences. In G.H.S. Singer & L.E. Powers (Eds.), *Families, disability, and empowerment: Active coping skills and strategies for family interventions* (pp. 89–118). Baltimore: Paul H. Brookes Publishing Co.

Eber, L., & Nelson, C.M. (1997). Integrating services for students with emotional and behavioral needs through school-based wraparound planning. *American Journal of Orthopsychiatry, 67,* 385–395.

Eber, L., Osuch, R., & Redditt, C.A. (1996). School-based applications of the wraparound process: Early results on service provision and student outcomes. *Journal of Child and Family Studies, 5,* 83–99.

Engelmann, S. (1980). *Direct instruction.* Englewood Cliffs, NJ: Educational Technology Publications.

Forehand, R., & Kotchick, B.A. (1996). Cultural diversity: A wake-up call for parent training. *Behavior Therapy, 27*(2), 187–206.

Forehand, R., Middlebrook, J., Rogers, T., & Steffe, M. (1983). Dropping out of parent training. *Behaviour Research and Therapy, 21*(6), 663–668.

Fujiara, G.T., & Yamaki, K. (2000). Trends in demography of childhood poverty and disabilities. *Exceptional Children, 66*(2), 187–199.

Gallimore, R., Weisner, T.S., Bernheimer, L.P., & Guthrie, D. (1993). Family responses to young children with developmental delays: Accommodation activity in ecological and cultural context. *American Journal on Mental Retardation, 98*(2), 185–206.

Griest, D.L., Forehand, R., Rogers, T., Breiner, J., Furey, W., & Williams, C.A. (1982). Effects of parent enhancement therapy on the treatment outcomes and generalization of a parent training program. *Behavior Research Therapy, 20,* 429–436.

Griest, D.L., Forehand, R., & Wells, K.C. (1981). Follow-up assessment of parent behavioral training: An analysis of who will participate. *Child Study Journal, 11,* 221–229.

Harris, T.A., Peterson, S.L., Filliben, T.L., Glassberg, M., & Favell, J.E. (1998). Evaluating a more cost-efficient alternative to providing in-home feedback to parents: The use of spousal feedback. *Journal of Applied Behavior Analysis, 31*(1), 131–134.

Hawkins, N.E., Singer, G.H.S., & Nixon, C.D. (1993). Short-term behavioral counseling for families of persons with disabilities. In G.H.S. Singer & L.E. Powers (Eds.), *Families, disability, and empowerment: Active coping skills and strategies for family interventions* (pp. 317–341). Baltimore: Paul H. Brookes Publishing Co.

Horner, R.H., & Albin, R.W. (1988). Research on general-case procedures for learners with severe disabilities. *Education and Treatment of Children, 11*(4), 375–388.

Horner, R.H., Dunlap, G., & Koegel, R.L. (Eds.). (1988). *Generalization and maintenance: Life-style changes in applied settings.* Baltimore: Paul H. Brookes Publishing Co.

Huynen, K.B., Lutzker, J.R., Bigelow, K.M., Touchette, P.E., & Campbell, R.V. (1996). Planned Activities Training for mothers of children with developmental disabilities: Community generalization and follow-up. *Behavior Modification, 20*(4), 406–427.

Kazdin, A.E. (2001). *Behavior modification in applied settings* (6th ed.). Pacific Grove, CA: Brooks/Cole Thomson Learning.

Kazdin, A.E., Siegel, T., & Bass, D. (1992). Cognitive-problem solving skills training and parent management training in the treatment of antisocial behavior in children. *Journal of Clinical and Consulting Psychology, 60,* 733–747.

Koegel, L.K., Koegel, R.L., & Dunlap, G. (Eds.). (1996). *Positive behavioral support: Including people with difficult behavior in the community.* Baltimore: Paul H. Brookes Publishing Co.

Koegel, R.L., Glahn, T.J., & Nieminen, G.S. (1978). Generalization of parent training results. *Journal of Applied Behavior Analysis, 11,* 95–109.

Koegel, R.L., Bimbela, A., & Schreibman, L. (1996). Collateral effects of parent training on family interactions. *Journal of Autism and Developmental Disorders, 26*(3), 347–359.

Lucyshyn, J.M., Albin, R.W., & Nixon, C.D. (1997). Embedding comprehensive behavioral support in family ecology: An experimental single-case study analysis. *Journal of Consulting and Clinical Psychology, 65*(2), 241–251.

Lundquist, L.M., & Hansen, D.J. (1998). Enhancing treatment adherence, social validity, and generalization of parent-training interventions with physically abusive and neglectful families. In J.R. Lutzker (Ed.), *Handbook of child abuse research and treatment* (pp. 449–471). New York: Kluwer Academic/Plenum Publishers.

Lutzker, J.R. (1984). A review of Project 12-Ways: An ecobehavioral approach to the treatment and prevention of child abuse and neglect. *Advances in Behavior Research and Therapy, 6,* 63–73.

Lutzker, J.R. (Ed.). (1998). *Handbook of child abuse research and treatment.* New York: Kluwer Academic/Plenum Publishers.

Lutzker, J.R., & Campbell, R. (1994). *Ecobehavioral family interventions in developmental disabilities.* Pacific Grove, CA: Brooks/Cole Thomson Learning.

Lutzker, J.R., & Steed, S. (1998). Parent training for families of children with developmental disabilities. In J.M. Briesmeister & C.E. Schaefer (Eds.), *Handbook of parent training: Parents as co-therapists for children's behavior problems* (pp. 281–307). New York: John Wiley & Sons.

Marquis, J.G., Horner, R.H., Carr, E.G., Turnbull, A.P., Thompson, M., Behrens, G.A., Magito-McLaughlin, D., McAtee, M.L., Smith, C.E., Ryan, K.A., & Doolabh, A. (2000). A meta-analysis of positive behavior support. In R. Gersten, E.P. Schiller, & S. Vaughn (Eds.), *Contemporary special education research: Syntheses of the knowledge base on critical instructional issues* (pp. 137–178). Mahwah, NJ: Lawrence Erlbaum Associates.

Neef, N.A. (1995). Pyramidal parent training by peers. *Journal of Applied Behavior Analysis, 28*(3), 333–337.

O'Dell, S., Flynn, J., & Benlolo, L.A. (1977). A comparison of parent training techniques in child behavior modification. *Journal of Behavior Therapy and Experimental Psychiatry, 8*(3), 261–268.

Sameroff, A., & Fiese, B.H. (2000). Transactional regulation: The developmental ecology of early intervention. In J.P. Shonkoff & S. J. Meisels (Eds.), *Handbook of early childhood intervention* (2nd ed., pp. 135–159). New York: Cambridge University Press.

Sanders, M.R. (1996). New directions in behavioral family intervention with children. In T.H. Ollendick & R.J. Prinz (Eds.), *Advances in clinical child psychology: Vol. 18* (pp. 283–329). New York: Kluwer Academic/Plenum Publishers.

Sanders, M.R., & Dadds, M.R. (1982). The effects of planned activities and child management procedures in parent training: An analysis of setting generality. *Behavior Therapy, 13*(4), 452–461.

Sanders, M.R., & Dadds, M.R. (1993). *Behavior family intervention.* Needham Heights, MA: Allyn & Bacon.

Sanders, M.R., & Glynn, T. (1981). Training parents in behavioural self-management: An analysis of generalization and maintenance. *Journal of Applied Behavior Analysis, 14*(3), 223–237.

Sanders, M.R., & Plant, K. (1989). Programming for generalization to high and low risk parenting situations in families with oppositional developmentally disabled preschoolers. *Behavior Modification, 13*(3), 283–305.

Serketich, W.J., & Dumas, J.E. (1996). The effectiveness of behavioral parent training to modify antisocial behavior in children: A meta-analysis. *Behavior Therapy, 27*(2), 171–186.

Sherman, A. (1994). *Wasting America's future: The Children's Defense Fund report on the costs of childhood poverty.* Boston: Beacon Press.

Simons, R.L., Lin, K.H., Gordon, L.C., Conger, R.D., & Lorenz, F.O. (1999). Explaining the higher incidence of adjustment problems among children of divorce compared with those in two-parent families. *Journal of Marriage and the Family, 61*(4), 1020–1033.

Singer, G.H.S. (1996). Introduction: Trends affecting home and community care for people with chronic conditions in the United States. In G.H.S. Singer, L.E. Powers, & A.L. Olsen (Vol. Eds.), *Redefining family support: Innovations in public–private partnerships* (pp. 3–38). Baltimore: Paul H. Brookes Publishing Co.

Singer, G.H.S., & Irvin L.K. (Eds.). (1989). *Support for caregiving families: Enabling positive adaptation to disability.* Baltimore: Paul H. Brookes Publishing Co.

Singer, G.H.S., Irvin, L.K., & Hawkins, N. (1988). Stress management training for parents of children with severe handicaps. *Mental Retardation, 26*(5), 269–277.

Singer, G.H.S., Irvin, L.K., Irvine, B., Hawkins, N.J., & Cooley, E. (1989). Evaluation of community-based support services for families of persons with developmental disabilities. *Journal of The Association for Persons with Severe Handicaps, 14*(4), 312–323.

Singer, G.H.S., Irvine, A.B., & Irvin, L.K. (1989). Expanding the focus of behavioral parent training: A contextual approach. In G.H.S. Singer & L.K. Irvin (Eds.) *Support for caregiving families: Enabling positive adaptation to disability* (pp. 85–102). Baltimore: Paul H. Brookes Publishing Co.

Singer, G.H.S., Marquis, J., Powers, L.K., Blanchard, L., Divenere, N., Santelli, B., Ainbinder, J.G., & Sharp, M. (1999). A multi-site evaluation of parent to parent programs for parents of children with disabilities. *Journal of Early Intervention, 22*(3), 217–229.

Singer, G.H.S., & Powers, L.E. (Eds.). (1993). *Families, disability, and empowerment: Active coping skills and strategies for family interventions.* Baltimore: Paul H. Brookes Publishing Co.

Singer, G.H.S., Powers, L.E., & Olsen, A.L. (Vol. Eds.). (1996). *Redefining family support: Innovations in public–private partnerships.* Baltimore: Paul H. Brookes Publishing Co.

Singer, G.H.S., & Yovanoff, P. (1993). *A meta analysis of depression in parents of children with developmental disabilities and parents of typical developing children.* Unpublished manuscript, Graduate School of Education, University of California at Santa Barbara.

Singer, J. (1993). *A qualitative study of the coping strategies and social support in the lives of parents having a child with a serious emotional or behavioral disorder.* Unpublished doctoral dissertation, University of Oregon, Eugene.

Smith, T.B., Innocenti, M.S., Boyce, G.C., & Smith, C.S. (1993). Depressive symptomology and interaction behaviors of mothers having a child with disabilities. *Psychological Report, 73*(3), 1184–1186.

Stokes, T.F., & Baer, D.M. (1977). An implicit technology of generalization. *Journal of Applied Behavior Analysis, 10,* 349–367.

Stokes, T.F., & Osnes, P.G. (1989). An operant pursuit of generalization. *Behavior Therapy, 20,* 337–355.

Strain, P.S., Young, C.C., & Horowitz, J. (1981). Generalized behavior change during oppositional child training: An examination of child and family demographic variables. *Behavior Modification, 5*(1), 15–26.

Turnbull, A.P., & Turnbull, R.H. (2001). *Families, professionals, and exceptionality: A special partnership.* Upper Saddle River, NJ: Prentice Hall.

Turnbull, H.R., Summers, J., & Poston, D. (2000, August). *Enhancing family quality of life through partnerships and core concepts of U.S. disability policy.* Paper presented at the Eloisa de Lorenzo family quality of life symposium, Seattle.

U.S. Census Bureau. (2000). *Poverty: 1999 highlights* [On line]. (Available: http://www.census.gov/hhes/poverty/poverty99/pov99hi.html)

VanDenBerg, J.E., & Grealish, E.M. (1996). Individualized services and supports through the wraparound process: Philosophy and procedures. *Journal of Child and Family Studies, 5*(1), 7–21.

Wahler, R.G. (1980). The insular mother: Her problems in parent–child treatment. *Journal of Applied Behavior Analysis, 13,* 207–208.

Wahler, R.G. (1988). Skill deficits and uncertainty: An interbehavioral view on the parenting problems of multi-stressed mothers. In R. DeV. Peters & R. McMahon (Eds.), *Social learning and systems approaches to marriage and the family* (pp. 45–71). Philadelphia: Brunner/Mazel.

Wahler, R.G., Cartor, P.G., Fleischman, J., & Lambert, W. (1993). The impact of synthesis teaching and parent training with mothers of conduct-disordered children. *Journal of Abnormal Child Psychology, 21*(4), 425–440.

Webster-Stratton, C. (1994). Advancing videotape parent training: A comparison study. *Journal of Consulting and Clinical Psychology, 62*(3), 583–593.

Webster-Stratton, C. (1997). From parent training to community building. *Families in Society, 78*(2), 156–171.

Webster-Stratton, C. (1998). Parent training with low-income families: Promoting parental engagement through a collaborative approach. In J.R. Lutzker (Ed.), *Handbook of child abuse research and treatment* (pp. 183–210). New York: Kluwer Academic/Plenum Publishers.

Webster-Stratton, C., & Hammond, M. (1990). Predictors of treatment outcome in parent training for families with conduct problem children. *Behavior Therapy, 21*(3), 319–337.

Webster-Stratton, C., & Hammond, M. (1997). Treating children with early-onset conduct problems: A comparison of child and parent training interventions. *Journal of Consulting and Clinical Psychology, 65*(1), 93–109.

Webster-Stratton, C., & Hancock, L. (1998). Training for parents of young children with conduct problems: Content, methods, and therapeutic processes. In J.M. Briesmeister & C.E. Schaefer (Eds.), *Handbook of parent training: Parents as co-therapists for children's behavior problems* (2nd ed., pp. 98–152). New York: John Wiley & Sons.

CHAPTER 8

Teaching Communication Skills for Behavioral Support in the Context of Family Life

Pat Mirenda, Teresa MacGregor, and Shannon Kelly-Keough

This chapter focuses on practical strategies and procedures that family members and others can use to design and implement a range of communication-based interventions for behavioral support in homes. To accomplish this, the chapter operates simultaneously on two levels: 1) the general level, with regard to practical strategies and principles that apply to home-based interventions for children who have difficulty communicating as a result of one or more developmental disabilities, and 2) the specific level, with regard to twin girls (Haley and Kelti) who both have pervasive developmental disorder (PDD) and profound hearing impairments. The chapter was written by a university professor who was employed from 1992 to 1996 as Director of Research and Training for CBI Consultants, the agency in British Columbia, Canada, that provided behavioral support to the twins' family (Pat Mirenda); the CBI consultant who was directly involved with the family (Teresa MacGregor); and the twins' mother (Shannon Kelly-Keough).

There are many unique challenges with regard to communication interventions implemented in homes, including those related to assessment (e.g., How does one determine which, if any, communication interventions are appropriate?), intervention design (e.g., Which communication interventions are appropriate, and what should they look like?), and implementation within the family context (e.g., How does one implement the intervention within natural home routines?). Basic principles and techniques, along with examples, are discussed for all three areas.

INTRODUCING THE TWINS

In February 1995, CBI Consultants, an agency providing behavior support services to children and adults in British Columbia, Canada, received a referral for 6-year-old twin girls, Haley and Kelti, who were experiencing severe behavior problems both at home and at school. The girls lived in a suburban neighborhood with their mother Shannon, who at the time was unemployed and was supported through social assistance (i.e., "welfare"). Both twins were profoundly deaf at birth and were diagnosed at 1 year of age. Immediately after the diagnosis, Shannon enrolled in sign language courses and quickly became a proficient signer. The girls attended a preschool class for deaf children from ages 3 to 5 and made some progress in learning to sign. However, their mother and their teachers were concerned about the twins' lack of social, communication, and language development despite the fact that they were in rich signing environments. Kelti began to have seizures at age 3 and was placed on medication to control them. Both girls were diagnosed at age $3\frac{1}{2}$ with PDD by an assessment team from the hearing disorders program at a large medical center near their home. At age 5, they began attending an inclusive school in which deaf students are provided with American Sign Language (ASL) translators and other supports.

Both girls are primarily visual learners and are easily distracted visually. Despite their commonalities, however, the girls have different personalities. Haley has been described as being funny, impatient, stubborn, determined, and independent. She is relatively more social than her sister and, prior to her referral to CBI, had invented many signs to represent objects and events for which she did not know the "correct" signs. In contrast, Kelti has been described as a "delicate flower" who is sensitive, easily upset, and very much prefers predictable routines. She loves physical activities such as running, swimming, bowling, and, above all, climbing. She is very determined and tries hard to do well at new activities, but she needs a lot of reassurance and is easily confused or frustrated by too much information or by information that is too complex.

When the twins were referred to CBI in 1995, they were in the same first-grade class. Haley's sign vocabulary was too large to count, and Kelti's repertoire consisted of approximately 80 signs. They had many similar, destructive behaviors: hitting, kicking, yelling and screaming, crying, and noncompliance (e.g., lying on the floor and covering their eyes). In addition, Haley often ran away from Shannon in public places to look at or touch unfamiliar items; Kelti engaged in self-injurious behavior (hitting her head with a closed fist), had frequent toileting accidents, and occasionally stopped signing at school for months at a time. Shannon estimated that Haley's behavioral outbursts, consisting of one or more of the just-mentioned behaviors, occurred approximately 15–20 times per day; Kelti's episodes, although somewhat less frequent (i.e., 10–15 times per day), were usually more intense and of longer duration. Shannon remembered their behavior as being both exhausting and challenging and also recalled being told that much of their behavior was her fault:

> It was like they were always trying to escape, they were always trying to get away. Kelti would eat books instead of reading them. She'd eat books, she'd eat plants, she'd fill her mouth full of rocks. They'd climb up on the furniture in someone's office or home, and Kelti still wasn't toilet trained. I didn't see anyone else's kids doing this, but I just kept getting told . . . that I wasn't signing well enough and so that's why they weren't learning.

FUNCTIONAL ASSESSMENT

The purpose of a functional assessment is to understand a person's strengths, preferences, and communication strategies in addition to the events and circumstances that influence his or her problem behavior (Koegel, Koegel, & Dunlap, 1996, p. xiv). Many useful processes and strategies have been devised over the years to accomplish this (e.g., Carr et al., 1994;

Meyer & Evans, 1989; Willis, LaVigna, & Donnellan, 1989). One of the most commonly used functional assessment approaches involves two primary assessment tools, the Functional Analysis Interview (FAI) and the Functional Analysis Observation (FAO), and a process for analyzing and summarizing them (O'Neill et al., 1997). The FAI provides information about ten aspects related to the problem behavior(s) of concern, including descriptions of the behaviors themselves, the setting events (i.e., ecological events) that predict or set up the behaviors, the specific immediate antecedent events that predict when the behaviors are likely and not likely to occur, and the consequences and functions of the behaviors. The FAI takes from 60 to 90 minutes to complete and can easily be conducted in the home. Although some family members may be able to complete it on their own, it is best to complete it though an interview between someone who is familiar with its use (e.g., a teacher, a behavior support consultant) and one or more individuals who know the person well (e.g., parents).

Haley and Kelti

Over the course of 2 days, Teresa conducted one FAI for Haley and one for Kelti by interviewing Shannon at home while the twins were in school. Separate interviews were completed for each girl to avoid the assumption that the twins' behaviors were similar in function, even though the behaviors were similar in topography (i.e., appearance). The interviews took approximately 75 minutes each; when asked about the experience 42 months later, Shannon remembered it well:

> *I remember the days that we were doing the assessment, when Teresa would leave, I'd be in tears. It was really a combination of feelings—I was so happy that this was finally happening, that I was getting some help, but I was also emotionally exhausted from having to talk about the girls' behavior problems so much. It was also a relief to find out that, no, it wasn't my fault; then, I started feeling guilty like, "Oh, my gosh, I should have done this years ago." It also made me realize that the deafness was this little, tiny thing that I had to deal with, but the PDD was this great big monster that was keeping me away from being able to deal with the deaf stuff, which is what I had focused on for so long. It really was grueling, but I also knew it was necessary so we could understand what was really going on.*

The results of the FAIs indicated that the twins' problem behaviors were similar but not identical in function. Haley's problem behaviors occurred most often when she was denied a preferred item or activity or when she was asked to stop a preferred activity. In such instances, the message of her behaviors was essentially, "I want that/I want to do that!" These were tangible-motivated behaviors, as they were done to obtain tangible items or activities. Second, Haley's problem behaviors occurred during transitions between activities or environments, when there were changes in an expected routine, when expectations or instructions were unclear to her, and when her signs were misunderstood. The goal of her problem behaviors in such instances was to escape from situations that she appeared to find confusing, frightening, or frustrating; the essential message was, "I don't like this!" The situations associated with Kelti's behaviors were similar but prioritized differently. Her challenging behaviors were primarily motivated by her desire to escape from any one of a number of situations, including nonpreferred activities, transitions between activities, activity interruptions or terminations, changes in routine, and/or unclear or confusing instructions or expectations. Second, Kelti's behaviors were tangible motivated and occurred when she wanted something and did not know how to ask for it. Neither twin engaged in behaviors that appeared to be attention or sensory motivated.

The results of the FAI suggested that Haley and Kelti both required communication interventions that provided augmented input to help them predict the sequences within and between activities. They also needed to be given clear input regarding instructions, expectations, activity schedules, and time lines. Because both girls were unable to make all of their wants and needs known, it also appeared that they would benefit from strategies to make specific requests. Finally, Haley needed a way to make herself understood when she did not know the conventional sign for an object or activity, as her use of idiosyncratic signs in such situations often resulted in communication breakdowns and associated behavior problems.

COMMUNICATION ASSESSMENT

Although the FAI includes questions related to the individual's strengths, preferences, and functional communication skills, it does not provide all of the specific information that may be necessary to design and implement a communication intervention for behavioral support. This may require additional assessment with regard to two issues: 1) the child's motor and visual skills, which affect the selection of a communication modality, and 2) the type(s) of symbols that the child can understand and use with minimal instruction.

Motor and Visual Skills Assessment

The basic motor assessment question that needs to be answered is, "From a motor perspective, in what ways does or could the child communicate?" For example, does the child speak adequately to meet all of his or her ongoing communication needs? Does or could the child point to an object or picture with a hand, finger, or fist? Hand an object or a picture to someone? Make a manual sign? Use eye gaze to look at objects or pictures? Answer "yes" and "no" questions clearly and accurately? Only if the answers to all of these questions are "no" will an extensive motor assessment be necessary, which will probably require the involvement of a professional team of occupational and physical therapists and is beyond the scope of this chapter. Fortunately, the vast majority of children who require communication interventions for problem behavior are able to use one or more of the previously listed motor techniques to communicate.

Similarly, the goal of a vision assessment is to determine how any visual impairments may affect the design of a communication intervention. For example, children with limited vision may need communication symbols to be enlarged, spread out with more space between them on a page, and/or placed within a particular visual field. They may need colored symbols or symbols placed on pages with a high contrast between the foreground and the background. Bailey and Downing (1994) articulated certain features of communication symbols that may help to gain an individual's visual attention when he or she has difficulty in this area. In general, vision assessment should be conducted by a qualified ophthalmologist.

Haley and Kelti   There were no motor or vision concerns for either of the twins. They both had good fine motor skills for manual signing and excellent gross motor skills. Neither of the girls wore or needed glasses.

Symbol Assessment

Many children with behavior problems are also unable to speak and may use one or more types of symbols to communicate. These include real objects, photographs, black-and-white line drawings (e.g., Picture Communication Symbols [PCSs], Mayer-Johnson Co., 1994), manual signs, or written words. The goal of a symbol assessment is to identify the type(s) of symbols that will meet a individual's current communication needs and match his or her current abilities, as well as to identify symbol options that might be used in the future.

Assessment of an individual's ability to use symbols usually involves several steps. Prior to the assessment, 10 or so functional items with which the child is familiar should be identified by family members, teachers, or other frequent communication partners. These might include items such as a cup, brush, washcloth, spoon, and so forth. Whenever possible, family members should be involved as "experts" on the child during this selection process, as one of the most common errors is to attempt a symbol assessment using items with which the child is unfamiliar. Next, sets of symbols representing the selected items should be compiled from a variety of sources. These might include sets of similar objects, colored photographs, one or more sets of commercially available symbols, and cards with written words on them.

Several formats can be used to conduct the assessment, including the receptive language, yes/no, and visual matching formats described by Beukelman and Mirenda (1998). (See Franklin, Mirenda, & Phillips, 1996, and Mirenda & Locke, 1989, for the research on which these formats were based.) In the receptive labeling format, the person conducting the assessment simply presents two or more symbols of a particular type to the child and, depending on the child's motor abilities, asks him or her to "Give me/point to/look at the (label for one of the symbols)." For example, the assessor holds up photographs of a cup and a shoe and says to the child, "Point to the shoe." If the child is able to clearly and accurately communicate "yes" and "no," then a yes/no format can be used. In this type of assessment, the assessor holds up one symbol at a time (e.g., one photograph) and asks, "Is this a (label of item)?" Trials should be arranged so that "yes" and "no" questions are presented randomly across all items. Regardless of the format used, each symbol should be presented two or three times to determine the consistency of the child's responses. The assessor can simply record which symbols the child identifies correctly and incorrectly, using a form such as the one provided in Figure 8.1.

Sometimes, symbol assessment cannot be conducted through either the receptive labeling or yes/no formats because individuals do not understand the task expectations and/or the language used. However, there is evidence that a visual matching format produces comparable results (Franklin et al., 1996); thus, this format may serve as a useful alternative. In a standard visual matching assessment, a single object is provided to the child, and two or more symbols (e.g., two photographs, two PCSs)—one of which matches the object—are laid out on a table. The child is asked to match his or her object to its corresponding symbol by placing it on, pointing to, or looking at the correct symbol. The task is repeated for each object in the symbol set, and the correct and incorrect responses are recorded. (For more detailed information about symbol assessment, see Beukelman & Mirenda, 1998.)

Symbol Assessment Form

Format used: _____ Receptive language   _____ Yes/No   _____ Visual matching

Number of items provided: _____

Instructions given to the child: _____

_____

Response accepted as correct (e.g., eye gaze, point): _____

_____

Indicate correct (+) or incorrect (-) in the appropriate column:

Item no.	Items used for the assessment	Real objects	Color photographs	Line drawings Type: _____	Written words	Other: _____
1						
2						
3						
4						
5						
6						
7						
8						
9						
10						

Figure 8.1.   Sample symbol assessment form. (From Beukelman, D.R., & Mirenda, P. [1998]. *Augmentative and alternative communication: Management of severe communication disorders in children and adults* [2nd ed., p. 200]. Baltimore: Paul H. Brookes Publishing Co.; adapted by permission.)

The results of the symbol assessment are analyzed to select one or more types of symbols that the child can likely use readily in communication interventions. To avoid frustration or confusion, it is critical to a select symbol set(s) with which the child is likely to give highly accurate responses, especially when communication interventions are designed in response to problem behaviors. This may mean that the type(s) of symbol used is other than that used in his or her primary communication system, which may be more cognitively demanding. Generally, it is wise to select a type of symbol for which the child scores at least 8 out of 10 correct responses. For example, if the child matches 9 of 10 objects with their corresponding photographs, 5 of 10 with their corresponding PCSs, and 4 of 10 with their corresponding written word cards, only photographs would be considered for use, as the other two types were recognized with considerably less accuracy.

Haley and Kelti   Teresa conducted the symbol assessment separately for each of the girls, and Shannon provided key assistance by acting as the ASL translator. Together, they identified a set of 10 objects with which both of the twins were both familiar and for which they knew the ASL signs; these included a ball, mirror, candle, cup, toothbrush, key, hairbrush, balloon, washcloth, and pair of sunglasses. They also compiled sets of 10 colored photographs, 10 PCSs, and 10 written word cards corresponding to the items, for a total of 30 symbols.

Teresa decided to use both the receptive labeling and the visual matching formats for the assessment because she wanted to ascertain the extent of both the girls' labeling and matching abilities. In the receptive labeling assessment, Teresa held up two symbols at a time (e.g., two PCSs) and Shannon signed, SHOW ME THE (SIGN FOR ONE OF THE ITEMS) (e.g., SHOW ME THE BALLOON). In the visual matching assessment, Teresa handed Kelti or Haley an object (e.g., a shoe) and placed two symbols on a table (e.g., word cards with CUP and SHOE written on them). Shannon signed, FIND THE SAME, and pointed to the object and the two symbols. Correct and incorrect responses were recorded on a form similar to the one in Figure 8.1.

Both Haley and Kelti identified and matched photographs and PCSs with high degrees of accuracy (between 80% and 100% correct). They were able to identify and match only 20%–40% of the written words. Based on this assessment, the PCSs were selected as the symbol set of choice because it is more convenient and less expensive to use than photographs.[1] Initially, Teresa and Shannon decided that Teresa would supply the necessary symbols because she had the Boardmaker software on her home computer. This saved Shannon both the time and the money that would have been required to produce the many symbols that were needed for the interventions.

COMMUNICATION INTERVENTIONS FOR BEHAVIORAL SUPPORT

In this chapter, the term *communication intervention* refers to a wide range of strategies and procedures with the common goal of facilitating an individual's ability either to understand communication from others (i.e., augmented input strategies; Wood, Lasker, Siegel-

---

[1]A binder of more than 3,000 PCSs in two different sizes (1" x 1" and 2" x 2") can be purchased from the manufacturer, Mayer-Johnson Co., and the complete symbol set is also available in a software program called Boardmaker for both PC and Macintosh computers. Contact information for Mayer-Johnson Co.: 800-588-4548 or 858-550-0084 (telephone); 858-550-0449 (fax); mayerj@mayer-johnson.com; www.mayer-johnson.com.

Causey, Beukelman, & Ball, 1998) or communicate more effectively to others (i.e., expressive communication strategies). A large body of research literature has demonstrated that both types of communication interventions can be effective components of individualized behavior support plans for children or youth with disabilities.

Augmented Input Strategies

One of the most common augmented input strategies involves the use of pictorial or written schedules to help the individual understand and follow predictable activity sequences in school and home settings (McClannahan & Krantz, 1999; Wood et al., 1998). In some research studies investigating this approach, children were taught to use within-task pictorial schedules to complete specific activities associated with their problem behaviors, such as hanging up a coat or putting away a favorite toy (e.g., Krantz, MacDuff, & McClannahan, 1993; MacDuff, Krantz, & McClannahan, 1993; Marshall & Mirenda, in press). In other studies, the participants used between-task schedules to predict what would happen next as they moved from one activity to the other (e.g., Flannery & Horner, 1994; Mirenda, Kandborg, & MacGregor, 1994; Robinson & Owens, 1995; Schmit, Alper, Raschke, & Ryndak, 2000). The results suggest that behavior problems can be reduced or eliminated completely through use of such schedules.

Expressive Communication Strategies

Perhaps the most extensively researched expressive communication strategy in the 1990s was functional communication training (FCT), which has been implemented successfully in homes and other settings. FCT involves "both the assessment of the function of the problem behavior and the teaching of a more appropriate form that serves the same function" (Durand, 1990, p. 23). For example, a child who has a tantrum to get his father to give him more juice might be taught to ask for juice verbally or to touch a picture of juice instead. Numerous studies have demonstrated that this strategy can effectively reduce or eliminate behavior problems in both children and adults, regardless of whether they communicate using speech or other forms of communication, such as manual signs or pictures (e.g., Carr & Durand, 1985; Mirenda, 1997; Tong, 1998).

Other reports have documented the successful use of concrete symbols, such as objects or line drawings, for choice making (e.g., Mirenda, 1995; Peterson, Bondy, Vincent, & Finnegan, 1995; Vaughn & Horner, 1995). For example, Vaughn and Horner provided food choices during mealtimes at home to Karl, a young man with autism. Sometimes, the choices were presented verbally (e.g., "Do you want X or Y?"); sometimes, they were presented verbally *and* with their corresponding photographs (e.g., "Do you want X [show photograph] or Y [show photograph]?"). With verbal choices only, Karl accepted about two thirds of the foods he chose, and he exhibited frequent disruptive and aggressive behaviors. When verbal and photograph choices were provided, Karl's acceptance rate for the foods he chose rose to about 85%, and there were many days on which he rejected no meals and exhibited no challenging behaviors at mealtime. From studies such as this, it is clear that choice-making interventions can substantially benefit some individuals with challenging behavior, probably because they clarify language input and/or increase predictability through the use of concrete symbols in addition to speech.

Finally, some children may benefit from the use of specialized expressive communication supports that may include symbol lists and/or monthly calendars (Hodgdon, 1996). Such supports may be needed to deal with idiosyncratic situational or individual needs. An example of one such strategy, a symbol dictionary, is provided later in this chapter.

COMMUNICATION INTERVENTIONS IN THE HOME

When the focus of implementation is on the home or other settings frequented by the family, it is critical to involve family members in decision making and to begin with issues that they deem priorities. Otherwise, family members may be asked to put considerable amounts of effort into implementing interventions that will have only minimal payoff for them on a day-to-day basis. For some children, this may mean that augmented input strategies will take precedence; for others, expressive communication strategies such as FCT may be more important initially. The sections that follow provide general information about when and how to implement a variety of communication interventions.

Within-Task Symbol Scripts

Within-task schedules, or symbol scripts, can be particularly useful when one or more problem behaviors occur predictably during specific activities that do not appear to be unpleasant, painful, frightening, or otherwise aversive. For example, a child might have a tantrum nightly when he is taking a bath or engage in aggressive behavior every morning while getting dressed for school. This is not the same as a behavior problem that occurs between activities or at the end of an activity; rather, the type of situation that calls for a symbol script is one in which merely participating in an activity seems to be problematic for the child. Functional assessment will usually indicate that the behaviors occurring in such situations are escape motivated; however, the reason why the child is trying to escape or avoid the activity is often unclear. In such cases, it may be that the child simply does not understand the sequence of steps that comprise the activity and attempts to escape from or avoid it. Thus, the intervention is designed to clarify the activity through the use of symbols that provide augmented input.

To design a symbol script, the activity should be analyzed on a step-by-step basis, as in a standard task analysis. Then, symbols of the appropriate type (i.e., photographs, PCSs, or written words, depending on the results of the symbol assessment) are produced for each of the key steps in the sequence. *Key steps* in this case means the steps in which the child is expected to actively participate or that have an impact on him or her in some way. The parent assembles the symbols sequentially on, for instance, the pages of a photograph album, a slide protector page, or a Velcro strip. Then, prior to the problem activity, the parent previews the activity with the child on a step-by-step basis, using the symbols for each step, as in the following example (words in small caps represent the symbols to which the parent points): "Now it's time to GET DRESSED for school. First, you need to TAKE OFF YOUR PAJAMAS. Then, you need to PUT ON YOUR UNDERWEAR," and so forth. Finally, during the activity itself, the parent uses the symbols before each step to tell the child what to do next, and provides assistance as needed: "Okay, let's TAKE OFF YOUR PAJAMAS now (assist). Great, your pajamas are off! Now, let's PUT ON CLEAN UNDERWEAR (assist)," and so on. Remember that the purpose of the script is not to teach independence but, rather, to clarify the sequence of the steps required.

Kelti   Shannon had no difficulty deciding that Kelti's evening hair washing routine was a top priority for intervention. Every evening, Kelti had a tantrum in the bathtub when it was time to wash her hair; the tantrum consisted of kicking, self-injurious behavior, attempts to bite and hit Shannon, and screaming. Teresa suggested that Shannon implement a within-activity symbol script, based on her hypothesis that Kelti's behavior occurred because she did not understand the sequence and/or the expectations inherent in the routine. She assembled a simples sequence of four PCSs depicting the key steps in the routine (see Figure 8.2): 1) take out the shampoo, 2) put some shampoo on Kelti's hair, 3) wash her hair to the count of eight (the upper limit of Kelti's counting ability at that time), and 4) rinse off the shampoo. The symbols were printed on a sheet of paper, which was laminated so that it could be fastened to the bathtub wall with Velcro and not get wet.

Teresa and Shannon role-played using the script prior to bath time and during the hair washing routine itself. Teresa suggested that they skip Kelti's hair washing altogether for a few days and simply role-play each step with Kelti so that Kelti would have several exposures to the script prior to actually using it during hair washing. Thus, armed with an empty shampoo bottle, Shannon and Kelti rehearsed the routine in their empty bathtub using the symbol script, with Kelti counting to eight at the appropriate step while Shannon pretended to wash her hair. Finally, after 3 days of practice, Shannon put water in the tub, had Kelti take her usual bath, and then pointed to the script to indicate that it was time to begin the activity. They proceeded as they had rehearsed, this time with real shampoo and real water—and Kelti had no tantrum whatsoever during hair washing for the first time in years! Shannon recalled the experience:

> *I had cut Kelti's hair because I couldn't comb it or wash it properly. She has a really sensitive scalp, and I thought, "Well, this is the way it's always going to be, I guess." But not only does she have a sensitive scalp, she didn't know what was expected of*

Figure 8.2.   Within-task PCS sequence used for Kelti's hair washing routine. (Picture Communication Symbols, Copyright 1981–2002, Mayer-Johnson, Incorporated, all rights reserved. The PCSs used in this chapter were taken from the Boardmaker software program and were used with permission [Mayer-Johnson, Inc., Post Office Box 1579, Solana Beach, CA 92075; 1-800-588-4548; www.mayer-johnson.com]).

her. So, when she didn't have a tantrum that first night, it was like magic, just like magic! For me, it was such a big success. It was really important to have success like that at the very beginning because it showed me, yes, this is the right move, this is the way to go, this is going to work! I just couldn't believe it!

Kelti's hair washing routine continued without any problem behavior for another 1½ years, at which point Shannon attempted to discontinue use of the symbol script. However, the problem behavior returned when the script was unavailable, so Shannon immediately reinstalled a smaller version of it on the bathroom wall, where it remains. Kelti is now able to wash her hair independently with the support of the script. Subsequently, she has also successfully used within-task symbol scripts during hand-washing and toothbrushing routines at home, with a similar reduction in problem behavior.

Rule Scripts

A variation of the standard within-activity script is one that is used to clarify the rules related to an activity rather than the sequence of steps that comprise it. For example, the rules for dinner time might be 1) eat what is on your plate/do not eat what is on other peoples' plates; 2) use your knife, fork, and spoon to eat/do not eat with your fingers; and 3) eat slowly and take small bites/don't eat quickly or take large bites. For some children, problem behaviors may occur because they are unaware of or uncertain about the rules that they are expected to follow, so within-activity rule scripts can be useful in providing augmented input.

As with standard within-task scripts, symbols must first be compiled to represent the rules of concern. The parent then rehearses the symbols and rules with the child prior to the activity itself. Next, the parent reviews the symbols representing the rules regularly during the activity and reinforces the child with praise or a preferred item or activity when the rules are followed (e.g., "You're doing a nice job of eating slowly and eating what's on your plate"). If a rule violation occurs, the rule script can also be used to provide feedback about the error and remind the child about the desired behaviors (e.g., "Whoops, you forgot to eat with your fork—remember, no eating with your fingers"). In effect, the symbols are used as instructional prompts to teach the child appropriate behaviors and what is expected of him or her in the situation.

Haley and Kelti   One of the primary contexts for both Haley's and Kelti's problem behaviors at home involved watching television or videotapes, highly preferred activities for both girls. Almost every time that Shannon interrupted either girl while engaged in these activities, a tantrum ensued. This was especially problematic on school mornings, when they preferred watching favorite programs or videotapes to getting ready for school, and on school nights, when the same was true for going to bed. Every school-day morning, Shannon would try to explain, "No TV because it's time for school," and every evening, "No TV because tomorrow is a school day," to no avail.

After 3 months of using symbols for other purposes, Shannon devised a "TV/No TV" rule script using PCSs. Shannon created enlarged PCS symbols for TV and NO TV and for SCHOOL and NO SCHOOL, as depicted in Figure 8.3. Every evening after the twins went to bed, she placed the appropriate TV and SCHOOL symbols directly on the television, depending on whether or not the next day was a school day and, thus, whether or not the twins were allowed to watch TV in the morning. When they woke up and headed for the

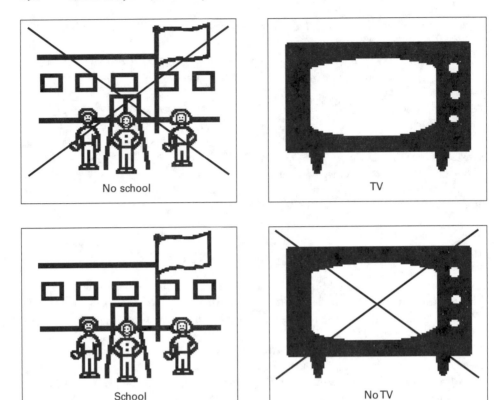

Figure 8.3.   Rule script for television used at home with Haley and Kelti. (Picture Communication Symbols, Copyright 1981–2002, Mayer-Johnson, Incorporated, all rights reserved. The PCSs used in this chapter were taken from the Boardmaker software program and were used with permission [Mayer-Johnson, Inc., Post Office Box 1579, Solana Beach, CA 92075; 1-800-588-4548; www.mayer-johnson.com]).

television, the rules were waiting for them, as was Shannon, who used the symbols to explain the rules to them. Initially, the symbols and her explanations met with the usual protests, but, within a week, the girls began to learn that not every morning was a "No TV" morning, and the tantrums gradually decreased in both frequency and intensity. Within a few weeks, the tantrums were eliminated completely. Subsequently, Shannon has successfully used rule scripts with one or both twins on numerous occasions, including "how to behave" scripts for the mall, for sitting in the front seat of the car, and at mom's wedding (to their new stepfather!).

Between-Task Symbol Schedules

Between-task schedules can be useful when one or more problem behaviors occur predictably at the end of specific activities and/or during transitions. For example, a child might exhibit challenging behaviors at home when moving from watching TV to eating dinner to brushing his teeth to playing outside. Again, a functional assessment usually indicates the presence of escape-motivated behaviors related to such situations. It appears that many children react very negatively to what they perceive to be a lack of predictability between activities and engage in problem behavior to escape from the resulting confusion. Indeed, it is not hard to imagine that children who have difficulty understanding and/or processing verbal or signed language input might find explanations in these modalities to be confusing and frustrating.

Many types of symbols can be used to construct a symbol schedule, depending on the results of the symbol assessment discussed previously. Once the appropriate type of symbol has been determined, specific symbols should be compiled for each of the activities or environments in which the child is expected to participate at home or in the community with the family. If real object or tangible symbols are used (see Rowland & Schweigert, 1989, 1996), then they can be collected in a large box to be readily available when needed. If photographs, PCSs, or printed words on cards are used, then they can be organized categorically (e.g., food, community activities, chores, things to do outside at home) and collected in a binder.

To construct a between-task symbol schedule, the parent and the child lay out a series of symbols in sequential order from the first to the last planned activity, with verbal or signed explanations, as appropriate. The number of symbols laid out at one time largely depends on two factors: 1) the nature and number of planned activities and 2) the child's ability to attend to the scheduling task itself. Often, short sequences of only three to five symbols may be used initially to introduce the concept to the child. For example, a series of symbols for a five-activity "going to the store" sequence might consist of PCSs representing 1) get in the CAR, 2) go to the STORE, 3) buy a DONUT, 4) get in the CAR, and 5) go HOME (the words in small caps are represented by symbols; see Figure 8.4). A series of containers (if real objects or tangible symbols are used) or a portable carrying case (e.g., a small photograph album) can be used to contain the symbols once they are sequenced.

Once the symbol sequence has been constructed, the parent helps the child use the schedule in a dynamic manner throughout the activity sequence. Table 8.1 presents an example of this assistance for the aforementioned "going to the store" sequence. As evidenced by Table 8.1, using a symbol schedule requires considerable preplanning on the parent's part. He or she must not only have the appropriate symbols available but must also insure that sufficient time is allotted to use them throughout the planned activity sequence. At first, it might seem that this strategy is "more trouble than it is worth." For many individuals who exhibit challenging behaviors during activity transitions or terminations, however, the results are usually well worth the time and effort spent. The strategy can result in dramatic reductions in problem behaviors, and it often teaches the person to manipulate, recognize, and use symbols to construct activity schedules independently.

Haley and Kelti The first strategy implemented with Haley and the second with Kelti was a symbol schedule that Shannon used to support their transitions between activities in the home. She created a list of all of the activities that might occur on a typical weekday or weekend. In the beginning, Teresa provided 2" x 2" laminated PCSs for each

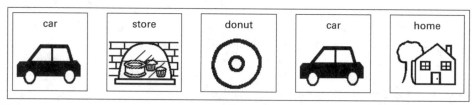

Figure 8.4. Between-task PCSs sequence for "going to the store" (from left to right): (1) get in the CAR, (2) go to the STORE, (3) buy a DONUT, (4) get in the CAR, and (5) go HOME. (Picture Communication Symbols, Copyright 1981–2002, Mayer-Johnson, Incorporated, all rights reserved. The PCSs used in this chapter were taken from the Boardmaker software program and were used with permission [Mayer-Johnson, Inc., Post Office Box 1579, Solana Beach, CA 92075; 1-800-588-4548; www.mayer-johnson.com]).

Table 8.1.   Example of a between-task symbol schedule for a five-activity sequence for going to the store[a][b]

Parent's comment	Child's action
AT HOME: "Okay, we're going to get in the CAR and drive to the STORE to buy a DONUT."	Follows along as the parent explains
"Let's go get in the CAR now."	Looks at the CAR symbol and gets in the car
UPON ARRIVING AT STORE: "We've finished the CAR ride now; let's turn over the symbol."	Turns over the CAR symbol, with assistance
"Now, let's go into the STORE."	Looks at the STORE symbol and walks into store with the parent
UPON REACHING THE STORE: "Here we are at the STORE."	Turns over the STORE symbol, with assistance
"Time to buy a DONUT; give this to the baker."	Takes the DONUT symbol and hands it to the counter person; receives donut and eats it
UPON FINISHING THE DONUT: "That was a good DONUT, right? Now it's all finished."	Turns over the DONUT symbol, with assistance
"Let's go back to the CAR."	Looks at the CAR symbol and walks to the car with the parent
UPON ARRIVING AT THE CAR: "Here's the CAR; it's time to get in and turn over the symbol."	Gets in the CAR and turns over the car symbol, with assistance
"Now it's time to go HOME."	Looks at HOME symbol
UPON ARRIVING AT HOME: "Here we are at HOME. Let's go inside and see what to do next."	Turns over the HOME symbol, with assistance, and enters the house

[a]Read table from left to right in rows.
[b]Words in small caps include the parent's point to the associated symbol.

activity. She organized the PCSs categorically in slide protector pages in a large binder so that Shannon could quickly locate the ones that she needed. Each weeknight after the twins went to bed, Shannon created short (i.e., three to five symbols) PCS sequences for their initial morning routines before school: get out of bed, go to the bathroom, eat breakfast, get dressed for school, and brush your teeth. Every morning, she went through the symbol sequences with the two girls, alternating between them for each activity. Shannon recalls, "I used to get up at 5 o'clock in the morning, it took so much time!" Yet, she also remembers, "I kept using the symbols because, for the first time, we could get through the morning without having a big scene!"

Soon, Shannon was creating symbol schedules for trips into the community—first with one of the girls at a time, then with both of them together, and, finally, for family special events, such as camping trips. Sometimes, the schedules were generic ("First we do A, then we do B, then we do C," and so on); other times, they were designed to solve specific problems. For example, Kelti had frequent toileting accidents whenever she was away from home—in the store, in the local swimming pool, at the skating rink, and so forth. After using generic symbol schedules with her for several months, Shannon and Teresa came up with a hypothesis about the nature of this problem behavior:

> We realized that maybe Kelti didn't know what to do. She would go to the bathroom at home, fine. She wouldn't go at school, she wouldn't go at the park, she wouldn't

go anywhere else. She would only go at home. If she was playing outside, she'd go outside; she wouldn't come in. One day, this light bulb went on: Every single time we go out in public, she pees herself. And what happens? She has to go home, the activity is finished—even activities she really enjoys, like skating. She thinks that if she goes to the toilet, the activity will end and the fun will be over! We have to show her that it's not over!

Shannon's solution was to use a symbol schedule to show Kelti that toileting could occur in the middle of an activity without the activity ending. Shannon recalled,

The next Sunday, off we went to the skating rink, but this time in her schedule book, we had symbols for SKATING, TOILET, and then SKATING again. We got her skates on, got her out on the ice, and let her do a couple of rounds. Then I said, "Come on, let's go to the bathroom," and showed her the symbol. She wasn't happy about it. She screamed all the way there because she thought we were going home, but she went to the bathroom, and I pointed to the SKATING symbol. Then, we went back to the rink— and boom! That was it! Toileting accidents just never happened again there! Then, we had to do it everywhere else—at the park, the swimming pool, the grocery store, school. We had to do it once in each place until we showed her in about a dozen places or so, then she got it: "I can go to the bathroom without having to go home!"

Currently, Kelti uses a symbol schedule at school and in the community, but she does not need this support at home. Haley has developed sufficient sign language such that she is able to understand activity sequence explanations without the support of a symbol schedule, except in novel situations (e.g., visits to new places, situations in which an expected community routine is altered in some way). Both girls have learned to construct and follow their own schedules as needed, and their transition-related behavior problems no longer occur.

Functional Communication Training

Within-task and between-task symbol schedules and rule scripts are examples of augmented input communication strategies that may be components of a behavior support plan. In addition, many individuals likely need one or more expressive communication techniques that are functionally related to their problem behaviors. For example, a child who hits herself to escape from an undesired activity might benefit from learning how to communicate the message, "Let me out of here!" instead. Another child who is predictably noncompliant when told what to do may be provided with a way to communicate a choice of activities when presented with two or three options. This type of intervention, FCT, can effectively both teach the child new communication skills and reduce problem behavior.

Preintervention Issues   To plan an FCT intervention, the function of the problem behavior must be identified. The functional assessment process described previously provides critical data in this regard; without such information, it is impossible to know which communicative message (or messages) to teach. In fact, there are often several problem behaviors that require one or more alternative communicative messages; these should be prioritized by family members so that the behaviors that they consider be the most disruptive can be addressed first.

The family should also be involved in deciding the exact form of the message that will be taught, based on the function(s) of the message. Messages should be constructed in ways that are culturally and logistically acceptable for family members so that when the child communicates, they are willing and able to respond (Durand, Berotti, & Weiner, 1993). For example, a child who engages in attention-motivated behavior could be taught to say, "Pay attention to me," but in a busy household, this request may be ignored sometimes despite a parent's good intentions. Alternative messages that are likely to result in parental attention and may also fit better with typical home life include, "Can I help you?" or "Can I watch you do that?" (Durand et al., 1993). Cultural acceptability is also important with regard to the form of the message. In some families, an escape-motivated message such as "Buzz off!" might be acceptable; in others, a more polite form (e.g., "Please leave me alone," "May I be excused?") is preferable. Family involvement in making such decisions is critical to the success of FCT interventions.

Another decision that must be made prior to beginning FCT is the communication mode that will be used. The options include those discussed previously—real object or tangible symbols, photographs, PCSs, and written word cards—as well as speech, vocalizations, simple gestures, manual signs, and even voice output communication aids if these are available (Mirenda, 1997). The communication mode should be selected with input from family members regarding their preferences. Often, even when symbol schedules are used for augmented input, FCT interventions may be implemented through modalities such as gestures, vocalizations, or manual signs. Because such communication modes do not require "external" symbols, they are always readily available to both the child and the family. Of course, it is important for the child to have the needed motor and sensory skills to use whatever mode is selected. Some examples of communication modes and messages that have been reported in the literature on FCT are summarized in Table 8.2.

To review, the pre-FCT issues that should be addressed include 1) identifing the function(s) of the problem behavior; 2) determining the form of the message to be taught, with particular attention to the family's cultural and practical preferences; and 3) deciding on the communication mode to be taught. Once these decisions have been made by the family, instruction can begin in the appropriate home or community setting.

Implementing Functional Communication Training   The goal of FCT is to teach the child to communicate by using a message form and mode that matches the function of the behavior. When instruction takes place at home and is provided by the family, it is best to use somewhat controlled but natural contexts initially to insure that adequate instructional support can be provided. The contexts in which the problem behavior occur should have been identified as part of the functional assessment. For example, the assessment may have indicated that a child's attention-motivated destructive behavior usually occurs when his mother is on the telephone or that another child's tangible-motivated self-injurious behavior occurs primarily during mealtimes at home when she wants more to eat or drink. During initial instruction, opportunities for the child to practice using the new communication form should be arranged in identical contexts at times that are convenient for the family. For instance, the first child's mother pretends to be on the telephone, and the father helps the child use his new communication form to ask for the mother's attention (e.g., the child hands her a symbol that means COME AND PLAY WITH ME). The second child's parent arranges a brief mid-afternoon snack time as a context for teaching the child to sign MORE food or drink to her brother.

Once the context has been arranged, the child is provided with instruction before the problem behavior occurs, through the use of hand-over-hand assistance, modeling, or ges-

Table 8.2. Examples of communication modes and messages reported in the functional communication training literature

Function of behavior	Mode/message	Reference(s)
Tangible motivated ("I want _____")	Manual sign (PLEASE or WANT + gesture (point to desired object)	Campbell & Lutzker, 1993; Day, Horner, & O'Neill, 1994
	Manual sign for desired items	Horner & Budd, 1985
	Voice output communication aid with a single MORE symbol on it	Durand, 1993
	Photographs or line drawing symbols for desired items	Lalli, Browder, Mace, & Brown, 1993; Sigafoos & Meikle, 1996
Attention motivated ("Pay attention to me")	Microswitch and tape recorder with single message tape that says, "Please come here," or "Somebody come here, please"	Northup et al., 1994; Peck et al., 1996
	Gesture (tap on adult's arm) that means, "Hello—pay attention to me"	Lalli et al., 1993
	Conversation books with colored photographs and line drawings to use during interactions with peers	Hunt, Alwell, & Goetz, 1988; Hunt, Alwell, Goetz, & Sailor, 1990
Escape/avoidance motivated ("I don't want _____")	Microswitch and tape recorder with single message tape that says, "I'd like a break now, please" or "Stop!"	Northup et al., 1994; Steege et al., 1990
	Manual sign for BREAK	Bird, Dores, Moniz, & Robinson, 1989
	Card with HELP, BREAK, or DONE printed on it	Day et al., 1994; Lalli, Casey, & Kates, 1995; Peck et al., 1996
	Voice output communication device with a single BREAK symbol on it	Durand, 1993

tural prompts to help the child use the new communication form. Table 8.3 displays how this support might look for the attention-motivated behavior described previously. In this example, one person (the communication partner) pretends to be on the telephone while a second person (the communication teacher) provides instructional assistance to the child.

From Table 8.3, it should be clear that in most cases, two people are needed during the initial phase of instruction. The most important requirement is that the communication teacher be very clear in providing assistance to the child to help him or her use the new communication form effectively before the problem behavior occurs. This person can be a parent, an older sibling, a friend, a teacher, a behavioral consultant, a child care worker, or any other individual who can provide clear and appropriate assistance. The communication partner should be an individual in whose presence the problem behavior usually occurs. In

Table 8.3.   Example of a functional communication training instructional sequence[a]

Communication partner	Communication teacher	Child
Picks up the telephone, says, "Hello," and pretends to have a conversation	Watches the child to see when he or she notices that the parent is on the telephone	Notices that the parent is on the telephone and begins to get agitated
Continues "talking" on the telephone	Provides hand-over-hand assistance to the child but no verbal prompt	With partner assistance, picks up the COME AND PLAY WITH ME symbol and hands it to parent on the telephone
Takes the symbol from the child, says, "Sorry—I need to go now," to the pretend telephone caller, hangs up the telephone, and plays briefly with the child	Not applicable	Plays with parent after he or she hangs up the telephone

[a]Read table from left to right in rows.

the previous scenario, for example, the partner was the child's mother, as the challenging behavior occurred primarily when she was on the telephone.

During practice teaching, the communication teacher should gradually reduce the directness of the prompts until the child is able to initiate the new communication form without assistance. Then, the child should be encouraged to use the new communication when these situations occur spontaneously (e.g., when the mother really is talking on the telephone). It is important that the communication partner be prepared to respond to the child's communication immediately and provide the desired outcome during initial instruction. Over time, brief delays can be inserted between the child's communication and the partner's response to teach the child to wait.

Many families may be unable to arrange initial practice instructional sessions because two people are not available at home. In this case, a creative solution might be to enlist the assistance of community members as communication partners if this is appropriate. That is what Shannon, as a single mother, did to teach Haley how to ask for permission to touch new things in the community, as described next.

Haley   Haley's most disruptive behaviors occurred in the community and were primarily tangible motivated: She often darted away from Shannon to touch or look at various objects, mannequins, store displays, or other visually interesting things. She did not want to own them as much as she wanted to look at and touch them and to have her adult partner tell her about them—what they were called, what they were for, and so forth. Haley's emerging curiosity was frightening to Shannon because Haley was unaware of danger and often ran away to look at something while Shannon's back was turned. Furthermore, when Shannon reprimanded Haley for running away, Haley responded by hitting her and yelling. Clearly, Haley needed a way to ask for permission to look at or touch things in the community in an appropriate manner. Shannon recalls implementing the intervention for the first time with the card depicted in Figure 8.5:

> *Teresa and I decided to use a card with a PCS symbol that meant "Can I touch this?" paired with YES and NO symbols, which Haley already understood. So Haley and I went to an interactive science museum for children, just the two of us, with this*

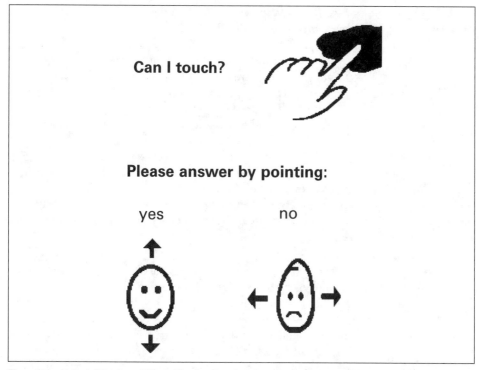

Figure 8.5. Haley's "Can I touch?" card for functional communication training. (Picture Communication Symbols, Copyright 1981–2002, Mayer-Johnson, Incorporated, all rights reserved. The PCSs used in this chapter were taken from the Boardmaker software program and were used with permission [Mayer-Johnson, Inc., Post Office Box 1579, Solana Beach, CA 92075; 1-800-588-4548; www.mayer-johnson.com]).

> CAN I TOUCH? *card. I helped Haley show it to the staff before she was allowed to touch any of the exhibits that were meant to be touched. The staff just touched the* YES *or* NO *symbol to answer her, as they couldn't sign. We started to use the card whenever we went out. If I saw that she was interested in something, I had her ask someone if she could look at or touch the object. She didn't hit the person when they said, "No," I guess because they were strangers. Eventually, she learned to take "no" for an answer from me, too.*

In this example, Shannon initially used the museum staff as Haley's communication partners, and she assumed the role of communication teacher. In other situations, she used shop clerks, waitstaff, or cashiers as partners by prompting Haley to ask them for permission to touch or look at novel items, until Haley could do so independently. Within a few weeks, Haley learned to ask for permission from someone rather than simply dart away and to understand that when Shannon or a community helper said "No," this did not always mean "No, never," but, rather, "No, not this time." As a result, Haley's hitting and yelling in public decreased dramatically.

Choice Making

Another way in which FCT can be implemented is to teach children to make choices related to food, drinks, activities, or people. This may be especially useful for problem behaviors that are either tangible or escape motivated. In either case, providing the child with a strategy for making choices may prevent the problem behavior from occurring.

Real objects, photographs or PCS symbols are used most commonly in choice-making interventions, as these are often easiest for the child to recognize with minimal exposure (Mirenda & Locke, 1989). Symbols are collected for a range of food, drink, and activity options that might be available to the child at various times in the home. Initially, the parent presents the symbols for two options to the child in an appropriate context. For example, a child who does not like being told what to do during her morning routine might be presented with the symbols WASH YOUR FACE and BRUSH YOUR HAIR and then asked, "Which do you want to do first?" A child whose behavior occurs when he or she is hungry after school might be shown GRANOLA BAR and RICE CAKE symbols and asked "Which do you want to eat?" Whatever the case, the idea is to teach the child to make choices using the symbols as an alternative to tangible- or escape-motivated behavior. Over time, the initial prompt (e.g., "Which do you want to eat?") should be faded gradually, and the child encouraged to initiate the choice him- or herself.

Kelti   Because Kelti understood and used so few manual signs, she frequently attempted to get what she wanted by hitting others and engaging in self-injurious behavior. Thus, an initial intervention for her involved using PCSs to help her make choices. Shannon and Teresa assembled a binder of approximately 100 symbols representing preferred foods, activities, and people. Throughout the day in a variety of contexts, Shannon offered Kelti two symbols at a time and asked her to choose between them—from symbols for breakfast foods to personal care routines (what to do first, next, on so on) to grocery items. Of course, Shannon simultaneously showed Kelti the manual signs that correspond to the symbol choices. Kelti soon began to enjoy making choices and to produce a greater number of manual signs, in addition to showing a marked decrease in problem behaviors.

Symbol Dictionaries

The symbol dictionary is an example of a specialized communication support that might be designed to meet a specific, idiosyncratic need. In the twins' case, the dictionary was designed for Haley because of frustration-related problem behaviors that occurred when people did not understand her manual signs. Over the years, when she did not know the correct ASL sign, she invented signs for objects, places, people, and actions. Unfortunately, most of these were not readily understood by Shannon or other communication partners. Haley engaged in frequent hitting, yelling, and other behavior when such communication breakdowns occurred.

The solution devised by Teresa and Shannon was to construct a symbol dictionary of PCSs representing the many foods, activities, places, animals, and people in Haley's life, as well as common colors, emotions, and action words. Whenever Haley used an invented sign, she was directed toward the dictionary and told, "Find it in the book." She quickly learned to flip through the pages, locate a symbol that at least approximated the word she wanted to communicate, and point to it. Shannon, in turn, provided her with the common manual sign for the word. Haley enjoyed the dictionary so much that she soon began looking through it on her own and pointing to symbols for Shannon to sign. Not surprisingly, her manual sign vocabulary increased rapidly, along with a reduction in communication breakdowns

and related problem behaviors. Although Haley's symbol dictionary is a unique intervention that may not be applicable to a wide range of children, it demonstrates the importance of examining individual child needs to design comprehensive communication supports.

CONCLUSION

Clearly, communication interventions to support children with problem behaviors can and should be implemented in home and other family settings. Often, parents are responsible for both designing and implementing such interventions, perhaps with support from consultants, teachers, speech-language pathologists, or others. This chapter has provided details to enable family members to initiate such interventions, at least at a basic level. Shannon, an extraordinary person in many ways, is no more extraordinary than most parents of children with developmental disabilities and problem behaviors who are committed to providing the communication, educational, and behavioral supports that their children need.

In September 2001, Haley and Kelti entered eighth grade. Neither has engaged in problem behaviors that exceed those of their peers for several years. Haley has made great progress in learning to read and write and has an extensive manual sign vocabulary. She still requires assistance at school to understand new concepts and tasks; this assistance is provided by an aide who draws pictures and diagrams for her during class discussions and lectures to illustrate the teachers' explanations and directions. Kelti is also doing well at school and has also made great progress in language and literacy development, although she still requires more support than her sister. At home, Kelti still uses augmented input strategies; in the community, both Kelti and Haley carry schedules and scripts, especially in new environments.

In 1996, as the girls' communication systems expanded and became increasingly awkward to transport, Shannon began sewing communication folders and waistband symbol displays for them. She now sells an entire line of home-sewn communication display products called the Portacom System through her business, Made by Mom Creations (www.por tacom.bc.ca). She regularly shares her family's story with parents and school personnel at workshops. It seems appropriate to give Shannon the final word: "If I can do it, you can do it. Once you start seeing the behavior as communication, it all starts to make sense!"

REFERENCES

Bailey, B., & Downing, J. (1994). Using visual accents to enhance attending to communication symbols for students with severe multiple disabilities. *RE:view, 26*, 101–118.

Beukelman, D.R., & Mirenda, P. (1998). *Augmentative and alternative communication: Management of severe communication disorders in children and adults* (2nd ed.). Baltimore: Paul H. Brookes Publishing Co.

Bird, F., Dores, P., Moniz, D., & Robinson, J. (1989). Reducing severe aggressive and self-injurious behaviors with functional communication training. *American Journal on Mental Retardation, 94*, 37–48.

Campbell, R., & Lutzker, J. (1993). Using functional equivalence training to reduce severe challenging behavior: A case study. *Journal of Developmental and Physical Disabilities, 5*, 203–216.

Carr, E.G., & Durand, V.M. (1985). Reducing behavior problems through functional communication training. *Journal of Applied Behavior Analysis, 18*, 111–126.

Carr, E.G., Levin, L., McConnachie, G., Carlson, J.I., Kemp, D.C., & Smith, C.E. (1994). *Communication-based intervention for problem behavior: A user's guide for producing positive change.* Baltimore: Paul H. Brookes Publishing Co.

Day, H.M., Horner, R., & O'Neill, R. (1994). Multiple functions of problem behaviors: Assessment and intervention. *Journal of Applied Behavior Analysis, 27*, 279–290.

Durand, V.M. (1990). *Severe behavior problems: A functional communication training approach.* New York: The Guilford Press.

Durand, V.M. (1993). Functional communication training using assistive devices: Effects on challenging behavior. *Augmentative and Alternative Communication, 9*, 168–176.

Durand, V.M., Berotti, D., & Weiner, J. (1993). Functional communication training: Factors affecting effectiveness, generalization, and maintenance. In S.F. Warren & J. Reichle (Series Eds.) & J. Reichle & D.P. Wacker (Vol. Eds.), *Communication and language intervention series: Vol. 3. Communicative alternatives to challenging behavior: Integrating functional assessment and intervention strategies* (pp. 317–340). Baltimore: Paul H. Brookes Publishing Co.

Durand, V.M., & Kishi, G. (1987). Reducing severe behavior problems among persons with dual sensory impairments: An evaluation of a technical assistance model. *Journal of The Association for Persons with Severe Handicaps, 12*, 2–10.

Flannery, B., & Horner, R. (1994). The relationship between predictability and problem behavior for students with severe disabilities. *Journal of Behavioral Education, 4*, 157–176.

Franklin, N.K., Mirenda, P., & Phillips, G. (1996). Comparisons of five symbol assessment protocols with nondisabled preschoolers and learners with severe intellectual disabilities. *Augmentative and Alternative Communication, 12*, 73–77.

Hodgdon, L. (1996). *Visual strategies for improving communication.* Troy, MI: QuirkRoberts Publishing.

Horner, R., & Budd, C. (1985). Acquisition of manual sign use: Collateral reduction of maladaptive behavior and factors limiting generalization. *Education and Training of the Mentally Retarded, 20*, 39–47.

Hunt, P., Alwell, M., & Goetz, L. (1988). Acquisition of conversation skills and the reduction of inappropriate social interaction behaviors. *Journal of The Association for Persons with Severe Handicaps, 13*, 20–27.

Hunt, P., Alwell, M., Goetz, L., & Sailor, W. (1990). Generalized effects of conversation skill training. *Journal of The Association for Persons with Severe Handicaps, 15*, 250–260.

Koegel, L.K., Koegel, R.L., & Dunlap, G. (Eds.) (1996). *Positive behavioral support: Including people with difficult behavior in the community.* Baltimore: Paul H. Brookes Publishing Co.

Krantz, P., MacDuff, M., & McClannahan, L. (1993). Programming participation in family activities for children with autism: Parents' use of photographic activity schedules. *Journal of Applied Behavior Analysis, 26*, 137–138.

Lalli, J., Browder, D., Mace, C., & Brown, D. (1993). Teacher use of descriptive analysis data to implement interventions to decrease students' problem behaviors. *Journal of Applied Behavior Analysis, 25*, 227–238.

Lalli, J., Casey, S., & Kates, K. (1995). Reducing escape behavior and increasing task completion with functional communication training, extinction, and response chaining. *Journal of Applied Behavior Analysis, 28,* 261–268.

MacDuff, M., Krantz, P., & McClannahan, L. (1993). Teaching children with autism to use photographic activity schedules: Maintenance and generalization of complex response chains. *Journal of Applied Behavior Analysis, 26,* 89–98.

Marshall, J., & Mirenda, P. (in press). Parent–professional collaboration for positive behavior support in the home. *Focus on Autism and Other Developmental Disabilities.*

Mayer-Johnson Co. (1994). *Picture Communication Symbols combination book.* Solana Beach, CA: Author.

McClannahan, L., & Krantz, P. (1999). *Activity schedules for children with autism.* Bethesda, MD: Woodbine House.

Meyer, L.H., & Evans, I.M. (1989). *Nonaversive intervention for behavior problems: A manual for home and community.* Baltimore: Paul H. Brookes Publishing Co.

Mirenda, P. (1995, November). *Schedule and choicemaking interventions for students with challenging behaviour.* Paper presented at the Annual Conference of The Association for Persons with Severe Handicaps (TASH), San Francisco, CA.

Mirenda, P. (1997). Functional communication training and AAC: A research review. *Augmentative and Alternative Communication, 13,* 207–225.

Mirenda, P., Kandborg, T., & MacGregor, T. (1994, October). *"What's next?": Activity schedule interventions for challenging behaviour.* Paper presented at the Sixth Biennial International Society for Augmentative and Alternative Communication (ISAAC) Conference, Maastricht, The Netherlands.

Mirenda, P., & Locke, P. (1989). A comparison of symbol transparency in nonspeaking persons with intellectual disabilities. *Journal of Speech and Hearing Disorders, 54,* 131–140.

Northup, J., Wacker, D., Berg, W., Kelly, L., Sasso, G., & DeRaad, A. (1994). The treatment of severe behavior problems in school settings using a technical assistance model. *Journal of Applied Behavior Analysis, 27,* 33–48.

O'Neill, R., Horner, R., Albin, R., Sprague, J., Storey, K., & Newton, S. (1997). *Functional assessment and program development for problem behavior: A practical handbook.* Pacific Grove, CA: Brooks/Cole Thomson Learning.

Peck, S., Wacker, D., Berg, W., Cooper, L., Brown, K., Richman, D., McComas, J., Frischmeyer, P., & Millard, T. (1996). Choice-making treatment of young children's severe behavior problems. *Journal of Applied Behavior Analysis, 29,* 263–290.

Peterson, S., Bondy, A., Vincent, Y., & Finnegan, C. (1995). Effects of altering communicative input for students with autism and no speech: Two case studies. *Augmentative and Alternative Communication, 11,* 93–100.

Robinson, L., & Owens, Jr., R., (1995). Clinical notes: Functional augmentative communication and positive behavior change. *Augmentative and Alternative Communication, 11,* 207–211.

Rowland, C., & Schweigert, P. (1989). Tangible symbols: Symbolic communication for individuals with multisensory impairments. *Augmentative and Alternative Communication, 5,* 226–234.

Rowland, C., & Schweigert, P. (1996). *Tangible symbol systems* (Rev. ed.) [Videotape]. San Antonio, TX: The Psychological Corporation.

Schmit, J., Alper, S., Raschke, D., & Ryndak, D. (2000). Effects of using a photographic cuing package during routine school transitions with a child who has autism. *Mental Retardation, 38,* 131–137.

Sigafoos, J., & Meikle, B. (1996). Functional communication training for the treatment of multiply determined challenging behavior in two boys with autism. *Behavior Modification, 20,* 60–84.

Steege, M., Wacker, D., Cigrand, K., Berg, W., Novak, C., Reimers, T., Sasso, G., & DeRaad, A. (1990). Use of negative reinforcement in the treatment of self-injurious behavior. *Journal of Applied Behavior Analysis, 23,* 459–468.

Tong, J. (1998). *Effects of functional communication training on reducing challenging behaviour in nonverbal individuals with developmental disabilities.* Unpublished master's thesis, University of British Columbia.

Vaughn, B., & Horner, R. (1995). Effects of concrete versus verbal choice systems on problem behavior. *Augmentative and Alternative Communication, 11,* 89–92.

Willis, T., LaVigna, G., & Donnellan, A. (1989). *Behavior assessment guide.* Los Angeles: Institute for Applied Behavior Analysis.

Wood, L., Lasker, J., Siegel-Causey, E., Beukelman, D., & Ball, L. (1998). Input framework for augmentative and alternative communication. *Augmentative and Alternative Communication, 14,* 261–267.

Learning to Collaborate as Colleagues

Our Key to Success

Susan Fake

My family's experience of positive behavior support (PBS) with my daughter Samantha has taught me many lessons. The one I wish to highlight in this essay is the tremendous power for change that is released when parents and professionals learn to collaborate and begin to work together as colleagues. The story of my daughter's development into a successful teenager and of my family's path to a happy life bears witness to the positive outcomes that can occur when home and school build a successful partnership. Samantha is 17 years old and attends high school. She enjoys her days at school, attending general education classes, singing in the school choir, and learning to support young children by taking child development courses. She has been on the honor roll for 4 consecutive years and, in fact, has been doing so well academically that she is now planning to attend college. When Sam—our family's affectionate name for her—is not being the diligent student, she is hanging out with her friends, talking about boys, gushing about favorite rock stars (e.g., 'NSync), and dreaming about the future. In many ways, she is very much the typical American teenager.

Samantha, however, is not like every teenager. She has autism, and our lives together were not always so pleasant. Before the fall of 1993, Samantha was extremely violent. My husband Ken and I lived in fear at home. Her teachers and aides dreaded her attendance at school. Neither we at home nor the educators at school knew what to do. Anger, resentment, and mutual recrimination soured communications between home and school. Fortunately, what began as a most grave situation turned out to be one of the most positive experiences of our lives.

Since Samantha's birth, our home life developed into a storm that did not abate. She began life as a colicky infant who cried constantly and almost never slept. She developed into an aggressive toddler and young child who was often completely uncontrollable. As she grew, she continued to kick, bite, spit, scratch, and head butt us for no apparent reason. When we tried to dress her in the morning, bathe her in the early evening, or put her to bed at night, she transformed into a tornado, rampaging through our small, cabin-like house. She knocked over lamps and tables, damaged doors, and smashed holes in walls. During these violent episodes, she grew stronger and more violent, and we feared for our safety. Her assaults left me bruised and battered at times. In three separate incidents, she cracked my ribs. The constant stress and repeated injuries so impaired my health that I began to experience daily anxiety attacks and eventually contracted arthritis.

My family had to find out what was causing Samantha to act this way. We had to find out how to calm this tempest. First, we turned to well-known behavior experts who tried to work with Sam. We watched as each told us in turn that they could not help us, that our daughter was too violent. We then worked with noted psychiatrists who prescribed various medications, most of which made Samantha's behavior worse. On the advice of other professionals, we placed her in a psychiatric ward for 8 weeks, where the staff tried new medications on her and put her into a straitjacket. In the end, it was a traumatic experience for both Sam and our family. They could not get her behavior under control and subsequently returned her to our care.

Back in our care, the storm raged on. During nonschool hours, we were trapped in our home. Outings to stores together were unthinkable, as she would run through aisles and knock items over. In the middle of the night, she would scream, waking our neighbors and fueling dark speculation about our parenting practices. When we saw our neighbors during the day, their troubled expressions betrayed the thought, "There but for the grace of God, go I." We were painfully aware that no one understood what we were going through. As my hope dwindled to a thread, I turned to God and asked for help. I prayed that some miracle would occur and that we would find a way to get through to her. I vowed that I would never give up on her. But for the time being, the storm raged on.

Samantha did not spare the school her wrath. Our tornado carved an indelible path through her classroom and school. On a daily basis, she bolted from rooms, ripped down displays, and destroyed school property. She often ran down hallways or out the doors onto school grounds, with aides and teachers running to catch up with her. She continually attacked her instructional aide, pulling her hair, putting her in a headlock, grabbing—and sometimes smashing—her glasses. These incessant and intense problem behaviors earned her the districtwide reputation of "The Wild Child." Almost every day, the school would call me or my husband and plead with us take her home. We often accommodated these requests. She was, after all, *our* wild child, and no matter how she behaved, we loved her.

As we continued our search for solutions, I did not know at the time that my prayer was about to be answered. The principal of Samantha's school had been informed by the district administrator that there were no other placement options available for Samantha, that his only choice was to make her current placement work. Soon after, we learned that the Experimental Education Unit (EEU) in the Department of Special Education at the University of Washington, Seattle, was helping to develop and test a new approach to problem behaviors called positive behavior support. We also learned that the school district had already contacted the EEU program and was planning to use this new approach with Samantha. We called the EEU and talked with Gigi DeVault, a doctoral student in special education. She explained PBS to us, emphasizing that it was a team approach in which we would first learn why our daughter engaged in problem behaviors and then, together with school staff, develop an individualized plan of support for Samantha. A functional assessment would be completed before the end of spring term, and key school staff would receive preliminary training in methods of PBS over the summer. Gigi was assigned the task of conducting summer training sessions and of facilitating a series of team meetings, which would begin at the start of the new school year. Another EEU program staff member, Cathy

Krug, was assigned the role of trainer to team members in the use of interventions. Cathy and Gigi would work together to complete the functional assessment and guide a group process toward developing a behavior support plan for Samantha. Cathy then would provide technical assistance to team members in the implementation of plan strategies.

During spring term while Samantha was still in second grade and over the summer, Gigi and Cathy completed the functional assessment. They interviewed school staff and conducted observations at the school. Cathy also visited our home and interviewed my husband, Ken, and me. She then completed observations in the home, as well as assessments of Sam's responses to various academic tasks. At the beginning of fall, after Gigi and Cathy had organized the results of the functional assessment, they scheduled the first meeting of Samantha's educational support team. Along with Ken and me and Cathy and Gigi, the team included Samantha's new fourth-grade teacher, the fourth-grade resource room teacher, Sam's instructional aide from the previous year, her speech-language pathologist, the school principal, and a district administrator. In the fall of 1993, with a nervousness borne of false starts, dead ends, and home–school conflict, we joined a process of PBS. For us at the time, it was, at best, an uncertain journey.

At the start of the first meeting, which was held at Sam's school, there was some evidence to justify my anxiety. The estrangement between home and school was immediately apparent in the seating arrangements around the table. The school staff sat opposite from Ken and me. Gigi and Cathy positioned themselves in the middle, appearing to ready themselves for the roles of facilitator and mediator. Everyone appeared tense and guarded. Some of the educators appeared angry. I speculated that they felt forced to do something they little understood or valued. I was scared because I saw this as our last option, our only hope. If this did not work, then we would be left with nothing.

The meeting began with a review of the functional assessment information. Gigi described what she and Cathy had learned about the reasons for Samantha's problem behaviors. Together, we learned how her lifestyle (e.g., little predictability or choice, the absence of friendships, difficult activities) set the stage for problem behaviors, how demands or the absence of attention or help triggered problem behaviors. Gigi emphasized the central fact that Sam's poor language skills (e.g., little meaningful speech, a few three-word phrases, nonfunctional signing) made it difficult for her to communicate her wants and needs. Finally, Gigi helped everyone see that bewildered attempts to assuage Sam's wants or fears and to stop or punish problem behaviors tended to reinforce these behaviors instead. Although these insights seem obvious now, they were a revelation then. I began to see rhyme and reason for the violent behavior that had engulfed our lives for so long.

As the meeting progressed, it became apparent that among the team members, there were a few skeptics. Gigi had to show much skill and grace under fire to build a consensus about why Samantha engaged in problem behaviors and to generate initial support strategies. Throughout the meeting, one skeptic interrupted her numerous times with questions that expressed strong doubt about the approach (e.g., "What is the basis of this hypothesis?" "What makes you think that this will work?" "How much work will this involve?"). Gigi answered each question politely and to the point. Other meeting participants also helped. Cathy explained the rationale for certain hypotheses. The speech-language pathologist offered strong encouragement for insights related to communication deficits and needs.

By the end of the meeting, most team members had gained a common understanding of the purposes of Samantha's problem behaviors and the situations and events that set off problem behaviors at home and at school. Over the course of the next few meetings, Gigi and Cathy led the team in developing support strategies that were based on the functional assessment. These strategies included:

- Creating a daily schedule and a weekly calendar to help Sam predict her activities and any changes or new events at school or home

- Teaching Sam that language is a more effective way to communicate wants and needs than problem behavior

- Modifying the curriculum to make tasks easier and to give her more choice

- Keeping a home–school notebook, in which Ken and I would inform the school about events at home the night before

During these plan development meetings, it was clear that Gigi's and Cathy's knowledge and sincerity, along with the goodwill of some other team members, created a feeling of trust and camaraderie among most of the team. Although Ken and I recognized these hopeful signs, we continued to harbor our own doubts. We wondered, "Can we really do this?" "Will the team really follow through?" "Will Samantha be able to understand what we are trying to do and stop fighting us?" Thankfully, over several additional team meetings, these doubts were put to rest. One hopeful sign was that team members sat around the table in a more integrated fashion. Some school staff sat next to Ken and me, and others sat near Cathy or Gigi. The seating arrangement, rather than revealing the fault lines of our estrangement, began reflecting a more open and collegial spirit. It became clear that in between meetings, some team members (e.g., Sam's aide, the speech-language pathologist) had begun implementing some of the strategies that we discussed during a prior meeting and the preliminary results were positive. Team members were heartened by these initial successes with Samantha and began viewing the approach as credible. Ken and I began to feel confidence and enthusiasm for the approach.

During one of these initial meetings, we developed an emergency plan for responding to Samantha's most violent and destructive escalations. This required considerable discussion to ensure that the strategies were feasible and safe at school and at home. As we scripted these procedures (e.g., giving Samantha a safe place to go, allowing her to run outside in a field within clearly defined boundaries), I noticed that the discussion was more lively, the contributions more constructive. Others who previously appeared skeptical joined in the group's effort to tackle problems and arrive at acceptable solutions. I also noticed that humor began to infiltrate the proceedings. Moments of light-heartedness and laughter began to leaven the serious nature of our discussions.

I found myself looking forward to driving to Sam's school for our meetings. Ken and I no longer felt like unwelcome intruders at a gathering of experts sanctioned with sole authority. Rather, we began to feel like equal partners in a shared endeavor to understand and help our daughter. At meetings, we collectively developed additional lifestyle supports, teaching strategies, and ways to de-escalate problem behaviors. One of the insights that we gained about Samantha was that she longed to have friendships with typical peers and that when she was supported in her lessons by typical peers, she was much more cooperative and willing to try. Based on this understanding, we generated strategies to enlist peer support at school and at home. We also developed strategies to teach Sam certain self-management skills: how to calm herself when she became anxious and how to complete self-care or work tasks on her own. To my great interest, we also agreed on strategies (e.g., modeling, behavior rehearsal) to teach Sam to engage in appropriate conversation and to verbally express her thoughts and feelings, both positive and negative. As I left the meeting, I had a tremendous feeling of relief and encouragement. We were ready to implement the plan in its totality. The invaluable link between home and school appeared to be clear to all team members. We felt a bond with members of the team that allowed us to gain, for the first time since our daughter was born, a positive view of the future. Through the storm clouds, we caught a glimpse of blue sky.

As the plan was implemented, with adept support from Cathy, Sam's behavior began to improve at home and at school. We were now able to understand the message of her problem behaviors. We began to teach her to talk to us, to use words instead of problem behaviors to gain some control over her world. Strategies to increase the predictability of activities and events in her life helped her remain calm. The introduction of friends and peer helpers and the increase in choice and meaningful tasks promoted tremendous growth in Sam's cooperation. The emergency procedure gave all of us a way to keep everyone and everything safe when Sam' behavior escalated out of control.

An important lifestyle change for Sam was placing her in a fourth-grade class, the grade that matched her chronological age. The previous, horrendous year, she was in a second-year class with students 1–2 years younger than her. During the first few team meetings, the fourth-grade teacher appeared apprehensive about including Sam in the class. The team, thankfully, did not let this fear prevail. Rather, key team members helped the teacher with Sam's successful transition into the class. Sam's speech-language therapist, in coordination with the fourth-grade teacher, talked to Sam's new classmates before Sam entered the class. The therapist and the teacher gave the children information about Sam, answered their questions, and encouraged members of the class to welcome Sam to the classroom and to help her succeed. We were encouraged to hear that several students raised their hands to volunteer to help. As Sam's mom, I offered to help the teacher in several ways. I agreed to work with Cathy to develop various self-management and data-gathering tools, including a goal-setting worksheet, a self-management checklist, and a daily points-earned sheet. Ken and I also agreed to make ourselves available during crisis situations. Rather than the school sending Sam home, which inadvertently reinforced problem behaviors, Ken or I came to the school and backed up staff in their use of emergency procedures. I believe that the teacher felt supported by the team and appreciated our collective devotion to helping her succeed with Sam in the classroom.

By the final meetings, we had been implementing the plan at home and at school for 4 weeks and were marveling at the changes in Sam's behavior. She was much calmer. Problem behaviors began to fall away. Her use of language began to blossom. From our perspective at home, we were getting to know our daughter for the first time. She began to express her thoughts and feelings, preferences and longings—all in a rush of speech that we had not heard before and that continues to this day. About our painful past together, she reflected, "I wanted to talk to you, but I couldn't find the words." On her new-found facility with the spoken word, she proclaimed, "I have a voice now" and "I really have a lot to say, Mom; sit down and listen!" She also began to explore her physical and social world as if she had been reborn into the body of a healthy and curious 10-year-old child. Sam had never really tasted food before because she could never calm down long enough to pay attention. She ate an apple and asked, "Is this what it is supposed to taste like?" She inquired earnestly, "What is love?"

Also, during the last few meetings, the team needed less facilitation. Gigi began to fade her involvement. Cathy and other team members carried on. We checked in with each other on how the plan implementation was going. When there were setbacks in behavior, we learned how to provide Sam with extra support and get her back on track. As we solved problems together, added new supports as needed, and shared Sam's accomplishments, our meetings grew more joyful. We laughed together and enjoyed each other's company. During one meeting, someone brought cookies. The struggle between home and school was over. We had learned to collaborate together as colleagues.

The sweetest fruit of this successful partnership was that Samantha had gotten beyond violence. She was finding her voice as a young person, and was being continually encouraged to do so by team members and by her peers and friends. By the spring of 1994, she had begun to thrive. She learned to self-manage her own behavior, controlling her anxieties and taking pride in independent action. She began to explore and enjoy new interests with her family and friends—bicycle riding, classical music, piano lessons, amusement park rides, and old TV shows such as *Happy Days*. She won a fourth-grade literature award for a poem she wrote and entered into the PTA's "Reflections Contest." She was blossoming into a lovely and lively girl with a good sense of humor. As her parents, we adored the girl she was becoming.

As Sam's life blossomed, our life together as a family began to open up as well. We purchased, for the first time in years, new furniture. We started to take Sam out with us. We went out to dinner, included her on shopping trips, and took her on a 5-day vacation to California. It was fun to be with Sam. For the first time, we felt that we were becoming a family.

The team's collaborative partnership also broadened that spring. The entire team attended a Council for Exceptional Children (CEC) conference in Olympia, Washington, and presented the results of our collaboration in PBS. Cathy and Gigi, along with Ken, the school principal, and other team members, captivated the audience with our tale of "The Wild Child" and her transformation into a vibrant and talkative child. The principal stole the show with his enthusiasm and humor. Ken brought tears to the eyes of many in the audience, including one person videotaping the presentation (me), as he shared a father's perspective on his daughter's transformation. The highlight was Sam's participation in a brief question-and-answer session with the audience. She informed the audience that her favorite class was choir and that she had a lot of friends. When asked, "How do you feel about yourself?" she replied, "I like myself. I really do!"

Also that spring, we bought and moved into a spacious new house in a new neighborhood. This meant that Sam had to change schools before the end of the school year. Given Sam's accomplishments, the team felt comfortable recommending that Sam transfer to the general education elementary school in her new neighborhood. At the same time, Sam's history of difficulty with changes and transitions did not make this an easy decision for us. After meeting the special education teacher assigned to help Sam make the transition to her new school, however, we knew that she would be in good hands. Michelle Corker, the special educator at the new school, expressed an immediate and wholehearted

interest in welcoming Sam to the school. She reassured us that she would work to make Sam's transition to her new school as comfortable and successful as possible. In fact, Michelle wanted to be an advocate for Sam. As we got to know Michelle, it became clear to us that she did not need to learn how to collaborate with parents. She simply collaborated. In doing this so well, Michelle taught us our second lesson about parent–professional relationships: When educators are committed from the start to collaborative partnership with families, the difficulties inherent in supporting and educating a child with disabilities and problem behaviors become easier and the effort becomes a lot more fun.

During the spring, several steps were taken to effect a smooth transition. First, Michelle and one of her instructional aides met with the support team and learned about Sam's behavior support plan. Both the teacher and aide were enthusiastic about mastering PBS. At a later date, Sam and her current instructional aide visited the new school for a day. They met with Michelle and the new general education teacher, spent time with her new aide, visited the classrooms in which Sam would work, and talked to a few of the students who would be her new classmates. Michelle spent time with me that spring, and I coached her in the use of plan strategies with Sam. In my mind, this was the most powerful expression of Michelle's collegial spirit: She let me show her how to work with my daughter. A professional recognized and respected a parent's expertise and consequently gained, in a very short time, the same level of expertise. For the last transition activity, Sam and her current aide spent an entire week at Sam's new school, and her current aide coached Sam's future aide in support plan strategies.

Thanks to these preparation activities, Sam's transition to her new school later that spring went smoothly. I agreed to back up the new teachers if Samantha's old behavior problems reemerged. The new team members had been coached in the crisis plan and were ready to use the procedures if needed. During the first couple of weeks at her new school, when Sam escalated into dangerous behavior, the new team implemented the crisis plan effectively; together, we worked through Sam's adjustment to this major change. By the third week of the transition, Samantha began to relax and problem behaviors subsided. With the continuity of support that Michelle and the new instructional aide provided, Sam grew into a successful member of her new school community. For my family, the sky cleared that year. The storm ended and blue skies extended to the horizon. New vistas of change appeared in Sam's life and in my life.

One of the first and most important positive changes that Michelle contributed to Sam's life was the development of a Circle of Friends (Snow & Forest, 1987). Michelle found six girls and two boys who truly liked Sam and wanted to become her friend. They oriented her to the school, assisted her in classes, and coached her in what to do and what not to do. Her new friends taught Sam common social skills such as greeting peers, contributing to a conversation, and handling stress. With the refrain, "You can do it!" they constantly encouraged her to do new things (e.g., taking the attendance list to the office, raising her hand to ask and answer questions, helping the teacher by writing other students' questions on the blackboard). That spring, Sam's new friends, along with a few old friends from her previous school, attended her 11th birthday party. As I watched her beam and laugh and talk with her friends, I could see something new in Sam—a sense of self-confidence. Thanks to her strong support system, by the end of the school year, Sam loved going to school and had become just "one of the kids."

Sam's accomplishments continued through the summer and the new school year. In the summer, she joined Special Olympics and participated in track events, for which she won a gold medal at the state level for the 200- and 400-meter sprint. In the fall, Michelle invited me to help develop goals for Sam's new individualized education program (IEP), and Sam contributed ideas (e.g., singing solo in choir, helping other students). Together, we agreed on appropriate curriculum adaptations and set high expectations for Sam. During her fifth-grade school year, Sam met these expectations. She completed all homework assignments and participated in school projects. During sixth grade, she exceeded expectations. She received an "A" on her science project at the schoolwide science fair, and in the spring, she was placed on the honor roll. For the first time in her life, she beamed with pride over her academic achievement.

During that year, my collaborative partnership with Michelle also grew. In addition to asking me to help write Sam's IEP, Michelle invited me to give talks to students about how they can help kids with disabilities become successful members of their school. I also volunteered in Michelle's classes, helping to teach and support other students with disabilities. As my relationship with Michelle deepened and Michelle's interest in and commitment to PBS grew, the school principal approached Michelle and me and asked us if we would be interested in helping another student in the school who was exhibiting problem behaviors. Together, we met with the family and developed the boy's behavior support plan for school. Michelle played a key role in implementing the plan at school, and the boy began to succeed in his general education classes.

An important outcome of this equal partnership with Michelle was that we began to conduct presentations together about PBS. We first did a presentation for the faculty at Sam's school. At that time, Michelle was teaching a course in special education at two local universities and invited me to present with her during several classes. By word of mouth, we were invited to present to local groups in our area, including an autism support group and an Arc group. Through these activities, we discovered that we really "clicked" as co-presenters. Parents and teachers at our presentations encouraged us by expressing the view that our partnership was unique and important to them.

At about this time, another colleague and I started our own educational and behavioral consultation business, and Michelle joined us soon afterward. We called the business P.A.C.T. The acronym reflects our activities: Positive behavior support, Advocacy, Consultation, and Transition services. Sam contributed our corporate image: P.A.C.T.'s logo is a drawing of Sam's face encircled by tiny hearts. P.A.C.T. began to serve a small clientele of schools and families through literature about Sam that was distributed by the staff of the Beach Center on Disability at The University of Kansas, on a web site that we created, and via informal networks. Since 1996, we have successfully guided a process of PBS with several schools and families. In doing so, we have helped other parents and educators follow the same path as the one that my family experienced a few years before: learning to collaborate, participating in a process of PBS, helping a child with disability overcome problem behaviors and gain a richer life, and experiencing the positive benefits of doing this together as equal partners.

Although I am grateful to God for answering my original prayer, I know that his work requires the helping hands of many people. Thus, I am also grateful to all of the educators (e.g., teaching assistants, teachers, speech-language specialists, administrators) who believed in my daughter, took risks to join us in a new approach to behavioral support, and saw the process through to its bright conclusion. I am glad that my family never gave up on Samantha. Her zest for life and determination has brought much to my family's life. Her success continually reminds me that together, we can succeed.

This book's editors have encouraged me to offer suggestions on how parents can help to promote home–school partnerships for PBS. Other families and educators have found the following tips helpful. I hope that you may find these suggestions helpful as well.

- Before attending a team meeting in which problem behavior is a primary topic, be knowledgeable about the law as it relates to behavioral support. Give your support to team members who recommend that a functional assessment be completed before the team decides exactly what to do to address problem behaviors. Be prepared to make this suggestion yourself. Also, give your support to team members who suggest positive behavior support strategies. Be prepared to advocate for the use of PBS.
- At the beginning of a process of PBS, help team members understand your child's physical needs and conditions. You and your physician are the most knowledgeable about these needs, and this information can be of great benefit for understanding the physiological conditions that may set the stage for problem behaviors. Examples of such physiological conditions include physical disabilities (e.g., visual impairment), common illnesses, allergies documented through testing, and sensory integration dysfunction.
- During meetings that are aimed at developing a behavior support plan, view members of your child's educational team as colleagues. Attend meetings with an open mind. Listen to and show respect for all team members' ideas.
- If you disagree with a team member, then work with the team to find a positive and mutually acceptable solution (a win-win solution). If you cannot come to agreement during the meeting, then amicably agree to disagree and move on to other points on which the team as a whole can agree; identify another time and place to work through the disagreement.
- If team members express frustration about or criticize your child's behavior, then do not contradict the team member or take offense. Trust that the behaviors they are experiencing at school are real, even if you are not experiencing them at home. Consider these comments as helpful because they provide the team with more information and give team members a chance to express their true feelings; this is often a first step in moving on to solving problems.
- If you find yourself beginning to show anger or beginning to cry at a meeting, it is useful to catch your breath and calm yourself. Consider excusing yourself from the meeting for a few minutes to regain your composure.
- When contributing to team discussions, keep your comments as concise as possible. Such comments will be better remembered and appreciated. Also, refrain from interrupting other team members when they are talking and from talking to the person sitting next to you while another team member is speaking to the group (i.e., "side-bar conversations"). Furthermore, honor meeting time limits set by the meeting coordinator by accepting the end of the meeting at the appointed time.
- When the team is developing intervention strategies, offer to assist and support school staff. This may include helping to make daily or weekly schedules, self-management checklists, and/or choice boards. Other supports to the school may include helping in the classroom or volunteering to assist during field trips. Whatever you agree to do in terms of helping your child's teacher and classroom, be sure to follow through.
- As friendship is so important to the social development of students with disabilities, consider helping school staff develop a Circle of Friends for your child.
- Because ongoing home–school communication is so important, consider establishing a home–school communication notebook. The notebook can be used by school staff or the family to inform each other of student successes and achievements. School staff also can use the notebook to provide the family with information about events (e.g., a field trip) or about homework and class projects. For problem behavior, parents can use the notebook to let school staff know when the student has a bad morning at home. The teacher can then take steps to prevent the student from having a bad day at school. Similarly, school staff

can use the notebook to keep the family informed about behavioral issues at school so that the family can take any necessary preventive steps at home.

• During team meetings, offer to take meeting minutes; bring refreshments. At the end of meetings, express your thanks to all meeting participants for taking time from their busy schedules to support your child.

• When you want to visit your child's classroom, schedule an appointment with his or her teacher and arrive at the appointed time. Do not show up unannounced. Although this may be your right, doing so does not promote trust.

• Throughout the school year, express your appreciation and encouragement for the efforts of school staff in tangible ways. Send a thank-you note to the teacher. Send the school principal a letter that praises the classroom staff. Make treats for the entire class and send them to school with your child.

• If you attend a special education conference, then make copies of relevant information and materials and share the information with classroom staff. Consider attending a conference with your child's teacher.

• Prior to an IEP meeting, schedule a meeting with your child's teacher to discuss the upcoming meeting. At this pre-IEP meeting, share with the teacher some of your ideas for goals and services for your child's IEP. Listen to the teacher's ideas. Try not to be demanding. Rather, try to reach a consensus of goals and ideas before the IEP meeting so that the meeting is a positive event for all involved. Doing so may actually save you and the teacher many hours of stress and conflict during the school year.

• Before your son or daughter makes a transition to a new classroom or school, make an appointment with new members of his or her educational support team, particularly the new teacher. At the meeting, give the teacher helpful information about your child, including specific tips on establishing rapport and ways to make teaching sessions successful. If your child responds well to peer support, then suggest ways that peers might help. Also, ask the teacher how you can support the classroom and the school. Given your own schedule and what is feasible for you, offer any additional assistance the teacher might find helpful.

> *Susan continues to provide behavioral consultation and support to school districts and to families through her private consultation business, P.A.C.T. She also serves as a co-coordinator of a state training team of PBS consultants in Washington state. Samantha continues to thrive in her community. Her schedule is full, including sports, traveling, and activities with friends. She will soon begin a part-time job at a baseball stadium near her home. She also has begun to assist Susan in her work as a behavioral consultant, providing support and insights to families and professionals about the experience of autism and the development of a Circle of Friends. Samantha's long-term goals are to attend college and develop a career working with children.*

REFERENCE

Snow, J., & Forest, M. (1987). Circles. In M. Forest (Ed.), *More education integration.* Downsview, Ontario, Canada: G. Allan Roeher Institute.

CHAPTER 9

Promoting Home–School Collaboration in Positive Behavior Support

Shridevi Rao and Maya Kalyanpur

DJ is a first-grade student at the Forest Hills Elementary School. DJ joined Forest Hills in late October, a week after he and his family moved into the neighborhood. As the days passed, DJ's behaviors drew marked attention from several of his teachers. DJ tended to curse a lot. He often got into fights with other students in the hallway or the playground. He also appeared to have difficulty focusing and paying attention. An initial strategy to address DJ's behavior was giving him "happy face" stickers when he had good days. When this did not seem to have any effect, DJ was sent to the principal's office. These trips to the principal's office eventually became a regular occurrence but also did not appear to have any effect on his behavior. Finally, DJ was suspended for a week in February. Things were peaceful for 3 days after DJ's return to school. Then, the same pattern started all over again.

DJ's story is not atypical. Across the United States of America, one finds stories of children like DJ. DJ has not yet been classified as being eligible for special education services, although he stands at the brink of classification. DJ attends a general education first-grade class, but his place in that class would have become tenuous if his teachers had not started asking some important questions. Why does DJ behave the way that he does? What are DJ's needs? What kinds of experiences did DJ go through in his early years? How does DJ learn? Although DJ's teachers had the answers to some of these questions, DJ's family provided valuable insights into many of these areas. For instance, a conversation with his adoptive family revealed that DJ had not had an easy life. He had been placed in several foster homes during early childhood. He was adopted a year ago, and his family believed that given the state of his behavior when he came to them, he had grown a lot since then. They believed that DJ's behavior might have something to do with the fact that he did not have an opportunity to establish strong bonding relationships in his early life. Perhaps his cursing was a way to communicate that he wanted to belong and be recognized by his peers, even a way of testing whether he would be accepted. Based on this information DJ's family and teachers jointly developed behavioral supports to be implemented both at home and at school. Thus, collaborating with DJ's family helped everyone begin to understand DJ and accommodate his needs as well as support each other through this process.

The purpose of this chapter is to describe ways in which school-based professionals can promote home–school collaboration with families during a process of functional assessment and positive behavior support (PBS). After a brief introduction to PBS, the process is framed as a form of inquiry that can lead to meaningful insights about child behavior and effective interventions. Then, common obstacles to home–school collaboration are discussed, and literature on best practice in home–school collaboration is summarized. This is followed by recommendations for strategies and practices that educators and parents can adopt to promote home–school collaboration. Most recommendations are illustrated by examples drawn from our experiences with schools and families. Each example revolves around a student with a disability. In the interest of highlighting the problem-solving process that is at the heart of PBS, however, the children's disability labels are not included. In describing home–school collaboration within the positive behavior support approach, attention is continually drawn to the ways in which the roles and participation of families within the approach differ from more traditional approaches to families. We believe that understanding this distinction is crucial in achieving home–school relationships that are truly collaborative.

POSITIVE BEHAVIOR SUPPORT

PBS is a comprehensive, research-based, proactive approach to behavioral support that is aimed at producing meaningful and durable behavioral and lifestyle changes for individuals with challenging behavior (Horner, Albin, Sprague, & Todd, 2000; Koegel, Koegel, & Dunlap, 1996; Ruef, Higgins, Glaeser, & Patnode, 1998). The process of PBS in schools has been described as being comprised of several steps (e.g., Horner et al., 2000; Sugai, Lewis-Palmer, & Hagan-Burke, 1999). For the purpose of this chapter, there are four significant stages of this process: 1) conducting a functional assessment interview, 2) conducting direct observations, 3) developing a behavior support plan, and 4) implementing and monitoring the support plan. Unlike traditional behavior management approaches, which tend to focus solely on the student and his or her problem behaviors, PBS focuses on various issues ranging from examining the teaching context and curriculum to long-term quality of life changes that need to be addressed (Knoster & Kincaid, 1999; Weigle, 1997). Based on a specific "line of inquiry" (O'Rourke, Knoster, & Llewellyn, 1999), PBS focuses on understanding the child, the message behind problem behavior, and the context that surrounds the child's behavior. PBS is especially relevant given the present context of special education and the emphasis on the inclusion of children with disabilities in general education classrooms, particularly children with challenging behavior who traditionally have been placed in the most restrictive settings, such as residential schools (Weigle, 1997). The emphasis on inclusion has resulted in increasing numbers of such students returning to their school districts and receiving opportunities to participate in the general curriculum with their peers without disabilities (Sailor, Gee, & Karasoff, 2000; Weigle, 1997).

The Individuals with Disabilities Education Act (IDEA) Amendments of 1997 (PL 105-17) provide new protections for students at risk of being subjected to exclusionary modes of discipline (Turnbull, Wilcox, Stowe, & Turnbull, 2001; Zurkowski, Kelly, & Griswold, 1998). The IDEA amendments further support this move toward inclusion of students with challenging behavior. The amendments also represent a shift from traditional reactive and punitive approaches to more proactive and positive approaches to problem behavior (Zurkowski et al., 1998). These changes place the burden of proof on schools to demonstrate that meaningful efforts have been made to address the student's behavior problem in the present environment, including the use of functional assessment and PBS (Turnbull et al., 2001). Given these changes, several questions arise. How should teachers address the needs of students who demonstrate challenging behaviors? What supports do teachers need from administrators? What skills do teachers need to acquire to be able to address the needs of these students? With whom should teachers collaborate? PBS addresses these and other questions.

Unlike traditional behavioral interventions, in which effectiveness often has been restricted to highly structured or artificial settings, PBS lends itself more easily to inclusive school environments. PBS is based on an in-depth understanding of the child, the environment, the curriculum, and the intertwined relationships among these components. Rather than resorting to removing a student from the classroom or school, educators have alternatives through PBS that enable them to implement changes within the environment and to develop the student's skill repertoire (Knoster & Kincaid, 1999). In addition, PBS rests on a collaborative approach that builds on the input of various stakeholders such as parents, teachers, therapists, and paraprofessionals (Anderson, 1999; Chapman, Kincaid, & Shannon, 1999; Janney & Snell, 2000; O'Rourke et al., 1999). This collaborative approach involves listening to the experiences and perspectives of stakeholders, facilitating the participation of stakeholders in regular team meetings, and building intervention strategies that include the input of stakeholders. Parents and other family members are crucial participants in this process (Ruef, Turnbull, Turnbull, & Poston, 1999). As Hieneman and Dunlap (1999) noted, such a team approach to problem solving has several advantages, including the development of more holistic and integrated interventions; an increased sense of commitment among individual support providers; the creation of a social and emotional support system for teachers and families; the development of new capacities among team members; and the opportunity for generalization across a wider range of home, school, and community environments.

FUNCTIONAL ASSSESSMENT AS A TOOL FOR CONDUCTING INQUIRY

Functional assessment is a critical tool for analyzing and understanding behavior. A *functional assessment* is a systematic process of examining problem behavior, identifying its function, and understanding its relationship to context (McConnell, Hilvitz, & Cox, 1998; O'Neill et al., 1997; O'Rourke et al., 1999). The purpose of a functional assessment is to develop hypotheses that explain the meaning of problem behavior (Carr et al., 1994; O'Rourke et al., 1999). Such hypotheses subsequently guide the development of a behavior support plan. Conducting a functional assessment requires the collection of data from different sources, including parents, general education teachers, special education teachers, paraprofessionals, and the student. Primary methods of data collection are structured interviews and direct observations (e.g., Demchak & Bossert, 1996; O'Neill et al., 1997).

The process of functional assessment, hypothesis development, and intervention planning is based on close collaboration among key stakeholders. Several studies of PBS recognize parents and family members as important participants (Carr et al., 1999; Lucyshyn, Albin, & Nixon, 1997; Vaughn, Dunlap, Fox, Clarke, & Bucy, 1997). During a functional assessment, family members participate by providing information and insights about the child, the behaviors of concern, the perceived purpose of problem, and the contexts in which such behaviors occur. Professionals do the same but take a posture of respect and reciprocity, not assuming that they are the sole source of knowledge and skill (Harry, Kalyanpur, & Day, 1999; Singh, 1995). Functional assessment, conducted with this sense of collaboration, becomes a form of joint inquiry in which educators and parents exchange information, examine current ways of responding to the child, gain valuable insights, and move forward together toward more positive and effective action (Eisner, 1991). Infused with this spirit of inquiry, the functional assessment and plan development process can guide professionals and families away from traditional patterns of assigning blame or of asserting control and toward forging new, constructive connections that lead to mutually acceptable, positive, and effective interventions.

CHALLENGES AND OBSTACLES TO HOME–SCHOOL COLLABORATION

Implementing home–school collaboration within a process of PBS, however, poses several challenges. Successful home–school collaboration is more likely to occur when team members are aware of these challenges and are familiar with practices and strategies that are aimed at overcoming them. The next section focuses on two significant challenges: 1) traditional approaches to behavioral intervention that focus on consequences to reduce problem behavior and 2) the "professional-as-expert" model of behavioral consultation.

Traditional "Consequence-Based" Intervention

PBS represents a relatively new approach to addressing challenging behavior. Deviating from traditional behavioral approaches that have tended to emphasize the use of consequences to reduce problem behavior, PBS focuses on understanding the person and the function behind such behavior and on the use of antecedent strategies to prevent it (Dunlap, Kern-Dunlap, Clarke, & Robbins, 1991; Sugai et al., 1999). Such an approach presents a challenge to the more common use of rewards and punishments as primary means for managing behavior within schools. Although IDEA (PL 101-476) and its 1997 amendments create a presumption for the use of PBS, educators and administrators may vary in their interest and commitment. Traditional interventions—such as token economies, time-out, or suspension—continue to be popular despite their limitations (Ringer, Doerr, Hollenshead, & Willis, 1993).

There may be several reasons for this. First, some teachers use behavioral interventions in a trial-and-error fashion, discarding one strategy when it does not appear to affect the targeted behavior and implementing another instead. Second, some teachers prefer interventions that require a minimum of effort and that result in a "quick-fix" of the problem. For example, a preferred option for a student who engages in head banging may be to have the student wear a protective helmet, rather than to investigate the antecedents of the behavior and to use more educative interventions (Anderson, Albin, Mesaros, Dunlap, & Morelli-Robbins, 1993). Time is an additional constraint that impedes teachers from considering more thoughtful, long-term approaches to solving behavior problems (Ayres, Meyer, Erevelles, & Park-Lee, 1994). Teachers often do not receive administrative support in terms of extra planning time for developing individualized interventions or for collaborating as a member of a team. Furthermore, administrative constraints may require teachers to follow standard procedures for addressing problem behavior rather than to rely on their own professional judgment (Gothelf, Petroff, & Teich, 1999). Finally, the absence of schoolwide behavior support systems in which the school as a whole is committed to positive, proactive approaches may add to a teacher's sense of isolation and, thus, further contribute to the use of short-term, consequence-based strategies (Ayres et al., 1994; Sugai et al., 2000).

Given this context, it is to be anticipated that PBS—a new approach that requires a substantial, up-front commitment of time and effort and does not promise immediate results—will be met with resistance. Working through this resistance may mean providing more support to teachers, administrators, and other professionals as they reconceptualize their roles, as well as the ways that they understand and approach problem behavior.

"Professional-as-Expert" Model of Behavioral Consultation

PBS encourages collaboration and communication between educators and family members. Parents are perceived as critical collaborators in all phases of assessment and plan development (Dunlap et al., 2000). Such an approach stands in stark contrast with traditional behavioral consultation approaches that are guided primarily by an expert–client model (see Table 9.1). Within this model, the clinician or professional is considered the sole authority or expert, while parents are perceived as "naïve" in their understanding and management of their child's behavior (Salisbury & Dunst, 1997). Such a traditional view of the parental role is strongly visible in first-person narratives (Barron & Barron, 1992) and qualitative studies that focus on parental perspectives about the long, arduous journey in trying to identify the meaning behind their child's baffling behaviors (Rao, 2000). In these accounts, parents report that their insights about their child's problem behavior often were undermined or dismissed during encounters with clinicians and other professionals. The professionals or clinicians designed the intervention plan and parents implemented the plans at home. These plans did not necessarily take into consideration the complexities of family life because consistency of implementation across environments was considered to

Table 9.1. Differences between parent–professional roles in traditional behavioral interventions and in positive behavioral interventions

Parent–professional roles in traditional behavioral interventions	Parent–professional roles in positive behavioral interventions
Interventions take place in clinical or experimental settings (Carr et al, 1999).	Interventions take place in natural contexts such as the home, school, or community (Carr et al., 1999).
Professionals and researchers are the key designers of intervention plans.	Families and professionals are the consultants and critical collaborators in all phases of the development of positive behavior support plans (Koegel, Koegel, Kellegrew, & Mullen, 1996).
Professionals and clinicians are the experts.	Professionals and families have shared expertise (Dunlap & Fox, 1996).
Professionals identify and define the goals for behavior change.	Families play an important role in defining priorities and long-term goals for behavior change (Ruef, Turnbull, Turnbull, & Poston, 1999).
Professionals are the primary stakeholders.	Families are significant stakeholders (Sugai et al., 2000).
The plans are child focused.	The plans are child and family focused (Albin, Lucyshyn, Horner, & Flannery, 1996).

be an important goal. Such traditional conceptions of family roles and professional authority pose a challenge to the implementation of PBS. Although there is a legal mandate for parental participation in a child's special education (Rothstein, 1990; Turnbull, 1994), parental participation often is interpreted by professionals as parental compliance (Harry, 1992). Traditional hierarchical school structures as well as traditional interpretations of family roles often prevent educators from viewing parents as equal decision-making partners. Especially disadvantaged in such situations are families of children with disabilities that have low incomes or cultural backgrounds that differ from the mainstream (Kalyanpur & Harry, 1999). Differing socioeconomic backgrounds and cultural values often make professionals and parents unwilling partners (Kemp & Parette, 2000; Lambie, 2000), and teachers' misinterpretations of behavior "differences" as behavior "disorders" can contribute to misunderstandings (Anderson, 1994). In addition, past interactions with professionals in which families have felt intimidated, unwelcomed, or judged may prevent them from building more trusting and productive relationships with professionals.

BEST PRACTICE LITERATURE ON HOME–SCHOOL COLLABORATION

To address the dual challenges described in the previous section, it is important to identify ways in which schools and families can collaborate within a process of PBS. PBS is based on the premise that home–school collaboration is integral to the process of supporting children and youth with challenging behaviors (Hieneman & Dunlap, 1999; Horner et al., 1999). The idea that home–school collaboration is a critical aspect in addressing the quality of educational outcomes for children with or without disabilities is not necessarily new. Indeed, there is a wide body of literature in general as well as special education that clearly provides evidence that good home–school relationships play a pivotal role in influencing the quality of educational outcomes for children (Christensen & Conoley, 1992; Deslandes, Royer, Potvin, & Leclerc, 1999; Rainforth & York-Barr, 1997; Turnbull & Turnbull, 2001).

Four significant themes have emerged from this literature. First is the recognition that the goals toward which educators strive are often complex and, thus, require a joint effort comprising a collaborative partnership between the home and school (Pugach, 1994; Zionts, 1997). Recognition of the importance of home–school collaboration has changed the traditional posture of professionals toward parents. Professionals must acknowledge that parents bring with them specific knowledge and skills that can provide crucial insights into the educational process (Pugach & Johnson, 1995; Stephenson & Dowrick, 2000). Valuing the insights of families and finding ways to accommodate those insights is a critical aspect of building relationships based on respect and reciprocity (Harry et al., 1999).

Second, the recognition of parents as key partners also has meant challenging the position of authority traditionally accorded to professionals (Biklen, 1992). Within the traditional conception of parent–professional relationships, professionals have been viewed as "experts" while parents often have been seen as "laypersons." The current literature urges us to go beyond this authority–layman gap to view the process as a cooperative venture based on shared authority (Bromwich, 1997; Turnbull & Turnbull, 2001).

Third, the literature focuses on the importance of facilitating opportunities for parents to participate actively and meaningfully rather than reducing their participation to one of mere consent or compliance (Harry, 1992). Home–school collaboration is much more effective when parents are willing participants, when they believe that they have a say in the process, and when their priorities and concerns are actively received. Instead of viewing family involvement as the responsibility of families, this literature draws attention to the need for professionals and schools to reexamine and restructure the ways in which they interact or communicate with families to create an atmosphere that is safe and conducive to meaningful family participation (Buzzell, 1996; Friend & Cook, 2000). Such a perspective has closely examined the conventional patterns of communication and forums for interaction, and it provides ways for professionals to systematically identify ways in which home–school collaboration is based on true teamwork and validation of parental perspectives (Harry et al., 1999; Kalyanpur & Harry, 1999). Family participation has broadened, not only involving families in learning activities at home but also including families in key decision-making roles such as governance and advocacy activities for schools (Deslandes et al., 1999; Epstein, Coates, Salinas, Sanders, & Simon, 1997).

The fourth theme underscores the importance of family-centered services (Salisbury & Dunst, 1997). In a family-centered approach to services, the inherent strengths of families are recognized and incorporated into plans of support. This stands in sharp contrast to a deficit-based view of families (Kroth & Edge, 1997). In addition, rather than solely focusing on the child, a family-centered approach includes attention to the family as a whole. When selecting goals and interventions, consideration is given to family priorities, values, and needs. Finally, services are provided in a flexible, responsive, and individualized manner, taking into account the preferences and schedules of families and professionals. Such an approach has been identified as one of the qualities of best practice in early intervention services as well as services for children and youth with emotional disorders (Hammond, 1999; Lourie, Stroul, & Friedman, 1998; Rao, 2000).

STRATEGIES FOR PROMOTING HOME–SCHOOL COLLABORATION

The following sections of the chapter describe and illustrate strategies and practices that are consistent with best practices literature by aiming to promote home–school collaboration during each stage in the process of PBS. What does it mean for professionals to listen to and value the perspectives of families during the behavior support process? In what ways do professionals need to communicate and interact with families to facilitate a truly collaborative process? How can professionals integrate family perspectives to develop an effective behavior support plan? These are some of the questions that are addressed in the next section. Table 9.2 presents a summary of strategies that we recommend.

Stage 1: Conduct a Functional Assessment Interview

The first stage of inquiry in a functional assessment, the functional assessment interview, focuses on generating broad information on the student, the behaviors of concern, the context, and other long-term issues (O'Rourke et al., 1999). This involves identifying key people who could provide the team with crucial information about the student and then conducting interviews with these key people. Key people may include parents and other family members, special education teachers, general education teachers, paraprofessionals, and related services professionals. The functional assessment interview has the potential to lay the preliminary foundation for developing tentative hypotheses about the purpose of problem behavior. For this reason, the quality and depth of the information and data generated by a functional assessment interview are crucial. Family members play a significant role at this stage of inquiry because of their valuable insights. They have a close relationship with the child, intimate knowledge about the child, and an overall holistic perspec-

Table 9.2.   Strategies for promoting home–school collaboration

Stage 1: Conduct a functional assessment interview

Use open-ended question formats to

Acquire a holistic view of the child

Focus on long-term and lifestyle issues

Identify family priorities

Listen to the family's account of its journey

Respect cultural differences

Stage 2: Conduct direct observations

Inform parents about the goals of direct observations

Determine the level and extent of parent participation

Designate one team member to serve as a home–school liaison

Stage 3: Plan and design intervention strategies

Develop plans with good contextual fit

Develop plans that are family focused

Stage 4: Implement and monitor effectiveness of the plan

Set up a mode of communication

Use proactive communication strategies

Arrange and facilitate periodic meetings with family

tive that extends beyond problem behavior. To utilize family perspectives as a building block for understanding the child's behavior, however, it is important that the assessment process be family centered. By this, we mean that during a functional assessment interview, the family's priorities for the child, understanding of the child, and vision for the child are included in the information and insights obtained.

Use Open-Ended Question Formats   One important way to conduct a family-centered functional assessment interview is to use open-ended questions that supplement or augment standard functional assessment interview protocols (e.g., O'Neill et al., 1997). Initial child-centered questions that focus on child strengths, interests, and idiosyncrasies can provide parents with an opportunity to offer a positive, holistic view of their child. Additional family-centered questions can help to identify family priorities, family strengths, and long-term issues related to the child and family. Through open-ended questions, professionals are more likely to elicit rich insights about the child and to gain a better understanding of cultural differences. Table 9.3 is an example interview protocol that may be used to supplement or augment a functional assessment interview. Illustrated next are the open-ended questions that have helped to promote home–school collaboration during a functional assessment.

Acquire a Holistic View of the Child   Child-centered, open-ended questions provide opportunities for families to talk about the child in depth and to offer a history and context for understanding and interpreting his or her behavior. Such a holistic understanding can help promote the identification of positive behavioral supports. This is evident in the following example:

Stacey, a 13-year-old, transferred from a residential school to a neighborhood school and was enrolled in a seventh-grade classroom with students without disabilities.

Table 9.3. Initial parent interview protocol

How would you describe your child? Please tell me a little bit about your child's strengths and interests.

Who are the key people with whom your child has strong relationships?

To what extent is your child a full member of the community? Are there settings or environments that you would like your child to be a part of in the future?

What are your visions for your child in the future? What are some strategies or supports that would help move toward that vision? What are your concerns for your child in the future?

What behaviors pose the strongest challenges and why? Could you describe the behaviors?

What situations or events appear to trigger challenging behaviors?

In your view, what could be the possible reasons for these behaviors?

Which behavior management or support strategies have you previously used? Which strategies have been successful? Which strategies do you believe will not work?

To which strategies or supports does your child appear to be most responsive?

What other strategies or supports might help you support your child at home and in the community?

Shortly after the school year began, Stacey's teacher and therapists noticed that she resisted any kind of physical prompting, whether it be a gentle touch that served as a cue or hand-over-hand assistance. When touched, Stacey would often cry and hit herself. During a functional assessment interview, the teacher asked Stacey's mother to share her view of Stacey and this emerging problem at school. Stacey's mother revealed the suspicion that Stacey had been physically abused in her prior residential program. Her mother thought that Stacey's resistance to any kind of physical assistance or prompting stemmed from her fear that she would be hit or made to do something against her will. This information from the interview helped the team understand Stacey's behavior in the larger context of her personal history. Although Stacey's team believed that she needed some physical assistance, they also came to understand that they needed to wait until they had built a more trusting relationship with her. Until then, they decided to use the more positive and effective strategies of peer modeling, teacher demonstrations, and picture prompts rather than direct physical assistance.

Focus on Long-Term and Lifestyle Issues Family-centered, open-ended questions may help families articulate their long-term goals for the child and lifestyle issues related to problem behavior. A qualitative study that explored various stakeholders' perspectives on behavioral support suggests that parents often place long-term goals involving lifestyle changes as a priority over short-term goals for reducing problem behavior (Ruef et al., 1999). The following example illustrates how educators can benefit from parental input on long-term goals and lifestyle issues related to problem behavior:

Larry, a 16-year-old junior in high school, had been in a job-sampling program for 6 months. When upset, Larry tended to hit himself, bite his hands, and scream. These behaviors had escalated in frequency and intensity since Larry had started working in an office supply store. The transition specialist contacted Larry's parents to alert them that Larry might lose his job because these behaviors were scaring his supervisor and the other store staff. She pointed out the need to identify consequences that would reduce these behaviors and suggested that a sheltered workshop might be a more suitable job site for Larry. Concerned at the recommendation of the transition specialist, Larry's parents requested that a functional assessment be conducted to further examine the situation.

During the functional assessment interview, Larry's parents shared their insights about why their son's behavior had worsened and offered ideas about new supports. Larry was now in new situations, such as his job in the office supply store, which placed new demands on his existing repertoire of communication skills. They believed that Larry's behavior had escalated because of these changes and that his repertoire of communication skills needed to be enhanced. They thought that a sole focus on problem behavior and negative consequences did not take into account the bigger picture of significant changes in Larry's life. Team members took these insights to heart. As part of the functional assessment process, they took a closer look at Larry's work situation and reevaluated his augmentative and alternative communication (AAC) system. They found that Larry's problem behaviors occurred when he was unable to lift heavy boxes onto a dolly to take them to their appropriate shelves. In response, the transition specialist arranged for Larry to unpack heavy boxes in the storeroom and carry their contents to the shelves in smaller loads. The support team also increased Larry's repertoire of signs on his communication board to allow him to ask his co-workers for help when needed.

Identify Family Priorities   Open-ended questions during a functional assessment interview can help the interviewer gain an in-depth understanding of the family's priorities and the behaviors that family members find most challenging. In their qualitative study of stakeholder perspectives, Ruef and colleagues (1999) also found that families and educators reported more successful outcomes when the priorities of parents, as well as those of teachers and caregivers, were taken into consideration. Developing plans that do not meet the needs of key people other than the child may fail because they do not fit the goals, resources, and environments of the people responsible for implementing the plan (Albin, Lucyshyn, Horner, & Flannery, 1996). An open-ended functional assessment interview can help clarify parents' priorities at the outset. A parent who believes that the objectives of a behavioral intervention are not a priority or do not address the long-term goals of the family for their child may not become invested in the plan. Having a voice in determining what behaviors and situations are challenging and need to be addressed as a priority gives parents a sense of plan ownership. The following example illustrates this point:

Sandy was a 16-year-old high school student. Sandy's behavior program at school focused primarily on reducing his stereotypic behaviors, such as his tendency to keep wiggling his head or clapping his hands. During a functional assessment interview in which his parents were asked about behaviors of concern, Sandy's parents stated that they did not consider changing this stereotypic behavior a priority. They believed that these behaviors were sporadic and really did not interrupt Sandy's daily life. However, they believed a priority that required immediate attention was Sandy's need to develop friendships with peers without disabilities and to participate in preferred activities in the community. They thought that Sandy's not having many friends probably contributed to his problem behavior because of boredom and social isolation. As a result of this family input, the team developed an action plan that focused not

on deceleration of Sandy's stereotypic behaviors but, rather, on enhancing his reper-
toire of leisure skills, providing Sandy with opportunities to be involved in more gen-
eral education classes in his high school, enrolling Sandy in recreational clubs and
other activities in the community, and developing a Circle of Friends for him (Falvey,
Forest, Pearpoint, & Rosenberg, 1994).

Listen to the Family's Account of Its Journey   Open-ended questions during
a functional assessment interview also can provide a forum for parents to share their own
history of struggle and success with their child over the years. Such questions encourage
parents to describe the strategies that they have used and whether these strategies have
worked. In the Ruef and colleagues (1999) study, parents often reported developing proactive interventions for their child with behavior problems. They also revealed a keen understanding of lifestyle changes that needed to be made to adequately address their child's
challenges. Other studies indicate that parents often are able to accurately identify the
communicative function of their child's behavior and to devise creative strategies that directly address the purpose of the problem behavior (Biklen, 1992; Frea & Hepburn, 1999).
These studies offer evidence of the growing view that parents are experts with respect to
their child and his or her behavior (Dunlap & Fox, 1996). Eliciting parent input on positive, effective strategies that are being used at home can have several advantages. First, educators gain a sense of the parents' journey in trying to address their child's challenging behavior. Second, team members avoid adopting strategies that have been tried before but
have not worked. Third, team members learn about a family's values with respect to discipline and behavior management and gain a better sense of the fit between proposed interventions and the family. The benefit of listening to a family's account of their journey is illustrated next:

According to Kwame's individualized education program (IEP), the speech-language
therapist was required to provide therapy during three 30-minute sessions per week.
The team agreed that to focus on developing Kwame's socialization skills, the thera-
pist would conduct two sessions in Kwame's classroom, where she could involve some
of his typically developing peers. The third session would be one-to-one in the speech-
language therapy room. Three weeks into the school year, the therapist noticed that
Kwame willingly participated in therapy sessions in the classroom, but he was very
uncooperative in the speech-language therapy room. At first, the therapist thought that
his reluctance was due to the solitary nature of these sessions; therefore, she brought a
classmate with Kwame. However, Kwame still refused to sit at the table next to his
friend in the speech-language therapy room. Asking his classroom teacher for possible
explanations yielded no answers, so the therapist decided to bring up the issue during
her end-of-the-month telephone call with Kwame's mother. "Is his chair facing the
window?" asked his mother immediately. "Yes," replied the therapist. "That's it,
then," continued Kwame's mother. "It took us years to figure out why he refused to sit
at the dining table at dinner time. You see, for the other meals, he got to choose where
he could sit and we hadn't noticed that he always sat with his back to the window.
Rather than fight it, we just let him sit separately. Then we moved to a new house.
There, the window in the dining room was behind his father's chair—and Kwame
joined us! That was when we realized what the problem had been. Now we don't even
think about it; we just make sure he has his back to the window when he's sitting at

a table. I didn't even think to mention it to his teacher because once I see that his chair is placed 'right' at school, I figure that his teacher won't have any problems!"

Respect Cultural Differences   When conducting a functional assessment, it also is important to consider a family's cultural identity. Parent perceptions of behavior may differ from professional perceptions because parents may use a different cultural "yardstick" to draw their conclusions. Before interpreting a behavior as a disorder or as deviant, it is important to know how such behaviors are perceived within the child's own home and community (Anderson, 1994; Rivera & Adkinson, 1997). Questions should focus on understanding how the family views the child's behavior at home and how the child's behavior and actions are perceived within his or her community. The following example illustrates this point:

Chunsong was a 10-year-old whose family had recently moved to the United States from Korea. Chunsong lived with his parents, sister, and grandparents. In September, when Chunsong entered Mary's fifth-grade class, her first impression was that he was very shy. Yet she grew increasingly concerned as the months passed and Chunsong's low class participation continued. At first, she thought Chunsong might have a problem with English and that he could not understand her directions. In a conversation with him, however, she realized that his language comprehension was at grade level. Nonetheless, she noticed that he still did not comply when asked to do certain things. Mary began to think that Chunsong was depressed, passive-aggressive, or emotionally disturbed. She wondered if she should refer him to the child study team. A colleague to whom Mary voiced her concerns suggested that Mary call Chunsong's parents and speak to them about his behavior at home. When Mary called Chunsong's mother and explained the situation, she was surprised that his mother did not see his behavior as problematic. Instead, Chunsong's mother expressed that he was a very polite child who showed a great deal of respect for his grandparents and other elders. Mary mentioned that at school Chunsong often did not comply with directions and remained silent. Chunsong's mother replied that silence was an acceptable way for a person to show that he or she had reservations about what was being asked and that this way of communicating was definitely preferable to arguing. She suggested that Chunsong's silence might be an indication that the activity or task was too difficult for him or that he would prefer to do it another way. This conversation with Chunsong's mother helped Mary understand his behavior. As a result, she saw Chunsong's behavior in a new and more culturally appropriate light. She began offering Chunsong choices, asking him if he needed directions clarified, and reminding him to request help if a task was too difficult. She was pleased to see that in time Chunsong became more willing to participate in classroom activities and complete assignments.

Stage 2: Conduct Direct Observations

The second stage of the functional assessment process is more focused. Drawing on the tentative hypothesis developed in the first stage of broad inquiry, the second stage focuses on closely examining environments in which problem behaviors tend to occur frequently

(O'Rourke et al., 1999). This stage of inquiry is crucial, as it helps to verify the relationship among the contextual factors, antecedent triggers, challenging behaviors, and consequences of the challenging behaviors. Because families can play an important role at this stage, several factors must be kept in mind for facilitating family participation. These factors are discussed in detail next.

Inform Parents About the Goals of Direct Observations   It is important at the outset to make parents aware of the goals embedded in this stage of the functional assessment process and to clarify its purpose and outcome. This stage of inquiry involves closely examining various contexts within which challenging behaviors occur, including the home. Although the child's behavior is supposedly the focus of behavioral observation, research indicates that parents often find their behavior, values, and parenting styles being judged or evaluated and, thus, may be hesitant or ambivalent about participating in this process (Kalyanpur & Rao, 1991). Behavior is a sensitive issue, and many families come to this stage often having encountered professionals who held them responsible for their child's difficulties. It is important to communicate to parents that the goal of collecting direct observation data is not to label or to blame but to confirm hypotheses about behavior so that effective supports and interventions can be identified.

Determine the Level and Extent of Parent Participation   It also is important to consider how and to what extent parents will participate in this stage of the process. Parent levels and intensity of participation may vary. If parents express willingness to contribute to this stage of inquiry, then it is important to clarify how often parents will be expected to collect data, what formats they will use, and with whom these data will be shared. Participation in descriptive data collection gives parents an opportunity to actively collaborate in the positive behavior support process (Berg, 1999; Chapman et al., 1999; Wacker, Peck, Derby, Berg, & Harding, 1996). Parents can contribute to data collection for the functional assessment in different ways. Families differ in terms of their literacy levels, the intensity of their daily routines, and the amount of time they can commit to data collection. Some parents might be willing and able to use standard functional assessment observation forms, such as those designed by Carr and colleagues (1994); O'Neill and colleagues (1997); or Vaughn, Dunlap, and Fox (1999). Other parents might prefer maintaining a journal to record their observations. Still others who have more demanding schedules may prefer to use a simple frequency chart or to make a brief audiotape recording that summarizes their experiences of the child's challenging behavior across a few days.

Designate One Team Member to Serve as Home–School Liaison   If families are going to be involved in the data collection process, then the team must consider who will communicate with families on a regular basis and how. This may be the team facilitator, the general education or special education teacher, or another team member who has an established relationship with the family. This decision may need to be made at the outset. Parents may want to share what they are observing with others on the team and also may want feedback on their data collection. The designated professional serves as a liaison between the family and the team. During this stage of the process, brief telephone conferences allow the liaison and parent member of the team to discuss the progress of home-based observations and to troubleshoot any difficulties with data gathering. If necessary and feasible, a team meeting at school can provide an opportunity for teachers to share with parents the emerging results of observations completed in the school.

Stage 3: Plan and Design Intervention Strategies

During the first two stages of a process of PBS, team members, including parents, generate hypotheses that explain the possible causes of problem behavior (Carr et al., 1994; O'Rourke et al., 1999). This is a necessary preliminary step for planning intervention strategies. The hypotheses generated by the team provide the information and analysis on which behavior support plans are based. In relation to home–school collaboration, a critical goal for school and family members of the team is to agree on the hypotheses that will guide the development of a behavior support plan. Doing so before proposing intervention options will increase the likelihood that interventions will be acceptable to the family and feasible to implement at home as well as at school. To facilitate this outcome, data gathered in the home and hypotheses offered by the parents should be part of the process of reaching a shared understanding of the functions of the challenging behavior and the lifestyle and antecedent events that are associated with it. Two additional considerations will further home–school collaboration at this stage in the positive behavior support process: 1) choosing interventions that are likely to have good contextual fit at home as well as at school; and 2) identifying interventions that are family focused as well as child focused.

Develop Plans with Good Contextual Fit   Studies in positive behavioral intervention suggest that the success of behavior support plans depends to some extent on the degree of contextual fit that plans have with the environments in which they are implemented (Lucyshyn et al., 1997; Moes & Frea, 2000; Steibel, 1999; Vaughn, Clarke, & Dunlap, 1997). Although some interventions are appropriate for school, they may not lend themselves to the home or the community. Thus, recommendations for interventions must consider the unique characteristics of the environment and the values of the people who work in it as well as the extent to which interventions can fit into the home and school environments (Albin et al., 1996; Sugai et al., 2000). For instance, tangible reinforcements (e.g., treats, stickers, small toys) are often used in school environments to motivate children. Professionals frequently recommend that parents provide such tangible reinforcement at home as well. Before making such a recommendation, however, it is important to consider how parents view discipline and if the recommended intervention is congruent with their cultural values or their personal understanding of good parenting. Interventions that do not consider parental values or resolve the differences between parents and professionals may not address the problem behavior at all. The following vignette illustrates this point:

> *Tanya's eighth-grade teachers felt that she needed to be responsible for submitting her homework assignments on time. Reminders did not work, so they suggested home use of the behavior management plan already in place for her at school, whereby Tanya earned or lost points depending on whether she submitted her assignments on time. Although Tanya's parents agreed that she needed to learn responsibility, they felt that this intervention was punitive. They also strongly felt that interventions carried out in the school did not fit within the home, as the two environments were entirely different. They wanted Tanya to learn to monitor herself and become more organized so that she could hand in her assignments without any external reinforcers. They were willing to provide the time and support at home for Tanya to learn to do so, and they also wanted the teachers to focus on this at school. In this case, both the parents and teachers agreed on the problem but disagreed on the approach. Through telephone calls and meetings, these differences were aired, and the team arrived at a compromise by*

which they could be sure that the recommended intervention would be implemented at home as well. Tanya's parents agreed to work with her to develop a schedule of activities for the evening that included time for homework. This would help her to monitor herself. Once she completed her homework, she would be permitted to engage in an activity that she enjoyed, such as watching her favorite television show or calling a friend. In school, the teachers would continue to implement the point system. This open discussion revealed that despite some difference in perspectives, common ground could work for Tanya's benefit by ensuring consistency between home and school.

Develop Plans that are Family Focused   Another consideration in promoting home–school collaboration in PBS is to ensure that intervention plans also are family focused rather than solely child focused. This is important given societal changes in traditional family structure (e.g., single-parent families) and the many stressors with which families have to cope (e.g., inadequate health insurance coverage, financial worries, difficulty in obtaining child care) (Singer et al., 1993; Turnbull & Turnbull, 2001). The school liaison must find out from parents the extent to which proposed interventions are feasible for home implementation. Do family members feel comfortable implementing the plan? Does it fit into their existing schedule, or do they have to make additional time for it? Does the plan impinge on the family's leisure time? Do they have other pressing concerns or priorities that weigh heavily on them? The following vignette illustrates what can happen when such questions are not asked before home-based interventions are recommended:

Randy, a 10-year-old, was learning to use sign language through a structured discrete trial program at school. This program focused on one particular skill at a time and provided massed trials in which he had to perform a specific skill several times over until he reached a specified criterion of performance. The school asked Randy's mother to conduct this program at home as well as at the YMCA center they attended and the mall where Randy loved to shop. Their rationale for this suggestion was based on the assumption that Randy needed numerous opportunities for practicing this skill. Nevertheless, his mother objected to their suggestion on two points. First, she felt that requiring Randy to publicly repeat the same sign 10 times merely made him seem conspicuous. Second, she preferred to focus on teachable moments at home and in the community. For instance, she encouraged him, through prompting or modeling, to use the appropriate signs in the right contexts, such as BURGER or DRINK in a restaurant. In this way, communication was both meaningful and interactive and also allowed her to enjoy her time with her son.

Stage 4: Implement and Monitor Effectiveness of the Plan

The final stage in a process of PBS involves implementing and monitoring the behavior support plan. This requires the team to put its plan into action as well as to continually evaluate its appropriateness and effectiveness. Families often are key team members, responsible for implementing the plan at home and in the community. Communication between the home and the school is crucial at this stage. We recommend three strategies to promote effective communication: 1) set up a mode of communication, 2) use proactive communication strategies, and 3) arrange and facilitate periodic meetings with families.

Set Up a Mode of Communication   Families may want to share the child's progress or discuss modification of the intervention plan. To facilitate this interaction, it is important that the designated liaison from school sets up a system to communicate regularly with families. The first step is to find out what mode of communication parents would prefer, as illustrated in the following vignette:

> *At the IEP meeting for 10-year-old Raju, an Asian Indian, his mother asked if Raju's special education teacher and speech-language therapist could communicate with her on a regular basis to keep her informed of his progress. Both professionals agreed; they decided that the special education teacher would send home a written note once per week and the speech-language therapist would call once per month. Raju's mother found that the written notes from the special education teacher, although more frequent, "told her nothing" because if she did not understand a word that the teacher used, she could not ask for clarification. Although the speech-language therapist's telephone calls were less frequent, they provided opportunities for immediate clarification, further questioning, developing a personal relationship, and exchanging stories. At the end of the year review, Raju's mother stated emphatically that she would prefer a telephone call, even if it were only monthly, to a weekly written note.*

Schools also should provide flexible conference schedules and consider alternatives to face-to-face meetings, such as written communications or e-mail. For some families, e-mail can be very effective, as is evident in the following case:

> *One of the interventions for Marty, a 14-year-old middle school student, was the introduction of an AAC device. Marty began using his AAC device to make simple requests at school and at home. Marty's teacher and his mother exchanged e-mail notes on his progress with the AAC device. This helped Marty's mother know when and how Marty used the device at school. It also kept her informed of Marty's progress so that she could decide when he should be required to use the device at home. At the same time, it gave Marty's teacher an idea of his ability to use the device in more natural contexts. For both Marty's mother and his teacher, monitoring the development of this skill was important because it was crucial in determining the success of his intervention plan.*

Although e-mail can be a very effective mode of communication, not all families have access to it. Some families may not have computers or be able to afford an Internet connection. In such instances, a home–school journal can be equally effective, as the following vignette illustrates:

> *Patti maintains home–school journals for many of the students in her preschool classroom. She makes daily journal entries describing each child's day. For some children, the journals go home at the end of the week. For others, the journal goes home every day. Parents read the journal and write their responses. Patti finds this exchange to be especially useful in monitoring the progress of a student in her class named Carl. The home–school journal is an important aspect of his behavior support plan, as it enables Carl's teachers as well as his family to understand his behavior in context and to apply appropriate strategies to address behavior problems. On one occasion,*

Carl was very upset when he came into the classroom, and he had a tantrum within minutes. When Patti read the journal, it turned out that his grandparents, who had been visiting over the weekend, had just left that morning. His parents had sent a photograph of his grandparents in his journal so that he could look at it and talk about it with his peers and teachers. Patti used her circle time to talk about grandparents and the relationships that the children had with their grandparents. With Patti's help, Carl shared the photograph and the fun things that he had done with his grandparents over the weekend. All of the children got to talk about their feelings about their grandparents and how much they missed their grandparents. Patti found that this strategy helped Carl relax, and he had a much better day after that.

Use Proactive Communication Strategies   New challenges might arise during the implementation of a behavior support plan. Professionals should use communication channels as proactively as possible to address issues that arise during implementation. Being proactive means contacting the family when things are going well, not only when there is a problem. It means anticipating potentially problematic situations (e.g., spring break; when child's aide is absent) and engaging in a problem-solving dialogue to prevent behavior problems. It also means working with parents to address new problem behaviors that develop at school rather than waiting until they reach crisis proportions. Parents can be wonderful resources for this, as evident in the next example:

Patrick is a student in Linda's second-grade classroom. Patrick had several challenging behaviors but has made considerable progress. Linda closely monitors his progress on his current behavior support plan. Lately, she has noticed that Patrick often gets up, makes loud noises, and coughs or asks for a drink of water several times throughout the day. Linda knows from past experience with Patrick that it is helpful to address this situation immediately and as proactively as possible, before a crisis situation arises. Before requesting support for modifying his present behavior support program, she decided to speak to Patrick's mother. Patrick's mother reported that he often behaved the same way at home, especially with activities that he does not like or finds boring. She said that when Patrick would act this way at home, she would say, "I understand that you don't like folding your laundry and that's why you're coughing, but I need you to finish this work and then you can play on your computer or do something else." She said that giving him a simple explanation and letting him know when he can do what he wants helps reduce this behavior. Linda and Patrick's mother then discussed how this intervention could be applied at school. A few days later, Linda reported that the strategy was working.

In this instance, it is important to note how Linda approached Patrick's mother. She did not call to talk about the behavior itself but to problem-solve and to ask Patrick's mother for her suggestions. By doing so, they jointly came up with a solution that could address the situation at school. This gesture from Linda not only helped address Patrick's behavior, but also enhanced her relationship with Patrick's mother.

Arrange and Facilitate Periodic Meetings with the Family   Team members may need to periodically meet with parents to discuss the student's progress on the behavior support plan or to solve new or ongoing problems. It is important for these meetings to be family friendly. Families who have collaborated in a process of PBS report that team meetings in which there is an atmosphere of openness and they feel their input is valued contribute to increased family participation and comfort level (Berg, 1999; Chapman et al., 1999). The traditionally impersonal means of communication that have existed between schools and families can discourage parent participation. For example, a school liaison may need to follow up on a written notice about a forthcoming meeting with a telephone call. This requires professionals to be prepared to talk at length and answer questions. If the parents have not yet received or read the letter, then the first call can be an opportunity to alert them to it. Following up the letter with a telephone call may involve briefly reviewing the letter's content and the specific responses that the school expects from the parents (e.g., calling to set up another time if the scheduled time does not suit them, attending the meeting, helping to improve the behavior support plan).

CONCLUSION

Collaboration between home and school is an integral part of the positive behavior support process. The first stage of this process is the functional assessment interview, a tool of inquiry that, if used with care, can illuminate family perspectives and insights about a child's challenging behavior. In a family-centered approach to functional assessment, using open-ended questions during the interview with parents helps professionals gain a holistic view of the child, identify family priorities and long-term issues, elicit family stories and insights, and respect cultural differences. The second stage of the positive behavior support process involves direct observations to closely examine the environments in which problem behaviors occur frequently. Family participation is facilitated by informing parents about the goals of the direct observations, determining the extent and level of parent participation, and designating a liaison between the school and the home. In the third stage, developing intervention plans that possess good contextual fit and are both family and child focused may strengthen parental investment. Finally, home–school collaboration in monitoring the effectiveness of a behavior support plan may be best accomplished by establishing a regular mode of home–school communication, using proactive communication strategies, and arranging and facilitating periodic meetings with parents. Home–school collaboration is a critical aspect of positive behavior support. Implementing good home–school collaboration can be the key to developing meaningful behavior support plans that are effective in the long run.

REFERENCES

Albin, R.W., Lucyshyn, J.M., Horner, R.H., & Flannery, K.B. (1996). Contextual fit for behavioral support plans: A model for "goodness of fit." In L.K. Koegel, R.L. Koegel, & G. Dunlap (Eds.), *Positive behavioral support: Including people with difficult behavior in the community* (pp. 81–98). Baltimore: Paul. H. Brookes Publishing Co.

Anderson, J. (1999, November). Reflections about positive behavioral supports. *TASH Newsletter,* 4–6.

Anderson, J.L., Albin, R.W., Mesaros, R.A., Dunlap, G., & Morelli-Robbins, M. (1993). Issues in providing training to achieve comprehensive behavioral support. In S.F. Warren & J. Reichle (Series Eds.) & J. Reichle & D.P. Wacker (Vol. Eds.), *Communication and Language intervention series: Vol. 3. Communicative alternative to challenging behavior: Integrating functional assessment and intervention strategies* (pp. 363–406). Baltimore: Paul H. Brookes Publishing Co.

Anderson, M.G. (1994). Perceptions about behavioral disorders in African-American cultures and communities. In R.L. Peterson & S. Ishii-Jordan (Eds.), *Multicultural issues in the education of students with behavioral disorders* (pp. 93–104). Cambridge, MA: Brookline.

Ayres, B.J., Meyer, L.H., Erevelles, N., & Park-Lee, S. (1994). Easy for you to say: Teacher perspectives on implementing most promising practices. *Journal of The Association for Persons with Severe Handicaps, 19,* 84–93.

Barron, J., & Barron, S. (1992). *There's a boy in here.* New York: Avon Books.

Berg, C. (1999, November). Positive behavioral supports or "if I had known then what I know now. . . ." *TASH Newsletter,* 25–26.

Biklen, D. (1992). The inclusion philosophy. In D. Biklen (Ed.), *Schooling without labels: Parents, educators and inclusive education* (pp. 20–48). Philadelphia: Temple University Press.

Bromwich, R. (1997). *Working with families and their infants at risk.* Austin, TX: PRO-ED.

Buzzell, J.B. (1996). *School and family partnerships: Case studies for regular and special educators.* Albany, NY: Delmar.

Carr, E.G., Levin, L., McConnachie, G., Carlson, J.I., Kemp, D.C., & Smith, C.E. (1994). *Communication-based intervention for problem behavior: A user's guide for producing positive change.* Baltimore: Paul H. Brookes Publishing Co.

Carr, E.G., Levin, L., McConnachie, G., Carlson, J.I., Kemp, D.C., Smith, C.E., McLaughlin, D.M. (1999). Comprehensive multi-situational intervention for problem behavior in the community: Long-term maintenance and social validation. *Journal of Positive Behavior Interventions, 1,* 5–25.

Chapman, C., Kincaid, D., & Shannon, P. (1999, November). The marketeers: A parent's perspective on positive behavioral support. *TASH Newsletter,* 13–16.

Christensen, S.L., & Conoley, J.C. (Eds.). (1992). *Home–school collaboration: Enhancing children's academic and social competence.* Bethesda, MD: National Association of School Psychologists.

Demchek, M., & Bossert, K.W. (1996). Assessing problem behavior. *Innovations* (No. 4). Washington, DC: American Association on Mental Retardation.

Deslandes, R., Royer, E., Potvin, P., & Leclerc, D. (1999). Patterns of home and school partnership for general and special education students at the secondary level. *Exceptional Children, 65,* 496–506.

Dunlap, G., & Fox, L. (1996). Early intervention and serious problem behaviors: A comprehensive approach. In L.K. Koegel, R.L. Koegel, & G. Dunlap (Eds.), *Positive behavioral support: Including people with difficult behavior in the community* (pp. 31–50). Baltimore: Paul H. Brookes Publishing Co.

Dunlap, G., Hieneman, M., Knoster, T., Fox, L., Anderson, J., & Albin, R.W. (2000). Essential elements of in-service training in positive behavior support. *Journal of Positive Behavior Interventions, 2,* 22–31.

Dunlap, G., Kern-Dunlap, L., Clarke, S., & Robbins, F.R. (1991). Functional assessment, curricular revision, and severe behavior problems. *Journal of Applied Behavior Analysis, 24,* 387–397.

Eisner, E.W. (1991). *The enlightened eye: Qualitative inquiry and the enhancement of educational practice.* New York: Macmillan.

Epstein, J.L., Coates, L., Salinas, K.C., Sanders, M.G., & Simon, B.S. (1997). *School, family, and community partnerships: Your handbook for action.* Thousand Oaks, CA: Corwin Press.

Falvey, M.A., Forest, M., Pearpoint, J., & Rosenberg, R.L. (1994). *All my life's a circle. Using the tools: Circles, MAPS, and PATH.* Toronto: Inclusion Press.

Frea, W.D., & Hepburn, S.L. (1999). Teaching parents of children with autism to perform functional assessments to plan interventions for extremely disruptive behavior. *Journal of Positive Behavior Interventions, 1,* 112–116.

Friend, M., & Cook, L. (2000). *Interactions: Collaboration skills for school professionals* (3rd ed.). New York: Addison Wesley Longman.

Gothelf, C.R., Petroff, J.G., & Teich, J. (1999, November). Positive behavioral support: Making it happen. *TASH Newsletter,* 17–18.

Hammond, H. (1999). Identifying best family-centered practice in early-intervention programs. *Teaching Exceptional Children 31,* 42–47.

Harry, B. (1992). Restructuring the participation of African-American parents in special education. *Exceptional Children, 59,* 123–131.

Harry, B., Kalyanpur, M., & Day, M. (1999). *Building cultural reciprocity with families: Case studies in special education.* Baltimore: Paul H. Brookes Publishing Co.

Hieneman, M., & Dunlap, G. (1999). Issues and challenges in implementing community-based behavioral support for two boys with severe behavioral difficulties. In J.R. Scotti & L.H. Meyer (Eds.), *Behavioral intervention: Principles, models, and practices* (pp. 363–384). Baltimore: Paul H. Brookes Publishing Co.

Horner, R.H., Albin, R.W., Sprague, J.R., & Todd, A.W. (2000). Positive behavior support. In M.E. Snell & F. Brown (Eds.), *Instruction of students with severe disabilities* (5th ed., pp. 207–243). Upper Saddle River, NJ: Prentice Hall.

Individuals with Disabilities Education Act (IDEA) Amendments of 1997, PL 105–17, 20 U.S.C. §§ 1400 *et seq.*

Individuals with Disabilities Education Act (IDEA) of 1990, PL 101–476, 20 U.S.C. §§ 1400 *et seq.*

Janney, R., & Snell, M.E. (2000). *Teachers' guides to inclusive practices: Behavioral support.* Baltimore: Paul H. Brookes Publishing Co.

Kalyanpur, M., & Harry, B. (1999). *Culture in special education: Building reciprocal family–professional relationships.* Baltimore: Paul H. Brookes Publishing Co.

Kalyanpur, M., & Rao, S. (1991). Empowering low-income black families of handicapped children. *American Journal of Orthopsychiatry, 61*(4), 523–532.

Kemp, C.K., & Parette, H.P. (2000). Barriers to minority family involvement in assistive technology decision-making processes. *Education and Training in Mental Retardation and Developmental Disabilities, 35,* 384–392.

Knoster, T., & Kincaid, D. (1999, November). Effective school practice in educating students with challenging behavior. *TASH Newsletter,* 8–11.

Koegel, L.K., Koegel, R.L., & Dunlap. G. (Eds.). (1996). *Positive behavioral support: Including people with difficult behavior in the community.* Baltimore: Paul. H. Brookes Publishing Co.

Kroth, R.L., & Edge, D. (1997). *Strategies for communicating with parents and families of exceptional children* (3rd ed.). Denver, CO: Love Publishing.

Lambie, R. (2000). *Family systems within educational contexts: Understanding at-risk and special needs students* (2nd ed.). Denver, CO: Love Publishing.

Lourie, I. S., Stroul, B. S., & Friedman, R. M. (1998). Community based systems of care: From advocacy to outcomes. In M. Epstein, K. Kutash, & A. Duchnowski (Eds.), *Outcomes for children and youth with behavioral and emotional disorders and their families: Programs and evaluation best practices.* Austin, TX: PRO-ED.

Lucyshyn, J.M., Albin, R., & Nixon, C.D. (1997). Embedding comprehensive behavioral support in family ecology: An experimental, single-case analysis. *Journal of Consulting and Clinical Psychology, 65,* 241–251.

McConnell, M.E., Hilvitz, P.B., & Cox, C.J. (1998). Functional assessment: A systematic process for assessment and intervention in general and special education classrooms. *Intervention in School and Clinic, 34,* 10–20.

Moes, D.R., & Frea, W.D. (2000). Using family context to inform intervention planning for the treatment of a child with autism. *Journal of Positive Behavior Interventions, 2,* 40–46.

O'Neill, R.E., Horner, R.H., Albin, R.W., Sprague, J.R., Storey, K., & Newton, J.S. (1997). *Functional assessment and program development for problem behavior* (2nd ed.). Pacific Grove, CA: Brooks/Cole Thomson Learning.

O'Rourke, S.L., Knoster, T., & Llewellyn, D. (1999). Screening for understanding: An initial line of inquiry for school-based settings. *Journal of Positive Behavioral Interventions, 1*(1), 35–42.

Pugach, M.C. (1994) *Collaborative practitioners, collaborative schools.* Denver, CO: Love Publishing.

Pugach, M.C., & Johnson, L.J. (1995). *Collaborative practitioners, collaborative schools.* Denver, CO: Love Publishing Co.

Rainforth, B., & York-Barr, J. (1997). *Collaborative teams for students with severe disabilities: Integrating therapy and educational services* (2nd ed.). Baltimore: Paul H. Brookes Publishing Co.

Rao, S. (2000). Perspectives of an African American mother on parent–professional relationships in special education. *Mental Retardation, 38,* 475–488.

Ringer, M.M., Doerr, P.F., Hollenshead, J.H., & Willis, G.D. (1993). Behavior problems in the classroom: A national survey of interventions used by classroom teachers. *Psychology in Schools, 30,* 168–175.

Rivera, B.D., & Adkinson, D.R. (1997). Culturally sensitive interventions: Social skills training with children and parents from culturally and linguistically diverse backgrounds. *Intervention in School and Clinic, 33,* 75–80.

Rothstein, L.F. (1990). *Special education law.* New York: Longman Publishing.

Ruef, M.B., Higgins, C., Glaeser, B.J., & Patnode, M. (1998). Positive behavioral support: Strategies for teachers. *Intervention in School and Clinic, 34,* 21–32.

Ruef, M.B., Turnbull, A.P., Turnbull, H.R., & Poston, D. (1999). Perspectives of five stakeholder groups: Challenging behavior of individuals with mental retardation and/or autism. *Journal of Positive Behavior Interventions, 1,* 43–58.

Salisbury, C.L., & Dunst, C.J. (1997). Home, school, and community partnerships: Building inclusive teams. In B. Rainforth & J. York-Barr, *Collaborative teams for students with severe disabilities: Integrating therapy and educational services* (2nd ed., pp. 57–87). Baltimore: Paul H. Brookes Publishing Co.

Sailor, W., Gee, K., & Karasoff, P. (2000). Inclusion and school restructuring. In M.E. Snell & F. Brown (Eds.), *Instruction of students with severe disabilities* (5th ed., pp. 1–29). Upper Saddle River, NJ: Prentice Hall.

Singer, G.H.S., Irvin, L.K., Irvine, B., Hawkins, N.E., Hegreness, J., & Jackson, R. (1993). Helping families adapt positively to disability: Overcoming demoralization through community supports. In G.H.S. Singer & L.E. Powers (Eds.), *Families, disability, and empowerment: Active coping skills and strategies for family intervention* (pp. 67–83). Baltimore: Paul H. Brookes Publishing Co.

Singh, N.N. (1995). In search of unity: Some thoughts on family–professional relationships in service delivery systems. *Journal of Child and Family Studies, 4,* 3–18.

Sugai, G., Horner, R.H., Dunlap, G., Hieneman, M., Lewis, T.J., Nelson, C.M., Scott, T., Liaupsin, C., Sailor, W., Turnbull, A.P., Turnbull, H.R., Wickham, D., Wilcox, B., & Ruef, M. (2000). Applying positive behavior support and functional behavioral assessment in schools. *Journal of Positive Behavior Interventions, 2,* 131–143.

Sugai, G., Lewis-Palmer, T., & Hagan-Burke, S. (1999). Overview of functional behavioral assessment process. *Exceptionality, 8,* 145–148.

Steibel, D. (1999). Promoting augmentative communication during daily family routines: A parent problem-solving intervention. *Journal of Positive Behavior Interventions, 1,* 159–169.

Stephenson, J.R., & Dowrick, M. (2000). Parent priorities in communication intervention for young students with severe disabilities. *Education and Training in Mental Retardation and Developmental Disabilities, 35,* 25–35.

Turnbull, A.P., & Turnbull, H.R. (2001). *Families, professionals and exceptionality: Collaborating for empowerment* (4th ed.). Upper Saddle River, NJ: Prentice Hall.

Turnbull, H.R. (1994). *Free appropriate public education: The law and children with disabilities* (4th ed.). Denver, CO: Love Publishing.

Turnbull, H.R., Wilcox, B.L., Stowe, M., & Turnbull, A.P. (2001). IDEA requirements for use of PBS: Guidelines for responsible agencies. *Journal of Positive Behavior Interventions, 3,* 11–18.

Vaughn, B.J., Clarke, S., & Dunlap, G. (1997). Assessment-based intervention for severe behavior problems in a natural family context. *Journal of Applied Behavioral Analysis, 30,* 713–716.

Vaughn, B.J., Dunlap, G., & Fox, L. (1999, December). *The family network project: Providing PBS to families from underserved communities.* Paper presented at the 25th annual meeting of The Association for Persons with Severe Handicaps, Chicago.

Vaughn, B.J., Dunlap, G., Fox, L., Clarke, S., & Bucy, M. (1997). Parent–professional partnership in behavioral support: A case study of community-based intervention. *The Journal of The Association for Persons with Severe Handicaps, 22,* 186–197.

Wacker, D.P., Peck, S., Derby, K.M., Berg, W., & Harding, J. (1996). Developing long-term reciprocal interactions between parents and their young children with problematic behavior. In L.K. Koegel, R.L. Koegel, & G. Dunlap (Eds.), *Positive behavioral support: Including people with difficult behavior in the community* (pp. 51–80). Baltimore: Paul. H. Brookes Publishing Co.

Weigle, K.L. (1997). Positive behavioral support as a model for promoting educational inclusion. *Journal of The Associations for Persons with Severe Handicaps, 22,* 36–48.

Zionts, P. (1997). Inclusion: Changing the impossible dream? Maybe. In P. Zionts (Ed.), *Inclusion strategies for students with learning and behavior problems: Perspectives, experiences and best practices* (pp. 3–26). Austin, TX: PRO-ED.

Zurkowski, J.K., Kelly, P.S., & Griswold, D. (1998). Discipline and IDEA 1997: Instituting a new balance. *Intervention in School and Clinic, 34,* 3–9.

Section III

Case Studies of Family-Centered Behavioral Support

They're Playing Our Song

Our Family's Involvement in the Individualized Support Project

Karen Scandariato

It was another beautiful, sunny, and bright October day in Spring Hill, Florida. The day was much like the one before and the one before that. My $2\frac{1}{2}$-year-old son Nicky had been referred to a pediatric specialist in Tampa. Nicky was an amazing child. There were things that Nicky could do that were no less than remarkable. He could put together a puzzle from the gray backside, without the benefit of the picture. He could anticipate the ninth song on his music box and press the button to bypass all the others so that he could hear "his" song again. Nicky was a strong baby with beautiful eyes and a great smile. He seemed to pay particular attention to details. In our eyes, he was gifted. As beautiful as he was, some things were going on that just did not seem right.

Nicky used to eat all kinds of foods, but he had suddenly stopped eating everything except Cheerios, graham crackers, and barbecue potato chips. He had almost completely stopped making sounds of any kind. He had developed a sort of guttural grunting sound. Even with the sun shining brightly over the rest of the state, the doctor's diagnosis hung over us like a dark cloud as we held our little boy in our arms.

THE REALITY OF BEING EDUCATED, CLUELESS, AND ALONE

Autism. The word alone seemed to conjure up negative images. How could it be that our little perfect baby might never be able to communicate verbally to us? How was it that he could have such out-of-control tantrums, when our hugs and kisses and lullabies did not soothe him at all? Surely two college-educated parents could handle one little baby's needs. Autism. This was a world of which we knew nothing. The truth is, we felt totally clueless.

243

Along with the diagnosis came another hard-to-deal-with situation. Our family and friends began disappearing. It was not that they meant to stop calling. It was more that they felt bad for us. They did not know what to say or how to help. They did not know how to support us. They too knew nothing about autism.

REACHING OUT: TAKING THE FIRST STEPS

My husband Mark had begun reading everything and anything that he could get his hands on that pertained to children with communication disorders. We were both pretty much numb and had not even talked about our feelings. I mean, what was there to say? I think Mark got stuck. Me? I just cried. After the diagnosis, almost 2 full weeks went by before I finally stopped crying long enough to follow up on a few calls that the doctor had suggested. It was then that I began to reach out for help.

Asking for help is not always easy. It is like admitting that you cannot manage your own world. We still were trying to accept the diagnosis. The days were very long for us. It was an extremely emotional time. We felt frustrated and alone. Nicky was still frustrated and having tantrums. I knew that we needed help with our son but had no idea what services were available or how to get access to them.

OUR INTRODUCTION TO POSITIVE BEHAVIOR SUPPORT

I remember the first time I spoke to Dr. Lise Fox at the University of South Florida. She explained the Individualized Support Project (ISP), which she was just starting. She described how she and her team were going to include a total of eighteen children over a period of 3 years in an early intervention program based on positive behavior support (PBS) (see Chapter 10). The idea seemed solid enough: Assess children's problem behaviors, teach them to use language to communicate their needs, decrease their problem behaviors, and then include them with their peers. The most amazing part was that the ISP believed in working with our child where his problem behaviors occurred . . . in OUR home! This was fortunate for us, because Nicky did not travel easily.

COMPLETING ASSESSMENTS
AND DEVELOPING A BEHAVIOR SUPPORT PLAN

One of the happiest moments in my life was the day I found out that Nicky had been selected to participate in the ISP. Anxious to get started, brimming with anticipation of a happier child and a quieter, more manageable home, we began the assessment phase. This involved formal and informal testing of our child and family, measuring everything from Nicky's performance on a single day to our level of parenting stress. I think I still hold the record for the parent with the highest stress score. My score indicated that I had more stress than 99% of parents in the United States!

Testing ended, and a review of the scores gave direction to the team on developing Nicky's personal intervention plan. The ISP support team worked with our family to help set up a more structured and predictable environment in our home and in his world. Photographs were taken of everything in our home, and a Velcro schedule board was put into place so that we could show Nicky what was going to happen next throughout the day. Two-item choice boards were developed to help Nicky make choices of things he wanted. We learned to minimize the stimuli in his environment so that he wasn't confused or overwhelmed. I relearned how to talk to Nicky, using fewer words, making simpler requests, and waiting a few seconds to give him a chance to respond. We also learned to prepare Nicky ahead of time for transitions out of the house (e.g., going by car to visit his grandma) by letting him know through words and pictures what we were going to do before we began to do it. We also learned how to help Nicky when he lost it big time. One family member, usually me, would stay with Nicky and calm him down while the other family members would disappear into another room until he was calm again.

MAKING THE PLAN FIT OUR LIFESTYLE AND VISION OF SUCCESS

Careful consideration of our personal family lifestyle guided the team in developing an appropriate individualized support plan. The plan took into consideration all of the things that we believed were important for our son and for our family—our lifestyle, our values, and the personal choices that we hold dear. Training and support activities were centered around routines that we deemed important to our family. As a Sicilian family, a large part of our life includes dining together, celebrating around the dinner table, and eating out at restaurants. Before the ISP, we could not do these activities with Nicky. It was socially stifling to be of Italian heritage but unable to do the things that most Italian families do. Community outings had become very stressful. I had pretty much decided that I would rather stay at home than face even one more judgmental stranger yelling at me, "Can't you control your child?!"

The ISP team members worked the schedule of training and support around our interests and Nicky's needs, as well as Nicky's deficits—what we all needed to know to help Nicky better fit into the whole family picture, including the ethnic character of our family. When we ventured out into the community with Nicky, we were forearmed with strategies for success, a carefully thought-out backup plan, and the direct support of an ISP team member. ISP team members showed tremendous respect for the particulars of our family. They helped make Nicky a successful member of our family in terms of our definition of success.

EDUCATING AND EMPOWERING OUR FAMILY

I have heard that autism occurs in approximately 4 out of every 15,000 births. The fact is, this statistic means nothing unless your child is one of the four. The information that is now available on autism is as diverse and as widely distributed as the children who have received the diagnosis. As a parent, I found the scope of information particularly overwhelming. Sorting through it all and selecting what feels right for your child takes time and patience. Sometimes you just have to go with your gut feelings. The ISP presented a viable option to us in that it considers the family a unit as opposed to just treating the child. We made a conscious decision to commit to one intervention approach. Members of the support team were teaching us behavior management through PBS, and it was working. Nicky was beginning to communicate with us functionally, making eye contact, pointing to what he wanted, and beginning to use language. His tantrums were decreasing. We seemed to be on our way.

Gradually, things began to shift for us at home. Our stress level began to decrease as Nicky began responding to the positive supports around him, such as his picture schedule. We learned methods that helped us increase Nicky's opportunities for success. We began to believe that our child had a future again.

COMING TO TERMS WITH A LOSS OF PRIVACY

There is truth in the saying that nothing comes without a price. The intervention process was intense, often involving up to 15 hours per week of support staff in our home, at our dinner table, in our bathrooms, in our car, and in our faces. There is no polite way to say this. It was invasive to our privacy. I personally went through a period when I felt like I had to be a hostess. These people were in our home, and it was dinner time, so I fed them. I wanted our "guests" to be happy, and so I catered to their likes and dislikes. It was like having house guests for months. In looking back, however, I realize that these feelings were my own and that members of the ISP team were committed to helping my family, regardless of my level of hospitality. They were sensitive to my personal limits and knew when they could press on and when to back off. The fact remained that I had made the decision that whatever it took to help Nicky, I would commit to it. I knew that we needed help and, thus, wanted to be as supportive of the team as possible.

LEARNING TO ACCEPT MODIFICATIONS TO OUR HOME

Imagine someone coming into your home and suggesting that you modify your family room into a playroom for the children. Not so bad, right? But what if everything in the room had to be in a clear container with a word label and a picture on it and all of those pictures had to correspond to individual photographs for use on a picture board? What if those containers had to be made so hard to open that a child would need to request your help to open them to get what was inside? What if you took the whole room and turned it into a classroom of sorts, with individual "centers," so that your child could understand where things go, how to use them, and how to get from one activity to another (e.g., pictures of toys on a shelf that help the child appropriately put toys back on the shelf)? Imagine how you would feel if you realized you had to teach your child all of the things that other children his age do quite naturally? What if someone suggested that you need to expand your own "play schemes," learning how to perform different types of imaginative and creative play? Sure you would do it. It seems like a small price to pay for such a worthwhile goal. After all, this is your child! So there we were: All of a sudden, I was the "Queen of Clear Contact Paper and Velcro," labeling everything in the house, and Mark was the "King of Pretend Play."

Does it change you as a family? You bet it does! We had consequence strategies printed in large type posted on our walls, with directions for each member of the family to follow in the case of a tantrum. Sometimes, Nicky would start to scream for some reason that was still unknown to us, and we would be caught off guard and react incorrectly. Later that day, in the aftermath of the tantrum, we would find ourselves spouting words of wisdom at each other such as, "You know, you didn't read the wall!"

BALANCING HOME, FAMILY, AND CAREGIVING RESPONSIBILITIES

Did you know that even if you have a child with a significant disability, you are still expected to manage other things? Well, it's true. It is the spice-of-life stuff that typical households have to manage, and families of children with disabilities are not immune (e.g., chauffeuring an older child to a school activity, picking up the dry cleaning). Learning to balance the needs of our other two children, as well as our own needs, had been getting increasingly difficult. Through careful planning, the ISP team provided us with support and guidance that enabled us to prioritize and manage our time more effectively. We learned to break up what seemed like huge problems into bite-size, more manageable pieces. I began to regain some of my personal independence and balance when I made two changes in my week. Every Thursday became "Autism-Free Day!" I would not do research, network, or advocate on that day. The second change was that I finally was able to accept the concept of respite!

Learning to give yourself breaks can be the single most important thing you do for your child. For a very long time, I simply would not allow myself a break at all. If I am the constant in an ever-changing line-up of interventionists, therapists, and educational staff, then I know that I have to keep up my endurance by allowing myself some regularly scheduled break times. Sometimes that means I have to leave my own house and sip coffee at the local bookstore so that I can rest and regain the energy necessary to start another day.

THE OUTCOMES OF EARLY INTERVENTION
AND POSITIVE BEHAVIOR SUPPORT FOR NICKY AND MY FAMILY

The ISP gave Nicky an effective way to communicate to those around him. I think Nicky's doors began to open once he was able to understand what was expected of him and he began to communicate successfully with us. As Nicky grows, he seems to be very aware of his place in the community and as part of our family unit. His problem behaviors appear to fade away as he attains more and more speech.

For the rest of the family, the ISP helped us to develop an early understanding and a healthier perspective on Nicky's diagnosis. The ISP helped us to accept Nicky for who he was. We learned to appreciate and enjoy his individual qualities without feeling the need to make him look and act like everyone else. It was no longer a matter of trying to fix Nicky. It became a matter of enhancing him and giving him his own way of becoming successful.

The program also helped us learn to recognize, document, and view real progress. Sometimes it is hard to see how very far you have come unless you capture vignettes along the way and take a few moments now and then to look back. ISP interventionists taught our whole family coping mechanisms and strategies not just for Nicky's success, but also for our own. PBS through early intervention was fast becoming a solid foundation for us to build on.

In the spring of 1996 we discovered that our daughter, Lara (who was $2\frac{1}{2}$ years old at the time), was also on the autism spectrum. The whole world looked a little different to me as I walked my little girl out of the doctor's office that day. In my mind, I felt as if someone had pulled the rug out from under me. I had hoped that Lara would be a good verbal role model for Nicky. I was noticeably shaken by the news, and it was a long, quiet ride home. The difference this time was that I already knew what to do for her. I was not shattered with the loss of the child I thought I had. Instead, in some small way, I was comforted by the fact that I knew how to reach her and I was confident that I could teach her to reach us.

Nicky is 10 years old now. He is fully included in a general education fourth-grade class with all typical peers. He has an assistant to support some of the more difficult challenges for him, such as creating written paragraphs, projecting his voice, and interacting with the other kids. He initiates conversation. He sometimes offers to read poems aloud to the class. He participates fully. He has expanded his food repertoire to more than 30 regular items including apples, carrots, ice cream, pizza, ham, and chicken. Last week he came in to wake up his father and said, "Come on, Dad, open your eyes, it's morning . . . it's time to get up." Just this morning he heard his little sister coughing badly from the bottom bunk, and he climbed down the ladder from the top bunk and asked, "Are you all right, Lara?" Nicky is able to tell us what hurts, what he wants, what he likes, and what happened yesterday. Nicky can hold conversations with his peers that often exceed three exchanges. He and his siblings argue, "It's my hot dog!" "It's not yours, it's mine!" I let them argue. It's music to my ears.

Lara is presently 8 years old. She is fully included in a typical second-grade class with 22 peers. She no longer needs support for her delayed fine motor skills or to stay on task. Sometimes, she uses a written schedule to help her stay on task and to ease transitions. Her classmates have fully and completely taken her in. Last week, I picked her up early at school to go to the state fair. Two classmates walked her downstairs to the office to me. I heard one little girl say, "Bye, Lara, have fun at the fair." Lara turned to them and replied, "I'll see you tomorrow, bye-bye." For her eighth birthday, she invited 14 classmates over for a slumber party, and 11 attended.

THE BEAT GOES ON

These days, our schedule at home for the children is still pretty intense. We continue to have our share of interventionists, therapists, and habilitation technicians who work with the children both together and individually toward their goals at home and at school. We are still working on better transitions, recounting and retelling events, answering concrete and abstract questions, maintaining eye contact, and going on a broader variety of community outings. We have built a strong team between home and school, and I think that makes all the difference in the world for the children's outcomes. The children are doing beautifully because of the carry-over effects between home and school and the collaborative partnerships that we have formed. We still use strategies from the ISP in all that we do with the children. As the children's issues change, we adapt the strategies and revise the plan around their needs. Most days, we are no more overwhelmed than any parents of three typical children might be. It does not get better than that.

Many positive experiences have grown from the challenges of raising two children with disabilities and from our involvement in the ISP. I consider myself fortunate to have had the opportunity to learn from some wonderful individuals and to have experienced all that I have with my children. I have grown into a more organized, accepting, and confident parent. Nicky and Lara are still the same beautiful children that they always were, only now we can all reach each other. This morning while I was in bed, I heard Lara ask Nicky, "Can I have the Koosh Ball?" Nicky replied emphatically, "No! It's mine. Get your own Koosh Ball." I just smiled at Mark, "Honey, they're playing our song!"

Karen Scandariato lives in Cary, North Carolina, with her husband Mark and their three children. Karen is an active advocate for children with communication disorders. Annually, she publishes a local directory of families of children with autism who live in her community. She completed a statewide parent empowerment program called Partners in Policy Making. She was also involved with the University of South Florida in the replication of the Individual Support Project. In this role, she shared her experiences to assist professionals in understanding the parent perspective.

CHAPTER 10

Early Intervention with Families of Young Children with Autism and Behavior Problems

Lise Fox, Nila Benito, and Glen Dunlap

Autism is a complex and puzzling disability that presents significant challenges to parents and professionals. Autism is typically identified during the second year of life. Children with autism often have uneventful births and unremarkable development during infancy, with delays becoming evident at the time that typically developing children begin to use language within social interactions. Children with autism appear to be socially disconnected from others; have limited understanding and use of language; and may exhibit serious behavior problems, ranging from incessant engagement in stereotypy to property destruction and self-injury.

The impact of autism on the family system is pervasive and often disruptive. In addition, the presence of problem behavior can affect many elements of family lifestyle, including relationships between siblings and among extended family members, the social life of family members, family participation in the community, and the quality of family routines (Bristol & Schopler, 1984; Dunlap & Fox, 1999; Moes, 1995; Sullivan, 1997; Turnbull & Ruef, 1996). Families often report that the early years following diagnosis are especially difficult, with emotional struggles to cope with the disability and the need to gain access to appropriate intervention and supports for the child.

Since the early 1980s, research and knowledge on providing effective interventions for children with autism have flourished. One significant advance in the field is the recognition that early intervention is vital to the achievement of long-term and meaningful outcomes (Dawson & Osterling, 1997; Rogers, 1996). Numerous studies attest to the pervasive and enduring benefits of specialized early intervention programs that address the specific challenges of autism (Campbell et al., 1998; Fenske, Zalenski, Krantz, & McClannahan, 1985; Handleman, Harris, Kristoff, Fuentes, & Alessandri, 1991; Hoyson, Jamieson, & Strain, 1984; Ozonoff & Cathcart, 1998; Rogers & Lewis, 1989; Smith & Lovaas, 1998). All of these programs have in common the use of systematic educational and behavioral interventions and family involvement in understanding and delivering intervention (Dawson & Osterling, 1997).

This chapter describes the structure of an early intervention program designed to meet the individual needs of young children with autism and their families. The program is designed specifically to offer features associated with effective early intervention programs (i.e., systematic and focused instruction, parent involvement) within the framework of family support and positive behavior support (PBS). The program is intended to support diverse families and children within their unique contexts; provide comprehensive behavioral support; and facilitate the provision of early intervention within the natural environments of the home, early education programs, and community environments by building the capacity of the family and community providers to support children with autism (Dunlap & Fox, 1996). The elements of the program, the Individualized Support Project (ISP), are described through an illustration of one family's participation in the program.

THE INDIVIDUALIZED SUPPORT PROJECT

The ISP was federally funded in 1995 to develop and replicate a model of early intervention focused on meeting the unique needs of young children with autism and challenging behavior and their families (Dunlap & Fox, 1999; Fox, Dunlap, & Philbrick, 1997). The model evolved through the 1990s from an earlier version of a parent-education program that focused on assisting family members to acquire skills for teaching their child and managing their child's problem behavior (Dunlap & Fox, 1996; Dunlap, Robbins, Dollman, & Plienis, 1988; Dunlap, Robbins, Morelli, & Dollman, 1988). The purpose of the ISP is to demonstrate the importance of communication-based intervention and family support, with a focus on promoting skill development within natural environments (home, community, and school) and preventing the occurrence of severe problem behavior. The ISP uses PBS as the framework for understanding the unique needs of the child and family and for developing interventions that promote meaningful outcomes.

The ISP is designed as an enhanced model of early intervention and is not intended to replace other early intervention efforts. Rather, it offers a structure for building a team of support providers who can intervene with the child's problem behavior and support the child in learning new skills and gaining access to new environments and experiences. The children involved in the program have problem behaviors that limit their ability to benefit from traditional early intervention and early education supports and interventions.

The components of the model are depicted in Figure 10.1. The first phase of model implementation is family-guided assessment. The family-guided assessment phase is used to develop an understanding of the child's capacities and instructional needs and the family's strengths, resources, and support needs. A major element of the assessment phase is the use of functional assessment strategies to develop an understanding of the functions of the child's problem behavior. The assessment process ends with the development of a circle of support for the child and family through person-centered planning. Person-centered planning brings together those who are central to supporting the child and facilitates a process in which they identify their vision for the child's future or intervention outcomes (Mount & Zwernik, 1988).

Focused intervention is the second phase of the model. Focused intervention includes providing communication-based intervention and evaluating the impact of the behavior support plan on the reduction of problem behavior and the development of new skills. During focused intervention, program staff demonstrate how to use the behavioral support strategies and coach family members and other support providers (e.g., child care providers, therapists) in using the strategies within planned and routine activities. Community inclusion is another element of the focused intervention phase. Program staff accompany family members as they take their child to community environments that are problematic

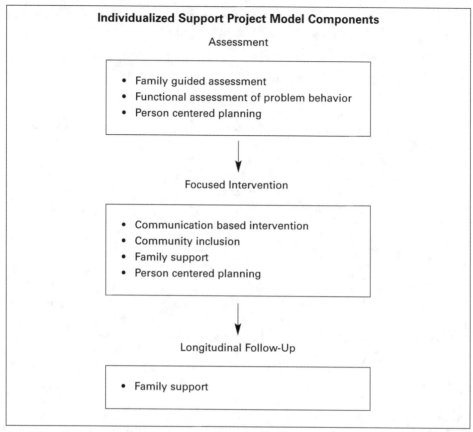

Individualized Support Project Model Components

Assessment

- Family guided assessment
- Functional assessment of problem behavior
- Person centered planning

Focused Intervention

- Communication based intervention
- Community inclusion
- Family support
- Person centered planning

Longitudinal Follow-Up

- Family support

Figure 10.1. Phases and components of the Individualized Support Project. (From Fox, L., Dunlap, G., & Philbrick, L.A. [1997]. Providing individualized supports to young children with autism and their families. *Journal of Early Intervention, 21*(1), 5; reprinted with permission.)

for the child (e.g., stores, restaurants, playgrounds). Program staff assist the family members in developing strategies for supporting their child within those environments and coach them to learn new ways to conduct routines so that problem behavior does not occur. In addition to teaching intervention strategies to family and other support providers, program staff spend a significant amount of time engaging in family support. Family support activities are individualized and specific to a family, although they typically include developing an understanding of the disability and providing information, emotional support, and strategies for negotiating services and advocacy. Focused intervention ends when the child is responding well to intervention efforts (i.e., problem behavior is reduced, communication has increased) and the family members and other providers feel confident about their abilities to support the child. At the end of focused intervention, person-centered planning is used again to expand the child's circle of support, develop new strategies, and/or plan for the child's transition to a new program.

The ISP continues to provide support for the family in the longitudinal follow-up phase of the model. Sometimes, families and their support teams need assistance as the child encounters new environments or situations. Some families continue to need information and support as their child grows older and gains access to new environments and circumstances.

In the following section, these ISP components are discussed with more detail. The story of one family, the Benitos, is provided to illustrate the program model and its impact on children and their family system.

SUPPORTING THE BENITOS

Many of the families supported by the ISP are struggling with the recent diagnosis of a child's disability and to cope with severe problem behavior. As project staff build rapport with families, family members reveal that their lives have been altered significantly in response to the child's behavior. Family members report that they no longer invite friends over, are unable to take their child into the community, and constantly fear that the child may have a tantrum. Project staff observe family routines that are developed solely around the need to make sure that the child does not exhibit challenging behavior. Disruptive behavior has altered family meals, recreational activities, friendships, and family members' health and emotional stability.

In the literature, there are many poignant personal accounts of how chronic and severe problem behavior can disrupt a family (Featherstone, 1980; Sullivan, 1997; Turnbull & Ruef, 1996, 1997; Turnbull & Turnbull, 1996). When families first enroll in ISP, project staff spend time with the family members to become familiar with their unique lifestyle and family construction. During the assessment phase, project staff seek to join the family in as many routines and activities as possible to achieve a vision of the family's daily life and challenges.

The staff of ISP first met Nila Benito at a parent support group meeting. Her sons Joseph and Vincent were diagnosed with autism. Vincent, a 3-year-old, had been placed in a public school classroom for preschoolers with disabilities and was making progress. Joseph, a 2-year-old, was a concern for the family. He had prolonged tantrums throughout the day and was inconsolable. During his tantrums he would cry, fall to the floor, and refuse to move. Nila and her husband expressed extreme frustration with the challenges of managing Joseph's behavior and their ability to understand what was causing the tantrums. Joseph attended a community preschool program in which he was having difficulty with engagement and peer interaction. Joseph liked to hold certain objects (e.g., a cracker, a cloth diaper that he chewed on), which often interfered with activity engagement and play. If those objects were taken away, he would engage in prolonged tantrum behavior.

The family was eager to work with the ISP team and expressed excitement at the possibility of beginning intervention. Nila had independently researched different treatment approaches once her children were diagnosed. As shown in the following excerpt, she expressed to the ISP team her desires to have her children included and treated as "children first," not "autistic children":

> Life was very hard. Our son Joseph was 2 years old and had just been diagnosed with autism. He was having severe tantrums. There were times he would work himself into such a state that he would hyperventilate and seem out of control. He had such tantrums throughout the day in many different situations. I felt like whatever I did would just make him more angry and frustrated. I was close to the end of my rope because I didn't know what to do.
>
> To compound the situation, my 3-year-old son, Vincent, was also diagnosed with autism. My husband was loving and supportive but in denial. All of my hopes and dreams for my family that I loved so much seemed to be falling apart. I was devastated. I had numerous moments when I didn't think life was worth living anymore.

Joseph was examined, observed, and tested by a variety of doctors and specialists. They prescribed medication that could sedate him and recommended that I take him to therapists who would "make" him learn how to behave appropriately. I voraciously read any information that I could find about intervention and autism. The articles that stressed strategies on extinguishing the child's problem behavior did not feel right to me. I had to find answers somewhere.

A simple trip to the grocery store had become a nightmare. Joseph would scream until he almost turned blue. After my mother took him to the store one time, she vowed that she would never take him again. Even visiting my family was overwhelming, as Joseph and Vincent did not seem to enjoy going to new places. Joseph would work himself into a frenzy when we would go somewhere new. Neither boy participated in any family holiday activities, such as opening gifts or eating dinner together. They preferred to hide out in a guest bedroom and watch videotapes. My family pressured us to try to get the boys to participate and join the rest of the family. By the end of a family visit, the boys and I were exhausted and frustrated. Finally, I began to ask my family to come to my house if they wanted to see us. Going to visit family had just become too much for us to handle.

ISP was the type of program that I needed. I felt comfortable with the information on positive behavior support, which involved a more natural way to address problem behavior. I wanted a program that would show my family and me how to support our boys.

Family-Guided Assessment

The program model begins with assessment activities that are conducted in partnership with the family in the child's natural environments. Through this process, program staff develop a richer understanding of the child, the family context, and the family's vision for the child's future.

Functional Assessment of Challenging Behavior   Functional assessment is used during the assessment phase to gain an understanding of the ways in which the child's problem behavior is related to the environment. Project staff conduct many observations of the child within routine activities noting the circumstances in which problem behavior is triggered or when it does not occur. When problem behavior occurs, project staff carefully observe how adults respond to the child's behavior. A structured interview (O'Neill, Horner, Albin, Storey, & Sprague, 1990; O'Neill et al., 1997) is used with family members and other support providers to gain more information about the behavior, possible setting events, the predictors of problem behavior occurrence and nonoccurrence, responses that may maintain the behavior, the child's communication abilities, and the history of previous intervention efforts.

The family members are important partners in the functional assessment process. Family members have the most knowledge about the idiosyncratic behavior patterns of their child and the events that are most likely to trigger problem behavior. It is important to acknowledge that the quality of the partnership with the family in conducting a functional assessment is directly influenced by the amount of rapport and trust that has been established between the family and the support provider. Families may be reluctant to be vulnerable with someone who appears detached or judgmental.

In ISP, families are involved in the functional assessment process by sharing observations, collecting setting event information, and identifying the routines and environments that are problematic for the child. Once the functional assessment process is completed, project staff meet with the family to collaboratively build hypothesis statements based on the gathered information. During the process of hypothesis development, family members often express a sense of relief when the function of behavior is first identified. It is comforting to identify the purpose of the behavior. Yet, that sense of relief frequently gives way to guilt as family members realize their role in providing maintaining consequences to the problem behavior. On these occasions, project staff must carefully guide the parents in realizing that they are not culpable for their child's problem behavior and reassure them about their parenting and responses to their child.

Person-Centered Planning   A person-centered planning meeting is the culminating event of the assessment phase. Person-centered planning processes are regarded by many professionals as an essential first step of PBS. The process of PBS emphasizes the importance of lifestyle change as an outcome. Person-centered planning provides a process in which a vision for the child's future and the dreams of a lifestyle can be expressed. Personal futures planning is one form of a variety of person-centered planning process that are used to bring together the people in a child's life who wish to support the child and family in achieving an optimal lifestyle (Mount & Zwernik, 1988; Turnbull & Turnbull, 1996). Personal futures planning is used to create a circle of support around the child and family and to articulate a vision for the child's future prior to the development of a support plan.

The process used in personal futures planning is informal and celebratory. Often, the families in ISP are moved by the caring attitude of the participants who attend the meeting. Frequently, family members and support providers express intimate feelings about their concern for the child and struggles with the disability. Families report feeling supported by those gathered in the meeting and express both hesitancy and excitement at articulating a vision for the child.

Joseph's person-centered planning meeting was attended by his immediate family, aunt, preschool teacher, and speech-language therapist, as well as the ISP team. It was heartening to see the outpouring of affection for Joseph and the interest in supporting him. The vision map for Joseph included goals that were critically important to the family, such as communicating, toileting, and celebrating holidays and birthdays. These goals were all achievable and assisted the ISP team in developing a focus for behavioral support and instruction. Nila's description of her experience with person-centered planning follows:

> As we worked with the ISP team through the functional assessment process, my overwhelming feelings of despair slowly began to diminish. I started to feel a sense of hope. On of the most fortifying experiences was the day of his personal futures planning. It was the first time that I actually realized I was not alone and that there were people who were going to ensure that I learned what I needed to know to help my sons.
>
> We talked about Joseph as a person who was not defined by autism. We identified Joseph's strengths, such as his knowledge of letters and numbers and how he loved being silly. We really focused on what Joseph can do rather than on his weaknesses. Then we looked at our vision and dreams for Joseph.
>
> My perspective on the future had been so grim that I hadn't even thought about what was possible for Joseph until I was asked about a vision for him at the personal

futures planning meeting. I felt safe enough to say that I wanted him to have friends, ride a bike, be toilet trained, and celebrate holidays. I felt like a weight was lifted when I told everybody that I was worried and afraid that these things would never happen for Joseph. Everyone responded that they would do all they could to help this vision happen. I had a new feeling of confidence in knowing that I was not alone!

I left the meeting that day with a more positive outlook. When I got home, I tacked the planning sheet titled "Our Vision for Joseph" on his bedroom wall, and it stayed there for 5 years as a reminder of what he was accomplishing and where we still wanted him to go.

Focused Intervention: Support Plan Development

Behavior support plan development begins with an identification of hypotheses about the function of problem behavior. Then, replacement skills are identified that may be taught to serve as a functional equivalent to the problem behavior. For Joseph, problem behavior was used to escape the demands of difficult activities or the transition to something that he did not want to do. He also had prolonged tantrums when he wanted the cloth diaper to chew on or a cracker to hold. Joseph's tantrums about transitions were maintained by most of the adults in his environment who did not follow through on the transition or activity once Joseph began a tantrum. When Joseph had a tantrum for his diaper or a cracker, adults reinforced his request by offering a variety of objects or food until he stopped crying.

His ISP interventionist and the family decided to teach Joseph how to cope with transitions and changes with activities, make choices, and engage in a variety of play activities. They hypothesized that his need to hold a cracker or chew on a diaper was related to his inability to become engaged in more purposeful activities or understand what other options were available.

In addition to identifying replacement skills, a support plan includes strategies that may be used to reduce the likelihood that problem behavior will occur. The strategies include modifications in the environment, interactions, and activities that reduce the need for the child to engage in the behavior. The prevention strategies listed in Joseph's behavior support plan included providing Joseph with a visual schedule of daily activities and with food and activity choice boards. These items gave Joseph information in a representational format that was concrete and easy to access. His family was also guided to establish rules for activities (e.g., "We eat at the table") that would be reinforced and to organize Joseph's environment in ways that would be predictable for him (e.g., snacks in the snack cabinet). Joseph's caregivers were taught to pair the visual representation of an activity with a transition warning to prepare him for activity changes. They were also taught to provide Joseph with many choices of activities, represented by visuals or objects, that would encourage Joseph to put down his diaper or cracker to engage in a more purposeful activity. The ISP interventionist examined some of the activities that Joseph avoided and helped his caregivers alter the activities to make them less confusing and to offer Joseph a simple role. For example, his parents were taught ways to make storybook reading less demanding by paraphrasing the text and offering Joseph turns to point to a picture and turn the page.

It was also important to include guidelines for ways to respond to Joseph's problem behavior in a manner that would not reinforce or maintain the behavior. Caregivers were provided with a script to respond to problem behavior when it occurred. For example, if Joseph had a tantrum about a transition even when the warning and visual aid were used, his parents were shown how to state the transition again and provide Joseph with physical assistance to complete the transition. When Joseph had a tantrum for his diaper or cracker, his parents used his visual choice board to show him the options of other activities.

In addition to these plan components, the family and the ISP interventionist discussed the vision for Joseph and his skill development needs, and they identified strategies that were described as long-term support strategies. *Long-term support strategies* are supports and skill development goals that assist the individual in achieving a desired lifestyle. For Joseph, long-term support strategies included learning to play with peers, toilet training, and other self-care skills.

Once the support plan is developed, it is written in simple language and distributed to all of the child's caregivers. Then ISP staff provide education and support to the family and other caregivers in learning how to implement the support plan in all environments. This means that ISP staff accompany the family at restaurants, on shopping trips, and in other community environments. ISP staff also went to Joseph's preschool program to demonstrate how to use the strategies and to provide coaching to the teaching staff as they began to implement the plan. Joseph's behavior support plan is presented in the appendix at the end of this chapter.

Communication-Based Intervention   The support plan was highly effective in reducing Joseph's problem behavior and promoting the use of conventional communication skills (e.g., the use of the visual choice boards). Evaluation data were collected on the effectiveness of the plan at home and school. The biggest challenge in the application of the support plan was to encourage all of the caregivers to use the plan with consistency. Figure 10.2 depicts the effect of the plan on Joseph's tantrum behavior.

As Joseph became more skilled and his caregivers were able to provide him with support, he was able to engage in new activities and new relationships. Occasionally, those new activities or environments presented challenges for Joseph that triggered new problem behavior. ISP staff guided Nila in identifying the predictors of the behaviors and the maintaining consequences for the behaviors and in developing new strategies that were functionally related to the behavior problems. As she describes next, Nila became adept at problem-solving new situations and developing strategies that were appropriate for Joseph's support:

> It was a relief to learn that Joseph's behavior had a purpose, that it was related to his inability to communicate effectively. Focusing on how we could prevent his tantrums and identifying the new skills to teach him was a very powerful experience. It was a new way of looking at behavior. Instead of only looking at ways to control and react to the behavior, we were looking at positive ways to prevent it.
>
> I remember examining the data and seeing a pattern with Joseph's tantrums in the kitchen. We hypothesized that he had tantrums there because he wanted a snack and didn't know where his snack foods were. I had been moving his favorite foods around because a doctor warned me to not let Joseph develop rigid behaviors. When I realized that my actions had resulted in Joseph's tantrums, I initially felt guilty that I had caused his frustration, but I was also grateful that I now understood how important predictability and consistency were for him. I chose a fixed location for his favorite foods so that he could always find them.
>
> Joseph was apraxic and his speech was unintelligible. We created a choice board, using visuals of foods so that he could let me know what he wanted in the refrigerator or freezer. It worked so well that we made choice boards for outside play activities and restaurant food selections.

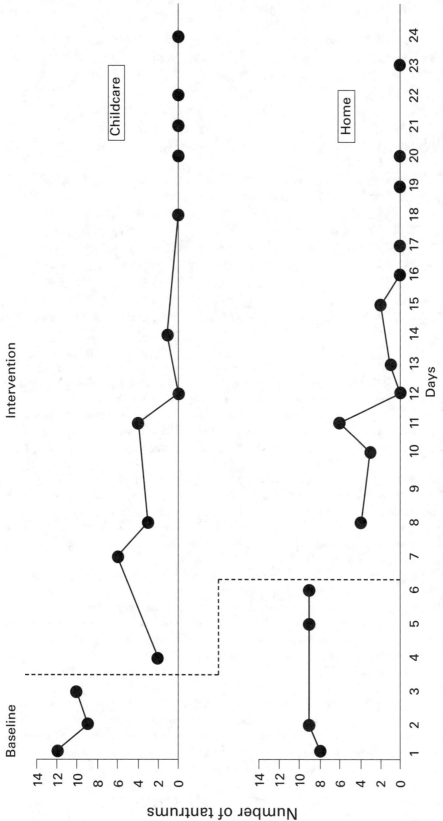

Figure 10.2. The number of tantrums exhibited by Joseph during the early stages of the behavior support plan implementation at home and child care. (From Dunlap, G., & Fox, L. [1999]. A demonstration of behavioral support for young children with autism. *Journal of Positive Behavior Interventions, 1*, 77–87. Copyright 1999 by PRO-ED, Inc. Reprinted with permission.)

Another issue for Joseph was having tantrums at bedtime. ISP helped me develop a consistent bedtime routine that was supported by an activity schedule. I was thrilled that within a month he was going to sleep without fussing. Once Joseph's tantrums had significantly diminished and he began sleeping well, I thought, "This really works; now he's got it and understands what is happening." So, I slacked off in using the support strategies. Guess what happened? Joseph's tantrums returned. This was a learning period for me. Our interventionist explained that Joseph couldn't have his supports suddenly taken away.

Intervention had a dramatic impact on Joseph and our family life. Joseph was learning many new skills. Having choices allowed Joseph to feel more in control of his life. Using visuals helped him understand what was expected and gave him a way to communicate with other people. As a family, we also could go visiting without the fear and anxiety that we used to experience. We would show Joseph a photograph of where we were going and who would be there. We always made sure that he brought along some of his favorite comfort items. We even started taking family vacations. The boys really enjoyed going to new places as long as they knew where they were going. Eventually, they began to feel comfortable and to trust us, and going out became fun.

Community Inclusion   The Benito family was always on the move! Both parents were determined that their sons' disability would not inhibit a full family life. Nila was an accomplished professional and her husband often traveled across the country for his job. The family loved going to the beach, parks, playgrounds, and restaurants and enjoyed family gatherings. On several occasions, the Benitos invited ISP staff to gatherings of family and friends that involved many young children, massive amounts of food, and delightful conversation.

ISP assisted the family in maintaining this important aspect of the family lifestyle. The ISP interventionist helped the family plan outings in ways that the boys' behavior could be managed. For example, on shopping trips Joseph would always insist on purchasing sidewalk chalk and would engage in a tantrum if he could not have it, or he would have a tantrum to stop at McDonald's for fries at times when it was not feasible to stop for a snack. The ISP interventionist observed these difficult situations and helped Nila understand the function of the behavior and then develop support strategies that could be used to prevent the behavior and teach new skills. Those strategies were often extensions or new applications of the strategies that worked for Joseph at home. For instance, Nila began using an activity schedule of the errands that she needed to complete. Joseph learned that if McDonald's was not on the schedule, they would not be stopping for a snack.

One of the most critical community environments for Joseph was his inclusion in preschool. The Benito family had enrolled Joseph in a community preschool program that was recognized in the community for providing high-quality early education. Joseph's teacher had limited experience in supporting children with disabilities but was enthusiastic about receiving support from ISP. When Joseph began ISP, his mother was very concerned about his participation in the preschool. The teacher had expressed deep frustration with Joseph's lack of participation with his peers, difficulty with transitions, limited play skills, and attachment to the objects that he liked to carry with him.

A functional assessment was conducted to examine some of the challenges that were presented at preschool and to identify the function of Joseph's difficult behavior in that environment. A behavior support plan was developed that was specifically tailored to the preschool classroom. The teacher was provided with a list of prevention strategies that easily fit into her instructional routine. She was also provided with information on how to facilitate development of Joseph's social, communication, and play skills. Finally, the behavior support plan for preschool included specific guidelines for responding to Joseph's problem behavior in ways that would not maintain the behavior. The ISP interventionist accompanied Joseph to preschool to model the implementation of the support plan in the classroom. Within 2 weeks, Joseph became more engaged in the classroom activities, was able to make transitions without having tantrums, and willingly put his diaper or cracker in his cubby before beginning the school day. In the following vignette, Nila describes implementation of ISP at Joseph's preschool:

> *Giving Joseph an opportunity to learn with and from his peers in the community was very important to me. I wanted him to learn how to cope and live in the real world and for others to learn to accept him. Shortly after he was diagnosed with autism, I decided to enroll him in a regular preschool. I wanted to get Joseph in the community and around typically developing children right away. I checked out many preschool programs that were associated with our county early intervention program. They were all segregated programs for children with disabilities. When I visited these programs, I took Joseph with me. Time and time again, he would take my hand and pull me out the door. We visited a neighborhood preschool and Joseph saw all of the children playing on the playground. He joined right in and immediately climbed to the top of the playground slide. He laughed and had a great time. Not only did Joseph "tell me" that this was where he wanted to be, but also the teacher was a wonderful person with an open mind and a willingness to learn how to support him.*
>
> *Joseph had a brief honeymoon period at his preschool and then began having intense tantrums and avoiding his peers. The ISP team offered to meet with his teacher and me to develop strategies to support Joseph. Initially, we decided that ISP would provide some in-class coaching for the adults to help them support Joseph. We also developed activities that would motivate Joseph. I developed a list of Joseph's interests and motivating activities such as trains, finger paints, and books. We also developed choice boards and activity schedules that could be used in the classroom.*
>
> *Joseph really enjoyed his 2 years in preschool, especially when he realized that his female peers liked to do things for him such as carry his lunchbox and clean up his toys. He showed us again and again just how smart he was and demonstrated that he was happy being with his peers.*
>
> *Other community issues were difficult. ISP helped me determine how to cope with shopping trips and waiting at the doctor's office. I learned strategies to support my boys and also ways to inform people in the community when I needed special assistance.*

Family Support   In ISP, family support is regarded as an essential component of the intervention model. Families are recognized as the most important influence in shaping a child's life (Dunlap & Fox, 1996). ISP's goal is to assist families in gaining access to the information and supports that they need to facilitate a child's development. ISP staff believe that it is critical to consider family needs, resources, and supports when developing a partnership to support a child with autism.

ISP's ability to provide family support hinges on the development of a trusting relationship with the family. The staff enter into family homes with an intention of under-

standing and listening to family concerns. Over time, the families realize that ISP's support is unconditional and unwavering. The staff's concern about the family extends beyond the child with autism to the entire family system. Each family visit includes inquiry about the entire family, family events, family concerns, and perspectives.

Families teach ISP staff that the work of examining and shaping the behavior of children may be emotionally difficult for the family system. Many issues are associated with a family's perspective about problem behavior and discipline that are rooted in a family's culture, perceptions of social expectations, and parenting style. As family members are asked to examine and change their responses to their child's problem behavior, it is critically important to listen as they share their feelings about the process.

ISP's goal is to help family members embrace PBS as a way to understand and support their child. Although the most immediate concern is to resolve issues with problem behavior, ISP's ultimate objective is to help families become confident in the ability to support and advocate for the child. The vehicle for achieving those goals is to spend time with the family members, to teach them, and to learn from them. Nila's experience in this area is recounted next:

> I wasn't sure whether I would ever know how to help my children. I turned to family members, who were very loving but unable to help me best support my children. I encountered many dead ends as I sought help in the community. I thought I had found an answer when the school district representative said, "We have a special program that is designed to teach children like yours." When I checked out the special program, I found dedicated teachers who were trying to do the best they could with students ages 5–12 under chaotic circumstances. These classrooms were based on the belief that children with disabilities had to be excluded from typically developing children until they were "ready" to be in the real world. I quickly realized that for many children "ready" actually meant never. I didn't see how these programs would be able to prepare my children for the real world.
>
> I kept hoping that someone would come along and tell me exactly what to do to help my boys. ISP helped me understand that those decisions would have to be mine. I remember the day they told me, "You are the expert." I thought, "Big deal—all

parents are experts about their kids." Then my interventionist explained that I knew better than anybody what motivates and frustrates my sons. She said that my input was the most important of any team member. It took a while for me to realize that my knowledge had that much value.

Realizing that my participation was pivotal for Vincent's and Joseph's progress changed my perspective and confidence level. I worked as a willing student and partner when we toilet trained the boys. Once I knew what to do, I needed ISP to encourage me and validate my feelings. Knowing that they understood what I was going through was fortifying.

I asked ISP to help me plan a meeting with my extended family. I wanted help in sharing our perspectives about the boys and to see if my family would be supportive. The big day came. There we were, my husband's family and my family. We talked about Vincent and Joseph and who they were. We shared with our families our hopes and dreams. We asked our families for support. Everyone was honest and caring. My brother-in-law was brutally honest when he said that his pediatrician had cautioned him to keep his children as far away from our children as possible. The whole family reacted to the statement and tried to help him understand that he should be more open-minded and that his pediatrician was reacting to a disability label without knowledge of our children.

I felt supported by ISP. It was a great comfort to know that I could call them if necessary. When no one else seemed to understand what my family was going through, ISP did. They were caring, patient, and helped us by teaching us strategies that we could use. On days when I wasn't coping well, just calling and leaving a message on the ISP office's voice mail gave me peace, knowing that they would call me back and help me figure out what to do.

Longitudinal Follow-Up

The ISP model is constructed so that focused intervention decreases after the following is achieved: A period of stability in the child's reduction of problem behavior, the child's use of conventional forms of communication, and the family members' and other caregivers' confidence in their ability to support the child. At that point in time, another person-centered planning meeting is held to bring together the child and family's circle of support. Often, the person-centered planning meeting is focused on the accomplishments that were achieved through PBS and on determining ways in which to continue supporting the child. The daily visits to coach the family and other caregivers stop at the end of focused intervention, although ISP staff are always available to support the family with new concerns or issues. ISP staff want to be viewed by the family as a resource that will always be there if needed.

Family Support   The most frequent requests for assistance that the program receives are for help as family members advocate for inclusive educational placements or appropriate intervention supports. Many of the families that complete ISP are ready to advocate for their child's right to be educated within inclusive placements. In addition, all of the families become very assertive about identifying the supports the child requires to develop social and communication skills and the need for educational programs to provide those supports. Many family members call ISP to request information that will help them as they advocate for their child. Often, project staff serve as a touchstone for the family as it develops a position or strategy for gaining access to appropriate supports.

There are occasions when children begin to exhibit challenging behavior and families call ISP for advice about moving forward. Through telephone conversations, ISP staff can generally guide the family members to address problems with family routines by using a functional approach. Those problems are often successfully and easily resolved. Unfortunately, some children exhibit problem behavior in classrooms in which traditional or coercive approaches to managing behavior are common practice. In these circumstances, ISP staff are available to provide consultation and training to school programs.

Over time, the families who participate in the program need it less and less. Several families have become parent leaders and now serve as a resource to other families. One parent has become a community leader in assisting parents in achieving in-home supports and inclusive educational placements. Another parent has written a newsletter that is internationally disseminated and targeted toward members of her faith community who have children with special needs and challenging behavior. Nila, whose story has been shared in this chapter, is the director of a program that provides training and experiences to pediatric residents and nursing students to assist them in understanding the needs of the family and its perspective on disability.

It is our experience that the provision of longitudinal support is necessary and important for families as they negotiate the array of support and entitlement programs. We believe that families on the challenging journey of achieving lifestyle change for a child with a disability need to know that there are supportive professionals available to provide them with assistance if necessary. Nila's perspective on this matter is shared next:

> It has always been important to me to have close relationships. After Vincent and Joseph were diagnosed with autism, some of my closer friends drifted away. I guess they didn't feel comfortable with our situation. It was very painful to lose friends whom I'd had for many years.
>
> Over time, I have developed new meaningful relationships, including those with the staff of ISP. It was inevitable that we would develop a close bond. How could you not bond with someone who helped with 3 days of toilet training? ISP was there for my family in our greatest time of need. My values and hopes matched theirs. Just like any friendship, I tried to not take advantage of their willingness to give. It was important to keep a balance.
>
> When I first met the ISP staff, I barely knew what "advocacy" meant. They gave me articles to read and contacts for advocacy and parent organizations. I soon realized that I was going to have to be a strong advocate in order to have my sons' needs met within any bureaucratic system.
>
> Inclusion with support has been the focus of my advocacy. When it was time for Joseph to make the transition from his child care center to a preschool, I chose a Head Start program. ISP staff and I met with the Head Start program staff to identify their needs and concerns about enrolling my son. ISP assisted by providing the teachers with training and in classroom support during Joseph's transition. Joseph blossomed in that placement. He enjoyed school and continued to use his visual supports consistently.

Then it became time for Joseph to make the transition to kindergarten. I was concerned. Vincent had been in the school for 2 years, and it had been very difficult. Although the district seemed willing to include the boys, the school was not committed to making inclusion work. Joseph's peers without disabilities were great, yet the adults had preconceived notions and resisted change.

ISP provided staff training and transition assistance, but it was clear to me that we were dealing with an entire system that did not understand the importance of inclusion. I began to teach the school personnel about PBS and inclusion with supports. Before I realized what had happened, I had become a strong advocate for my boys. My advocacy skills had developed from the seeds that ISP had planted in those early days. ISP had given me knowledge that was transformed into my confidence.

I highly respect ISP's knowledge, commitment, and values. I am grateful to them for so much. Their sincere belief in me has given me the strength and courage to do all I can to help Vincent and Joseph have the best quality of life possible.

CONCLUSION

This chapter has described the ISP model's adjunctive approach to early intervention for young children who have autism and significant behavioral difficulties. The model emphasizes support for the family system with elements that are designed to reduce problem behaviors, increase conventional communication and other functional skills, and promote socially active lifestyles in home and community environments. The goal of the ISP approach is to help families address the challenges of autism and to become the strong, cohesive, confident, and competent systems that are necessary for young children to experience optimal cognitive, emotional, and social development. The model's approach has been illustrated by the story of the Benitos. Their experiences represent many of the struggles and achievements that are characteristic of many of the families with whom ISP has worked to construct meaningful family supports.

Family support, and the process of helping families to confront the challenges of autism and problem behaviors, is a complex undertaking. Our experience indicates that efficacy depends on a commitment to an individualized and family-centered approach. Yet, we also recognize that such a commitment by itself can be hollow without the availability of flexible resources and wise support providers who can work with families to identify the most appropriate interventions. The ISP model offers a useful framework, but it does not necessarily provide solutions for the various challenges (e.g., poverty, chronic illness, competing sources of stress) that can affect a family's ability to implement positive behavioral interventions.

Despite the variety and depth of the presenting challenges, we have nevertheless seen many children and families who have participated in the ISP achieve gratifying progress. The Benitos are one of many examples. A chief reason underlying this progress is the nature of the partnerships that have been established between the families and the ISP support providers and, more generally, the ISP program itself. A partnership implies reciprocity, and it is this concept that inspires optimism. As long as service providers can learn from the families with whom they work, they should be able to improve their responsivity and effectiveness. A continued ability to hone family-centered interventions will inevitably lead to improved outcomes for children.

REFERENCES

Bristol, M.M., & Schopler, E. (1984). Developmental perspective on stress and coping in families of autistic children. In J. Blacher (Ed.), *Families of severely handicapped children: Review of research* (pp. 91–141). San Diego: Academic Press.

Campbell, S., Cannon, B., Ellis, J.T., Lifter, K., Luiselli, J.K., Navalta, C.P., & Taras, M. (1998). The May Center for early childhood education: Description of a continuum of services model for children with autism. *International Journal of Disability, Development, and Education, 45,* 173–187.

Dawson, G., & Osterling, J. (1997). Early intervention in autism. In M.J. Guralnick (Ed.), *The effectiveness of early intervention* (pp. 307–326). Baltimore: Paul H. Brookes Publishing Co.

Dunlap, G., & Fox, L. (1996). Early intervention and serious problem behaviors: A comprehensive approach. In L.K. Koegel, R.L. Koegel, & G. Dunlap (Eds.), *Positive behavioral support: Including people with difficult behavior in the community* (pp. 31–50). Baltimore: Paul H. Brookes Publishing Co.

Dunlap, G., & Fox, L. (1999). A demonstration of behavioral support for young children with autism. *Journal of Positive Behavior Interventions, 1,* 77–87.

Dunlap, G., & Fox, L. (1999). Supporting families of young children with autism. *Infants and Young Children, 12,* 48–54.

Dunlap, G., Robbins, F.R., Dollman, C., & Plienis, A.J. (1988). *Early intervention for young children with autism: A regional training approach.* Huntington, WV: Marshall University.

Dunlap, G., Robbins, F.R., Morelli, M.A., & Dollman, C. (1988). Team training for young children with autism: A regional model for service delivery. *Journal of the Division for Early Childhood, 12,* 147–160.

Featherstone, H. (1980). *A difference in the family.* New York: Viking.

Fenske, E.C., Zalenski, S., Krantz, P.J., & McClannahan, L.E. (1985). Age at intervention and treatment outcome for autistic children in a comprehensive intervention program. *Analysis and Intervention in Developmental Disabilities, 5,* 49–58.

Fox, L., Dunlap, G., & Philbrick, L.A. (1997). Providing individualized supports to young children with autism and their families. *Journal of Early Intervention, 21,* 1–14.

Handleman, J.S., Harris, S.L., Kristoff, B., Fuentes, F., & Alessandri, M. (1991). A specialized program for preschool children with autism. *Language, Speech, and Hearing Services in Schools, 22,* 107–110.

Hoyson, M., Jamieson, B., & Strain, P.S. (1984). Individualized group instruction of normally developing and autistic-like children: The LEAP curriculum model. *Journal of the Division of Early Childhood, 8,* 157–172.

Moes, D. (1995). Parent education and parenting stress. In R.L. Koegel & L.K. Koegel (Eds.), *Teaching children with autism: Strategies for initiating positive interactions and improving learning opportunities* (pp. 79–93). Baltimore: Paul H. Brookes Publishing Co.

Mount, B., & Zwernik, K. (1988). *It's never too early it's never too late: A booklet about personal futures planning.* St. Paul, MN: Metropolitan Council.

O'Neill, R.E., Horner, R.H., Albin, R.W., Storey, K., & Sprague, J.R. (1990). *Functional analysis of problem behavior: A practical assessment guide.* Sycamore, IL: Sycamore Publishing Co.

O'Neill, R.E., Horner, R.H., Albin, R.W., Storey, K., Sprague, J.R., & Newton, J.S. (1997). *Functional assessment of problem behavior: A practical assessment guide.* Pacific Grove, CA: Brooks/Cole Thomson Learning.

Ozonoff, S., & Cathcart, K. (1998). Effectiveness of a home program intervention for young children with autism. *Journal of Autism and Developmental Disorders, 28,* 25–32.

Rogers, S.J. (1996). Brief report: Early intervention in autism. *Journal of Autism and Developmental Disorders, 26,* 243–246.

Rogers, S.J., & Lewis, H. (1989). An effective day treatment model for young children with pervasive developmental disorders. *Journal of the American Academy of Child and Adolescent Psychiatry, 28,* 207–214.

Smith, T., & Lovaas, O.I. (1998). Intensive and early behavioral intervention with autism: The UCLA Young Autism Project. *Seminar on Applied Behavior Analysis Treatment for Autism, 10,* 67–78.

Sullivan, R.C. (1997). Diagnosis autism: You can handle it! In D.J. Cohen & F.R. Volkmar (Eds.), *Handbook of autism and pervasive developmental disorders* (2nd ed., pp. 1007–1020). New York: John Wiley & Sons.

Turnbull, A.P., & Ruef, M. (1996). Family perspectives on problem behavior. *Mental Retardation, 34,* 280–293.

Turnbull, A.P., & Ruef, M. (1997). Family perspectives on inclusive lifestyle issues for people with problem behavior. *Exceptional Children, 63,* 211–227.

Turnbull, A.P., & Turnbull, H.R. (1996). Group action planning as a strategy for providing comprehensive family support. In L.K. Koegel, R.L. Koegel, & G. Dunlap (Eds.), *Positive behavioral support: Including people with difficult behavior in the community* (pp. 99–114). Baltimore: Paul H. Brookes Publishing Co.

Joseph's Behavior Support Plan

CHALLENGING BEHAVIOR

Joseph often screams and pulls away from adults in an attempt to escape difficult or undesirable situations (e.g., transitions). Adults often respond to his challenging behavior by decreasing demands, cuddling, and consoling him. Joseph screams and cries to request his cloth diaper or a cracker to hold. When Joseph screams and cries, adults offer him the diaper or a cracker to see if it reduces his distress. Joseph rarely has tantrums when he is looking at books, is watching videotapes, or is engaged in an activity that he has selected.

REPLACEMENT SKILLS

1. Joseph will be taught to use a photo activity schedule to anticipate the routines and activities of the day.

2. Joseph will be taught to make choices of activities or objects. Adults will show Joseph a photo choice board or objects for him to indicate his selection before engaging in an activity. Joseph's choice board will be available to him throughout the day so that he can indicate his requests and preferences.

3. Joseph will be taught a variety of play schemes and activities that are simple and pleasurable to him. During those activities, Joseph will be asked to put his diaper or cracker away.

PREVENTION STRATEGIES

1. Photo choice boards will be available to Joseph throughout the day. Joseph will be encouraged to point to a picture on the board to communicate his requests and preferences.

2. The family will establish predictable expectations for Joseph and communicate them in simple language. For example, if the rule is to eat at the table, Joseph will be told, "Eat at table," and be guided back to the table. Predictable rules must be established about when Joseph will be allowed to hold his diaper or cracker. At school, Joseph should be asked to put the diaper or cracker in his cubby and then immediately be offered a choice of two desirable activities.

3. Joseph's environment will be organized so that it is predictable for him. Visuals will be used to mark cabinets and toy bins where desired objects are stored.

4. When adults want Joseph to make a transition (e.g., go in the car, go inside the house), they will present the visual from the activity schedule and warn Joseph of the upcoming transition (e.g., "In a few minutes, time to go in"). After warning him, the adult will approach Joseph with the visual and state the transition using simple language (e.g., "Time to go in—all done swing").

5. Games, activities, and play will be simplified for Joseph so that they will be easier for him to complete while providing him with an active role. ISP staff will assist Joseph's caregivers in developing play sequences and simplifying family activities so that Joseph can participate more easily.

6. Adults will provide Joseph with frequent reinforcement for play engagement and communication throughout the day (e.g., "You are playing cars—good for you," "You showed me juice—good boy; Joseph wants juice").

CONSEQUENCES

1. If Joseph is having a tantrum for a cracker or his diaper at a time when he cannot have the object, the adult will first acknowledge his request (e.g., "You want your diaper"). Then he or she will state the rule and the alternatives ("No diaper during bath time—you can play with the boat or the duck").

2. If Joseph is having a tantrum for a cracker or his diaper and it is permissible for him to have it, the adult will ask Joseph to show what he wants (e.g., "Joseph, show me—do you want diaper or cracker?"). He or she will provide the object after he has pointed to the picture.

3. If Joseph is having a tantrum because he does not want to make a transition, the adult will restate the transition cue while pointing to the visual. He or she will tell Joseph, "I'll help you," and then physically guide Joseph to make the transition.

4. If Joseph is having a tantrum because the activity is difficult and he wishes to stop, the adult will state, "This is hard. One more time." He or she will guide Joseph to complete one more step or turn and then say, "All done. You can stop."

LONG-TERM SUPPORT STRATEGIES

1. ISP staff will assist Joseph's caregivers in identifying ways to facilitate peer interactions and promote the development of friendships with children in the neighborhood and at school.

2. ISP staff will teach Joseph's caregivers strategies for teaching Joseph self-care routines, including toileting.

3. ISP staff will teach Joseph's caregivers strategies for embedding communication instruction within daily routines and activities.

CHAPTER 11

On the Road to an Extraordinary Life

Supporting a Daughter with
Autism Using Positive Behavior Support

Sharleen Tifft with Lisa S. Cushing

My family embarked on a great adventure. In 1998, my husband Gary and I sold our home, purchased a travel trailer, and began touring the country with our three children—Daniel (then age 14), Ashley (then age 11), and Shawndell (then age 7). It had been our dream to travel around the United States. This dream was finally realized. Our travels took us to various campgrounds across the states of Oregon, Idaho, Utah, Wyoming, Colorado, Nebraska, and Kansas, landing us in Missouri. We consider St. Charles, Missouri, our new home . . . for now.

CAUTION: HAZARDOUS CONDITIONS

We have not been able always to dream of great adventures, and it is only recently that such dreams could be fulfilled. We once yearned to lead an "ordinary" family life. This vision of a normal life included sharing pleasant dinners together, having our children go to bed at a decent hour, and attending church as a family. Instead, our lives revolved around our daughter Ashley, who had been diagnosed with autism and was displaying high levels of aggression and self-injurious behavior. Ashley's problem behaviors prevented us from functioning as an ordinary family. These behaviors were so pervasive that they permeated every context—occurring at home, in the community, and at school. Her outbursts controlled what we did and where we went. I became housebound for close to 2 years. As we dealt with aggression in the morning and self-injury well into the night, Ashley's behaviors became a central theme in our lives.

At home, problem behaviors occurred often. Mealtimes were challenging. Ashley only sat at the table briefly. The rest of the time she was up and running around the house. Her table manners were atrocious. She grabbed the food she wanted, no matter whose plate it was on. She became aggressive if we told her that she could not have a particular item.

Playing with her sister or neighborhood children often ended in Ashley's causing harm to someone. She hit any child who played with something she wanted. Ashley hit

Shawndell when they bathed together. This was especially confusing because Ashley asked Shawndell to join her. Within seconds of getting in the tub, Shawndell screamed and cried because Ashley had hit her.

Another problematic daily routine was bedtime. Ashley yelled and hit me if I told her to brush her teeth. Bedtime was a constant battle. It became so bad that I stopped making her brush her teeth. It just wasn't worth the effort. When we tried to put her to bed, she cried and hurt herself. She sat at the edge of her bed and kicked the walls or banged her forehead into the corner of the headboard. A large yellow welt formed on her forehead. I feared that this welt would never go away.

Problem behaviors in the community made it very difficult for us to go out as a family. We often were unable to make it to a destination because Ashley's behaviors would escalate to crisis levels while in the car. This did not happen all the time. Sometimes she was fine, but other times she hit and kicked Daniel or Shawndell or continuously banged her head against the window with such force that I was afraid she would cause herself permanent injury.

Due to these problems, we were unable to attend church on a regular basis for 2 years. Our church was 30 minutes away and had a Sunday school class for "special needs" children. By the time we arrived at church, we were emotionally unable to go inside because of the traumatic ordeal we experienced in the car. Despite our efforts each week, we rarely made it through the sanctuary doors, so we stopped trying.

The frequency and intensity of aggression and self-injury limited all of our activities. Before a shopping trip, I had to find someone either to stay with Ashley at home or accompany me in case she acted out. Because of Ashley's aggression, I could not allow my son, Daniel, to babysit her. I needed skilled respite care providers trained in supporting children with disabilities. However, quality respite care was difficult to find. I resorted to recruiting people who already knew and liked Ashley. Still, good care was not completely reliable, as care providers inevitably called in sick or could not always work when I needed them. Consequently, there was little spontaneity in our family. Every event had to be planned 3–7 weeks in advance.

Looking back, I realize that we were living an abnormally limited life. It took a lot more effort and planning to do the everyday tasks that ordinary families did naturally. We were coping, but we were stuck. Life was not getting better for us or for Ashley. We were so immersed in the daily struggle that we never had time to consider a better way of living.

CONSTRUCTION AHEAD

Although things were bad at home, they were considerably worse at school. The school was in crisis. In October 1995, when Ashley was 7 years old, her teacher reported that Ashley engaged in aggressive behaviors up to 50 times in a single school day. She screamed, hit other students, and reportedly picked up one student and threw her to the floor.

I am thankful that the school called that day. It was that telephone call that started us on the road from merely existing to really living. I received the call from the school principal, who asked that I attend an emergency meeting. At the meeting, the principal and the special education teacher informed me that Ashley was out of control and that they were concerned about the safety of other children and the staff. They recommended pulling her out at noon every day, as Ashley seemed to act out more in the afternoons. I agreed that there was a problem and that safety was a very important concern, but I disagreed with the solution. I suggested that an outside consultant, knowledgeable in positive behavior support (PBS), provide assistance. Coincidentally, just 1 month before, I had attended a workshop on PBS and was impressed with the information that the presenter had shared. Fortunately, the director of special services at Ashley's school had attended the same workshop and was equally interested in PBS. Consequently, we were able to get services both at home and school. The school district agreed to hire a behavioral consultant to guide the process of PBS at school. The Arc of Clark County agreed to apply our unused respite care funds to pay for home-based positive behavior support services.

Beneath the surface of these decisions, however, was a river of tension and mistrust between home and school. Although the school district agreed to positive behavior support services, I was not altogether certain that this would have occurred if I had not strongly advocated for the approach. The meeting with the principal and special education teacher had created a deep schism. I left the meeting feeling that they viewed me as an overbearing and ignorant parent who was unwilling to comply with the school's recommendations. I wanted the teacher and principal to see me as a colleague and partner, but I could not imagine this happening after the meeting. In the midst of these adversarial feelings, the school district hired a behavioral consultant who was recommended by an expert in PBS, and the process of PBS began.

ON OUR WAY

The process of PBS took place in the home and across a series of meetings at school with Ashley's educational support team, from November 1995 to April 1996. The process involved approximately 40 hours of direct service by the consultant. A functional assessment was completed, a comprehensive behavior support plan was developed, and implementation support was provided both at home and school. It took time for everyone to grasp the philosophy, procedures, and strategies of PBS. Although the work was long, detailed, and difficult, the lasting outcomes that we achieved made the entire process worthwhile. With each success at home and at school, the time and effort seemed minuscule compared with what we accomplished. I was certainly never going back to the way it had been when we were just coping.

Positive Behavior Support at Home

On the same day that functional assessment activities were completed at school, Jim, the behavioral consultant, met with us that evening in our home. I wasn't sure of what to expect when Jim asked that we meet and develop a plan to support Ashley at home. I wasn't prepared for such a family-oriented approach. Sitting around the dining room table, Jim went through the functional assessment interview again, but this time with a focus on problem behaviors at home. He also explored with us different qualities and experiences of our family life. We discussed our strengths as a family, Ashley's positive contributions to the family, our resources and social supports, the stressors we experienced, and our goals for Ashley and for our family. It was a great experience . . . but odd. I expected that Jim would have his own agenda. As such, I found it highly unusual for a professional, especially one with a Ph.D., to ask us about *our* experiences, *our* views and *our* concerns. We were in control and, thus, able freely to divulge our wants and needs for Ashley and for ourselves. Jim was willing to spend as much time as necessary to find out what our family needed and to develop a plan that would work for Ashley and the rest of us.

Jim asked us to describe family routines that were not working and to choose a routine that we most wanted to improve. We decided to work on the bedtime routine, which directly affected all of us. Ashley was falling asleep between the hours of midnight and 3 A.M. She cried, screamed, and injured herself. We weren't sleeping well, and our patience was wearing thin. We also believed that she may have had a difficult time functioning at school due to lack of sleep.

Once we agreed to begin with this routine, Jim asked us to describe the ideal bedtime routine. I never really thought about what I wanted. I just knew I wanted something better. This makes a lot of sense to me now. We needed to know what we wanted out of each routine before we could know how to get there and when we had achieved it. Together, we created a vision of a successful bedtime routine. It involved Ashley putting on her pajamas, brushing her teeth, using the toilet, giving Gary and I a kiss and hug, and toddling off to bed. Then Gary and I would come to her room, tuck her in, and turn off the light, and she would fall asleep. Once we created this vision, we used insights gained from the functional assessment to build a specific plan.

The functional assessment led us to believe that there were multiple functions to problem behaviors embedded in the bedtime routine. Each function needed to be addressed separately. First, Ashley screamed or engaged in self-injury to get attention, particularly when she was alone in her room. She didn't want to be alone in her room, especially when other family members were in the living room. Second, we hypothesized that Ashley engaged in problem behaviors when she was feeling hungry. Third, we speculated that Ashley might be afraid to go to bed due to her poor grasp of time and limited knowledge about the natural world (e.g., seeing her parents in the morning, knowing that morning always returns).

We developed a plan that dealt with each issue. First, we created a climate that was conducive to going to bed and falling asleep. We developed a consistent routine for Ashley that began with a soothing bedtime snack—yogurt and herbal tea. Activity and noise emanating from the living room was reduced to a minimum. We asked our other children to go to bed at the same time as Ashley. We made hygiene tasks more motivating by letting her choose the flavor of toothpaste she used to brush her teeth and having her wash her hands with watermelon-scented pump soap after using the toilet. We addressed her desire for attention by making it contingent on completion of her bathroom duties. After Ashley completed hygiene tasks, she came to the living room and cuddled with me. At first, "cuddle time" lasted for 30 minutes. I gradually dropped this time to 20 minutes and then to 10 minutes. While cuddling, I tried to soothe any fears she might have about being alone in a darkened room for 9–10 hours. I reassured her that although the sun went down, it would show up again and a new day would come. I promised her that in the morning, she would see her mom, dad, sister, and brother again.

Once Ashley was comforted, Gary walked with her to the bedroom, tucked her in, and said her prayers with her. He turned on a night-light and helped her choose a quiet bedtime activity (e.g., listening to soft music on a cassette tape, snuggling with a favorite stuffed animal). Before leaving the room, turning off the light, and closing the door, Gary used a "safety signal" to alert Ashley that he was leaving but would return. The safety signal maintained Ashley's trust and comfort. He said, "Now, I'm going to go, but I will be back in 1 minute." Gary then went to the kitchen and set the timer for 1 minute. Once the timer sounded, Gary or I went into her room and praised Ashley for lying in bed quietly. We gave her a kiss, told her we would return in 1 minute, and left the room. Again, the timer was set and the procedure repeated. This process continued for about a week, until we were able to help Ashley feel secure during the anxious time between going to bed and falling asleep. Then gradually, we increased the amount of time we waited before returning to her room. Within 2 weeks, we were able to return to her room after a 20-minute delay. By that time, she was fast asleep.

Our plan also included procedures to deal with times when Ashley was having a bad night. If she screamed, we prompted her to use language or we used a safety signal. We knew that we needed to attend to her immediately or her behavior would escalate into self-injury. Rather than offering help or reassurance at that time, we prompted her to say, "I need you," and to say it three times. Once she said the words, we made a big fuss over her, smothering her with attention. If she escalated into more screaming, we calmly but firmly told her that once she was calm, we would talk with her. We then waited until she calmed down, prompted her to say, "I need you," and provided her with the attention or the help she wanted. The whole idea was to teach Ashley that screaming and crying no longer worked at obtaining our attention. We taught her that saying "I need you" was a much easier and quicker way to get our attention. Over time, Ashley screamed less and asked for help more often.

If Ashley was in crisis and engaging in self-injury, we physically blocked or restrained her from hurting herself. We did so as silently and calmly as possible because we did not want to provide attention for self-injury. We then told her, "When you have quiet hands, we can talk." We refrained from making any other comments until she was calm and had stopped hurting herself. Once she was calm and safe, we prompted her to say, "I need you," three times and then satisfied her want or need. Self-injury is dangerous and cannot be ignored. Nevertheless, these last-resort strategies allowed us to minimize attention maintained by self-injurious behavior while still keeping Ashley safe.

These strategies were so successful that Ashley embraced the bedtime routine and was able to establish a consistent sleep schedule. This helped the entire family, as Ashley was no longer keeping us up until all hours of the night. We were all rested and better able to tackle what the next day brought. Bedtime was no longer the stressor that it had been for years. I began to look forward to it. Cuddle time was my special time with my daughter. Afterward, Gary and I were able to spend quality time together.

The knowledge and strategies that lead to a successful bedtime routine were then transferred to other home and community routines. My new understanding of PBS made it easy for me to figure out why Ashley was engaging in problem behaviors and then decide which support strategies from the behavior support plan would work best in other routines. Most important, I realized that if I wanted Ashley's behavior to improve, I had to improve my parenting skills. I had to be more proactive in my support. I had to reinforce desired behavior and make sure that problem behavior did not achieve its aim or purpose. Above all, I had to be consistent. If I was tired and let something go, then I could not really expect Ashley to behave appropriately next time. I remembered a powerful statement from the workshop on PBS that I had attended. The workshop leader said that all immediate responses to all behaviors strengthen or weaken the behaviors; the behaviors never stay the same. That is the beauty of PBS; it emphasizes the need to teach new skills as well as to reduce problem behavior. Other methods that emphasized negative consequences actually taught Ashley new problem behaviors as she persisted in trying to achieve her unmet want or need.

By combining several powerful strategies, I could almost ensure success. Strategies that worked well with Ashley involved building trust, teaching communication skills, making things interesting and motivating by embedding reinforcers in less preferred activities, using positive contingencies (i.e., "making deals"), and starting with easy tasks or activities and gradually building to more difficult ones.

One of the most important strategies I learned was to build trust with Ashley by being more careful about how I communicated with her. I realized that sometimes Ashley engaged in problem behaviors because I spoke vaguely about a future event of interest to her, changed my mind after making a promise to her, or simply became distracted and forgot to do what she was expecting. Based on this insight, we created a much clearer and more predictable family life for Ashley. If I told her that we would go swimming at 3:00 P.M., I made sure that I followed through. If I told her we were going to have tacos for dinner, I did not change the menu at the last minute. I stopped using phrases such as "in a while," "later," or "give me a minute." I used a timer to help her predict the length of a delay and to help me remember to follow through. Once the family made a decision together (e.g., a new household rule, a family outing) and Ashley was informed, it was carved in stone. Over time, this created a peace in Ashley. Her daily life at home made more sense to her; we kept our promises, and there were far fewer surprises.

Many of the routines at home or in the community required new communication skills. The bathing routine mentioned previously is a good example. For Ashley to bathe successfully with her younger sister, she needed to learn what sharing meant and how to use words to indicate her desire for a toy. Whenever Ashley took a bath, she always asked that Shawndell join her; however, Ashley considered all of the toys in the tub her own. If Shawndell began playing with a toy, Ashley would inevitably hit her to retrieve it. I taught Ashley and Shawndell to use the word *trade*. Before Shawndell entered the tub, I told Ashley that if she wanted a toy that Shawndell was playing with, she needed to say, "Trade." I also taught Shawndell to respond immediately to Ashley's request by handing her the toy. Eventually, I taught Ashley to do the same and switch toys with Shawndell if her sister said, "Trade." Now when they take a bath together, they have all kinds of toys in the water and are able to bathe together without incident.

I changed the car-riding routine from being aversive to Ashley to being enjoyable by embedding highly preferred items in the routine. Success in the car was essential for moving on to other more complex routines in the community. During the functional assessment of the routine, we came up with the hypothesis that Ashley was bored in the car. For Ashley, there was absolutely no purpose to getting in the car and riding to a destination. She did not find the scenery interesting, there was nothing to do, and no one talked with her. With suggestions from Jim, we decided to make car rides more interesting to Ashley. First, we purchased special toys that were solely for use in the car. The toys included button books, Barbie dolls, and hair bands. These toys were placed in a laundry basket and kept in the car. The toys were changed regularly so that they remained novel and interesting to Ashley. Once in the car, we said, "Sit nicely, keep your seat belt on, and you can play with the toys." We also made sure that we spoke with Ashley. We asked her what she was doing and made an effort to include her in conversations. If she unbuckled her seat belt, we stopped the car, took the toy away, and waited until she buckled her seat belt. At first she screamed, but quickly learned what was expected of her. Riding in the car was no longer boring or aversive to Ashley. She could play with her toys or chat with us. Soon, we were able to take Ashley on a variety of errands and family outings (e.g., the grocery store, short day trips). Now, Ashley loves to go places in the car.

Strategies that we used to help Ashley attend church included gradually building endurance, embedding reinforcers in the routine, and using positive contingencies. To get Ashley accustomed to going to church, we began by staying for the worship band's music. She loved the contemporary sound of the band. Once the music was over, one of us would escort Ashley out of the church and let her play until the service was over. Slowly, she endured longer periods in the church. To satisfy hunger, I gave her a little bag of Cheerios or another quiet snack. To alleviate boredom, I allowed her to doodle. For this activity, I had to teach her to whisper so that she did not distract other parishioners while she explained a drawing or requested more paper. A positive contingency was in place for the length of the service. If Ashley behaved well, the family would go out for a treat on the way home.

If Ashley behaved poorly, one of us would go out to the car and sit with her until the end of the service. During this time, she was given little attention and was not allowed to play with any toys. We also did not stop for a treat on the way home. Now, Ashley regularly attends church with all of us on Sunday mornings and accompanies her father to a Bible study group Sunday evenings.

To build a successful grocery shopping routine, I used positive contingencies and gradually increased the level of difficulty of the task. Before we went to the store, I talked to her about how I expected her to behave. When we entered the store, I first made a beeline for the produce section. Ashley loves bananas, so I selected a bunch of bananas, separated one, and put it where she could see it. I told her, "I am going to set this banana aside for you. If we make it the entire way through the store and through the checkout line, you can have the banana." While shopping, I constantly talked to her, reminding her of the contingency and prompting and praising appropriate behavior. To ensure success, we took very short trips at first. I only looked for six or seven items and we went through the express line. If she behaved well, she received the banana (or another treat) that we had discussed at the start of shopping. Now, Ashley loves to go to the grocery store. The treats are no longer necessary for her success. She is sufficiently reinforced by pats on the back and praise. Sometimes at home, she'll come to me with her shoes and say, "Go store, go grocery store?"

We ensured the success of other community routines by focusing on a favorite activity, such as swimming. Ashley has always loved to swim, but the only pools in the winter are indoor pools with lots of people. Nevertheless, we found that Ashley would endure adverse stimulation while swimming. We decided to go to a huge indoor swimming facility and see how she would do. The crowds, the noise, the chlorine smell—things that could potentially set her off before—didn't even faze her. She discovered the water slide and was able to climb the stairs, wait her turn, and slide down by herself. At the bottom of the slide, we waited with enthusiasm and praise. We can now take Ashley to all types of pools and water recreation areas.

Another activity we learned that Ashley loves is traveling. A few years ago, we purchased a 32-foot travel trailer and began taking trips to regional vacation spots. Had we not developed a successful car-riding routine, we would never have discovered her love for this type of travel. The destinations were carefully selected to ensure Ashley's success. We made sure that the places were interesting to her. We always stayed in campgrounds. We also made sure that the campgrounds had access to swimming pools or other types of water recreation. To build Ashley's endurance, we started with very short trips. Before heading out, we prepared her by explaining to her where we were going and the fun things we would do when we got there. One of the things we learned along the way was that the trailer itself was interesting to her. She loved it!

As the boundaries of Ashley's life expanded beyond our home to our immediate community and to our region of the United States, Gary and I made a momentous decision. We decided to do something that we had dreamed of doing but never thought possible. For many years, we had wanted to explore the United States in a travel trailer and homeschool our children along the way. Fortified by Ashley's successes, we sold our house and took to the road.

Ashley likes living in the trailer. There are things for her to play with, and we refresh the toys regularly so she doesn't tire of them. Before we stopped in St. Charles, we went from place to place and Ashley experienced many changes. However, we made sure that her support followed her. Wherever we went, we supported her proactively and positively. The act of going somewhere was filled with intrinsic and embedded reinforcers (e.g., swimming pools, restaurants, parks along a river). When we arrived at our destination, she experienced things that we knew she liked. We made sure that we brought these things to her attention and we arranged the environment so that she was successful.

Positive Behavior Support in School

On the same day that assessment activities began at home, Jim facilitated a meeting at school. Several people attended: the principal, the special education teacher, three instructional assistants, the communication specialist, the occupational therapist, a district supervisor, a school psychologist, and Gary and I. I remember the thick sense of apprehension that permeated the room. Gary and I felt excluded from the team; our ideas for supporting our daughter had been unwelcome and disregarded. For everyone, this was a new experience. No one knew what to expect. I felt nervous yet also excited about an approach that made so much sense to me.

The first meeting was long, and much information was gathered. Jim began by conducting a functional assessment interview. An array of questions were asked. Some were about Ashley's problem behaviors (e.g., what they were like, how frequently they occurred, when they were likely to occur), but Jim also asked about alternative behaviors that might successfully replace problem behaviors. He also asked us to describe Ashley's positive qualities and skills, strategies that prevented problem behaviors from occurring, and items or activities that motivated her.

From the functional assessment interview and direct observations of Ashley in school, the consultant surmised that Ashley engaged in challenging behaviors, particularly aggression, for several reasons: She was able to avoid nonpreferred tasks and events, get preferred items or activities, and get and maximize adult attention while minimizing adult attention to peers. If Ashley was presented with a demand or a task that she did not like, then she would show aggression. This would result in a time-out that actually allowed her to get away from the aversive demand or task. If Ashley was denied a preferred item or activity, then she would hit others or scream until she obtained the item or activity. Ashley also used challenging behaviors to get adult attention. When she was aggressive, peers moved away from her and adults moved toward her to stop the assault. If Ashley was involved in a group activity and another peer was getting adult attention, then aggression brought adult attention back to her. The assessment showed us that Ashley effectively used problem behaviors to control her environment.

Two more lengthy team meetings were held to review the functional assessment findings, discuss recommendations for a behavior support plan, and finalize the plan. Because of the complexity of Ashley's problem behaviors, Jim proposed a multicomponent support plan. Much like the behavior plan created for the home environment, this plan addressed each of the issues that surrounded Ashley's problem behaviors. The final plan included ecological procedures, proactive strategies, skills and behaviors to be taught, positive reinforcement strategies, de-escalation procedures, and emergency procedures. This plan is briefly outlined in the appendix at the end of this chapter.

By the end of November, each team member received a copy of the plan and began to implement it. By February 1996, Ashley's school team had made significant progress in building an effective school environment for Ashley. Aggression, self-injury, and screaming behaviors had become, for the most part, inefficient and ineffective at achieving her wants and needs. By understanding and proactively addressing her wants and needs for adult attention, minimizing nonpreferred tasks or irritating sounds, and embedding preferred tasks and reinforcers into her day, the team had reduced the events that triggered the occurrence of problem behaviors. Teaching Ashley to use language (e.g., "I need help," "I'm hungry," "Break please") to achieve her wants and needs lessened the need for her to engage in problem behaviors. The communication skills that were taught at school matched those taught at home. The staff created lessons and outcomes that were meaningful to Ashley.

The use of interesting materials increased Ashley's ability to attend to and follow directions in class. She readily attempted new tasks and remained engaged for longer periods of time. Because many tasks had become fun and interesting, she had fewer reasons to resort to problem behaviors for attention or removal from boring or aversive tasks.

BUILDING BRIDGES BETWEEN HOME AND SCHOOL

The school staff worked hard at implementing the behavior support plan. By concentrating their efforts on the plan and Ashley's needs, communication between home and school improved. We realized that we needed to humbly put our differences aside and collaborate to make the plan work. Every one of us had been trying to prove that we knew more than the other. Fortunately, we overcame this obstacle of pride. Team members began to listen and to respect my ideas. I began to appreciate the teacher's challenges and efforts. With every success that we experienced together, the belief that we all needed each other to make the plan work grew stronger.

Communication between home and school was a vital component to making Ashley's plan work. For this end, we used a home–school communication notebook. In the morning, I wrote a note summarizing Ashley's emotional and physical state before going to school: whether she had gotten enough rest the night before, had an adequate breakfast, or was on edge for any reason. Events at home alerted school staff on how to proceed. If Ashley had a good night's sleep and everything went smoothly the morning before going to school, then the staff would proceed with Schedule A, which involved implementing the regular school day. If Ashley did not sleep well or something else caused her to start the day poorly, then the school would switch to a revised schedule, which started things off slowly for her. Schedule B alerted staff to shorten the duration of requests, make tasks easier, and give her more rest time. Ashley was given time to do what she wanted, even if this meant crawling into a quiet area, set up specifically for Ashley, and sleeping. After about an hour of Schedule B, Ashley was often ready to cooperate with the demands of the regular school schedule.

Thanks to the home–school notebook and Schedule B, a bad morning at home did not necessarily lead to a bad day at school. The staff had a method for starting her school day on positive footing. Rather than a lost morning of education, I viewed it as the gain of a positive and productive afternoon. Before PBS, the whole day would have been lost. Ashley's successes continued. She learned how to sit through and participate in circle time. She also began to monitor her own behavior. A quiet area was created in the corner of the classroom for which Ashley could request a retreat anytime she felt overwhelmed or needed a break.

Home and School: Becoming Partners

As Ashley began to experience success, she received glowing daily school reports. Home–school notebook entries changed from mostly descriptions of bad days and problem behaviors to positive stories and notes about her day. Notes from school to home about Ashley's achievements affected the home–school relationship. Rapport and trust grew where once there had been conflict and mistrust. We had come a long way from my first meeting with the school principal and the special education teacher. My relationship with the school had changed into a collegial partnership. As we began to pursue common goals and strategies across school and home environments, we realized how much we needed to share information for Ashley's success to continue. We then saw notable improvements at home and school. By working together, we were succeeding together. Cooperation paid off, and home–school communication blossomed.

An incident illustrating our changing roles involved a problem on the school bus. The principal informed me that the school bus driver was concerned about Ashley's behavior on the bus. While buckled in a safety harness, she screamed, kicked other students as they passed, and banged her head against the window. As the behaviors were severe, the bus driver would pull the bus to the side of the road and attempt to calm Ashley. This was a major safety issue and it seriously delayed the bus driver's completion of her route.

Rather than inform me of the school's solution to the problem, the principal asked me to meet with her and the bus driver to solve the problem together. The principal treated me as a colleague. During the meeting with the bus driver, I told her about our car-riding routine and suggested that Ashley's problem behaviors were for attention. The more the bus driver stopped the bus and gave Ashley individualized attention, the more Ashley would scream, kick, and bang her head. I suggested a simple solution: Give Ashley something to do that she enjoyed while riding the bus. I offered to purchase an interactive book and attach it to her harness so that she had continuous access to it. From the day we implemented this strategy, Ashley had no more incidents on the bus. The following school year, she no longer needed to be harnessed into her seat.

Another event that marked our transition from adversaries to colleagues was an end-of-the-year luau, a Hawaiian celebration. Ashley's teacher had accepted a new teaching position at a different school. To honor her teacher and to celebrate a successful year, the teaching assistants and I organized the surprise luau. The teaching assistants made paper grass skirts and murals of palm trees. The assistants wore bikini tops and grass skirts. During the luau, we ate skewers of pineapple and listened to the Beach Boys. Earlier in the year, I had taken pictures of Ashley with her teacher, and I made a framed collage as a going-away present. Tears of thanks suggested that Ashley's teacher was moved by our regard for her work with Ashley. We had come a long way together.

By the end of the school year, Ashley had gone from 50 or more reported aggressions per school day to fewer than three reported aggressions per week. These improvements endured at home during summer vacation and perhaps lulled me into complacency. It wasn't until the final day of summer vacation that I realized that Ashley would be going back to school with a brand-new teacher. I immediately called the teacher and met her on the day she was setting up her room. She was happy to meet with me and wrote four pages of notes as we sat and talked about Ashley. She treated me as the expert on Ashley. A bridge among Ashley, the behavior support plan, and the school had been built.

Ashley and Peers: Becoming Friends

The second year of PBS was much easier. The plan had been implemented, and we all knew that the strategies worked. My relationship with school staff had dramatically improved. Above all, Ashley was happy, more confident, and better trusted those around her. That second year, Ashley was very successful. By the end of the school year, Ashley was spending up to 50 minutes in a general education classroom engaged in academic work, with an instructional assistant on hand outside the classroom if needed. Ashley had developed friendships with typical peers, who would save a seat for her during lunch and school assemblies. She also was able to move about the school on her own.

The support that had made Ashley so successful in the self-contained classroom was carried over into the general education classroom. This support was essential because we added difficult tasks and activities and a new environment to her school day. All of these situations had previously triggered aggressive and self-injurious behavior. We felt that Ashley needed to learn how to work with other students and see them as an important part of her life. Ashley had experienced difficulty sharing adult attention in the self-contained class room. Now, we wanted her to share the attention of one adult with 30 peers! The strategies used in this environment were peer support, praise, and reinforcement. The general education teacher kept treats for Ashley in her desk. Ashley also had her own desk with her name on it, right next to other desks, which were clustered in threes. The teacher handed out Ashley's classwork and provided any necessary instructions. The student sitting next to Ashley that day was her "buddy." The buddy was taught to provide encouragement and reinforcement (e.g., "You're not hitting," "I'm glad you're my friend," "You're doing your work"). When Ashley finished her work, she and her buddy would approach the teacher, say that Ashley's work was done, and place her completed work in the finished box. Her peer then gave her a treat before Ashley left to return to the resource room. By the end of the second school year, Ashley was completing two or three pages of school work in a 50-minute period. Many of her peer buddies would visit Ashley in her special needs classroom during recess.

IMPROVEMENTS IN BEHAVIOR AND LIFESTYLE ALONG THE WAY

Our first successes with Ashley involved fairly simple routines such as going to bed, taking a bath with Shawndell, and riding in a car. These routines provided the foundation for accomplishing more complex routines, such as going grocery shopping, swimming at a public pool, attending church, and traveling. Starting with simple routines and slowly building up to more complex routines ensured Ashley's success. These successes have created a higher quality of life for Ashley and the entire family.

Along the way, we have seen improvements in many areas of Ashley's life: behavior, life skills, communication skills, and social skills. Above all, Ashley is no longer engaging in self-injury. We no longer have to worry about her safety, which is a great relief! Ashley is now able to dress herself. In addition, her hygiene has improved. Ashley brushes her teeth, and she tolerates wearing her hair in ponytails or pigtails. This is a big deal, as her scalp is very sensitive. In addition, she sits at the table for an entire meal. She also likes going to nice restaurants and can even navigate a buffet line with minimal assistance.

Ashley's language skills have improved dramatically. She now uses language to communicate what she wants or needs rather than resort to aggression or self-injury. Once she realized that saying, "I need help," was more efficient and effective at meeting her needs, she began to ask for help more often. Ashley now answers questions accurately with "yes" or "no." Her vocabulary has increased, and she has begun to use complete sentences. She initiates conversations and also accurately answers questions that are posed to her.

One of the things that I have found is that all things build on each other. Not only do specific skills relate to each other, but also little improvements become bigger, affecting more areas of her life. I really enjoy conversation time with Ashley. While driving, shopping, or just sitting together, we talk. At first, I had to prompt her replies, but now she typically replies on her own. The more she uses language, the more excited we become and the more we encourage her to talk. The more we encourage her, the more practice she gets, and the better she becomes. I remember when we used to wonder whether she was deaf. Now we are no longer walking around on eggshells, waiting for the next outburst to occur. We have relaxed and can spend quality time together.

Currently, we put Ashley in situations that offer new opportunities for her to practice language and learn new words. At the grocery store, I will say, "I need two milks. I need two of them. How many is two?" I remember a family walk while we were still living in Washington. We let Ashley pick the route to a park. At each corner, we would stop and ask her, "Which way?" She would have to say "straight" or "right." She was not used to this. She was used to pointing the direction, but now we asked her to verbalize the direction. Eventually, she used the words, and we ended up at the park.

Ashley seems to be getting more comfortable with language. She says her prayers at night and even generates her own meanings. She began with rote phrases such as, "Dear Jesus, thank you for our day, thank you for our food." She then added, "Thank you for our school." She can also sing songs in their entirety. Previously, she didn't have the endurance for this. She also has begun to engage in imaginative play. While we were packing for our trip, Ashley tore into the living room, ran to the telephone, picked up the receiver, and politely replied to an imaginary caller, "Hello? Aha. Aha, aha. Really? Really? Tank. Bye." We were stunned!

Many times, Ashley says a word that I do not understand due to articulation problems. She is incredibly patient and persistent, saying the word over and over until I figure it out. As soon as I understand the word, an "I can't believe it took you this long to understand!" look appears on her face. We respect what she says and encourage her to persist. We never ignore her attempts.

Dramatic improvements have been seen in her social skills as well. Ashley has learned to ask for things rather than to grab them. She has learned to share. We are able to give things to Ashley and say, "Here's one for Shawndell; go give Shawndell hers," and she'll do it. She no longer feels deprived when other people have things that she doesn't have. She has also learned how to wait. For instance, she has been waiting a week for me to make Malaysian chicken curry. She loves it and recently asked if I would make it. I told her that I didn't have it on the menu for this week, but I would be sure to make it next week. She went away happily with that answer. A little later, she came back to check, "Mommy will make chicken curry?" I answered, "Yes. When?" She replied, "Next week." She wanted to make sure I had not forgotten.

Ashley seems more comfortable in a variety of situations and trusts that things will work out. She is not fearful or expecting the worst in new situations. She assumes that things will go well. She does not expect to be bored or ridiculed. She continues to push herself, expecting more of herself. Ashley has been placed in situations where the support is weak, but she can still draw on her knowledge and skills for quite a while without falling apart. She seems to understand that she will wake up and a new day will come. Gary and I have worked hard at building her trust. During the bedtime routine, we told her that we would be back in a minute and came back each time. This melted away a lot of mistrust and fear. Now, Ashley knows that her fundamental wants and needs for comfort, nourishment, rest, and love will always be met.

These improvements in life skills, language skills, social skills, and self-confidence have allowed us to expand Ashley's and our horizons. Her successes have made us more courageous in attempting new activities. One activity that I once thought Ashley would never experience is horseback riding. I signed her up to take riding lessons. She had to learn how to groom the horse before riding it, making a highly preferred activity (riding) contingent on a less preferred one (grooming). Ashley loved to ride. She especially liked to gallop, which made it important to teach her how to stop her horse. I asked myself, "Why in the world would Ashley stop her horse when she loved to gallop?" I knew that she would break for a treat, so I embedded it within the horse riding activity. We put a knot in the reins and let Ashley gallop. When it was time for a break, I said, "Knot to chest." She then pulled the knot up to her chest and the horse stopped. I reinforced her by saying, "Look, you stopped your horse. Right on! Here's your treat."

As Ashley's quality of life improved, so did the entire family's. The children are much closer to each other. Shawndell chooses to play with Ashley and is no longer on her guard for fear of being hit. Daniel has learned how to support Ashley and enjoys interacting with her. He likes to make her laugh and she trusts him. They play and roughhouse together and tease each other. Daniel babysits for us now. This allows Gary and me to spend some quality time together away from the trailer home. Gary has always enjoyed spending time with Ashley, either roughhousing with her or videotaping her activities. Now, though, their relationship has a deeper and more mature dimension to it.

Prior to PBS, we were too busy putting out fires to enjoy Ashley or each other. My relationship with Gary has improved. We have a lot of fun together and have dared to dream again. Before, our only desire was to get through each day. We were so tired by everyday events that we did not have time to look to the future. That has changed. Of course, our parenting skills have improved immensely. My new understanding of Ashley and her behavior problems has helped me to recognize the effectiveness and ineffectiveness of my actions and to use effective parenting strategies more often. As we came to understand why we did what we did, we were able to dissect it for Shawndell and Daniel so they could understand. I now incorporate PBS into the way I parent all three of our children.

CONCLUSION: JOURNEY TO AN EXTRAORDINARY LIFE

Many changes have occurred since we began using positive behavior support. Ashley has blossomed into a young lady and continues to amaze us. Many wonderful characteristics are emerging. Ask me to describe my daughter now and her autism is not the first thing that comes to mind. I will tell you that she is a beautiful girl with curly brown hair and big blue eyes. She has a great sense of humor, a zest for life, and a growing sense of self-confidence. She loves the comedian Nathan Lane and will watch anything he is in. She loves music, picnics, swimming, fireworks, horseback riding, air shows, car rides, and camping. She enjoys going to church and school, looking at trailers and model homes, trying on shoes and clothes, having her hair styled, cuddling, playing with her siblings and friends, and going to restaurants. I feel like I am really getting to know my daughter and can see that she has a rich inner life. We may have never discovered the many aspects of this complex, wonderful child had it not been for positive behavior support.

When we started on the road of positive behavior support with Ashley, our aim was to get beyond coping with problem behaviors and to attain an ordinary life. We yearned to be like ordinary families. What we did not know at the time was that this journey would lead us to quite an extraordinary life. At one time, our world consisted of the family room, the bathroom, and Ashley's room. Now, our world extends to the continental shorelines.

We have chosen to stay in Missouri for a while. Our trailer is in the most beautiful of spots, surrounded by huge trees and a large grassy knoll that overlooks three lakes. Ashley has her own "thinking spot" on one lake and often sits at the shore's edge, staring into the water. The school district has welcomed us with open arms and has asked that I help in Ashley's education. I have been encouraged to help other families establish healthy home–school relationships. God only knows what is in our future. We do know that Ashley will continue to grow and be supported through the strategies of positive behavior support. Our plans currently match our extraordinary life; they are filled with dreams and hopes that carry us further into new, grander adventures. We are grateful for the freedom we have had to explore the United States with our children. More important, we are glad for the knowledge and tools that have helped us experience the depth and beauty of our daughter Ashley.

Ashley's Behavior Support Plan

ECOLOGICAL STRATEGIES

1. Embed preferred items, activities, events, and outcomes in nonpreferred or difficult tasks and activities (e.g., use Ashley's favorite toothpaste during the hygiene routine, provide toys to use while she rides in the car, give her a snack break at school).

2. Use a personal schedule that helps Ashley predict daily tasks and activities; weekly or monthly events; and important changes in task, activities, or events.

3. Help Ashley develop a positive rapport with classmates and friendships with typically developing peers at school.

4. Increase positive, supportive experiences early in the morning at home and school (e.g., a few extra minutes in bed before getting up, a conversation with Mom while waiting for bus, one-to-one support during first period, a review of her daily school schedule to start the day).

5. Use an alternative schedule ("Schedule B") if Ashley is having a bad morning. During Schedule B, increase choices, shorten the length of lessons, offer more breaks, and provide more access to reinforcing events.

PREVENTIVE STRATEGIES

1. Use positive contingencies that are natural to the situation to increase motivation and cooperation (e.g., say, "Wait calmly and then I will help you" or "After you wash up in the bathroom, let's visit together on the sofa")

2. Provide information about what she will be doing and how long a task or activity will last. Highlight the reinforcers she will experience during or after the task or activity.

3. Offer Ashley reasonable and feasible choices to increase motivation. Choices can include the materials that she uses, the length of a task or an activity, and/or the reinforcers that she will receive.

4. Intersperse easy or fun tasks with new or difficult tasks. Sequences that increase success include fun task, easy task, hard task, break and easy task, new task, fun task.

TEACHING STRATEGIES

1. Teach Ashley to use language to communicate her wants and needs for attention (e.g., "I need you"), for a break (e.g., "Go to quiet place"), or for an item or activity (e.g., "I want rice cracker").

2. Use safety signals to teach Ashley to endure delays in having her wants and needs met (e.g., say, "Let's do three more and then take a break" or "Wait here quietly and I will be back in 1 minute").

CONSEQUENCE STRATEGIES

1. Reinforce positive behavior by making breaks, adult attention, and preferred items and activities contingent on positive behavior.

2. When minor challenging behaviors occur, de-escalate them by actively ignoring and redirecting Ashley to the task or activity, prompting her to use language to get what she wants and honoring her use of language, or using safety signals to encourage her to accept a delay in getting what she wants.

3. When aggression occurs, minimize reinforcement by blocking the behavior, briefly but firmly reprimanding her, redirecting her to the task or activity, and using a safety signal that addresses her want or need (e.g., say, "You need to do three more, then you can have a break.").

EMERGENCY PROCEDURE

1. When aggression or self-injury escalates, prevent injury by immediately using appropriate nonaggressive restraint procedures in a careful and calm manner.

CHAPTER 12

Behavioral Support for School-Age Children with Developmental Disabilities and Problem Behavior

Stephanie M. Peck Peterson, K. Mark Derby,
Jay W. Harding, Tom Weddle, and Anjali Barretto

Since the early 1990s, we have had the privilege of jointly working with several families to develop behavioral intervention plans for their children. We assume that most challenging behaviors serve a communicative function for children. That is, children often use their challenging behavior to communicate something—whether that something is the desire to escape or avoid a particular task; to gain attention from a parent, sibling, or peer; or to gain access to preferred toys and materials. Thus, when collaborating with families of young children to provide behavioral support, we have found that it is helpful to utilize a multiphase assessment and intervention process to identify the purpose of challenging behavior and to provide interventions that match these purposes. For example, interventions to match a child's challenging behavior that occurs to escape or avoid difficult tasks might involve decreasing the task demands (i.e., make the task easier), teaching the child to request task breaks, or teaching the child to request assistance. Throughout the entire process, families and caregivers play an integral role in implementing assessments and interventions and in making decisions based on the outcomes of each phase.

Phase 1 of this multiphase functional assessment process consists of a descriptive assessment, in which parents or teachers identify and record naturally occurring events that are associated with problem behavior. Phase 2 involves manipulating antecedent events to identify situations that set the occasion for problem behavior. Both of these phases are used to formulate hypotheses regarding the function of problem behavior. Phase 3 involves an experimental analysis of either antecedent or consequence events (i.e., a functional analysis) to test the hypotheses generated in the first two phases. In Phase 4, parents implement functional communication training (FCT) based on the assessment results. Follow-up intervention

The research projects for Cal and Billy were funded in part by Grant R01-HD 29402 from the National Institute of Child Health and Human Development of the National Institutes of Health. The opinions expressed herein do not necessarily reflect the position or policy of that agency.

We gratefully acknowledge the assistance of Cal's, Billy's, and Jolene's parents in conducting these studies. Our lives have been enriched through our collaboration with them. We also express our appreciation to David P. Wacker and Wendy K. Berg for their assistance in preparing this manuscript.

probes are then conducted weekly and monthly to evaluate the effectiveness and durability of intervention outcome over time. When an intervention has been selected, the care providers implement it while the interventionists continue to collect assessment data on its effectiveness and potential side effects. Based on these data, modifications are made as necessary to improve the success of the intervention. Throughout the process, a collaborative effort is made to capitalize on the strengths and skills of each individual involved in the assessment and intervention phases. We refer readers to Derby and colleagues (1997) for a more thorough description of these procedures.

We have found that this model of assessment and intervention is useful because it allows for active collaboration among behavioral consultants, parents, and teachers. This form of collaboration often results in concurrent positive changes in parent, teacher, and child behavior. In addition, through this form of collaboration, parents may become more confident in their behavior management skills. As a result, they may also become experts in the implementation of their child's intervention plan. When this occurs, parents are viewed as equal partners with school personnel, and they may even show teachers how to implement the intervention effectively to assist in generalization.

This chapter provides three vignettes that illustrate this collaborative behavior support process. Cal's story provides an overview of the multiphase assessment and intervention process. This example specifically demonstrates the role that parents play throughout the process. In addition, the reciprocal changes that occur in both parent and child responses are discussed. Billy's story provides an example of how parents can become experts in their child's intervention procedures through this collaborative process. In doing so, parents can assist teachers and school staff in transferring the intervention's success at home to school. Jolene's story illustrates the integral role that parents can play in the assessment and intervention process, even when intervention is initially conducted in the school.

CAL: PROMOTING POSITIVE, RECIPROCAL INTERACTIONS BETWEEN PARENTS AND CHILD

Cal and his parents were participants in a federally funded research project that used the previously described multiphase assessment procedure in home environments to develop individualized intervention programs for young children with developmental disabilities who displayed severe behavior problems (e.g., self-injury, aggression) (Wacker & Berg, 1992). All assessment and intervention procedures were conducted by the children's parents, with coaching from the researchers.

Participants and Environment

Cal was 5 years old when he was enrolled in the project. He lived with his mother and father in a rural area and attended a local early childhood special education program. He was diagnosed as having pervasive developmental disorder, microcephaly, and moderate mental retardation. Cal displayed no recognizable verbal language but had learned the manual sign MORE and could use it independently to request additional snack items. Cal displayed severe aggression and destruction, which occurred most frequently during self-care activities, such as getting dressed, brushing his teeth, washing, and sitting at the table for meals. These behaviors occurred at home and school. Although Cal had many toys, he rarely engaged in age-appropriate toy play. Cal enjoyed active play, however, such as wrestling with his father and jumping on a trampoline. Cal's parents were committed to working as a team to help Cal learn to use more appropriate behavior for meeting his needs.

Assessment

The first assessment objective was to identify the situations associated with problem behavior. Cal's parents used a scatterplot to record Cal's behavior for 1 week within 30-minute intervals throughout each day (Touchette, MacDonald, & Langer, 1985). After each problem behavior was displayed, Cal's parents recorded a brief description of the events that preceded the behavior, the specific behavior that Cal displayed, and their response to his behavior (i.e., an A-B-C analysis; Bijou, Peterson, & Ault, 1968). The results of the scatterplot and A-B-C analyses were used to clarify concerns about Cal's behavior and to generate initial hypotheses regarding events that controlled the occurrence of his problem behavior.

Following the descriptive assessment, the interventionists observed Cal's behavior under specific antecedent conditions that Cal's parents believed would result in either high or low rates of problem behavior (i.e., structural analysis; Carr & Durand, 1985). This analysis of antecedent variables enabled the interventionists to observe how both Cal and his parents responded in various situations. First, the effects of high and low task demands on Cal's problem behavior were evaluated. Next, the role of high and low attention on Cal's problem behavior was evaluated. The results of this analysis showed that Cal's problem behavior consistently increased when task demands were made of him. Very little problem behavior was observed when no task demands were placed on Cal, regardless of whether he received parental attention.

Although the results of the antecedent analysis suggested that Cal's problem behavior was related primarily to task demands, Cal's parents hypothesized that Cal also engaged in such behavior to gain parental attention. Thus, the interventionists decided to continue the assessment process by conducting a functional analysis (Iwata, Dorsey, Slifer, Bauman, & Richman, 1982/1994) to test directly whether escape from task demands or access to parental attention (or both) maintained Cal's problem behavior. To do this, Cal's behavior was evaluated across a series of test conditions: contingent attention, contingent escape, and free play. All test sessions were 5 minutes in length. During the contingent attention condition, which tested whether Cal's problem behavior was maintained by access to parental attention, Cal was told to play with his toys by himself. His mother's attention was diverted unless Cal engaged in problem behavior. If Cal displayed a problem behavior, then his mother provided verbal attention in the form of reprimands and redirection to his toys (e.g., "Don't do that, Cal. Play with your toys."). During the contingent escape condition, which tested whether Cal's problem behavior was maintained by escape from task demands, Cal's mother prompted him to sort his blocks by color. As long as Cal complied, his mother continued to deliver task prompts. If Cal displayed problem behavior, then the task items and prompts were withdrawn and he was given a brief "break." The free play condition was designed to maintain the best behavior possible and to serve as a control condition against which the other two conditions would be compared. During this condition, Cal was allowed to play with his toys, no demands were placed on him, and his mother provided continuous attention.

Throughout the functional analysis, a 6-second partial interval recording procedure was used to measure child and parent behaviors. In this procedure, a social behavior was recorded if it occurred at any time during the 6-second interval. The percentage of intervals in which the behavior occurred during a session was then calculated to provide an approximation of the frequency or duration of the behavior.

The results of the functional analysis are shown in Figure 12.1. Cal consistently showed increased levels of problem behavior during the contingent escape condition. As predicted by Cal's parents, he also displayed low levels of problem behavior during the contingent attention conditions. Very little problem behavior was observed during the free play condition. The results of the functional analysis suggested that Cal's problem behavior functioned as a means of escaping from adult demands and, to a lesser degree, gaining parental attention. Given these results, Cal's parents agreed to implement two (FCT) programs, one to address the escape function and one to address the attention function.

Intervention

The first training program (Demand Program) focused on teaching Cal to complete task requests and request breaks from demands appropriately. Because Cal resisted many task requests both at home and school, his parents decided to work with him on educational tasks. These tasks included having Cal sort objects by color and shape. Cal's parents placed a desk in his playroom and labeled it with a WORK sign. During training sessions, Cal was given a WORK picture card and directed to place the card in a folder at his desk. His par-

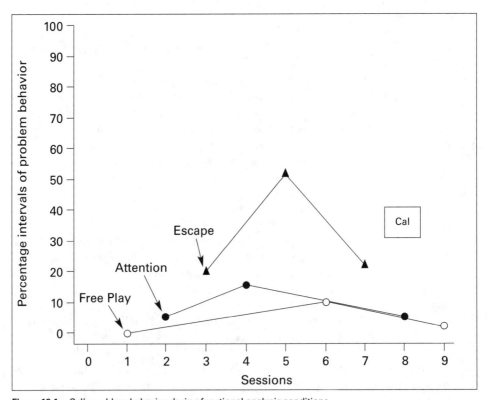

Figure 12.1.   Cal's problem behavior during functional analysis conditions.

ents sat on either side of Cal and presented him with a series of work tasks. Cal was not allowed to leave his desk during the session. If Cal refused to comply with a request (e.g., he began to destroy the materials), then his parents used gentle hand-over-hand guidance to assist him in completing the task. After Cal had completed several requests, his parents placed a DONE card on his desk and prompted him by saying, "Touch the card if you want to play." When he touched the card, the task was removed and Cal was given toys and enthusiastic attention for 1 minute. Problem behavior during his break resulted in his parents removing the toys and presenting another work task to Cal.

The results of the demand training program over a 6-month period are displayed in Figure 12.2. The top panel shows Cal's problem behavior (e.g., task refusal, aggression, destruction), appropriate social behavior (e.g., laughing, verbalizations, toy play), and requesting a break independently during intervention probes. Initially, Cal displayed high levels of problem behavior and low levels of appropriate social behavior. Over time, Cal's problem behavior decreased and his appropriate social behavior increased. He also learned to request a break with minimal parent prompting. The bottom panel of Figure 12.2 shows positive parent social behavior (e.g., praise, physical affection) and negative parent social behavior (e.g., reprimands, physical redirection). At first, Cal's parents used reprimands and physical redirection frequently to direct Cal to his desk, to keep him seated, and to block problem behavior. As Cal learned to follow directions, parent reprimands and redirection decreased.

The primary objective of the second training program (Attention Program) was to teach Cal to request his parent's attention and desired toys in an appropriate way. A secondary objective of this program was to increase Cal's age-appropriate toy play. During these sessions, one of Cal's parents played with him but initially kept all of the toys. If Cal attempted to obtain a toy, then his parent prompted him to sign MORE. Signing MORE resulted in Cal's receiving the desired toy, enthusiastic praise, and continued parental attention. Minor inappropriate behavior was ignored or redirected during these sessions. For example, if Cal engaged in a repetitive behavior (e.g., spinning a block), then his parent modeled an appropriate play activity (e.g., "Look, Cal, let's build a tower"). More severe problem challenging (e.g., toy destruction) resulted in brief removal of toys and parental attention.

The results of the attention training program are shown in Figure 12.3. The top panel shows Cal's problem behavior, independent signing of MORE, and appropriate social behavior during intervention probes. Cal's problem behavior remained at zero or near-zero levels throughout the sessions. Initially, Cal signed MORE primarily to obtain desired toys. Over time, Cal also signed MORE to maintain parent interaction. The bottom panel of Figure 12.3 shows positive and negative parent social behavior during sessions. These results show that negative parent social behavior decreased to zero levels after the first session, and positive parent social behavior remained high throughout all sessions.

The extent of family satisfaction with the intervention was assessed indirectly via a treatment acceptability checklist (Treatment Acceptability Rating Form–Revised; Reimers & Wacker, 1988) at the conclusion of involvement with the family. For example, in response to the question, "How acceptable do you find the treatment to be regarding your concerns about your child?" parents can rate the treatment on a scale of 1 (not at all acceptable) to 7 (very acceptable). Cal's answered this question with a 6, which suggests that they were satisfied with the intervention procedures. His parents noted that Cal seemed happier and less frustrated because he was now able to communicate his needs more readily. Cal's parents were also happier and less frustrated because Cal's behavior had improved. As a result, Cal and his parents developed a more positive relationship.

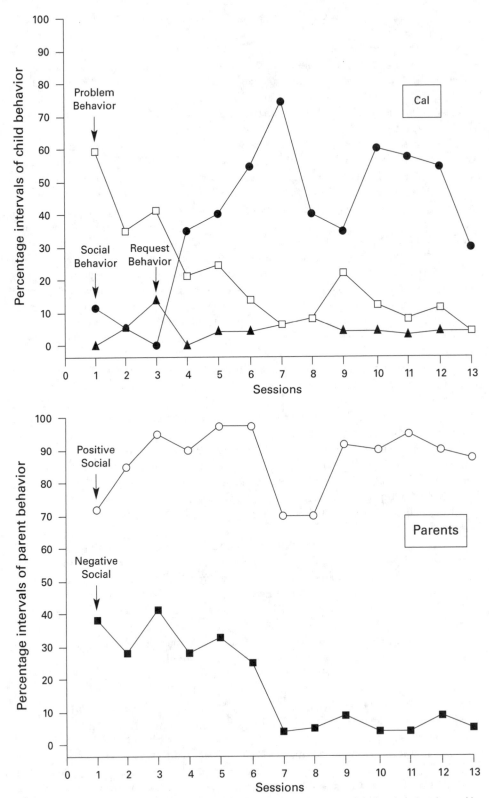

Figure 12.2. Top panel: Cal's problem behavior, social behavior, and requests for a break during demand intervention probes. Bottom panel: Positive parent social behavior and negative parent social behavior during Cal's demand intervention probes.

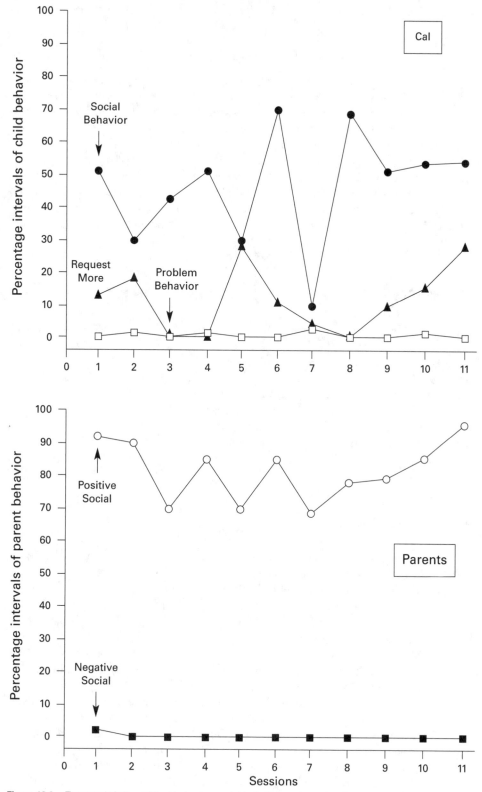

Figure 12.3. Top panel: Cal's problem behavior, social behavior, and requests for toys or attention during attention intervention probes. Bottom panel: Positive parent social behavior and negative parent social behavior during Cal's attention intervention probes.

Summary

Cal's story provides a model of systematic assessment in the home for young children who display severe behavior problems. It also illustrates that parents can collaborate actively with behavioral consultants throughout the assessment process and successfully implement individualized intervention programs at home. For Cal, intervention resulted in decreases in behavior problems and increases in appropriate social behavior across two social contexts: completing parent requests and gaining attention or toys. Positive changes in Cal's behavior were associated with decreases in the amount of negative attention (e.g., reprimands, redirection) that he received from his parents. Thus, as Cal learned to complete parent requests and communicate appropriately for desired outcomes (e.g., breaks from demands, toys, attention), his parents were able to spend more time engaging in pleasant interactions with him.

BILLY: PARENTS AS EXPERTS IN THE INTERVENTION PROCESS

The utility of interventions for challenging problem behavior are typically evaluated only within a single context. Studies have shown that stimulus generalization can occur (i.e., intervention gains can generalize to new tasks or environments and across novel tasks; Cooper et al., 1992; Dunlap, Kern-Dunlap, Clarke, & Robbins, 1991; Durand & Carr, 1992; Mace & Belfiore, 1990; Mace & Lalli, 1992; Sasso et al., 1992); however, generalization is often not assessed. In the few studies that have demonstrated generalization of intervention gains across environments (Durand & Carr, 1991; Parrish, Iwata, Dorsey, Bunck, & Slifer, 1985), additional training has been needed to promote stimulus generalization. Billy's story demonstrates how parents can facilitate the generalization of intervention gains from the home to the school.

Participants and Environment

Billy was enrolled in the same federally funded research project as Cal (Wacker & Berg, 1992). Because Billy was enrolled in the project at 2 years of age, however, his parents and therapists were faced with the task of transferring intervention gains from home to school during long-term follow-up evaluations. Billy was referred for participation in the project because of his self-injurious behavior (head banging), destruction (throwing objects), and tantrums (crying and screaming for up to 2 hours). His parents reported that these behaviors had been occurring several times per day for approximately a year. Billy was diagnosed with developmental delay, visual impairment, and asthma. He greatly enjoyed interacting with his parents. When the interventionists first met Billy, he used only gestures for communication. The initial assessment and intervention sessions were implemented at home, and follow-up sessions were conducted in Billy's classroom when he was 3 years old.

Billy had two siblings, one of whom had Down syndrome and another who was diagnosed as having attention-deficit/hyperactivity disorder. Billy's parents had worked hard with school staff and personnel for many years to improve their children's skills. They were committed to collaborating with school personnel to provide the best education possible for their children. However, they had never visited their children's classrooms prior to Billy's enrollment in this project.

Assessment

The initial in-home assessment of Billy's problem behavior consisted of the same multi-phase assessment procedures that were used with Cal. The assessment indicated that Billy's problem behavior was maintained by parental attention. Billy's mother reported that she allowed Billy to sit on her lap throughout the entire day to avoid problem behavior. When she attempted to remove Billy from her lap to complete household chores, he engaged in high intensity self-injury that resulted in bruises and abrasions. Given the intensity of Billy's problem behaviors, his mother was often unable to accomplish routine chores or interact with her other children.

Intervention

There were two primary purposes for the intervention: 1) to teach Billy an alternative to sitting on his mother's lap all day (e.g., playing with toys) and 2) to teach Billy communication skills that he could use to gain parental attention. To accomplish these goals, FCT was implemented by Billy's mother with consultation from the interventionists. To implement FCT, Billy's mother allowed him to sit on her lap while playing with a preferred toy. She slowly moved him off her lap and then prompted him to sign PLEASE to get back on her lap. If he signed PLEASE, he was allowed to sit on her lap again. If Billy displayed problem behavior, however, his mother left the room until he stopped his tantrum. Another adult remained in the room to ensure Billy's safety. The implementation of FCT resulted in a dramatic decrease in Billy's problem behaviors, and he began to sign PLEASE consistently to gain his mother's attention. In addition, Billy began to display a number of new social behaviors, such as verbalizing new words and displaying novel toy play skills, within 6 months of in-home intervention.

Generalization Promotion

At the age of 3, and after 10 months of in-home FCT, Billy was placed in a preschool classroom for children with developmental delays. Billy's preschool teacher reported she did not observe any problem behaviors. In fact, she was surprised to learn that Billy had been a participant in a federally funded project to reduce problem behavior at home. Although this was encouraging news, she also reported that Billy was very shy, rarely used spoken words, and typically avoided group activities. This was certainly not the case at home, where Billy had become very social and verbal. It was disappointing to learn that the gains in social skill development Billy displayed at home had not generalized to school.

Given his teacher's anecdotal reports, the interventionists decided to observe Billy's behavior at school. To evaluate generalization at school, a series of observations were conducted in both Billy's home and classroom. The first one was a home baseline, in which Billy's positive social behavior was observed in both free play and FCT conditions. The 6-second recording procedure that was used for Cal was also used to measure Billy's social and challenging behaviors. During free play, Billy was provided with continuous adult attention and toys. As shown in Figure 12.4, Billy was very sociable during free play, and he never signed PLEASE. During FCT, Billy was allowed to play with toys, but adult attention was diverted from him. Billy's signing dramatically increased, and he continued to socialize with his parents while he played with his toys.

Next, a school baseline observation took place. Baseline conditions were conducted during one-to-one instructional activities. Billy's teacher was told to interact with him in a natural manner, give Billy a task on which to work, and intermittently check to see how he was doing. As shown in Figure 12.4, Billy never signed PLEASE, and he engaged in very low levels of social interaction.

Following the school baseline measures, teacher education was implemented. This was the first time Billy's mother had ever been to the classroom, even though Billy had attended the school for 4 months. During the teacher education, Billy's mother demonstrated FCT for the teacher, using the same procedures that she used at home. Compared with previous sessions conducted in the school by Billy's teacher, a moderate increase in signing and a substantial increase in social interaction occurred (see Figure 12.4).

After 10 minutes of modeling, FCT was then implemented by Billy's teacher. Billy continued to sign PLEASE, and he interacted socially with his teacher, which he had rarely done previously. To demonstrate that the change in Billy's behavior was due to the use of FCT, the FCT plan was briefly discontinued at school, and a return to the one-to-one instructional activity was reinstated. This resulted in a decreased level of signing and social interaction. When FCT was reinstated, an increase in both signing and social interaction occurred. The decrease in signing and social interaction when FCT was removed and the subsequent increase in signing and social interaction when FCT was reinstated suggested a causal relationship between the FCT plan and improved behavior for Billy.

Follow-up probes of teacher-implemented intervention were conducted at 6 and 8 weeks. As can be seen in Figure 12.4, Billy continued to display social interaction more than 60% of the time, and he rarely signed PLEASE. Billy's teacher reported that the sign was rarely needed because Billy used verbalizations throughout the day to communicate his needs.

Summary

For Billy, the gains in social and communicative behavior that were observed following 10 months of in-home intervention did not generalize to the preschool. Fortunately, the problem behaviors that were originally targeted for intervention were not observed at school. In this case, generalization of social skills was facilitated by Billy's mother, who was the expert and demonstrated the intervention procedures for the teacher. Given the limited effort involved (10 minutes of modeling by Billy's mother), the outcomes were very satisfying.

JOLENE: INTEGRAL ROLE OF PARENTS IN SCHOOL-BASED ASSESSMENT AND INTERVENTION

As children grow up, they spend less time at home and more time in other environments during the day. For example, a child is at home in the morning, rides the bus to school, attends before-school child care, is at school for the entire day, attends after-school child care, and then goes home again. Thus, the term *caregiver* often encompasses more than just biological parents. Caregivers also include child care workers, school staff, and transportation staff who care for the child throughout the day. Children who are involved in such routines must make several transitions across environments and people during the day, which can make it difficult to implement interventions for severe problem behavior. The next vignette demonstrates how functional assessments and positive behavioral interventions can be conducted by using input from a variety of caregivers.

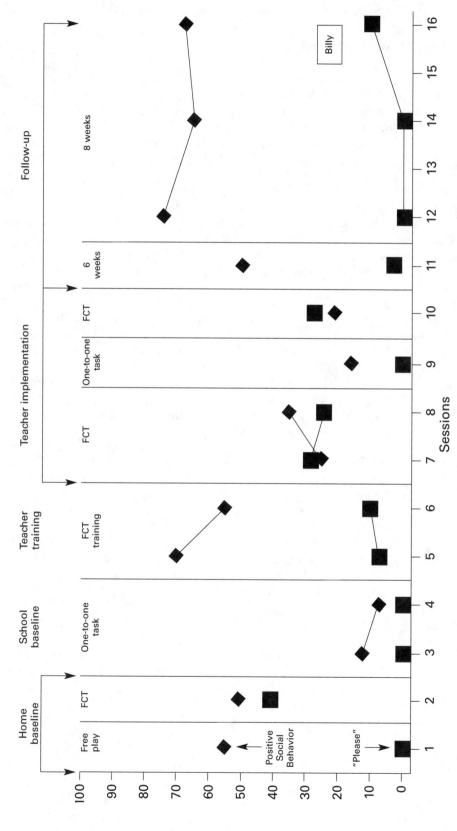

Figure 12.4. Social behavior and signing displayed by Billy at home and school before and after Billy's mother educated his teacher about Billy's intervention.

Participants and Environment

Jolene was 10 years old and had been diagnosed with pervasive developmental disorder-not otherwise specified (PDD-NOS). Her cognitive and language skills were moderately delayed, but her functional use of language and social skills was significantly delayed. When the interventionists first met Jolene, Jolene's greeting was an expletive and a swift kick to one of the therapist's shins. This was not atypical, given that Jolene engaged in high rates of challenging behavior (e.g., swearing, hitting, kicking, throwing objects) across multiple environments and individuals.

Jolene lived with her mother and two brothers. Jolene's mother had established an excellent relationship with Jolene's teacher via regular telephone contact to discuss medication issues and home events that might affect Jolene's behavior at school. Jolene's mother made a point of taking Jolene along whenever she went shopping or to at a restaurant with Jolene's brothers. Although this sometimes resulted in embarrassing episodes, Jolene's mother felt that Jolene needed to be with the family, go places, and have a "normal" life. As a result of Jolene's problem behavior, however, her access to family and integrated school activities (e.g., dining out, music class) decreased over time due to safety concerns and social stress. Jolene participated in a school-sponsored child care program for 1 hour before school and 2 hours after school each day, during which she frequently displayed problem behavior, especially on the bus ride. As a result of her behavior on the bus, Jolene received several bus citations, which threatened a loss of her bus-riding privileges. Jolene's mother had worked diligently over the preceding years in an attempt to decrease her problem behavior. She had tried several intervention programs in multiple contexts, including both punishment and reward programs. However, these programs were unsuccessful in addressing Jolene's needs and improving her behavior.

At the beginning of the new school year, a multidisciplinary team meeting was held to discuss Jolene's behavior, her preferred activities, and the possible reasons for her problem behavior. At this meeting, it was agreed that an intervention conducted in one environment alone would have limited overall impact. Furthermore, because Jolene made numerous transitions between environments every day, the child care staff and school bus driver needed to be incorporated into the plan. The school was the environment where the most structure and staff support was available. Therefore, it was decided that assessment and intervention would begin there, with input and assistance from Jolene's mother, child care staff, and bus driver. Over time, the intervention would be extended to other environments.

Assessment

First, a functional assessment interview was conducted (O'Neill et al., 1997). The purpose of this assessment was to define the problem behaviors, identify the interventions that had been attempted previously, and form a hypothesis regarding the purpose of Jolene's behavior. In addition to her mother, the school, child care, and bus staff were interviewed. A communication notebook that consisted of anecdotal information was also established so that Jolene's mother and the school staff could regularly exchange information.

The interview results indicated that Jolene's interests in leisure activities had diminished over time. During the previous school year, she displayed a relatively typical range of leisure interests that included using the computer, singing, listening to audiotapes of favorite songs, playing on the outdoor play equipment, jumping rope, watching videotapes, blowing bubbles, playing in water, dancing, having books read to her, and going out to restaurants. At the time of this evaluation, however, her leisure interests dwindled to going outdoors and playing with water. Restricted access to activities, due to Jolene's behavior problems, was hypothesized to be the cause of this change.

Staff working with Jolene noted that the frequency of Jolene's problem behavior increased when she was asked to stop engaging in a leisure activity to perform a work task. They also noted that she often ran away and hit others even when she was engaged in preferred activities, such as snack time or water play. It was hypothesized that Jolene engaged in problem behavior during these times to gain attention. This hypothesis was supported by staff reports that she did not remain in time-out unless an adult sat next to her. If an adult sat next to her, then Jolene sat calmly. The hypothesis was further supported by her mother's report that she had successfully used time-out as a consequence for Jolene's problem behavior. The child care staff noted that they, too, had successfully used time-out from attention and activities to address Jolene's swearing. As a result of these reports, it was hypothesized that Jolene's problem behavior was maintained by attention and access to preferred activities.

Next, Jolene was observed within her daily routine to identify when she engaged in problem behavior most frequently (i.e., functional assessment observation; O'Neill et al., 1997). Jolene rarely played or worked independently for more than a few minutes at a time before engaging in problem behavior. She typically displayed such behavior in group activities that required waiting or attending to group instruction. She also engaged in problem behavior in the presence of task demands, especially when the task demands were not part of her normal routine. She usually performed best when she had a very structured schedule. It was noted that she rarely engaged in problem behavior when a staff member sat next to her and that she frequently asked preferred staff members to work with her. Finally, it was observed that the choices for preferred activities were often determined by staff routines and not what Jolene desired at the moment.

Based on the interviews and direct observations of Jolene's problem behavior, it was hypothesized that Jolene engaged in problem behavior for multiple reasons. The primary hypothesis was that she engaged in problem behavior to gain adult attention, especially if adult assistance was part of the routine. In addition, she appeared to engage in problem behavior to gain access to preferred activities that were not currently provided as a choice and to escape tasks that were not part of her routine.

Then, the interventionists conducted a more formal, experimental assessment to test these hypotheses. During this assessment, Jolene worked appropriately for short periods of time if she received immediate access to highly preferred activities contingent on work completion. Within these test conditions, she appropriately requested attention when she needed help with her work. In contrast, Jolene often kicked and swore at those who approached her or spoke to her when she was engaged with a preferred activity (e.g., swinging during one of her work breaks). These results appeared to confirm the initial hypotheses.

Intervention

The initial intervention goal was to reduce the frequency of Jolene's swearing and aggression. As the assessment was implemented, however, it was hypothesized that Jolene's communication delays were a primary reason for her problem behavior. Therefore, the intervention included developing a comprehensive augmentative and alternative communication (AAC) system that Jolene could use to express her needs. A communication board was devised that consisted of line drawings to indicate tangible items, feelings, and activities (see

Figure 12.5). In addition, improved social skill acquisition was sought via the AAC system. Social skills were practiced by using conversational scripts, which Jolene's mother and the child care staff developed for staff interaction with Jolene. These scripts contained information that the teachers would not otherwise know without the scripts. For example, Jolene's mother might write a script regarding a special trip that the family took to a fastfood restaurant. The script might contain questions such as, "Where did you go last night?" (answer: "McDonald's"), "What did you have to eat?" (answer: "Hamburger and fries"), and "Did you see anyone you know?" (answer: "Donna"). Jolene answered the questions by using verbalizations and her AAC picture system when necessary. Pictures were added to her AAC picture system as needed for conversational topics.

In addition to the communication training component, the team, including Jolene's mother, also decided to include a time-out component in the intervention. This decision was based on two factors. First, time-out had been somewhat successful in reducing Jolene's problem behavior across environments in the past. Second, the research literature suggests that it is often necessary to include a reductive component (e.g., extinction, time-out, guided compliance) in reinforcement-based interventions to achieve maximum effectiveness (Fisher et al., 1993; Wacker et al., 1990). Given that the primary intervention procedure for Jolene was reinforcement based, the team felt that the time-out contingency would constitute only a small part of the intervention. In addition, safeguards were implemented to ensure that the process was not abused. The therapist implementing the intervention routinely took data on the effectiveness of intervention and the number of times that time-out was implemented. Furthermore, the team met regularly to reevaluate intervention procedures and the necessity of the time-out procedure.

Daily 1-hour intervention sessions were implemented to help Jolene acquire communication, choice making, leisure, and conversational skills. First, Jolene was prompted to choose an activity from her communication board. Second, two rules—"Friendly talking" and "Hands and feet to self"—were established for maintaining access to the activity. Jolene was required to repeat these rules before she was allowed access to her chosen activity. Third, upon beginning the activity, Jolene was asked whether she wanted the interventionists to stay and talk to her or to go away. Regardless of her choice, a timer was then set for 3 minutes. When the timer went off, Jolene was asked whether she wanted to continue the activity in which she was currently engaged or to choose a new activity. As long as she did not display problem behavior, she could continue engaging in her preferred activities. If any problem behavior occurred, then the activity was stopped and Jolene was placed in time-out for 1–3 minutes. The interventionists lightly held Jolene's arms to her side to keep her in time-out but provided no other attention. As Jolene's communication skills improved, the need to hold her in time-out decreased because she no longer tried to escape. At the end of the time-out period, Jolene had to return to her communication board to make another choice. She was allowed to select the same activity but was required to rehearse the rules before gaining access to her choice.

Interestingly, it was only necessary to implement the time-out contingency for a very short period of time. During the first week of intervention, time-out was implemented approximately ten times during each 1-hour session. By the second week of intervention, however, time-out was implemented three to five times per 1-hour session. By the third week of intervention, the time-out component was unnecessary because Jolene's behavior had improved so dramatically. This remained the case for the remainder of intervention.

After 2 months, the intervention was modified to include academic tasks as choices on the communication board. If Jolene chose to work on an academic task, then she was

Figure 12.5. Jolene's communication board. (Picture Communication Symbols, Copyright 1981–2002, Mayer-Johnson, Incorporated, all rights reserved. The PCSs used in this chapter were taken from the Boardmaker software program and were used with permission [Mayer-Johnson, Inc., Post Office Box 1579, Solana Beach, CA 92075; 1-800-588-4548; www.mayer-johnson.com]).

prompted to touch the I'M ALL DONE picture or to say, "I'm done!" whenever she wanted to take a break to engage in a preferred activity. If she said, "I'm done!" or touched the picture card, then she was allowed to choose an activity of her choice.

Throughout intervention, improving Jolene's social skills was addressed by implementing the conversation scripts while Jolene was engaged in preferred activities. Conversations were initiated by the interventionists during intervention sessions and by school, bus, and child care staff during daily activities. These conversation scripts were developed by Jolene's mother, who provided details of activities in which Jolene had participated outside of school (e.g., trips to restaurants). At first, Jolene was simply asked these questions while she was engaged in preferred activities. For example, someone might have said, "So, I hear you went out to eat at _____ last night. Tell me what you had to eat." At first,

Jolene ignored these conversational gambits and did not respond. When provided with her own verbal script (e.g., prompted to say, "I had a hamburger!"), however, she began to answer. In addition, she also began to initiate questions on her own.

After 2 months of intervention, the rate of Jolene's problem behavior decreased from an average of 60 occurrences per hour to an average of three occurrences per hour. In addition, her communication skills improved dramatically. She began to initiate choice making and to set the timer herself. The timer became a means for her to control her interactions with others. She would say, "Set the timer. You come back when the timer goes off." Control over her activities and interactions seemed to be an important component in her improved behavior.

Generalization Promotion

After several months of intervention, the next issue was to train others to work with Jolene throughout the day rather than implementing the intervention for only 1 hour of the school day. First, the school staff participated in the 1-hour intervention sessions to learn the intervention procedures and to use the scripts provided by Jolene's mother. Then, the school staff implemented the intervention throughout the school day.

Next, the interventionists worked with Jolene's mother to implement the intervention at home. First, the communication board was modified to include the preferred home activities: watching videotapes, cooking with her mother, and engaging in water play. The interventionists then worked with Jolene's mother to modify the intervention procedures for the home environment. Jolene's mother chose to shorten the intervention session to 15 minutes per day and incorporated the same demands, choice making, and consequences for problem behavior that were used at school. The school developed conversation scripts about preferred activities, which were similar to the scripts that Jolene's mother had previously developed for the school. Thus, Jolene's mother could discuss with Jolene what she had done at school each day. Jolene's mother also was encouraged to take a portable communication board with her whenever she and Jolene were in the community to teach Jolene appropriate scripts as the need arose.

In addition, the child care staff attended Jolene's intervention sessions at school and developed the manner in which the communication board and choice-making procedures would be used in the child care program. Furthermore, the bus driver was invited to observe Jolene at school and meet with the intervention team to discuss Jolene's use of her communication board on the bus.

Summary

Jolene's story provides an example of how school staff, family members, and other care providers can work hand in hand to build a comprehensive behavior support plan. In this case, Jolene's appropriate behavior while engaged in preferred activities was used to teach her conversational scripts and improve her social and communication skills. With this approach, Jolene quickly learned to use her communication board to express her needs and exert control over her environment in an appropriate manner.

Incorporating other environments and significant adults into the intervention plan led to a generalized reduction in Jolene's problem behavior, especially during transitions and changes in routine. In addition, an increase was observed in Jolene's self-initiated use of communication to seek information about her day and adjust to change. For example, when music class was canceled one day and a conversational script to this effect was provided, Jolene said to a staff member, "No music today. Music next Thursday." In the past, this change in schedule typically resulted in increased problem behavior. The communication board and conversational script, however, gave her a method for dealing with changes more appropriately.

The plan has been implemented across all environments in which Jolene interacts, and she has even moved to a new classroom. Everyone involved feels that the first step has been taken for a less restrictive lifestyle for Jolene. Active intervention is no longer in place for Jolene's behavior because she is not viewed as a student with significant behavior problems. She is performing well under typical classroom management procedures. To everyone's delight, Jolene was even able to participate with her general education classroom's music program. Her special education teacher cried as Jolene smiled and waved to her from the stage during the dress rehearsal. The teacher telephoned Jolene's mother to encourage her to bring Jolene to the evening show for parents and guests. At this event, Jolene performed flawlessly during both songs, and she did so without supervision or intervention. After the dress rehearsal, as Jolene's teacher had been walking with her back to the special education classroom, Jolene had beamed and stated repeatedly, "I did a good job in music! I did a good job in music!"

CONCLUSION

This chapter has provided three vignettes that demonstrate the integral role parents play in the assessment and treatment of their children's problem behavior. Cal's example demonstrates that parents can effectively treat their children's problem behavior at home. Billy's example illustrates how parents can educate teachers and other professionals to provide intervention at school. Jolene's example shows how parents, school staff, child care providers, and transportation staff can work together to provide an effective and comprehensive behavior support plan.

Through our partnerships with parents, we have found that parents add an important dimension to the assessment and intervention process. Facilitating parental input in behavior support plans is especially valuable when children reach school age because of the variety of settings in which they must participate (e.g., home, classroom, bus, child care). Good communication among home, school, and other environments provides consistent implementation of behavior support plans and can improve the social validity of intervention results. For example, when teaching appropriate social skills, such as conversational skills, it is often helpful for teachers to have information on what the child had for dinner last night, the leisure activities in which the family participated the previous night, and the family's upcoming activities. Similarly, it is helpful for parents to know what the child did at school that day, what special events took place at school, and the school's upcoming special events. This information can provide conversational topics that are socially relevant and valid for the child. Without good communication between parents and school personnel, social skill training requires contrived conversational topics, which may limit the social validity of intervention.

Parents should be viewed as equal, if not primary, partners in the assessment and intervention process. We believe that the multiphase assessment and intervention procedure described in this chapter helps promote parents as experts in their child's behavior and intervention. When parents and teachers of young children work as equal partners, positive changes in adult behavior often occur simultaneously with positive changes in child behavior. These reciprocal changes in adult and child behavior may be the key to socially valid intervention approaches that are durable over time and promote generalization across multiple environments.

REFERENCES

Bijou, S.W., Peterson, R.F., & Ault, M.H. (1968). A method to integrate descriptive and experimental field studies at the level of data and empirical concepts. *Journal of Applied Behavior Analysis, 1,* 175–191.

Carr, E.G., & Durand, V.M. (1985). Reducing behavior problems through functional communication training. *Journal of Applied Behavior Analysis, 18,* 111–126.

Cooper, L.J., Wacker, D.P., Thursby, D., Plagmann, L.A., Harding, J., Millard, T., & Derby, M. (1992). A functional analysis of the role of task preferences, task demands, and adult attention on child behavior: Application to an outpatient and classroom setting. *Journal of Applied Behavior Analysis, 25,* 823–840.

Derby, K.M., Wacker, D.P., Berg, W., DeRaad, A., Ulrich, S., Asmus, J., Harding, J., Prouty, A., Laffey, P., & Stoner, E.A. (1997). The long-term effects of functional communication training in home settings. *Journal of Applied Behavior Analysis, 30,* 507–531.

Dunlap, G., Kern-Dunlap, L., Clarke, S., & Robbins, F.R. (1991). Functional assessment, curricular revision, and severe behavior problems. *Journal of Applied Behavior Analysis, 24,* 387–397.

Durand, V.M., & Carr, E.G. (1991). Functional communication training to reduce challenging behavior: Maintenance and application in new settings. *Journal of Applied Behavior Analysis, 24,* 251–264.

Durand, V.M., & Carr, E.G. (1992). An analysis of maintenance following functional communication training. *Journal of Applied Behavior Analysis, 25,* 777–794.

Fisher, W., Piazza, C., Cataldo, M., Harrell, R., Jefferson, G., & Conner, R. (1993). Functional communication training with and without extinction and punishment. *Journal of Applied Behavior Analysis, 26,* 23–36.

Iwata, B.A., Dorsey, M.F., Slifer, K.J., Bauman, K.E., & Richman, G.S. (1994). Toward a functional analysis of self-injury. *Journal of Applied Behavior Analysis, 27,* 197–209. (Reprinted from *Analysis and Intervention in Developmental Disabilities, 2,* 3–20, 1982).

Mace, F.C., & Belfiore, P. (1990). Behavioral momentum in the treatment of escape-motivated stereotypy. *Journal of Applied Behavior Analysis, 23,* 507–514.

Mace, F.C., & Lalli, J.S. (1992). Linking descriptive and experimental analysis in the treatment of bizarre speech. *Journal of Applied Behavior Analysis, 24,* 553–562.

O'Neill, R.E., Horner, R.H., Albin, R.W., Sprague, J.R., Storey, K., & Newton, J.S. (1997). *Functional assessment and program development for problem behavior: A practical handbook* (2nd ed.). Pacific Grove: Brooks/Cole Thomson Learning.

Parrish, J.M., Iwata, B.A., Dorsey, M.F., Bunck, T.J., & Slifer, K. (1985). Behavior analysis, program development, and transfer of control in self-injury. *Journal of Behavior Therapy and Experimental Psychiatry, 16,* 159–68.

Reimers, T., & Wacker, D. (1988). Parents' ratings of the acceptability of behavioral treatment recommendations made in an outpatient clinic: A preliminary analysis of the influence of treatment effectiveness. *Behavioral Disorders, 14,* 7–15.

Sasso, G.M., Reimers, T.M., Cooper, L., Wacker, D.P., Berg, W., Steege, M., Kelly, L., & Allaire, A. (1992). Assessing the functional properties of behavior in natural environments. *Journal of Applied Behavior Analysis, 25,* 809–821.

Touchette, P.E., MacDonald, R.F., & Langer, S.N. (1985). A scatter plot for identifying stimulus control of problem behavior. *Journal of Applied Behavior Analysis, 18,* 343–351.

Wacker, D.P., & Berg, W.K. (1992). *Inducing reciprocal parent–child interactions.* Washington, DC: Department of Health and Human Services, National Institute of Child Health and Human Development.

Wacker, D.P., Steege, M.W., Northup, J., Sasso, G., Berg, W., Reimers, T., Cooper, L., Cigrand, K., & Donn, L. (1990). A component analysis of functional communication training across three topographies of severe behavior problems. *Journal of Applied Behavior Analysis, 23,* 417–429.

Team-Based Training in Positive Behavior Support

A Parent's Perspective on the Process

Terry Williams with Meme Hieneman

DESCRIPTION OF JORDAN, THE TEAM, AND THE SETTINGS

In many ways, Jordan is a typical little girl. She is a member of a loving family, attends school, and participates in the community. She is usually happy and carefree. She loves to watch Disney movies, ride her bike, dress up, have tea parties, and roughhouse with her big brother. She's an eager learner and is caring and friendly toward people she knows. Jordan also has pervasive developmental disorder and a history of behavioral and social difficulties. Her greatest challenges have been using her verbal skills and adapting to changes and new situations.

Our family consists of Jordan; her father, Anthony; her brother, Alexander; and me (Terry), her mother. Church and religion play a major role in our family household. We are active in the community and enjoy going to the beach, restaurants, the park, and "junk hunting" (e.g., flea markets, garage sales). At school, Jordan participates in a special education program that focuses on communication and functional skills. She receives support from her special education teacher, her speech-language therapist, her counselor, and other professionals.

STATUS AT THE TIME OF TEAM ESTABLISHMENT

When our training in positive behavior support (PBS) was initiated in 1998, Jordan was 6 years old and was having behavior problems at home and at school, particularly during transitions between activities. Almost every day, she had tantrums that involved screaming, kicking, and scratching. She also made "raspberry" noises. Her teacher and I dealt with these problems by offering Jordan choices and extra time to respond but did not find these strategies to be consistently effective. In our household, I was the family member who was best able to cope with Jordan's special needs. I usually took my cues from Jordan as to how far I could push her to do anything—from toilet training to learning her ABC's. Following her lead was very important, but it wasn't enough.

Jordan's teacher, her counselor, a program specialist, and I were invited to participate in a team training session on PBS delivered by Florida's PBS Project, of which Meme Hieneman was part. Although members of the group had worked together previously, the entire team had not been established until this point. Over the course of the training, Jordan's team would be expected to work together in order to develop a plan to address her behavior.

SUMMARY OF THE TEAM TRAINING PROCESS

The team training on PBS involved a structured process. Our team began by setting goals. We then gathered information through interviews and observations, developed hypotheses about what influenced Jordan's behavior, and generated ideas for intervention. We isolated the incidents or behaviors of concern and established goals. We engaged in a person-centered planning process to map out where Jordan was and where we wanted her to be at certain points in her future. We spent time learning about Jordan's preferences and needs and used antecedent-behavior-consequence (A-B-C) analysis to gather data on causes of Jordan's behavior. We compared notes and shared our concerns for Jordan. Then, based on all of this information, we developed strategies to help Jordan. These strategies included preventing problems by talking to her about expectations and orienting her to new places. We also learned to redirect Jordan to more acceptable activities. For example, we diverted her attention away from repeatedly picking lint, clothes, socks, or her hair to popping bubble wrap or something totally different. Our plan also focused on teaching Jordan replacement skills to help her communicate her needs and interact with her peers more effectively (e.g., using small talk).

KEY FEATURES OF TRAINING

This training program had several unique features. Our team worked together to address Jordan's specific needs as well as to learn and practice skills to better understand and support her behavior. The most important element of the training was the inclusion of people who have a direct impact on Jordan every day. Bringing all of these people together and choosing particular goals got everyone on the same wavelength. One of the main things about the process that worked well was actually identifying particular target behaviors. In many cases, we found that some smaller fragments of concern could be eliminated through finding solutions to our target behaviors.

Another important feature was that the training was broken down into several sessions so that the participants got a chance to apply the information that they learned. During each session, we were able to present our ideas in front of the other groups, which gave everyone a chance to bounce ideas off each other and to eliminate any weak points in the interventions. Key steps of the training were trying to prove or disprove our hypotheses and actually coming up with workable solutions to change or improve the targeted behaviors.

I really liked the way that the training was presented. First, we were given an information base from which to work to achieve a positive outcome. Second, the trainers interjected stories and videotapes about children with similar problems. It was comforting to me as a parent to know that others could understand how I felt. Third, the trainers had us work in our teams (e.g., on our hypotheses) while they went from table to table to offer advice. Fourth, they were able to keep everything in precise order, even when everyone's hypotheses kept changing and we seemed to be rambling along. Finally, the humor was helpful—it lightened the mood when things were challenging.

One of the things that didn't work too well for me was collecting data. I don't think the problem was with the program as much as it was that Jordan decided that she no longer wanted to exhibit the behaviors we targeted! Coming up with working hypotheses isn't as easy as it sounds when someone has many different facets to his or her personality and behavior. Although the data collection was difficult, it became clear as time went on that this information was important in guiding our decisions.

REFLECTIONS ON THE TEAM TRAINING EXPERIENCE

I can't stress enough how much I learned from the training. Doing the person-centered planning gave me a realistic view of the type of future that I want Jordan to have. It also helped to point out that some things may take a little longer for her to achieve than others. One of the most positive outcomes for me was learning how to diffuse problems before they occur. We learned how powerful the spoken word is. We found that talking to Jordan about a concern or before a new situation really worked wonders. It helped to reduce her stress and discomfort. Jordan responds much better to transitions if she is informed of them beforehand. We do this by creating and reading a social story about the upcoming change. This has been a real blessing to her new teachers and our family.

Jordan now feels that she has some control and can make choices when options are presented to her. That empowerment makes it easier to get her to do less desirable tasks. Another skill that Jordan has acquired through our participation in the training is learning to calm herself. Now, when she feels herself getting overwrought, she can stop herself! We've also learned to help Jordan replace behavior that was becoming obsessive (e.g., picking at something repetitively) with acceptable behavior (e.g., engaging in appropriate hands-on activities). These solutions can work in any situation and, most of the time, work like a charm.

In addition to direct benefits for Jordan, I've learned more about the people who were on Jordan's team. The progress that Jordan has made would not have been possible without the assistance and support of teachers and therapists from her school. In addition, getting to know the people who work closely with her in the school system has opened lines of communication. I found that simply talking to the team members from school has had a dramatic impact on how we handle situations that arise at home and at school. As a parent, it was refreshing to learn that there are different avenues available to me. For our team, an open mind and a willingness to learn something different was a definite requirement (actually, the most important one). We've had additional meetings since our last training session and plan to pass the information along to Jordan's next teacher.

What I learned in the training on PBS is vital in helping Jordan to achieve many life goals. Some have been met; others are coming along fine. I want to supply Jordan with as many social and life skills as possible. The broader the base from which she can draw, the better equipped she will be to someday live in a group home or on her own with some as-

sistance. To other families with special children, I must stress early intervention that includes PBS. It is one of the most important things that parents can use because it carries over to other problem areas and can be useful for children well before they reach school age.

Terry Williams lives with her family in the panhandle of Florida. Since this essay was written, they have moved into another school district. This transition triggered a reemergence of Jordan's problem behavior. However, Terry worked with the school to problem-solve and reinitiate interventions that had been effective in the past (e.g., preparing Jordan for transitions, encouraging the use of words to express her needs). With this support, Jordan has adjusted to her new school and continues to make wonderful progress.

CHAPTER 13

Families and the Tri-State Consortium for Positive Behavior Support

A Unique Collaboration for People with Challenging Behavior

Don Kincaid, Claire Chapman,
Patrick Shannon, Carol Schall, and Joshua K. Harrower

My name is Claire Chapman. My husband Bob and I make our home in Stafford, Virginia, with our sons Mark, age 24, and Brian, age 20. I'm a homemaker who does some volunteer work, including serving on Stafford County Public School's Special Education Advisory Committee (SEAC). The events of this story took place when Mark was a student at Brooke Point High School, where he flourished. Mark worked two periods per day in the school's library and completed most of his academic lessons independently. His school day included job exploration. At home, self-help and independent living skills enabled Mark to do things for himself with minimal supervision. We credit Mark's ongoing success to the opportunities that were afforded to us through person-centered planning and positive behavior support training. This training enabled us to explore the various techniques that would help Mark to handle changing situations and environments. We were also encouraged to ask a lot of questions and to expand Mark's horizons. Our family also is fortunate to have an extensive support system that offers constant encouragement. Our family is grateful for the chance to have taken part in person-centered planning and behavior support training. It has truly made a difference in our lives.

THE TRI-STATE CONSORTIUM

Claire is just one of the many parents of children with challenging behavior who was involved in positive behavior support (PBS) activities in Virginia, Pennsylvania, and West Virginia. From 1991 to 1996, these states received training from the Rehabilitation Research and Training Center (RRTC) on Positive Behavior Support (Anderson, Russo, Dunlap, & Albin, 1996; Dunlap et al., 2000). Each state developed a PBS state training team that implemented a "train-the-trainer" model. As a result of this initial training, the state coordinators began to embed behavior support training and technical assistance within their existing service structures for families, schools, and community agencies.

Although all three state training teams laid the foundation for PBS within their own state, their ability to assist families, schools, and agencies was tremendously enhanced when they began to collaborate on positive behavior support activities within the larger RRTC state training team network. Through planning sessions, discussions about ongoing activities in each state, and the sharing of resources across programs, the three state teams began to consider the possibility of collaborating in a more formal and effective manner.

As a result of this initial collaboration, Virginia, Pennsylvania, and West Virginia received grant funding from the U.S. Department of Education in 1996 for an outreach training project called the Tri-State Consortium for Positive Behavior Support. The Tri-State Consortium was a unique collaboration among different agencies across the three states: the Pennsylvania state education agency, Pennsylvania regional service providers (intermediate units), West Virginia's University Affiliated Center for Developmental Disabilities, and the Virginia Institute for Developmental Disabilities.

The abilities of these programs were enhanced because they shared a very similar philosophy about providing PBS to children, families, schools, and community agencies. This philosophy included a commitment to the following:

1. *Provide person- and family-centered support.* All three states' teams realized that frequently decisions were made and services were determined based on agency- or system-centered priorities, not on the particular needs of the individual or the family. As an alternative to this traditional approach to service delivery, all three state teams were committed to person- and family-centered approaches that are effective in local schools and agencies and larger statewide systems.

2. *Emphasize a broad ecological approach for behavioral support.* This value follows directly from being person and family centered within local agencies and broader systems. Included in this perspective is the idea that challenging behavior has to be seen within the context of a person's life—his or her home, school, workplace, and community. Team members were also committed to making adaptations or accommodations in these environments to better support the family and the child's educational and/or behavioral needs.

3. *Commit to a team approach involving an array of support.* Because of PBS's broad ecological approach, it is essential that a variety of individuals commit to collaborating and participating in a team process. These commitments must be gathered at the individual, family, teacher, agency, and system levels. In addition, a positive behavior support approach also must examine each level to determine which outcomes and supports need to be in place to reinforce participation and collaboration. For instance, why should a school participate in an individual's or a schoolwide positive behavior support program? Why should a family participate? Why should an individual teacher or classroom aide participate? Why should a system change to provide behavior support services and technical assistance? Answers to these questions are essential for families, professionals, and agencies to commit fully to a team process of positive behavior support.

4. *Emphasize positive and effective supports for all children.* The Tri-State Consortium initially believed that the bulk of referrals and supports would center around children with severe disabilities because they are traditionally identified as requiring intensive posi-

tive behavior support approaches. However, the Tri-State Consortium also committed itself to the prospect that behavioral support should be available for all children in all environments. For this reason, systemic change at the individual, classroom, school, and system levels was necessary to bring the technology and philosophy of PBS to all students, teachers, and schools.

5. *Increase local capacity.* The Tri-State Consortium also realized from the beginning that no grant or ongoing positive behavior support activities in the three states provided sufficient resources to meet the needs of every school, classroom, or student with challenging behavior. Therefore, an overriding philosophy of the Tri-State Consortium was to pursue activities that increase the local capacity of families and providers to learn a positive behavior support philosophy, technology, and problem-solving approach, which can be applied to all children and all environments.

The Tri-State Consortium had a shared commitment to family, school, and community collaboration. It also had a shared commitment to disseminating an effective process for positive behavior support training and technical assistance. The five-step process included the following:

1. Establish collaboration among a family, school, and community.

2. Initiate a broad assessment of the child and the family environment.

3. Complete specific assessments through direct and indirect functional assessment methods.

4. Combine broad and specific assessment information into a comprehensive behavior support plan.

5. Evaluate and revise the behavior support plan.

Although this process appears simple, there are many different ways to accomplish the five steps. There also are many barriers to their successful implementation. The five-step process forms the background and context for the chapter, which tells Mark's story through his mother Claire's eyes. Claire describes what happened during each step of the process and how Mark, the family, and the team were affected. This is followed by a discussion of family themes and issues as they relate to the unfolding story, with particular focus on opportunities and barriers to the effective implementation of the positive behavior support process at the family, school, and community levels. We also discuss what we have learned about an effective process from interviews with Claire's family, other families, and team participants.

STEP 1: ESTABLISH A COLLABORATION
AMONG A FAMILY, SCHOOL, AND COMMUNITY

> *Mark had a behavior problem that was becoming excessive and would surely get in the way of his school success. We definitely needed to get some sort of help. At this point, the Virginia Institute for Developmental Disabilities was offering positive behavior support training in our county, and we were selected to be a part of this training.*
>
> *A group was formed that included people who were part of Mark's daily life and would be familiar with the behavior that was of concern. This group that came to-*

gether for the training soon became known as "Mark's Team" and, later, "The Mar-keteers." My husband and I, his teacher, his speech-language therapist, a transition specialist, a representative from the local community services board, and a classroom aide were invited to be a part of this training. The county school system also offered this training to individuals who knew little or nothing about Mark. The county school system felt that others could benefit and learn about PBS by participating in the training. They then could take this new knowledge and apply it to individuals in other environments. Although we planned to focus on Mark's particular targeted behavior, the knowledge gained from the training could be adapted to anyone else's situation.

I think that one of the keys to parent and professional collaboration was creating an environment for open communication. It was clear to me from the beginning of the process that we were a team. The positive behavior support trainers communicated to me that I was an equal member of this team and that the team was going to work closely to support Mark and our family. It was also communicated that everybody on the team needed to be open and willing to share information. I felt free to ask questions and was never made to feel dumb. The positive behavior support trainers were primarily concerned with whether I understood what they were telling me. I think that the person-centered planning process helped to build some trust between us.

Team trust was tested right from the start. The school system was being a little rigid about committing staff time to the process. The team came together to ask the administrators to release staff for participation in the process. This was no small ac-complishment—we met once per month for 10 months! This meant that the school system had to pay substitute staff for each of those days. Another thing that we did was meet in Mark's school so that it was easier for his teachers to attend. This also allowed the team members who did not work with Mark in the classroom to observe his class.

Family Themes and Issues

Claire's story makes evident several critical themes that are related to forming strong part-nerships among parents, professionals, and the community. These themes include the par-ents working with other parents to promote PBS, the family feeling overwhelmed by the scope of the process, and the parents' willingness to share information.

Parents Working with Other Parents   Parents who have been through the pos-itive behavior support process can help forge partnerships with other parents by telling their positive behavior support stories and providing support and guidance. Claire men-tioned that she talks to parents about PBS every chance she gets:

We had a special education advisory board meeting last night. Afterward, I spoke with a woman who was clearly at her wit's end. She didn't know what to do about her son's behavior problems, so I talked with her about person-centered planning and PBS and how they helped Mark and our family. She asked me to explain everything to her, especially how she could participate.

Other members of the team agreed with Claire regarding the importance of family support. Mark's special education teacher believed that Claire had been a valuable resource for other parents who were in similar situations. The speech-language therapist, the transition specialist, and the leisure and recreation specialist have asked for permission to refer families to Claire for consultation. Claire stated that she would have benefited from having another parent to talk to when she started the process. Yet, as Claire said, "We were the first parents in the county to go through the Tri-State Consortium's positive behavior support process; we paved the way for other families." She believed that support from other families at the beginning of the process is critical to ensure family involvement in the positive behavior support process.

Family Feeling Overwhelmed by the Process   Strategies for seeking family "buy-in" to the process emerged as another theme. Claire reported that initial buy-in was difficult for her to achieve. She stated,

> I think the first time {the trainer} and I met to discuss person-centered planning and PBS, I was completely overwhelmed about the scope of what we were talking about. I didn't believe that anyone could do what they said they were going to do. I thought they were crazy.

She also said that she was so overwhelmed when she came back from the first few meetings that she did not think she could continue. She said, "It was so much information to take in and try to process." She also said that she did not believe that a team was actually there to support her. She felt that it was Mark, her husband, and herself. As a result, Claire was skeptical about engaging in the positive behavior support process. Both positive behavior support trainers recall Claire's initial skepticism. They felt that they needed to take steps to "sell the concept to her." One of the trainers said that she had to keep reassuring Claire that the process was going to work even though it was going to be difficult. Claire acknowledged that it was this reassurance that made her finally agree to commit herself and Mark to the process. She said, "Even though I was skeptical, I remember thinking that this would really be neat if it all worked out the way they said it was going to work."

After the initial buy-in, Claire said she and her husband committed themselves to the process. It wasn't until the process began that they realized how much of a commitment was truly required:

> Together with Mark, we set out to determine his future and how we could best help to prepare him. We worked hard and did everything the team asked us to do. We did our homework. I think that was what really set the groundwork for everything that followed. Yet, nothing could have prepared us for how much work it was going to be. It is hard for a family to commit this kind of time and energy to anything, let alone to something as stressful as your child's behavior problems.

Other members of Mark's team commented on Claire's strong commitment to the process. One team member said that they were "a cohesive team, largely due to the commitment and influence of Claire." Another team member observed, "Claire worked very hard and she held everyone else accountable for his or her part." Still another team member stated, "This team worked, it worked very well, all because of Claire. She drove that team." A team member summed up her experience working with Claire: "Claire's presence was amazing.

We watched her blossom. She has a natural propensity to facilitate teamwork. She is caring, funny, introspective, and painfully honest."

Parents Sharing Information   The final theme related to building strong partnerships among parents, professionals, and the community is related to the openness of the team environment. Claire felt that sharing with the team was the most difficult task that she faced:

> *This meant that I had to open myself up completely and let everyone analyze me and tell me things that made me feel like I was a bad mother. That is what you feel like when you see that some of your child's behavior problems happen because of things that you are doing. This is not something that is easy to share with people. It was against my nature to let other people look at us so closely. It was a very hard thing for me to do, but I did it.*

Several other team members observed this conflict. One team member reflected, "Claire is a very strong person who was able to look at her family with a critical eye, accept what she saw, and change what needed to change to help Mark." Another team member stated, "She really struggled with herself initially, but I think that an open enough environment was created for her to work through these issues and to support her when she needed it."

Claire's story is an excellent example of how a positive behavior support approach can build a strong collaboration among parents, professionals, and community members. However, a strong partnership and collaboration cannot be presumed to occur without significant effort and commitment by a positive behavior support facilitator and other team members. Building and maintaining a strong team may be one of the most critical components of effective positive behavior support training and technical assistance. For this reason, an initial effort must be made to establish this collaboration and an understanding of its necessity.

Functioning within a team approach is a unique experience for many professionals. They are accustomed to having their activities restricted to their areas of expertise. A positive behavior support approach strips away the "expert" role and attempts to bring all team members together equally to pursue more effective supports for an individual. Within this context, several important strategies help form a strong partnership: building respect, setting the ground rules for collaboration, involving all of the players, and leveling the playing field.

Building Respect   Positive behavior support teams seldom form when there are no problem behaviors, everyone is getting along, and everyone knows what to do and how to do it. Positive behavior support teams generally are formed in situations that are in or close to crisis. As a result, the main team participants often want to lay the blame at someone else's feet. The school is ready to blame the parents. The parents are ready to blame the school. Both the school and the parents are upset with the community support agencies.

For a team to form a strong partnership, respect and communication must be built among team members. Building respect does not occur as the result of a single respect-building activity. Rather, it is achieved through an entire process. Nonetheless, we have found that effective outside support and facilitation can help address this issue. Team members who do not respect one another are unlikely to maintain a collaboration without having a savvy facilitator point out and address issues of disrespect, as well as model and reinforce appropriate respectful attitudes. The most effective facilitator also plans and identifies opportunities for people to develop respect for one another. He or she identifies team members' strengths, supports their participation in the process, and makes their strengths evident to all team members.

Setting the Ground Rules for Collaboration

Before starting the positive behavior support process, it is essential that all team members understand each step of the process. It is also important that they understand how they are to function together as a team. This includes setting the ground rules for collaboration even before the team begins meeting and can be accomplished through contracts, memorandums of agreement, or formal or informal discussions. All of the team members, as well as representatives of the agencies supporting their participation, first meet to determine whether there is a commitment to the process. It also is extremely important that each participant knows what is expected from him or her and from his or her supporting agency. Agency commitment may include time, funds, programmatic changes, or other means of support. We have found that an informal or a formal memorandum of agreement is essential for establishing individuals' commitment to the process and to the team. When a memorandum of agreement is not written, some participants may be completely unaware of the purpose and process of the positive behavior support team meetings. For instance, some team participants may indicate during the first team meeting that they did not know there would be a second meeting and would not commit to a long-term team process. These impediments to forming a strong partnership can be avoided through initial planning with each team member and supporting agency.

Involving All of the Players

We believe that in the initial steps of a positive behavior support process, it is important to receive input and information from a variety of different sources. This may mean that the initial team will be substantially larger than the team that actually meets to begin the positive behavior support work. The initial team may consist of 15–20 people. All of the initial participants need to be made aware of the length and value of their involvement. Nonetheless, some agencies, for example, may want limited or short-term involvement. Thus, the initial team may then be reduced to a more manageable number of participants who know the child and family best and can commit time, energy, and resources to making the behavior support plan work.

When the team begins to meet about the actual behavior support plan, it is the facilitator's responsibility to ensure that information is gathered from all participants and that each person is prompted to contribute to this process. Some people require very little prompting. In fact, some people need to be prompted to allow others to share their ideas, opinions, and information. However, it is the facilitator's responsibility to occasionally prompt individuals directly with questions, such as, "What do you think of this?" "How do you see this situation?" "What do you think of the process so far?" or "Is there anything you'd like to add?" This involvement is extremely important for all team participants, but especially for those who have not had their input and information valued during other school- or agency-based meetings. Sometimes these individuals actually know the child and the family the best, but their input has never been solicited. Therefore, they are not likely to share information initially without prompting and support.

Leveling the Playing Field

It is important to realize that teams, by their nature, do not always allow for equal and full member participation. The team facilitator should closely examine the team composition and participation during initial team activities to determine whether situations need to be adjusted or addressed to increase team effectiveness. During the earliest stages of team formation, attention to issues such as the following provides for a more effective collaboration:

- Meeting site: It is essential to consider convenience and emotional safety when selecting the meeting space. Some teams agree to alternate the meeting space to provide an encouraging atmosphere for all team members.

- Team composition: The composition and membership of the team is an important consideration as well. This requires sensitivity to family, community, and agency needs. The goal is to avoid over- or underrepresentation of agencies or family and community members.

- Information sharing: Facilitators must be aware of strategies to encourage all team members' participation.

The ability to form a strong partnership is further affected by the participants' histories regarding team participation. First, it is important to realize that when multiple agencies and individuals provide support to children with challenging behavior, there may be a significant history of failure, fatigue, and frustration. Prior to beginning an individual's behavior support plan, some team members need to be supported and heard before they are willing to commit their time and energy to complete the five steps of the positive behavior support process. The facilitator's skills in functional assessment and positive behavior support strategies are no more important than his or her skills in creating a team environment that promotes true collaboration.

STEP 2: INITIATE A BROAD ASSESSMENT OF THE CHILD AND THE FAMILY ENVIRONMENT

We were already a team before we began the positive behavior support process. We were a good team and we worked well together because we went through the person-centered planning process before PBS. To me, PATH {Planning Alternative Tomorrows with Hope (Pearpoint, O'Brien, & Forrest, 1993)} was essential for Mark. I was asked to describe any problems that could get in the way of Mark's success in life, and we put them on his PATH. PBS was mentioned as a strategy on Mark's PATH.

When the team first came together, we went through various exercises to "break the ice." For example, we played games to help each team member learn things about others. These games were meant to show the team members that we were all on equal ground. For me, it soon became apparent that although some may have had titles or degrees to go along with their initial introductions, we were all coming together on the human level. We were all going to go through the positive behavior support training as a team, with the goal of addressing Mark's needs.

Any predetermined views about never questioning a professional's suggestions needed to be set aside. I became an equal partner, and my voice was just as important to the team as other team members' voices. I realized that these people wouldn't judge me by what I told them. I needed to feel safe in telling them everything and letting them closely observe me and my family. I needed to be honest with them and relate times when Mark's behaviors were at their worst. The more knowledge that they had of Mark and our family, the more helpful they could be.

Family Themes and Issues

Several strategies emerged for getting to know Mark and his family better. First, communicating commitment to the family through support and team action was essential. Second, all team members considered person-centered planning to be an integral component in the team's success.

Initial Skepticism Followed by Growing Commitment

As mentioned previously, Claire was initially skeptical about the team process. She assumed that the team would exist in name only:

> *I didn't believe that there was actually a team. I thought it was Mark, my husband, and I. Then there were the others who would be doing their own things but not necessarily helping us. I didn't think we were all going to actually work as a team, but we did.*

Other team members felt the same way. Although the positive behavior support trainers said that they were all going to work as a team, they were skeptical. One team member said, "I had never worked on a team that worked this closely and this well before, and so I didn't think this team was going to be any different." Another team member said, "I thought it was all hype and that the positive behavior support people were out of touch with reality."

The key for Claire was the support she felt from other team members. She said, "What helped me was for the team to say that what had been happening at home was okay." This support was further communicated through team action that led to change. For example, Claire relayed the following activity that helped build her trust of the team process:

> *With the help of positive behavior support training and the team, we were able to set up a communication system with {picture} cards of feelings for Mark to use to express himself. This made my husband and I so happy, and it reinforced my faith in the process.*

One of the most unique features of this team is their sustained, long-term commitment to Mark. Two years after beginning the positive behavior support process, they still considered themselves a functioning team. Claire stated, "While our frequency of meeting as a team has dropped off, we still meet, and I know that I can call the team together whenever I need them." Another team member said, "The team has just moved to a different level now; we are a team even if we don't see each other anymore."

Importance of Person-Centered Planning

Most team members attributed the team's success to the person-centered planning process in which they engaged as an initial step in the positive behavior support process. Several members of Mark's team were excited about PBS when they were told that they were selected for the process. For example, Mark's teacher remarked about the opportunity to help Mark plan his future. Claire added that she and her husband "would now be able to show others that Mark was smart." Prior to addressing Mark's challenging behaviors, person-centered planning already had contributed to the formation of a well-functioning and cohesive team. Everyone on the team knew each other, they had worked through issues of trust and commitment, and they began to think about Mark as an individual rather than as a behavior problem. Regarding the process, Claire stated the following:

When we conducted person-centered planning, we gathered, dreamed, and envisioned what Mark would be doing in 10 years. These dreams were colorfully displayed on Mark's PATH. This became a constant reference for us.

Team consensus was that the process of person-centered planning helped them to view Mark holistically as an individual with strengths, needs, and dreams. For example, one member of Mark's team said, "One of Mark's dreams was a job gardening or working with computers/typing, so we enrolled him in the horticulture and basic business classes in our county. Before person-centered planning, I would have thought this was a crazy idea." Another member thought that person-centered planning "helped us become a team. PBS challenges everyone involved to think about themselves critically, related to how they interact with Mark. You need to trust everybody on your team to open yourself up at that level."

Person-centered planning assisted Claire and her husband in getting to know Mark as well. Claire said that she learned a lot about what Mark wanted and was capable of accomplishing. She added,

It probably changed me more than it changed the other people on the team. In fact, in the beginning they spent a lot of time trying to convince me that Mark was capable of doing the things that he was talking about. I was the one who was skeptical.

Many practitioners believe that the essential feature of a behavior support plan is gathering specific information about challenging behavior, which is the process of functional assessment. Although functional assessment is an essential element of PBS, gathering information needs to go beyond analyzing the antecedents, behaviors, and consequences for a particular child. For this reason, the positive behavior support teams in the Tri-State Consortium emphasize the need to gather broader information about the child and family so that the behavior support plan can be fit into the context of the child, family, classroom, school, and community. Sometimes a traditional behavior management approach misses this information. The result is that plans fail to capture the richness of the child, family, and school environments and miss some critical aspects that may determine whether a plan succeeds or fails.

This broader information can be gathered through a number of methods that depend on the team and their time commitment, as well as the specific issues that are unique to each team. Sometimes, all of the team members are interviewed to gather information about the context of the child's life and the environments in which behavior problems occur. Other times, a team can begin addressing these issues by having the members answer a series of questions about their knowledge of what works or does not work with a child.

Finally, person-centered planning processes, such as PATH, are useful for gathering information about the ecology of a person's life. Other approaches include MAPS (Making Action Plans; Vandercook, York, & Forrest, 1989) and Personal Profiling and Futures Planning (Kincaid, 1996; Mount, 1987). These approaches gather information from the individual, his or her family, and those who know that person best to learn about his or her past, present, and future.

In addition to providing broad information about the individual and establishing a context for a comprehensive and more effective behavior support plan, person-centered planning processes also have the capacity to improve team members' collaboration and partnership. Initially, this process allows people to see things that they may never have seen before. It may also quickly address misperceptions and misunderstandings about the individual's behavior and environment that may impede true collaboration. It is not uncommon to hear people say in a meeting, "I just now understand what's going on" or "I didn't realize that what I was doing in the classroom was inconsistent with what was going on at home."

Many team members come together in this process never knowing anything about a given child's life outside of their experiences with him or her in the classroom. Person-centered planning begins to give the team a broader perspective on the child, the family, and the major issues that the team needs to address.

In the long run, person-centered planning also sets the stage for a real change in team commitment, direction, and mutual respect. For instance, when family members share how often they have been disappointed by service providers in the past, agencies may step forward and make a longer and stronger commitment to the family. Parents may say that they have realized for the first time that school personnel actually like their child because they have never attended a meeting in which anybody said anything positive about their child. Person-centered planning activities allow opportunities for information to be shared in a comfortable, straightforward, and respectful manner, and they set the stage for developing true trust and collaboration.

Person-centered planning approaches do present some issues in the positive behavior support process, most notably the required time commitment. Although person-centered planning sessions may only last an hour, others may last an entire day, depending on the complexity of information gathered and the team composition. Scheduling a number of people to meet together for an extended period of time requires a significant commitment of time, resources, and funds for agency personnel.

In addition, it is critical that team members realize that person-centered planning and PBS may not produce a "quick fix" for problem behavior. Often, teams want to solve the problem quickly. A positive behavior support approach that utilizes person-centered planning will not solve the identified problems immediately, but the plan will be more effective in the long term.

Furthermore, a person-centered planning process requires that team members be willing to change their view of the person. Team members also must be open to changing their own behavior with the individual. A person-centered planning process seldom has a direct impact on the individual's challenging behavior. These processes set the stage for behavior change within the team that will result in behavior change for the individual.

STEP 3: CONDUCT SPECIFIC ASSESSMENTS THROUGH DIRECT AND INDIRECT FUNCTIONAL ASSESSMENT METHODS

Functional assessments can be time consuming and very detailed; however, parents usually need immediate help. They want to see results right away, and just talking about the long-term benefits of PBS may not work with families. I think it is important to begin by first building a family's confidence in the whole process. I think families need to hear that things are going to improve very soon. Before beginning a functional assessment, one way to build confidence in the process would be for families to talk with other families about their experiences. I try to talk with other families every chance I get. It helps me, and I know it helps them.

Once parents understand the value of a functional assessment, probably the most important approach is observation. For us, observations came in various forms. We used a journal to record what we observed when the negative behavior was present.

We also used a behavior chart, which related the environment, who else was present, and the antecedents and consequences of the behavior. We were to be very specific in recording the events surrounding a particular incident. These observation approaches taught me to be very attentive to what was happening around Mark's behavior. I began to notice things that I would not have noticed beforehand.

It also was helpful for individuals who were not on Mark's team to assist us in our data collection. "Constants" in Mark's life were asked to help us, and we readily accepted their cooperation. For example, if the bus driver saw something negative, she would contact us. Likewise, if something positive occurred, we always welcomed those comments. When Mark visited with his aunt, she reported a behavior that was easily redirected, and an "incident" was avoided. It was a team effort that went beyond the team.

A strategy that proved both useful and problematic was using a journal to record Mark's behaviors. Right after a behavior incident, I would write down everything that happened before, during, and after it occurred. This relieved some of the pressure of having team members in my house observing everything I did, and it helped me gain my own insights about Mark's behavior. I was able to diligently record everything that happened and communicate it to the rest of the team. It wasn't always easy for me to do and it required a lot of training, but it was worth it. I wasn't the only one who wrote in the journal. Mark's teachers did as well. In this way, we could communicate on a daily basis about how Mark was doing. If he had an incident at school, I would know about it. I liked this because I felt like I had a better sense of what Mark's day was like and that—surprise, surprise—most of the days he did not have any problems. There was, however, a major problem with the journal. Mark knew the purpose of the journal. If he had a bad day at school, Mark knew that his teacher would write in the journal and send it home with him. Mark did not want to get in trouble twice for one incident so he became obsessed with the journal. He wanted to know what we were writing. So we turned it around and asked him to write in the notebook when he had a bad day. This worked so well that when he had bad days, he wanted to come home and read to me what he wrote in the journal. Short of filming everything, I think the journal was the best way to collect the information the team needed.

Family Themes and Issues

Mark's team learned that the transition from a personal futures planning process to a process of functional assessment and behavior support plan development can be difficult for families. For Claire, it was uncomfortable to change from a process of dreaming of a better future for Mark to a process of looking in great detail at problem behaviors and their causes. During a functional assessment, families are forced to look critically at themselves and how they interact with their child with challenging behaviors. In Claire's case, she was hurt by the realization that her interactions with her son sometimes led to his challenging behaviors. Claire stated, "It is a hard thing to admit to yourself and to a group of people that, in some way, your behaviors as a parent were leading to your child's problems."

She also mentioned feeling totally overwhelmed by the first few meetings because of the intensity of this new process. Other members of Mark's team recognized Claire's struggle and offered her emotional support. In addition, they felt that it was important to emphasize the benefits of PBS to Claire as quickly as possible. Claire indicated that team members told her things such as, "Stick with it; you will be amazed at where Mark is in a few months," "We are here for you and your family as much as we are for Mark," and "We are not here to fail; we are here to improve Mark's life." Claire stated that this support was invaluable to her during the initial meetings.

Claire was the primary reason for the team's success in reducing Mark's challenging behaviors and improving his quality of life. Claire committed herself whole-heartedly to the process. She struggled through her own issues, was open with the team, diligently completed every task required of her, fought with the school system, and assumed leadership of the team. Several team members commented that it was Claire's personality that led to the success of the team. These team members acknowledged that this often is not the case; families who do not have the same ability or willingness to commit to the process often have negative experiences. They suggested that as part of the initial stage of conducting a functional assessment, the team should have an open discussion with the family about the best way to work together. This may mean giving total control to the family or total control to the rest of team; the point is that the family should decide.

Team flexibility is important when conducting a functional assessment. Claire stated, "It was helpful that the team was flexible in how they collected their data. For example, trusting me to take detailed and honest notes was helpful. I was uncomfortable with being observed at home." One team member reflected, "We spent a little extra time preparing Claire and Mark for the functional assessment. We could tell that she was unsure about PBS, so we took our time." This implies moving at a different pace with each family to ensure commitment to the process. Families that are pushed too quickly into a thorough functional assessment may withdraw from the process.

As the broad information gathered through person-centered planning is the foundation for a behavior support plan, the functional assessment information is the cornerstone—the support around which the entire structure of a positive and effective plan is built. If the functional assessment information is gathered appropriately and the information is correct, then the ensuing plan will have a greater likelihood of success. Developing the functional assessment requires teaching the team 1) a rationale for the importance of functional assessment, 2) the different ways to collect functional assessment information, and 3) the meaning of functional assessment results.

These three features are critical to the entire positive behavior support process. First, team members must understand why a functional assessment is important. Second, they must also understand why they are conducting observations, collecting data, being interviewed, and participating in other functional assessment activities. Team members who do not understand the need for such information may begin to ask, "Why do we have to collect this data?" or "Shouldn't we be putting together a plan instead of spending all of this time collecting information?" Third, it is essential that team members understand the meaning of the information that has been gathered. One of the facilitator's critical roles is to present the gathered information to the team members in a manner that they can understand, process, and act on. To develop an effective behavior support plan for an individual, it is important that all team members understand the functions of that person's behavior. If they do not understand the purpose of the person's problem behavior, then they are unlikely to view the ensuing behavior support plan as the most effective approach to supporting the child and his or her family. They also are less likely to implement the plan accurately and consistently.

Because the Tri-State Consortium positive behavior support teams tended to operate within typical community environments—such as homes, schools, and agencies—including team members in all aspects of a functional assessment was emphasized. The Tri-State Consortium's functional assessment approaches included indirect functional assessments such as rating scales (Durand, 1988), checklists, and interviews of family and team participants (O'Neill et al., 1997) as well as a group facilitated process, the Initial Line of Inquiry (Llewellyn & Knoster, 1997). In addition to these indirect methods, direct methods of functional assessment included antecedent-behavior-consequence (A-B-C) analyses (Bijou, Peterson, & Alt, 1968), scatter plots (Touchette, MacDonald, & Langer, 1985), and other formal systems for direct observation. Direct and indirect methods can be time efficient, accurate, and reliable in identifying the functions of behavior for a particular person. However, the Tri-State Consortium also sometimes utilized direct analog or functional analysis manipulations. For the most part, these processes require a trained consultant or support individual to implement them in home, school, and community environments.

Functional assessment requires team participants to change their view of the individual. Participants must understand that behavior is influenced by its environment and accept responsibility for some aspects of that child's environment. Ultimately, it requires the team to stop blaming the child for challenging behavior and to start understanding how the child's past and current environments have shaped and maintained his or her behavior.

One critical issue for teams is how much functional assessment information is necessary. Questions may include, "If I do this interview, will that be enough?" or "If I collect this much data, will that be sufficient?" Team members want clear guidelines for conducting a functional assessment. The Tri-State Consortium's teams would begin with indirect methods, move to direct methods, and end with functional analysis manipulations, if necessary. Yet, it really comes down to the consistency, reliability, and accuracy of the information collected. If interviews yield consistent findings about the predictors and functions of behavior and observations are consistent with the interviews, then further information may not be necessary. If there are great discrepancies, however, further interviews, observations, and, perhaps, manipulations may be necessary. For the team to proceed with the next step of the process, members have to be confident about the identified functions of the behavior. This does not necessarily mean that the team members are always accurate, only that they are confident in the accuracy of the information that they have gathered to this point.

STEP 4: COMBINE BROAD AND SPECIFIC ASSESSMENT INFORMATION INTO A COMPREHENSIVE BEHAVIOR SUPPORT PLAN

With the complete cooperation of all those directly involved with Mark, we found effective ways to help Mark with his behaviors. Those new to Mark's environment were informed of the best ways to help Mark perform to his full potential. We have always reminded ourselves that our aim is to "set Mark up for success." We were able to show, through our comprehensive record-keeping, what worked in the past and what we should continue to keep in place. We were always ready to adjust or initiate new methods of handling various situations. What didn't work before may be helpful now, and what was already in place may need to be reevaluated.

Flexibility on the part of our family and the team was essential. To make the plan work, I had to be willing to let people into our home, think critically about being a parent, and change my schedule when necessary. The team had to be willing to live by rules. I wanted their help and I believed in what we were doing, but that didn't mean I wanted our lives turned upside down. They respected that, and we never had any conflicts. I think that is because we were able to be open and honest with each other.

Family Themes and Issues

At this point in the process, the team has gathered enough broad and specific information to come to an understanding of the person and his or her environment. For example, broad information about Mark included health issues and his likes, dislikes, strengths, and challenges. Specific information for Mark included the results of the functional behavior assessment. In general, this information takes the form of a hypothesis such as "When (predictor) occurs, Mark engages in (problem behaviors); as a result, (maintaining consequence) occurs." There may be numerous hypotheses, because the person likely has numerous behaviors that occur under different conditions and produce different outcomes. Generally, a comprehensive support plan addresses more than one specific hypothesis for an individual.

By this point in the process, the team also has gained additional information from evaluating curricula or other aspects of the environment, such as activity patterns in the home and community. As a result, the team is now able to move from the hypotheses about why an individual's behavior is occurring to evaluating possible interventions. Teachers, parents, and team members can write about 80% of any plan based on the information that is provided in Steps 1–3. A skilled facilitator with experience in positive behavior support interventions and how they fit with the functions of behavior can augment the team's ideas with additional approaches that may not have been considered.

This step in the process is exciting for team members, who can now use their areas of expertise in developing a behavior support plan. They are not looking for an expert to give them a plan. Rather, they are able to see how curriculum, environmental, antecedent, consequence, and lifestyle changes can provide multiple effective interventions. Many of these interventions are very simple and can be combined into one comprehensive behavior support plan. In addition, the information gathered up to this point allows for the development of a plan that better fits into the context of the child's family, classroom, school, and community (Albin, Lucyshyn, Horner, & Flannery, 1996).

For the process to work and a plan to be implemented appropriately, at least one team member must be willing to be the team "champion." A champion is a team member who is fully knowledgeable about and committed to the plan. He or she understands the process, the function(s) of the behavior(s), and how the plan works. If the champion is a family member, then at least one additional team member within the service system must also be fully dedicated to the plan and its implementation. This "ally" ensures that the intervention is implemented within the classroom, school, and community. For school-age children and youth, the best possible situation is that a family member and the classroom teacher are allied. In our experience, this results in the most effective behavior support plans—those that are implemented consistently at home and school.

This step in the process is critical in that all the team members must address issues that affect whether the plan will be implemented. Developing a comprehensive plan identifies systems issues, such as resources and time, that need to be addressed for the plan to be effective. In addition, the team needs to determine how all members will confidently and consistently apply the plan components. The team members also must decide how to support one another. The family and the teacher should not be expected to "just do it" on their own. What resources from the community or the school can support the family, the teacher, and other team members in implementing a plan that may require additional time, energy, and follow-through? If the plan is developed without the necessary team support, then it is unlikely that critical team members will successfully implement the plan.

Finally, one of the critical elements of a behavior support plan is that it reflects a comprehensive and multicomponent approach (Koegel, Koegel, & Dunlap, 1996). The positive behavior support process identifies a number of ways to accomplish the same goal for a child and a family; by Step 4 of the process, the team begins to realize multiple roads can lead to the same outcomes. For example, there may be many ways to teach communication and social skills. There are certainly different ways to develop more effective social relationships for the child and the family. Supports also can be provided in many various ways for different families, children, and schools. This flexibility contributes to the effectiveness and acceptability of positive behavior support compared with a single intervention or a more narrowly constructed approach.

STEP 5: EVALUATE AND REVISE THE BEHAVIOR SUPPORT PLAN

I regularly need to remind myself of the outstanding progress that Mark has made. I see how he easily handles a stressful situation now, when before he would have exhibited an unsuitable behavior. Our home environment doesn't contain the same stresses. Before, we almost never knew when a behavior would present itself. We learned that one way to deal with the unexpected was to prepare Mark the best that we could. Change was never easy for Mark, and he did best when his routine stayed the same. Yet, we needed to help Mark adjust to the possibility that our plans might change abruptly and that everything would be okay anyway. We said things like "I'm not sure when we will get there," "We'll see what happens," or "Maybe tomorrow." Mark is able to accept it when our plans change. Now, if he asks for something in particular and we don't have it, he is easily satisfied with something else. He surely has made strides in adjusting to changes in his home and school environments. We have learned how to speak to Mark and how to calm him when the change is hard. We use reassuring words to let him know what a wonderful job he is doing and how well he has handled a new or different situation. We allow ourselves the choice to not do something if we believe it might be too stressful for Mark. Why push him into a new situation with a lot of variables over which we have no control?

Mark is a happier person now. I think that is the best measure of the success of a comprehensive behavior support plan. We have talked about how the team worked really hard, but Mark did too. I give him most of the credit. There was something in him that really wanted to improve, and we showed him the way. Even though Mark did not attend our team meetings, I truly believe that he was part of the team because he worked just as hard as everyone else, if not harder. He has matured, and he is more independent. I have changed, too. I now have the ability to analyze a situation and can prevent a problem behavior or at least understand what went wrong to cause

one. It is a skill that has changed how I think about Mark's behavior. Another way to assess the success of a comprehensive plan is to imagine what the behaviors would be like if nothing had changed. I am sure that Mark would not be doing this well. Some time ago, I ran into someone who knew Mark when his behaviors were at their worst. She was stunned at how well behaved he was when she saw him. She only knew Mark in terms of his behaviors, and now she knows Mark for who he really is.

Family Themes and Issues

One of the central issues of the Tri-State Consortium was how to document and evaluate quality of life outcomes that are achieved from its positive behavior support training and technical assistance. Since the early 1990s, the vision of outcomes in the area of positive behavior support has expanded. This expanded vision goes beyond simple improvements in targeted problem behavior to include the acquisition of alternative appropriate behavior; the absence of side effects; and quality of life improvements such as less restrictive school and living placements, greater participation in the community, and expanded social relationships (Meyer & Evans, 1989).

One of the Tri-State Consortium's first tasks was to look at the quality of life domains that PBS affects. Its initial attempt looked at eight quality of life domains: 1) emotional well-being, 2) material well-being, 3) physical well-being (i.e., health), 4) interpersonal relations, 5) personal development, 6) self-determination, 7) social inclusion, and 8) civil rights. Following on these domains, the Tri-State Consortium developed various measures that utilized rating scales, interviews, direct observation, and other approaches to assess quality of life. The initial attempts at gathering this information resulted in an evaluation process that required several hours to complete and was tedious for team members, particularly family members, teachers, and other team participants. In fact, several team members indicated that the quality of life assessment process actually reduced the team's and the family's quality of life! Therefore, the Tri-State Consortium developed a more time-efficient evaluation process that captures unique, significant, and rich information about how PBS affected the lives of consumers, families, and professionals. The Tri-State Consortium's positive behavior support state training teams continued to emphasize the use of multiple methods of data collection to measure progress for individuals with problem behaviors. These methods included interviews, anecdotal reports, rating scales, natural documents, and direct observation of behavior (Meyer & Janney, 1989).

The Tri-State Consortium evaluation approach measured the following:

1. Changes in educational or residential arrangements

2. Changes in an individual's quality of life

3. Objective measures of behavior change

4. A behavioral outcomes survey (a subjective evaluation of change)

5. A satisfaction survey of team functioning and support

6. Ethnographic research interviews

7. Individual outcomes measures for a child and his or her family (e.g., being able to take a family vacation)

These multiple evaluation approaches and measurement areas for each child, family, and team reflect the need for PBS to document outcomes that go beyond simple behavior change. For many years, PBS has resulted in changes at the family, professional, classroom, school, and even larger systems levels when the approach is embedded within training, technical assistance, teaching, and support. It has become commonplace to see individuals not only show significant changes in their challenging behavior but also learn more effective and appropriate alternative behaviors, develop true friendships, begin to spend more time in inclusive environments, and begin to make more choices about their personal and educational life. In the same way, families value the development of trusting, collaborative relationships with other team members. They see that there are other individuals who understand them and on whom they can depend. Families also are supported in developing social and personal relationships that are of value for dealing with the stresses, frustrations, joys, and celebrations of supporting a child with challenging behavior. Finally, parents become more effective self-advocates. They promote the use of PBS in their home and community and strive to further expand the quality of their child's and family's life.

PBS for one child also yields significant outcomes at the school and agency levels. Teachers may begin to use and adapt functional assessment and behavior support interventions for other children within their classrooms. Teachers also may develop approaches that address the inappropriate behavior of all students in their classroom by promoting the attainment of social and academic skills. Administrators may investigate how to apply PBS information to developing effective, positive schoolwide programs for all children. Finally, system administrators—such as special education directors, superintendents, or state education agency representatives—may embed PBS within teacher training in-services and adopt statewide policies and procedures that promote best practices in PBS at individual student and schoolwide levels.

CONCLUSION

Claire's story addresses many of the issues that are common when developing a comprehensive behavior support plan. It demonstrates the need for a five-step process to develop an effective plan. Although there are a variety of ways to address each component in the process, it is essential to 1) establish collaboration among the family, school, and community; 2) initiate a broad assessment of the child's and family's environment; 3) complete specific assessments through direct and indirect functional assessment approaches; 4) combine the broad and specific assessment information into a hypothesis-driven, comprehensive behavior support plan; and 5) evaluate and revise the plan to ensure its long-term effectiveness. Furthermore, Clare's story indicates the need to continually account for and address potential barriers to the success of the positive behavior support process.

Claire's story also shows how the Tri-State Consortium's philosophy was directly incorporated into a team-planning process. First the Tri-State Consortium's commitment to providing person- and family-centered support was reflected in the use of a person-centered planning process. Similarly, the ecological and environmental variables that affect behavior were emphasized by utilizing a variety of direct and indirect functional behavioral assessment data. Team-building activities, such as icebreakers, were examples of the Tri-State Consortium's commitment to a team approach. Assisting the team to develop a behavior support plan based on the functional assessment results taught a problem-solving approach that can be positive and effective for all students. Finally, this example demonstrates how supporting the team with periodic input from an outside facilitator may result in an increased capacity to understand and implement the philosophy, technology, and problem-solving approach of positive behavior support without the assistance of an external expert. In turn, this can lead to self-sufficient teams that are capable of meeting the individual behavior support needs of all children in all environments.

REFERENCES

Albin, R.W., Lucyshyn, J.M., Horner, R.H., & Flannery, K.B. (1996). Contextual fit for behavioral support plans: A model for "goodness of fit." In L.K. Koegel, R.L. Koegel, & G. Dunlap (Eds.), *Positive behavioral support: Including people with difficult behavior in the community* (pp. 81–98). Baltimore: Paul H. Brookes Publishing Co.

Anderson, J.L., Russo, A., Dunlap, G., & Albin, R.W. (1996). A team training model for building the capacity to provide positive behavioral supports in inclusive settings. In L.K. Koegel, R.L. Koegel, & G. Dunlap (Eds.), *Positive behavioral support: Including people with difficult behavior in the community* (pp. 467–490). Baltimore: Paul H. Brookes Publishing Co.

Bijou, S.W., Peterson, R.F., & Ault, M.H. (1968). A method to integrate descriptive and experimental field studies at the level of data and empirical concepts. *Journal of Applied Behavior Analysis, 1,* 175–191.

Dunlap, G. Hieneman, M., Knoster, T., Fox, L., Anderson, J., & Albin, R.W. (2000). Essential elements of inservice training in positive behavior support. *Journal of Positive Behavior Interventions, 2,* 22–32.

Durand, V.M. (1988). Motivation assessment scale. In M. Herson & A. Bellack (Eds.), *Dictionary of behavioral assessment techniques* (pp. 309–310). Elmsford, NY: Pergamon.

Kincaid, D. (1996). Person-centered planning. In L.K. Koegel, R.L. Koegel, & G. Dunlap (Eds.), *Positive behavioral support: Including people with difficult behavior in the community* (pp. 439–465). Baltimore: Paul H. Brookes Publishing Co.

Koegel, L.K., Koegel, R.L., & Dunlap, G. (Eds.). (1996). *Positive behavioral support: Including people with difficult behavior in the community.* Baltimore: Paul H. Brookes Publishing Co.

Llewellyn, G., & Knoster, T. (1997). Screening for understanding of student problem behavior: An initial line of inquiry. Harrisburg: Pennsylvania Department of Education, Instructional Support System of Pennsylvania.

Meyer, L.H., & Evans, I.M. (1989). *Nonaversive intervention for behavior problems: A manual for home and community*. Baltimore: Paul H. Brookes Publishing Co.

Meyer, L.H., & Janney, R.E. (1989). User-friendly measures of meaningful outcomes: Evaluating behavioral interventions. *Journal of The Association for Persons with Severe Handicaps, 14,* 263–270.

Mount, B. (1987). *Personal futures planning: Finding directions for change* (Doctoral Dissertation, University of Georgia). Ann Arbor: University of Michigan Dissertation Information Service.

O'Neill, R.E., Horner, R.H., Albin, R.W., Sprague, J.R., Storey, K., & Newton, J.S. (1997). *Functional assessment and program development for problem behavior: A practical handbook.* Pacific Grove, CA: Brooks/ Cole Thomson Learning.

Pearpoint, J., O'Brien, J., & Forrest, M. (1993). *PATH (Planning Alternative Tomorrows with Hope): A workbook for planning better futures.* Toronto: Inclusion Press.

Touchette, P.E., MacDonald, R.F., & Langer, S.N. (1985). A scatterplot for identifying stimulus control of problem behavior. *Journal of Applied Behavior Analysis, 18,* 343–351.

Vandercook, T., York, J., & Forrest, M. (1989). The McGill Action Planning System (MAPS): A strategy for building the vision. *Journal of The Association for Persons with Severe Handicaps, 14,* 205–215.

CHAPTER 14

Climbing the Mountain, Walking the Ridge

More than a Decade of Positive Behavior Support with Jesse

Kathy R. Ben with Catherine C. O'Leary

Our family has spent many years surrounded by the rugged terrain of the Pacific Northwest and Alaska. Through the years we have encountered many mountains, both literal and figurative. Some seemed insurmountable at times, but with perseverance we found that they could be conquered. One such mountain has been my son Jesse's severe behavior problems. This is the story of my family's journey through this rugged terrain, the successes and challenges we have experienced, and the way in which positive behavior support (PBS) has provided essential and enduring tools for overcoming many of the difficulties that we have faced. We have been using PBS with Jesse since the fall of 1990. Through the years, the knowledge and tools that we have gained has helped us climb this mountain, walk a "ridge line of success," and regain our footing after a series of setbacks and falls.

My son Jesse was born 19 years ago in Homer, Alaska. He is an affectionate, handsome, and fun-loving young adult who enjoys an active life filled with school, family, and community activities. He finds pleasure in his surroundings, enjoying nature, taking photographs, viewing wildlife, camping, and traveling. In addition to these pursuits, Jesse likes to cook, swim, and spend time with family and friends.

Jesse also faces multiple challenges. He has developmental disabilities as a result of neonatal meningitis, which he contracted as a 1-day-old infant. Jesse has autism and profound deafness as a result of his early illness, and he uses American Sign Language (ASL) to communicate his needs and desires and to carry on basic conversations.

Jesse lives with my partner, Scott, and me in Tucson, Arizona. I work full time at the University of Arizona as a retention specialist, advising and counseling in academic domains. Scott does restoration ecology, research, and grant writing in conservation biology, and he has been Jesse's co-parent since early 1997.

BASE CAMP: FACING THE MOUNTAIN

Before moving to Arizona, I lived in Alaska for 20 years. Until the time Jesse was 4 years old, we lived in Homer, Alaska, a small fishing village of about 10,000 people. Homer was a wonderful place to live, but it had limited resources for Jesse. To be closer to educational services and a deaf community, we moved to Anchorage—Alaska's largest city. At that time, Jesse's birth father, Steve, and I had been separated for 2 years, so Steve did not move to Anchorage with us. However, Steve was very involved in Jesse's life and continued to have a close relationship with him. When Jesse was 6 years old, Steve was diagnosed with inoperable cancer and died in a short span of time.

At this time in Jesse's life, I met Stanley, who shared our lives and home for the following 8 years. Commonly referred to as "Jesse's Dad," the two formed a strong bond and loving relationship. At that time, Stanley was teaching elementary special education and was a strong advocate for Jesse and his educational needs. Stanley was with us through many transitions throughout those 8 years. Jesse continues to see Stanley at least twice per year, and the bond between them remains strong.

THE MOUNTAIN

Jesse was at home with me until he reached his preschool years. Even at this young age Jesse could be quite aggressive and was prone to tantrums, especially during transition times. Due to his small size, Jesse's tantrums weren't as dramatically intense in the preschool years as they would later become. When he entered school, I found that different teachers had varying ideas about how to address Jesse's behavior. As a result, we endured a variety of behavior programs that did not have a positive impact. At times, the behavior programs even led to more difficult behavior. Punitive time-outs, for example, often escalated Jesse's behavior in school.

In the early school years in Anchorage, Jesse's days were split between a school for deaf students and a self-contained special education classroom within a general education public school. This split was due, in part, to the lack of behavioral expertise among the staff at the school for deaf students. I advocated for Jesse to be in school with teachers and peers who signed fluently so that his language development would not be lost, but his behavior was difficult for the staff to handle, leading to the decision to split his time.

By the time that Jesse was 7 years old, he was big and strong for his age, and his aggressive behaviors and tantrums were becoming more frequent, scary, and downright draining. At that time, there were no diagnostic or special support services for students with autism in Anchorage. In the summer of 1989, Stanley and I decided to move with Jesse to Monmouth, Oregon, for 2 years to enroll Jesse in a school with services for deaf students with developmental disabilities. Through the school, he was assessed by the Mid-Oregon Regional Autism Program. He tested in the range of mild to moderate autism. By the spring of 1990, when Jesse was 8 years old, he and staff in his school program began to receive additional training and support services from an autism specialist.

Although support from the school was somewhat helpful, it was not sufficient to overcome Jesse's problem behaviors. During the summer and fall of 1990, I often considered an out-of-home placement (or suicide!) as my whole existence revolved around structuring every waking minute of Jesse's day and trying without success to "manage" his behavior. At the time, I was terrified by how he became truly wild at times, almost like an animal.

I felt ashamed of myself for the inability to "be a better parent." I dreaded going anywhere alone with Jesse, as his tantrums were unpredictable and were getting to be more than I could physically or emotionally handle.

The most difficult situations were transitions, such as leaving a friend's house, the child care center, or the zoo to drive home. These became long, drawn-out scenes, often with Jesse hitting others, biting himself, running away, and screaming. One time in particular, I remember fearing for our lives when we had returned from a vacation and were driving home from the airport in Portland. Transitions were difficult for Jesse, and this proved to be too much. Jesse climbed into the front seat and grabbed me, causing me to almost lose control of the car as I drove 55 miles per hour on a busy interstate highway. Thank God we were close to a rest stop, where we were able to cool down from the frenzy, and Jesse finally crashed into an exhausted sleep.

Although that is an extreme example, our daily routines were filled with struggles and frequent tantrums. The most difficult situations were getting out the door and onto the school bus in the morning, leaving the child care facility in the afternoon, and trying to supervise Jesse and cook dinner simultaneously. The most common behaviors were yelling, hitting, pinching, or kicking others; hitting himself; and running away. More severe but less frequent behaviors included biting himself and breaking household items such as furniture and windows. The morning school bus pick-up at our home sometimes lasted as long as 15 minutes, as Jesse would run around the block or lie down in the street to avoid getting on the bus.

Needless to say, these behaviors caused serious problems in our family life. Recruiting, training, and retaining respite care providers was extremely difficult. Thus, Stanley and I typically resorted to giving each other breaks and getting very little time alone as a couple. When we did receive respite care, I was so emotionally and physically exhausted from the challenges and demands of caring for Jesse that I experienced little benefit from this extra time. Instead, I would experience a myriad of emotions such as guilt, shame, resentment, helplessness, sadness, anger, and fear. Rather than be supportive and helpful to each other, Stanley and I tended to be overly critical of each other's parenting styles and methods of dealing with Jesse's challenging behavior. Naturally, this was not healthy for our relationship, but we were stuck in these negative patterns and seemed unable to change them.

FINDING A GUIDE AND CREATING A TEAM

Because Jesse's behavior continued to be very difficult to manage, I searched for other sources of support outside of the school program. In the fall of 1990, I contacted the Specialized Training Program of the University of Oregon and was encouraged by the understanding and empathetic response that I received over the telephone. The faculty member with whom I spoke offered to provide behavioral assessment and support resources if Jesse's school program was also willing to participate. After gaining the consent of the administrator and teacher from the school program, we collectively scheduled initial meetings and assessment dates for the beginning of November.

As part of the initial agreement, two behavioral consultants from the university began the functional assessment process by interviewing Stanley and I as well as the educational staff at Jesse's school and child care programs. They took care and time to truly get to know our family and to gain a thorough understanding of Jesse through a comprehensive assessment. Early on, I noticed three things that set this process apart from other evaluations that we had experienced. First, the consultants held unconditional respect for our insights and expertise as Jesse's parents. They viewed our role on the team as implicitly valued and essential. Second, this was the first time that we had worked with professionals who stressed the importance of developing a comprehensive support plan across all environments. Third, these professionals also offered to provide the training, support, and follow-through necessary for successful implementation of the plan.

MAPPING THE ASCENT

Following the initial assessment, one of the consultants, a graduate student, continued to work directly with my family and the school. The other consultant, a university faculty member, provided supervisory support. Over the course of the following 3 months, the consultant facilitated a series of meetings in which the support team—consisting of me, Jesse's teacher, the special education program administrator, and related services specialists—met and developed a comprehensive behavior support plan. After the plan was developed, we met a few additional times to provide support to each other for the plan's implementation. During this time period, the consultant began meeting with us in our home once per week to help us implement the plan.

In the home environment, Stanley and I identified so many problem areas and negative behaviors that we wanted to change that it was hard to choose what to focus on first. The consultant helped us prioritize specific routines in which problem behaviors occurred. We decided to work on the times of day that were the most difficult for Jesse: Waking up, getting dressed, and eating breakfast; getting on and off the school bus; and leaving child care and returning home in the afternoon.

For each of these routines and transitions, we developed and implemented behavioral supports. First, we broke down each activity into a series of steps and designed "picture schedules" that illustrated each step with drawings or photographs. We chose items that would be used as reinforcers or rewards (e.g., healthy snacks, extra time using the computer) when Jesse successfully completed difficult transitions or routines. We also made a "menu of rewards" from which Jesse could choose when he calmly and smoothly completed the steps in an activity.

We also directly taught Jesse the receptive language he needed to better understand his world and the way that things worked. The following concepts were essential to Jesse's success: "More good things will happen in the next environment," "You will come here, see friends, and do this AGAIN tomorrow (or next week)," and "With calm, good behavior, you have choices, and you can choose." The concrete visual images of the picture schedules gave Jesse the security and predictability he needed. Equally important was the great increase in choice-making opportunities that we consciously gave Jesse every day within most activities. He became less anxious, began to show more self-control, and exhibited more appropriate behaviors.

Included in the intervention was a plan for fading the use of tangible rewards (e.g., healthy snacks) while continuing to rely on social reinforcers (e.g., signed praise with a hug, a "high-five"). For instance, when we went on hikes in the old growth forests near our home, we first used healthy snacks to motivate Jesse to calmly walk back to the car and return home. As he began to complete these difficult transitions without a problem, we faded out the use of the tangible rewards but continued to praise him for leaving cooperatively. We also learned to accentuate our positive facial expressions and body language when we praised Jesse because this was very reinforcing to him. We also learned to "actively ignore" and redirect minor negative behaviors. During home meetings with the behavioral consultant, we role-played common scenarios and videotaped our role plays so we could learn from our own actions. For example, it was difficult for me to avoid eye contact with Jesse and to remain calm with flat affect when I was feeling frustrated or angry. The use of active ignoring was an important skill to learn because Jesse was good at reading facial expressions and seemed to thrive on these reactions. His negative behaviors escalated when he saw that he was getting on my nerves. Through role playing, I learned to mask negative emotions and stay calm, not allowing Jesse to see that he was pushing my buttons. I learned to avoid eye contact at times when a sudden glare might reveal my frustration.

The consultant helped us to focus not only on Jesse's negative behaviors but also to identify and appreciate Jesse's strengths, gifts, and positive contributions to the family. I hate to admit it, but at first it was difficult to enumerate many positive qualities or contributions. After giving this some serious thought, however, I began to recognize several of Jesse's strengths and contributions to my life. For example, I realized that the skills that I had developed up to that time as an advocate and educator were partly due to my efforts to provide Jesse with the best possible life that I could. Also, his incredible energy and curiosity prompted us to participate in many interesting and energetic activities, such as hiking, cross-country skiing, and mountain climbing.

REACHING THE SUMMIT

During the process of PBS in Oregon, we became empowered. Instead of the deficit-based "fix-it" approach that marked our past, we experienced the holistic "ecology of change" approach that is associated with PBS. Throughout the process, I never once felt the old blaming-shaming-guilt that I had previously experienced. I recall professionals asking, "What's wrong with Jesse today?" "Is there something wrong at home?" "Jesse kicked and hit others today. Did you have a bad night?" or "Jesse punched a peer today. Is there too much sugar in his diet?" In each instance, my interpretation of these inquiries was, "What did you do to cause this child to be so bad?!"

In contrast, the functional assessment, the development of interventions, and the ongoing support was family centered and empowering. We received praise and support for each positive step taken and for every success, no matter how small. These words of encouragement were combined with a sincere respect for all of our hard work. I deeply appreciated this unconditional positive support. It boosted my morale and strengthened my determination.

It was hard work. It was not always easy or preferable to be proactive and to take time to complete self-assessments of our implementation of support strategies. I clearly remember wishing it was easier and resenting the time and energy it took to make it all work smoothly. Occasionally, there still were problems. After all, PBS is not a cure for autism! As with anything, practice makes perfect. Eventually, the use of PBS became easier and even began to feel like second nature.

The consultant's weekly visits to our home were filled with animated discussions of what was and wasn't working and real-life problem solving as we worked through each problematic routine. Through this hands-on guidance, the consultant became not only a trusted support person but also a friend. I knew I could count on him to listen nonjudgmentally and humbly offer support through the problem-solving process. His willingness to work through difficult situations with us made an enormous difference in the quality and durability of the outcomes of support. The consultant never doled out advice but instead gently insisted that we were the experts and ensured our active involvement in designing and implementing each intervention. In so doing, the experiences that we had during those initial 5 months of intensive support became invaluable to us in the future, serving as basic tools that we could utilize and expand on as we encountered new situations and obstacles.

THE VIEW FROM THE TOP

At this stage in our journey, the payoffs were incredible. The strides that Jesse made in language skills and communication and the overall impact on his entire life (and mine!) were tremendous. I would not trade any part of the process of support for anything—not one day of meetings or designing another picture schedule or completing another self-assessment form. I feel incredibly fortunate that we were able to learn these positive strategies, gain skills and confidence, and receive in-depth support. PBS was and is a lifesaver and a godsend to my family and me!

As planned, we returned to Alaska in the summer of 1991 after receiving 5 months of intensive support and training in implementing Jesse's behavior support plan. The trip back to Alaska entailed 3 weeks of driving, visiting family, staying with friends, and camping out, as well as an unplanned stay for 2 nights in British Columbia as we struggled to fix our car during the Canadian Independence Day holiday. Overall, Jesse managed the journey and unanticipated upheaval quite well. Upon arrival in Anchorage, we stayed at a friend's house while searching for a house to rent. We also spent a couple of weeks in Homer at our old cabin prior to settling in to our new home and lives in Anchorage.

The multiple transitions and lack of structure would not have been possible for Jesse just months prior. Our newly acquired skills and confidence from training in positive behavior support made such a trip feasible. We were able to proactively support Jesse and prevent any major problems from developing.

In the fall of 1991, Jesse reentered the school for deaf children that he had previously attended, as well as his former after-school child care program. During the first few months of our return, the teachers and other staff who knew Jesse often greeted us with both surprise and pleasure: "Wow! Jesse has really changed!" "Jesse is doing great. He is so much fun to be with now!" "Is this the same kid that kicked out the school bus window?" Jesse went from having a terrible reputation and severe behavior problems to being liked, accepted, and included in a wider range of community activities with more children without disabilities. Our initial challenge in moving back to Alaska was not our ability to provide behavioral support to Jesse. At home, we were doing this just fine. The real challenge we faced was advocating for training and supporting the use of behavioral supports in the school system. We experienced some resistance to the changes we suggested. To be sure, some aspects of Jesse's behavior support plan were quickly incorporated into his school program, such as the picture schedule system and the provision of choice for Jesse within the academic curriculum (e.g., choosing a particular task to work on within a math lesson). However, teachers still tended to use time-out procedures in a punitive way rather than as a way that allowed Jesse to take a couple of minutes to calm down. Despite these challenges with implementation at school, Jesse did not have nearly as many problems as he did before our trip to Oregon.

Having reached the summit with Jesse, we found ourselves walking along a ridge line of success with a remarkable view. There were many positive outcomes for Jesse and our family. Jesse moved on to do many things that he was not able to do before our involvement in PBS. Jesse became more able to manage himself in the community. As a result, Jesse was able to switch from an after-school program for children with special needs and their siblings to a community-based Camp Fire Program at his own elementary school. Jesse also made a change from the special education bus to a regular school bus. He attended a sixth-grade camp with deaf and hearing students, which he truly enjoyed. He also participated, with support, in environmental education overnight camps in the Alaskan wilderness for three consecutive summers. These camps lasted from 3–7 days. In addition, Jesse had a friend for almost 2 years who called, visited, and invited Jesse to spend the night at his house. (When Jesse's friend made the transition to a charter school and relocated, it became difficult to get together and they eventually lost touch.) In addition, during seventh grade, Jesse joined the cross-country ski team and participated fully in practice and ski meets.

During Jesse's first 4 years back in Alaska, he continued to make great strides. In the fall of 1992, he successfully made the transition into the middle school program. As a family, we visited relatives and friends in various parts of the United States and Mexico. We were able return home with minimal to no "readjusting-to-routine" problems. Jesse was able to stay overnight, for weekends, and for longer periods of time at various respite care providers' homes and to make a successful transition back home. In the summer of 1993, Stanley and I were able to leave Jesse with a competent respite care provider and travel to Africa for a month. A flexible daily picture schedule, a calendar that reassured Jesse of our eventual return, and a couple of postcards from Africa helped to mediate this separation. Prior to the positive changes in Jesse's behavior and life, I would never have dreamed that I would be willing or able to travel so far and for such a length of time.

As part of Jesse's behavior support plan, much effort was made to improve his language skills—both what he could understand and what he could express. As he developed the ability to discuss past, present, and future events, he grew more able to calmly accept changes and manage daily transitions. The picture schedule proved to be an essential tool for developing Jesse's language skills. What a lifesaver that was! Wall schedules showed the week at a glance both at home and at school. Smaller, portable schedules were put together for daily or weekend transitions. His schedules were filled with visual reminders and choice opportunities, giving him the ability to predict daily and weekly events in his life and to share control over his routines and environment.

Several support strategies were essential for improving Jesse's behavior. Increasing Jesse's choice-making opportunities and building his language skills gave him more control over his life. Rather than becoming anxious and upset at the end of a favorite daily activity (e.g., time spent at child care) or weekly event (e.g., a visit with a family friend), he began to look forward to the next activity on his schedule. For weekly or monthly events, he began to trust that within a week's or month's time, he would have another opportunity to participate in the event again. Jesse also became better at negotiating with us and at accepting compromises and limits. We used, to good effect, multiple alternatives to signing NO, such as NO, NOT NOW; LATER; NEXT WEEK; OOPS! FRIEND NOT HOME NOW. TRY AGAIN TOMORROW; MAYBE, BUT YOU NEED TO ASK (NAME OF TEACHER OR FRIEND); and SORRY, NOT TODAY. The language of positive contingencies also became a strong and helpful part of our repertoire of parenting skills. For example, if early on a Sunday morning Jesse wanted to go the zoo but had not gotten ready yet, then we might say, "Take your bath, get dressed, and make your bed; then we will go to the zoo."

In the summer of 1995, Jesse's school-based team, including Stanley and me, participated in a person-centered planning process referred to as MAPS (Making Action Plans, formerly known as the McGill Action Planning System; Pearpoint, Forest, & O'Brien). The

MAPS process provided an opportunity for members of Jesse's team to build on his accomplishments and create a broader support network for Jesse both at school and in the community. For school-based goals, the team focused on enhancing Jesse's academic inclusion and effecting a successful transition to high school. For home- and community-based goals, the team focused on developing a larger circle of support for Jesse and expanding his involvement in the community. MAPS also provided a context for Stanley and me to transmit the knowledge of PBS. During the meeting, we easily enumerated Jesse's numerous talents and positive qualities, as well as the strategies that worked and did not work! We were finally bringing together the resources and providers in Alaska, and the knowledge and skills that we had gained, in a way that would build a strong community of support around Jesse. Little did we suspect how important that network was going to be in the next few months and years.

FALLING OFF THE MOUNTAIN

In the fall of 1995, and then again in spring of 1997, two health crises severely impeded our collective vision of a richer and more inclusive life for Jesse. Up until this time, Jesse had experienced excellent health and was well coordinated and physically fit. In September of 1995, he experienced a stroke, precipitated by a seizure, that severely altered his physical capabilities. He developed a mild hemiparesis on his right side. He also began to take seizure medication. Although Jesse remained ambulatory, he became left-hand dominant and virtually a one-handed signer. This affected his ability to communicate using ASL, his writing and keyboarding skills, his vocational capacities, and his ability to participate in leisure activities.

Thanks to the MAPS process that took place over the summer, however, there were more people who were aware of his capabilities and needs and were willing and able to support him. He could have been much more isolated in the middle school deaf education classroom, but that did not happen. There was a team in place that was ready and able to solve a lot of new problems quickly. His circle of support, including family members, respite care providers, and school staff, provided a tremendous amount of support to Jesse in this crucial time. They really helped him get through it. As a result, he regressed only slightly in his academic progress. The team decided to hold him back in middle school and planned a much more gradual transition to high school.

In May of 1997, Jesse was attending high school half days, and had 2 weeks of school left before summer break. Suddenly, he had a major subdural hematoma. He fell into a coma and entered the intensive care unit of a hospital in Anchorage. The doctors there, however, were unable to diagnose the problem. He was then medevaced to a children's hospital in Seattle that has a program for epilepsy. The lead neurologist there was wonderful. He consulted with a pediatric neurosurgeon in Sacramento, and they diagnosed the specific problem as low-pressure hydrocephalic syndrome and recommended surgery. Jesse was then medevaced to a hospital in Sacramento, where the surgery was performed. After the surgery, Jesse briefly came out of the coma, but then a series of complications occurred that resulted in several more neurosurgeries, reentry into a coma, and lengthy hospitalizations during the summer and fall of 1997. It was a nightmare.

The final shunt revision surgery occurred in September of 1997. Jesse was then flown back Seattle, this time to a children's hospital. He came out of the coma for good and started rehabilitation. Just after Thanksgiving of the same year, he returned with me to Alaska. The plan was for Jesse to return to school and enter the high school program in January of 1998. In addition to multiple shunt surgeries, he also had major hip surgery. Consequently, Jesse had to relearn how to walk and at first used a wheelchair most of the time. Jesse made slow but steady progress in his ability to get around and in his other physical skills. However, what had been set in place the previous year for his education and quality of life no longer seemed appropriate. His short-term memory was severely affected by the neurological and cognitive damage that he sustained. Compared to the previous problems, Jesse faced a much more serious set of difficulties at school and in doing the things he loved in the community. It was clear to us that his high school teacher needed a lot of support. She did not know what to do. Also, there was no team established in the high school. When I tried to help establish a new support team for Jesse, it became clear that in this high school, parent–professional partnership, collaborative teaming, and inclusion were new and unwelcome concepts. It was not a good situation. In addition, the Alaskan snow and ice of winter made it very difficult for Jesse to stand and walk outside, least of all hike on his favorite trails. This severely limited the quality of his life.

At this time, I began to consider a better place for Jesse to live and go to school. After conducting some research, I learned that Tucson, Arizona, was one of the most accessible cities in the United States for people with physical disabilities. It had, in fact, become a mecca for people with physical disabilities. I also learned that Tucson is the home of a school for students who are deaf and that it has an excellent program for students with multiple disabilities. Scott and I visited Tucson for 5 days and confirmed this information. I also visited developmental disability services in Tucson and saw how much easier it would be to find skilled respite providers and people fluent in ASL to support Jesse. Although it was a very difficult decision, with Jesse's best interests at heart, we decided to move to Arizona.

FINDING OUR FOOTING IN A NEW AND ARID LAND

We moved to Arizona in April of 1999. The move has been a major transition for all of us. Being so far away from family and friends and adjusting to a new environment has been quite a challenge. One of the challenges that Scott and I faced was finding meaningful and gainful employment. This took several months for me and more than a year for Scott to find a position in his highly competitive field. Along with these personal challenges, Jesse's behavior regressed. The sudden loss of so many supports (e.g., beloved friends, favorite respite care providers) and the major changes in his environment and lifestyle (e.g., days that were hot instead of cold, no forest hiking trails, fewer opportunities for skiing) were too much for Jesse to bear at one time. Tantrums and aggression resurfaced. Since Summer 1999, we have worked to build a new support system and valued life for Jesse in Tucson.

Jesse misses the closeness and familiarity of old family friends. He expresses it by looking at picture albums and home videotapes, as well as talking about people whom he misses and how he wants to visit with them. With time, we have added new activities and dimensions to Jesse's life, helping him to feel more secure and supported in his new environment. As time has passed and we have been able to get a new support system into place, Jesse has been exhibiting decreasing levels of problem behavior.

Jesse is one of the only students in his high school program who has mild autism and challenging behaviors *in addition* to deafness and physical disabilities. He seems to be well accepted and liked, and the school appears to be a good fit for him. He is currently involved in after-school sports such as swimming, bowling, and weight training. He has peers with whom he participates in these activities, and his teachers and coaches all have the ability to sign. This alone is a great benefit. Jesse also enjoys being an active member of the

YMCA, where he swims and works out 2–3 days per week. In addition, he is participating in art classes and horseback riding lessons. He goes to physical therapy once per week. Most of his activities in the community take place under the supervision of either his parents or care providers.

Because of the stroke, comas, brain surgeries, shunt insertions, and medical complications, Jesse has had more difficulty with physical activity. He continues to have balance problems; walking on uneven terrain is challenging for him, even when he uses a cane. This has been hard for our family because we like to be physically active and spend time outdoors. We continue to go camping together, but hiking is difficult for Jesse, who can walk only about 1 mile each way. We have been seeking additional respite care so that Scott and I can enjoy some of the more physically demanding outdoor activities that Jesse is no longer able to do.

The physiological changes continue to be very trying for Jesse. He is on a low dosage of a medication that has taken the edge off of his behavior. It has helped him become calmer and has given him more self-control. Medication prescribed by a psychiatrist was something that we never thought that we would want or need to utilize, but it became a necessity. We are hopeful that it will be a temporary measure. We have been told that Jesse's medication is commonly prescribed for people with neurological complications that are similar to Jesse's. To us, this measure does not feel like we have failed in our support to Jesse. Rather, it feels like we have added, for the time being, another component to the comprehensive ecology of support that we are in the midst of rebuilding for Jesse. We remain thankful that despite the complications, most people still describe Jesse as an affectionate, friendly, curious, and loving young man.

We continue to use picture schedules, particularly during times of transition. We take his schedules with us on trips; the schedules include images that depict the activities in which we will engage and the return home. In general, this process is not as necessary as it used to be. In years past, we used a full-page schedule each day. Now, Jesse has a wall schedule at home and does not need such intensive support for transitions throughout the day. We do use more intensive picture schedules during weeks off from school and on vacations.

As we continue to build a new life for Jesse in this beautiful, austere, desert valley, his behavior and lifestyle continues to improve. Recently, Jesse had a wonderful winter vacation. He took a trip to Mexico with Stanley and then accompanied us on a 5-day visit to Scott's mother's home in Scottsdale, Arizona. He handled all of the transitions very well, meeting and visiting with many new relatives, then returning home and back to school. His monthly calendar and weekly picture schedules continue to make all the difference in the world. He requests them before trips and helps put them together. He also actively chooses what goes on the weekly wall schedule at home. It really is remarkable what a critical and positive support this has become for him. Now, when we finish an activity that he really enjoys, Jesse asks upon our arrival home if he can put it on the calendar for a future date so that he can be sure of when to look forward to that activity again!

Our journey in supporting Jesse has included many ups and downs. At times, we have had to take one or two steps back for every two or three steps forward. I know how strenuous and even painful the journey can be. I also know how incredible life can be when you get beyond problem behaviors and experience the joy of watching your child grow and live a happier and more successful life. When you walk that ridge line of success and take in the view, you feel that you are on top of the world. From that place, it is easy to forget the effort and pain involved in getting there. We have been involved in PBS with Jesse for more than a decade now. The philosophy, insights, and tools that PBS has given us have helped to fortify and sustain us in the face of many challenges and setbacks. As we take in the beau-

tiful view before us and apply our skills to present circumstances and challenges, we are mindful that new valleys and peaks lie ahead. We face these prospects with confidence, knowing that however Jesse and our circumstances may change, we can find our way back up the mountain.

> *Jesse turned 20 in January 2002. Although he still lives at home with his parents, his mother is actively building support to create a positive, successful living situation in the community for Jesse. This is his last year at school, and after experience and training at a variety of job sites, Jesse has determined his strong preference for working in the food services arena. His mother continues striving to help Jesse enjoy a full, rewarding, high-quality life.*

REFERENCE

Pearpoint, J., Forest, M., & O'Brien, J. (1996). MAPS, Circles of Friends, and PATH: Powerful tools to help build caring communities. In S. Stainback & W. Stainback (Eds.), *Inclusion: A guide for educators* (pp. 67–86). Baltimore: Paul H. Brookes Publishing Co.

A Legacy of Love

Our Path to Freedom Through Behavioral Support

Ursula Arceneaux Markey

I live in New Orleans, the Big Easy, where life is literally a festival. Louisiana holds more festivals than there are days in the year. There are festivals to celebrate music—jazz, blues, zydeco, reggae, gospel; festivals to celebrate food—gumbo, shrimp, crawfish, Creole tomatoes, strawberries, oranges, peaches, poke salad; and festivals to celebrate events—Bastille Day, the Battle of New Orleans, the blessing of the shrimp boats, the Crescent City Classic race, pirogue races. You name it! And each year, we host that wildest of all festivals—Mardi Gras!

My family is African American, and we were not always welcomed at Louisiana's festivals. During my childhood, we lived under the legal mandates of racial segregation. I can remember the anguish in my parents' eyes each time they had to introduce another of the many restrictions placed upon us because of the color of our skin. "Uh, we can't go to the amusement park . . . besides, those rides are dangerous." "You don't need to ride those ol' dirty ponies anyway. Climb up on my back; I'm a bucking bronco!" "Let's go home and we'll play with the hose. It'll be just as much fun as swimming in their ol' pool."

Every family outing had to be planned carefully because there were so few public accommodations available to us. The shortest trip could end abruptly because of this: "You can't drink from that water fountain," "We can't eat at this lunch counter," and "There's no 'colored' restroom here, so we'll have to go back home." There was no relief from the Jim Crow laws anytime or anywhere, not even on Sundays. We had to walk a mile past the neighborhood church, which was reserved for white parishioners, to attend the "colored" church where people of our race were allowed to worship.

All of these restrictions were especially difficult to understand and accept because they did not apply to all of the families in our neighborhood. In the steamy, rain-washed afternoons of summer, my two brothers and I, bathed and talcum powdered in the Creole tradition, would sit on our front steps in our racially mixed neighborhood and listen to the adventures of white children who knew no such restrictions. Their fascinating accounts of roller coasters, first-run movies, and spontaneous family outings weighed heavy on our young hearts. It was through those front-step stories that we came to understand the meaning of exclusion.

Our parents and extended family worked hard to make us feel valued in a society that did not value us. They created opportunities for us to experience success in protective, self-contained environments. They held backyard parties, officiated at sidewalk games, and hand-crafted Mardi Gras costumes—princess gowns and cowboy vests—to indulge our fantasies. They staged talent shows in which aunts, uncles, cousins, *nanans, parans,* and neighbors tolerated and even applauded our fledgling singing, stiff recitations, and awkward dance routines.

We met new friends at multifamily picnics held on the "colored" end of the shore of a local lake. I remember us all together on that end of the lake; playing baseball; racing each other; listening to family stories; eating the best of each other's cooking; and laughing, hugging, and laughing. "One of y'all gonna be President one day," my father used to tell us. Our parents expected us to do well in spite of everything.

I love those memories. The ones that I cherish most are of the times when my parents would give us a hug or a kiss for no reason at all or for doing some little thing—an errand we did for a neighbor; kindnesses shown to each other; a household chore completed; reading, writing, or drawing something. I remember smiling broadly whenever they let us overhear them praising our good deeds and accomplishments.

As my siblings and I grew older, we began to recognize the effects of exclusion and second-class citizenship on our people. We saw the disparity between their talents and the menial work they had to accept in order to make a living. We heard their discussions on philosophy, politics, justice, and peace. We saw the brilliance that the outside world refused to acknowledge. We felt the sadness of their own deferred dreams of education, employment, entrepreneurship, and home ownership. We also sometimes heard what we didn't want to hear—whispered accounts of the insults, indignities, and dangerous situations that they endured. So even as our parents supported our progress in our segregated schools, they knew that they had to do their part in giving us access to the unlimited possibilities associated with first-class citizenship in the United States. To gain these rights and privileges, they became active in the American Civil Rights movement, and they supported the involvement of my brothers and I in voter education, demonstrations, boycotts, and marches even before we were teenagers.

I was in high school when integration came to the public schools in Louisiana. The negative response to the inclusion of African American students in previously all-white schools was so intense and violent that many African American parents had second thoughts about sending their children to integrated schools. Yet, for my family and the majority of others, there were no thoughts of turning back. Integration had become a legal reality, and the truth we had known all along was exposed for all to see—that "separate-but-equal" had never been equal and that full inclusion was our only hope of receiving quality education and equal rights.

In 1970, 6 years after Congress passed the Civil Rights Act, I entered into married life and parenthood with a partner who had shared the struggles and victories of the movement. Together, D.J. and I were happy to leave the sit-ins, boycotts, marches, and pain in the past and to move on to a future filled with promise for ourselves and our children—a place we had played an active role in shaping.

Then, in 1972, a gifted teacher entered our lives—our son, Duane, who had autism. As a preschooler, Duane was singled out by teachers as a child who did not "fit in." We would get a laundry list of problem behaviors from teachers and few positive reports. Various forms of exclusion were suggested and imposed by school administrators to control Duane's challenging behaviors. Family and friends knew nothing about the characteristic behaviors of autism and offered advice based on their experiences with typical children. When one after another of their suggestions failed, they eventually left us alone to cope with our fear and frustration.

Some of Duane's behaviors were extremely troubling. One day when he was 5 years old, we were visiting my brother and his family. My brother's children and several of the neighborhood kids were playing outside. Duane joined them, but we were keeping a close eye on him, unable to concentrate on the adult conversation. After a while, the kids were called in for a snack. Every child rushed in for the treats—every child except Duane. Instead, he darted toward the street.

We ran after him. He didn't respond when we shouted and begged him to stop. We caught him just as he was about to run out into a busy street. Everyone was relieved that Duane was okay; however, my husband and I were not okay. Although we tried not to show it, we were still deeply frightened because it was just one of the many times Duane had not listened to us or anyone, even in the face of imminent danger. We were terrified that there might be a time when we would not be able to stop him before something terrible happened. As we collected our coats to leave, my nephew came up to me and asked, "Auntie, why does Duane act like that?" I didn't have an answer, and the question was too painful to deal with at the time, so I just fought back my tears, hugged my nephew, and left. Later we would learn just how important our young nephew's question was. At the time, we just knew we wanted those horrible, frightening behaviors to stop. We wanted Duane to stop running off. We wanted him to stop humming the same tune over and over again. We wanted him to play with other children instead of choosing to be alone all of the time. We wanted him to stop having temper tantrums.

All of these behaviors prevented our son and us from participating fully in activities that other young families were enjoying. Addressing our child's behavior became increasingly more difficult. We often decided to stay home to avoid the stress. When we did venture out, it was for activities that allowed us to be self-contained. Movies, video arcades, long drives, and picnics were standard fare. Thus, although our family was visible in the community, there was no real interaction. We had won the right to participate in the many festivals and other activities that we had heard about as children, but we still found ourselves excluded because of Duane's challenging behavior.

Doctors and school officials encouraged us to start Duane on Ritalin. They explained that the drug would calm Duane and allow him to benefit from instruction at school. We were hesitant. We had no doubt that the medication would make life easier for the teachers and us, but what would it mean in the long run? He was only 5 years old. We wanted him to stop throwing things, but we didn't want him to stop laughing. We wanted him to stop running off, but we didn't want him to stop running to us with a hug. We wanted him to stop repeating meaningless words and phrases, but we didn't want him to stop talking to us. We wanted to know our son. Would the medication interfere with that?

We decided to try something else. It was called *behavior management,* and training was being offered through our community mental health center at a small cost. My mother and father attended the training with us, and we learned several useful strategies to get Duane's behaviors under control. Through it all, however, nobody ever asked the question my nephew had asked that day: "Why does Duane act like that?" Instead, behavior management started with the objective of shaping and controlling Duane's behaviors through contingency planning and reward systems.

Over the years, we strove to learn how to best support Duane and to advocate for the best possible education and the best possible life for him. When he was in junior high school and engaging in serious challenging behaviors, we went through due process to get Duane placed in a residential school program. During this struggle, we learned about the importance of normalization, inclusion, and community-based instruction. These concepts had not surfaced in any of our numerous meetings with doctors, mental health professionals, or educators. We were horrified that in our ignorance of these important concepts, we had almost succeeded in removing our son from his community to somehow prepare him to live in it.

Thus, we rejected the residential school placement that we had won in due process and turned toward inclusion. We placed Duane in a group home in our community. Staff used a point system to encourage desired behaviors. Meanwhile, we participated in the development of an inclusive individualized education program to meet his needs. We knew that it would be difficult to send Duane to a general education campus, where he immediately would be identified as "different" and subjected to the cruelty of other children. Yet, for the first time we understood what our parents must have gone through in helping us face those days when racial integration first came to public schools. We had come to understand now what they understood then—that total inclusion and full participation are rights worth fighting for.

We celebrated Duane's 18th birthday the same year (1990) that we celebrated the passage of the Americans with Disabilities Act (ADA). I thought about these milestones and reflected on our lifelong struggle to achieve civil rights as African Americans and as parents of a child with a disability. Duane appeared to be progressing well. He spent every weekend, holiday, and vacation with us. He was attending the neighborhood high school and participating in school activities as well as in special and general education classes. He was receiving training in the use of public transportation and gaining work experience as part of his transition to an adult life plan. Also, with the support of a dedicated teacher, Duane went on his first date.

Our first indication that Duane was not as happy as we were with his program came when he shocked us by eloping from the group home. It was the materialization of a parent's worst fear. He was out in the world alone and without the supports that we thought were necessary for his survival. The next 24 hours were nightmarish, with family, friends, and group home staff frantically searching for him. During those hours, two people offered insights that would forever change the way I viewed my son. One was Duane's teacher, who reassured me that Duane had acquired many skills that he could call on if needed. The other was my brother. When I called him to tell him Duane was missing, I was shocked and baffled by his response. He immediately joined the search team, but first he said, "I feel good for him. He's taken control. He's making his own decisions."

In my distress, I couldn't see how my brother could suggest that Duane's running off could be a positive thing. I saw nothing positive about my child's being out in the city alone after dark. When he returned safely the next morning, however, I thought about how my brother had characterized Duane's leaving as a means of taking control of his life. I knew then that there was indeed a great deal of truth in my brother's words. Duane wanted to have some control over his life; he wanted to make his own decisions. I realized then that his teacher was also right. Duane had command of many skills that I had not imagined until that moment. This was a turning point for me. For the first time, I saw my son as his own person with his own mind and his own thoughts and dreams. I realized that by his actions, he was telling us that he wanted to be free. I realized the behavior management techniques that we were using with him were aimed at controlling him. These strategies were not empowering him or giving him greater freedom. Having lived under the apartheid of the Deep South, I understood in my heart and soul the desire not to be controlled and limited.

Soon after that realization, when Duane was still 18 years old, we bought a house and brought him home. Many of the old behaviors that were controlled by behavior management strategies resurfaced, and we struggled to relearn how to support him. During this effort, we came to see more and more of his behaviors as his way of communicating his needs and desires. In the same year, our family began a support and advocacy group called Pyramid Parent Training. We did so based on the encouragement of friends and neighbors who admired Duane and also to share with our community what we were learning about how to support Duane. A year after bringing Duane home, we were introduced to positive behavior support (PBS). Our community parent program received a donation of books from Paul H. Brookes Publishing Co., and my attention was drawn to the title *Positive Behavioral Support: Including People with Difficult Behavior in the Community* (Koegel, Koegel, & Dunlap, 1996). D.J. and I read it together. We immediately recognized PBS as being important and relevant to Duane's life and to our efforts to support him. Our son's behavior and his lifestyle improved when we began to adopt principles and strategies that were consistent with PBS. We were amazed at how much we were already doing intuitively that was part of the approach. For example, we had already asked and answered many of the questions that are part of a functional assessment. We knew that good support had to include praising our son for his courage and accomplishments, providing opportunities for success, and offering meaningful choices. We knew that the best context for support was inclusion in one's neighborhood, school, and community.

All that we had learned and accomplished up to that point had led us to PBS. The approach validated what we had been striving to learn and what we had been fighting to create in our lives together. We began to see that behavior management strategies we had learned when he was a child, including token and point systems, had accomplished little toward building Duane's sense of his own power and personhood. We had learned to control some of his behaviors some of the time, but we had placed more emphasis on control than on communication. Once we read the theoretical basis and importance of functional assessment, we understood the profound meaning of my nephew's query, "Why does Duane act like that?" We saw the truth in the concept that all behavior is communication.

We read the theory and validated it as we recalled the times that we had used PBS without knowing it had a name and a body of research and theory. I reflected on my own most cherished childhood memories, and invariably my mind returned to those times my parents would reward us with a hug or a kiss for no apparent reason. Those noncontingent, nonjudgmental displays of affection were fuel for our positive sense of self. I began to understand how my parents had structured the environment for us. They offered us choices that we would ordinarily not have. Whenever we began to feel bitter or experienced something negative, they redirected us to the positive. They taught us the skills we needed to respond to others in a way that drew respect toward us. I realized that PBS had been in our family for generations. This insight awakened in me a deep sense of connection to my family and my ancestors in all that they had taught through the generations.

As we continued to follow a PBS approach with our son, his need for challenging behaviors decreased significantly. Our communication partnership deepened to a level beyond our most optimistic imaginings. I began to ask Duane about his childhood memories. To my surprise, he had vivid memories. I began to explain the various events and strategies that we experienced together throughout his life—the different schools that he attended, our move to California for 6 years, and the "star charts" that we had used in our home. He appeared to understand. Then he began to ask the questions: "Why wasn't I allowed to eat hot dogs and candy?" "Why did they make me use Dial soap?" and "Why couldn't I go dancing?" This became a daily ritual for nearly a year. Each morning Duane would choose a year in his life and ask about something that happened during that year that he did not understand. I would explain the reasons behind the event or situation. I explained to Duane, for example, that he had not been allowed to eat hot dogs or candy because the sugar or chemicals in these foods appeared to have a negative effect on his behavior.

Reviewing Duane's personal history with him served as a means of evaluating the systems and environments in which he had grown up. His troubling memories were almost always about how others had treated him or how people had reacted to his behaviors. They were about his feelings concerning how he fit in within systems—schools, social services, community institutions such as churches, our own family—and about his interactions with elements of his environment. Often, they were about restrictions that others placed on him, things that he was not allowed to do, or feelings of isolation and confusion.

With each new understanding, Duane evidenced a palpable release, a centeredness. Duane's personhood was emerging. After his most pressing questions were answered, we continued our talks once per week over Sunday brunch. The positive effect of this dialogue usually lasted all week. He was more relaxed, content, and tolerant of the irritations of daily life.

Duane finished high school at age 21, and for the next several years served as a volunteer in many programs that held meaning for him. He enjoyed working and performed well in the positions that he held. He struggled for years to gain the competitive employment promised by the Civil Rights Act and the ADA, but lingering negative attitudes about race and disability continued to present obstacles to this goal. When paying jobs failed to materialize, Duane created work for himself. He became a writer. He documented his favorite moments in the history of the National Basketball Association (NBA). He established regular hours for writing and kept to his schedule. Our family delighted in seeing him sit at the computer every day, creating chapters for his book on the NBA. We began to refer to him as a writer, and his self-esteem soared.

One evening at dinner, Duane's younger brother, Teiko, told us that he was having problems with concentrating on his schoolwork. He said that he believed he would have to give up watching movies, a favorite pastime. We were astonished when Duane told Teiko about a time when he thought he would have to give up watching his beloved NBA games. Whenever players got into fights on the court, Duane would find himself acting out those fights and getting out of control. He told Teiko that he learned to walk away from the TV when he saw that a fight was about to happen—that was how he solved the problem and still got to see the games. "If I could do it, you can, too," he told his brother. Duane was demonstrating a new-found ability to reflect on another's experience and to offer sound advice based on his experience and personal accomplishments. Duane was moving past all limitations.

At age 26, Duane applied to the Home of My Own program, a supported homeownership program for adults with disabilities. Two months later, Duane died after having a seizure. His notice of acceptance in the Home of My Own program arrived in the mail on the day of his funeral.

Losing our son has been devastating, a loss that is difficult to express even now. Yet, we are compelled to continue the work that Duane inspired. Images of his smiling face remind us of his breakthrough. The example of his life honors all of our ancestors—those wise, early practitioners of PBS—and offers hope for generations to come.

I spend a lot of time reflecting on Duane's life. I think of the withdrawn little boy he was; the troubled teen with difficult behaviors; and the young man who somehow got it together, recognized his calling, and summoned his skills and talents to achieve his dreams. How did he get there? I have to say that as we read and practiced the concepts of PBS, we saw over and over again the wisdom of its principles—inclusion, noncontingent rewards, positive reinforcement, empowerment, and fixing systems rather than people.

As a mother, I longed to see my son included as one of the gang, grouped together with cousins, schoolmates, and neighbors for some outing or activity. Yet, when it came to activities with his peers, the norm was usually exclusion. When Duane was about 13 years old, one of his cousins invited several youngsters to a dance. Duane was not asked to go. I know that no one had any intentions of hurting Duane by excluding him. They probably thought that it would be inappropriate for him to go to a dance. After all, Duane was special, and sometimes others didn't understand his actions. Nevertheless, it was painful for Duane and for us. He looked at me with bewilderment and hurt on his face and said, "I like to dance." This was his way of asking me why he had not been invited.

Some years later, after we embraced the wisdom of PBS, Duane became empowered rather than controlled. With an enhanced sense of his own power, he gained the confidence that helped him build on his skills. He traveled independently in the city using public transportation, he developed friendships, and he made valuable contributions as a volunteer in several community programs. Some years ago, there was an evening when I felt immeasurable happiness for my son. He danced all night at his cousin's wedding, wearing out one dance partner after another. Other young people gathered around him to clap and cheer his energy. Several young men said things such as, "Look at that dude go!" and "That dude is somethin' else." My son, who had always liked to dance, was one of the guys that night. I was seeing the transformation—Duane had become "that dude" whom the other young people accepted and befriended. He belonged.

Ursula Arceneaux Markey and her husband D.J. co-direct Pyramid Parent Training, a Community Parent Resource Center in New Orleans. The center is funded by the U.S. Department of Education. The Markeys, along with parent associates and staff, also provide support to families of children and youth with behavior challenges through Operation Positive Change. This program, funded by the Institute of Mental Hygiene of New Orleans, is designed to bring the best research-based practices in positive behavior support to families in traditionally underserved communities.

REFERENCES

Americans with Disabilities Act (ADA) of 1990, PL 101-336, 42 U.S.C. §§ 12101 *et seq.*

Civil Rights Act of 1964, PL 88-352, 20 U.S.C. §§ 241 *et seq.*

Koegel, L.K., Koegel, R.L., & Dunlap, G. (Eds.). (1996). *Positive behavioral support: Including people with difficult behavior in the community.* Baltimore: Paul H. Brookes Publishing Co.

CHAPTER *15*

Comprehensive Lifestyle Support

From Rhetoric to Reality

Ann P. Turnbull and H. Rutherford Turnbull, III

Authors' Note

We wrote the following chapter in 1998, describing JT's and our lives at that time. Since then, there have been some changes. JT has qualified for three kinds of federal-state benefits: Medicaid (Home Community Based Services), housing (Section 8 rent subsidies), and Social Security Disability Insurance. These make it possible to secure some of the outcomes that we only envisioned in this chapter and that we could not otherwise afford.

None of the benefits, however, change our basic messages: To assist JT and others to "get a life," families must marshal a wide range of reliable allies and must employ multiple strategies. Moreover, the service delivery and research communities must adapt their policies and practices, just as they ask people with disabilities and families to adapt to their frameworks.

Can the "family context" accommodate behavioral challenges? Of course. It always has and always will. But the family and the person who present those challenges should not be asked to go it alone; few families can, and none wants to.

As a family we have made a sustained effort, expanded on a daily basis since 1988, to support our son, JT, to "get a life" outside of the established service delivery systems where we live. Nothing that we have done in our professional work has been as challenging or as rewarding as discovering the authentic meaning of *comprehensive lifestyle support* that is present on a day-to-day basis. Our journey toward attaining this goal has been both harder and easier than we ever imagined. In this chapter, we describe JT's life as it is today and review the lessons we have learned, hopeful that our successes and failures, and our process, will be useful to others.

This chapter is adapted from a previously published article: From Comprehensive lifestyle support for adults with challenging behavior: From rhetoric to reality by A.P. Turnbull & R. Turnbull, *Education and Training in Mental Retardation and Developmental Disabilities*, 34(4), 1999, 373–394. Copyright 1999 by The Council for Exceptional Children. Reprinted with permission.

WHO IS JT?

JT is (if we may say so) a handsome 31-year-old man. His love of life—his *joie de vivre*—derives from his relationships with his family and friends and from his soulful love of music. These facts are often obscured under his four "labels." When JT was an infant, he received the label of low-moderate mental retardation. In his adolescence he acquired the label of autism. In 1997, he acquired the labels of bipolar disorder and obsessive-compulsive disorder (OCD). Much is written today about people with a dual diagnosis, and JT definitely has challenges related to cognition and mental health. When he is at the stable point of his bipolar cycle, JT is cheerful, relational with others, and self-determined. He derives genuine pleasure from his many activities. When he slips from that stable state into depression, he becomes sad, socially aloof, and nearly incapable of making a decision. When he accelerates into the opposite polarity, he can be excessively cheerful, often silly and babyish; he engages in extensive self-talk rather than interacting with others, has difficulty sleeping, and is unyieldingly insistent on having his own way. One of our greatest challenges is to choreograph and calibrate his supports in light of his rapidly changing moods and anxiety levels, which vary not just week to week but sometimes as often as hour to hour.

Although JT is 31 years old, we continue to be challenged by mood and anxiety states that we do not fully understand. Mental retardation seems "simple"; we shudder when bipolarity captures JT or when OCD imprisons him. The bottom line is that JT presents enormous complexity.

WHAT IS COMPREHENSIVE LIFESTYLE SUPPORT?

Comprehensive lifestyle support often is the purported goal of positive behavior support (PBS). As stated by Carr and colleagues, "The goal of positive behavior support . . . is to apply behavioral principles in the community in order to reduce problem behaviors and build appropriate behaviors that result in durable behavior change and a rich lifestyle" (1999, p. 3). There is, no consensus about the meaning of a *rich lifestyle*. There is, however, a consensus on the technique to achieve it, namely through comprehensive intervention. As Horner and Carr noted,

> An intervention is comprehensive when it (a) addresses all problem behaviors performed by an individual; (b) is driven by the functional assessment; (c) is applied throughout the day; (d) blends multiple intervention procedures (change in structure, instruction, consequences); and (e) incorporates procedures that are consistent with the values, skills, and resources of the implementers. (1997, p. 94).

Implicit in the Carr and colleagues (1999) and Horner and Carr (1997) approaches is the premise that an intervention, or several of them, can indeed address all behaviors. In JT's case, interventions would address impairments associated with the rather stable condition of mental retardation and the variable conditions associated with autism, bipolarity, and OCD. Also implicit is the premise that the interventions are applied throughout the day. In JT's case, they are integral parts of his daily routines and of the routines of those who interact with him, such as his family, housemates, co-workers, and friends. Those two premises should be put under the microscope, for they are formidable to achieve.

PRELUDE TO GETTING A LIFE

When we first started working on comprehensive interventions, we had no idea how encompassing our task would be. Creating comprehensive supports 24 hours per day, 7 days per week, 52 weeks per year, is a daunting task in and of itself. We have learned over the years, however, that JT does not just need one all-purpose comprehensive lifestyle support plan. Rather, he needs plans that are calibrated according to his mood and anxiety cycles and to the interaction of those two cycles. Allow us to recount how we learned this lesson.

In 1987, when JT was 19 years old, he was terminated from the only adult agency in our community because of a mismatch between the program's services and his challenging behavior. His program involved being at the high school for half of the day and being at the local adult agency the other half of the day. He did not believe that he "had a life" in either place. Within the adult agency, his behavioral challenges escalated to daily occurrences. He frequently was aggressive toward others, refused to get up in the morning, and destroyed his personal belongings. It was a nightmarish experience for him and for us as a family. We were getting daily telephone calls reporting in excruciating detail his most recent behavior. We dreaded hearing the telephone ring, for it always seemed to herald another round of devastating news.

A moment of reckoning came for us when a good family friend commented, "No matter how far down the wrong road you go, if it's the wrong road, turn around." We realized that the road of traditional services would never lead us to the destination of our visions. No matter how hard we and the agency staff worked or wanted things to work out for JT, he and we were simply on the wrong road.

Indelibly imprinted in our memories is our last meeting with the agency director. That meeting resulted in JT's withdrawal from the agency program. We quit and the program expelled JT, simultaneously. That parting being a given, we described for the agency director our vision of JT having a home, a job, friends, and places where he could hang out in the community. After listening to our visions, the administrator asked, "What are you going to do when you fail?" This was his not-too-subtle way of reminding us that his agency was the only program in town and that we probably would have to return to it, put our names on the bottom of the waiting list, and wait for traditional services. At that point, his dad Rud responded, "We're not going to fail; we're going to succeed. And that's not a threat, it's a promise." Making the promise, however, proved much easier than keeping it. How we tried—how we keep on trying—is worthy of extended discussion, for therein lie the lessons for others.

GENERAL COMPONENTS OF JT'S LIFE

It is impossible to capture on paper the many compositional nuances of JT's lifestyle. Figure 15.1 provides a snapshot of his daily and weekly schedule. The key components are friends, home, work, "*Cheers* connections," and family.

Friends

As we recall JT's life before he left the adult agency, we remember how very few peer friendships he had. True, he had many family friends and participated in numerous social out-

Time	Monday	Tuesday	Wednesday	Thursday	Friday	Saturday	Sunday
7:00 A.M.–8:00 A.M.	Morning routine with Stacie	Morning routine with Anne	Morning routine with Stacie	Morning routine with Anne	Morning routine with Stacie	Morning routine with his father	Morning routine with his father
8:30 A.M.–9:00 A.M.	Breakfast at a restaurant with Stacie	Breakfast at home	Breakfast at home	Breakfast at home	Breakfast at home	Breakfast with his father	Breakfast at home
9:00 A.M.–9:45 A.M.	Bus ride to work	Bus ride to work	Bus ride to work	Bus ride to work	Bus ride to work	Workout with Katie S.	
10:00 A.M.–12:00 P.M.	Work	Work	Work	Work	Work	Errands with his parents	Church with his parents and grandfather
12:00 P.M.–12:30 P.M.	12:00 P.M.–1:00 P.M. speech-language therapy and lunch with Loren	Lunch with Kate T.	Lunch with Katie S.	Lunch with Marilyn	Lunch with his co-workers	Lunch with his parents	Lunch with his parents and grandfather
12:30 P.M.–2:00 P.M.	Work	Work	Work	Work	Work	Visit with his grandfather	Visit with his parents
2:00 P.M.–3:00 P.M.	Bus ride home	Bus ride home	Bus ride home	Bus ride home	Bus ride home	Visit with his grandfather	Visit with his parents
3:00 P.M.–6:00 P.M.	3:30 P.M.–4:20 P.M. Music class	Workout with Jennifer	3:30 P.M.–4:20 P.M. Music class	Speech-language therapy with Loren; Workout with Jennifer	3:30 P.M.–4:20 P.M. Music class	Visit with his parents	Visit and dinner with his parents, sisters, and grandfather
6:00 P.M.–9:00 P.M.	Dinner with housemates and guests	Dinner with his housemates	Natural Ties	Dinner and music with Mike	Dinner and music with Terrie	Dinner with his parents; watch Statler Brothers	Grocery shopping with Richard
9:00 P.M.–9:30 P.M.	Evening walk	Evening walk	Evening walk	Evening walk	Dinner and music with Terrie	Visit with his parents	Evening walk

Figure 15.1. JT's weekly schedule. (From Comprehensive lifestyle support for adults with challenging behavior: From rhetoric to reality by A.P. Turnbull & R. Turnbull, *Education and Training in Mental Retardation and Developmental Disabilities, 34*[4], 1999, 373–394. Copyright 1999 by The Council for Exceptional Children. Reprinted with permission.)

ings with people who were paid or who were receiving practicum credit for being with him, but he had few peer friendships during his childhood and youth.

Because friendship necessarily involves a give-and-receive exchange, we were determined to create friendships; we were dissatisfied with JT being a "client." That was not fulfilling for JT; us; or, in most cases, the dedicated and lively young people who were his "providers." There is nothing inherently wrong with a client– or practicum–recipient relationship, but there is vaster richness and fulfillment in a friendship.

Since JT's exit from the established service delivery system in 1988, we have placed a high priority on creating opportunities for JT to have friends and to be a friend. Because friends are people who have a common ground, a number of his friends are musicians who share his passion for music. One of our most valuable friendship facilitators is Dr. Alice-Ann Darrow, a member of the music therapy faculty at The University of Kansas (KU).

For 10 years, Dr. Darrow has been the link between her students and JT. She has selected students for practicum experiences with JT, and, over time, many have become his friends. Over the years, JT has hung out with these friends, has gone to community musical events with them, has received formal music therapy from them, and has had dinner with them on a regular basis. Some of these music therapy students and friends have even been JT's housemates.

The lesson that JT, Dr. Darrow, and her students have taught us is twofold. First, find a "door opener." A *door opener* is a person or an entity that can identify the common interests that those with disabilities and those without disabilities have so that friendships can evolve; friendship requires an open-door policy. Second, connect the door openers to one of JT's passions (in his case, music); friendship requires a common ground. Mike Brownell, a music therapy graduate student, describes how he and JT combined music therapy and friendship facilitation:

> *There are two major foci to JT's involvement with music therapy: decreasing problem behaviors and increasing overall quality of life. Because of the ease with which JT memorizes song lyrics, it becomes natural to use this modality to impart important information by changing lyrics to familiar songs or creating new songs. The lyrics might include a simple task analysis of what JT is or is not supposed to be doing in a given situation. Some behaviors that we have addressed include pouring mouthwash down the sink (to the tune of "Let It Be"), getting up in the morning (to the tune of "Wake Up Little Susie"), and hair pulling, using original lyrics that JT helped create. To increase quality of life, my goal as a music therapist is to increase the breadth of JT's relationship with music. One of JT's greatest accomplishments since I have been working with him has been learning to play the guitar. With minimal cuing, JT is able to play simple folk songs on his guitar and sing simultaneously. This provides the opportunity for success in a medium in which he feels intense pride, and it can be used as a basis for interaction with his other friends. As one of the most capable individuals in his group music therapy sessions, JT is able to put his musical facility to work as a model and leader to others in the group, a position he might not frequently be afforded.*
>
> *As much as I have tried to teach and do for JT, he has returned as much in kind. JT's musical abilities are every musical therapist's dream. His enthusiasm and passion for the medium is both inspiring and instructive. He has demonstrated to me, more than any other client or friend, the capacity of music to change behaviors and*

to forge friendships. JT's affinity for music has enabled him to relate on some common ground with old and new friends, co-workers, and family members alike.

Friendship for JT is like friendships among people who do not have disabilities; it spans various types of people and is multidimensional. Entry into friendship does not have to be based on a single set of door openers, a single set of people. For example, JT has lunch each Wednesday with a college student, Katie Schwartzburg, who was our next-door neighbor during her elementary through high school years. She emphasizes the reciprocity of their friendship as follows:

> *I've known JT since I was a little girl, so being a part of his life came very naturally to me. JT and I have had our good days and not-so-good days together, but we usually have good times. I have lunch with JT on Wednesdays and work out and/or have a snack with him on Saturday mornings. I have found the time I spend with JT to be of great value. He has inspired me to become a special educator. He has taught me patience, because I have had to wait for him to answer me or to catch up to my speed of doing everything. Although I am there to be JT's friend and helper, I have found I am the one who has been helped. For example, some elementary school students once teased JT when we were taking a walk near his home. I wanted to chastise them, but JT just ignored them. He taught me about hostile and forgiving attitudes and about the security of being comfortable with one's self. I have found JT to be totally honest and amazingly aware of his surroundings. The more time I spend with JT, the more I learn about him and myself. I truly value the time I get to spend with JT.*

Friendships based on a one-to-one ratio—such as those we have just described—are perfectly fine, but they do not exclude the group friendships that many people without disabilities experience through membership in various organizations. For JT, the group friendship that he most values occurs each Wednesday night (and on other occasions) when he participates in Natural Ties.

Natural Ties is a student-directed organization in which KU students and adults with disabilities get together on a regular basis to share friendship and enjoy themselves. Although most of the adults with disabilities in Natural Ties are matched with KU campus organizations, JT has a match with five students (nicknamed "The Jackson Five" because they all love music) rather than an organization. Their Wednesday night activities include country line dancing (JT's favorite), bowling, movies, dinners, and similar group activities. Sarah Ellestad is a KU student who is JT's friend in Natural Ties:

I guess describing my relationship with JT would be the same as if someone had asked me to describe my relationship with any of my other friends. When I think of true friendship, I think that it means being able to love someone for all of their good qualities and then being able to love them even more for their not-so-good qualities. So, I will describe my relationship with JT based on this definition.

First of all, I know that JT is a good friend because when I am with him, I can sing old, goofy songs as loud as I want and "dance" around in my truck while driving down the street and JT will not make fun of me. In fact, he joins right in with me, and if I listen closely enough while he sings, I can catch all of the words to the songs that I could never for the life of me figure out. But this is just one reason why JT is my friend. I could talk about JT's sense of humor or how he has the ability to cheer me up without even knowing it, just by giving me a soft-five {a handshake that is his variation of a high-five} or saying, "You look nice today, Sarah."

However, like everyone, JT also has his faults. For example, I guess I never will understand why some days JT will not get out of bed even if he knows that it is Wednesday, the day we go to Natural Ties together. Although I do not understand why he does this, I do know how much he loves Natural Ties. Furthermore, I know that if JT misses Natural Ties, he must really be going through some rough times. There were also a few days in the last months when I went to pick JT up that his roommates warned me that he recently pulled someone's hair. This information is always followed by strict orders to bring JT home if I see even the slightest sign of such behaviors. Again, I don't understand why he sometimes pulls people's hair because I know that he is not the kind of person who would purposely try to hurt someone. I have never seen this side of JT, but I know that it does exist. Of course, I hope that I never see the day that JT pulls my hair. However, I do know that if it does happen, there is no way that I would ever stop being JT's friend.

When it comes down to it, my friendship with JT really does not differ from any of my other friendships. Like all of my friends, JT has his share of faults. Of course his faults may differ from others'; then again, not one of my friends is like the other. Furthermore, I know that JT is my friend because all of the things that I like about JT allow me to truly accept him for who he is despite our differences.

Challenging behavior can impair friendships. On a few occasions, JT has pulled his friends' hair, and on more occasions he has broken their glasses. His friends need information and support in how to handle these behaviors, especially when he becomes fixated on hair and ponytails. There are times when we worry at our innermost core about JT's hurting his friends when his mood, anxiety, and behaviors are at a very difficult place. We also worry about how open to be with his friends from the outset. When he is having very few challenging behaviors, we don't want to share information with friends that will make them afraid of or put off by him. It is difficult to balance the equation of how much to tell people and how much to withhold.

Pointers for Facilitating Friendships at the Individual Level   The development of friendships should not be left to chance. Everyone in JT's network needs (and truly wants) to be on the lookout for people who might be interested in being friends with JT and to think about how to introduce those people to JT. Before several of JT's longtime friends moved out of his life, they "recruited" people who might be interested in being JT's friends and brought them along on outings for a couple of months before departing. In this way, they took personal responsibility for replenishing his social network.

People who are new in JT's friendship network often have questions about how they can best support JT when he engages in unusual behavior. It is helpful if newly introduced people can get to know JT by hanging out with him and one of his longtime friends during the "warm-up process." In addition, we have parties several times per year, each one attended by many of JT's friends. These happenings help them get to know and become friends with each other. The more we build a sense of community around JT, the more the communal sense gratifies everyone else.

Each semester, a speech-language student works with JT in a practicum arrangement. Several of these students have worked with JT in learning important information about his friends (e.g., their birthdays, the names of their pets, their favorite television shows, their upcoming plans) so that JT can more easily engage in reciprocal conversations with them. This makes him a more interesting conversation partner and also lightens the conversational load because JT can help carry it.

With the assistance of his housemate, Anne Guthrie, JT e-mails his friends daily. He dictates what he wants to say, and Anne types his words. Nearly everyone likes to receive a cheerful note; JT and Anne make that possible, and, by so doing, they invite others to reciprocate. We also support JT in remembering his friends on special occasions through gifts or other thoughtful gestures. Being a friend means acting like one, and giving on others' special occasions is an especially memorable way of demonstrating friendship.

Pointers for Facilitating Friendships at the Systems Level   Research is needed to document best practices in friendship facilitation starting at the early intervention level. The reciprocity related to companionship, informational support between friends, and emotional support between friends must be emphasized (Turnbull, Blue-Banning, & Pereira, 2000). A rich friendship literature exists for typical children and increasingly for individuals with severe disabilities, which should serve as a guide in providing supports and services related to the strengths, needs, and preferences of individuals with problem behavior.

In addition, friendship facilitation is not an integral part of most educational programs for individuals with behavior problems. This important quality-of-life aspect needs to be a priority outcome of instructional effectiveness. It should be incorporated in educational and rehabilitation programs across the life span for individuals with problem behavior who want more rewarding friendships. Funding is also needed for friendship facilitators to be companions of individuals with behavior problems. These facilitators can then link such individuals with others who have similar interests and foster relationships that move from the level of acquaintance to intimate friend.

A Home of His Own

JT has lived in his own home since 1989. We have been in the most fortunate position of being able to purchase a three-bedroom ranch-style house in a neighborhood that is near

KU. It is in a stable neighborhood, and his home is on a bus route to the university, where he works.

The title and mortgage are in our names, so we receive a tax deduction for the interest on the mortgage and for the real estate property taxes. Yet, JT earns enough to pay the mortgage (principal, interest, taxes, and insurance) with his monthly salary, and he makes his net income available to us for that purpose.

JT has two housemates who live with him without paying rent or utilities. They do not receive any wages, but their basic housing expenses are covered. Each provides JT with approximately 12–15 hours of personal support a week. We do not have any formal "job description" or "duty list." Each set of roommates individually negotiates with each other, JT, and us to develop a routine with which everyone feels comfortable.

To date, JT has had 15 housemates—always two at a time. The shortest stay was for a couple of months, the longest was for 2 years. On two different occasions, the housemates have been a married couple; at other times, they have been two single people. We have found housemates through friends in the community who provide services to individuals with developmental disabilities, through JT's friendship network, and through word of mouth.

JT's week, as reflected in Figure 15.1, includes being at his home throughout the work week and then coming to our home on the weekend. The weekend change allows JT to connect closely with us and provides his housemates an opportunity to pursue their own interests. If and when JT qualifies for the Medicaid waiver in the future and we have additional financial resources to pay for support, he may well stay at his own home on most weekends with weekend companionship paid for through his financial resources.

All of JT's housemates have had unique strengths, preferences, and needs. JT's current housemates, Anne Guthrie and Richard Gaeta, excel in creating a home with warmth, caring, hospitality, and delicious food. Richard is an outstanding cook, and JT and his friends are extremely fortunate to reap the benefits of Richard's culinary talents. In addition to preparing wonderful food for the three of them, Richard, Anne, and JT also routinely invite guests over on Monday nights. They have an enjoyable evening of friendship, conversation, laughter, and delicious food. This is a way for JT reciprocate with his friends, providing unique opportunities for their enjoyment.

We have tried to avoid having JT's housemates become "residential staff." Yet, we also have tried to make it possible for them to support JT in a professionally competent way, for he needs various kinds of support in daily-living skills. He especially needs emotional/behavioral support at those times when his bipolarity or OCD behaviors become problematic.

The role of housemates of people with challenging behavior has received scant attention, although it is critically important. As we learned from JT's original housemates, Jesus and Shahla, and as we learned again and again from subsequent housemates, the fundamental issue is how to develop a relationship so that the housemates and JT are truly in tune and have a relationship that fosters JT's self-determination and sense of security. Housemates also have to be prepared to assist JT with some personal needs, go through the phases of challenging behavior, problem-solve with his family and friends, and help schedule and coordinate his multiple activities. Anne Guthrie described the relationship that she and Richard have with JT:

> *After nearly 2 years of sharing JT's home, Richard and I think the three of us almost have the rhythms of our co-existence down. We hope that JT shares our opinion. What has been essential for all of us is the continuous availability and support of*

JT's family and longtime friends. This was especially critical during our first few months as housemates when we were still learning to interpret JT's verbal and non-verbal communications. The process of negotiating shared space and routines, providing pertinent information, and honoring preferences is most easily accomplished through clear communications. Although JT is more than capable of recalling complex song lyrics and the names of long-lost friends, as well as their favorite expressions, his ability to express his feelings, describe a situation, or explain an action are limited and unreliable. Thus, it was important to have his circle of friends and family available to JT to help him explain his preferences for such things as furniture arrangement, assistance in personal care, and relaxation activities. JT's adjustment to having two new people "intrude upon his home and routines" would surely have been more tumultuous without this support.

Although we all seem to be more adept now at understanding each other's spoken and unspoken languages now, JT's inability to verbally communicate his needs during episodes of especially challenging behavior—times when he is typically less responsive—still causes great frustration for us and all who know him. At such times, the support of a second housemate and/or others close to JT is vital. Housemates' negotiations with each other are essential. We have done this through establishing a routine whereby Richard typically is available to JT for certain parts of the day, while JT and I typically spend other times of the day together. While we frequently do things altogether, or individually, it is helpful to have a routine to fall back on at difficult times, both for JT's reassurance and for our own need for respite.

The most chronic and problematic of JT's challenging behaviors at home is his extreme difficulty in getting up in the morning. When he is depressed or anxious, he often simply will not budge from bed. He now has a "morning coach" who goes to his house 3 days per week, and Anne coaches him the other 2 days. They use a very specific behavioral program of prompting, which is usually but not always successful. About once per week, JT refuses to get up. On that day, he does not come to work and he also loses all of his special daily activities. This is hard on his housemates because he typically stays in bed for the major portion of the day. It also means that we receive "SOS" calls from his housemates and usually have to intervene to get JT up and moving. If his morning coach, housemates, and parents fail to help JT overcome his biobehavioral shutdown, JT is at loose ends in the afternoon and evening, having no organized activities.

Pointers for Living in and Enjoying a Home of One's Own at the Individual Level   Given JT's wide-ranging needs and his and our vision of a rich lifestyle characterized by independence from his parents and achievement of his own home, we have learned at least the following lessons. First, all housemates have their own strengths, preferences, and needs. The focus has to be on building a home that is responsive to them as well as to JT. Second, we try to be as flexible as possible in backing up the housemates when they need to be away because of an emergency or when they want some time off. Likewise, they support us when we are not able to be home on the weekends. Flexibility and informality are the ingredients of mutually responsive collective living. Third, we need to explore creative ways of providing compensation to housemates if we want to be able to retain them for a long period of time. When JT qualifies for the Medicaid waiver, we will be able to provide more attractive compensation to regular housemates. In addition, we will have funding for someone to provide more intensive support in the mornings for the wake-up routine and to cover weekend support. This will mean that JT will not need to stay at our house every weekend and that his housemates can have a more spontaneous schedule.

Pointers for Living in and Enjoying a Home of One's Own at the Systems Level Researchers should interview housemates of individuals with problem behavior to codify what they have learned about their important role. Veteran housemates might be available to support new housemates in learning the ropes of sharing a home with an individual with autism, for example. Research is also needed to document the most effective way to provide supports and services within a home to build on strengths and preferences and to enhance quality of life to the greatest possible degree.

Federal and state policies are needed that subsidize community living and home ownership for people with problem behavior. Families need policy assistance, whether in the form of subsidized rent, tax credits, heightened tax deductions, and/or Medicaid Waiver allotments. Other policies are needed to create funding strands that can be used to provide compensation to housemates, home consultants, home coaches (similar to job coaches), and other personnel who enable people with challenging behavior to have a home of their own. In addition to salary, attention needs to be directed at benefit packages.

Finally, from the earliest years, educational and rehabilitation programs should focus on developing knowledge and skills that enhance successful home living. Major changes are needed in preservice and in-service development so that educators and service providers are prepared to provide this training and an infrastructure of training and consultation support for housemates.

Work

We must be candid at the outset: We make it possible for JT to have a job because we co-direct the Beach Center on Disability at KU, where JT is an employee. To comply with university rules, we do not supervise and evaluate his work. The fact is, however, that JT works with our support. The university does not object to this situation; without JT as our "best professor" and inspiration, we would not have had the wisdom and courage to create the Beach Center, nor the determination for it to be a force for change on behalf of families with children who have disabilities. In addition, our federal funding agencies give any applicant for grant money some bonus points in scoring the application if the applicant employs people with disabilities. Thus, JT's employment has an additional value to our university.

JT works from 10:00 A.M. until 2:00 P.M. 5 days per week as a clerical aide. He copies, collates, staples, folds mail, stuffs envelopes, stamps mail, and delivers the mail and the huge amount of materials that the Beach Center disseminates each week. JT has a job coach who provides him with instruction on new tasks, supports him through his mood and anxiety cycles, and helps staff know how to best provide support to JT. Jaimie Swanger, his current job coach, described JT's work situation as follows:

> JT's work at the Beach Center is essential to everyone who works here. JT's main role at the Beach Center is to collect and distribute the large amount of mail that comes in and goes out every day. There are more than 25 people employed at the Beach Center, and JT is responsible for all of their mail, including federal mail, international mail, and KU campus mail. JT's mail routes keep him quite busy for the majority

of his employment here. When JT has completed his morning and afternoon mail routes, time is allotted for JT to assist the office staff by doing clerical activities like copying, stapling, collating, and putting together dissemination materials that are distributed by the Beach Center on a daily basis.

My main role as JT's job coach is to motivate JT to come to work on a daily basis and to keep him busy learning new tasks and interacting with his co-workers. The Beach Center staff have been very supportive of JT through the years and consistently support him through his different moods and anxiety cycles. Many staff members regularly ask JT for assistance on specific tasks, some mail related and others not. The staff interact with him daily and count on JT's being there for assistance, support, or a friendly soft-five.

Although JT is employed at the same organization as his parents, the central office supervisor and his immediate supervisor delegate his office work and monitor his work-related behavior. When inappropriate work behaviors occur, it is up to the central office supervisor to decide whether JT can work the rest of the day or needs a half day off to go home. When JT has a difficult mood and/or anxiety cycle, the Beach Center staff pull together to increase JT's work support by talking with him more, giving him more positive feedback, or even taking him out to breakfast or lunch. JT's employment at the Beach Center is an ongoing learning experience for all of us who work with him. He enriches our lives in ways that only he is capable of. He works hard, giggles at our jokes, and is continually available for assistance or a soft-five.

Would JT have a job like this if we were not his parents and in a position to hire him? Almost certainly not. We are acutely aware of how unusual it is for us to be able to make this opportunity available to our son. Providing this opportunity, though, also has downsides for us. JT's performance and his behavior are always on our minds, given that we share the same work setting 5 days per week. When JT encounters problems at work or displays challenging behaviors, we have the ultimate responsibility for problem resolution. It would be refreshing to have respite from these employer and parent responsibilities, but, overall, we accept the downsides for JT to have this opportunity.

JT has been aggressive only a few times while working at the Beach Center. That is problematic for staff; however, they are alerted by us and JT's job coach when JT may be on the cusp of aggression. With this alert comes accommodations from staff to JT—always simple accommodations that do not inconvenience staff or disrupt anyone's work. Yet, there are others in the building where JT works who are not so easily alerted or are not able (as our Beach Center staff are) to detect the early warning signs that JT is apt to be aggressive.

It seems paradoxical—an unexpected outcome—that from the hard times JT faces at work, there comes a solidarity of the Beach Center staff, a cohesiveness that only JT creates, a recommitment to him personally and, thus, to the collective mission of the Beach Center. When all of us do something to benefit JT at the times he is most challenged and challenging, it benefits us individually and collectively by teaching us more about challenging behaviors and by causing us to rise to meet and overcome the obstacles of those behaviors. We all benefit, as do our friends and colleagues throughout the special education field. We learn what we have not learned before, we relearn what we have forgotten, or we learn what no research yet seems to be able to teach. More than that, we acquire a sense of shared adventure as all of us—JT, parents, and co-workers—embark on a journey of mutual life enrichment.

Pointers for Increasing Work Success at the Individual Level   Because JT's work productivity depends in part on his mood and anxiety cycles, job coaching and work accommodations need to respond accordingly. A static and uniform approach simply will not work. In addition, we try to teach JT new skills continually so that monotony does not become part of his work. It is extremely difficult, however, to find new jobs that he can learn given his cognitive, motor, emotional, and communicative impairments.

It is also extremely difficult to find qualified job coaches who can work from 10:00 A.M. until 2:00 P.M. each day. The problem is that most people interested in such a job are students or often have other part-time employment and it is difficult for them to be available for four consecutive hours in the middle of the day.

To the extent that is possible, we ensure that the work setting does not escalate JT's behaviors or create inordinate tension for his co-workers when JT is at difficult points of his mood and anxiety cycles. We constantly have to balance being caring and sensitive to his needs without our own moods and anxiety levels cycling with his. There also is a fine line between supporting JT when he may be close to aggressive outbursts and ensuring the safety and security of his co-workers. By being candid with everyone in his workplace about his anxiety and behaviors, enlisting their support, and alerting them when JT is in a "hard" cycle, we try to balance these competing interests. Privacy is foregone, work is retained, and community is built.

Pointers for Increasing Work Success at the Systems Level   Wehman, Revell, and Kregel (1997) estimated that approximately 140,000 individuals with developmental disabilities are in supported employment making a mean average wage of $4.70 per hour and working an average of 24 hours per week. Wehman and colleagues reported specifically on individuals with mental retardation, mental illness, physical disabilities, and other disabilities. Of these individuals with disabilities, it is likely that individuals with challenging behavior have the hardest time maintaining competitive employment. Aside from that fact, however, is the systemic problem of low wages and the part-time work that characterizes supported employment for individuals with developmental disabilities. Greater attention needs to be given to increasing income by expanding the number of hours and career advancement opportunities that are available, especially for individuals with problem behavior.

Less than .5% of individuals with disabilities who receive Social Security join the work force and are removed from the Social Security rolls on an annual basis (Wehman et al., 1997). Hundreds of thousands of people with disabilities still remain in segregated workshops. Long-term job coaching and enhanced natural supports are critical for individuals with challenging behavior to be successful in competitive work and to maintain their jobs. Greater attention needs to be given to recruiting, training, and compensating job coaches.

Greater attention also needs to be given to government-mediated supports, including Social Security work incentives, the use of the Medicaid waiver for long-term job coach support, and tax credits. Families need assistance in understanding what is available and in easing the tremendous investments of time and energy that are now required to receive benefits.

Facilitating *Cheers* Connections

We use the term "*Cheers* connections" to recall the type of chemistry that happened on the television program *Cheers,* in which people had a place to go where everyone knew their names. It is especially important to JT to have places in the community where he is considered to be a regular. We think about *Cheers* connections as part of the evolutionary process of having friends. Once you have friends, you start going places and hanging out. Once you start hanging out regularly, relationships typically evolve so that you can indeed become a regular.

JT's schedule (see Figure 15.1) shows that he has many different *Cheers* connections, including a community mercantile cooperative, his church, a fitness club, several restaurants, a video store, and a barber shop. JT is a regular because he knows what to do, how to behave, where the restroom is, and so forth. He also is a regular because many of the people in these places know him and his idiosyncrasies. They greet him by using his soft-five handshake and the fraternity grip that he learned while associated with the Sigma Alpha Epsilon chapter at KU, both of which he gives to nearly everyone (often to their dismay at first and later to their pleasure).

The incredible value of having *Cheers* connections was illustrated during an incident that Anne, JT's housemate, reported to us. She and JT were at a local brewery having dinner. JT needed to go to the restroom and ended up staying there for an inordinate length of time. Anne became worried and was about to ask one of the waiters to check on him when JT came out of the restroom. Later on during dinner, a waiter came by the table and asked JT if he was doing okay. He then explained to Anne that he had gone in the restroom when a man was about to grab JT and push him into the wall. The man felt that JT was staring at him inappropriately, and he perceived that JT was propositioning him for a homosexual encounter. When the waiter walked in and saw this incident, he quickly defended JT and explained to the man that JT was not propositioning him. That's the essence of a *Cheers* connection—when the regulars look out for you and vouch for you when problems arise that cannot be fully anticipated.

Pointers for Facilitating Cheers *Connections at the Individual Level* It is critical to make friends with the staff and regular patrons of various *Cheers* connections and to provide them the information and support that they need to be comfortable with JT. We tell these individuals how much they contribute to JT's quality of life and how grateful he is and we are to them. We also invite them to JT's parties as a way of bringing them into his community of support.

Because there are often new people in these settings, Anne made a wallet-size fold-out card that JT can give to people. The information provides a foundation so that people can begin to get to know him personally and determine how to best provide support and friendship. This card is presented in Figure 15.2.

When JT seems to be edging close to challenging behavior, we encourage him to not go to the various *Cheers* connections. Sometimes, we simply divert him from going to these places to avoid an untenable situation.

Pointers for Facilitating Cheers *Connections at the Systems Level* Research is needed on best practices for facilitating *Cheers* connections in a variety of community locations—especially those where the regulars share the same interests as the individual with behavior problems. Funding streams must be flexible so that *Cheers* connections companions can be compensated for serving as facilitators in the individual's becoming a "regular." Policies are needed that enable community establishments to welcome individuals with problem behavior.

Hi. I'm glad to have you as a new friend, and I look forward to having some great times with you!

Because I sometimes have difficulty letting new friends know some things that are important to me, my friends and I wrote this for you to read and keep.

$$$$$$$$$ Money $$$$$$$$$

I usually have cash in my wallet but need help counting it. I also have a checkbook that I like to use when I'm shopping or paying for a meal. You can help by filling out the check, then I will sign it and give it to the cashier.

!!!!!!!!!! My Favorite Things to Do !!!!!!!!!!!!

Music is my main love—listening, singing, and dancing to it. I also like exercising, walking, playing catch, going to stores or movies, and eating out.

#%#! Things that I Really Don't Like #%#!

I don't like bad weather and slippery sidewalks, big hugs and hard handshakes, or being talked to lots when I am trying to make a decision or am upset.

" " " " How I Show that I'm Upset " " " "

I show that I'm upset by saying, "No" or "I don't want to" or making a face, laughing a lot, clapping my hands fast, or maybe saying that my forehead is hot or my throat is sore.

~~~ Things that Help Me Calm Down ~~~

Remind me to take some deep breaths. Other things that help me calm down are listening to quiet music, singing a slow song, and *sometimes* getting a hug (ask me first).

+ + + Things I Need to Avoid Doing + + + (Please Remind Me if I Forget)

I need to avoid drinking lots of caffeinated drinks, touching and pulling people's hair, touching and breaking people's eyeglasses, touching people's car stereos without asking, shutting and locking people's car or room doors, talking about baby things (like baby powder), taking down posters, and ripping up papers.

Like you, most of the time I'm in a great mood—especially when I'm with my friends. If you ever have any questions, please call!

*** Important Telephone Numbers ***

My telephone number is_____.
(Anne and Richard are my housemates)

My parents' telephone number is _____.
(Ann and Rud Turnbull)

My work telephone number is _____.
(Jaimie is my job coach, and my parents work there, too)

Figure 15.2. JT's fold-out card. (From Comprehensive lifestyle support for adults with challenging behavior: From rhetoric to reality by A.P. Turnbull & R. Turnbull, *Education and Training in Mental Retardation and Developmental Disabilities, 34*[4], 1999, 373–394. Copyright 1999 by The Council for Exceptional Children. Reprinted with permission.)

Family

Family is definitely the bedrock of JT's support system. When JT left the service system in 1988, we all started down this new road of supporting JT to "get a life" through person-centered planning. Our version of person-centered planning is called *Group Action Planning (GAP)*. GAP involves a reiterative and long-term process of envisioning great expectations and working together through group support to transform these expectations into daily and weekly supports (Turnbull et al., 1996; Turnbull & Turnbull, 1996; Turnbull, Turnbull, & Blue-Banning, 1994).

For several years, JT's action group met on a regular basis. Now, we have evolved into a highly informal and flexible group. We gather the critical people across all of JT's environments when new or recurring issues need to be addressed. On a fairly regular basis, we meet with his housemates, job coach, morning coach, behavior specialists, co-workers, and close friends to steer the overall efforts and troubleshoot the problems that arise.

As JT's service coordinators, we help orchestrate all of the previously described components. We are also JT's support on weekends and holidays. The advantage of this approach is that we have maximum flexibility to design his PBS and to advance his and our great expectations.

The downside of our approach is that it is extremely time consuming. Most of his service coordination and support falls on us. Given that we both have jobs that take about 150% effort from each of us, in addition to having two other children and an elderly parent for whom we provide daily caregiving, there is rarely an unclaimed minute in our lives. It is often hard to keep our energy levels sufficiently high to give JT's comprehensive lifestyle support network the time and attention that it requires.

Aside from the sheer number of hours that it takes to plan, implement, and monitor comprehensive lifestyle support, the emotional toll of challenging behavior on families is often overlooked in the professional literature (Turnbull & Ruef, 1996, 1997). A critical issue for families is learning to cope emotionally with the ambiguity of not knowing when or how the challenging behavior is going to occur and what potentially serious circumstances may be on the horizon.

One key of coping is learning to handle both the pessimistic and optimistic possibilities that could accrue so that one can still have great expectations without undue risks. People often say, sometimes rather tritely, "There is dignity in risk"; yet, too much risk that results in a dangerous and hurtful situation is anything but dignifying. As much as we always want to support JT's self-determination, there are times when we have to restrict it by having an ever-present support person available to ensure his safety and the safety of others.

JT spends almost every weekend at our family home. He joins us on Saturday for errands and on Sunday for church and family chores. He spends Saturday afternoon at his grandfather's apartment, and his grandfather joins us at our home on Sunday for a day of family meals, conversation, and shared activity.

We take great delight in the reciprocal caregiving that JT and his grandfather provide each other. Of the five grandchildren, JT is the one who calls his grandfather every day and visits with him every week. JT's grandfather, who never took an active role in child care himself, is always eager to help in any way that he can with JT's support needs.

JT's sisters, Amy and Kate, are now 23 and 20, respectively. Kate has 1 year left of college and Amy will receive her master's degree in May and will be married in June 1999. Because they have attended KU, Amy and Kate have not only been siblings but also friends to JT. They have also been an ever-present back-up system for us whenever we needed help and they could provide it. They learned early on about JT's challenging behavior and what they and others can do to help decrease the likelihood of its occurrence. They worry when he goes through the cycles of depression and heightened anxiety, and their own moods sometimes fluctuate according to JT's emotional state.

In addition, Amy and Kate are aware of the enormous responsibilities that they might need to assume if we die before a person-centered support system with longevity can be created for JT. It is also inevitable that some day they will have a greater responsibility for decision making than they do now, as we will most likely predecease our children. On the one hand, we believe very strongly that Amy and Kate deserve the freedom to live their own lives and pursue their own dreams without being restricted by their brother's comprehensive lifestyle needs. On the other hand, we worry JT's state-of-art comprehensive lifestyle support is at risk without the safety net and structure of an agency. If something happened to us as the service coordinators and convenors of JT's action group, then an enormous hole would be left in his support system, and someone would need to fill it.

What are their perspectives on their relationship with their brother? Kate commented as follows:

> My lunches with JT on Tuesdays are usually the saving grace of my week. If he is in good spirits, then we listen and sing along to James Taylor and John Denver, chitchat over Wendy's Frosties and fries, and laugh a lot. On other days, when he is not in such good spirits, he nervously cleans my car and consistently asks about his schedule or other worries on his mind. Some days, he does not even make it to lunch, as he does not make it out of bed to go to work. I love my brother, perhaps more than anything in the world. His anxieties sometimes tire me, often frustrate me, and always concern me. See, I just want him to be happy, as we all do. So, when I think about what will happen after my parents die, and my sister and I "take on JT's life," I think about doing whatever it takes to continue those good days at Wendy's when he is courteous, affable, and happy. Lunch with my brother, loving and caring for my brother, has always been and will always be my first priority.

Although we are grateful for our daughter's lifelong commitment to JT, we also know Kate's aspirations for theater performance and the call to experience New York City's theater scene. We have cherished, nurtured, and delighted in her performance talents since she was a preschooler. How Kate will balance her priorities for a career (in which mobility is inherent), artistic expression, a committed relationship with a significant other, and her love for her brother will be part of our family's future journey and adventure. Like comprehensive lifestyle support, the rhetoric of family support is easy; the implementation is incredibly complex, with a multitude of potential conflicts of interest.

Pointers for Family Resilience at the Individual Level   Our family's quality of life will be substantially enhanced when JT receives the Medicaid waiver and services characterized by self-determination. This means that his action group will be able to develop a budget and receive direct funding to implement the budget in a way that will maximize JT's quality of life. The day that we can do that cannot come soon enough. We hope that within the next several months we will have funding to purchase the services and supports for which we have been paying as a family and to arrange for service coordination from providers other than ourselves.

We have found that it is critically important for us to communicate honestly with each other (and with other members of JT's action group) about our great expectations, what is working, and what needs to be improved. We also need to discuss our individual and collective capacities for investing time and energy or to acknowledge when we are at the end of our rope and need a break.

We need opportunities to totally get away from responsibilities, and we need to learn not to worry while we are jettisoning our duties. Over the years, we have taken family vacations without JT. That made us feel guilty at times, but we also knew that we needed opportunities to be together and to be free from the constant vigilance that JT requires. On some vacations, we found that JT was physically absent but emotionally present: We simply could not stop worrying about him. As family members, it is critically important to take mental vacations, knowing that for a certain amount of time, whatever happens is not part of our immediate responsibility.

Pointers for Family Resilience at the Systems Level

Pointers for Family Resilience at the Systems Level   The vast majority of family research is not particularly helpful to families. A participatory action research model is needed in which families and researchers work together on research questions and answers that truly make a significant and sustainable difference in the quality of family life (Turnbull, Friesen, & Ramirez, 1998). Then, families and researchers can work together in planning and implementing the research, as well as in partnering, disseminating research, and utilization of the research in service delivery agencies and policy-making forums. The problem is not so much a research-to-practice gap but that research is not related to the questions and issues that are relevant to families.

In addition, service providers must provide quality, state-of-art services. Families across the United States say that they are exhausted and frustrated from frequently having to take the initiative in requiring agencies to implement practices such as inclusion, self-determination instruction, and friendship facilitation. Families are resoundingly saying that major change only comes when they mount an incredible advocacy effort to hold service providers accountable. The fields of special education, psychology, and related services need to ensure that state-of-art practices exist within their own spheres. They should not be required by families to do their jobs well.

Families also need increased funding to purchase services from agencies and an array of informal community support options that best meet their needs. The most significant catalyst for family-centered services will come when families rather than agencies have purchasing power.

For a long time, we as a family have made the basic assumption that people in typical environments would not know how to address JT's challenging behavior. We have been surprised and delighted over the years with how many "ordinary people" have demonstrated fantastically good judgement and problem-solving abilities in handling situations that were totally new to them. We are learning to trust the community safety net, which at its most fundamental level is a web of human relationships, and the kindness of strangers—the "good Samaritans" in our midst.

SUMMARY OF JT'S SUPPORTS AND A VISION FOR THE FUTURE

This chapter highlights JT's comprehensive lifestyle but in no way covers all of the involved complexities and responsibilities. We have six professional degrees between us; sufficient financial resources to purchase the necessary help for JT; and an extensive network of caring family, friends, and professional colleagues who have gone the second, fifth, and even tenth mile in providing support to JT and to us. Nevertheless, it is still extremely demanding to "keep all of the balls juggling" for comprehensive behavioral support and to constantly calibrate the support in light of JT's changing mood and anxiety cycles. If it is a challenge for us, then how do single parents living in "challenged environments" with no financial or health care resources even begin to support their children with similar disabilities and challenging behavior?

Reconfigured Supports

What, then, are the desiderata for JT's enviable life? What, in the ultimate analysis, will make the greatest difference for him, his family (his parents and two sisters for as long as they outlive him), and society? In answering this question, we must bear in mind—and also bear in the sense of accommodating to the fact—that

- JT is 31 years old.

- It has taken him, us, his friends, the law, and society that long to achieve as much as he and we all have achieved so far.

- He will probably live for 30–40 more years.

- Regardless of the research that has been and will be done to address his inherent complexities or how laws and societal attitudes change over the next three to four decades (assuming the changes are favorable to JT, which is always debatable), research does not easily translate into policy, policy does not easily translate into practice, and progress can be made or delayed concerning the unknowns in JT's world.

Given these considerations, we are deeply disappointed by the data reported by Carr and colleagues (1999): Only 13% of the outcomes measured in research on PBS between the years 1988 and 1998 followed someone for 6 months or longer, and only 1% of the outcomes tracked people for 13 months or longer. Despite the rhetoric that the goal of PBS is to improve lifestyle outcomes, Carr and colleagues (1999) reported that lifestyle outcomes were measured for fewer than 3% of the participants.

The bottom line is that a huge disparity exists between the rhetoric about providing comprehensive lifestyle outcomes and the research that documents efficacious ways to achieve that goal. Research must catch up with innovative "family-directed models" such as JT's support system and illuminate resolutions to the many difficult issues that arise. In addition, research is needed on the biochemical interaction among JT's mental retardation, autism, bipolarity, and OCD. We are convinced that the next major improvements in eliminating his rapid mood and anxiety cycling will have to come through psychopharmacological advances because on a 1–10 scale, his environmental support is a 15.

Now, in 1998 and for not much longer than the next decade, the following items will contribute the most to JT's comprehensive lifestyle support. We wish that research and model demonstration programs would illuminate the most efficacious support strategies because we grow weary of "making it up as we go."

Family   First and foremost, JT depends on his family for creating, sustaining, monitoring, and adjusting his lifestyle support. All that is good about his life comes from his family's efforts, and all that is limiting comes from them as well. Since JT left the formal service system in 1988, his support has come from outside the formal service delivery system. Support for JT's family—his parents and his sisters—is the sine qua non of both public policy and comprehensive lifestyle support. We can imagine what his life would have been like without his family's participation over the last ten years; that is not, however, something we want to ponder, for the fact is that JT's life would be impoverished were it not for his family. Likewise, it is imaginable what his life would be like for the next decade without his family; it is not pleasant to conjure. We desperately want a system in which agencies and service providers offer person- and family-centered supported living. We do not want JT's support to depend on us nearly as much in the future.

Friends   JT's life is leavened—made to rise like bread—when he has friends. Friendship requires inclusion. Segregation is the enemy of inclusion, of a leavened life. That is why magnificent programs such as Natural Ties at KU are so important to him. Citizens such as JT need young people in their lives, whether in schools under the auspices of the Individuals with Disabilities Education Act (IDEA) of 1990 or in a community's rhythms through activities such as the music therapy program at KU. This also contributes to the lives of those who do not have disabilities. Any policy that advances inclusion is meritorious; any retreat from inclusion must be fought, tooth and nail. We want support from agencies and service providers that place high priority on friendship facilitation.

Home of His Own   JT regards himself as a man, and to him, being a man means living in his own home with people who like him and whom he enjoys. That is why family support, tax, antidiscrimination, and other policies have to support "home-of-my-own" approaches. What JT needs, however, is not just the physical setting and the means to afford it. He also needs housemates who will be with him for 3–5 years. At the longest, his past housemates have been with him for 2 years. JT needs the stability, predictability, understanding, and nurturance derived from long-term, communal living. We need the service system to help JT and us sustain it.

Work   JT is proud that he works. He also benefits from work. First, there is the matter of his salary and significant fringe benefits such as a good health insurance policy (i.e., one that avoids many of the cost and reimbursement limitations of Medicaid and the stigmatization that comes with being a Medicaid beneficiary). Second, there is the matter of psychic compensation—that sense that comes from making a contribution. JT needs both. Sheltered employment is not an option: He failed at that long ago. Supported employment is the only option: He needs the support as much as he needs the work itself. Only one change would enhance his Beach Center work—namely, the extension of his workday by about 2 hours daily.

Cheers *Connections*   Having places where everyone knows JT (and all who are involved in his life) assures him that he is both in and of our community—that he has his own special places to shop, have his hair cut, get his physical checkups, do his banking, enjoy music, and participate in other meaningful community activities. For as long as his family and his housemates are able, we create and sometimes re-create these *Cheers* connections. Law in itself cannot change public attitudes, nor can exemplary practices such as the ones we have launched on JT's behalf. Yet, law that does not facilitate inclusion and research and practice that are based on segregated individuals are simply unacceptable.

Money   JT is among the many people with developmental disabilities who are sometimes classified as "WLs"—people on the waiting list for Medicaid services (essentially, home and community-based services). Despite lawsuits in states such as New York and Massachusetts, as well as the advocacy efforts of organizations such as The Arc and the Judge David L. Bazelon Center for Mental Health Law, nearly every state has its "WLs." The promise of Medicaid reform—namely, the home and community-based services waiver—is great; however, the reality of waiting is not. If JT comes off the waiting list and is declassified from being a "WL" and made an active beneficiary, then he will receive sufficient funds to purchase nearly all of the services and supports that he now uses.

CONCLUSION

There are phases of human life. In *As You Like It,* Shakespeare referred to them as seven ages. JT is now well into the young man age. Within a decade, he will begin middle age; within three decades, he will begin his last age.

Likewise, there are phases for the field of developmental disabilities and mental health. Nearly 30 years have passed if the field's beginning is dated as being the late 1960s or early 1970s. Laws have been initiated or enacted. Many millions of dollars have been invested in research as well as demonstration programs and in practice based on them. In the 1990s alone, millions of research, demonstration, and training dollars have been invested in addressing challenging behaviors.

Have those investments been worthwhile? Yes, if the question subsumes the premise that the investments would not have been made anyway. It is better to have had something potentially good than nothing at all or something bad (i.e., the perpetuation of the institutional, medical model). Yet, the question about the worth of the investments can be answered without the categorical, assumption-premised "Yes." It can be answered, "Yes, but. . . ." Yes, the investments have been important and have initiated and justified much that has helped people with disabilities, but they have not helped enough.

We have the sense that the rights revolution that began in the late 1960s and early 1970s is, like JT, in the young man age, but we also have the sense that the field—the rights advocates, the researchers, the practitioners, and the families—are not fully prepared for middle age, the next phase. Of course, some leaders in the field are anticipating and setting the future. They seem to be saying that what they and their colleagues created to address the problems at the end of the 20th century was suitable for then but is not suitable for tomorrow. We ourselves believe that to be the case.

Making marginal improvements on what is already known and tweaking systems that were devised to fit the horrific problems of the early 1970s (e.g., the propensity for institutionalization, the exclusion of children with disabilities from schools) seem to us to simply be ways of solidifying a system that is already too ripe with shortcomings. We fail to see the sense of improving a system that is already outmoded. Why is that system of research, demonstration, service delivery, and training outmoded? As we have tried to make clear in this chapter, it does not work well enough for JT and his family, friends, and community. It most likely does not work well enough for others, either.

We ourselves seek to recapture the revolution—to experience again the sense of adventure in the pursuit of a different way to live joyfully and productively. Nonetheless, we are cautious. Indeed, we are skeptical, concerned that the field may try to sustain the prevalent models created from a 1970 rather than a 2002 mentality.

Something is amiss in JT's life, in the lives of people like him, in the lives of families like ours. We search for it and in this chapter gave some pointers that may guide everyone toward it. Yet, the comprehensive vision—the Camelot that we see when we shut our eyes and free ourselves of the fetters of today—has yet to be captured. It is time—yes, it is past time—to recapture the revolution. It has to be a different revolution, however, one focused on helping JT and other individuals with disabilities to "get a life" with the same standard and rhythm of living as enjoyed by citizens without disabilities. The revolution also must value knowledge from families and self-advocates as much as that from professionals. The revolutionary agenda will not succeed if it is dominated by professionals. It requires authentic and equal partnerships. Comprehensive lifestyle support—we are overdue in moving from rhetoric to reality for the benefit of individuals with challenging behavior and their families.

REFERENCES

Carr, E.G., Horner, R.H., Turnbull, A.P., Marquis, J.G., McLaughlin, D.M., McAtee, M.L., Smith, C.E., Ryan, K.A., & Ruef, M.B. (1999). *Positive behavior support for people with developmental disabilities: A research synthesis.* Washington, DC: American Association on Mental Retardation.

Horner, R.H., & Carr, E.G. (1997). Behavioral support for students with severe disabilities: Functional assessment and comprehensive intervention. *The Journal of Special Education, 31*(1), 84–104.

Individuals with Disabilities Education Act (IDEA) of 1990, PL 101-476, 20 U.S.C. §§ 1400 *et seq.*

Turnbull, A.P., Blue-Banning, M.J., Anderson, E.L., Seaton, K.A., Turnbull, H.R., & Dinas, P.A. (1996). Enhancing self-determination through Group Action Planning: A holistic perspective. In D.J. Sands & M.L. Wehmeyer (Eds.), *Self-determination across the life span: Theory and practice* (pp. 237–256). Baltimore: Paul H. Brookes Publishing Co.

Turnbull, A.P., Blue-Banning, M., & Pereira, L. (2000). Successful friendships of Hispanic children and youth with disabilities: An exploratory study. *Mental Retardation, 38*(2), 138–143.

Turnbull, A.P., Friesen, B.J., & Ramirez, C. (1998). Participatory action research as a model for conducting family research. *Journal of The Association for Persons with Severe Handicaps, 23*(3), 178–188.

Turnbull, A.P., & Ruef, M. (1996). Family perspective on problem behavior. *Mental Retardation, 34*(5), 280–293.

Turnbull, A.P., & Ruef, M. (1997). Family perspectives on inclusive lifestyle issues for individuals with problem behavior. *Exceptional Children, 63*(2), 211–227.

Turnbull, A.P., & Turnbull, H.R. (1996). Group action planning as a strategy for providing comprehensive family support. In L.K. Koegel, R.L. Koegel, & G. Dunlap (Eds.), *Positive behavioral support: Including people with difficult behavior in the community* (pp. 99–114). Baltimore: Paul H. Brookes Publishing Co.

Turnbull, A.P., Turnbull, H.R., & Blue-Banning, M.J. (1994). Enhancing inclusion of infants and toddlers with disabilities and their families: A theoretical and programmatic analysis. *Infants and Young Children, 7*(2), 1–14.

Wehman, P., Revell, W.G., & Kregel, J. (1997). Supported employment: A decade of rapid growth and impact. In P. Wehman, J. Kregel, & M. West (Eds.), *Supported employment research: Expanding competitive employment opportunities for persons with significant disabilities.* Richmond: Virginia Commonwealth University, Rehabilitation Research and Training Center.

Section IV

COLLABORATIVE
RESEARCH WITH FAMILIES

CHAPTER 16

Collaborative Research with Families on Positive Behavior Support

Richard W. Albin, Glen Dunlap, and Joseph M. Lucyshyn

The message of this chapter is simple: Families are important and willing collaborative partners in research on positive behavior support (PBS). The capacity to conduct meaningful and socially valid research on PBS procedures depends on the continued development and use of collaborative research partnerships between professionals and families. The preceding chapters in this book have emphasized and illustrated the essential role of collaborative partnerships with families in the development and implementation of effective behavior support plans and procedures. Collaboration with families has been increasingly recognized as a key element in the clinical application of effective and sustainable behavioral support. The premise of this chapter is that families also must be viewed as key partners in conducting the research that provides the information that 1) is required as a foundation for the effective application of PBS in homes and community environments and 2) validates and confirms the effectiveness and value of behavioral support procedures used by and with families and other stakeholders. Conducting collaborative research with families makes it easier to gain important knowledge about PBS from typical users and from natural settings.

This chapter describes the following: 1) the need and rationale for conducting collaborative research with families, 2) the foundations for conducting collaborative research with families, 3) specific quantitative research methods in collaborative research with families, and 4) issues related to conducting collaborative research with families.

NEED AND RATIONALE FOR
COLLABORATIVE RESEARCH WITH FAMILIES

An extensive body of literature, including the chapters in this book, documents the value and effectiveness of PBS (Carr et al., 1999; Horner et al., 1990). PBS has gained broad ac-

Preparation of this chapter was supported in part by the U.S. Department of Education National Institute on Disability and Rehabilitation Research through Grant No. H133B98005. The opinions expressed in this chapter are those of the authors, and no endorsement from the U.S. Department of Education should be inferred.

ceptance among practitioners and policy makers in disability and educational arenas. Increasingly, PBS is recommended in the professional literature as the desired approach to supporting children and adults with problem behaviors in homes, schools, and communities (Bambara & Knoster, 1998; Carr et al., 2002; Fox, Dunlap, & Buschbacher, 2000; Horner, 1999; Horner, Albin, Sprague, & Todd, 2000; Koegel, Koegel, & Dunlap, 1996; Scotti & Meyer, 1999; Sugai et al., 2000). Also, since the 1990s, federal education legislation such as the Individuals with Disabilities Education Act Amendments of 1997 (PL 105-17) and statutes or administrative rules and regulations in many states (e.g., Nevada Department of Education, 1999; Oregon Technical Assistance Corporation, 1998; Pennsylvania Department of Education, 1995; Wright, Gurman, & The California Association, 1998) have specifically identified PBS as a strategy for supporting students and adults with disabilities and problem behavior (Turnbull, Wilcox, Stowe, Raper, & Hedges, 2000; Wilcox, Turnbull, & Turnbull, 1999–2000; see also Chapter 2).

The prevalence of local, state, and national policies that identify PBS as either desired or required practice has heightened interest in what constitutes PBS and in the application and effectiveness of positive behavior support procedures. This rise in interest is particularly true for the families; practitioners; and program, agency, and school administrators who are only now becoming aware of PBS. Although the research base underlying PBS dates back to the 1960s, only at the end of the 20th century did the gap begin to close between the research base and the practice of PBS by typical families and practitioners (e.g., teachers, service providers). PBS has become the expected practice.

Need for More Research on Positive Behavior Support

Some may argue that the current research base related to PBS is adequate and sufficient and that attention should now be turned from research to widespread implementation, dissemination, and training. However, from our perspective, now is a time when additional research on PBS is important and needed to facilitate the widespread adoption of PBS. The existing research base supporting the efficacy of PBS is strong (for meta-analyses and reviews see Carr et al., 1999; Carr, Robinson, Taylor, & Carlson, 1990; Didden, Duker, & Korzilius, 1997; Scotti, Evans, Meyer, & Walker, 1991; Scotti, Ujcich, Weigle, Holland, & Kirk, 1996). This body of research clearly warrants and supports policy and systems change efforts aimed at systemwide adoption and implementation of PBS. As PBS becomes a more widespread and expected practice, however, the necessary and desired features of research on PBS change. Many research questions remain unanswered, and much needs to be learned about the use of PBS by typical families and practitioners in homes, inclusive schools, and community environments over extended time periods.

This book and other sources describe strategies for the application of PBS with families (e.g., Fox et al., 2000; Lucyshyn & Albin, 1993; Lucyshyn, Nixon, Glang, & Cooley, 1996). A small number of experimental and quasi-experimental research studies document and illustrate how providing PBS has positive effects on children with behavior problems and their families (e.g., Clarke, Dunlap, & Vaughn, 1999; Fox, Vaughn, Dunlap, & Bucy, 1997; Lucyshyn, Albin, & Nixon, 1997; Moes & Frea, 2000; Vaughn, Clarke, & Dunlap, 1997; Vaughn, Dunlap, et al., 1997; Vaughn, Wilson, & Dunlap, 2002; see Chapter 1 for a summary of several of these studies). One critical feature of these studies is the research collaboration between the family members and university-based researchers. Although few in number, the studies provide good models for collaborative research with families.

Specific Research Needs

Two literature reviews—Carr and colleagues (1999) and Dunlap, Clarke, and Steiner (1999)—have provided descriptive analyses of the research literature on behavior intervention and PBS between 1980 and 1997. These analyses yielded information that is helpful in identifying needs and gaps in the research base on PBS. Both analyses found that most of the research studies on PBS and behavioral intervention involved what are considered traditional research procedures. Three findings of interest were related to the widespread application of PBS by families and other typical care providers. First, interventions were more likely implemented by "atypical agents" (e.g., researchers, behavior specialists, psychologists) than by "typical agents" (e.g., parents, family members, teachers, direct support providers, caregivers). Second, interventions were more likely implemented in "atypical settings" (e.g., clinics, state institutions, segregated schools, sheltered workshops) than in "typical settings" (e.g., family homes, supported living environments, inclusive schools, job sites). Third, interventions were more likely to be implemented only in some relevant contexts rather than in all relevant living contexts. In addition to these three findings, these analyses noted that only a small percentage of studies looked at the maintenance of outcomes beyond 6 months, the lifestyle changes resulting from intervention, or the social validity of outcomes. Trends in the research data showed changes in key features of research studies conducted over the review period, with studies published since 1992 being more consistent and relevant to family's and other typical practitioners' use of PBS. However, a clear message of both analyses is that although PBS has clearly documented effectiveness, important gaps remain in the research base on its use within typical conditions. Researchers have an obligation to extend research on PBS and to further establish the external, social, and ecological validity of research outcomes on PBS (Fawcett, 1991; Gaylord-Ross, 1979; Meyer, 1991; Schwartz & Baer, 1991; Wolf, 1978).

If PBS procedures are to be used effectively on a broad scale by families and other typical support providers, then there exists a significant need for rigorous socially and ecologically valid research that meets several criteria. The research must document the effectiveness of comprehensive, multicomponent behavior support plans rather than single intervention procedures. It should involve interventions that are implemented by natural caregivers across all relevant support settings on a 24-hour basis. The research needs to document intervention effects across many years rather than across several weeks or months. It must measure intervention effects across multiple dependent variables, including behavioral gains, child lifestyle, social validity, and broader family variables (e.g., family wellness, parent stress, family lifestyle, patterns of parent–child interactions) in addition to changes in problem behaviors. Finally, the research should address the processes of providing support to and measuring the effects of PBS on families as units, not just the child with problem behaviors.

Why Research Collaboration with Families Is Important for Researchers

Meeting the need for socially and ecologically valid research on PBS is possible only with the collaboration of families of children with problem behaviors. From a traditional research perspective, families are needed as participants in such research. Researchers cannot learn about what works for and with families unless families are involved in the research. However, the purpose of this chapter is to emphasize the involvement of families as collaborative research partners, not simply as participants. Partners have an active voice in the research process and in the decisions made.

Families can provide information, participate in decisions, and conduct activities that strengthen research on PBS, thereby enhancing all aspects of research design validity. Collaboration allows for the collection of more types of data in more settings and across longer periods of time. Collaboration facilitates development, implementation, and evaluation of comprehensive behavior support plans that are a good contextual fit for families—that is, support plans that are likely to be used and sustained faithfully over long time periods (Albin, Lucyshyn, Horner, & Flannery, 1996). Furthermore, collaboration promotes interest and willingness on the part of families to get and stay involved in a process that can be time consuming, distracting, intrusive, and—at times—downright annoying. Our message to researchers is this: Do not collaborate with families simply because family members are good people who may need assistance and are willing to serve as participants in a research study. Rather, collaborate with families because collaboration is key to producing research that meets criteria for the delivery of effective behavioral support and is both rigorous and meaningful (Baer, Wolf, & Risley, 1968; Carr et al., 2002; Schwartz & Baer, 1991; Wolf, 1978).

Why Collaboration in Research Is Important to Some Families

All families are unique. Families members likely have their own reasons for collaborating in a research study. In our experience, however, discussions with families have identified two noteworthy reasons for their willingness to participate in a research study on PBS, despite the additional demands involved. First, some families have expressed a sincere value of science and the systematic development of new knowledge. These families view participation in a collaborative research study as meaningful because in addition to helping their own child, participation offers an opportunity to provide help to other families in similar circumstances through the dissemination of research results.

The second reason relates to the practical reality of implementing PBS. It takes time, effort, and resources to design and implement behavior support plans. New skills may need to be learned. Changes may be necessary in family or personal routines, activities, and interactions. Implementing PBS represents a significant and substantial family endeavor and investment. Researchers view experimental results as the ultimate standard for knowing that an intervention works. Similarly, some families also want to know in the strongest possible way that the time, effort, and expense involved is truly worth it. As one parent stated,

> The primary goal of the research methods was to show that the support plan effected the changes in [my daughter's] behavior. This goal was no less meaningful and important to me as a father. If I am going to commit to a plan of action that may become a lifetime effort, then I want to know that the interventions that I am using are actually working. (Lucyshyn, Albin, Horner, Mann, & Mann, 1997)

To make informed choices and decisions among procedure options or to make plan modifications or adjustments, families, like professionals, often want clear and convincing information. Many families are committed to making decisions based on information that meets the standards of good science.

FOUNDATIONS FOR COLLABORATIVE RESEARCH WITH FAMILIES

There are two foundations on which to build the methods for conducting collaborative research on PBS with families. Participatory action research (PAR) provides a conceptual foundation (Bruyère, 1993; Turnbull, Friesen, & Ramirez, 1998). Collaboration with families in the clinical application (i.e., nonresearch use of PBS in natural conditions) of comprehensive behavior support plans provides a practical foundation (Lucyshyn & Albin, 1993; Lucyshyn et al., 1996).

Participatory Action Research

Park, Meyer, and Goetz characterized PAR as "an umbrella of research approaches encompassing a variety of involvements of participants in the research process" (1998, p. 163). According to Turnbull and colleagues,

> Participatory action research refers to a process whereby the researchers and stakeholders (those who potentially benefit from research results) collaborate in the design and conduct of all phases (e.g., specification of questions, design, data collection, data analysis, dissemination, utilization) of the research process. (1998, p. 178)

Turnbull and colleagues emphasized that PAR provides a model for conducting *family research*—that is, research focused on family issues and support. Bruyère (1993) noted that PAR results in data and outcomes that are more useful and relevant to consumers (i.e., families and practitioners).

A primary goal of PAR is to more fully involve in the research process key stakeholders who have been traditionally viewed only as consumers or users of research knowledge. In this way, families and typical practitioners (e.g., teachers, residential and work support providers) may directly collaborate in the processes of developing knowledge and collecting information that they will utilize in delivering best practice (Bruyère, 1993; Meyer, Park, Grenot-Scheyer, Schwartz, & Harry, 1998; Park et al., 1998; Turnbull et al., 1998). PAR breaks down traditional distinctions between those who conduct research and those who use it. Research is likely to benefit from input that makes it more relevant to the perceived needs of the field. Turning research into practice is likely facilitated because the users of the research are involved in conducting it. For example, stakeholders collaborate with researchers to frame research questions; select research methods and designs; plan independent variables (i.e., interventions); decide on dependent variables and measurement procedures; and analyze, interpret, and present results and conclusions. Also, the external and social validity of research is enhanced through PAR and collaborative research processes because the research is conducted in conditions and settings that are typical of actual practices (Meyer, 1991; Meyer et al., 1998; Turnbull et al., 1998).

Clinical Application of PBS with Families

The application of PBS with families in typical living conditions shares many features of collaborative research on PBS and provides a practical foundation for collaborative research. Best practice for using PBS under typical circumstances involves a collaborative, transdisciplinary team process to develop, implement, and evaluate the effects of a comprehensive, multicomponent behavior support plan. This team process is based on mutual respect and collaborative decision making among team members. Descriptions of how to apply PBS with families are presented in this book (see Chapter 5) and elsewhere (e.g., Lucyshyn & Albin, 1993; Lucyshyn et al., 1996). Typical implementation strategies for providing comprehensive PBS to families lend themselves to research designs. Although the leap from typical practice to research should not be underestimated, the differences are limited to the following: the factors considered when decisions are made regarding the implementation or modification of support procedures, the types of data and data-collection procedures used, and the timing and processes used in sharing information on the effects and outcomes of support. See Chapters 12, 17, and 18 for illustrations of how different researchers have made the leap from clinical practice to research.

QUANTITATIVE RESEARCH METHODS
IN COLLABORATIVE RESEARCH WITH FAMILIES

PAR guidelines focus on research processes, including collaboration and communication among research participants, rather than on specific research methodologies (Turnbull et al., 1998). Although often associated with qualitative research methods, PAR guidelines may be followed in conducting either quantitative or qualitative research methodologies. Both research methodologies are represented in the literature base that describes, illustrates, and supports the use of PBS by documenting its effectiveness. Both methodologies also offer examples of collaborative research on PBS with families (e.g., Fox et al., 1997; Lucyshyn, Albin, & Nixon, 1997; Moes & Frea, 2000; Vaughn, Clarke, & Dunlap, 1997; Vaughn, Dunlap, Fox, Clarke, & Bucy, 1997; Vaughn et al., 2002).

This section focuses on conducting collaborative research by using quantitative methods that are particularly well suited for research on the use of PBS by families and other stakeholders. Procedures and opportunities for collaboration are described in conducting experimental single subject research (Barlow & Hersen, 1984; Kazdin, 1982; Richards, Taylor, Ramasamy, & Richards, 1999; Tawney & Gast, 1984) and quantitative case study methods (Yin, 1994).

Single subject research methods provide options for conducting experimental research that is rigorous in documenting experimental control (i.e., has good internal validity) and can be generalized to other individuals with problem behaviors and their families (i.e., has good external and social validity). Generalizability in single subject research is established through direct and systematic replication of research findings across multiple studies (Barlow & Hersen, 1984; Sidman, 1960). Collaboration with families as co-researchers facilitates the replication of research across children with problem behaviors and families as well as across home and community intervention settings, activities, routines, and support conditions. The option of being a co-researcher may increase a family member's willingness to participate in research on PBS. Also, when research is conducted collaboratively with families, social and ecological validity are enhanced because family members and other typical support agents in natural environments are the PBS implementors.

Single subject research methodology is a popular and common research paradigm within the field of behavioral support (Meyer, 1991). A substantial portion of the experimental research literature documenting the effectiveness and utility of PBS utilized single subject methods. When single subject experimental research designs are not appropriate or desirable, however, quantitative case study methods can be used for collaborative research with families (Yin, 1994). Case studies may employ quasi-experimental or nonexperimental designs to produce empirical data and results that go beyond anecdotal experiences in documenting the impact of PBS. Single subject and case study research procedures are highly suitable for a PAR approach to research with families because the procedures and decision-making processes that characterize these two methods may be strengthened by collaboration with families. In both methods, decisions are made continually throughout the process of designing and conducting a study. The inclusion of family members and their perspectives in making these decisions creates a better research study—that is, a study with increased research validity and real-life applicability.

Points for Joint Decision Making in Collaborative Research

The first decision to make is whether to conduct a research study at all. Most families receive comprehensive PBS in the context of clinical practice and technical assistance, not a research study. As noted previously in this chapter, however, some families are interested in participating in research and receiving PBS within the context of a research study. Professionals may seek and approach families with the idea of their participating in a research study on PBS, or professionals may respond to a family's request for assistance with an offer to deliver PBS in the context of a research study. Either way, professionals must assist families in making an informed and voluntary decision regarding whether to consent to participate in a research study. Delivering PBS in the context of research has implications for the support process that must be understood before a truly informed decision can be made. For example, a research study may involve activities that occur solely or primarily for research purposes, less flexibility in the implementation of PBS and in the modification of its procedures, increased requirements or responsibilities related to data collection, and information sharing that is adapted or even temporarily limited for research purposes. Potential risks and benefits must be discussed. Not all family situations that require PBS are suitable for research, especially research that involves an experimental design.

If a family is willing to participate in a research study on PBS, then the researchers and family members should jointly consider and decide on the role of the family in the research process and the degree to which the research will utilize a PAR approach. Will the research process follow a traditional "Professional Expert Model" (Bruyère, 1993), with the family members participating only as research participants (subjects), or will it follow the PAR model, with family members participating as research collaborators, actively involved in making research decisions? In this chapter we encourage the latter option, and the remainder of this section describes procedural aspects of the quantitative research process in which collaboration and joint decision making may occur.

Research Questions   In the PAR model, families and other stakeholders are involved in the development of the research questions that a study seeks to answer. In collaborative research on PBS, families help to frame specific research questions. Although professional researchers may provide a starting point or an initial, broad research question of interest, the collaborative research team considers the appropriateness and scope of research questions. The team also arrives at a consensus on specific questions to be answered prior to conducting a study.

Research Method and Design   A decision to implement PBS in the context of a research study sets up the need for the next set of decisions: What research method and design should be used? In conducting a quantitative study, researchers must consider whether to use an experimental single subject research design or a quasi-experimental case study design. Experimental single subject designs require time-staggered implementation of an intervention across multiple conditions (i.e., a multiple-baseline design), systematic implementation and withdrawal of an intervention (i.e., a withdrawal or ABAB design), or alternating implementation of two or more interventions (i.e., an alternating treatments design) (Barlow & Hersen, 1984; Richards et al., 1999). Each of these designs raises logistical and ethical issues for consideration. If no option is logistically and ethically possible, or if no option is desirable even if possible, then a quasi-experimental case study design may offer an appropriate alternative (Yin, 1994). For example, based on the desires and concerns of the family, Vaughn, Dunlap, and colleagues (1997; see Chapter 17) decided on a quasi-experimental design involving the concurrent implementation of PBS across three community settings and activities without time-staggered implementation phases. In the study conducted by Lucyshyn, Albin, and Nixon (1997), however, a mutual decision was made that an experimental multiple-baseline design across settings and activities was both desirable and possible, so the experimental single subject design was used (see also Chapter 17).

Settings, Routines, and Activities   These two design examples (i.e., Lucyshyn, Albin, & Nixon, 1997; Vaughn, Dunlap, et al., 1997) highlight the fact that PBS is implemented and research is conducted within the contexts of specific settings, routines, or activities (see Chapters 1 and 5). Regardless of the type of research design used, the research collaborators must select the contexts in which PBS will be implemented and data will be collected to measure effects. Even if the ultimate goal is the implementation of PBS across all contexts, for logistical and research purposes implementation of an intervention typically begins in one context or setting or a limited number of contexts and then is extended systematically to additional contexts and settings. Selection of the settings, routines, and activities in which a research study will be conducted provides an opportunity for collaborative decision making.

Families should lead in identifying the contexts in which they will learn and be supported in the implementation of PBS. The contexts may be existing routines, such as during a family dinner, getting ready for school, or getting ready for bed. With existing routines, research team members need to define and agree on the activities or steps in the routine so that the routine is consistently conducted across the research sessions. In some cases, however, families and professional researchers may need or want to define and construct new or adapted routines or activities. For example, a family that has never eaten at a restaurant because of a child's severe problem behaviors may decide that going out to eat is a desired community activity, and eating at a restaurant should be included as one setting in a multiple-baseline across settings design. The research team must collaboratively define the steps that constitute this particular activity. Again, families should lead in defining the steps of new activities and routines.

When multiple settings or routines are identified for intervention, as in a multiple-baseline across settings design, collaborative decisions are also made regarding the order across settings in which PBS will be implemented. Families may prioritize intervention sequencing. Alternatively, the team may mutually agree to base sequencing on factors such as the ease of PBS implementation, the availability of opportunities or resources, training needs or issues (e.g., which new skills are needed, from which routine training will best generalize), research design considerations (e.g., which sequence may best document experimental control), or the likelihood of the fastest or broadest positive effects.

Dependent Variables and Measurement Procedures Identifying and defining dependent variables (behaviors to be measured in a research study) and specifying measurement procedures are key elements of the research process. Decisions on what to measure and how to measure it are made collaboratively with families. Families assist in identifying the following:

- Behaviors of concern

- Appropriate alternative and replacement behaviors to be increased or taught

- Lifestyle and quality-of-life outcomes or indicators to measure (e.g., activity patterns, social networks)

- Other measures of child and family improvement and effects (e.g., improved health and safety, generalization and maintenance of effects, family use of PBS procedures, family stress indicators, positive and negative side effects of intervention)

- Social validity measures (e.g., family satisfaction, goodness of contextual fit)

A collaborative research approach facilitates the identification and definition of measures that are relevant and meaningful to family members and other practitioners as well as to professional researchers.

In addition to deciding what to measure, a collaborative research team also determines measurement procedures and responsibilities for collecting data. A benefit of collaborative research is the capacity to collect multiple measures, across many natural contexts, for extended periods of time. This is possible because of the participation of family members in data collection. Although having family members or other typical support providers (e.g., teachers, educational assistants) collect some data raises concerns related to reliability or lack of observer agreement, it allows for the collection and analysis of data that reflect behavior and the effects of PBS across all living contexts for the whole day. Such data represent more than snapshots of behavior in limited contexts for relatively brief measurement sessions. An advantage of collaborative research is that by including multiple measures, both data that meet traditional observer agreement standards and data taken by typical support providers can be collected and analyzed to more fully evaluate the effects and associated outcomes of PBS. A strategy that has worked well in the chapter authors' collaborative research studies is developing a mutually agreed on schedule that identifies the data collection time cycle and the person responsible for collecting each dependent variable measure. For example, in one study researchers made direct observations of specific routines at agreed-on times to measure changes in the child's problem behaviors and the parents' use of intervention procedures. The parents participated in a monthly schedule of reporting major behavior incidents and a yearly schedule of reporting the child's activity patterns in the home and community (see Chapter 17).

Finally, with comprehensive measurement on the effects of PBS implementation with families, qualitative research methods (e.g., open-ended interviews, maintaining a journal) may be incorporated into single subject experimental and case study research designs to complement and augment quantitative measurement procedures (e.g., Lucyshyn, Olson, & Horner, 1995). The family research on PBS conducted by Fox and colleagues (1997) and Vaughn, Dunlap, and colleagues (1997) illustrated a collaborative research effort that incorporated both quantitative and qualitative methods and measures to provide a comprehensive analysis of the effects of implementation of PBS with a family. Although published as separate articles, these two studies represented a single comprehensive research collaboration in which combined quantitative and qualitative methods offered compelling evidence of the efficacy of the intervention with the family.

Intervention   In collaborative research, family members have input regarding the intervention or the manipulation that serves as the independent variable of the study. As in any application of PBS, developing a comprehensive, multicomponent support plan or selecting specific intervention procedures occurs in the context of a collaborative team process, involving all relevant stakeholders and support providers. Unlike in a purely clinical application of PBS, a professional researcher may initiate the collaborative research process with a specific intervention in mind. However, the collaborative process helps ensure that all stakeholders who are implementing a support plan or intervention have a voice and some ownership in the intervention. In finalizing the support plan or intervention prior to initial implementation, family members, professional researchers, and other members of a person's support team should reach a consensus regarding the specific procedures that constitute the study's independent variable. As with any PBS intervention, the support plan procedures should be logically based on functional assessment summary hypotheses and should be a good contextual fit for the family and other team members who are implementing the intervention (Albin et al., 1996; Horner et al., 2000; Lucyshyn & Albin, 1993).

Procedural Details and Logistics of Conducting Research with Families

In conducting any research study, researchers must address many procedural and logistical details. Decisions related to these details must be made regularly throughout a study. Collaborative research on PBS with families can be relatively complicated in terms of logistics. The study is conducted in family homes and natural community settings (where approvals may be needed for research activities), with family members and other typical support providers who are implementing the intervention. Professional researchers must provide training and support on the implementation of the intervention while also coordinating and providing support on key elements of the research process, such as data collection. Therefore, conducting a collaborative study with families involves attention to many details and decisions, including the following:

- Scheduling research and data collection sessions

- Determining the length of the sessions

- Setting criteria for terminating a research or data collection session due to problem behaviors

- Ensuring fidelity in implementing the intervention that serves as the study's independent variable

- Ensuring the reliability and consistency of data collection

- Deciding on research phase changes and modifications to the intervention, if needed

- Establishing guidelines and procedures for sharing information on many aspects of the study while it is in progress (e.g., how the professionals respond to family questions regarding what to do in specific situations, either within or outside of research contexts)

Decisions related to many of these details must be handled in ways that give strong consideration to the family's preferences, needs, and concerns while honoring the requirements of research. If family members are truly partners in the research, then their preferences, needs, and concerns are well represented and respected in the decision-making process. Having a research study conducted with one's family and in one's home is intrusive; while the study is in progress, it is likely to affect greatly the lives of all family members. Having a voice, choice, and control in the decisions related to the logistics and details of the study makes collaboration easier for families and also ensures a sense of true partnership. In our experience, when family members are treated as partners with a voice in the logistical decisions, they are more willing to consider and accommodate the needs of the research study.

We have found that deference to the family's considerations and wishes is especially important in scheduling research-related activities (e.g., sessions for training or data collection, meetings for problem solving or providing feedback) as well as in determining the length of research sessions. Families have lives and needs outside of the research study and appreciate flexibility and understanding from professional researchers when it comes to scheduling and timing. Although it may take longer to complete a study, allowing families control over scheduling and timing promotes sustained involvement in the research while showing respect for the family's needs.

It is not necessary in research on PBS for a child to engage in dangerous or stigmatizing behaviors. Sometimes research sessions will need to be terminated due to a child's problem behaviors or the possibility of problem behaviors. Involving the family in setting criteria for this termination is key to assuring families of their child's and other family members' safety in the study. Termination criteria also help to avoid embarrassment and stigmatization during research sessions in the community. Mutually agreed on criteria for immediately ending a session should be set in advance and strictly respected throughout the study. Families can identify their own limits and tolerance levels so that termination criteria reflect the family's perspective and wishes. In addition, dependent variable measures, such as latency to meeting the termination criteria or the number of steps in an activity completed before termination, can be used rather than a measure such as rate of problem behaviors. By mutually agreeing on session termination criteria and selecting appropriate dependent variable measures, researchers and families can ensure the safety and dignity of a child and family participating in collaborative research on PBS.

Finally, it is important to set clear guidelines at the beginning of a study regarding what information will be freely shared throughout the study. It may be that all information will be shared freely among all collaborators in a particular study. Depending on the research design used, however, there may be some limits to sharing information during the course of a collaborative study. For example, in the Lucyshyn, Albin, and Nixon study (1997), the research design was a multiple-baseline design across settings (routines) with multiple measurement probes in each routine. At the start of the study, the professional researchers and family members agreed that during and immediately after observation probes in the home or community, the researcher would not provide the family with feedback or share with the family the results of the probe observations. The purpose of this procedure was to maintain the consistency of observation probe sessions across baseline, intervention, and follow-up conditions. The family also consented to a second constraint in the sharing of intervention information that was related to the multiple-baseline design. The family understood that due to design considerations, the researchers could only provide information and support to the family in the routine or routines that were currently targeted for intervention (i.e., during initial training and support or maintenance support phases; see Chapter 17). For routines still in the baseline phase, information and support would not be provided unless a behavioral crisis in these settings required immediate protection of the family from psychological or physical risk (as required by human subjects protection procedures).

During the course of the $2\frac{1}{2}$ year study, these research design considerations and constraints were acceptable to the family and worked well. Information and support were provided to family members in each routine during an initial training and support phase and continued to be provided during a subsequent maintenance support phase. Across the course of the study, family members received a total of 67 hours of training and support. They successfully implemented PBS and improved the behavior and lifestyle of their daughter with severe disabilities. The family actively collaborated in many aspects of the study and, based on collected consumer satisfaction data, was highly satisfied with the process of PBS and the study's outcomes. In our experiences, when family members and researchers respect and trust one another and share common goals in the conduct of a research study, mutual agreements can be reached that promote the integrity of the research process and study results.

ISSUES RELATED TO COLLABORATIVE RESEARCH WITH FAMILIES

Research is a systematic process of inquiry that involves long-established traditions and methods. Professional researchers tend to be conservative and to move cautiously regarding changes and new developments in methodology and procedures for conducting research (Kuhn, 1970). Following a PAR model and bringing families into the research process as co-researchers, rather than as research subjects, may pose a challenge for some researchers. There may be concerns regarding weakened experimental control—that is, control in the sense of experimental rigor (Johnston, 1996). There also may be concerns regarding weakened control over the mechanics and logistics of the research process itself. Professional researchers who are trained in the professional expert model are accustomed to calling all of the shots in their research studies. Collaborative research requires shared control and decision making. In our experience, the benefits of collaboration are well worth any increased threats to experimental control and lessened researcher control. This section addresses issues that arise from collaborative research with families.

Internal Validity

A major issue related to the collaborative research process is perceived threat to the internal validity of research findings. One particular concern is the knowledge related to the research study that family members may possess as co-researchers. In the traditional professional expert research model, family members, as participants, are likely to be relatively naïve regarding research questions and hypotheses, manipulation of the independent variable(s), and expected results. As co-researchers, family members usually are not naïve regarding many aspects of the research process, although some limits on information sharing may be maintained in a collaborative research study. A concern about sharing information is that family members may act in a biased manner or may purposely control their behavior to affect results in ways that are consistent with the researchers' hypotheses or expectations. Researcher bias, demand characteristics related to participating in research, and even fabrication or falsification of results are concerns in all research studies and must be addressed by all researchers (McMillan & Schumacher, 2001). These concerns are not unique to the participation of family members as co-researchers. Questions have been raised about potential bias and expectations even within the classic double-blind design for evaluating psychotropic drugs (Fisher & Greenberg, 1993). There are no data to suggest nor reasons to believe that family members would be any more likely than traditional research collaborators (e.g., professional researchers, paid research assistants, graduate and undergraduate students) to be susceptible to bias or to engage in unethical research practices. In fact, families are likely to have strong personal interests in finding procedures that are successful in supporting their child with severe problem behaviors. In our experience, this strong personal interest motivates families to act scrupulously in collaborating in research on PBS. Families that participate as research collaborators are committed to honestly documenting practices that are effective with their child. Their goal is finding effective intervention and support for their child and themselves, not pleasing researchers and producing "good" research data.

Reliable Measurement

Measurement issues also are a concern in any type of research and may raise particular concerns in collaborative research with families. Clinical data collected by family members is a potential strength of collaborative research. However, the possible influences of observer bias and lack of reliability (i.e., observer agreement) in clinical measurement are issues that must be addressed. Collaborative research on PBS with families utilizes the same measurement safeguards and precautions as used in any research study. Collaborative researchers establish the reliability and validity of measurement instruments and procedures. Collaborative studies include traditional observer agreement procedures and report observer agreement calculations when appropriate and possible. Videotaping can be used in collecting research data in specific routines and activities at home or in the community (with permission). Videotapes are especially useful for establishing and calculating observer agreement because of the opportunity that they provide for repeated viewing of observation sessions. Studies can utilize multiple measures of behavior, including both research and clinical data on occurrence of problem and other behaviors. The reliability and validity of data sources then can be established by showing similarity of performance across multiple measures or by showing consistency among different measures—some with and some without observer agreement established (e.g., see Durand & Kishi, 1987).

Clearly delineated and scripted measurement procedures also can help to establish the reliability and believability of clinical data. For example, families may be asked to collect data on the daily frequency of moderate to severe behavioral incidents (see Lucyshyn, Albin, & Nixon, 1997). Such incidents are clearly defined, obvious, and easily remembered by family members. Specific behaviors of interest can be mutually determined and defined by the research team. Recall of incidents to report can be prompted using a consistent script during nightly calls by a researcher or assistant, who prompts the responding family member(s) to recall incidents within specified time periods across the day (e.g., "Remember this morning before _____ left for school. Were there any incidents involving aggression? How many incidents? Any involving self-injury? How many?").

Adequacy of Traditional Research Designs

Some professionals and family members have proposed that there is a need to develop new and more user-friendly research methods and designs that meet the needs of collaborative researchers working in family and community settings (Carr, 1997; Carr et al., 1999; Dunlap, Fox, Vaughn, Bucy, & Clarke, 1997; Horner, 1997). Carr and colleagues (2002) described

PBS as an evolving applied science in which researchers must adopt more flexibility with respect to what constitutes acceptable data and adequate research designs. This need for increased flexibility in scientific practices stems in large part from a shift in emphasis from conducting research in more controlled and artificial settings, such as laboratories, clinics, and institutional settings, to less controlled but more natural settings, such as family and community homes, inclusive schools, and typical community work and leisure settings (Carr et al., 2002). Collaborative research on PBS with families is a prime example of this shift in research focus.

Increased respect for and use of case study methods in collaborative research with families is one way in which researchers have responded to the need for more flexibility in methods. Although it is possible to use experimental research designs in collaborative research with families, case study methods can be responsive to logistical, ethical, and research validity concerns. Case studies do not use the single subject experimental design convention of documenting a functional relationship between variables by demonstrating a minimum of three changes in behavior at three different points in time. However, case studies can document clear and convincing changes in behavior associated with implementation of an intervention. Particularly in research that addresses long-standing and intractable problem behaviors, changes within a case study that are clearly associated with implementation of PBS are not readily explained by alternative hypotheses, fortuitous covariation of extraneous variables, or random chance.

Acceptance of and confidence in research depends on both the integrity of research designs and the credibility of individual researchers to conduct ethical research. As increasing numbers of collaborative family research studies on PBS—using both experimental and case study designs—are published in peer-reviewed sources, researchers and practitioners in the field will see and appreciate that high-quality research is being conducted with families in natural settings and contexts. This research will have strong social and ecological validity, and it will meet the goals and guidelines proposed for applied behavior analysis (Baer et al., 1968) and good behavioral community research and intervention (Fawcett, 1991). As with all research, the direct and systematic replication represented in multiple published studies will ultimately establish the internal and external validity of collaborative research.

CONCLUSION

The relationship between research and practice is bidirectional. Research should guide and validate best practice. Practice and the needs and concerns of practitioners should inform and shape research. Collaborative family research on positive behavior support provides the opportunity to meet these two goals. Research collaboration with families provides numerous benefits to the field. First, such research demonstrates the effectiveness of positive behavior support in real homes and in natural performance conditions. Second, it shows that positive behavior support can be used successfully by typical family members and other direct support providers. Third, collaboration with families demonstrates that the effects of positive behavior support occur across the entire day and last for extended periods of time. Fourth, it illustrates the generalization and maintenance of positive behavior support by family members, as well as the generalization and maintenance of effects on a child's behavior across new and nontrained contexts. Fifth, collaboration with families demonstrates that comprehensive positive behavior support processes can be carried out and sustained over time by families and other typical practitioners in the community. Research must be rigorous, but it also must be applicable to the everyday needs of families and practitioners. Collaborative family research on positive behavior support allows for an effective and meaningful balancing of the internal, external, ecological, and social validity of the research process and results.

REFERENCES

Albin, R.W., Lucyshyn, J.M., Horner, R.H., & Flannery, K.B. (1996). Contextual fit for behavioral support plans: A model for "goodness of fit." In L.K. Koegel, R.L. Koegel, & G. Dunlap (Eds.), *Positive behavioral support: Including people with difficult behavior in the community* (pp. 81–98). Baltimore: Paul H. Brookes Publishing Co.

Baer, D.M., Wolf, M.M., & Risley, T.R. (1968). Some current dimensions of applied behavior analysis. *Journal of Applied Behavior Analysis, 1,* 91–97.

Bambara, L., & Knoster, T. (1998). Designing positive behavior support plans. *Innovations* (No. 13). Washington, DC: American Association on Mental Retardation.

Barlow, D.H., & Hersen, M. (1984). *Single case experimental design: Strategies for studying behavior change* (2nd ed.). New York: Pergamon.

Bruyère, S.M. (1993). Participatory action research: Overview and implications for family members of persons with disabilities. *Journal of Vocational Rehabilitation, 3,* 62–68.

Carr, E.G. (1997). The evolution of applied behavior analysis into positive behavior support. *Journal of The Association for Persons with Severe Handicaps, 22,* 208–209.

Carr, E.G., Dunlap, G., Horner, R.H., Koegel, R.L., Turnbull, A.P., Sailor, W., Anderson, J.L., Albin, R.W., Koegel, L.K., & Fox, L. (2002). Positive behavior support: Evolution of an applied science. *Journal of Positive Behavior Interventions,4,* 4–16, 20.

Carr, E.G., Horner, R.H., Turnbull, A.P., Marquis, J.G., Magito-McLaughlan, D., McAtee, M.L., Smith, C.E., Anderson-Ryan, K., Ruef, M.B., & Doolabh, A. (1999). *Positive behavior support for people with developmental disabilities: A research synthesis.* Washington, DC: American Association on Mental Retardation.

Carr, E.G., Robinson, S., Taylor, J.C., & Carlson, J.I. (1990). *Positive approaches to the treatment of severe behavior problems in persons with developmental disabilities: A review and analysis of reinforcement and stimulus-based procedures.* (Monograph No. 4). Baltimore: The Association for Persons with Severe Handicaps.

Clarke, S., Dunlap, G., & Vaughn, B.J. (1999). Family-centered, assessment-based intervention to improve behavior during an early morning routine. *Journal of Positive Behavior Interventions, 1,* 235–241.

Didden, R., Duker, P.C., & Korzilius, H. (1997). Meta-analytic study on treatment effectiveness for problem behaviors with individuals who have mental retardation. *American Journal on Mental Retardation, 101,* 387–399.

Dunlap, G., Clarke, S., & Steiner, M. (1999). Intervention research in behavioral and developmental disabilities: 1980 to 1997. *Journal of Positive Behavior Interventions, 1,* 170–180.

Dunlap, G., Fox, L., Vaughn, B.J., Bucy, M., & Clarke, S. (1997). In quest of meaningful perspectives and outcomes: A response to five commentaries. *Journal of The Association for Persons with Severe Handicaps, 22,* 221–223.

Durand, V.M., & Kishi, G. (1987). Reducing severe behavior problems among persons with dual sensory impairments: An evaluation of a technical assistance model. *Journal of The Association for Persons with Severe Handicaps, 12,* 2–10.

Fawcett, S.B. (1991). Some values guiding community research and action. *Journal of Applied Behavior Analysis, 24,* 621–626.

Fisher, S., & Greenberg, R.P. (1993). How sound is the double-blind design for evaluating psychotropic drugs? *The Journal of Nervous and Mental Disease, 181,* 345–350.

Fox, L., Dunlap, G., & Buschbacher, P. (2000). Understanding and intervening with young children's problem behavior: A comprehensive approach. In S.F. Warren & J. Reichle (Series Eds.) & A.M. Wetherby & B.M. Prizant (Vol. Eds.), *Commication and language intervention series: Vol. 9. Autism spectrum disorders: A transactional developmental perspective* (pp. 307–331). Baltimore: Paul H. Brookes Publishing Co.

Fox, L., Vaughn, B.J., Dunlap, G., & Bucy, M. (1997). Parent–professional partnership in behavioral support: A qualitative analysis of one family's experience. *Journal of The Association for Persons with Severe Handicaps, 22,* 198–207.

Gaylord-Ross, R. (1979). Mental retardation research, ecological validity, and the delivery of longitudinal education programs. *Journal of Special Education, 13,* 69–80.

Horner, R.H. (1997). Encouraging a new applied science: A commentary on two papers addressing par-ent–professional partnerships in behavioral support. *Journal of The Association for Persons with Severe Handicaps, 22,* 210–212.

Horner, R.H. (1999). Positive behavior supports. In M.L. Wehmeyer & J.R. Patton (Eds.), *Mental retar-dation in the 21st century* (pp. 181–196). Austin, TX: PRO-ED.

Horner, R.H., Albin, R.W., Sprague, J.R., & Todd, A.W. (2000). Positive behavior support. In M.E. Snell & F. Brown (Eds.), *Instruction of students with severe disabilities* (5th ed., pp. 207–243). Upper Saddle River, NJ: Prentice Hall.

Horner, R.H., Dunlap, G., Koegel, R.L., Carr, E.G., Sailor, W., Anderson, J., Albin, R.W., & O'Neill, R.E. (1990). Toward a technology of "nonaversive" behavioral support. *Journal of The Association for Per-sons with Severe Handicaps, 15,* 125–132.

Individuals with Disabilities Education Act Amendments of 1997, PL 105-17, 20 U.S.C. §§ 1400 *et seq.*

Johnston, J.M. (1996). Distinguishing between applied research and practice. *The Behavior Analyst, 19,* 35–47.

Kazdin, A.E. (1982). *Single case research designs.* New York: Oxford University Press.

Koegel L.K., Koegel, R.L., & Dunlap, G. (Eds.). (1996). *Positive behavioral support: Including people with dif-ficult behavior in the community.* Baltimore: Paul H. Brookes Publishing Co.

Kuhn, T.S. (1970). *The structure of scientific revolutions* (2nd ed., enlarged). Chicago: The University of Chicago Press.

Lucyshyn, J.M., & Albin, R.W. (1993). Comprehensive support to families of children with disabilities and behavior problems: Keeping it "friendly." In G.H.S. Singer & L.E. Powers (Eds.), *Families, disabil-ity, and empowerment: Active coping skills and strategies for family interventions* (pp. 365–407). Baltimore: Paul H. Brookes Publishing Co.

Lucyshyn, J.M., Albin, R.W., Horner, R.H., Mann, J.C., & Mann, J.A. (1997, May). *Collaborative positive behavioral support research with families: Longitudinal, single-case analyses with two families of children with disabilities and problem behaviors.* Presentation at the Association for Behavior Analysis Convention, Chicago.

Lucyshyn, J.M., Albin, R.W., & Nixon, C.D. (1997). Embedding comprehensive behavioral support in family ecology: An experimental, single-case analysis. *Journal of Consulting and Clinical Psychology, 65,* 241–251.

Lucyshyn, J.M., Nixon, C.D., Glang, A., & Cooley, E. (1996). Comprehensive family support for be-havioral change in children with traumatic brain injury. In G.H.S. Singer & A. Glang, & J. Williams (Vol. Eds.), *Children with acquired brain injury: Educating and supporting families* (pp. 99–136). Baltimore: Paul H. Brookes Publishing Co.

Lucyshyn, J.M., Olson, D., & Horner, R.H. (1995). Building an ecology of support: A case study of one young woman with severe problem behaviors living in the community. *Journal of The Association for Per-sons with Severe Handicaps, 20,* 16–30.

McMillan, J.H., & Schumacher, S. (2001). *Research in education: A conceptual introduction* (5th ed.). New York: Addison Wesley Longman.

Meyer, L.H. (1991). Advocacy, research, and typical practices: A call for the reduction of discrepancies be-tween what is and what ought to be, and how to get there. In L.H. Meyer, C.A. Peck, & L. Brown (Eds.), *Critical issues in the lives of people with severe disabilities* (pp. 629–649). Baltimore: Paul H. Brookes Pub-lishing Co.

Meyer, L.H., Park, H.S., Grenot-Scheyer, M., Schwartz, I., & Harry, B. (1998). Participatory research: New approaches to the research to practice dilemma. *Journal of The Association for Persons with Severe Handicaps, 23,* 165–177.

Moes, D.R., & Frea, W.D. (2000). Using family context to inform intervention planning for the treatment of a child with autism. *Journal of Positive Behavior Interventions, 2,* 40–46.

Nevada Department of Education. (1999). *Positive behavioral interventions and supports: A model program of education.* Carson City: Author.

Oregon Technical Assistance Corporation. (1998). *The Oregon Intervention System: Behavior support in the com-munity* (Version 2.3). Salem: Oregon Technical Assistance Corporation and Oregon Office of Develop-mental Disability Services.

Park, H.S., Meyer, L.H., & Goetz, L. (1998). Introduction to the special series on participatory action re-search. *Journal of The Association for Persons with Severe Handicaps, 23,* 163–164.

Pennsylvania Department of Education. (1995). *Guidelines: Effective behavioral support.* Harrisburg: Author.

Richards, S.B., Taylor, R.C., Ramasamy, R., & Richards, R.Y. (1999). *Single subject research: Applications in educational and clinical settings.* San Diego: Singular Publishing Group.

Schwartz, S., & Baer, D.M. (1991). Social validity assessments: Is current practice state of the art? *Journal of Applied Behavior Analysis, 24,* 189–204.

Scotti, J.R., Evans, I.M., Meyer, L.H., & Walker, P. (1991). A meta-analysis of intervention research with problem behavior: Treatment validity and standards of practice. *American Journal on Mental Retardation, 96,* 233–256.

Scotti, J.R., & Meyer, L.H. (Eds.). (1999). *Behavioral intervention: Principles, models, and practices.* Baltimore: Paul H. Brookes Publishing Co.

Scotti, J.R., Ujcich, K.J., Weigle, K.L., Holland, C.M., & Kirk, K.S. (1996). Interventions with challenging behavior of persons with developmental disabilities: A review of current research practices. *Journal of The Association for Persons with Severe Handicaps, 21,* 123–134.

Sidman, M. (1960). *Tactics of scientific research: Evaluating experimental data in psychology.* New York: Basic Books.

Sugai, G., Horner, R.H., Dunlap, G., Hieneman, M., Lewis, T.J., Nelson, C.M., Scott, T., Liaupsin, C., Sailor, W., Turnbull, A.P., Turnbull, H.R., Wickham, D., Wilcox, B., & Ruef, M. (2000). Applying positive behavioral support and functional behavioral assessment in schools. *Journal of Positive Behavior Interventions, 2,* 131–143.

Tawney, J.W., & Gast, D.L. (1984). *Single subject research in special education.* Columbus, OH: Charles E. Merrill.

Turnbull, A.P., Friesen, B.J., & Ramirez, C. (1998). Participatory action research as a model for conducting family research. *Journal of The Association for Persons with Severe Handicaps, 23,* 178–188.

Turnbull, H.R., Wilcox, B.L., Stowe, M., Raper, C., & Hedges, L.P. (2000). Public policy foundations for positive behavioral interventions, strategies, and supports. *Journal of Positive Behavior Interventions, 2,* 218–230.

Vaughn, B.J., Clarke, S., & Dunlap, G. (1997). Assessment-based intervention for severe behavior problems in a natural family context. *Journal of Applied Behavior Analysis, 30,* 713–716.

Vaughn, B.J., Dunlap, G., Fox, L., Clarke, S., & Bucy, M. (1997). Parent–professional partnership in behavioral support: A case study of community-based intervention. *Journal of The Association for Persons with Severe Handicaps, 22,* 186–197.

Vaughn, B.J., Wilson, D., & Dunlap, G. (2002). Family-centered intervention to resolve problem behaviors in a fast food restaurant. *Journal of Positive Behavior Interventions,4,* 38–45.

Wilcox, B.L., Turnbull, H.R., & Turnbull, A.P. (1999–2000). Behavioral issues and IDEA: Positive behavioral interventions and supports and the functional behavioral assessment in the disciplinary context. *Exceptionality, 8,* 173–187.

Wolf, M.M. (1978). Social validity: The case for subjective measurement, or how applied behavior analysis is finding its heart. *Journal of Applied Behavior Analysis, 11,* 203–214.

Wright, D.B., Gurman, H.B., & The California Association of School Psychologists/Diagnostic Center, Southern California Positive Intervention Task Force. (1998). *Positive intervention for serious behavior problems: Best practices in implementing the Hughes Bill (A.B. 2586) and the positive behavioral intervention regulations* (Rev. ed.). Sacramento: California Department of Education.

Yin, R.K. (1994). *Case study research: Design and methods* (2nd ed.). Thousand Oaks, CA: Sage Publications.

CHAPTER 17

Family Implementation of Comprehensive Behavioral Support

An Experimental, Single Case Analysis

Joseph M. Lucyshyn, Richard W. Albin, and Charles D. Nixon

Authors' Note

This chapter presents an expanded version of an experimental research article first published in 1997.[1] At the time that the study was conducted, it represented one of the first research demonstrations of the implementation of comprehensive positive behavior support with a family. The study also represented one of the first examples of collaborative, experimental research on positive behavior support with families in which parents served as research partners. The chapter provides a richer and more complete description of the assessment and intervention process and its outcomes with the child and family. Shortly after the article was published, the third author, Dr. Charles D. Nixon, passed away. Dr. Nixon was a gifted counseling psychologist who dedicated his career to helping families of children with disabilities. He played a key role in the development of the collaborative family intervention process. We dedicate the chapter to his memory.

---

[1]An early version of this chapter was previously published in the following: Lucyshyn, J.M., Albin, R.W., & Nixon, C.D. (1997). Embedding comprehensive behavioral support in family ecology: An experimental, single-case analysis. *Journal of Consulting and Clinical Psychology, 65,* 241–251. Copyright © 1997 by the American Psychological Association. Adapted with permission.

This study was supported in part by Grant Nos. H133C20114 and H133B20004 from the U.S. Department of Education to the Specialized Training Program of the University of Oregon. The opinions expressed herein do not necessarily reflect the position or policy of the U.S. Department of Education, and no official endorsement by the Department of Education should be inferred.

We gratefully thank the participating family for their collaboration throughout the study. We thank Dr. Robert Horner for his many contributions to the research methodology, support process, and editing of the original manuscript. In addition, we gratefully acknowledge the contributions of the following individuals to the development or refinement of the support process and research methodology: Dr. George H.S. Singer, Dr. Ann P. Turnbull, Dr. Glen Dunlap, Dr. Philip Ferguson, and Dr. John Reid. Furthermore, we thank Carol Knobbe, Sue Mathison, Ron Williams, Dr. Marv Wilkerson, and Dr. Linda Carnine for their support and collaboration.

Children and adolescents with severe disabilities living at home present significant care-giving challenges to their families (Hawkins & Singer, 1989). Foremost among these challenges are problem behaviors such as aggression, self-injury, and property destruction. Problem behaviors comprise a serious source of stress for family members and strongly influence out-of-home placement decisions by parents (Blacher & Hanneman, 1993). Consequently, families of children with disabilities and problem behaviors are a significant source of referral for behavioral family intervention services (Lutzker & Campbell, 1994).

The ecology of social interactions (Patterson, Reid, & Dishion, 1992), of family structure (Egel & Powers, 1989), of child activity settings (O'Donnell, Tharp, & Wilson, 1993), and of social supports and stressors (Singer & Irvin, 1991) have been viewed as relevant to the design of behavioral family interventions. Two significant challenges exist. The first is to design individualized, multicomponent interventions that are logically linked to a comprehensive functional assessment of problem behaviors (Horner & Carr, 1997). Such an assessment includes attention to ecological variables (e.g., activity patterns, opportunities for preference and choice) in addition to a focus on the antecedent and consequent events that occasion or maintain problem behaviors (Horner et al., 1990). This expanded ecological view recognizes that single interventions are rarely sufficient for producing generalized and durable behavior change. The second challenge is to assess the family contexts in which interventions will be implemented and to integrate interventions into this larger ecology. In addition to a focus on the child, there is concern about the effects of intervention on implementors and implementation settings (O'Donnell & Tharp, 1990; Willems, 1974). Lack of treatment adherence, side effects, and loss of maintenance all may result from inattention to these variables (Witt & Elliot, 1984). This is particularly relevant for families of children with disabilities and problem behaviors because of the diversity of child and family characteristics (Turnbull & Turnbull, 1997) and the potential for multiple presenting problems (Griest & Forehand, 1982). For multicomponent interventions to have any chance of success in family settings, they need to be individualized to the child but also tailored to the social and physical ecology of the family.

The term *contextual fit* is used in this chapter to define multicomponent support plans that are congruent with relevant child, implementor, and setting variables and, therefore, are likely to be effective and socially valid (Albin, Lucyshyn, Horner, & Flannery, 1996). We developed a comprehensive, ecological approach to behavioral support for families of children with disabilities and problem behaviors that adopts this heuristic. In this approach, a functional assessment of problem behaviors is integrated with an ethnographic assessment of family ecology for the purpose of building effective and contextually appropriate multicomponent behavior support plans (Lucyshyn & Albin, 1993). Implementor variables taken into consideration include family goals and values, strengths, and stressors (Singer & Irvin, 1991). Setting variables include the structure of child activity settings (i.e., daily routines) (O'Donnell et al., 1993) and available resources and social supports (Harris, 1994). The approach also is highly collaborative, recognizing the expert knowledge that families possess about their ecology and the role of families as "their children's most powerful, valuable, and durable resource" (Dunlap & Robbins, 1991, p. 188). The goals of the approach are to improve the child's behavior and lifestyle, to augment parenting and problem-solving skills, and to strengthen the family as a whole.

Descriptive results from preliminary applications of the comprehensive approach have been encouraging (Lucyshyn & Albin, 1993; Lucyshyn, Nixon, Glang, & Cooley, 1996). The study described in this chapter provides a more rigorously controlled experimental and descriptive single case analysis to evaluate the efficacy of the approach. The study addresses three themes: 1) the need for empirical examples of multicomponent interventions that are linked to a functional assessment and designed to promote durable behavior and lifestyle changes (Horner & Carr, 1997); 2) the value of collaborative research that includes consumers in the selection of research goals and in the design of independent and dependent variables (Fawcett, 1991; Turnbull & Turnbull, 1993); and 3) the design of empirically based, context-sensitive, single case studies that illustrate the process of change and the variables that are associated with change over the entire course of intervention (Hilliard, 1993).

The primary goal of the study was to evaluate the functional relationship between implementation of the comprehensive family support process and child behavioral improvement in valued family routines. A second goal was to document parent implementation of a multicomponent intervention following the introduction of training and support activities and to evaluate implementation fidelity pre- and postintervention. The third goal was to assess the relationship between implementation of the support process and generalized improvements in child behavior and lifestyle. A family report measure of daily indicator behaviors illustrated a novel method for assessing generalization to nontrained settings. Additional goals were to assess the contextual fit of the multicomponent support plan and the social validity of the support effort.

METHODS

This section describes the research participants and settings and the methods that were used during the conduct of the study. These methods include 1) procedures for measuring independent variables (i.e., the comprehensive intervention) and dependent variables (i.e., the effects of intervention), 2) procedures to measure agreement between observers, 3) research designs used, and 4) specific research procedures and steps in the conduct of the study.

Participants

The family of a 14-year-old girl with multiple disabilities participated in the study. The teenager, Helen, was selected for the study because she represented an extreme case of someone for whom comprehensive family support is appropriate. Helen was diagnosed as having severe mental retardation, functional blindness, and severe forefoot pronation. Her adaptive behavior was ranked in the severe deficit range of the Vineland Adaptive Behavior Scales (Standard score 24, <1 percentile rank) (Sparrow, Balla, & Cicchetti, 1984). She did not use formal speech to communicate but often vocalized sounds and sometimes uttered words. Helen attended a self-contained classroom for students with moderate and severe disabilities in a general education public secondary school.

Helen had a long history of problem behaviors including self-injury, aggression, property destruction, and disruptive behaviors. Severe problem behaviors occurred primarily at home with family members. Family reports indicated that she engaged in intense episodes of eye poking that sometimes caused tissue damage and that were potentially life threatening. She hit, kicked, and head butted family members, sometimes inflicting physical injury on them. Severe problem behaviors occurred many times every day and were a chronic source of stress for the family. Helen lived at home with her mother, Katharine, and her father, Jacob, both 37 years of age. Also living at home were her older sister and brother, Ashley and Michael, ages 15 and 16 respectively. Katharine worked primarily as a homemaker, and Jacob worked at a warehouse of a national hardware chain. The family lived in a three-bedroom ranch-style house in a middle-class neighborhood of a moderate sized city (population 43,000).

Settings

Four family routines in the home and community were collaboratively selected and defined with Helen's parents. Each routine represented an activity setting (Gallimore, Goldenberg, & Weisner, 1993; O'Donnell et al., 1993) that the family valued but rarely or never did with Helen because of her problem behaviors. These routines were

1.   Helen and her parents having dinner together in the dining area of the house

2.   Helen going out with her parents for dinner at the family's favorite pizza restaurant

3.   Helen participating in a leisure routine composed of simple chore and leisure tasks (e.g., giving her father a beverage, engaging in independent play)

4.   Helen accompanying one or both parents on a grocery shopping errand to a neighborhood supermarket

The selection and definition of routines were guided by an interview protocol administered by the first author. Definitions were based on the concept of the activity setting and its elements as described by Gallimore and colleagues (1993) and O'Donnell and colleagues (1993). For each setting, Helen's parents first described the current routine, and then envisioned what a meaningful, feasible, and successful routine would look like. Each description was composed of six elements: 1) time and place; 2) people; 3) material resources; 4) tasks and organization; 5) family goals, values, and beliefs; and 6) common patterns of interaction. Envisioned routines were then summarized into a one-page operational definition of each setting.

Measurement

The study used multiple measurement procedures to monitor the dependent variables and to document implementation of the independent variables. The primary measurement procedure and the dependent variables are described next.

Microcomputer Direct Observation Data Collection   Observation sessions in the home and community were videotaped using an 8-millimeter camcorder, and data were collected in a data room using a video monitor and two IBM-compatible desktop computers. A computer software observation program, Portable Computer Systems for Observational Use (PCS; Repp, Karsch, Van Acker, Felce, & Harman, 1989), was used to record rate and duration data from videotapes in real-time (i.e., recording the exact time, in seconds, of the onset and/or offset of target behavior) and to compute interobserver agreement. Observation sessions in the four family settings were planned to conform with a multiple-baseline design. Two kinds of observation sessions were conducted: observation probes and training probes. Observation probes were conducted during baseline, maintenance, generalization, and follow-up phases. During such probes, an observer videotaped child and family participation across all four routines. Probe sessions were repeated until stable behavioral patterns were evidenced in the data. Training probes were conducted only during the initial training and support phases of the dinner, restaurant, and leisure routines. The observer videotaped family participation in only one setting, the routine in which initial training and support was being provided. Training probe sessions were repeated every 1–4 weeks until stable improvement was evidenced in the data.

Before a probe, Helen's parents reviewed the operational definition of the routine and ensured that the materials and structure of the routine were present. The family initiated the routine by telling Helen what they would do together and by prompting her to do the first step in the routine. During a probe, an observer videotaped child–parent interaction until the routine was completed or until a criterion level of problem behavior was reached.

Dependent Variables   Seven dependent variables were measured: 1) rate of problem behaviors, 2) latency in minutes either to termination of a routine because of problem behaviors or to the successful completion of a routine, 3) rate and occurrence or nonoccurrence of parents' accurate use of support plan procedures, 4) frequency of parent-reported indicator behaviors, 5) child activity patterns in the community, 6) average index of the support plan's contextual fit with family ecology, and 7) average rating of social validity of the support effort. Each dependent variable is described in detail next.

Rate of Problem Behaviors   Four categories of problem behaviors were defined for Helen. The first category was self-injurious behaviors, including eye and temple poking, hair pulling, and pinching. The second was aggression toward others, including slapping, kicking, head butting, pinching, grabbing eyeglasses, and pulling hair. The third was disruptive-destructive behaviors directed at objects, including grabbing and throwing items, opening and spilling containers, tearing or crumpling items, pushing or knocking things over, and pounding items against floor. The fourth was disruptive body movements, including falling to the ground or floor or lying down on a booth seat. A behavioral event ranged in intensity from low to high and in duration from a second to a few seconds.

Latency in Minutes   Because Helen's problem behaviors placed her and her parents at physical and psychological risk, a criterion level of problem behaviors for terminating a routine was collaboratively defined with her parents (Carr & Carlson, 1993). *Latency to termination* was defined as the number of minutes that elapsed from the initiation of the routine to 1) the first instance of untolerated problem behaviors, 2) the second instance of tolerated problem behaviors, or 3) the third instance of immediate physical restraint of Helen's hands or arms by a parent. *Latency to successful completion of a routine* was defined as the number of minutes to completion of all critical task steps in a routine without the occurrence of the termination criterion.

Parents' Accurate Use of Support Procedures   Eight positive behavior support (PBS) procedures were defined: 1) embedded reinforcers, 2) proactive information giving, 3) proactive positive contingency statements, 4) proactive task prompts, 5) proactive language prompts, 6) contingent praise for prosocial behavior, 7) a contingent de-escalation procedure for problem behavior, and 8) a contingent emergency procedure for high-intensity problem behavior. These procedures constituted the core of the multicomponent behavior support plan that Helen's parents implemented in each setting. Embedded reinforcers (a setting event procedure) were assessed using a nominal scale of measurement (i.e., a measure of qualitatively different categories). The *occurrence or nonoccurrence of the procedure* was defined as a critical number of tangible reinforcers present and available during a routine.

Instances of proactive information giving, positive contingency statements, task prompts, language prompts, and contingent praise for prosocial behavior were determined by attending to discrete phrases or sentences and by evaluating whether the phrase or sentence was a positive or negative example of the procedure. De-escalation and emergency procedures involved between two and five procedural steps that extended in duration from a few seconds to 2 minutes. Definitions specified the statements and/or actions that initiated, sustained, and terminated a procedure. An error in any step of a de-escalation or an emergency procedure resulted in the procedure not being scored as an instance of accurate use.

Parent Daily Report of Indicator Behaviors   *Indicator behaviors* were defined as incidents of moderate- to high-intensity aggression or self-injury. Each incident was separated by 1 minute in which moderate- or high-intensity self-injury or aggression did not occur. These behaviors were associated with high rates of low-intensity problem behaviors across a variety of family settings; thus, they served as a rough measure of the generalization of behavioral improvement across a wide range of settings not directly observed. A standard interview protocol was used to assess the time, frequency, intensity level, and setting of indicator behaviors during nonschool hours (16.5 hours per weekday). Helen's family reported daily indicator behaviors in the early evening of weeks in which probes were conducted. Procedural steps taken to enhance the reliability and validity of the verbal-report data included prior training on definitions, practice reporting sessions, and monthly reviews of definitions.

Child Activity Patterns in the Community   The Resident Lifestyle Inventory (RLI; Kennedy, Horner, Newton, & Kanda, 1990) was used as a quality-of-life index to assess Helen's participation in home and community activities during baseline, intervention, and follow-up phases. The RLI is an 18-page interview form that provides information about an individual's participation in 144 different leisure and personal-management activities during the previous 30 days. The RLI measures the frequency of activities performed, the number of different activities performed, and the number of different activities identified as preferred activities. Helen's parents completed RLI interviews once during baseline, twice during the intervention phase, and twice during follow-up.

Contextual Fit Evaluation   Helen's parents evaluated the contextual fit of the behavior support plan with their family's ecology using an assessment instrument specifically developed for this purpose (Albin et al., 1996). The instrument was composed of 20 items that sample parameters relevant to contextual fit (e.g., goals and expectations, congruence with family lifestyle, sustainability). Family members rated each item using a five-point Likert scale. The evaluation was completed four times during the intervention phase and twice during follow-up. Average ratings for each parent were used as indices of contextual fit.

Social Validity Evaluation   Helen's parents evaluated the social validity (Schwartz & Baer, 1991) of the comprehensive support effort using a ten-item instrument with a six-point Likert scale (Schwartz & Baer, 1991). An evaluation was completed at the end of the initial training phase for the dinner, restaurant, and leisure routines, at the end of the generalization promotion phase, and twice during follow-up. Average ratings for each person served as formative and summative indices of social validity.

Interobserver Agreement   An undergraduate psychology student conducted observations in the home and collected data using the video monitor and computer observation system. The first author served as interobserver agreement data collector. Observers participated in 25 hours of training prior to the collection of child behavioral data and 40 hours of training prior to the collection of the parents' use of support procedure data. Data collection began after the observers achieved 90% agreement for each problem behavior category across two pilot observations and 85% agreement for each support procedure category across two pilot observations for each setting. Observers maintained coding skills by scoring previously coded tapes 1–2 hours per month for the duration of the study.

For Helen's problem behaviors and her parents' accurate use of support procedures, observer agreement was measured using PCS observation software (Repp et al., 1989). Two observers simultaneously viewed videotapes of probe sessions and coded behaviors using computers separated by 1 meter and a visual barrier. A tolerance of ±3 seconds was used to calculate agreement. Observer agreement was calculated by dividing the number of agreements by the number of agreements plus disagreements, then multiplying this number by 100%.

Observer agreement for latency to termination or successful completion of routine was measured with checklists for criterion problem behavior categories and for task steps in each routine. Two observers, separated by 1 meter and a visual barrier, simultaneously observed the videotape of a probe session and noted the time of occurrence of criterion behavior. If the criterion was not met, then the observers checked off which task steps were completed and noted the time of successful routine completion. A margin of ±5 seconds was used to assess the agreement of time(s) noted by observers. Observer agreement for latency to termination or successful completion of routines and for steps completed was calculated by dividing the number of agreements by the number of agreements plus disagreements, then multiplying this number by 100%.

Observer agreement checks were completed in 30%–49% of probe sessions for each dependent variable, balanced across settings and phases. The average agreement across all problem behavior categories was 94% (range = 75%–100%). The average agreement for disruptive-destructive behaviors was 95% (range = 75%–100%). The average observer agreement across all categories for parents' accurate use of support procedures was 94% (range = 56%–100%). The average agreement for latency to termination due to problem behavior was 98% (range = 67%–100%). The average agreement for latency to successful completion of routines and for steps completed was 100% and 98% (range = 67%–100%), respectively.

Research Design

This subsection describes the research designs that were employed to answer the study's research questions and the specific procedural steps that were followed in the conduct of the study.

Single Subject Research Methods   The study employed a multiple-baseline design across four settings (Barlow & Hersen, 1984). A multiple-probe measurement strategy (Horner & Baer, 1978) was utilized to reduce the amount of time that the family spent in data collection activities and to maximize time in training and support activities. The design involved 5 phases: 1) baseline, 2) initial training and support, 3) maintenance support, 4) generalization promotion, and 5) follow-up. An alternating treatment design (Iwata, Dorsey, Slifer, Bauman, & Richman, 1982/1994) was used during a functional analysis to verify hypotheses about the functions of problem behaviors. A single-baseline, time-series design (Campbell & Stanley, 1966) was employed to describe the correlation between baseline, intervention, and follow-up phases and the reported daily frequency of indicator behaviors.

Participatory Action Research Methods   During the longitudinal study, participatory action research (PAR) principles and practices were adopted to ensure that the research process was acceptable and feasible to the family (Bruyère, 1993; Fawcett, 1991;

Turnbull, Friesen, & Ramirez, 1998). Helen's parents participated in the study as collaborative partners, sharing in decisions related to research and family support activities. Specifically, Katherine and Jacob selected and defined the research settings (i.e., family routines), helped to define the primary independent variable (i.e., positive behavior support plan) and dependent variables (e.g., Helen's problem behaviors), and implemented the behavior support plan with Helen. Helen's parents also shared control over the pace of the study by participating in decisions about the scheduling of observation sessions and support activities. In addition, they participated in the collection of data and the interpretation of results through evaluations of contextual fit and social validity.

Procedures

The first author served as the primary interventionist throughout the study, conducting or coordinating all assessments and collaborating with the family on intervention development and implementation activities. The second and third authors served as research and clinical supervisors of the study. The procedures that were used in the study are described in the following subsections.

Baseline   Observation probes in each routine measured preintervention rates of problem behaviors, latency in minutes to termination or successful completion of routines, and rates of parent implementation of support procedures. Operational definitions of routines guided the implementation of a structured baseline whose physical elements (e.g., time and place, people, material resources, tasks) remained consistent throughout subsequent phases of the study (Davis, Turner, Rolider, & Cartwright, 1994; Gallimore et al., 1993). Observation probes were conducted in each routine until a stable rate of problem behaviors was evidenced in the graphed data. Baseline probe data were gathered across 5 weeks. The preintervention level of indicator behaviors was measured across 13 interviews with Helen's family members, spanning the same 5-week period as direct observation data. The RLI was administered once to assess Helen's activity patterns during the 30 days preceding baseline probe sessions.

Comprehensive Assessment   The comprehensive assessment included an assessment of family ecology and a functional analysis of Helen's problem behavior. These assessment and analysis procedures are described in the following subsections.

Family Ecology Assessment   The clinical goal of the assessment was to gather information about the family's ecology relevant to the design of a contextually appropriate behavior support plan. Across two interview sessions, Helen's parents answered open-ended questions about family goals, family strengths, resources and social support available to the family, and sources of stress, including the effect of problem behaviors on family members. A summary of family ecology assessment results is presented in Table 17.1.

Functional Analysis   The functional analysis consisted of two activities: 1) descriptive assessment to generate hypotheses about the functions of problem behaviors and the conditions that promoted adaptive behavior and 2) experimental manipulations to verify hypotheses about the functions of problem behaviors.

A descriptive assessment of Helen's problem behaviors was completed using the functional analysis interview and observation protocols described by O'Neill, Horner, Albin,

Table 17.1. Family ecology assessment

Family strengths

Strong religious values (e.g., loving kindness, patience)

True partnership between parents

Family's optimism and "can do" spirit

Older brother's and sister's knowledge and skill with Helen

Resources and social supports

Excellent support from classroom teacher and teaching assistants

Help and support from brother and sister (e.g., respite)

Local respite care services available

Sources of stress

Effect of problem behaviors on family members (e.g., anxiety attacks, physical injury, easy to anger)

Helen's domination of her parents' lifestyle (e.g., parents do not get away enough, little respite from caregiving)

The absence of any progress in Helen's behavior or level of independence

Child and family goals

Helen participating in tasks and activities in the home and community more independently

Helen learning to self-manage free time in the home

Increasing communication skills and decreasing problem behavior

Family receiving skilled respite care services

Parents getting away to relax at least one evening each week

Storey, and Sprague (1990). The functional analysis interview was completed across three meetings with core members of Helen's education team. Functional analysis observations also were conducted in the home and school. Five hypotheses about the functions of Helen's problem behaviors emerged from the assessment. First, Helen engaged in problem behaviors—in particular, disruptive-destructive behavior—to get attention. Second, Helen engaged in self-injurious behavior and aggression to escape or avoid nonpreferred tasks and activities and transitions between activities. Third, Helen engaged in self-injurious behavior or aggression to escape unanticipated interruptions or physical discomfort or pain. Fourth, Helen engaged in problem behaviors to obtain an item or an activity. Fifth, Helen engaged in stereotypic behaviors to get automatic reinforcement (i.e., self-stimulation). A summary of the functional assessment is presented in Table 17.2.

The validity of the five hypotheses was tested during a series of experimental manipulations conducted in the family's home, with Helen's parents serving as the interventionists. Five conditions in the home were designed in collaboration with Helen's parents to verify the hypothesized functions of problem behaviors. These conditions were 1) attention for problem behaviors, 2) demand, 3) interrupt preferred activity, 4) removal of a reinforcing activity, and 5) alone with no activity. A sixth condition, noncontingent attention, predicted the absence of problem behaviors and served as a control condition.

The six conditions were counterbalanced across three to four sessions in an alternating-treatment design (Iwata et al., 1982/1994). During the hypothesis testing sessions, Helen's parents read a procedural description of each condition, then implemented the condition with Helen. Each condition was implemented for 5 minutes or until the criterion level of problem behaviors was reached. An observer videotaped each session, and the data were later coded using the PCS computer software program.

Table 17.2. Functional analysis summary

Setting event conditions associated with problem behavior

Ecological factors
  Participating in home routines largely shaped by problem behaviors
  Little to no community participation
  Absence of age-appropriate leisure materials
Medical/physical factors
  Physical pain in ankles and feet
  Physical discomfort due to constipation
Educational/skill factors
  Little to no formal language to communicate wants/needs
  Unable to perform simple tasks independently

Antecedent triggers

Preferred person nearby but not giving attention
Attention to Helen interrupted
Sitting near or walking past items
Abrupt, unpredicted interactions
Transition from preferred activity
Non-preferred foods offered

Hypotheses about the functions of problem behaviors

Helen engages in disruptive/destructive behaviors, aggression, and self-injurious behavior (SIB) to get attention (e.g., preferred person, intense verbal interaction, physical contact).

Helen engages in SIB and aggression to avoid/escape: (a) non-preferred task, activity, or person; (b) transitions from preferred to non-preferred activities; (c) interruptions, abrupt interactions, or harsh interactions; and (d) physical pain or discomfort.

Helen engages in disruptive/destructive behavior, aggression, or SIB to obtain an item (e.g., food) or activity (e.g., use bathroom).

Helen engages in mild SIB to get self-stimulation.

___

Preliminary Plan Design   This section briefly describes the process by which a preliminary positive behavior support plan and an implementation plan were developed.

Positive Behavior Support Plan   Following the comprehensive assessment, a preliminary multicomponent support plan was developed. Two goals were sought. The first goal was to build an effective environment for Helen. Using the competing behavior analysis framework described by Horner, O'Neill, and Flannery (1993), the authors selected setting event, antecedent, teaching, and consequence strategies to make problem behaviors "irrelevant, ineffective, and inefficient" at achieving their functions (O'Neill et al., 1997, p. 66). The second goal was to design a behavior support plan that fit well with the family's social and physical ecology. To generate a contextual fit with the family's ecology, support procedures were retained or proposed that reflected family goals, enhanced family strengths, incorporated informal or formal resources or social supports available to the family, and diminished stressors (Albin et al., 1996).

Implementation Plan   An action plan proposal for implementing the multicomponent behavior support plan in the home and community was designed. The proposal included recommendations for parent training and support activities and the delineation of support roles and responsibilities. Proposed training and support activities included a written positive behavior support plan, routine-specific implementation checklists, in vivo modeling and coaching, behavioral rehearsal, and problem-solving discussions (Sanders & Dadds, 1993).

Team Meetings and Plan Finalization   Members of Helen's support team met twice (4 hours total) to review the assessment information and finalize the positive behavior support plan and the implementation plan. Meeting participants included Helen's parents, teacher, school-based behavior consultant, communication specialist, physical therapist, occupational therapist, and service coordinator. Team members reviewed and reached a consensus on functional assessment hypotheses, proposed intervention procedures, and implementation support activities. Team member input was solicited during the meeting and incorporated into the finalized plan. Helen's comprehensive behavior support plan is summarized in Table 17.3.

Table 17.3.   Helen's behavior support plan

Ecological procedures

1. Enhance family activity patterns in the home and community. Build Helen's ability to participate in valued home and community routines.
2. During setting events (e.g., constipation, illness, change in daily routine): (a) increase preferred activities; (b) decrease demands and nonpreferred interactions; and (c) minimize confusion, pain, or discomfort.
3. Provide a diet and/or medication that minimizes pain or physical discomfort due to constipation or illness.

Antecedent procedures

1. Give Helen information that helps her predict interactions, tasks/activities, assistance, and changes.
2. Use an instructional style that promotes attention, cooperation, and success: (a) offer choices where possible; (b) keep attention on the task; (c) use proactive assistance to assure success, (d) use one-step directions; and (e) go at her pace.

Teaching new behaviors/skills

1. Teach Helen to use communicative signals for (a) wanting attention, (b) wanting a break/to stop, (c) wanting food/drink, and (d) wanting to use bathroom.
2. Teach Helen to tolerate an absence or interruption of attention.

Positive reinforcement strategies

1. Embed natural reinforcers in functional tasks and activities.
2. Give social and physical attention *contingently* for trying, improvement, and independent actions.
3. Use positive contingencies and natural reinforcers to ease transitions.

De-escalation procedures

1. Actively ignore and positively redirect minor problem behaviors.
2. Minimize reinforcement for moderate/high intensity behaviors: (a) step away from aggression; (b) quietly block self-injury and redirect when calm; (c) interrupt grabbing with "Let go," prompt hands down for 3–10 seconds without touching hands, and redirect when calm; (d) ignore throwing, prompt hands down, and redirect; (e) interrupt destructive behavior, prompt "let go" and "hands down," and redirect; (f) verbally redirect falling to ground/floor.

Emergency procedures

1. Use nonaggressive physical restraint to prevent injury.
2. Wrap Helen in a blanket as a last resort.

Implementation Support During implementation support Helen's parents were taught to implement the behavior support plan. Implementation support and training activities were introduced in a multiple-baseline design across family routines in the following order: 1) dinner routine, 2) restaurant routine, 3) leisure routine, and 4) grocery shopping routine. Two phases of implementation support were sequentially introduced for the dinner, restaurant, and leisure routines: initial training and support and maintenance support. One phase of implementation support was introduced to the grocery shopping routine: generalization promotion. These three phases are described in the following subsections.

Initial Training and Support Intensive training and support were provided in only one routine. Training sessions occurred in the home or community one to three times per week (mean [M] = 2.3 days per week) and lasted 20–75 minutes per session (M = 33.4 minutes). Initial training and support for the dinner routine required 29 sessions across 12 weeks for a total of 17 hours. Initial training and support for the restaurant routine involved 12 sessions across 4 weeks for a total of 8 hours. Training and support for the leisure routine involved 25 sessions across 11 weeks for a total of 13 hours. Training activities included 1) providing direct training with Helen, 2) modeling interventions for her parents, 3) coaching her parents in the use of interventions, 4) conducting problem-solving discussions, 5) role playing the use of interventions, and 6) teaching her parents to self-monitor and self-evaluate the use of interventions. As Helen and her parents became successful at participating in the routine together, the consultant faded training and support activities (Sanders & Dadds, 1993).

Maintenance Support Maintenance support was sequentially introduced to the dinner, restaurant, and leisure routines after training probes in each routine indicated meaningful and stable improvement in Helen's behavior. During maintenance support, the schedule of training and support sessions was decreased to one session every 1 or 2 weeks (M = 1 session every 1.5 weeks). For the dinner routine, 15 sessions ($\cong$ 8.5 hours) of maintenance support occurred across 21 weeks. For the restaurant routine, 14 sessions ($\cong$ 7.5 hours) were provided across 23 weeks. For the leisure routine, 3 sessions ($\cong$ 1.4 hours) were provided across 4 weeks. Session length remained about the same as the first intervention phase (M = 31 minutes; range = 20–55 minutes), but the amount of training and support during a session decreased. Implementation support was faded to brief coaching before a routine began, little or no coaching during a routine, and debriefing meetings that included acknowledgement of accomplishments, concept-building activities, and problem-solving discussions.

During maintenance support, training and support activities focused on overcoming three obstacles to the continued success of the routines: 1) recurring parent errors in implementation fidelity (e.g., attention contingent on disruptive behavior), 2) adverse child effects on parent effectiveness (e.g., child prompts for affection that thwarted the parents' use of de-escalation procedures; see Carr, Taylor, & Robinson, 1991), and 3) setting events that negatively influenced child or parent performance (e.g., Helen's loss of appetite due to illness, her father's stressful day at work; see Horner, Vaughn, Day, & Ard, 1996; Wahler & Graves, 1983). When behavioral data indicated deterioration in Helen's behavior or her parents' responses, the consultant and the family assessed problems and collaboratively generated solutions. Such solutions were written as addenda to the support plan following regression in the dinner and restaurant routines. These solutions were designed specifically to help Helen's parents overcome common errors in implementation, to circumvent child effects, or to prevent or neutralize detrimental setting events.

Generalization Promotion   After the first training probe in the leisure routine, meetings were held with Helen's parents in the home to promote generalization of support plan effects to nontrained settings (Dunlap, 1993). Meetings occurred twice a month across a 4-month period and lasted 30 minutes to 2 hours (M = 1.3 hours). Generalization promotion activities included parent use of an implementation checklist to self-monitor and self-evaluate the implementation of support procedures in nontrained settings (Sanders & Dadds, 1993) and guided practice in the use of a problem-solving strategy for adapting support procedures to novel settings. The steps in the problem solving strategy were 1) identify a problem setting, 2) assess the functions of problem behavior, 3) select relevant procedures from the implementation checklist, and 4) adapt the procedures to fit the setting. The grocery store routine was used to directly assess generalization effects. No direct training occurred for this setting; rather, we implemented generalization promotion activities with the family before assessing generalized effects in the grocery store.

Follow-Up   At 3 and 9 months after the termination of all support, data were collected across dependent measures. Before follow-up measurement, Helen's parents were encouraged to review the behavior support plan. After observation sessions, brief consultative assistance was provided as needed.

RESULTS

This section summarizes the results of the functional analysis and the implementation of the family support approach.

Functional Analysis

The results of the functional analysis are presented in Figure 17.1. These results confirmed four of the six hypotheses identified from interviews. The data indicate that Helen engaged in high rates of problem behaviors to get attention (M = 34.3 per minute), to escape an abrupt interruption (M = 21 per minute), and to escape a demand (M = 13 per minute). The noncontingent attention condition confirmed that Helen engaged in zero to low rates of problem behaviors during nondemanding, preferred interactions (M = 1.8 per minute). Two hypotheses were not confirmed by this initial analysis. During the removal of a reinforcer (a preferred activity with her father), Helen engaged in zero to low rates of problem behaviors (M = 0.8 per minute). During the alone without an activity condition, she did not engage in stereotypic behavior.

Implementation of Family Support Approach

Seven dependent variables were used to evaluate the impact of the intervention: 1) Helen's problem behaviors, 2) latency in minutes, 3) the parents' accurate use of support procedures, 4) Helen's indicator behaviors, 5) activity patterns, 6) contextual fit indices, and 7) social validity ratings. Because normative comparative data did not exist for children with or without disabilities in situations that were identical to Helen's (Kendall & Grove, 1988), the chapter authors defined the characteristics of a socially valid (i.e., important and acceptable) effect for problem behavior results rather than a clinically significant one. A socially valid effect required 1) near-zero levels of disruptive-destructive behaviors; 2) low

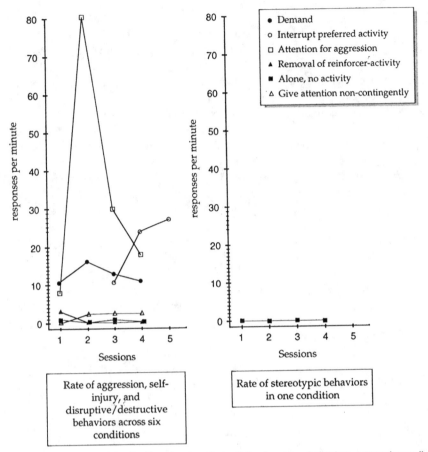

Figure 17.1.   Results of the first functional analysis: Rate of problem behaviors across six conditions and of stereotypic behavior in one condition. (From Lucyshyn, J.M., Albin, R.W., & Nixon, C.D. [1997]. Embedding comprehensive behavioral support in family ecology: An experimental, single-case analysis. *Journal of Consulting and Clinical Psychology, 65,* 241–251. Copyright © 1997 by the American Psychological Association. Reprinted with permission.)

levels of gentle eye or temple poking; 3) covariation with the successful completion of routines; and 4) high parent ratings of social validity during intervention and follow-up phases.

Problem Behaviors   Figure 17.2 shows the rate of total problem behaviors and disruptive-destructive behaviors across four routines. Overall, the data documented a functional relationship between the implementation of family support and training and socially valid reductions in both total problem behaviors and the more intense subset of disruptive-destructive behaviors. These effects largely endured across maintenance and follow-up conditions. During baseline across four routines, total problem behaviors averaged 10 behaviors per minute (range = 2.8–33.2 per minute). This declined to an average of 3.8 behaviors per minute during the initial training and support phase in the dinner, restaurant, and leisure routines (range = 1.0–7.7 per minute); an average of 2.4 behaviors per minute during the maintenance phase for three routines (range = 1.1–5.5 per minute); and an average of 2.3 behaviors per minute during generalization promotion for the grocery shopping routine (range = 1.2–5.0 per minute). Disruptive-destructive destructive behaviors averaged 4.1 per minute during baseline (range = 0.4–18 per minute) but declined to an average of 0.5 per minute during the initial training phase (range = 0.0–3.4 per minute), 0.4 per

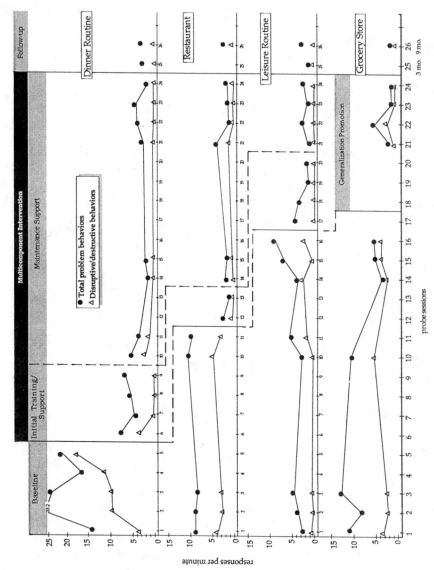

Figure 17.2. Rate of total problem behaviors and disruptive-destructive behaviors across four family settings. (From Lucyshyn, J.M., Albin, R.W., & Nixon, C.D. [1997]. Embedding comprehensive behavioral support in family ecology: An experimental, single-case analysis. *Journal of Consulting and Clinical Psychology, 65,* 241–251. Copyright © 1997 by the American Psychological Association. Reprinted with permission.)

405

minute during the maintenance phase (range = 0.0–2.1 per minute), and 1.1 per minute in the generalization phase (range = 0.5–2.2 per minute). By the end of the maintenance and generalization phases, problem behaviors involved low-intensity grabbing and eye poking that were easily redirected and irrelevant to Helen's successful participation in each setting. During 3- and 9-month follow-up, further improvement was evidenced. Total problem behaviors across four routines averaged 2.1 per minute (range = 1.5–2.9 per minute), and disruptive-destructive behaviors averaged 0.2 per minute (range = 0.0–0.3).

Latency in Minutes   Figure 17.3 summarizes latency in minutes to the termination or successful completion of a routine. Overall, these data indicate socially valid improvements in latency from baseline to intervention phases. During baseline across settings, Helen spent an average of 4.3 minutes in routines (range = 0.3–16 minutes). No routines (0 of 25) were completed successfully, with the termination criterion occurring before completion of tasks during each observation probe. Across initial training in the dinner, restaurant, and leisure routines, latency improved to an average of 15.2 minutes (range = 1.2–22.3 minutes). During maintenance and follow-up phases for the three routines, latency for successful completion decreased (maintenance phase: M = 12.7 minutes, range = 3.8–19.1 minutes; follow-up phase: M = 14.7 minutes, range = 12.5–16 minutes). During generalization promotion, latency improved to an average of 6.5 minutes in the grocery store and maintained during follow-up. Across training, maintenance, generalization, and follow-up phases, Helen successfully completed 33 of 38 routines (87%).

Parents' Accurate Use of Support Plan Procedures   Table 17.4 shows the average rate of the parents' accurate use of support procedures across the baseline, intervention (including initial training and support, maintenance support, and generalization promotion), and follow-up phases. Overall, the data indicate a threefold increase in the use of procedures from the baseline to intervention phases. During baseline across four routines, Helen's parents implemented support plan procedures at an average rate of 4.5 per minute (range = 0.0–10.4 per minute). Following initial training and support in the dinner, restaurant, and leisure routines, the average rate increased to 12.7 procedures per minute (range = 9.1–18.3 per minute) and remained stable at 12.7 per minute (range = 9.3–17.5 per minute) during the maintenance phase. Following generalization promotion, the average rate increased to 13.9 per minute (range = 10.2–16.7 per minute) in the grocery shopping routine. During follow-up, procedure use averaged 12.5 per minute (range = 10.0–15.3 per minute), indicating substantial maintenance. Specific procedures that evidenced higher average rates postintervention were proactive information giving (preintervention M = 0.5 per minute, postintervention M = 1.2 per minute), proactive positive contingency statements (preintervention M = 0.0, postintervention M = 0.7 per minute), proactive task prompts (preintervention M = 2.9 per minute; postintervention M = 5.4 per minute), and contingent praise for prosocial behavior (preintervention M = 0.3 per minute, postintervention M = 4.8 per minute). In terms of embedded reinforcers, during baseline an average of 37.5% of routines included embedded reinforcers (range = 0%–100%). This increased to an average of 100% of routines across intervention and follow-up phases.

Indicator Behaviors   Figure 17.4 displays the frequency of indicator behaviors reported by Helen's parents across a 26-month period from July 1993 to August 1995. Overall, these data provide a complex pattern. Baseline averaged 18 incidents per day with an increasing trend. Implementation of training in the dinner routine was associated with a reduction in the frequency of incidents and the reversal of the baseline trend. In April 1994,

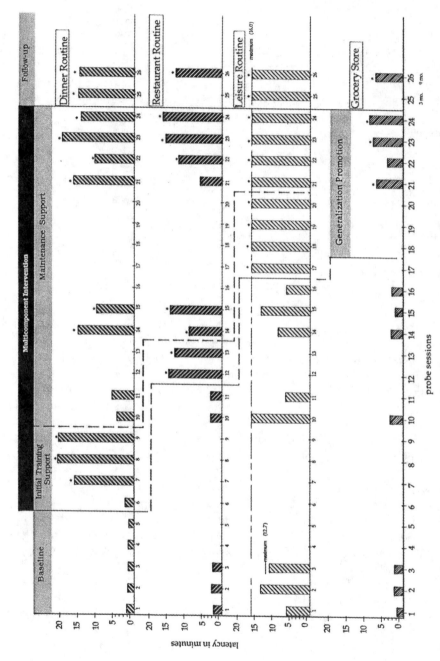

Figure 17.3. Latency in minutes of problem behaviors or to successful completion of a routine across four family settings. (* = A successfully completed routine; mo. = months.) (From Lucyshyn, J.M., Albin, R.W., & Nixon, C.D. [1997]. Embedding comprehensive behavioral support in family ecology: An experimental, single-case analysis. *Journal of Consulting and Clinical Psychology, 65*, 241–251. Copyright © 1997 by the American Psychological Association. Reprinted with permission.)

Table 17.4. Average rate per minute of parents' accurate use of behavior support plan procedures across baseline, intervention, and follow-up

Behavior support plan procedures	Baseline[a]	Initial training and support[b]	Maintenance support[b]	Generalization promotion[c]	Follow-up[a]
		Phases			
Information giving	0.5	1.3	1.0	1.3	1.2
Positive contingency statement	0.0	0.4	0.9	0.2	1.3
Language prompt	0.5	0.7	0.9	0.3	0.7
Task prompt	2.9	4.5	4.7	7.9	4.5
Contingent praise	0.3	5.7	4.9	3.9	4.7
De-escalation procedure	0.3	0.1	0.3	0.3	0.1
Emergency procedure	0.0	0.01	0.0	0.0	0.0
Total	4.5	12.71	12.7	13.9	12.5

[a]Average rate across four settings

[b]Average rate across three settings (dinner, restaurant, and leisure routines)

[c]Average rate for one setting (grocery store routine)

Helen had an eye operation and training began in the restaurant routine. Across May 1994, there was a dramatic increase in indicator behaviors. Many of these were associated with reactive attempts by family members to stop Helen from touching the eye that had received surgery. As this regression involved life-threatening behavior, immediate consultative support was provided. Helen's family implemented strategies aimed at decreasing intensive eye poking, and the behavior subsided within 2 weeks. Training in the leisure routine and in the final maintenance and follow-up phases were associated with progressively decreasing levels of indicator behaviors ($M = 4.7$ incidents per day, range = 2–7 incidents).

Activity Patterns   RLI data indicate that after intervention, Helen's community activity patterns increased. Helen's baseline RLI showed participation in 98 community activities during a 1-month period. After intervention, community activities increased to 122 and 138 during assessed months. These improvements largely maintained during the 3-month and 9-month follow-ups (120 and 135 activities, respectively). Also, during baseline, Helen engaged in six different community activities per assessed month, all of which her parents perceived as Helen's preferred activities. After intervention, different and preferred activities doubled to 12 and 13 per assessed months. At follow-up, these improvements maintained.

Contextual Fit   A contextual fit index was devised in which 1 represented a poor fit and 5 represented a good fit with the family's ecology. For Helen's mother, the average contextual fit index across six evaluations, distributed across intervention and follow-up phases, was 4.8 (range = 4.6–4.9). For Helen's father, the average contextual fit index was 4.7 (range = 4.6–4.8). Overall, Helen's mother and father believed that the support plan fit well with the family's ecology. One exception occurred during leisure routine training

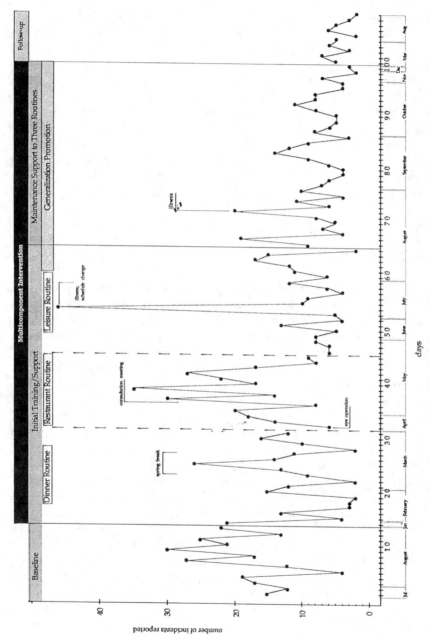

Figure 17.4. Frequency of indicator behaviors per day reported by the family during baseline, intervention, and follow-up (over a course of 26 months). (From Lucyshyn, J.M., Albin, R.W., & Nixon, C.D. [1997]. Embedding comprehensive behavioral support in family ecology: An experimental, single-case analysis. *Journal of Consulting and Clinical Psychology, 65*, 241–251. Copyright © 1997 by the American Psychological Association. Reprinted with permission.)

in the spring and summer of 1994. The index for Jacob dropped somewhat, and critical comments were written on the instrument. Because Jacob began working overtime in the summer, starting the leisure routine immediately after arriving home from work became stressful. During problem-solving discussions, the family agreed to adjust the time element of the routine so that Jacob could rest for 15–30 minutes before initiating the routine with his daughter. This change was associated with a somewhat higher index of contextual fit by Helen's father during the fourth evaluation. Follow-up indices and comments (e.g., "We have proven the plan works for all of us") suggest that the family continued to believe that the support plan fit well with their ecology.

Social Validity   Ratings and parent comments largely coincide with goodness of fit evaluative data. Across 6 evaluations (in which 1 = *unacceptable* and 6 = *acceptable*), Helen's mother's average social validity rating was 5.8 (range = 5.5–6.0), and Helen's father's average social validity rating was 5.7 (range = 5.3–5.8). Overall, Helen's parents perceived the plan goals, procedures, and outcomes as acceptable (e.g., "We have and continue to see major improvements in Helen's behavior," "We are all better equipped to support each other").

DISCUSSION

After Helen's parents implemented a multicomponent positive behavior support plan in four family routines, her problem behaviors decreased to low, socially valid levels. Disruptive-destructive behaviors, the major behavior of concern in each setting, fell to zero or a near-zero level in three of the four routines. These behavioral improvements maintained with little to no regression across a 1- to 5-month period and during follow-up at 3 and 9 months postintervention. Most important, after implementing the support plan, Helen and her parents participated together successfully in 87% of valued routines observed in the home and community across a 10- to 14-month period of maintenance support and follow-up. Taken together, these data illustrate the effectiveness of the comprehensive family support process for promoting meaningful and durable changes in Helen's behavior and participation in family routines.

Paralleling these improvements in child behavior, Helen's parents demonstrated marked increases in their use of positive behavior support procedures following introduction of an implementation plan consisting of several training and support activities. These data document parent implementation of the behavior support plan (i.e., the primary independent variable; Gresham, Gansle, & Noell, 1993). The data also suggest the efficacy of implementation support activities for developing the parents' capacity to ameliorate problem behaviors and build successful routines with their daughter.

In addition, implementation of the support process was associated with a broader range of improvements in child behavior and lifestyle. By the conclusion of implementation support, Helen's parents reported generalized improvements in Helen's self-injurious and aggressive behaviors to low, stable, and acceptable levels. Improvements in Helen's activity patterns in the community also were reported. At follow-up, these improvements largely maintained. Additional validation of the effectiveness of the support process was found in high parent indices of contextual fit and social validity.

During follow-up, Helen's parents also reported collateral effects on Helen, themselves, and other family members. For example, Katharine and Jacob reported that even though Helen had become ill with influenza, she did not experience her typical setback in behavior due to illness. Katharine reported that rather than physically help put Helen through tasks and activities without any advance notice, she more often gave Helen information and negotiated with Helen about the timing of tasks and activities. Katharine also noted that the anxiety attacks that she experienced prior to intervention had diminished from one or two per day to no more than one or two per month. She reported that she was considerably less afraid and much more confident about supporting Helen. Helen's parents also reported that their older children had begun to emulate the use of support procedures and that Helen's brother was more interactive and positive with Helen than he had been preintervention.

Although the support process was clearly effective with Helen and her family, it required considerable time and effort. The intervention involved 67 hours of direct support distributed across 106 sessions and 47 weeks. This level of effort is consistent with research on parent training for children with severe clinical disorders, which indicates that positive outcomes are more likely to occur through intensive training programs (i.e., 50–60 hours) involving direct contact with the child (Bergan & Kratochwill, 1990).

Contributions to the Literature

The study described in this chapter contributes to and extends several findings in the literature on behavior analysis and treatment. It provides further evidence for the efficacy of functional assessment technology for understanding problem behaviors and for designing effective interventions that are logically linked to the functions of problem behavior (Kennedy & Souza, 1995). The study also extends the use of functional analysis procedures into home settings, with parents as collaborators in the design and implementation of naturalistic conditions that test hypotheses about the functions of problem behaviors (Wacker, Cooper, Peck, Derby, & Berg, 1999).

The study adds to a growing body of evidence for the importance of multicomponent support plans that address each function of problem behavior and the ecological or antecedent variables associated with problem behaviors (Carr & Carlson, 1993; Dunlap, Kern-Dunlap, Clarke, & Robbins, 1991). The study extends this evidence into family settings with parents as interventionists. Finally, the study extends to family settings the use of multiple methods to measure meaningful outcomes of comprehensive behavioral intervention (Lucyshyn, Olson, & Horner, 1995; Meyer & Evans, 1993). Direct observation data, parent report of indicator behaviors to assess generalization, an empirically validated lifestyle instrument, and subjective indices were combined to document effects, associated changes, and parent perceptions following comprehensive family intervention.

Three unique contributions to the literature on behavioral family intervention are represented by the study. First, it illustrates an approach to collaborative intervention research in home and community settings with families of children with disabilities and problem behaviors (Fawcett, 1991). Helen's parents collaborated with the researchers to define each setting in terms of the goals, values, resources, and tasks that were present or available in the family's ecology. They participated in the design of natural conditions in the home to test hypotheses about the purposes of their daughter's problem behaviors, and they implemented these conditions within an alternating-treatment design. During assessment and plan development, family members and education professionals contributed knowledge about Helen's problem behaviors and collaborated in the design of behavior support plan procedures. During intervention, Helen's parents implemented the primary independent variable. From a research perspective, the immediate consumers of the research participated in defining the independent and dependent variables of the study (Faw-cett, 1991), and they served as knowledgeable partners throughout the research process (Bruyère, 1993; Turnbull et al., 1998; Turnbull & Turnbull, 1993).

A second contribution is the use of a structured baseline and a multiple baseline across valued family routines that were acceptable to one family and compatible with one partic-ular comprehensive family support approach. The structured baseline (Davis et al., 1994), which was organized by the theorized elements of daily routines (e.g., time, place, goals, people, resources, tasks; Gallimore et al., 1993; O'Donnell et al., 1993), allowed for mean-ingful comparisons between baseline and intervention phases. The lagged introduction of training and support to one routine at a time appeared to be compatible with the family support process. For Helen's parents, intervention in one routine at a time simplified the complexity of the support effort and thus made it more feasible to the family. We encour-age further attention to routines as a unit of analysis for family interventions.

A third contribution is the integration of two logical frameworks for the design of an effective, acceptable, and contextually appropriate multicomponent behavior support plans. The competing behavior analysis framework described by Horner and colleagues (1993) was used to generate interventions that were logically linked to the functions of Helen's problem behaviors. Then, a contextual-fit framework, described by Albin and colleagues (1996), was employed to select interventions that fit well with several relevant features of the family's ecology.

Results of the study offer several implications for practitioners and researchers who are involved in behavioral family intervention. The study demonstrates that it is possible for parents of children with severe disabilities and problem behaviors to collaborate in a comprehensive family support process and effectively implement a multicomponent beha-vior support plan. Results also suggest that generalized improvement in child behavior throughout the child's and family's day together may be associated with direct training in specific routines, paired with generalization promotion activities for nontrained settings.

Because children with severe disabilities often engage in problem behaviors for mul-tiple purposes and these purposes will be asserted in a variety of family settings, behavior support plans need to include multiple components. Also, the obstacles that Helen's par-ents faced in effectively supporting Helen suggest the importance of direct consultative support in natural family settings for children with extensive repertoires and histories of problem behaviors (Carr et al., 1994).

Limitations and Cautions

A limitation of the study is that the multicomponent nature of the intervention does not permit comment about the unique contribution of each component to improvement in Helen's behavior. In addition, inferences of causality between generalized improvement in indicator behaviors and implementation of the support process cannot be made. The single baseline, time-series design (see Figure 17.4) does not control for alternative explanations for results such as history or maturation effects.

Although the results of the study are encouraging, five cautions merit consideration. First, outcomes reflect support to one family and one child. For this reason, the ability to draw conclusions about the external validity of the family support process with other fam-ilies of children with severe disabilities and problem behaviors is limited. Second, indica-tor behavior data need to be interpreted cautiously. Interobserver agreement was not meas-ured, so the reliability and validity of these data may be questioned. Efforts to increase the believability of the data included training and practice in reporting indicator behavior incidents before actual data collection, monthly reviews of definitions, and requests for detailed information about each incident. Third, as part of the collaborative nature of the research effort, Helen's parents were informed of the research design and expected results. This information may have introduced a bias; that is, parent implementation fidelity may have improved at the point of intervention for each setting due to implementation support activities paired with parental expectations about when to initiate procedures. Helen's extensive history of problem behavior and the amount of time required during initial training and support (M = 12. 8 hours and 9 weeks per routine) suggest that any influence of bias was minimal. Nevertheless, caution is required when interpreting changes in parent behavior as a function of training and support activities. Fourth, results do not indicate that Helen was "cured" of problem behaviors. She continued to engage in problem behaviors, albeit at low levels of frequency and intensity. Thus, the possibility of regression is present. Finally, although preliminary follow-up data are encouraging, the durability of contextually appropriate, multicomponent support plans should be measured in years, not months, postintervention.

Future Research

Future research should consider three areas. First, because of the need to establish external validity, the family support process should be replicated with other families of children with developmental disabilities and problem behaviors. Second, the integration of PAR procedures with single subject research methods holds promise for increasing family participation in intervention research and for advancing knowledge about the use of positive behavior support by families. For these reasons, replication and extension of the collaborative procedures employed in this study should be considered. Finally, the concept of contextual fit as a guide to developing effective, feasible, and durable behavior support plans, although promising, requires further empirical validation.

CONCLUSION

The study described in this chapter provides behavioral family interventionists and researchers with three central messages and one challenge. First, a comprehensive, ecological approach to behavioral family intervention that integrates functional assessment and family ecology assessment may contribute to the design of effective, contextually appropriate, and durable multicomponent support plans. Second, the emerging technology of positive behavior support, delivered to families in a collaborative framework, can empower parents to successfully include children with disabilities into valued family routines and to transform the quality of family life. Third, parents of children with disabilities and problem behaviors can actively contribute to the development of knowledge about behavioral family intervention in the role of equal partners in the research endeavor. Family participation in the design of independent and dependent measures, the selection of assessment and intervention activities, and the collection of outcome data can help to shape a research process and to develop knowledge that is meaningful and useful to families. The challenge is to join with families as partners in a shared research agenda to build knowledge that is reliable and valid from a research perspective and is accessible and vital to families raising children with disabilities and problem behaviors.

REFERENCES

Albin, R.W., Lucyshyn, J.M., Horner, R.H., & Flannery, K.B. (1996). Contextual fit for behavior support plans: A model for "goodness of fit." In L.K. Koegel, R.L. Koegel, & G. Dunlap (Eds.), *Positive behavioral support: Including people with difficult behavior in the community* (pp. 81–98). Baltimore: Paul H. Brookes Publishing Co.

Barlow, D.H., & Hersen, M. (1984). *Single case experimental design: Strategies for studying behavior change* (2nd ed.). New York: Pergamon.

Bergan, J.R., & Kratochwill, T.R. (1990). *Behavioral consultation and therapy.* New York: Kluwer Academic/Plenum Publishers.

Blacher, J., & Hanneman, R. (1993). Out-of-home placement of children and adolescents with severe handicaps: Behavioral intentions and behavior. *Research in Developmental Disabilities, 14,* 145–160.

Bruyère, S.M. (1993). Participatory action research: Overview and implications for family members of persons with disabilities. *Journal of Vocational Rehabilitation, 3,* 62–88.

Campbell, D.T., & Stanley, J.C. (1966). *Experimental and quasi-experimental designs for research.* Chicago: Rand McNally.

Carr, E.G., & Carlson, J.I. (1993). Reduction of severe behavior problems in the community using a multicomponent treatment approach. *Journal of Applied Behavior Analysis, 26,* 157–172.

Carr, E.G., Levin, L., McConnachie, G., Carlson, J.I., Kemp, D.C., & Smith, C.E. (1994). *Communication-based intervention for problem behaviors: A user's guide for producing positive change.* Baltimore: Paul H. Brookes Publishing Co.

Carr, E.G., Taylor, J.C., & Robinson, S. (1991). The effects of severe problem behaviors in children on the teaching behavior of adults. *Journal of Applied Behavior Analysis, 24,* 523–535.

Davis, J.R., Turner, W., Rolider, A., & Cartwright, T. (1994). Natural and structured baselines in the treatment of aggression following brain injury. *Brain Injury, 8,* 589–598.

Dunlap, G. (1993). Promoting generalization: Current status and functional considerations. In R. Van Houten & S. Axelrod (Eds.), *Behavior analysis and treatment* (pp. 269–296). New York: Kluwer Academic/Plenum Publishers.

Dunlap, G., Kern-Dunlap, L., Clarke, S., & Robbins, F.R. (1991). Functional assessment, curricular revision, and severe behavior problems. *Journal of Applied Behavior Analysis, 24,* 387–397.

Dunlap, G., & Robbins, F.R. (1991). Current perspectives in service delivery for young children with autism. *Comprehensive Mental Health Care, 1,* 177–194.

Egel, A.L., & Powers, M.D. (1989). Behavioral parent training: A view of the past and suggestions for the future. In E. Cipani (Ed.), Treatment of severe behavior disorders: Behavior analysis approaches. *Monographs of the American Association on Mental Retardation, No. 12.*

Fawcett, S.B. (1991). Some values guiding community research and action. *Journal of Applied Behavior Analysis, 24,* 621–626.

Gallimore, R., Goldenberg, C.N., & Weisner, T.S. (1993). The social construction and subjective reality of activity settings: Implications for community psychology. *American Journal of Community Psychology, 21,* 537–559.

Gresham, F.M., Gansle, K.A., & Noell, G.H. (1993). Treatment integrity in applied behavior analysis with children. *Journal of Applied Behavior Analysis, 26,* 257–263.

Griest, D.L., & Forehand, K.C. (1982). How can I get any parent training done with all these other problems going on? The role of family variables in child behavior therapy. *Child and Family Behavior Therapy, 14,* 37–53.

Harris, S.L. (1994). Treatment of family problems in autism. In E. Schopler & G. B. Mesibov (Eds.), *Behavioral issues in autism* (pp. 161–175). New York: Kluwer Academic/Plenum Publishers.

Hawkins, N.E., & Singer, G.H.S. (1989). A skills training approach for assisting parents to cope with stress. In G.H.S. Singer & L.K. Irvin (Eds.), *Support for caregiving families: Enabling positive adaptation to disability* (pp. 71–83). Baltimore: Paul H. Brookes Publishing Co.

Hilliard, R.B. (1993). Single-case methodology in psychotherapy process and outcome research. *Journal of Consulting and Clinical Psychology, 61,* 373–380.

Horner, R.D., & Baer, D.M. (1978). Multiple-probe technique: A variation of the multiple baseline. *Journal of Applied Behavior Analysis, 11,* 189–196.

Horner, R.H., & Carr, E. (1997). Behavioral support for students with severe disabilities: Functional assessment and comprehensive intervention. *The Journal of Special Education, 31,* 84–104.

Horner, R.H., Dunlap, G., Koegel, R.L., Carr, E.G., Sailor, W., Anderson, J., Albin, R.W., & O'Neill,

R.E. (1990). Toward a technology of "non-aversive" behavioral support. *Journal of The Association for Persons with Severe Handicaps, 15,* 125–132.

Horner, R.H., O'Neill, R.E., & Flannery, K.B. (1993). Effective behavior support plans. In M. Snell (Ed.), *Instruction of students with severe disabilities* (4th ed., pp. 184–214). Columbus, OH: Charles E. Merrill.

Horner, R.H., Vaughn, B.J., Day, H.M., & Ard, W.R. (1996). The relationship between setting events and problem behavior: Expanding our understanding of behavioral support. In L.K. Koegel, R.L. Koegel, & G. Dunlap (Eds.), *Positive behavioral support: Including people with difficult behavior in the community* (pp.381–402). Baltimore: Paul H. Brookes Publishing Co.

Iwata, B.A., Dorsey, M.F., Slifer, K.J., Bauman, K.E., & Richman, G.S. (1994). Toward a functional analysis of self-injury. *Journal of Applied Behavior Analysis, 27,* 197–209. (Reprinted from *Analysis and Intervention in Developmental Disabilities, 2,* 3–20, 1982).

Kendall, P.C., & Grove, W.M. (1988). Normative comparisons in therapy outcomes. *Behavioral Assessment, 10,* 147–158.

Kennedy, C.H., Horner, R.H., Newton, J.S., & Kanda, E. (1990). Measuring the activity patterns of adults with severe disabilities using the Resident Lifestyle Inventory. *Journal of The Association for Persons with Severe Handicaps, 15,* 79–85.

Kennedy, C.H., & Souza, G. (1995). Functional analysis and treatment of eye poking. *Journal of Applied Behavior Analysis, 28,* 27–37.

Koegel, L.K., Koegel, R.L., & Dunlap, G. (Eds.). (1996). *Positive behavioral support: Including people with difficult behavior in the community.* Baltimore: Paul H. Brookes Publishing Co.

Lucyshyn, J.M., & Albin, R.W. (1993). Comprehensive support to families of children with disabilities and problem behaviors: Keeping it "friendly." In G.H.S. Singer & L.E. Powers (Eds.), *Families, disability, and empowerment: Active coping skills and strategies for family intervention* (pp. 365–407). Baltimore: Paul H. Brookes Publishing Co

Lucyshyn, J.M., Albin, R.W., & Nixon, C.D. (1997). Embedding comprehensive behavioral support in family ecology: An experimental, single-case analysis. *Journal of Consulting and Clinical Psychology, 65,* 241–251.

Lucyshyn, J.M., Nixon, C., Glang, A., & Cooley, E. (1996). Comprehensive family support for behavior change in children with ABI. In G.H.S. Singer, A. Glang, & J. Williams (Vol. Eds.), *Children with acquired brain injury: Educating and supporting families* (pp. 99–136). Baltimore: Paul H. Brookes Publishing Co.

Lucyshyn, J.M., Olson, D., & Horner, R.H. (1995). Building an ecology of support: A case study of one young woman with severe problem behaviors living in the community. *Journal of The Association for Persons with Severe Handicaps, 20,* 16–30.

Lutzker, J.R., & Campbell, R. (1994). *Ecobehavioral family interventions in developmental disabilities.* Pacific Grove, CA: Brooks/Cole Thomson Learning.

Meyer, L.H., & Evans, I.M. (1993). Meaningful outcomes in behavioral intervention: Evaluating positive approaches to the remediation of challenging behavior. In S.F. Warren & J. Reichle (Series Eds.) & J. Reichle & D.P. Wacker (Vol. Eds.), *Communication and language intervention series: Vol. 3. Communicative alternatives to challenging behavior: Integrating functional assessment and intervention strategies* (pp. 407–428). Baltimore: Paul H. Brookes Publishing Co.

O'Donnell, C.R., & Tharp, R.G. (1990). Community intervention guided by theoretical development. In A.S. Bellack & A.E. Kazdin (Eds.), *International handbook of behavior modification and therapy* (2nd ed., pp. 251–266). New York: Kluwer Academic/Plenum Publishers.

O'Donnell, C.R., Tharp, R.G., & Wilson, K. (1993). Activity settings as the unit of analysis: A theoretical basis for community intervention and development. *American Journal of Community Psychology, 21,* 501–520.

O'Neill, R.E., Horner, R.H., Albin, R.W., Sprague, J.R., Storey, K., & Newton, J.S. (1997). *Functional assessment and program development for problem behavior: A practical handbook.* Pacific Grove, CA: Brooks/Cole Thomson Learning.

O'Neill, R.E., Horner, R.H., Albin, R.W., Storey, K., & Sprague, J.R. (1990). *Functional analysis of problem behavior: A practical assessment guide.* Pacific Grove, CA: Brooks/Cole Thomson Learning.

Patterson, G.R., Reid, J.B., & Dishion, T.J. (1992). *Antisocial boys.* Eugene, OR: Castalia.

Repp, A.C., Karsh, K.G., Van Acker, R., Felce, D., & Harman, M.L. (1989). A computer-based system for collecting and analyzing observational data. *Journal of Special Education Technology, 9,* 207–217.

Sanders, M.R., & Dadds, M.R. (1993). *Behavioral family intervention.* Upper Saddle River: Prentice Hall.

Schwartz, I.S., & Baer, D.M. (1991). Social validity assessments: Is current practice state of the art? *Journal of Applied Behavior Analysis, 24,* 189–204.

Singer, G.H.S., & Irvin, L.K. (1991). Supporting families of persons with severe disabilities: Emerging findings, practices, and questions. In L.H. Meyer, C.A. Peck, & L. Brown (Eds.), *Critical issues in the lives of people with severe disabilities* (pp. 271–312). Baltimore: Paul H. Brookes Publishing Co.

Sparrow, S., Balla, D., & Cicchetti, D. (1984). *Vineland Adaptive Behavior Scales (VABS)*. Circle Pines, MN: American Guidance Service.

Turnbull, A.P., Friesen, B.J., & Ramirez, C. (1998). Participatory action research as a model for conducting family research. *Journal of The Association for Persons with Severe Handicaps, 23*, 178–188.

Turnbull, A.P., & Turnbull, H.R. (1993). Participatory research on cognitive coping: From concepts to research planning. In A.P. Turnbull, J.M. Patterson, S.K. Behr, D.L. Murphy, J.G. Marquis, & M.J. Blue-Banning (Eds.), *Cognitive coping, families, and disability* (pp. 1–14). Baltimore: Paul H. Brookes Publishing Co.

Turnbull, A.P., & Turnbull, H.R., (1997). *Families, professionals and exceptionality: A special partnership* (3rd ed.). Upper Saddle River, NJ: Prentice Hall.

Wacker, D.P., Cooper, L.J., Peck, S., Derby, K.M., & Berg, W. (1999). Community-based functional assessment. In A.C. Repp & R.H. Horner (Eds.), *Functional analysis of problem behaviors: From effective assessment to effective support* (pp. 32–56). Belmont, CA: Wadsworth.

Wahler, R.G., & Graves, M.G. (1983). Setting events in social networks: Ally or enemy in child behavior therapy? *Behavior Therapy, 14,* 19–36.

Willems, E.P. (1974). Behavioral technology and behavioral ecology. *Journal of Applied Behavior Analysis, 7*, 151–165.

Witt, J.C., & Elliott, S.N. (1984). Acceptability of classroom intervention strategies. In T.R. Kratochwill (Ed.), *Advances in school psychology* (pp. 251–288). Mahwah, NJ: Lawrence Erlbaum Associates.

CHAPTER 18

Research Partnership

One Family's Experience
with Positive Behavior Support

Lise Fox, Bobbie J. Vaughn, and Glen Dunlap

Positive behavior support (PBS) has been described as an approach to behavioral support that may be considered a new applied science (Carr, 1997; Carr et al., 1999). PBS, as a new applied science, is built on the foundation of applied behavior analysis and extends the traditional parameters of measurement, procedures, and dependent variables. PBS challenges researchers and interventionists to understand and work within complex natural community settings and to implement interventions through partnerships with the people who are most relevant to the individual with problem behavior. In addition, the intention of PBS has stretched far beyond seeking behavior reduction as a meaningful goal by embracing the importance of broad lifestyle changes for individuals with challenging behavior.

In many ways, this applied science is in its infancy. A synthesis of research indicates that although the use of PBS has shown steady and dramatic growth from 1985 to 1996, research in PBS has yet to provide demonstrations of successful lifestyle change or the need for lifestyle support (Carr et al., 1999). Furthermore, research in PBS continues to focus on demonstrations of experimental control and has failed to focus on the larger goals of the relevance, practicality, and importance of interventions within complex social systems (Carr et al., 1999).

As PBS evolves, there is a need to address new research issues and to pose questions in new ways. The goals of PBS that include the delivery of comprehensive support in natural environments to achieve broad lifestyle outcomes are impressive and important. In the real world of practical PBS applications, professionals and stakeholders are implementing interventions, assessing issues, problem-solving challenges, celebrating outcomes, and creating communities of support. In addition, good applications of PBS often fail due to overwhelming challenges that impede the implementation or fidelity of the process (Hieneman & Dun-

Preparation of this chapter was supported by the Rehabilitation Research and Training Center on Positive Behavior Support Grant No. H133B980005, funded by the U.S. Department of Education's National Institute on Disability and Rehabilitation Research. Opinions expressed herein are those of the authors, and no endorsement by the funding agency should be inferred.

We express our deep gratitude and appreciation to Millie Bucy for her numerous and generous contributions to the work described in this chapter. We also thank Shelley Clarke, who was instrumental in conducting the research and collecting and organizing the data throughout this project.

lap, 1999). These real-world experiences in applying and sustaining PBS must be considered, studied, and used to enhance the knowledge and current practice of PBS. Although existing foundations for PBS are substantial, additional learning and experience are needed to enhance applications of PBS and the field's ability to respond to the complex needs of individuals with problem behavior (Duchnowski, 2000; Horner, 1997; Singer, 2000).

In many ways, PBS encourages viewing problem behavior through new lenses. We are challenged as researchers and practitioners to grow in our understanding of how we shape and influence problem behavior, how problem behavior influences ourselves and systems of care, and how the technology of PBS can be implemented and sustained within complex ecologies. These challenges precipitate a need to conduct research that does not solely focus on the efficacy of PBS in changing an individual's behavior or lifestyle; multiple types of research using multiple methodologies are needed to enhance the field's understanding of the vast implications of PBS and its implementation (Dunlap, Fox, Vaughn, Bucy, & Clarke, 1997; Meyer & Evans, 1993).

COLLABORATIVE RESEARCH PARTNERSHIP

In the social and behavioral sciences, researchers are becoming increasingly interested in research approaches that actively involve constituents in every phase of the research process (Turnbull, Friesen, & Ramirez, 1998; Whyte, 1991). In collaborative research, sometimes referred to as *participatory action research,* stakeholders are involved in developing the research question, designing the research study, collecting data, interpreting the findings, and using research. Involving stakeholders as research partners, rather than treating them as study subjects, constructs a framework for research that promotes the pursuit of practical and ecologically valid research questions, strategies, and outcomes (Park, Gonsier-Gerden, Hoffman, Whaley, & Yount, 1998).

Collaborative research provides a mechanism for research to produce an understanding of social phenomena in a different way. It broadens the researchers' perspective through partnerships with the people who are most affected by research practice and its resulting outcomes. In the process of collaborative research, researchers and stakeholders enter into a partnership with diverse perspectives and approaches that are grounded in problem solving or seeking answers to the research question. In this endeavor, subjective experiences and the messy real-life contexts can be important quantitative data that are collected to capture objectively defined phenomena. The research that is conducted through partnerships with stakeholders is richly grounded in the context and typically achieves strong ecological validity (Graves, 1991).

In collaborative research endeavors, multiple research methodologies are often required to examine both changes in behavior, and the impact of those changes on the beliefs, attitudes, and social climate of people involved in the research process. In many investigations, researchers often employ both quantitative and qualitative research methodologies to capture a holistic evaluation. The use of multiple methodologies creates a structure for understanding phenomena from the perspectives of measurable change and change as perceived by people within the research context (Meyer, Park, Grenot-Scheyer, Schwartz, & Harry, 1998).

When investigating issues related to PBS, a collaborative research approach may enhance the development of relevant research questions and the use of ecologically valid procedures. Much of the research in PBS has been conducted by scientists who are studying the efficacy of PBS with problem behavior. Few studies have involved the interventionists, teachers, and families who are the ultimate implementors of PBS research. In addition, research has largely involved the application of PBS by researchers rather than by teachers, family members, and other practitioners whose daily work includes many competing tasks (Dunlap, Clarke, & Steiner, 1999). Collaborative research partnerships with family members or interventionists offer an approach to research that will provide a deeper understanding of how PBS may be used effectively within natural environments by the people who are most involved with the individual who has problem behavior (Lucyshyn, Albin, & Nixon, 1997). In addition, collaborative research may provide stakeholders who are involved in the research with a better understanding of how they may continue to implement and use PBS long after the research project is completed.

This chapter chronicles a family's experience with the process of PBS that was conducted as a research partnership. Previously published research reports used quantitative and qualitative methods to describe this process (Fox, Vaughn, Dunlap, & Bucy, 1997; Vaughn, Dunlap, Fox, Clarke, & Bucy, 1997). This chapter provides the complete story of the collaborative research partnership and the team members' perspectives. We are sharing this story with the hope that our experience illustrates the importance of partnering with families to acquire deeper understanding of the family's experience and the value of PBS to researchers, families, and professionals.

The following section describes how this particular research project was launched and who was involved in the partnership. We explain how we decided to conduct a collaborative research partnership and the goals of our research endeavor.

THE RESEARCH PROCESS

We are researchers and educators in a university setting, conducting applied research, training professional personnel, and operating model programs. In our work, we have intentionally involved family members of individuals with disabilities as staff members and advisors to reap the benefit of their insights and experiences. Millie Bucy, the mother of a child with significant disabilities and challenging behavior, was employed by an early intervention model demonstration program operated by our division. She served as an early intervention team member, providing family support and guidance to families of young children with autism and problem behavior. Other team members noticed that Millie often came to work on Monday feeling stressed about her weekend and bearing scratches on her arms. Millie reluctantly shared that her 9-year-old son displayed extreme problem behavior over the weekend. Millie, in her effort to portray herself as a confident staff member, quickly assured her concerned team members that these were temporary issues that she would be able to resolve. After several weeks passed without change, Millie's colleagues gently suggested that she seek help from individuals in the division who were skilled with PBS.

When Millie approached us for assistance, we asked if she would like to participate in a formal research project to identify a solution for her family and provide a vehicle for sharing this solution with others. Millie was excited about the prospect. She had seen the power of PBS as it was applied with the children in the early intervention project and was eager to experience similar outcomes for her son, Jeffrey. In addition, she wanted to do what she could to help others understand the impact and importance of PBS.

The Bucy Family

Millie discussed the potential of the research project with her family members to gain their approval and investment. Millie's husband, Bob, worked as a truck driver, which required him to be away from home for a week at a time. Their children Jeffrey, 9 years old, and Chris, 10 years old, attended public school. The Bucy family lived in a rural area of southwest Florida and enjoyed close contact with Bob's family, who lived nearby and who often cared for the boys.

Jeffrey was diagnosed with Cornelia de Lange syndrome at 4 years of age. He was very small, had severe cognitive impairments, and had a history of difficult behavior that began at age 2 with self-injury. He had a complex medical history, which included many hospitalizations and the persisting, painful condition of gastroesophageal reflux.

At the time that the project began, Jeffrey was enrolled in a special education classroom in a public elementary school. Jeffery was nonverbal and used gestures, some simple signs, and physical guidance to communicate his needs. He expressed his pleasure through an infectious laugh and broad smile. Jeffrey's problem behaviors included aggression, head banging, scratching, biting, and screaming. He also had an intense preoccupation with watching doors open and close and often refused to enter or exit through doors. These behaviors were evident in all of his environments, but were especially difficult in the community.

Jeffrey loved outdoor activities, sitting in his dad's truck and on the family patio, playing Frisbee, and swimming. He had a keen interest in music and often requested his audiotape recorder. Jeffrey was also interested in toys that included bright lights and made noise or played music.

Developing the Partnership

We began the research process by forming a collaborative research team that would partner with Millie. During the initial meetings, we focused on developing a collaborative vision for the purpose and outcomes of the research. As the research partnership was formed, we began to keep careful records of our meetings, correspondence with each other, and the discussions that surrounded decisions we made. The reflections that are shared in this chapter come from those records as well as from the data that were collected through the research (Fox et al., 1997; Vaughn et al., 1997). Millie was emphatic about achieving a change for Jeffrey and her family and documenting the process in a way that would benefit other families. She noted that the first issue to address was Jeffrey's problem behavior in the community. She said that it was extremely important for the family to be able to take Jeffrey into the community with ease. She shared, "You will need to teach me how to interact with Jeffrey and manage his behavior in a new way. I need someone objective to show me and give me feedback." In addition to stating her desire to manage Jeffrey's problem behavior, Millie said that her ultimate goal for Jeffrey was to help him gain communication skills and interact more with his peers.

We followed those initial discussions with planned observations and home visits to build relationships with Jeffrey and the other family members and to observe the contexts in which problem behavior did and did not occur. Those observations and home visits offered us rich opportunities to build rapport with the family and to develop a deeper knowledge of Jeffrey and his capacities and challenges. The family guided us in identifying the most difficult circumstances for Jeffrey. We captured some of these activities on videotape to better understand the context and nature of the problem behavior.

For a few weeks, the research team's activities focused on developing a relationship with Jeffrey and the family within their daily routines. During this period of time, Millie was an informant and guide to the team members in furthering their understanding of Jeffrey and his family life. We met as a collaborative team to develop the research plan and move forward with the process of PBS. The process of collaborative research was an evolving endeavor. All of the research team members wanted to create a partnership that included and valued all members' perspectives. In addition, we wanted to proceed carefully and take advantage of the opportunity to continually reflect on and learn from the collaborative relationship. Nonetheless, this resulted in some tension. Millie's family was challenged by Jeffrey's behavior, and we were anxious to offer a solution. The lead interventionist on the research team shared with the team her concern that "in the process of establishing collaboration, we may be halting the flow of support, which may make this a more agonizing process." Sharing tensions and honestly expressing hopes and desires became the glue of the collaborative process. It served as the basis for discussions about the research progress and the team members' roles and responsibilities, as well as the foundation for reflective inquiry.

A research plan was developed that included a single subject time series design to assess the impact of intervention on Jeffrey's problem behavior, engagement, and skill acquisition. The research team wanted to demonstrate the efficacy of PBS when applied by family members within community routines. In addition, the research team decided to conduct a qualitative investigation to develop a richer understanding of the impact and outcomes of PBS on Jeffrey and his family. Millie agreed to begin keeping an audiotape journal of her impressions and experiences, and we developed a plan for interviewing immediate family members at key points in the process.

IMPLEMENTING POSITIVE BEHAVIOR SUPPORT

The process of developing and providing PBS began with building rapport with Jeffrey and his family. Research team members spent many hours observing Jeffrey at home, during activities with his brother and mother, and during community routines. Through these contacts, we were able to acquire a better understanding of the routines that were challenging for Jeffrey and his family, as well as Jeffrey's skills, capacities, and interests.

Person-Centered Planning

Person-centered planning (Mount & Zwernik, 1988) was used to gather together the people important in Jeffrey's life to discuss their understanding of Jeffrey, his strengths and gifts, and their vision for Jeffrey's future. The person-centered planning meeting involved Jeffrey's paternal grandparents; his teacher; Jeffrey's brother, Chris; and the research team members. Jeffrey's father, Bob, was unable to attend the meeting.

This meeting was critically important for understanding Jeffrey and others' thoughts about his present and future. The process offered mechanisms for celebrating Jeffrey's gifts and strengths (e.g., "funny," "playful," "determined," "curious") and discussing his challenges (e.g., "stubborn," "annoying," "clumsy," "frustrated"). Millie described Jeffrey's background, history of health problems, and developmental delays, as well as the family's experiences negotiating the maze of medical and educational services. The meeting also included a discussion about the places in the community that Jeffrey frequented and his relationships with others. The people who attended the meeting identified Jeffrey's preferences and opportunities for making choices in his daily life. The discussion ended with the development of a vision for Jeffrey's future. A vision for Jeffrey at 12 years of age included having friends his own age, participating in the community, contributing more at home through helping and chores, becoming independent in self-care routines, communicating effectively, and expanding his independent leisure interests and skills. The discussion of first steps toward those goals established everyone's commitment to achieving Jeffrey's vision.

The research team was pleased with the person-centered planning meeting. Everyone who attended expressed interest in working together to improve Jeffrey's lifestyle. Chris was an active participant at the meeting. He gave great insight into the world of pre-adolescents and suggested strategies for helping Jeffrey become more independent and connected to peers. Millie was thrilled by the commitment to her son and family that was expressed during the meeting. She was even more pleased when she overheard Jeffrey's grandparents describe to Bob the power and importance of the meeting.

Functional Assessment

The functional assessment process involved structured interviews with family members (O'Neill et al., 1997) and multiple observations of Jeffrey within family routines. The research team reviewed the functional assessment information and selected three important family routines that were difficult for Jeffrey: 1) going to the bank's drive-through, 2) going grocery shopping, and 3) eating in fast-food restaurants. Jeffrey exhibited serious problem behaviors in each of these settings, which made it difficult and often unsafe for his family members as they engaged in the associated routines.

Because of Bob's pay schedule, it was necessary for Millie to go to the bank's drive-through on a weekly basis. During these trips, Jeffrey screamed, yelled, and often banged his head against the car window while they waited. Needless to say, Millie, Chris, and Jeffrey could not complete this activity without incredible stress.

The grocery store offered different challenges to the Bucy family. Jeffrey's preoccupation with doors made entering and exiting the store extremely challenging. His screaming and flailing interfered with other customers' access to the doors. Once Jeffrey was inside the store, Millie put him in the cart to prevent him from running around. He often continued screaming and tried to scratch or bite Millie. This created an embarrassing spectacle. At the checkout, Jeffrey screamed until he was taken from the cart, then screamed again as they approached the door.

On evenings when Bob traveled and Chris had Boy Scout meetings and other activities, it often was more convenient for Millie and the boys to eat dinner at a fast-food restaurant. During these outings, Jeffrey exhibited severe behavior problems entering and exiting the restaurant. Once inside the restaurant, Jeffrey and Chris sat in a booth, and Chris attempted to entertain Jeffrey while Millie ordered the food. However, Jeffrey often crawled under the table, ran around in the restaurant, and went to the doors. Under these circumstances, meals were not relaxing, and the family often left the restaurant without Millie and Chris finishing their food.

Hypothesis Development

The functional assessment process became focused on the three community routines and identifying the predictors, maintaining consequences, and purposes of the problem behaviors within each routine. Jeffrey's problem behaviors at the drive-through began as soon as Millie stopped the car. Jeffrey engaged in self-injurious and aggressive behaviors (face slapping, hand biting, and scratching) whether he was alone or with his brother in the back seat. These behaviors continued to occur when Millie and Chris attempted to calm him. Once Millie finished her banking and drove away, Jeffrey's problem behaviors stopped.

The problems in the grocery store began with entering the store. Jeffrey loved to stand at the doors and watch them open and close. Millie had to physically guide him to enter the store. Jeffrey screamed, threw himself on the floor, kicked, and scratched his mother when he had to leave the doors. He stopped his aggression only if he was allowed to stare at the doors. Millie struggled to put Jeffrey in the shopping cart. Once in the cart, Jeffrey often continued yelling and scratching. If these behaviors abated during shopping, then they resumed while he waited in the cart for Millie to complete the checkout process. These behaviors persisted until he reached the doors, at which time he smiled and stopped. He then resisted going through the doors by throwing himself on the pavement or street, and he scratched and bit whomever attempted to assist him.

Jeffrey's fixation with doors was also a problem in fast-food restaurants. Jeffrey sat on the floor between the two sets of doors and refused to stand up, which created problems when other customers attempted to enter the restaurant. No amount of coaxing from Millie or Chris would get him to stand; he had to be physically lifted and guided through the doors. He often became aggressive during these episodes. Once he and Chris sat down, Jeffrey often stood in the booth or crawled out to see the doors. He scratched his brother when Chris attempted to keep Jeffrey seated and in the booth. Jeffrey ate his food quickly, then resumed his mission to gain access to the doors. He again engaged in problem behavior when exiting the restaurant through the doors.

The research team reviewed the functional assessment information and began building hypotheses about the function of the problem behavior within each routine. The discussions of behavioral hypotheses were centered on identifying the predictors of problem behavior onset and the maintaining consequences that followed problem behavior. Millie's participation in these discussions was important for two reasons. First, she had tremendous insight about Jeffrey's problem behavior and was able to guide the team in identifying the triggers. Second, these discussions helped Millie understand the meaning of Jeffrey's problem behavior within each routine and how she or Chris responded in ways that reinforced problem behavior. As we discussed the behavioral hypotheses for the targeted routines, Millie started making associations about the possible functions of problem behavior within other routines at home and school. Millie began to shift her thinking about Jeffrey's problem behavior from it being uninterpretable and uncontrollable to it expressing his requests and needs.

The functional assessment identified variables common to each of the three settings. The predictors of problem behavior seemed to be associated with waiting. As revealed by the functional assessment, problem behaviors occurred while waiting in the car at the bank's drive-through, in line and during shopping at the grocery store, and for food at the fast-food restaurant. In each of these instances, ending or changing the activity, rather than receiving attention from Millie or Chris, stopped the problem behavior. For instance, Jeffrey's behaviors subsided when Millie finished banking and drove off and when he received food at the restaurant. Escape from waiting was one variable that maintained his problem behaviors.

The second variable was that Jeffrey was content as long as he could stare at doors. The longer he was allowed access to the doors, the more difficult it became to move him. Jeffrey would calm down again when he was afforded a few more minutes at the doors. No amount of attention from Millie or Chris could compete with Jeffrey's interest in the doors; only access to the doors eliminated his problem behavior. It was clear that access to the doors reinforced and maintained his problem behavior.

Intervention Assessment

We collaborated with Millie to develop purpose statements, or hypotheses, about the function of and the variables associated with Jeffrey's behavior in each of the settings. These hypotheses provided the research team's best guess about the events that set off and maintained Jeffrey's problem behavior. As we discussed the behavioral hypotheses, research team members began considering possible interventions for preventing the problem behavior or providing Jeffrey with alternatives to express his needs and requests. Much of our discussion focused on making the targeted family routines meaningful and purposeful for Jeffrey. This discussion resulted in possible interventions that would compete with the reinforcing properties of the doors or by provide Jeffrey with alternative activities to waiting. Table 18.1 summarizes the problem behaviors, the hypotheses about each, and the corresponding interventions.

We wanted to determine whether these interventions could contribute to a behavior support plan that would include additional prevention strategies, replacement skills, and more effective ways to respond to Jeffrey's problem behavior. We decided to conduct brief assessment sessions to examine the impact of the intervention components on the problem behavior. At this time, the research team felt that it was best to demonstrate the efficacy of the interventions before asking Millie to use them.

The lead interventionist conducted two 2-minute probe sessions in each setting. The data in Figure 18.1 indicate that the use of the interventions resulted in increased participatory behavior and positive affect. Moreover, Jeffrey's disruptive and aggressive behaviors diminished significantly when the interventions were used. Using the toy while at the bank's drive-through, the picture schedule while in the grocery store, and the picture book while in the fast-food restaurant diminished Jeffrey's disruptive behavior in these settings. Although the assessment was brief, it confirmed the potential efficacy of the planned interventions.

Developing the Plan

We met with Millie to outline and develop a support plan. Plan development involved determining efficient and socially acceptable strategies for implementing the interventions and defining the necessary replacement skills for Jeffrey. Although the team members knew that the interventions decreased Jeffrey's behaviors in the 2-minute probes, we did not know how easily Millie could implement them. The next steps involved Millie's confirmation of the viability of the components, as well as the team's assessing and discussing the most efficient way for her to implement the intervention.

We believed that the efficiency of implementation posed the biggest challenge for intervention success. Neither Millie nor her family had used a picture schedule or picture book or had encouraged Jeffrey's active involvement in the targeted routines. If the intervention components were to be effective, then the use of the materials would need to fit with the family's routines and style of interaction. In meetings, we developed step-by-step procedures for how the routine would be implemented and how intervention components would be used. Table 18.2 presents the key features of the support plan for each of the community routines.

Implementing and Evaluating the Plan

Millie agreed to implement the behavior support plan with Jeffrey in all three settings. It was important for Millie to evaluate how well the intervention components fit with her interaction style and comfort level in addition to Jeffrey's behavioral needs. The team dis-

Table 18.1. Problem behaviors, hypotheses, and interventions for each routine

Routine	Problem behavior	Hypothesis	Intervention
Bank drive-through	Jeffrey engages in tantrums and aggression while waiting in the car during transactions.	Waiting in a stationary vehicle is aversive because of the absence of reinforcing stimulation.	Provide preferred toys one at a time in the order of preference to produce engagement with the reinforcement activity and promote pleasurable and manageable interactions while waiting for transactions to be completed.
Grocery store	Jeffrey engages in severe tantrums during transitions through doorways.	Doors are highly reinforcing stimuli for Jeffrey; tantrums postpone removal of the stimuli.	Provide a competing reinforcer: Show Jeffrey a picture of a preferred toy before the transition, and provide the toy after leaving the store to compete with the reinforcement of the doors.
	Jeffrey screams and is aggressive while Millie is completing the store routine.	Shopping is aversive because of the absence of reinforcers and a means for Jeffrey to participate.	Provide a picture schedule depicting the routine, offer Jeffrey a means for participation, and provide a picture book for Jeffrey to occupy himself during periods when active participation is unlikely (e.g., during checkout).
Fast-food restaurant	Jeffrey engages in severe tantrums when going through doorways.	Doors are highly reinforcing stimuli for Jeffrey; tantrums postpone removal of the stimuli.	Provide a competing reinforcer: Show Jeffrey a picture of a preferred toy before the transition, and provide the toy after leaving the restaurant to compete with the reinforcement of the doors.
	Jeffrey screams and is aggressive while waiting in the restaurant.	Waiting for food is aversive because of the absence of reinforcers.	Provide a picture book as a reinforcing and contextually appropriate way for Jeffrey to occupy himself.

From Vaughn, B.J., Dunlap, G., Fox, L., Clarke, S., & Bucy, M. (1997). Parent-professional partnership in behavioral support: A case study of community-based intervention. *The Journal of The Association for Persons with Severe Handicaps, 22*(4), 190. Copyright © *The Journal of The Association for Persons with Severe Handicaps*; adapted by permission.

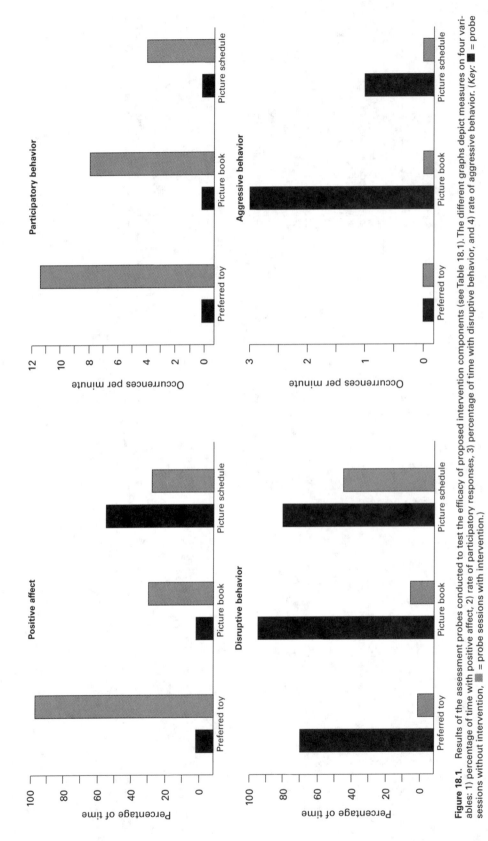

Figure 18.1. Results of the assessment probes conducted to test the efficacy of proposed intervention components (see Table 18.1). The different graphs depict measures on four variables: 1) percentage of time with positive affect, 2) rate of participatory responses, 3) percentage of time with disruptive behavior, and 4) rate of aggressive behavior. (*Key:* ■ = probe sessions without intervention, ■ = probe sessions with intervention.)

426

cussed the drawbacks and advantages of certain research designs to evaluate the effectiveness of the behavioral support strategies. The issue of time efficiency in relation to the severity of Jeffrey's problem behavior warranted a simple, efficient research design such as baseline and intervention phases with a follow-up design.

We decided that the plan's effectiveness would be documented primarily by the effect of the behavior support plan on disruptive behavior and cooperative responding. The team was interested in not only addressing Jeffrey's challenging behavior but also in the impact of the support plan on the quality of Jeffrey's engagement in community routines. We decided to collect all data by videotaping the routines rather than through direct observation. This decision was made because the videotapes would serve as valuable tools for further analyses. The team agreed to use a small hand-held videocamera to diminish intrusiveness. Millie supported this approach and being videotaped in public settings.

Baseline   During the baseline phase of each routine, Jeffrey was videotaped several times in each setting to show the consistency and frequency of his behavior before the intervention components were introduced. Millie performed the routines as she did during a typical week without coaching or feedback. All of the data were collected from videotapes of the sessions, and the results were displayed on a graph that delineated baseline from intervention. The graph permitted us to evaluate the progression of the research by using session-by-session visual analysis.

Intervention   During the first three sessions of intervention, members of the research team coached Millie in the use of the intervention procedures. Coaching involved a two-part process. The first step of the process involved four activities that occurred prior to going into the community setting: 1) reviewing the written intervention procedures, 2) reviewing videotaped sequences that depicted the use of the intervention components, 3) discussing how to respond to problem behaviors if they occur, and 4) discussing any concerns about the use of the support procedures. The second part of the coaching process occurred in the community setting by providing Millie with reminders if she forgot or hesitated in using intervention procedures. Following three intervention sessions with coaching, Millie implemented all of the strategies in subsequent sessions without assistance. Upon completion of a community outing, we returned to Millie's house to discuss any adjustments in the strategies or in her interactions with Jeffrey.

Follow-Up   Follow-up occurred 6 months after the last intervention session. Team members remained in the background during these sessions as the family conducted the targeted community routines. The intervention procedures remained the same as those in earlier intervention sessions, with one exception in the grocery store routine. As indicated in Table 18.2, Millie now had Jeffrey walk through the store with her instead of placing him in the shopping cart, which she did during baseline and at the beginning of intervention. During intervention, Millie chose to leave Jeffrey in the cart while she learned the new intervention strategies.

UNDERSTANDING THE OUTCOMES AND IMPACT

We had worked together for several months to establish the team membership, conduct the functional assessment and component validation, and develop the intervention plan. Thus, the team was excited about observing the plan's impact on Jeffrey's behavior and the family's routines.

Table 18.2.   Description of activities in each routine

Routine	Activity summary	Intervention process
Bank drive-through	Jeffrey sits in the car's back seat during the drive to the bank.	During the waiting time at the bank, Millie gives Jeffrey three to four toys one at a time, in order of least to most preferred.
	Millie pulls up to the drive-through window and conducts her banking. Jeffrey is expected to sit appropriately in his seat.	Millie intermittently interacts with Jeffrey until the banking is completed.
	Millie completes the banking and exits the drive-through, and Jeffrey sits in the back seat until the family gets home.	Jeffrey plays with the last toy during the ride home.
Grocery store	Jeffrey enters the store holding Millie's hand.	Once inside the store, Millie places Jeffrey in the shopping cart and shows Jeffrey the picture schedule for shopping.
	Millie puts Jeffrey in the grocery cart.	
	Millie pushes the cart down the aisles and selects four to eight items to buy, while Jeffrey remains in the cart.	Millie shows the first item on the picture schedule (yogurt) and says, "Let's go get yogurt."
	After the items are selected, Millie waits in line at the checkout.	Millie pushes the cart to the dairy section and asks Jeffrey to put the yogurt in the cart. If he resists, then she provides hand-over-hand assistance.
	Millie puts the items on the conveyor belt while Jeffrey remains seated in the cart.	
	Millie pays for the groceries.	At the same spot, Jeffrey is given an opportunity to select another item on the schedule as part of the transition.
	Millie removes Jeffrey from the cart.	
	The bagged groceries are put in the cart, and a store employee pushes the cart through the store's doors to the family's car.	As Jeffrey walks down the aisles holding his mother's hand, Millie continues to give him the opportunity to select items on the shopping picture schedule. In between stops, Millie uses the schedule to remind him of the next stop.
	Millie holds Jeffrey's hand while walking through the doors and across the parking lot.	After the last item is selected, Millie shows Jeffrey the picture schedule, removes the item's picture, and states, "We're done shopping now."
		They walk to the checkout line, and Millie offers a picture book to Jeffrey to look at while waiting.
		Jeffrey looks at the picture book while Millie unloads the groceries.
		After the groceries are purchased and bagged, Millie puts the book away, shows Jeffrey a picture of a preferred toy, and states, "Let's go get the toy; it's in the car."
		Millie places Jeffrey in the back seat of the car and hands him the toy.

Routine	Activity summary	Intervention process
Fast-food restaurant	Jeffrey enters the restaurant holding Millie's hand and walks with her to a booth.	After Jeffrey is seated in the restaurant booth, Millie takes out the picture book and looks at it with him.
	Millie instructs Jeffrey to sit in the booth, then sits next to him.	Once Jeffrey is engaged, Chris takes Millie's place looking at the book with Jeffrey. This continues until Millie returns with the food.
	Chris then takes Millie's place in the booth while Millie orders food at the counter.	
	Once Millie returns with food, she takes Chris's spot in the booth, and Chris sits across from Millie and Jeffrey.	Millie prepares a serving of mashed potatoes in an adaptive bowl brought from home and asks Jeffrey to eat.
	Millie prepares a plate of mashed potatoes and prompts Jeffrey to eat.	Millie provides hand-over-hand assistance if Jeffrey does not pick up the spoon and start eating.
	Millie feeds Jeffrey the first bite and instructs him to take the spoon and feed himself.	If Jeffrey requests more food, then Millie refills his bowl and praises him.
	Once everyone finishes eating, Millie states, "It's time to go."	If Jeffrey finishes his meal first, then he is given the picture book and Millie looks at it with him.
	Millie assists Jeffrey out of the booth.	When everyone finishes eating, Chris clears the table and Millie verbally cues Jeffrey to put the book away by saying, "It's time to go."
	Jeffrey holds Millie's hand and walks through the doors and to the car.	Millie then shows Jeffrey a picture of a preferred toy and states, "Let's go get the toy; it's in the car."
		Millie places Jeffrey in the back seat of the car and hands him the toy.

From Vaughn, B.J., Dunlap, G., Fox, L., Clarke, S., & Bucy, M. (1997). Parent–professional partnership in behavioral support: A case study of community-based intervention. *The Journal of The Association for Persons with Severe Handicaps, 22*(4), 192. Copyright © *The Journal of The Association for Persons with Severe Handicaps*; adapted by permission.

Throughout this process, Millie audiotaped her impressions of the research collaboration and the impact of the project on her family (see Fox et al., 1997). Millie stated in her audiotaped journal:

> *I'm really excited to get started finally because I feel like we are really moving toward our goals. But even as comfortable as I feel with the team and the process, I'm a little nervous because now the focus is on me a little bit more and how I interact with Jeffrey.*

These impressions were also reflected by the other research team members. We anxiously coded each intervention session and were pleased by the rapid changes in Jeffrey's challenging behavior. Most important, Jeffrey was happily engaged in these routines, as evidenced by his smiling, laughing, and following his mother's directions.

Data

This chapter does not provide the details of the research procedures (see Vaughn et al., 1997, for more information). Rather, the following discussion summarizes the impact of the intervention on Jeffrey's behavior. Figure 18.2 demonstrates the effectiveness of the intervention in reducing disruptive behavior across all three settings.

As shown in Figure 18.2, challenging behavior at the bank's drive-through and in the fast-food restaurant dramatically decreased with the intervention and remained stable through follow-up. The results of the interventions for the grocery store were less clear. This may be explained in part by the fact that this setting involved Jeffrey's learning new skills and greater activity participation. For example, by follow-up, Jeffrey no longer rode in the cart but walked and helped select grocery items.

We also measured Jeffrey's cooperative responses to Millie's activity-related requests and instructions (see Table 18.3). As shown in the first data column of Table 18.3, Millie's average of activity-related instructions increased in all phases across all three settings except for the follow-up in the restaurant. In keeping with her activity-related instructions, Jeffrey's average cooperative responses also increased. The third column reflects the percentage of Millie's instructions with cooperative responses from Jeffrey. For the most part, the trends noted in the percentage of cooperative responses coincide with those in the previous two columns.

We examined Jeffrey's transition through the doors of the restaurant and store separately by asking raters—who were unaware of the research process or participants—to watch the videotaped sessions and rate the level of difficulty that they observed. As described previously, Jeffrey's problem behaviors entering and exiting these settings were often dangerous as well as embarrassing, and they posed difficulties for other customers who were entering and exiting. Table 18.4 shows the percentage of entering and exiting transitions across the three phases of the research (baseline, intervention, and follow-up) that the observers rated as having significant problems.

Experiences

Using PBS was a positive experience for all involved. The data do not portray the significant difference in the emotional tenor of the targeted routines. Jeffrey was now smiling and happily interacting with his family during the targeted activities. Jeffrey's brother, Chris, became more willing to go out to eat or to the bank with Millie and Jeffrey. Millie was able to go to the bank drive-through, grocery store, and fast-food restaurant without fear and embarrassment. She reflected in her journal:

> Jeffrey doesn't have any problems at all; he's laughing the whole time, enjoying it. It's been just wonderful. It's a big help; it sounds like a little thing, going through a bank drive-through. I have to do drive-throughs, and they were just a stressful time. Jeffrey would bang his head and scratch or bite.

Millie was excited about how the intervention affected Jeffrey's behavior; as a result, she felt more hopeful about Jeffrey's future. In her journal, she described her dreams for Jeffrey: "Through our efforts, our new strategies, and so forth Jeffrey will eventually be able to communicate on some level with typically developing peers and begin to have friendships, which is one of our major goals." In addition, as intervention progressed, Millie became interested in sharing the success of the research with other family members. She believed that they should be informed of how the behavior support strategies helped Jeffrey.

The research team was also excited about the impact of the intervention and the videotapes of routines that were qualitatively different from baseline sessions. We discussed

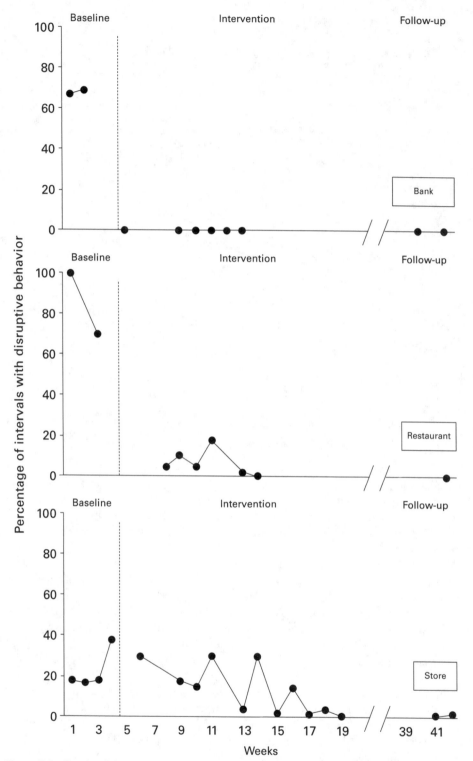

Figure 18.2. Results of the intervention process implemented across three community settings. The graphs show the percentage of intervals with disruptive behavior. (*Key:* ● = intervals with disruptive behavior; / = time break in data collection.) (From Vaughn, B.J., Dunlap, G., Fox, L., Clarke, S., & Bucy, M. [1997]. Parent–professional partnership in behavioral support: A case study of community-based intervention. *The Journal of The Association for Persons with Severe Handicaps, 22*[4], 193. Copyright © *The Journal of The Association for Persons with Severe Handicaps*; reprinted by permission.)

Table 18.3.   Mean number of Millie's activity-related instructions and Jeffrey's cooperative responses per session

Session	Number of Millie's activity-related instructions	Number of Jeffrey's cooperative responses	Percentage of Millie's activity-related instructions and Jeffrey's cooperative responses
Bank drive-through			
Baseline	2	0	0
Intervention	17	15	89
Follow-up	11	10	96
Grocery store			
Baseline	6	3	55
Intervention	24	19	82
Follow-up	23	15	64
Fast-food restaurant			
Baseline	17	7	53
Intervention	25	19	75
Follow-up	4	4	100

From Vaughn, B.J., Dunlap, G., Fox, L., Clarke, S., & Bucy, M. (1997). Parent–professional partnership in behavioral support: A case study of community-based intervention. *The Journal of The Association for Persons with Severe Handicaps, 22*(4), 194. Copyright © *The Journal of The Association for Persons with Severe Handicaps*; adapted by permission.

the changes in Jeffrey's behavior and noted that Millie appeared more relaxed and able to facilitate Jeffrey's active engagement in the routines. Thus, the research team decided that it was time to conduct another person-centered planning meeting to share Jeffrey's successes and begin discussing how PBS could be used to assist Jeffrey within other difficult routines.

A second person-centered planning meeting was held during the last few days of intervention. We showed the family videotape vignettes from the study so that they could see the difference in Jeffrey's behavior and the effective use of support strategies. The family immediately began to think of other routines that were problematic and brainstormed ideas for support strategies. Millie was excited about the family's enthusiasm and eagerness to support Jeffrey. In Millie's journal she described the meeting by saying, "It was nice to see how family members just clicked right in, were offering good suggestions, and really understood it much better than I gave them credit for."

The process of conducting collaborative research as team members also had an impact on our understanding and behavior as university researchers. This was the first time that we had developed this kind of research partnership for PBS with a family member. The experience provided us with valuable insight into variables and conditions that were not formally measured. We became familiar with the family's capacities and challenges through our developing relationship as friends and advocates. As researchers, we became much more aware of the complexity of family history, relationships, and needs and how these variables affect family functioning. We became more comfortable with relinquishing experimental control and more willing to accommodate the "messy" context of family and community life.

Table 18.4. Percentage of entering and exiting transitions that were rated with significant problems

Session	Entering	Exiting	Total
Baseline			
Grocery store	100	33	67
Fast-food restaurant	50	100	75
Intervention			
Grocery store	13	0	7
Fast-food restaurant	0	0	0
Follow-up			
Grocery store	0	50	25
Fast-food restaurant	0	0	0

From Vaughn, B.J., Dunlap, G., Fox, L., Clarke, S., & Bucy, M. (1997). Parent–professional partnership in behavioral support: A case study of community-based intervention. *The Journal of The Association for Persons with Severe Handicaps, 22*(4), 194. Copyright © *The Journal of The Association for Persons with Severe Handicaps*; adapted by permission.

REFLECTIONS

Millie's audiotape journal contained many entries about the process of conducting collaborative research. She expressed her hope that the research would demonstrate to other families that the PBS approach can help support children with problem behavior. Again, Millie was excited about the outcomes of the collaboration:

> *I think that all of us will grow in some way from this project in addition to the outcome that we all hope to achieve of helping Jeffrey. I think that we will all grow from it and that's just as important to me.*

As a collaborative partner in the research process, Millie was included in all decisions concerning the research design and measurement procedures. She was able to describe the way that the research imposed on her and family life. She was aware that at times the progress of the behavior support process may have been slowed by the need to follow research procedures. The assessment and baseline period was especially difficult for a family that wanted and needed immediate solutions. Millie shared this comment that her husband made: "You've been working on this research project for a long time. When are we going to get to the good part? When are we going to get to the intervention part when all of these changes are going to happen?" Other research impositions that Millie described were the loss of family privacy and the inconvenience of scheduling her community trips so that the research could be conducted.

It was interesting to note Millie's shift from using the phrase "the researchers" to "we" when discussing the progress of the research process in her audiotape journal. In her comments on the process of collaboration, Millie described her enjoyment at being included as an "insider" in the research process. She felt as though there was a shared responsibility among the team members and that the research team entered into the project with a clearly articulated shared purpose. She also discussed the importance of reciprocity in the collaborative teaming process. She described the team's interactions as being a "give-and-take relationship," with the team members respecting each other's perspective.

Beyond the Support Process

We interviewed Millie approximately 1 year after the research project ended to capture her perspective on the importance of PBS. In this interview, she elaborated on the essential elements of the behavior support process that remained intact for Jeffrey. She provided advice for families embarking on collaborative research partnerships for PBS.

In our interview, Millie emphasized the need for families to be open to the possibilities that await them. She encouraged family members to view their situation as objectively as possible and to describe what they want the support and intervention process to accomplish: "Be very honest with the people involved about what you would like to achieve and how your family operates. Just be very open." She further relayed the need for the family members to take stock of how they have changed or not changed by having a child with a disability in the family: "Everybody gets in a rut with what they've been doing. You've gotten into a place and you don't even know how you got there, but it's not very comfortable and you want to change it."

She cautioned families on how easy it is to talk about the need for change in relation to the challenges associated with the change process. She found that the first step to change is to trust what professionals say about how they will support the family. Again, Millie believed that the family and the professional need to establish an honest relationship. She discouraged the professional from interpreting family needs as family failure:

> I think having an open, trusting relationship is very key to the process, as opposed to saying, "Oh, well, you've been doing this wrong and this wrong and this wrong. Let me show you the right way to do things."

She proposed that the professional take the role of the guide who facilitates a change in the family's focus from the past to the present and helps the family assess its unique needs.

Millie described the next step as moving from "a quick-fix or Band-Aid approach" to building a commitment to achieving a more permanent change. She felt that families, including her own, need to understand that permanent change involves a more lengthy process. She described it this way:

> It's not like a medicine that a doctor's going to give that's going to take away everything. It means a lifestyle change most of the time—for everyone, not just the mother. If it's going to work, it's got to be a lifestyle change. That's not easy for folks.

Millie identified family attitudes toward Jeffrey's problem behaviors as an essential element of the behavior support process. The family began to understand why Jeffrey exhibited difficult behaviors. They understood that his behavior was based on his inability to express his needs in more traditional ways and that how family members interacted with him directly affected his responses. To illustrate her point, Millie relayed how she overheard Chris explaining Jeffrey's problem behavior to a friend. He said, "Well, Jeffrey isn't able to talk and so he does a lot of these behaviors because it's a way of him trying to communicate. He's trying to help us understand that he's upset." Millie stated, "Before PBS, Chris would have said, 'He's just a pain.'" The family addressed Jeffrey's behaviors more effectively because they understood them better.

Millie discussed how the family's altered approach to Jeffrey's problem behavior resulted in pivotal family changes. She stated, "I think that started the metamorphosis, if you want to call it that, of bringing our family out of a dark place and into a better world." Mil-

lie and her family realized that they bore the responsibility of change because Jeffrey would continue to have a disability and need support.

Millie encouraged parents to step back and give themselves permission to ease up on intervention when they are going through difficult times. She elaborated that her family could not use all of the strategies during these times; they needed to pull back and not pressure themselves or Jeffrey to continually work on achieving new skills. However, Millie acknowledged that once the difficulties or stressful events passed, the family returned to the support plan.

Millie felt that she and the family maintained and expanded Jeffrey's support over time. They have taken Jeffrey into new environments, developed new support strategies, and refined the strategies that were developed through the research. Millie reflected that the lesson of PBS that has remained the most stable is the family's different attitude. She stated:

> I think the thing that has carried forward is our attitude, our reaction to what he does. Whenever we're going into a new situation, we ask, "How can we prepare Jeffrey? How can we set this up so it's going to be easier?"

Words of Wisdom

Millie offered final words of wisdom to families as they launch the process of lifestyle change. She encouraged family to view themselves as competent and to accept help without a sense of inadequacy. She proposed that families let go of past experiences and welcome new ideas without merely placating professionals. She advised families to "look at it as something different and as a different avenue opening to you." She emphasized honesty, trust, and teamwork as major building blocks in the support process. As a part of the honesty and team effort, Millie felt that families need to assess what works and does not work for them and to clearly state their feelings to professionals. She indicated that if families feel obligated to blindly accept recommended strategies, then the effects of those strategies will be short lived. She described the importance of honest expression in this way:

> *If it's not really what is going to work for you, you're not going to carry it with you. It's not going to be long lasting. What you gather has got to be something that's useful and works for you and your family. It's not trying to say what you think a professional might want to hear, but it's really saying what you need and what you want from this, honestly.*

In our interview, Millie promoted PBS as a learning process for everyone in spite of the challenges involved. She emphasized that all family members need to become a part of the process, that support cannot be achieved in isolation. She felt that the process of PBS can provide the family members with successful experiences that bolster their confidence in the process and their investment in the intervention. She stated, "It's a learning process. You just have to hang in there and it can be done. The first time you experience success, it's going to make that worth it and make you realize that you can do it."

CONCLUSION

We strongly believe that many vital future developments in the emerging applied science of positive behavior support will come from collaborative research partnerships with stakeholders. If the field is to make meaningful differences in people's lives, then the people who are most directly affected and invested must provide the insights and guidance. In this respect, Millie Bucy and her family contributed greatly in our efforts to develop new, holistic approaches to research and practice in behavioral support. In particular, Millie's generous contributions to the research team offered data and direction that were unavailable from any other source.

The purpose of this chapter has been to convey our experiences with a single research partnership, and we recognize and emphasize that this is a single exemplar. The Bucy family and the nature of our relationships with its members are unique in many ways. The exact features of our research experience with the Bucy family cannot be directly replicated, nor should they be. Instead, we advocate numerous and individualized efforts to establish close and functional research partnerships, to adopt multifaceted research methodologies, and to expand the realm of experiences and perceptions related to positive behavior support. These are the kinds of partnerships that will bridge the gap between research and practice and bring a richer and more meaningful source of support to children, families, and all others who are affected by the challenge of problem behaviors.

REFERENCES

Albin, R.W., Lucyshyn, J.M., Horner, R.H., & Flannery, K.B. (1996). Contextual fit for behavioral support plans: A model for "goodness of fit." In L.K. Koegel, R.L. Koegel, & G. Dunlap (Eds.), *Positive behavioral support: Including people with difficult behavior in the community* (pp. 81–98). Baltimore: Paul H. Brookes Publishing Co.

Bailey, D.B., Simeonsson, R.J., Huntington, G.S., Comfort, M., Isbell, P., O'Donnell, K.J., & Helm, J.M. (1990). Family-focused intervention: A functional model for planning, implementing, and evaluating individualized family services in early intervention. *Topics in Early Childhood Special Education, 10,* 156–171.

Carr, E.G. (1997). Invited commentary. The evolution of applied behavior analysis into positive behavior support. *The Journal of The Association for Persons with Severe Handicaps, 22,* 208–209.

Carr, E.G., Horner, R.H., Turnbull, A.P., Marquis, J.G., McLaughlin, D.M., McAtee, M.L., Smith, C.E., Ryan, K.A., Ruef, M.B., Doolabh, A., & Braddock, D. (1999). *Positive behavior support for people with developmental disabilities: A research synthesis.* Washington, DC: American Association on Mental Retardation.

Duchnowski, A.J. (2000). Improving family support: An agenda for the next decade. *Journal of Positive Behavior Interventions, 2,* 117–118.

Dunlap, G., Clarke, S., & Steiner, M. (1999). Intervention research in behavioral and developmental disabilities: 1980 to 1997. *Journal of Positive Behavior Interventions, 1,* 170–180.

Dunlap, G., Fox, L., Vaughn, B.J., Bucy, M., & Clarke, S. (1997). In quest of meaningful perspectives and outcomes: A response to five commentaries. *The Journal of The Association for Persons with Severe Handicaps, 22,* 221–223.

Fox, L., Vaughn, B.J., Dunlap, G., & Bucy, M. (1997). Parent–professional partnership in behavioral support: A qualitative analysis of one family's experience. *The Journal of The Association for Persons with Severe Handicaps, 22,* 198–207.

Graves, W.H. (1991, September). Participatory action research: A new paradigm for disability and rehabilitation research. *ARCA Newsletter, 19,* 9–10.

Hieneman, M., & Dunlap, G. (1999). Issues and challenges in implementing community-based behavioral support for two boys with severe behavioral difficulties. In J.R. Scotti & L.H. Meyer (Eds.), *Behavioral intervention: Principles, models, and practices* (pp. 363–384). Baltimore: Paul H. Brookes Publishing Co.

Horner, R.H. (1997). Invited commentary. Encouraging a new applied science: A commentary on two papers addressing parent–professional partnerships in behavioral support. *The Journal of The Association for Persons with Severe Handicaps, 22,* 210–212.

Lucyshyn, J.M., Albin, R.W., & Nixon, C.D. (1997). Embedding comprehensive behavioral support in family ecology: An experimental, single-case analysis. *Journal of Consulting and Clinical Psychology, 65,* 241–251.

Meyer, L.H., & Evans, I.M. (1993). Science and practice in behavioral intervention: Meaningful outcomes, research validity, and usable knowledge. *The Journal of The Association for Persons with Severe Handicaps, 18,* 224–234.

Meyer, L.H., Park, H., Grenot-Scheyer, M., Schwartz, I., & Harry, B. (1998). Participatory research: New approaches to the research to practice dilemma. *The Journal of The Association for Persons with Severe Handicaps, 23,* 165–177.

Mount, B., & Zwernik, K. (1988). *It's never too early, it's never too late: A booklet about Personal Futures Planning.* St. Paul, MN: Metropolitan Council.

O'Neill, R.E., Horner, R.H., Albin, R.W., Storey, K., Sprague, J.R., & Newton, J.S. (1997). *Functional assessment of problem behavior: A practical assessment guide.* Pacific Grove, CA: Brooks/Cole Thomson Learning.

Park, H., Gonsier-Gerdin, J., Hoffman, S., Whaley, S., & Yount, M. (1998). Applying the participatory action research model to the study of social inclusion at worksites. *The Journal of the Association for Persons with Severe Handicaps, 23,* 189–202.

Singer, G.H.S. (2000). Ecological validity. *Journal of Positive Behavior Interventions, 2,* 122–124.

Turnbull, A.P., Friesen, B.J., & Ramirez, C. (1998). Participatory action research as a model for conducting family research. *Journal of The Association for Persons with Severe Handicaps, 23*(3), 178–188.

Vaughn, B.J., Dunlap, G., Fox, L., Clarke, S., & Bucy, M. (1997). Parent–professional partnership in behavioral support: A case study of community-based intervention. *The Journal of The Association for Persons with Severe Handicaps, 22*(4), 186–197.

Whyte, W.F. (Ed.). (1991). *Participatory action research.* Thousand Oaks, CA: Sage Publications.

19

A Collaborative Study of Parent to Parent Programs

Implications for Positive Behavior Support

Betsy Santelli, Connie Ginsberg, Steve Sullivan, and Carol Niederhauser

For parents who have children with disabilities, chronic illnesses, and other special health care needs, Parent to Parent programs offer the opportunity to be carefully matched in an one-to-one relationship with another parent who has had similar experiences. The informational and emotional support is broad based and responsive to the needs and preferences of the parent seeking the support. Parent matches are community based and flexible, offering parents the chance to benefit from support that is nearby and accessible 24 hours per day. This unique support from another parent may mean that the child with challenging behaviors and his or her family benefit from best practices in behavioral supports and receive the understanding and compassion that can only come from those who have "been there." Parents know that it works, and research conducted by a participatory action research (PAR) team of parents and researchers validates the effectiveness of parent to parent support (Singer et al., 1999).

This chapter provides the following:

- An overview of Parent to Parent programs

- A discussion of PAR as an important approach to research

- A summary of the PAR experience of the team of parents and researchers who worked as equal partners to carry out the Parent to Parent efficacy study

- A discussion of the results and implications of the Parent to Parent efficacy study for families who have children with challenging behaviors and for professionals who work with families

---

This chapter is adapted from the following previously published article: Santelli, B., Singer, G.H.S., DiVenere, N., Ginsberg, C., & Powers, L.E. (1998). Participatory action research: Reflections on critical incidents in a PAR project. *The Journal of The Association for Persons with Severe Handicaps, 23*(3), 211–222. Copyright ©*The Journal of The Association for Persons with Severe Handicaps*; adapted by permission.

The chapter begins with two of the authors, Steve Sullivan and Carol Niederhauser, relating experiences with Family Connection of South Carolina, a statewide Parent to Parent program in Columbia, South Carolina.

OVERVIEW OF PARENT TO PARENT PROGRAMS

On Halloween night in 1990 in Columbia, South Carolina, the neighborhood streets were filled with children in costumes and choruses of "Trick or treat!" We responded to the doorbell as parents typically do and thought ahead to when our 7-month-old, Danny, would join the ranks of the neighborhood trick or treaters. Just as we were enjoying this shared vision, Danny's arms and legs tightened to his tummy and his eyes rolled back into his head. He relaxed, then repeated the spasms dozens of times. Our lives changed forever that night.

The first bout of seizures was short—it passed almost as quickly as it came—but, in a panic, we called Danny's pediatrician. We took Danny to the pediatrician's office the next morning. Danny also had seizures in the examining room, so the pediatrician referred Danny to a neurologist. He also referred us to Family Connection—a brand new Parent to Parent program in our area. Although our lives had changed forever the night before, receiving these two referrals the next day gave us the hope and courage we needed to deal with our new reality—Danny had a seizure disorder.

We called Family Connection and spoke with a parent about our son, our visit with the pediatrician, and our fears. This parent listened carefully as we explained our situation, and because she has a child with a disability, she knew only too well the emotional roller coaster that we were experiencing. She offered to match us with one of Family Connection's trained support parents, and she comforted us with the notion that parents who share similar experiences are often unique sources of emotional and informational support. She was right.

Our first match through the Family Connection was with a support parent whose son also had neurological issues. Her little boy was being monitored for sleep apnea, and she knew all about living with unpredictability and the feelings of helplessness that come with each episode. She gently introduced us to the world of disability and provided us with a road map for finding services for Danny and for ourselves. By the time that Danny was 18 months old, he was in a special preschool program for children with developmental disabilities.

Along with the seizures that still were a part of Danny's reality as well as our own, we began to notice that Danny was missing many developmental milestones and developing some very challenging behaviors. He didn't talk. He also wouldn't look at us when we tried to play with him; rather, he looked through and beyond us. In addition, he often bolted away from us when we were running errands or participating in community events. When Danny was 3 years old, he was diagnosed with autism. We were back at square one and needed to learn about a whole new disability.

Because our support parent had been so helpful to us as we learned to live with Danny's seizures, we called Family Connection again, hoping that we might be matched this time with a support parent who had a child with autism—another parent who could help us learn to deal with Danny's challenging behaviors. We were matched almost right away with a support parent whose daughter was 3 years older than Danny and also had autism. This parent knew firsthand how frustrating it can be to have your child screaming in public or striking other children who get too close. She also had some helpful tips for us. When Danny begins to scream, we now know to whisper. When Danny started locking himself in the bathroom and dumping laundry detergent all over the laundry room, our support parent suggested swapping the doorknobs. Now our laundry room door locks and our bathroom door does not! Our link with Family Connection and our support parent match have not changed Danny's diagnosis, but they have given us reliable allies who are walking the same road, friends who know what we face every day and who can help us discover strategies for encouraging positive behaviors and reducing challenging ones.

Caring for a family member who has a disability is an experience that few parents anticipate and plan for, and it comes with many strong emotional responses and day-to-day challenges. Families that have a relative with a disability must not only cope with the typical demands of family life but also with a host of disability-related issues. Family members must learn about the disability itself and what it means for the individual as well as for the whole family; they must learn the languages of the medical, legal, financial, and special education worlds, and they must find their way in a service system that may or may not provide appropriate support opportunities. When the nature of the child's disability means that the child exhibits challenging behaviors, the family often must cope with such additional stressors as being blamed by others for the child's behaviors, expulsion from school and community programs, and the physical and emotional exhaustion that accompanies addressing difficult behaviors day in and day out.

At one time, strong family networks existed that helped families to meet the challenges of family life, but increased mobility over the course of the 20th century means that extended family members often live far away. Moreover, finding another family with a child who also has challenging behaviors is often very difficult because most families prefer to keep their child's disability and challenging behaviors to themselves. Thus, many families deal with their child's difficult behaviors alone. Yet, parents are often the best resources for other parents, particularly when the two parents have children with challenging behaviors. How do these parents find one another? Perhaps they can connect through a Parent to Parent program.

Parent to Parent programs have evolved to meet the special needs of families that have a family member with a disability (including challenging behaviors) and want to connect with others who share their experiences. These community-based parent support and information programs emerged in the United States in the early 1970s. The first organized Parent to Parent program, the Pilot Parents Program, at the Greater Omaha Arc in Omaha, Nebraska, grew out of a parent's wish to make it easier for parents to connect with each other. As of 2001, more than 700 local and 32 statewide Parent to Parent programs modeled after the Pilot Parents program exist throughout the United States, and these programs are serving more than 100,000 families nationally.

Parent to Parent programs provide emotional and informational support to parents who wish to talk with other parents who have "been there." A parent who connects with a Parent to Parent program is carefully matched in a one-to-one relationship with a trained and experienced supporting parent. Often, at the time of the match, the referred parent's child has just been diagnosed or the parent is beginning a new era in the life of the child with a disability. For parents of children with challenging behaviors, perhaps the match is made at the time a diagnosis of autism is confirmed or when the school system is considering whether to remove the child from the general education classroom. A parent to parent match can be made at any time that a parent would like to talk with another parent who has had similar experiences.

Parent to parent matches are made usually very quickly, often within 24 hours of the referral, so that the support can begin immediately. Because the quality of support that is offered in the match is so dependent on the relationship between the referred parent and the supporting parent, program coordinators carefully consider a whole host of disability and family issues to ensure the best possible fit between the two parents. The supporting parent knows from personal experience the challenges and special joys that come with parenting a son or daughter with a disability and through the match is able to provide informational and emotional support in ways that only another parent can. In addition, before they are matched with another parent, supporting parents receive orientation or training to help them understand their role as a supporting parent and to equip them with communication and listening skills. Once supporting parents are matched with newly referred parents, many programs also offer supporting parents ongoing training opportunities and informal support from the program coordinator.

Each parent to parent relationship evolves individually, depending on the needs and preferences of the referred parent. For some parents, the match is short term and primarily involves the exchange of information; for others, the match endures for years and develops into a lifelong friendship. As noted by Santelli, Turnbull, Marquis, and Lerner (1995), parents who have participated in Parent to Parent programs report that the match provided them with 1) someone to listen and understand, 2) information about the disability, 3) information about community resources, 4) assistance with referrals, and 5) problem-solving support. These key support opportunities, delivered through a carefully made one-to-one match between a trained supporting parent and a newly referred parent, are the very essence of Parent to Parent programs. Although many Parent to Parent programs offer other program activities beyond the one-to-one match, providing these key support opportunities is the common denominator among all Parent to Parent programs (Santelli, Turnbull, Marquis, & Lerner, 1997).

Parent to Parent programs carefully document and follow each match to ensure that it is comfortable for both parents and that it meets the needs of the referred parent. Because the two parents share so many common experiences, the match offers a unique form of support that is different from that provided by professionals. Furthermore, because the relationship between the parents is one to one, the nature of the support is different from that found in parent support groups.

Parents and professionals who participate in or connect parents to Parent to Parent programs have also provided compelling anecdotal evidence of the importance of the emotional and informational supports that are offered through the one-to-one match between parents. As Steve and Carol recounted,

> Raising a child with autism can be almost overwhelming in the times of crisis. We feel like sponges sometimes, soaking up any scrap of information that might be useful in the next challenge. Yet, you cannot store emotional support for later. The emotional load is always lighter after talking with our support parent. We have a bond born of shared experience, and that is what makes the emotional support so relevant and the informational support so credible.

A professional added,

Professionals often find that when a Parent to Parent program is available to families receiving services from their agency, the Parent to Parent program is a resource for the professionals as well as for the families. Professionals who are not also parents of children with disabilities cannot truly understand the disability experience, and they appreciate being able to offer parents the opportunity to be matched with a support parent who provides the emotional support that they as professionals cannot.

Research Needs for Parent to Parent Programs

At the request of Parent to Parent programs, the Beach Center on Disability at The University of Kansas conducted multiple national surveys of local and statewide Parent to Parent program coordinators and of the supporting and referred parents who participate in these programs. Data from the surveys provided a great deal of descriptive information about 1) the organizational and administrative structure of Parent to Parent programs; 2) the ways that programs are funded and staffed; 3) the services they provide to parents, family members, and professionals; 4) the training for supporting parents; and 5) the resources that are available from the programs. The vast majority of Parent to Parent programs are local, community-based programs that are cross disability and match parents whose children have a wide range of physical, cognitive, and emotional disabilities, including chronic illness, acquired disabilities, and disabilities that are accompanied by challenging behaviors (Santelli, Turnbull, Marquis, & Lerner, 1993). Parents and program directors at the local, state, and national levels also requested efficacy data on Parent to Parent programs. As a result, a PAR team consisting of parents, Parent to Parent program directors, and researchers conducted a national study to determine the effectiveness of parent to parent support for parents who were referred to Parent to Parent programs for emotional and informational support (Singer et al., 1999). The results of the study indicate that parent to parent support is an effective means of providing emotional and informational support to parents of children with disabilities. Although the results of the study validate the efficacy of parent to parent support, equally important is the use of PAR to carry out the study. The next section discusses PAR and how parents and researchers worked together to plan, fund, carry out, and disseminate the results of this national study. The study's specific results appear on page 452.

OVERVIEW OF PARTICIPATORY ACTION RESEARCH

The majority of families that have a family member with a disability report that they most often need information about the disability, disability-related services, and best practices for supporting the individual as well as the whole family (Santelli et al., 1995). Although a wealth of research-based information is available in the disability field, families report that they have a difficult time finding meaningful, relevant, and useful information (Turnbull, Friesen, & Ramirez, 1995). Sadly, there appears to be a gap between the research-based knowledge that disability researchers generate and the information that families—as the intended beneficiaries of the research—receive and find helpful. PAR provides a viable alternative for closing this gap.

When used in the family and disability field, PAR is an approach to applied social research that seeks to 1) define relevant issues for individuals with disabilities and their families; 2) find solutions to the identified problems; and 3) ensure that the research-based solutions are meaningful, useful, and actually make a difference in the lives of families affected by the disability experience (Bruyère, 1993). With its special emphasis on useful outcomes, PAR is a research approach that encourages researchers and beneficiaries (in this case, individuals with disabilities and their families) to jointly identify the problem and then to collaborate throughout every phase of the research, dissemination, and utilization process.

In the field of disability and rehabilitation research, involving the beneficiaries in the process is not an entirely new concept. Leaders of the independent living movement in the early 1970s demanded greater participation by individuals with disabilities in a whole variety of areas that affected their lives, including research (DeJong, 1979). Over time, the field of disability and rehabilitation research moved from the traditional model, almost entirely directed by the researcher, toward a model that facilitated and encouraged greater participation by beneficiaries in all phases of the research (Fenton, Batavia, & Roody, 1993).

With the passage of the Rehabilitation Act Amendments of 1992 (PL 102-569), Congress sought to empower individuals with disabilities and their families by requiring research and training supported by federal funds to be "relevant and responsive to the self-identified needs of individuals with disabilities, and those of their families and guardians" (Fenton et al., 1993, p. 2). In 1993, the National Institute on Disability and Rehabilitation Research (NIDRR), the federal funding agency for research and training centers that conduct disability and rehabilitation research, proposed that PAR be implemented in all phases of NIDRR-funded research. NIDRR defined PAR as follows: "disability and rehabilitation research, including training, dissemination, and utilization, and its evaluation, that entails meaningful participation by relevant constituencies in all stages of the NIDRR research and training process" (Fenton et al., 1993). NIDRR thus endorses full participation by all parties in the design and conduct of all research phases. Participation in the research process supports and empowers all parties and leads to research outcomes that are more relevant, more meaningful, and more useful (Lather, 1986).

PAR moves away from the traditional notion of the researcher as the technical expert who directs the investigation to a model in which "groups of people can organize the conditions under which they can learn from their own experiences and make this experience accessible to others" (McTaggart, 1991, p. 170). In traditional research, the researchers alone decide what is studied, and research is often conducted as its own end rather than as a means for any practical application of the findings. In PAR, those expected to benefit from the research influence the research agenda, and research is a means for changing the system. Because it is an approach to identifying the research questions, implementing the investigation, and ensuring that the relevance between the findings and practical needs are strong, PAR is an organizational framework rather than a specific research methodology (Whitney-Thomas, 1997). Whyte and Doe (1995) described some characteristics of PAR:

- PAR seeks to link the research process to the process of social change. Efforts to change social systems are enhanced through the gathering of new knowledge that is shared by the participants in the PAR process. Yet, research is seen not only as a process of gathering and creating knowledge but also as a vehicle for developing consciousness and mobilizing change.

- Participants can be from any stakeholder group, assuming that they have personal experiences or an insider's perspective to share. PAR participants should be people whose lives will be most affected by the research outcomes.

- A balance of team members is needed to ensure that nonresearchers are not overshadowed by researchers but instead feel empowered to be a part of the change effort. PAR turns the paternalistic relationships that can exist between researcher and the researched into a collaborative adventure to work for change.

- The constituency participants (i.e., nonresearchers) should be experts on the topic being studied, whereas the research participants should be experts on research methodologies. PAR requires researchers to enter and understand the world of the people being studied. PAR also requires the nonresearchers to enter and understand the world of research.

Chesler (1991) noted that PAR is particularly relevant for inquiry with self-help groups. As issues of personal and collective empowerment are crucial in self-help groups, PAR inquiry methods that explicitly seek to empower participants are extremely relevant and important. Self-help groups tend generally to have a highly participatory membership with a grassroots orientation and a great respect for experience-based knowledge. PAR efforts often use research methodologies (e.g., self-assessments, focus groups) that fit well with the reliance on local wisdom that runs through the self-help movement. Many self-help groups develop to fill gaps or create change in the service delivery system, so the ways in which PAR efforts use research findings for systems change are congruent with the action orientation of most self-help groups. Because the activities that occur in self-help groups are often private interactions among the participants, PAR teams involving representatives of the self-help groups themselves give the team a better understanding of the conditions at hand. Moreover, because these interactions cannot be known or directed ahead of time or from the outside, the highly controlled research designs that may be developed by researchers working in isolation may not be feasible with self-help groups. A PAR team that includes members of a self-help group most likely will develop a more flexible set of procedures. Many self-help groups that are struggling for legitimacy or were involved in research that did not generate meaningful results may not trust establishment-based researchers. The use of a PAR team may allow for easier access to self-help group participants. In summary, research with self-help groups may require the development and use of different methods of social inquiry and action. Thus, the principles underlying PAR fit quite well with the interactive style and goals of self-help groups.

As the field of disability and rehabilitation research strengthens its commitment to PAR and PAR becomes more widespread, the field's knowledge of best practices will increase. Whitney-Thomas (1997) stressed the need to document strategies and disseminate success stories to facilitate the growth of PAR. The next section shares the success story and the strategies of a national PAR team working together to document the effectiveness of parent to parent support.

National Study of Parent to Parent Programs: Successful Use of Participatory Action Research

In July 1996, a PAR team of parents and researchers completed a 3-year study to examine the effectiveness of the one-to-one parent to parent match as a form of support for parents who have a child with a disability, chronic illness, or other special needs, including challenging behaviors. We believe that research on positive behavior support strategies is more relevant and beneficial to parents who have children with challenging behaviors if parents have participated in all phases of the research. Therefore, we hope that the PAR experiences of the team of parents and researchers that conducted the efficacy study of parent to parent support provides a model for others to replicate. The next sections discuss this PAR team's procedures:

- Determining membership and responsibilities

- Understanding Parent to Parent programs

- Choosing the research questions

- Developing the research design

- Choosing the evaluation measures

- Preparing the grant application and funding the study

- Conducting the study

- Disseminating and utilizing the results

Determining Membership and Responsibilities   At the seventh International Parent to Parent Conference in April 1992, a small group of parents and researchers talked about the need for evaluative research on the effectiveness of the one-to-one parent to parent match. The parents at this initial meeting were all directors of Parent to Parent programs. They knew that data that validated what parents had been saying informally about the value of parent to parent support would be useful in convincing potential funding sources and referral sources of the importance of one-to-one parent to parent support. Perhaps such data would mean that parent to parent support would become more widely available to families. The researchers were all committed to family research as a way of creating a system of family support that is responsive to the needs of families affected by the disability experience. The researchers listened carefully to the parents' hopes and visions, and they believed that research might play a pivotal role in clarifying the significance of one-to-one parent to parent support. This initial and shared commitment to the importance of the research united the group in its purpose.

Chesler (1991), Hall (1984), Turnbull and Turnbull (1996), and Whitney-Thomas (1997) all spoke to the importance of mergers between researchers and constituencies and of establishing shared commitment and trust before these groups even specify the research questions. Turnbull and Turnbull (1996) pointed out that early involvement of all parties leads to shared ownership and attention to the developing partnership; these factors then heighten commitment, intensify collaboration, and bring about more immediate and meaningful use of the research results. The PAR team soon discovered these realities.

We met again 2 months after the conference to design a research study to determine the effectiveness of parent to parent support. Our team membership grew to more than a dozen participants, with equal representation of parents and researchers. Whyte and Doe (1995) stressed the importance of achieving a balance in PAR team membership—both in numbers and perspective and in expertise brought to the PAR effort. Everyone on our PAR team brought his or her own unique skills to the team effort, and roles and responsibilities were established based on these abilities and preferences. The parents on the team had first-hand knowledge of Parent to Parent programs, both as program directors and as parents themselves of children with special needs. The researchers brought many years of professional training and experience in conducting quantitative research. Although team members recognized that their roles and responsibilities would vary somewhat depending on the tasks at hand, they anticipated that the researchers would take on the following roles and responsibilities:

- Provide information about research design and research methods—what makes for solid research

- Suggest/lead the development of instruments that might be used in the study

- Run all of the statistical analyses and summarize the data

- Submit the findings for publication in professional journals

The team also decided that the parents would take on these roles and responsibilities:

- Provide information about Parent to Parent programs—how they work and what they do for parents.

- Suggest modifications to the research design and research methods so that the study would be more comfortable for parents.

- Recruit parents to participate in the study.

- Write about the findings in a way that parents would clearly understand.

Menz (1995), Morningstar (1994), and Whitney-Thomas (1997) stressed the need to acknowledge the diverse perspectives and skills that each PAR team member brings to the process and recommended that PAR teams identify preferred roles and responsibilities for each PAR team member. Researchers are dedicated to scientific rigor and are trained in technical areas. Parents' direct life experiences offer a different perspective to the PAR team effort (Fenton et al., 1993). When these areas of expertise are clearly defined, the PAR team as a whole may make better use of the diverse skills represented on the team.

One of the researchers on this particular PAR team, Janet Marquis, spoke about the benefits of having parents involved from the outset: "Sometimes research is esoteric and not really relevant to the family experience. A parent–researcher team that has input from parents from the very start helps to ensure that the resulting research will indeed be meaningful to families."

Understanding Parent to Parent Programs
To define the research questions, we started by looking carefully at the goals and objectives of Parent to Parent programs and their perceived outcomes. The parents initiated a discussion about the impact of parent to parent support on referred parents, sharing their own and many other parents' personal experiences. The researchers listened carefully and asked questions to enhance their own understanding about the perceived importance of parent to parent support.

From this discussion, we agreed on three goals of parent to parent support. First, increase emotional support for parents who have a child with a disability. Second, increase informational support for parents who have a child with a disability (including parents whose children exhibit challenging behaviors). Third, offer parents a one-to-one match with a veteran parent who can provide emotional and informational support around common disability issues. Based on the parents' descriptions of parent to parent support, *emotional support* and *informational support* were defined as follows:

- *Emotional support*—1) a sense of having a reliable ally; 2) a sense of empowerment; 3) a sense of social support; 4) a sense of being able to cope; and 5) a sense of greater acceptance of the disability circumstances

- *Informational support*—1) knowledge about services for the child with a disability and 2) knowledge about services for the family

From the beginning, we had talked about measuring the impact of a one-to-one parent to parent match, but now we needed to define exactly what was meant by a *one-to-one par-*

ent to parent match. From a researcher's perspective, we needed to be sure that we measured the same experience for each participating parent, yet no two parent to parent matches are the same. Thus, the challenge was to determine how to impose the necessary consistency required by research on the intimate, flexible, individualized, and personalized experiences that are at the heart of Parent to Parent programs. The parents talked about what typically happens in a parent to parent match and mentioned that most matches have at least four contacts over an 8-week period. Therefore, if the research study required a minimum of four contacts during the first 8 weeks of the match, the study would not change what typically happens in most matches. So we agreed on the last definition:

- *One-to-one match*—at least four contacts from a veteran parent during an 8-week period

Through continued reflection, we identified parent to parent outcomes for parents receiving support (see Table 19.1).

Choosing the Research Questions   We considered the definitions of the program goals, the key terms in Parent to Parent programs, and the perceived outcomes of the programs. We then identified several different evaluation questions to answer:

- What is the impact of the one-to-one match on referred parents' 1) sense of having a reliable ally, 2) sense of empowerment, 3) sense of social support, 4) sense of being able to cope, and 5) sense of greater acceptance of the disability circumstances?

- What is the impact of the one-to-one matched experience on referred parents' knowledge about services for the child with a disability?

- What is the impact of the one-to-one match on referred parents' satisfaction with Parent to Parent programs?

- What is the impact of the one-to-one match on referred parents' sense that their needs have been met?

- How does the number of contacts with the supporting parent affect the referred parents' satisfaction with Parent to Parent programs?

Developing the Research Design   With the research questions determined, we turned our attention to research design. We knew that the research design needed to be rigorous so that the findings would be convincing and useful. We needed to determine how we were going to carry out this study to yield data that would be respected by other researchers, funding sources for Parent to Parent programs, and those who might refer parents to Parent to Parent programs. Determining the research design was our biggest challenge.

Based on their formal training and experience in research methods, the researchers presented what they thought would be the strongest research design: an experimental group and a control group, with parents being randomly assigned to one of the two groups. The parents in the experimental group would be matched with another parent immediately. The parents in the control group would not. Our team would follow each group of parents for 1 year, asking them to complete written questionnaires several times during the year. The researchers could then look for any differences between the groups' responses to the questionnaires and attribute these differences to whether the parent had participated in a one-to-one parent to parent match.

The parents on the PAR team were concerned about this type of research design, believing that it would be unethical to deny parents in the control group parent to parent

Table 19.1. Outcomes of parent to parent support

Emotional outcomes	Informational outcomes
Sense of having a reliable ally	Knowledge about services for the child with a disability
Sense of empowerment	Knowledge about services for the family
Sense of social support	
Sense of being able to cope	
Sense of greater adjustment to the disability circumstances	

support for the sake of the research. From their own experiences, they knew how important parent to parent support could be, and they were uncomfortable with denying this support to parents who wanted it. One parent on the PAR team clearly demonstrated the central importance of the control-group issue when she indicated that if the research design required some parents to be denied the parent to parent experience, then the Parent to Parent program that she directed would not be able to participate in the study. Without a research design that was family sensitive, the study would not have the backing of the parents and their Parent to Parent programs. Yet, without a well-respected research design, the study would probably not receive the funding needed to carry it out, and the results might not be viewed as credible. The tension between what was best for researchers and what was best for families brought the team to a difficult place.

Each participant's commitment to Parent to Parent programs and high-quality research was appreciated. In addition, because all of the team members' expertise and perspectives were respected, we were able to develop a creative compromise to the dilemma. We decided that parents in the control group would not need to wait a full year before being matched with a veteran parent. The parents on the team advised the researchers that most parents report a significant impact during the first 8 weeks of the match, so the researchers agreed to a shorter waiting period for parents in the control group, even though they recognized that a 1-year time period to compare the responses of parents in the experimental and control groups would make a stronger study.

We also decided that no parent who wanted to be matched right away would be denied that opportunity. If a parent did not want to risk being assigned to the control group that waited for 8 weeks before being matched, then that parent would not be a part of the study and would be matched right away. We recognized that this solution meant that the study would not include parents for whom parent to parent support might make the most difference; ethically, however, we believed in the greater importance of a study that would not harm parents.

Furthermore, we decided to add a qualitative study to hear directly from the parents about their matched experiences. To gather qualitative data, the researchers used a standardized interview protocol to conduct 24 telephone interviews with parents. This group included 12 parents who reported that parent to parent support was helpful and 12 who reported that parent to parent support was not helpful.

Some individuals express concerns about the validity, reliability, and objectivity of PAR efforts. They fear that nonresearchers do not have the relevant training to decide about research design; thus, research design issues may be decided more on sensitivity-to-constituency issues than on scientific rigor. Yet, as Whitney-Thomas suggested, "Issues of validity and reliability are addressed in any research and have more to do with how one carries out methodology than who is involved in deciding what methods are used" (1997, p. 191). Bruyère (1993) and Whyte and Doe (1995) pointed out that an effective PAR team addresses questions of scientific rigor just as any team of researchers would—balancing the ideals of traditional standards of research with the enhanced sensitivity and relevance of the project outcome. Reason (1994) added,

> A key notion here is dialogue, because it is through dialogue that the subject–object relationship gives way to a subject–subject one, in which academic knowledge of formally educated people works in a dialectic tension with the popular knowledge of the people to produce a more profound understanding of the situation. (p. 328)

Choosing the Evaluation Measures   Once we had determined the basic research design, we went on to consider evaluation measures. Based on what was learned from the parents about the perceived outcomes of parent to parent support, the researchers on the PAR team presented a number of instruments that could be used to measure these kinds of outcomes. The researchers recommended which of these instruments were the most psychometrically sound, and the team reviewed all of these instruments. Some were long, with seemingly repetitive questions; others were depressing to complete.

In reviewing each instrument, the researchers stressed the importance of having enough questions on each instrument to ensure consistent answers from the respondents. The researchers noted that some of the most well-respected instruments have been used for many years but do not incorporate a positive perspective of the family. Once again, we struggled with the competing preferences for using respected and validated instruments or for choosing measures that were family friendly and would not leave families feeling depressed and confused. We also wrestled with how to include paper-and-pencil research instruments into the otherwise intimate way that parent to parent matches are made.

We settled on six instruments—three well-established instruments that are often used in family research and three new instruments. The three published instruments were 1) The Kansas Inventory of Parental Perceptions (KIPP; Behr, Murphy, & Summers, 1992), a measure of parental attitudes about a child with a disability in the family; 2) The Family Empowerment Scale (FES; Koren, DeChillo, & Friesen, 1992), a measure of perceived changes in parent empowerment; and 3) the Social Provisions Scale (Cutrona & Russell, 1990), a measure of perceived social support. The researchers also developed the three new instruments based on what the PAR team parents said about the impact of Parent to Parent programs: 1) the Parent Coping Efficacy Scale (PCES; Blanchard, Powers, Ginsberg, Marquis, & Singer, 1996), a measure of perceived coping with disability-related challenges; 2) The Reliable Alliance Scale, a measure of the perceived sense of having a reliable ally— someone who knows and understands; and 3) an informal questionnaire that asks parents about the helpfulness of Parent to Parent programs, specifically to what extent parent to parent support helped meet parents' needs. This collaborative effort resulted in a packet of instruments that was both scientifically rigorous and comfortable for parents to complete. We hoped that the three new instruments would particularly help Parent to Parent programs in their own program evaluations.

Preparing the Grant Application and Funding the Study   The next 2 months were spent working collaboratively by telephone, fax, and e-mail to prepare the proposal to apply for funding for the study. Researchers and parents worked together to prepare all sections of the grant application. We discovered that because PAR had been used as a process for planning the study and preparing the proposal, obtaining letters of support from key parent leaders was much easier. Parent leaders who were not on the PAR team had the same uneasy feelings about the design of the study; however, because parents were a part of the PAR team, parent leaders outside the team were willing to write support letters. The proposal was submitted in October 1992, and funding began in July 1993.

Conducting the Study   In July 1993, we met again to spell out the details of the study and the procedures for working together across sites. Over a course of 2 days, we mapped out specific procedures for recruitment, developed protocols and letters for enrolling parents and communicating with them, and designed the data collection system.

After discussing a variety of ways to recruit parents to participate in the study, we decided to recruit parents through existing parent to parent channels (e.g., posters and flyers in the offices of service providers for children with disabilities and their families, parent presentations about Parent to Parent programs, Parent to Parent program newsletters). The parent team members were sure that these channels would yield enough parents. The researchers, who had more experience in recruiting parents for research studies and knew how hard it can be to find willing participants, were not so sure. In fact, one of the researchers and one of the parents each felt so confident of their projections that they entered into a bet about the number of parents that could be recruited into the study by using only the existing parent to parent channels. The parent won—perhaps because Parent to Parent program directors recruit parents all the time and they know which recruitment strategies work. To the surprise of the team's researchers, recruitment was much easier than when research is conducted by researchers alone. Eventual participants lived in Kansas, New Hampshire, Vermont, North Carolina, and South Carolina. They were parents, foster parents, or grandparents of children with a disability or chronic illness and were willing to wait for support for up to 2 months if they were randomly assigned to the waiting list comparison group. Parents who already received support through a Parent to Parent program were not eligible, and parents who wished to be matched right away were not selected for the study but were referred immediately to a Parent to Parent program.

We determined the content of letters to and telephone conversations with parents. The parents urged the group to develop telephone and written protocols that were less formal and free of jargon. Yet, the researchers pointed out that they did not want protocols to be so family friendly that the interactions became a support that might contaminate the data. The team members thought long and hard about what was ideal and what was practical and then jointly prepared all of the questionnaire packets, informed-consent forms, cover letters, and promotional materials. These materials differed in appearance from those typically prepared by researchers, and this new look may have made it easier for parents to agree to participate. One of the researchers noted,

> Not only do parents help the researcher with the substance of the research, but also with the style or tone of the research. Our telephone protocol, our cover letters, and indeed some of our instruments themselves have a much friendlier feel to them because of the input of the parents on our team.

The data collection methods included the six written questionnaires for all participating parents. Parents in both the experimental and the control groups completed these questionnaires before having contact with a Parent to Parent program, 2 weeks after the match was made (for parents in the experimental group), 2 weeks into the waiting period (for parents in the control group), and 2 months later. Demographic information about the families was also collected so the researchers could learn more about potential participants in Parent to Parent programs. At the beginning and the end of the study, the study participants were asked to describe their needs, how well their needs had been met, and their level of satisfaction with Parent to Parent programs.

The statistical analyses of the quantitative data helped the researchers to draw precise conclusions about the nature of the contacts in parent to parent matches and the impact of parent to parent support. Each time the researchers completed a round of preliminary data analyses, they explained the meaning of the statistical analyses to the parent team members. The parents, with their intimate understanding of the nuances of parent to parent support, provided valuable input for the data interpretation. This mutual education process provided the perspectives of both the researchers and the parents and fostered a more accurate interpretation of the findings.

Study Results   Because the researchers believed that the dependent variables were conceptually distinct, they conducted separate analyses for each measure. They used an ANCOVA (analysis of covariance) for each dependent variable, with the pretest score serving as a covariant for each posttest measure.

The quantitative study yielded many findings. First, parent to parent support makes a significant difference in the parents' acceptance level of family and disability, as indicated by a pattern of statistically significant gains on the Source of Strength and Family Closeness subscale of the KIPP. Second, parent to parent support makes a notable difference in how much progress parents feel they have made in getting their needs met. This finding was revealed when parents were asked at posttest, "How much progress have you made on meeting your primary need?" The question yielded statistically significant differences in parent responses between the groups when the pretest scores were used as the covariant. Third, parent to parent support makes a significant difference in parents' perceptions of their ability to cope with their child's disability, as indicated by a pattern of statistically significant gains on the PCES. Fourth, parent to parent support helps parents feel better able to solve problems pertaining to their child's disability. Fifth, a strong relationship exists between the number of contacts that a parent has with a supporting parent and how helpful the parent finds Parent to Parent programs. Sixth, more than 80% of the parents in the study found Parent to Parent programs to be helpful (Singer et al., 1999).

The qualitative interviews with parents suggested that parent to parent support is helpful for many reasons. First, the supporting parent has had similar experiences as the referred parent. Second, the referred parent is able to compare his or her feelings with those of the supporting parent, thereby learning that these feelings are normal and gaining a sense of hope for the future. Third, the supporting parent is available by telephone around the clock. Fourth, the referred parent and the supporting parent are in an equal relationship that is based on similar life experiences, and the support is often reciprocal (Ainbinder et al., 1998).

For a parent of a child with challenging behaviors, a parent to parent match with a support parent whose child has similar challenging behaviors may reduce feelings of shame, isolation, and frustration. Second, the match may provide some creative and practical tips for managing difficult behaviors. Third, it can offer personalized support that is available 24 hours per day. Fourth, such a match can provide a comfortable context for sharing research-based information on positive behavior support strategies. Finally, this match offers an opportunity for giving, not just receiving, information and support regarding challenging behavior.

Disseminating and Utilizing the Results   Our PAR team's results have been shared in joint presentations, with the parents and the researchers presenting side by side. The parents are getting more comfortable with talking about research methodology, and the researchers are getting more comfortable with discussing the finer points of Parent to

Parent programs. Interest in the results has been widespread because the research effort met a real need for Parent to Parent programs.

The products that we developed were also based on input from parents and researchers. These products are both traditional and functional. The traditional products include journal articles and conference presentations that fulfill researchers' needs for publication and professional contribution. The functional products include a manual on program evaluation that is specific to Parent to Parent programs, a packet of materials for parents and researchers to use in presenting the findings and discussing their implications for Parent to Parent programs nationwide, and an easy-to-use summary of the results for public awareness efforts by Parent to Parent programs.

From the data analyses, we learned a great deal about the efficacy of the one-to-one parent to parent match and about parent to parent programmatic issues. The precision that research demands has documented exactly what is happening in parent to parent matches, as one of the Parent to Parent program directors, Bev Parry, described,

> *One of the neat aspects of this parent–research team effort is that I always come away from our meetings feeling as though I have attended "Parent to Parent school." The fact that researchers need to know precisely what is being measured is helping us to be more thorough in how we run Parent to Parent programs. We helped to define for the research what typically happens in a parent to parent match, and now the research is helping us to maintain and improve the quality of the support that we at Parent to Parent programs want to provide to parents through the match.*

These program coordinators have already initiated new procedures to ensure that matches do indeed begin as quickly as possible after the initial referral and that at least four contacts occur during the first 8 weeks. The data also suggested ways in which the training for supporting parents might be modified to add to the overall quality of the matched experience. New questions for further research have been identified, such as "What is the impact of the one-to-one match on the supporting parent?" "What are best practices in implementing and supporting the one-to-one match and for training the veteran parents?" Our PAR team hopes to continue working together to answer these questions.

IMPLICATIONS OF THE
PARTICIPATORY ACTION RESEARCH STUDY RESULTS

In a mutual effort to determine the efficacy of the one-to-one parent to parent match, our PAR team members reflected on the advantages and challenges of PAR. The advantages were numerous. Using PAR involved shared visions, and shared visions led to the sense of a shared commitment to the study. Shared visions strengthened our PAR team as well. Using PAR from the beginning also meant that our initial steps were indeed taken jointly. Having equal numbers of parents and researchers on the team led to equal empowerment and greater participation by all. Furthermore, PAR involved careful listening by all team members, which helped all involved to thoroughly understand the content of the research area. Listening also helped each person to feel as though he or she really was a valued and contributing member of the PAR team. On a practical note, PAR led to the development of new and more relevant instruments, as well as questionnaires that were more comfortable for families. PAR also involved compromises. Although this meant that the needs of parents and researchers were not completely met, making compromises ensured that the study moved ahead. In addition, using PAR resulted in a proposal that most likely was stronger and more relevant than a proposal prepared by either researchers or parents alone and, perhaps, a grant that was funded in part because of the PAR preparation process. The PAR process also meant that it was easier to obtain parent support letters for the project. In turn, because the researchers and parents jointly designed the study and family-friendly forms, it was easier to recruit study participants. PAR had the added benefit of increasing the knowledge base of all team members. Researchers learned firsthand about the families participating in Parent to Parent programs and about the importance of support for families. Parents benefited from a thorough orientation to the research process. Finally, the PAR team developed presentations, products, and journal articles that were nontraditional, interesting, and pertinent to a wider audience.

A primary challenge that our PAR team faced was that PAR efforts, because they are democratic, take more time to complete than projects that are conducted in isolation. Group decisions can only be made after the team has had time to process and learn from each member's diverse perspectives. When planning a PAR project, teams must build in sufficient time for the group consensus process. Funding agencies that seek to encourage PAR projects will need to allow more time for proposal preparation as well as project implementation. Because of this added time, additional funding is also necessary to support the extra planning meetings and conference calls that are crucial to the ongoing communication. In addition, budgets need to include funding to support PAR-related activities as well as the actual research activities. Challenges for the PAR team members themselves include beginning the PAR experience with a willingness to listen, consider different perspectives, and compromise. This willingness needs to be discussed and assessed as team members are recruited. In addition, PAR efforts should have a built-in mechanism for the mutual education that is needed for the group to make informed decisions. PAR team members must also be willing to share not only the work of the project but also the rewards. Presentations and papers with multiple authors often are the results of a PAR effort, and PAR team members need to be comfortable with this reality. Furthermore, universities need to support and reward the efforts and products of faculty members who are involved in PAR research. Thus, products of PAR efforts need to be available in a variety of formats; journal articles and conference presentations are not accessible to most families. Finally, for PAR to be replicated more widely, there is a need for comprehensive documentation and validation of PAR efforts and best practices.

Implications for Disseminating Knowledge About Positive Behavior Support

This chapter has described the results of a carefully designed and conducted evaluative study of parent to parent support, which was conducted by a PAR team of parents and researchers working as equal partners. The findings provide the first evidence of the efficacy of Parent to Parent programs. Based on these significant quantitative and qualitative data, our PAR team members recommend that parent to parent support be included as an essential component of a comprehensive family support system. Supporting parents in Parent to Parent programs provide emotional support as well as a great deal of practical information to the parents with whom they are matched. Therefore, the more than 700 Parent to Parent programs in the United States that are training and matching supporting parents are efficient vehicles for knowledge dissemination about positive behavior support strategies. Many Parent to Parent programs are also beginning to work collaboratively with universities in disseminating research-based information to parents.

If Parent to Parent programs have information about best practices for addressing challenging behaviors, they can include it in their training sessions for the supporting parents. Supporting parents can then share these best practices through their matches, passing the information from parent to parent. The information will be shared in a comfortable, informal way, and the supporting parent will be readily available to help the parent personalize the information as necessary. Steve and Carol, for example, learned many effective behavior support strategies (e.g., modifying the environment by changing the doorknobs on their bathroom and laundry room doors) through their match with the parent whose daughter also had autism.

Supporting parents who have received training in behavior support strategies (through their Parent to Parent program or another environment) may be resources to professionals as well. Training teams composed of both parents and professionals are beginning to train school personnel in the use of behavior support strategies. When these training teams include parents, the importance of a family perspective will be reflected in the training and technical assistance that the school personnel receive. Moreover, many of the larger Parent to Parent programs host annual conferences and publish newsletters for parents—both of which are also efficient means for reaching the hundreds of parents on Parent to Parent program mailing lists.

CONCLUSION

We encourage parents of children with behavior problems to contact a local or statewide Parent to Parent program to determine whether a supporting parent with knowledge of positive behavior support can serve as a parent match. If you are a professional who plays a leadership role in your state regarding the dissemination of knowledge about positive behavior support, we also encourage you to contact Parent to Parent programs in your area. Professionals and program leaders can then discuss ways to collaborate for the purpose of embedding positive behavior support in the support activities of Parent to Parent programs. Empowering parents to support parents in the use of positive behavior support in their homes and communities may greatly strengthen dissemination efforts throughout the United States.

REFERENCES

Ainbinder, J., Blanchard, L., Singer, G.H.S., Sullivan, M., Powers, L., Marquis, L., & Santelli, B. (1998). How parents help one another: A qualitative study of Parent to Parent self-help. *Journal of Pediatric Psychology, 23,* 99–109.

Behr, S.K., Murphy, D.L., & Summers, J.A. (1992). *Kansas Inventory of Parental Perceptions: Measures of perceptions of parents who have children with special needs.* Lawrence, KS: Beach Center on Disability, The University of Kansas.

The Beach Center on Disability maintains a current listing of all Parent to Parent programs and has a number of products and resources for Parent to Parent programs. For further information, please contact the Beach Center:

Beach Center on Disability
The University of Kansas
Haworth Hall, Room 3136
1200 Sunnyside Avenue
Lawrence, KS 66045-7534
785-864-7600
beach@dole.lsi.ukans.edu

Blanchard, L., Powers, L., Ginsberg, C., Marquis, J. & Singer, G.H.S. (1996). *The Parent Coping Efficacy Scale: Measuring parents' perceptions of coping with a child with a disability and family problems.* Unpublished manuscript, University of North Carolina Medical School, Chapel Hill.

Bruyère, S. (1993). PAR: Overview and implications for family members of persons with disabilities. *Journal of Vocational Rehabilitation, 3*(2), 62–68.

Chesler, M.A. (1991). Participatory action research with self-help groups: An alternative paradigm for inquiry and action. *American Journal of Community Psychology, 19*(5), 757–768.

Cutrona, C.E., & Russell, D.W. (1990). Type of social support and specific stress: Toward a theory of optimal matching. In B.R. Sarason, I.G. Sarason, & G.R. Pierce. (Eds.), *Social support: An interactional view* (pp. 319–366). New York: John Wiley & Sons.

DeJong, G. (1979). Independent living: From social movement to analytic paradigm. *Archives of Physical Medicine and Rehabilitation, 60,* 435–446.

Fenton, J., Batavia, A., & Roody, D. (1993). *Proposed policy statement for NIDRR on constituency-oriented research and dissemination (CORD).* Washington, DC: National Institute on Disability and Rehabilitation Research.

Hall, B. (1984). Research commitment and action: The role of participatory research. *International Review of Education, 30,* 289–299.

Koren, P.E., DeChillo, N., & Friesen, B. (1992). Measuring empowerment in families whose children have emotional disabilities: A brief questionnaire. *Rehabilitation Psychology, 37*(4), 305–321.

Lather, P. (1986). Research as praxis. *Harvard Educational Review, 56*(3), 257–277.

McTaggart, R. (1991). Principles for participatory action research. *Adult Education Quarterly, 41,* 168–187.

Menz, F.E. (1995). *Constituents make the difference: Improving the value of rehabilitation research.* Menomonie: Research, Rehabilitation and Training Center on Improving Community-Based Rehabilitation Programs, University of Wisconsin–Stout.

Morningstar, M.E. (1994, April). *PAR: Whose research is it anyway?* Paper presented at the Syracuse University Consortium for Collaborative Research on Social Relations, Syracuse, NY.

Reason, P. (1994). *Participation in human inquiry.* Thousand Oaks, CA: Sage Publications.

Rehabilitation Act Amendments of 1992, PL 102-569, 29 U.S.C. §§ 701 *et seq.*

Santelli, B., Singer, G.H.S., DiVenere, N., Ginsberg, C., & Powers, L.E. (1998). Participatory action research: Reflections on critical incidents in a PAR project. *Journal of The Association of Persons with Severe Handicaps, 23*(3), 211–222.

Santelli, B., Turnbull, A.P., Marquis, J.G., & Lerner, E.P. (1993). Parent to parent programs: Ongoing support for parents of young adults with special needs. *Journal of Vocational Rehabilitation, 3*(2), 25–37.

Santelli, B., Turnbull, A.P., Marquis, J.G., & Lerner, E.P. (1995). Parent to Parent programs: A unique form of mutual support. *Infants and Young Children, 8*(2), 48–57.

Santelli, B., Turnbull, A.P., Marquis, J.G., & Lerner, E.P. (1997). Parent to Parent programs: A resource for parents and professionals. *Journal of Early Intervention, 21*(1), 73–83.

Singer, G.H.S., Marquis, J., Powers, L., Blanchard, L., DiVenere, N., Santelli, B., Ainbinder, J.G., & Sharp, M. (1999). A multi-site evaluation of parent to parent programs for parents of children with disabilities. *Journal of Early Intervention, 22*(3), 217–229.

Turnbull, A.P., Friesen, B.J., & Ramirez, C. (1995, April). *Participatory action research: Forging collaborative partnerships with families in the study of disability.* Paper presented at National Institute on Disability and Rehabilitation Research Conference on Participatory Action Research, Washington, DC.

Turnbull, A.P., & Turnbull, H.R. (1996). Participatory action research. In National Council on Disability (Ed.), *Improving the implementation of the Individuals with Disabilities Act: Making schools work for all of America's children* (pp. 685–710). Washington, DC: National Council on Disability.

Whitney-Thomas, J. (1997). Participatory action research as an approach to enhancing quality of life for individuals with disabilities. In R. Schalock (Ed.), *Quality of life: Applications to persons with disabilities: Vol. II* (pp. 181–198). Washington, DC: American Association on Mental Retardation.

Whyte, J., & Doe, T. (1995, April). *Participatory action research: Forging collaborative partnerships.* Paper presented at National Institute on Disability and Rehabilitation Research Conference on Participatory Action Research, Washington, DC.

Index

Page numbers followed by *t* or *f* indicate tables or figures, respectively.